HANDBOOK OF INTERNATIONAL FINANCIAL MANAGEMENT

HANDBOOK OF INTERNATIONAL FINANCIAL MANAGEMENT

Michael Z. Brooke

M

First published by
MACMILLAN PUBLISHERS LTD

Distributed by Globe Book Services Ltd
Brunel Road, Houndmills
Basingstoke, Hants RG21 2XS

British Library Cataloguing in Publication Data

Brooke, Michael Z. (Michael Zachary) 1921-
Handbook of international financial management.
1. International financial management
I. Title
658.15

ISBN 0-333-53203-1

Typeset and printed in Great Britain

Contents

How to use the International Financial Management Handbook

LOOKING FOR FUNDING FOR PROJECTS ABROAD?

Chapter 2.6 gives you the basic information and a list of addresses and telephone numbers.

HAVING TROUBLE WITH CREDIT RISKS?

Chapter 3.4 lists insurance opportunities and 3.5 lists credit control techniques for difficult areas, with addresses and telephone numbers. These chapters are full of information for companies large and small. Smaller companies may find themselves particularly interested in exporting to regions where competition is less and margins are higher, but the risks are too great without good cover. How to cope is explained here.

CONFUSED BY CROSS-BORDER TAXATION?

Chapters 6.1 and 6.2 will help to chart a path through the maze. Of course you need expert advice as well but these chapters (written by an expert adviser) are designed to help readers talk intelligently to their tax consultants — a case of a little knowledge that can save a lot of fees.

UNSURE WHAT TO EXPECT FROM YOUR INTERNATIONAL BANKER?

Chapter 2.3 explains what the client can expect from an international banking service, giving hints in depth about the best use to be made of the banks.

These are just four of the many questions tackled in this book. Its role is that of a practical working tool to provide profit-boosting insights for international finance managers and their advisers.

Part 1 is introductory, a broad look at the world in which financial decisions have to be taken. Useful for reading before those endless corporate planning meetings.

One chapter in this part (1.5) demonstrates opportunities for international portfolio management and lists a number of independent consultants who provide further advice.

Part 2 deals with capital structures, international banking and financing. A final chapter (2.7) provides a guide to cross-frontier mergers and acquisitions.

Part 3 expands on other aspects of financing from long-term projects to trade and from there to compensation trading. This part also contains a chapter (3.6) listing investment opportunities in European Community countries.

Part 4 looks at investment appraisal and control across frontiers.

Part 5 examines in detail the question of risk and how to reduce it. The first five chapters give advice on the main kinds of risk — currency exchange and political — and how to manage them actively. The other three chapters chart a way through the complexities of financial futures, swap financing, options and equity derivatives.

Part 6 is devoted to taxation, starting with international tax planning, followed by a chapter (6.2) on European taxation systems, and concluding with a look at tax havens; for different purposes, this chapter concludes, most countries may be tax efficient places for holding funds.

Many topics, naturally, cut across the chapter boundaries; and an index of subjects signposts arm's length, debt, exchange, finance and much else. This index is selective there are no time wasting references to pages without significant information.

Take **Government** as an example of how the index can help by pointing to a summary of relationships between companies and countries (pages 45-46 and 56-59), support for major projects and investment incentives (143-145, 256-264, and project appraisal on 381–390 and for regulations on foreign shareholdings (395–387).

The index of names is more comprehensive; most references to a country or a company may provide a useful clue to a searcher for information.

Lists of useful names and addresses (which are not indexed) can be found at the end of the following chapters: 1.5 (fund management consultants), 2.6 (funding organizations), 3.4 (credit insurance organizations), 3.6 (sources of information on country risk)

HOTLINE

For any questions arising from the book, do not hesitate to 'phone the editor. He will be more than glad to help when he can and to point you to sources of further information.

Contact: Michael Z Brooke, Brooke Associates (Manchester) Ltd, 21 Barnfield, Urmston, Manchester M31 1EW. Telephone: 061-746 8140, Fax: 061-746 8132.

The contributors

Robert Arnold
Director and Head of Mergers and Acquisitions, WestLB UK Ltd
Robert Arnold began his career in Los Angeles with a manufacturer of construction chemicals. After holding various positions in both sales and manufacturing, he moved to Europe in 1984.

Based in Switzerland, he completed his MBA at IMEDE and his first German cross border Mergers and Acquisitions transaction in 1985. The next year, he moved to London and subsequently became Head of Mergers and Acquisitions for BHF Capital Markets Ltd. In 1989, he joined WestLB UK Ltd as a Director and Head of its Mergers and Acquisitions Group. He has experience in a wide range of manufacturing and service industries including food, leisure, packaging, and distribution services.

Michael Z Brooke, MA, PhD, FIEx.
Author and consultant, Managing Director, Brooke Associates (Manchester) Ltd
Fellow of the Academy of International Business. Formerly, senior lecturer in Management Sciences and Director of the International Business Unit, University of Manchester Institute of Science and Technology. He has published 17 books on international business, including *Centralization and Autonomy, Selling Management Services Contracts in International Business, International Management*, and *Profits from Abroad.* He has lectured on the subject in fourteen countries and has acted as consultant for numerous companies.

Robert Z Brooke, MA, MBA
Director, BZW International Equities Ltd
Robert Brooke is a graduate of Cambridge University and has an MBA from INSEAD (the European Institute of Business Administration). He has studied and taught in Germany, France, Canada and Japan. He is now a Director of BZW International Equities Ltd, working as an analyst of the Tokyo equity market.

Jack Broyles, BSc, MSc, PhD
Association of Corporate Treasurers Professor of Treasury Management at the Cranfield Institute of Management. Director of the Research Centre for Treasury Management at Cranfield.
Author and co-author of three textbooks on corporate finance and numerous articles on finance, financial planning and acquisitions and mergers. Formerly, Harold W Siebens Fellow in Finance at Templeton College, Oxford and Lecturer in Finance at the London Business School where he was Director of the Corporate Finance Programme.

Mark Burges Watson, MA
Barclays de Zoete Wedd International Securities Ltd
After graduating in history at St John's College, Cambridge, Mark Burges Watson took up his present appointment as research assistant at BZW.

David Challen
Head of Investment Banking Division, J. Henry Schroder Wagg & Company Ltd
David Challen has been at Schroder's for eighteen years, always in the corporate finance division apart from one year at Schroder's in New York.

Among major clients he has advised in M & A transactions are Pilkington in its defence against BTR and Rowntree during the competing bids from Suchard and Nestlé. He also led Schroder's water privatization team.

Brian Clarke MICM
Credit Training Associates
Brian Clarke has spent over 30 years in credit and finance, for much of this time responsible for international credit management at Imperial Chemical Industries plc. In 1986 he established Credit Training Associates, specializing in training courses and consultancy to meet the international credit and finance needs of companies. He runs training seminars, both public and in-house, for a number of organizations, including the Department of Trade and Industry (British Overseas Trade Board), and Dun & Bradstreet. A member of the British Institute of Credit Management; an honorary life member of FCIB (Finance, Credit and International Business), formerly European Director and Chairman of their largest common interest industry group. Editor of the *Handbook of International Credit Management.*

Denis C Cross, MA, DPhil
Executive Director, Hambros Bank Ltd
Joined Hambros in 1961 after a post-graduate degree in mathematics at Oxford. Appointed a director in 1972 and an executive director in 1985. Experience in the bank has included portfolio investment, corporate finance, venture capital and project lending. A member of Aims of Industry.

Hans Dahm, Dipl.-Kfm, Dr.rer.pol.
Senior Vice President and Head of the Mergers and Acquisitions Department, Westdeutsche Landesbank, Düsseldorf
Dr Dahm obtained his degree in business administration and his doctorate at Cologne University. After completing a number of traineeships and study terms abroad, he joined Booz, Allen and Hamilton as a consultant in 1967. He joined the Westdeutsche Landesbank (WestLB) in 1975 after holding management posts in Peek and Cloppenburg, European Enterprises Development and Reuter Technologie.

Ken Duker, MBA
Midland Montagu, New York
Recently moved to the Treasury Section, Midland Montagu, New York, he was previously responsible for both the Treasury Marketing Department and Special Product Group at Nomura Bank International plc.

Malcolm J Finney, BSc, MSc (Bus Admin), AFIMA, MBIM
Senior Partner of Malcolm J Finney & Partners, International Tax Consultants
Graduated with a first class honours degree in pure and applied mathematics from the University of Hull in 1969, and with a master's degree in business administration from the University of Bradford Management Centre in 1972. Previous experience has included working as an international tax consultant with the City firm of J F Chown & Co Ltd. For six years he was head of international tax with the accounting firm of Grant Thornton. Publications are many and he is a frequent speaker at conferences both in the United Kingdom and overseas.

Jenny Foster-Smith, BSc, MSc
Director, Fixpoint Ltd, economic and marketing consultants
She has specialized in the analysis of exchange rate and interest movements for the past ten years. Following a commercial career, she read economics at City University and later undertook a Master's Degree (specializing in econometrics) at London University. Between 1979 and 1986, she worked as an International Economist at the Henley Centre for Forecasting, latterly as Manager of its International Forecasting Group. She is Executive Editor of *European Business*.

Brigitte Granville
Research Associate, The Royal Institute of International Affairs
She has studied at the University of Dijon, University of Sussex and the European University Institute, Florence. Has worked at the World Bank and the OECD. Has recently coauthored a book entitled *The New Eastern Europe: Western Responses*, published by Pinter. Her current research is on exchange rate reform in Eastern Europe.

Jeremy J A Howarth, MA, MBA, FCA, FCT
Deputy Chairman and Finance Director, European Leisure plc
After graduating in history, qualifying as a chartered accountant and graduating from INSEAD, has had treasury experience with Rowntree Mackintosh, Haden BICC and the Ladbroke Group before joining European Leisure plc in October 1987. European Leisure has since developed from shell status to being one of Europe's leading consumer leisure companies. He has contributed to *The Treasurer* on funding policy and addressed treasury conferences in the United Kingdom and Australia.

P H A Kenyon, MA, FCA, FCT
Visiting Professor, City University Business School
After graduating in Politics, Philosophy and Economics (PPE) at Oxford, worked for AEI, Deloittes and Plessey in various finance positions, mainly as treasurer. Specialized in export finance. Contributed to *The Control of Working Capital* (ed. M Grass) and is author of *Currency Risk Management* (Wiley 1981) and *Currency Risk and Business Management* (Blackwell, Autumn 1990). Since 1982 he has taught financial management and treasury topics on the City University Business School's MBA programme in international business and export management. Research interests include risk management and competitive and corporate strategy. Has served on the education committee of the Association of Corporate Treasurers.

Andrew Leasor, MA
Director, Lloyd Thompson Ltd
After graduating in Politics, Philosophy and Economics (PPE) from Oriel College, Oxford in 1978, joined Investment Insurance International (Managers) Ltd, the political risk insurance subsidiary of Hogg Robinson and Gardner Mountain plc. As a Director developing overseas business he played a key role in winning the Queen's Award for Export Achievement in 1983. He was made an executive director of Hogg Robinson (Credit and Political) Ltd in 1985. Besides his substantial experience of export credit and political risk insurance, he specializes in alternative financing techniques such as leasing, securitization, forfaiting and debt swaps as well as financial risks, including credit enhancement and asset guarantees. He has addressed a number of international conferences on these subjects, and has contributed articles to, or been interviewed by, *The Financial Times*, *Wall Street Journal*, *Euromoney Trade Finance*, *Airfinance Journal* and many other publications. He has served on the CBI Investment Protection Panel. In November 1987 he joined Lloyd Thompson Ltd, the Lloyd's broking subsidiary of Lloyd Thompson plc, where he is now a Director. He is also a Director of the Philippine Long Term Equity Fund Ltd and the Emerging Eastern Europe Fund Ltd.

John A Ledger
Coordinator United Kingdom Trade Finance, Standard Chartered Bank
Joined the Bank from school in 1961 and has held a number of posts in a number of cities, he was Area Manager North West before taking up his present position.

Tracey McHugh, BA
Commercial Union Risk Management Ltd
Graduated from Glasgow College with a BA in Risk Management and is also a graduate member of the Institute of Risk Management; she has worked with Commercial Union Risk Management for two years and her current position is technical assistant.

Phedon Nicholaides
Research Fellow, The Royal Institute of International Affairs
Has studied at the London School of Economics, University of Amsterdam and Clark University, Massachusetts. Has worked at the Trade Policy Research Centre and the London Business School. Has recently written a book entitled *Liberalising Service Trade: Strategies for Success*, published by Routledge. His current research is on foreign direct investment in Europe.

Stanley Paliwoda, BA, MSc, PhD
Professor of Marketing, University of Calgary, Alberta
Before taking up his present post in 1990, Stanley Paliwoda was a lecturer at the Manchester School of Management (in the University of Manchester Institute of Science and Technology). He has published 5 books including *International Marketing*, and contributed to 10 others. He has specialized in industrial marketing to Eastern Europe and the Soviet Union and on the growing phenomenon of countertrade.

Adam Parkin, MPhil(Oxon)
Director, John Govett & Co Ltd
Responsible for currency, fixed interest and derivative investments at John Govett & Co Ltd, which manages £20bn of discretionary funds. Previously an economist at American Express Bank, a director of AEIBC Asset Management Ltd, a director of Foreign & Colonial Management Ltd. Currently a board member of the Association for Futures Investment and The Options and Futures Society.

Bob A Rand
Credit Insurance Broker
Joined the Export Credits Guarantee Department (ECGD) in 1966 and progressed through various posts to Regional Director at the Cambridge regional office. Moved to Jardine Credit Insurance Limited in 1982 as Director of their East Anglia Division handling all forms of credit insurance and related facilities. Now working for Bain Clarkson Credit and Political Risks Limited.

Keith Redhead, BSc, MA, MSc, MPhil

Principal Lecturer in Economics, Coventry Polytechnic

He has more than thirty publications in the area of financial risk management. He was the first Chief Examiner for the Securities Industry (Stock Exchange) examinations in Financial Futures and Options. He is course leader for the City University Business School securities industry programme for financial futures and options and has carried out in-house training in a number of major city institutions.

T M Rybczynski, MSc(Econ), BCom, Hon.DSc, FIB, FSBE

Visiting Professor, The City University

Formerly economic adviser, Lazard Bros and Director of Lazard Securities. A graduate of London University, he has spent his working life in the City but has also maintained active interest and involvement in academic, industrial and other areas. Governor and member of the executive committee of the National Institute of Economic and Social Resources; member of the governing body Institute for Fiscal Studies; member of the Scientific Committee, International Centre for Monetary and Business Studies, Geneva; Chairman Finance Markets Groups, Centre for Economic Policy Studies.

Colin R B Smith, MA, MBA

Senior Consultant, KPMG Peat Marwick McLintock

Graduated in engineering from Cambridge University, and worked for four years as an engineer in the oil industry. Obtained an MBA (with distinction) at INSEAD, Fontainebleau, France, before joining Samuel Montagu and Co. Ltd (later Midland Montagu) where he worked first on interest rate simulation and option theory, then on the trading of interest rate and currency swaps and options, and later on the creation of structured transactions. Moved to KPMG Peat Marwick McLintock in 1988, since when he has worked with the management of a wide range of banks and financial institutions on risk management processes and techniques.

I N Spurgeon, CA

Formerly Deputy Head, Finance Department, British-American Tobacco

Joined British-American Tobacco shortly after qualifying as a member of the Institute of Chartered Accountants of Scotland in 1956. After a spell as a travelling auditor, principally in the Far East, became an assistant accountant in BAT's head office in Millbank, London, where he was involved, among other things, in the development of management accounting systems. In 1967 was appointed finance director of a group of companies in the perfumery and cosmetics business, returning to head office at the end of 1969 to help set up group corporate planning. Subsequently became finance adviser for the BAT companies in the Indian subcontinent, then for Latin America and the Caribbean, corporate finance adviser and finally finance adviser for Africa. He was deputy head of the finance department from 1980 to retirement in 1987. He is currently a non-executive director of a privately owned engineering group.

Tom Stonier, AB, MS, PhD, FRSA
Professor of Science and Society, University of Bradford
After obtaining his doctorate from Yale, held scientific posts at Brookhaven National Laboratory, Rockefeller University and at Manhattan College. In 1975 he moved to the north of England to take up his present post. He has been involved with strategic forecasting and as consultant or lecturer to numerous companies, trade unions, and government bodies. His speciality is studying the impact of science and technology on society. He is author of over 100 articles in a wide range of scientific, technical, professional and business journals as well as the lay press. He has appeared on numerous radio and TV programmes in three continents. Author of *The Wealth of Information: A Profile of the Post-Industrial Economy* (1983).

Julian Sturdy-Morton
Director, Crédit-Lyonnais Securities
After graduating from King's College, London, Julian Sturdy-Morton joined Williams and Glyns Bank; he moved, in 1982, to Morgan Grenfell where he later took charge of European marketing for the capital markets division and became Director, Morgan Grenfell International Ltd. He took up his present post as Director responsible for origination of international equities business with the Crédit Lyonnais Group in 1988.

Christopher H Taylor
Senior Manager, Price Waterhouse
Christopher H Taylor is a senior manager in the captal markets and treasury management groups of Price Waterhouse in London. He was educated at Manchester University where he read mathematics obtaining a first class honours degree. He joined Price Waterhouse in 1980 where he specialized in the banking and capital markets industries. In 1988 he was seconded to Price Waterhouse New York for a short period.

Andrew Thompson, BA(Econ)
Secretary, Equipment Leasing Association
Andrew Thompson is secretary to the Equipment Leasing Association. He is responsible for advising the Association, servicing committees, contact with authorities on taxation and accounting matters and banking supervision.

Ira Vater, Diplom Betriebswirt, BA(Hons)
Consultant in European Affairs, Price Waterhouse, Brussels
After graduating in European Business Studies at the Fachhochschule Münster and Humberside College of Higher Education, Ms Vater joined the Financial Institution Division of Directorate General XV of the European Commission in 1986; after a period with C and L Belmont, she joined Price Waterhouse in 1988.

Brian A Walsh
Finance Director, GKN plc
Brian Walsh was born in London in 1944. He graduated with an MBA from the London Business School, and he is a Fellow of the Chartered Institute of Management Accountants.

His first employment was with Ford of Europe in financial management. In 1973 he joined British Steel International as Finance Director. He moved to First Boston Corporation in 1976 as Vice-President, later becoming Executive Director of Crédit Suisse First Boston. In 1980 he was appointed Vice-President and Director of Finance and Business Planning, Europe for the Singer Corporation. In 1982 he joined General Ford Corporation as Assistant Corporate Controller and Treasurer, subsequently Finance Director of its US grocery business. He moved from America to London in 1987 to become Finance Director of GKN plc.

1
STRATEGIC ISSUES

Part 1 deals with general and strategic issues that face the international trader. In particular the environment is scanned for landmarks and guidelines that may help in decision-making, both long and short term.

The first two chapters look at the economic, political and technological changes which are likely to influence future directions of business. The always topical question of relationships between companies and national governments — at home and abroad — is the theme of chapter three.

After these chapters on the environment, chapter four analyses the international options open to finance managers, while the last chapter advises on portfolio management.

1.1 Structural Changes in the World Economy

MAY YOU LIVE IN INTERESTING TIMES

'May you live in interesting times' runs the Oriental curse. We certainly do. This analysis of changes in the world economy looks at the world in three ways. The first is by focussing on the changes, the generators of uncertainty and opportunity. The second is by highlighting trends which will carry those changes forward and which offer reference points for action. The third is by breaking the world into its three major economic blocs: the United States, Japan and Europe.

The review is split into two sections, and each section is guided by the three dimensions of the analytical framework. Section one takes as a starting point the growth of the Tokyo equity market to overtake that of New York in size, and projects the continuing growth in importance of the Japanese economy. For the next decade at least Japan is likely to be the dominant factor in world cash flow.

Section two examines the renewed vigour in the drive to create a single market in the European Community. Strategy has been changed and so have tactics. Political will now seems to have pushed events far enough to take the motive force out of the hands of politicians with national sovereignty on their minds. Instead it has been passed into the hands of businessmen who will be obliged to force the pace by the imperative of a fast-changing competitive environment. A case study is presented of developments in the European automobile industry.

The two sections also exemplify the concentration on changes. Comparing Japan with the United States highlights long-term changes in performance. Relative decline, if it continues unchecked, sooner or later becomes absolute decline. The dramatic growth in the United States budget and trade deficits confirms the climax of relative United States decline just as the surge in overseas investment by Japan confirms the climax of relative Japanese improvement. Both countries now have to adjust to a more sustainable acceptance of their relative positions.

FROM LIBERALIZATION THROUGH COMPETITION TO REGULATION

Focusing on the development of the Common Market highlights a series of changes in regulations which will alter forever the structure of countless product markets. In a way this adventure in deregulation is the culmination of a process which has been at work throughout the 1980s. The privatization and liberalization wave was identified closely with the high-profile personalities and political ideologies of Ronald Reagan, Yasuhiro Nakasone and Margaret Thatcher. By the beginning of 1989, only Mrs Thatcher was left in power, and the new Japanese and American leaders are guaranteed to be of a lower profile than their predecessors. As a result, it is time to consider where the next political wave will lead.

The natural sequence of events is for liberalization to lead to greater competition. This competition throws up new questions which had not existed under the previous market structure, so a new set of regulations is needed to establish a new order. A cursory glance at the state of the telecommunications markets in Britain, Japan and the United States shows how this works. In each of these three countries a monopoly has been broken and its services opened to competition. In each case, though, the former monopolist is so large by comparison with its competitors that a competitive position has to be regulated into existence for them. This is certainly true in both Japan and the United Kingdom, where NTT and BT (the telecommunications companies in the two countries) are the largest and second-largest stocks in their respective stockmarkets, let alone the largest providers of telecommunications. Even in the United States the baby Bells, the broken-down parts of the old AT&T, are still dominant in their regions, and the rump of AT&T itself is the fifth largest stock in the market.

Taking the British example, competition has been brought into basic network provision and into pay telephones. New product markets — cellular telephones, telepoint, personal communication networks — are now born licensed but competitive. The trend will continue as 1989 brings more open access to the pay telephone market and 1990 a review of the duopoly between Mercury and BT in a wide range of basic services. At the same time, after public outcry in 1987 over the quality of service provided by BT, more attention is being paid to the details of its operating licence. Already the pricing formula — previously retail price index minus 3% average across all services — has been altered to force BT to improve operating efficiency and eliminate cross-subsidization of services.

It seems inevitable therefore that two strands will develop at the same time. The first is the liberalization of product markets which is the focus of attention as the Common Market develops. As liberalization picks up momentum and the direction passes more into the hands of businessmen than politicians, the focus of attention will shift towards new forms of regulation for the more competitive markets. The pace of events will differ market by market for three reasons. The first reason is the speed of introduction (and complexity) of new legislation. The automobile market, for all its protectionism, is still more influenced by continent-wide, even worldwide, determinants of success than is the retail banking market for instance. There are therefore more potentially far-reaching changes which can be applied to banking than there are to automobiles.

The second reason is the structure of the market itself. A local and fragmented market such as the construction industry is more likely to respond quickly, but on a small scale and continuously, to new initiatives than is, for instance, the telecommunications market which is dominated by a handful of large, wealthy and government-backed national monopolies.

The third reason is foreign competition. One part of the liberalization package which is still outstanding is the treatment of non-European Community companies. In theory, if a single European market open to all-comers from Europe is to the benefit of all Europeans, there should be no reason that this cannot be extended to include all-comers from outside Europe as well. To believe that, however, is to ignore the track record in protectionism of most European countries. In the run-up to 1992 therefore greater attention will be paid to the competitive position and regulatory treatment of non-European companies.

RISING PRODUCTION, RISING AGE

Unspoken in these discussions, but assumed throughout, are two dominant trends whose influence will determine the direction of the world economy until the end of the century at the earliest. The first is the move from primary to secondary to tertiary industries in the West. There was much anguish in the early 1980s over the loss of manufacturing jobs which have not been replaced. In fact, though the adjustment may have been harsh, this is now seen as being part of a similar trend to that which has affected agriculture since the industrial revolution. Rapid increases in productivity have meant continuing increases in production by a decreasing workforce. The agricultural surpluses in the European Community bear testimony to the ability of a small — and falling — section of the population to provide the basic foodstuffs of the entire region. This is now applying to manufacturing. The 1979 peak in manufacturing output has now been matched in Britain by a dramatically reduced workforce which shows no sign of real increase. Increases in employment have instead been in service areas such as banking and tourism — the areas reviewed at the end of this chapter — where there have been far lower rates of productivity growth. Even within the service industries the same shifts can be seen. Airline executives are fond of valuing the computer networks which drive their booking systems more highly than the airlines themselves. All they are doing is reflecting the shift towards greater value being added by processing information than by moving people.

The second dominant trend is that of the population itself. Whereas the nightmare of the 1980s has been high unemployment, and particularly high youth unemployment, that of the 1990s is likely to be just the opposite. By the mid 1990s, the number of school-leavers in Britain is expected to fall by 30% as the baby boom comes to an end. The projections of the Norwich Union Insurance company suggest that it might need to employ all the school-leavers in the city of Norwich in 1995. At the other end of the spectrum, the number of elderly is set to grow, and their percentage of the total population to grow even more rapidly as life expectancy increases and the baby boom ends. The average member country of the Organization for Economic Cooperation and Development (OECD) used 12% of its gross domestic product for social expenditure in 1960, and 24% in 1985. In 1985 an average 12% of the population was aged over 65, but by 2000 this is projected to rise to 15%, and to continue rising to 30% by 2050. Over the next fifty years therefore no western country will be able to escape the pressure to radically overhaul its employment systems, pension provisions and health services. Pensions and health will be hit hard and fast. In France, for example, it is rare to find pensions which are capitalized — that is where the contributor is building up capital to pay for his own future pension, as against paying into a fund which immediately pays out his contribution to a present pensioner.

Health services around the world, from state-provided Britain to private United States, are already suffering from constant increases in demand for more and more costly services. Add to this the growth in old people — whose health needs are greater — and a relative decline in the number of young people — whose health care provision is cheaper, and who are contributors of revenue to the system — and the scene is set for a major funding crisis.

JAPAN OVERTAKES THE UNITED STATES

In April 1987 the market value of the Tokyo stock exchange overtook that of the New York stock exchange. Not since the United States took over from the United Kingdom as the world's leading economic power in the late nineteenth century has so portentous a change taken place in the world's financial markets. Part of the change in relative values has been caused by the rise in the value of the Yen against the Dollar, and part by the inflow of funds into the Tokyo stock market. On 12 September 1985 the Dollar would have bought 244 Yen. A little more than two years later, on 1 January 1988, it would have bought no more than 122 Yen. In other words, the Dollar lost fifty percent of its value against the Yen. At the same time, the amount of money flowing into the Tokyo stock market surged. Average daily turnover on the Tokyo stock exchange was Y264bn in 1985. This more than doubled to Y560bn in 1986 and then rose by another sixty percent to Y890bn in 1987, the October crash notwithstanding. At the same time, the Nikkei Stock Average, the headline Japanese index, rose from 11,558 at the beginning of 1985 to 26,646 in October 1987, immediately before the crash. The market value of corporate Japan had risen fourfold in Dollar terms.

Both of these surges in value reflected the same phenomenon — a worldwide belief in the strength of the Japanese economy compared with that of the United States. Hand-in-hand with the rise of the Yen went a rise in Japanese money supply growth. Throughout 1987 M2+ Certificates of Deposit, the Bank of Japan's preferred broad measure of money supply, rose by more than 12% year-on-year. This compared with an average nominal growth of 4.2% in gross national product. At the same time, interest rates fell. The average yield on a long-term bond started 1987 at 5.5%. By the end of April it was at 4.0%. The stage was set for sustained price rises in the equity market. At the same time corporate Japan was finding little new room for extra investment; financial instruments were becoming more attractive. The most significant aspect of these largely domestic considerations was the impact on the self-image of the Japanese. The country had been accustomed, since its comprehensive defeat in the second world war, to thinking of itself as a small, isolated island which had to fight every single day for its existence. Now, suddenly, forty years after the war, the realization has hit that the country is in fact wealthy (with a per capita gross national product of $16,300 compared with the United States of $17,500 in March 1988). The swaggering financial markets knew no bounds in the recovery from the October crash. From the first day of trading in 1988 to the end of March 1988, the Nikkei Stock Average rose by more than 25%. This was better than any other first quarter performance of the previous twenty years, and made Tokyo the only major stock market to pass its pre-October high. By the end of 1989 the Nikkei Stock Average was just short of 39,000, nearly 50% higher than in October 1987.

Neither the relative valuation of the Tokyo equity market compared with that of New York (including the exchange rate effect), nor the absolute valuation of the Tokyo market is sustainable. Both represent extremes which are sure to be corrected over time. Indeed there are already chinks in the armour. By March 1990 the Dollar had recovered to 150 Yen, 25% above its lowest value. In the stockmarket the index may have risen by 50%, but the share prices of the major stockbrokers had fallen by 50% in the preceding three years. The psychological significance should not be overlooked, however. The Japanese set of expectations has been irreversibly altered. The Yen is a strong currency, inward Japanese investment much coveted in the West, and corporate Japanese paper a powerful buying weapon.

FUNDS FLOW OUT OF JAPAN

The motivating force which will bring on the longer, more subtle and more lasting effects of this Japanese financial predominance is the excess supply of funds available for investment compared with the demand for funds, or opportunities for investment. The funds come from two major sources. The external source is the trade account. In Japan's case, this has been a trade surplus since the early 1980s. The balancing item has been increasing investment overseas. In fiscal 1986 (April 1986 to March 1987) there was a net outflow of $145bn of long-term capital. Of this $100bn went into overseas bond markets, some 90% into United States treasury bonds. The internal source is the high domestic savings ratio. In fact, both savings and investment have been falling as a percentage of gross national product since the 1970s, but investment has fallen more rapidly over the last five years. In 1970, total savings were 40% of gross national product, and investment was 39%. By 1980 this had fallen to 31% for savings and 32% for investment. Since then a gap has opened up and remained, so that savings at the end of 1987 were still 31% of gross national product, but investment only 28%. The high savings ratio is unlikely to disappear.

Japanese individuals contribute a higher proportion of funds to their own pension payments, and to fund children's education than is the case in European countries. This provides an inbuilt tendency to higher savings by the present generation to fund future spending.

In trade terms there is enormous pressure from a high Yen on the one hand, and from protectionist policies on the other, for action to redress the imbalance. The most likely way the trade account will be balanced is by more production overseas. The supply and demand dynamics of investment imply better returns overseas than at home. Though the trade account may return to balance, the current account is unlikely to do so as quickly. Japan is at the beginning of a lengthy period of net investment overseas. As this continues, income from overseas assets will grow also, increasing the total amount available for investment. It is a virtuous cycle of a kind that was enjoyed by Britain in the nineteenth century and by the United States in the twentieth. In the style of Britain and the United States, Japan will become rentier to the world, the dominant factor at the margin of world cash flows.

Evidence, both anecdotal and substantial, abounds that this trend is already firmly established. Sony's purchase of CBS Records and of Columbia Pictures, Bridgestone's of Firestone Tires and Sumitomo Life Insurance's of part of Goldman Sachs are major acquisitions, unthinkable a few years ago. Each has important commercial logic behind it, but together they represent a large investment in American industry. Honda is now exporting cars from the United States to Japan (it already sells more cars in the United States than in Japan), and in early 1990 the Accord became the first non-American car to be a best seller in the American market. In late 1988 Nissan started exporting cars from the United Kingdom to other European countries. Symbolic ? Yes, but not just a symbolic gesture to defuse trade friction. More symbolic of a new attitude of mind. Japan now thinks of itself as the wealthiest nation in the world.

The best evidence of this, however, is anecdotal. Press reports from the Toronto summit of the seven largest industrial economies included stories — in American newspapers — of the Japanese outspending the Americans in North America. Japanese television companies had a camera stand twice as high as any other country's. The same television companies had hired two of the three available sets of studios for the duration of the summit, leaving all the other participants to fight over the one remaining. The Japanese contingent had hired all the hire cars in Toronto fitted with mobile telephones. The others had to do without.

In 1987 Japanese capital investment was focused on the United States. Japan exports twice as much as to the United States as to the European Community, but the level of investment in the States is running at four times that in Europe. That balance will be redressed as the initial surge of investment matures. A pick-up in investment in Europe can be expected as 1992 and the Common Market approach, leaving Japan the major motivator and the major beneficiary of the initial move to create the common market. A later section of this chapter uses developments in the auto industry as a case study of how this set of factors is shaping investment decisions.

The counterpoint to the rapid build-up in Japanese wealth and financial holdings overseas has been the rapid growth of the United States trade deficit and its slide into net debtor status. External debt for the United States is now $264bn, 6% of gross national product. This compares with 41% for Australia, but American reserves are only 11% of imports, whereas Australian reserves are 47% of imports. There are serious doubts over the creditworthiness of the United States system, even before looking closely at horror stories like the Texan banking system and the savings and loans institutions.

THE DRAGONS AT THE SAMURAI'S HEEL

While Japan is investing in the United States and Europe to produce high-margin products in the wealthy developed country markets, there is a further shift going on closer to home. Investment in south-east Asian countries continues apace as Japanese manufacturers push component supplies off-shore. Countries like Korea, Taiwan and Thailand have currencies closely related to the US Dollar, so their labour costs have fallen sharply relative to Japanese as the Dollar has fallen. Japanese wealth is thus being spread among its satellites in a trend which is likely to continue, and to continue adding greater weight to the economies of the south-east Asian countries.

Those countries are, of course, not insignificant in their own right. Taiwan, Hong Kong, Singapore and South Korea all have gross national products per head greater than Portugal, for instance ($3,400, $6,800, $7,300 and $2,300 against $2,200). In the twenty-one years from 1965 to 1986, gross national product per head in Taiwan and South Korea rose at a compound rate of more than 6.5% per annum. Moreover, if the exports of those four countries are added together they amount to some 75% of total Japanese exports. If their imports are added together, they are greater than total Japanese imports. They are already major trading nations in their own right, and with the increasingly powerful role of Japan, they are set to become more so.

This implies a growing role for Japan as a major importer of manufactured goods. Indeed, part of the adjustment to a high yen has been a rapid growth in imports from neighbouring countries — a near doubling of imports from Hong Kong in 1987 — a growth which can be expected to continue. Although the United States has not benefited greatly in the Japanese market from a weaker dollar, European countries have done so. Purveyors of traditional European luxury goods like cars, clothing, perfume, jewellery and drinks have all prospered. This again is a sign of a nouveau riche, but it is a sure sign that there will be larger markets as the less well-off Japanese realise that they can buy imported products which are cheaper than home-made.

THE OLD WORLD REVIVES

THE WINDS OF CHANGE

As portentous and as historical as the growth of Japanese financial muscle is the development of the European Common Market. The closest parallel is that of the Zollverein among the German states of the nineteenth century, but the parallel is inadequate. The European Community includes four of the six largest non-Communist economies and, when a single market develops, will represent the largest consumer market in the world. The implications are breathtaking for the balance of economic and political power, and for the competitive strategy of every European enterprise.

Such changes have been sought since the Treaty of Rome was signed in 1957. Progress has been limited to date, so what has changed to make success a likelihood now? Two elements have changed to combine in the Commission's 'new approach'.

Previously the watchword was harmonization. This meant all states agreeing on industrial standards, on health and safety standards, on lawmaking. Endless detailed discussions meant a long and tortuous procedure for establishing standards that would be out of date by the time they were written. The new approach establishes the principles of mutual recognition rather than harmonization and of majority voting rather than consensus.

In the first place, the need for unanimity has been taken out of the equation. Whereas it used to be the case that a single state had the right of veto — the empty chair created by de Gaulle in the 1960s — that right has now been abrogated by the Single European Act passed in 1987. Henceforward decision-making is to be by qualified majority voting. One of the most sclerotic parts of the system has been revitalised.

In the second place, harmonization of standards has given way to a lowest common denominator approach. Since all countries have authorities which determine industrial and commercial standards for products and practices and, as a result, already have huge numbers of such standards, the Commission has decided that any product which meets the standards of its home country should be acceptable for sale in any of the other Community countries.

There are two major implications of this new approach. The first is that the gains it represents are irreversible. Having agreed to majority voting, member states are not able to backpedal to consensus. Having agreed to minimum standards, they have unleashed competitive market forces which create commercial imperatives that will take the initiative away from policy makers. This is the second major implication. There is now a framework for commercial enterprises to determine their strategic responses to the new environment, and it is one that is legally enforceable.

As early as 1978 a German company, Rewe Zentral AG, took the West German government to the European Court of Justice over its refusal to allow the import of Creme de Cassis. The reason given was that it did not contain enough alcohol to be deemed a liqueur. Effectively the court found that Germany was discriminating against foreign products. This principle has recently been reaffirmed twice in the European Court. The first case again involved West Germany and alcohol. This time the point at issue was the Reinheitsgebot, a mediaeval Bavarian law prohibiting beer from containing anything but hops and water.

Whereas German brewers were allowed to add preservatives to their own brew and export it, non-Germans could not do likewise in Germany for fear of damaging German health. Again, the court found effectively that this was a trade barrier rather than a health matter, so the German beer market was opened to foreign competition. In 1988 this finding was followed by one against the Italian government and its refusal to allow pasta sold in Italy to be made from anything but hard durum wheat. Once again the net effect was to find Italian standards protectionist, and to open the Italian pasta market to non-Italian companies with different products.

What is interesting about these last two cases is that they open up markets at the very core of the traditions and emotions of the two countries concerned. The principle has been well and truly established that only bona fide reasons of health and consumer protection will prevent the free passage of goods.

The adoption of a new strategic approach to the grand objective of a Common Market has lent new impetus to its achievement. It has gone hand-in-hand with the equally successful adoption of new tactics. To begin with, a specific date has been set for the Common Market. 1992 has become synonymous with the single European market. It is an indication of the successful presentation of the project that the British Government has spent millions of pounds advertising the 1992 project — even down to having a hotline with the number 1992 — without mentioning that the target is actually the end of 1992. To go with this specific date, precise targets have been defined. To be exact, there are 279 directives proposed, of which about 130 have been agreed. Each of these directives has a practical objective such as the liberalization of the road haulage industry, of the air transport industry, of the insurance industry.

To sum up, there is: a new approach through mutual recognition rather than harmonization; a new framework thanks to majority voting rather than consensus; and new tactics in the form of specific, detailed objectives with a clear deadline. This is the dynamic executive stuff of the new Europe.

MANAGING THE UNCERTAINTIES

The European Community has set out on an exhilarating adventure in the liberalization of markets, but what does this mean in the commercial market place? There can be only one certainty, and that is that change will be a constant for many years to come. The claim that the changes will affect the competitive strategy for every European enterprise may turn out to be too conservative, rather than too dramatic. It would be better to include in that claim any corporation that has aspirations to international business. This period of big changes brings with it big challenges, but also big opportunities, opportunities the like of which are seen only once in a lifetime. They depend on the kind of underlying changes which are more normally wrought by a disaster like war. The theme of this section is therefore managing the uncertainties, in the belief that it is one of the tasks of managers to identify the uncertainties and manipulate them by their own actions to increase the chances in their favour. To make their own luck.

The momentum built up behind the 1992 project is now unstoppable. The gains will not be reversed and their influence will grow rather than diminish. Sovereignty may fight back temporarily, but the most important point is that the changes are at the level of micro markets, not macro economic policy. Success and failure will be determined by a company's present competitive position and its response to the changes in the competitive environment in its own particular industry. This implies a need to focus in strategic terms, to decide what businesses the company should be in, and to build a strong competitive position in each of them. This is not as simple as it sounds, for it demands a new definition of what the market will be, and therefore what a strong competitive position will be. In the analysis of competitive position, it is essential to identify the determining factor behind the structure of the market. In the case of the European market that factor is now the regulatory changes coming out of Brussels. Foot-dragging will only delay the inevitable, not prevent it.

The nature of the changes is such that they affect the supply side of the market and the structure of the market. Liberalization of road haulage and reduction of paperwork at borders mean that it will be cheaper and quicker to get products to market. The removal of the need to alter a product for each of the twelve national markets will reduce the unit cost of production, and will allow further cost savings from economies of scale. Moreover, for new products, it will no longer be necessary to get certification from twelve different sources, and it will be possible to plan to sell into a single large market. This will make it considerably more attractive to bring new products to market more rapidly. Costs are set to fall and availability to increase. These benefits are not automatic, but they are made possible. They are now there for the taking and the rewards will go to those who do take them.

That is not the end of the story, however. While there may be considerable gains on the supply side of the market,it is not necessarily the case that anything will change on the demand side. Simply allowing any beer into Germany or any pasta into Italy does not of itself mean that German taste will take to foreign beer, or the Italian palate to foreign pasta. The normal determinants of success — the price factors in the quality/price ratio, and the non-price factors of design, snob-appeal, image — will continue to apply. The rewards will go to those with the marketing skills necessary to combine the supply side benefits with the demands of the market place, to meet present demand and to fashion new markets. Since this is a time of major change, there will also be considerable opportunity to develop new markets, to develop new competitive positions. It is here that the management of the uncertainties becomes a key competitive advantage.

The other side of this equation is the response of the competition. Since it only takes one company to change the competitive environment, there is only one possible aggressive strategy, and that is to act first. Since it only takes one competitor to realise this and to act on it, that means that virtually every European company is going to be affected. There are two main defensive strategies — to plan growth to become a large player in a large market, or to identify a niche market. Stasis will not be an option, since the definition of niche is almost certain to change. At the moment it can still be defined geographically in terms of a country, but it is highly unlikely that this will continue to be the case. Never has it been truer to say that the choice is to grow or to perish.

This analysis focuses on the immediate effects of the changes that are already in train as the Common Market develops. There will be a second stage that begins as the initial hectic pace of change starts to slow down. This is the longer-term series of effects resulting from having a large home market which is the real pot of gold that the European countries are searching for. As the single market takes hold of thinking, planning and acting industry by industry, it will have a decisive impact on the expectations of European businessmen. At such point as it becomes as instinctive to a European to consider all twelve countries as his home market as it is to an American to think in terms of the fifty states, then a new generation of European businesses will emerge. Their competitors will be less other Europeans than the corporate giants of Japan and the United States. It is for this reason that the development of the Common Market promises to have an impact on every enterprise with international ambitions.

GLOBAL COMPETITION

Just how strong the forces behind the European Common Market are is shown by a case study from an unlikely source. Rather than look at what European companies are doing, let us take the example of a Japanese manufacturer. The opportunities presented by the rapid development of the Common Market could scarcely come at a better time for Japanese companies. The corporate sector is facing global pressure to invest overseas as a result of both protectionism in foreign markets and extreme competition at home. The second half of the 1980s saw a big increase in capital investment in the United States. That wave is now maturing and the next largest market, Europe, beckons.

In February 1984 Nissan decided to build its Bluebird cars in Northern England. This decision has had profound repercussions and suggests the way that the Common Market is most likely to develop. It is a case study in the way businessmen have become the driving force behind its development. Nissan's decision was not originally inspired by the move to unify the European market. It was, in fact, taken before the 1985 White Paper was published. But it has played an important role in that unification. Nissan's search for a European base started in 1981 as part of management's strategy of establishing sales, production and design facilities in each of the three major Western markets — Europe, Japan and the United States.

Of the four large European economies, only Germany has no quantitative restrictions on imports of Japanese cars. The United Kingdom has a bilateral voluntary restraint agreement limiting Japanese car imports to 11% of the United Kingdom market. In France, Japanese imports account for 3% of the market and in Italy less than 1% with a quota of 2,500. In Ireland, by contrast, where there is no domestic car industry to protect, Japanese imports account for as much as 30% of the market. On average, imports from Japan represent about 10% of the European Community car market. Prospects for growth in market share were therefore good in Europe provided the important step of becoming an insider was taken. Here was the opportunity to carve a new market position, with the added advantage of British government assistance in the aftermath of the 1981 to 1982 recession.

Nissan's original targets have been revised upwards as the project has developed. By 1991 production of 100,000 Bluebirds a year is planned. This will double in 1993, the additional 100,000 coming from the Micra range of small cars. The initial intention was to produce only Bluebirds. Of the 200,000 cars, 50% are to be exported to the rest of Europe, with the British plant the sole source of Bluebirds for 12 European markets. The question of local content had been agreed at the outset with the United Kingdom government. The target was for Bluebirds to contain 60% local content by 1988 and 80% by 1991, thus making possible their export as British products to other European Community member countries, and thereby escaping the restrictions on Japanese imports.

United Kingdom production by Nissan has put pressure on rival manufacturers. Both Honda and Toyota have been forced to follow Nissan into production in the European Community because Nissan's production in Britain will enable it to gain market share unhampered by the various bilateral agreements that set ceilings on Japan's car exports there. Not only that. Manufacturing in the Community gives Nissan access to highly protected markets like France and Italy, assuming it will be relatively easy to increase its share of these markets. Nissan would thus be in a stronger market position and with better growth prospects than would be available to either of its main domestic rivals. In retrospect, Nissan's decision unilaterally changed the whole competitive structure of the European car market.

From the European point of view the situation is more complex. Outside competition will threaten the strategic base of European car manufacturers for the first time. There are already too many producers with too much capacity in the European car industry, despite several years of record sales. The pressure to rationalize is already growing, as demonstrated by Ford's take-over of Jaguar, GM's of Saab, and the Volvo-Renault tie-up. The most vulnerable to Japanese competition is Fiat of Italy. It has the second largest share of the European car market after Volkswagen, but that share is heavily dependent on the Italian market — the most protected from Japanese competition. Fiat has 60% of the Italian market and this accounts for 70% of the company's sales. This has been its strength, but in a new competitive environment it could become its Achilles heel.

The move also puts pressure on the governments of France and Italy. Their first response was to count Nissan's British-built cars as part of the Japanese quota. This was a direct challenge to the British government's support of Nissan and it duly accepted the challenge, fighting on behalf of the company for free access to European markets. A stand-off was inevitable while the argument shifted through specific definitions of local content to general questions of the European Community's view of the structure of the post-1992 car market. But the whole picture changed following three announcements. The first was a decision that the argument over local content was largely spurious. If an integrated market was to have any meaning, cars built in the United Kingdom should be sold freely throughout Europe. The second and third announcements were by Honda and Toyota that they too would build plants in Britain. It had become painfully clear to France and Italy that they were facing the worst of all worlds, namely that there would be European-built

Japanese cars which they could not keep out of their markets, without their having any benefit of the manufacturing plants in their own countries. This threat promptly became reality when Toyota further announced that it was to build its European engine plant in the United Kingdom also (both Honda and Nissan already had engine plants in the country).

The British government has made a clean sweep of the big three Japanese auto makers' investment and governments are being put on notice that further obstructionism will not only prove futile, but even damaging to the very industries they are trying to protect. There is also likely to be a painful lesson for the European car industry as Japanese production in Europe increases in the 1990s. Market success will go to companies that produce quality cars at affordable prices. This is the simple but powerful lesson of 1992.

The factors behind the decisions by Toyota and Honda to build in Britain were complex, but an important one was the willingness of the British government to fight on behalf of Nissan. Effectively it was also a fight for a freely functioning market and the outcome has changed both its regulatory and its competitive structure. It is important to remember that these developments in the Community reflect the dynamics of the global car market. Despite all the protectionism, the car industry is more influenced by worldwide factors than most other industries, and any developments in the European market must first fit into that global framework. The pace and scale of change caused by the 1992 process will vary from product to product, depending on the structure of each different product market.

The issue of market access for Japanese cars produced within Europe seems to be resolved, so the discussion has moved on to the even more vexing question of how to respond to imports from outside the Community. It will, of course, no longer be possible to maintain bilateral or unilateral restrictions on imports. They will be rendered obsolete by leakage from one country to another. So what should replace them? Should targets be set as a percentage of the total European market? Should European cars built in the United States be included in the import quotas on Japan?

Discussions of such tough issues continue with the European Commission leaning toward open markets and national governments toward preserving some form of protection, even if only for a limited period. Meanwhile in the car industry the battle for markets has moved on to details of competitive strategy. In January 1990 Toyota announced it would set up a trading subsidiary in Italy — no doubt further concentrating the minds of Fiat's executives.

MARKET FORCES

The 1980s were ushered in after a decade of oil shocks and stagflation. They started with new political personalities, a new political economy in the form of monetarism and a sharp recession in the West. The 1990s start with political upheaval, the end of a political economy and (for Poland at least) a massive recession in the East. The political agenda is being set by the collapse of Communist governments in Eastern Europe. Just when superlatives had been exhausted on the change of relative status between Japan and the United States, then revivified for use on the European Community, unthinkable changes pull the Soviet bloc apart. The scale and speed of the changes have been breathtaking. How to make sense of the world being turned upside down in this way? The one great consolation is that the changes can be approached in a pragmatic way. What the new business environment amounts to is letting markets operate. So many of the changes in the West were aimed at precisely this in the 1980s, that it is possible to see the same pattern emerging in the East.

Regardless of the personalities, who seem to change by the day, there is one constant which allows rational analysis. Micro markets — product markets — are where change is really generated for business corporations. Political and macroeconomic factors fertilise the ground, but the sowing, reaping and marketing is still done by businessmen. Japan's ability to grow faster than the United States has been achieved by competition in a series of individual markets. Even today, average productivity in the United States is virtually twice that in Japan — but not in the auto industry or in consumer electronics. The development of the European Common Market will evolve through a host of common product markets. The example of Nissan shows how the developing common market in cars is inextricably linked to the existing world car market. So as the Eastern Europe pot boils over into the fire which is forging the European Community, sanity lies in a cold analysis of how the market is changing.

BEST OF TIMES, WORST OF TIMES

These interesting times in which we live are also the best of times and the worst of times. Major changes are taking place which promise to alter the face of the economic world. They are also major opportunities for those who identify them and, at the detailed level, help to fashion them. Japan has arrived in manufacturing terms, now comes the financial strength. Europe is rearranging itself in a series of changes whose implications will only become clear over many years. The trend to worldwide competition will continue, focussing at the industry level on the relative changes in national competitiveness.

ROBERT Z. BROOKE

BZW International Equities

1.2 The Changing International Order

Global society is changing at an accelerating pace. It is doing so under the impact of accelerating technological and scientific advances.

Any forecasting which relies on financial trends or political analyses, yet fails to take into account technological developments, is bound to assess the future wrongly. The continuing advances in biomedical, photovoltaic, information and communications technology, for example, mean that pension funds are under threat, the value of oil will continue to decline, and the Soviet bloc countries, and others, will continue to democratize.

This chapter will look at the following areas:

(1) the democratization of the communicative society and its relation to the Soviet Union;
(2) the shift in confrontation from an East-West axis to a North-South axis;
(3) the problems for OPEC countries as the price of oil continues to erode;
(4) the general improvement in global productivity;
(5) the China factor;
(6) Sub-Sahara — the global black spot;
(7) the continued integration of the global economy and its political consequences.

THE DEMOCRATIZATION OF THE COMMUNICATIVE SOCIETY

Overview. The extent to which a country's political organization democratizes reflects three major factors:

(1) the extent and efficiency of its communications systems;
(2) the extent and efficiency of its education system; and, related to that,
(3) the rise of the information operative as the dominant form of labour.

These factors are technologically based. The technological base of the Southern European states — Greece, Portugal and Spain — was such that, in the 1970s, they democratized. Similar developments have overtaken Soviet bloc countries and countries such as Korea.

THE COMMUNICATIVE ERA

The increase in the availability to state authorities of ever more sophisticated computers, sensors and a wide variety of monitoring devices would appear to favour the view that the world might slip into the 1984 condition foreseen by George Orwell. For example, Soviet authorities had at their command increasingly efficient electronic devices for monitoring dissident activities. However the organization of society, including its political system, involves much more than the electronic gadgetry available to its police forces.

Orwell got it wrong: Television, instead of becoming a device whereby Big Brother spied on his people, became a device enabling citizens to spy on their leaders. In the West every night of the week one sees politicians, trade union leaders, corporation executives, government officials, foundation heads, film makers and many others, explaining their decisions or actions. Leaders have become accountable to the public via the media, and the most powerful of the media is television. Television is not only national, and increasingly transnational, but it allows the viewer to monitor the facial expressions and other components of the human signalling system.

If microelectronics has provided computers and electronic eaves-dropping to facilitate state control, it has also changed the flows of information to such an extent that the state itself, as an institution, has become unable to control the system from the centre. This is one of the paradoxes of the communicative era.

During the second half of the twentieth century — beginning with the United States, Japan and the more affluent European states — Western society slipped into this new historical era. It is not the purpose of this chapter to review all the cultural aspects of this phenomenon. These have been covered by both the present and other authors (see the bibliography at the end of this chapter), as have the economic consequences — the rise of a post-industrial or, more accurately, the information economy.

THE EVOLVING STATE

From the point of view of the state as an institution, there are three factors which force its further democratization:

(1) the creation of an extensive, powerful yet leaky communications network;
(2) the rise of the information operative as the dominant form of labour;
(3) the emergence of an advanced education system in response to the needs of the above which, in turn, fosters the evolution towards democratization.

The communications infrastructure can be measured quantitatively in terms of the per capita number of radios, television sets, telephones, telex and fax machines, tape recorders, record players, newspapers, periodicals, books, radio and television stations, photocopying machines and communications satellites as well as the number of hours spent watching television, the attendances at theatres or concerts, the number of private automobiles, the passengers on intercity railways, the number of tourists moving into and out of the country, the number of books published, the radio broadcasts and the television programmes.

As countries evolve from an agrarian to a mechanical and then to the communicative era, the communications infrastructure continues to grow, both in size and complexity. At the same time it becomes more and more difficult to control the flows of information from the centre. Sometimes a new technology enters a pre-communicative society with remarkable consequences. For example, the Shah of Iran kept a tight control over the press, radio and television. He overlooked cheap, portable tape recorders which carried the Ayatollah's message from mosque to mosque. The microelectronic revolution has provided not only cheap tape recorders, but also relatively cheap citizen's radio, cheap photocopiers, cheap computers and cheap printers — a range of cheap information providers.

When it is no longer possible to control information flows from the centre it becomes almost impossible to control public opinion. The emergence of a significant body of public opinion opposing a regime on any specific issue places an authoritarian regime in a predicament. Either it follows public opinion or it becomes repressive. In the first instance it cedes decision-making power, in the second it alienates support and, as the Greek colonels discovered in the early 1970s, there is a limit to how often one can do that. A good, first-order approximation of a country's communications infrastructure may be obtained by noting the number of telephones per capita. With minor exceptions (such as Bermuda) the figure normally represents a first-order indicator of the extent to which a country has moved from a mechanical era society to a communicative one. For example the United States has close to ten times the number of telephones per capita as the Soviet Union. Given an approximate doubling of the telephones in about a decade, the United States is about three decades ahead of the Soviet Union in terms of its communications infrastructure. The United States began to show signs of moving into the communicative era during the 1950s while the Soviet Union is only now entering this era.

The second, and even more important factor in the evolution of the modern state is the nature of a country's workforce. Is it made up principally of farm workers and domestic servants, of factory workers, or of information operatives? It is the rise of the information operatives as the largest group of labour which, coupled to an extensive communications infrastructure, makes it impossible to control the flows of information from the centre. Mechanical era organizations tend to be hierarchical, with one person at the top and various levels of authority and responsibility below. The flows of information tend to move vertically from bottom to top and back. Lateral information flows are only sporadic and often discouraged. It is because one group or department does not know what the other is doing that each group must rely on the chief for decision-making. A good chief instils loyalty to the organization, as well as a trust in his wisdom to make the correct decisions for the benefit of the organization as a whole. Underlings, kept in the dark, have no way of judging the chief's wisdom or even his honesty. If they feel their welfare is tied to the welfare of the organization, they will accede to the chief's decision and may challenge it only if such a decision affects them directly in an adverse manner. Even then, in their ignorance, they may be wholly ineffective in knowing whether or what to challenge. Communicative era organizations depend on the effective interactions of specialists and other high-level information operatives forming a pool of information. Flows of information tend to be lateral and the organization is much more egalitarian, with leadership changing in response to the need to solve different types of problems or to achieve different tasks. These changes in information flows occur at the national state level as well as at the small company level. They are the consequence of the information explosion and the pre-eminence of information as the most important single input into the modern production system, more important than land, labour or capital, or even materials and energy. It is the pre-eminence of information as an input which accounts for the rise of information operatives as the dominant form of labour.

Modern productive systems involve a complex interaction of land, labour, capital, machinery, energy and material inputs, coupled to equally complex transport, communication and distribution systems. To get these various factors properly organized required a host of *organization* operatives, that is, managers. They represent one kind of information operative. Another kind is involved with the *transmission of information* — secretaries, telephone operators, postal workers, journalists and others working in the mass media, educators of all sorts, and technical salesmen. A third category is involved with *information storage and retrieval* — filing clerks, librarians, computer programmers. A relatively small number is involved in *creating new information* or patterns of information — scientists, artists, statisticians, architects, designers. A fifth category *applies information* in order to solve specific problems — lawyers, doctors, counsellors, accountants. Lastly there is a large group of information operatives who are not normally considered part of the labour force (but historically used to be) — people who make their living *receiving information* — students.

The rise of the information operative as the dominant form of labour has profound political implications. It is not merely that white collar workers, managers, technicians and professionals may vote differently from farmers or manual works. It is more basic than that. The whole fibre of society has changed and, as a result, so have its political institutions. For example, contrast the educational level of peasants with that of the post-industrial operatives. Today's modern farmer tends to be a manager with a university degree, running an agri-business. Similarly, the blue collar worker on the factory floor is becoming a white-coated engineer qualified to supervise a robotized assembly line. Nor do the levels of education tell the whole story. A peasant ploughing his field has very little reason to communicate with another peasant in order to get his job done. A machine operative on the factory floor may need to confer with his mates on the assembly line, but there is no need to go beyond that. In contrast, information operatives are continuously writing each other letters and memoranda, calling each other on the telephone, sending faxes, attending committee meetings, seminars and conferences. Their tools are the pencil and the telephone, or their extensions — pens, chalk, typewriter, word processor, teletext, radio, TV, printing press, satellites and the rest.

It is easy to mystify and bully peasants. It is less easy to do so with factory workers, and it becomes very difficult to mystify information operatives — one can only bully them. No one wants to be sent into exile, go to jail or face torture or death; therefore most people play by the rules of the official game. The rules, however, become increasingly corrupted because they are backed neither by informed judgment nor by a social consensus.

Authoritarianism thrives on ignorance. It is probable that, for pre-industrial and early industrial societies, large, heterogeneous populations can be welded into a single state only by means of a coercive, central authority. For Third World countries, moving from agrarian to mechanical era societies, one can expect only more authoritarianism — some progressive, some benign, some purely predatory or parasitic. If a country is lucky it gets a Jawaharlal Nehru, if unlucky an Idi Amin. For countries moving out of the mechanical into the communicative era, the opposite holds. Their condition is incompatible with authoritarianism — they democratize.

During the 1970s, the Southern European states of Greece, Portugal and Spain were overtaken by the communicative era. They democratized. In each case the trigger for change differed. For Greece it was the confrontation with Turkey over Cyprus; for Portugal the revolt of army officers exposed to a no-win war in Angola and Mozambique; and for Spain the death of Franco. One should not confuse the trigger for a change of *administration* with the deeper causes which change political *institutions*. If the evolutionary processes affected the political institutions of Southern Europe in the 1970s, they affected countries such as Korea and those of the Soviet bloc in the 1980s.

IMPACT ON THE SOVIET UNION

The author has for some time forecast the liberalization of the Soviet political system in the late 1980s. The forecast was based on the argument presented above that societies evolve as a result of the basic changes in technology which force people to do things differently and which impose changes upon all existing cultural institutions.

THE DEMOCRATIZATION OF THE SOVIET UNION

In the late 1980s Western analysts were still trying to decide whether the rise of Gorbachev merely represented a stroke of luck, or whether he was here to stay. Such ambivalent analyses overlooked the fundamental historical dynamic which, over the long run, in spite of temporary setbacks, favoured the progressive forces.

In the 1990s, as forecast earlier, the Soviet Union will be buffeted by two opposing sets of forces: One integrative, the other destabilizing. The integrative forces are dependent on the move into a communicative-era style, post-industrial economy. It was these same forces which, in the 1970s, democratized the Southern tier European states and, in the 1980s, forced the nation states of Western Europe into an ever more integrated European Community — a process which is accelerating in the 1990s.

A parallel situation is developing in the Soviet Union. The various Republics comprising the Union are becoming economically, increasingly interdependent. At the same time, in many of these republics, the nationalism — suppressed for so long — is re-emerging with a fervour bordering on fanaticism.

This is the destabilizing force: The Soviet Union is not an integrated country like the United States or China. Tribalism and nationalism are endemic in the Republics and in Soviet society. The Baltic States, deprived of independent nationhood only a generation ago, the 30 to 50 million Moslems and an equal number of Russian Orthodox Christians, the Armenians, Azerbaijanis, Georgians, Kazakhs, Mongols, Tartars, Ukrainians, Uzbekis and so forth, all are capable of exhibiting intense nationalistic feelings.

The second instability inherent in the Soviet political system is what has been termed intra-structural dissent. Structural dissent reflects the general demoralization of a country and exhibits itself in absenteeism, alcoholism, corruption, nepotism, petty crimes such as pilfering, a generally indifferent or poor performance at work and in other similar ways. It is both aggravated by, and contributes to, a country's poor economic performance. Structural dissent may be so widespread that, if there develops any kind of crisis which challenges the authority of the government, no one will lift a finger to save it. As with the expulsion of Khrushchev, or of the Greek colonels, loss of power can occur in a matter of hours as a new regime or structure appears.

Ironically, it was the desire to combat structural dissent and a decaying economy which provided the rationale for *glasnost* and *perestroika*. Gorbachev understood the need to reverse the economic stagnation of the Brezhnev era. In his book, *Perestroika*, he pointed out that: 'In the last fifteen years the national income growth rates had declined by more than half and by the beginning of the eighties had fallen to a level close to economic stagnation.' Part of his strategy involved drastically reducing Soviet military spending by reversing the arms race, normalizing relations with the West, pulling out of Afghanistan and Eastern Europe, and improving relations with China. These foreign policy initiatives, coupled to his enlightened leadership at home made him immensely popular with the West.

Unfortunately, the continuing poor performance of the Soviet Union's economy during the transition from state capitalism to a private market economy, has cost Gorbachev dearly at home. The author revisited the Soviet Union in January 1990. His impression of developments, at that time, were that *glasnost* was working while *perestroika* was not.

Glasnost was easy to observe — even to a casual tourist in Moscow. Whereas in earlier years it was almost impossible to get the *Intourist* guides to talk about anything controversial, even in private, now they were prepared to discuss a wide range of topics with the rest of the tourists on the coach, using their microphone, apparently not inhibited in the slightest by the presence of the driver and, on occasion, other guides. The epitome was the joke told as the Intourist bus passed the KGB headquarters: 'And on your right hand, ladies and gentlemen are the Headquarters of the KGB. This is the tallest building in Moscow.' The guide paused to let the puzzled tourists peer at a building that didn't seem any taller than a lot of other buildings around the square before adding: 'This may not be immediately apparent — but they say you can see Siberia from the basement!'

It was interesting to find out the attitude of the guides; when asked about the possible secession of various Republics from the Soviet Union, their reaction ranged from indifference, to strong support. One guide suggested that Russia itself should secede from the Soviet Union. 'We'd all be a lot better off', was her comment.

Guides may not represent the opinions of the average Muscovite. They are better educated, must speak at least one foreign language and are in continuous contact with foreigners. Nevertheless, it is significant that none of the guides expressed shock or horror at the idea of various Republics leaving the Soviet Union. When asked about *perestroika*, and whether it was working, all the guides replied that it was *not*. This was also true in Leningrad. There were fewer goods in the shops than ever before, and the queues were longer than ever. One person complained: 'I'm tired of spending most of my life waiting in a queue.'

When it came to explaining the reason for this failure, everybody had a different answer, although two major themes emerged. One was sabotage. Under the old guard, all the people involved in transporting and distributing foodstuffs, and other goods, got a cut. Under the new system, they did not. So they were very slow in unloading wagons and lorries, causing much rotting and spoilage. The other theme blamed Gorbachev for incompetence. This attitude was illustrated by the following story.

'Imagine a train carrying the Soviet leadership comes to a halt because a flash flood has washed away the tracks. What would have been the response of the various leaders? Lenin would have organized a series of working parties to get the tracks repaired as quickly as possible. Stalin would have had the crew shot. Brezhnev would have pulled down the shades and said: "Comrades, let's pretend the train is still moving", and Gorbachev would have pulled the shades back up and shouted: "Help, help! The train has stopped." But that is all.'

By 1990, Gorbachev was a lot less popular at home than he was abroad. The extent of economic chaos was plainly visible to any observant tourist. Several incidents illustrate this. The official exchange rate in Moscow in January 1990 was approximately 1 ruble = 1 pound sterling. At the *Intourist* hotel, however, the author regularly received 10 rubles per pound — even though the paperwork appeared to indicate a 1:1 ratio. On the street, it would have been possible to get 15:1, or even 20:1, for a British pound. All hard currency was sought after; however, US dollars were most popular. Another powerful form of currency proved to be packs of cigarettes — particularly, for some reason, Marlboro. Taxi drivers didn't want rubles, only hard currency (or cigarettes). At all the usual tourist spots, tourists were accompanied by numerous touts trying to change money, sell watches, rabbit fur hats, T-shirts, caviar and much else. Moscow had become as bad as Marrakech.

The quest for hard currency is so pervasive that, on numerous occasions, fellow tourists bought what was clearly pilfered state property from a variety of enterprises. Such pilfered property was not only bought from black marketeers, or other middle-men, but directly from the employees working at such state-run enterprises. Organized crime is rampant, involving extensive inter-city syndicates, probably with international connections. The author witnessed one arrest of a member of a tourist organization who, apparently, was using her inter-city business travelling as a cover for transporting illicit goods.

If one remembers that the economic chaos in Europe in the 1920s led to Mussolini and Hitler, one cannot but feel uncomfortable about all this. In fact, the perceived turmoil in the Soviet Union is so great that some Western analysts are suggesting the possibility of civil war. A report in the *International Herald Tribune* (21 March 1990) quotes Peter Frank, a Sovietologist at Essex University, as saying that '*perestroika* is at an end' and suggests three scenarios: (1) Gorbachev manages to hold together a Soviet Union, with some republics breaking away; (2) The Soviet Union disintegrates slowly with political authority and the economy collapsing; and (3) Factional rivalries escalate into civil war. Frank considers the first of these the least likely.

The present author, for reasons indicated above, believes that although some republics, in particular the Baltic Republics, may leave the Union, the majority have nowhere to go. Who is Azerbaijan going to trade with? Iran? That is, even if certain Republics achieve political autonomy, post-industrial economic pressures will continue to drive them back into a collective, just as the traditional European nation states are being driven into a collective (the European Community). Ultimately, in fact, the Soviet bloc countries and the European Community will integrate, but not until we are well into the 21st century.

The present author also rejects the historical analogy: The Soviet Union of the 1980s and 1990s is not equivalent to the Europe of the 1920s and 1930s. The half century, or so, beginning with World War I, in which Western Europe moved from the Mechanical to the Communicative Era represents a 'Little Dark Age'. The Soviet bloc countries are now leaving this period behind and entering the Communicative Era. The historical dynamics are entirely different. Given Gorbachev's new presidential powers, and given his innate managerial and political competence, he stands a good chance of surviving. At least part of that survival will depend on his ability to persuade the Soviet people of two things: (1) that he *is* an effective leader able to achieve the generally desired goals of *perestroika*; and (2) that they must be patient. If he fails on either count he will be displaced. But who, or what, would displace him?

Not Ligachev or his partocratic supporters; there will be no going back. But the way forward could become very messy. The worst scenario is a series of ineffectual liberal leaders creating further disorganization until, finally, the system breaks down to the extent that there would be a take-over by the military (already disgruntled by their down-grading), or some other right-wing group. Such an authoritarian system (though of limited life span) could regenerate a whole new spiral of East-West mistrust and a renewed arms race.

The most desirable scenario would be the emergence of a competent technocratic leadership — with or without Gorbachev — which manages to solve the economic problems and create a truly democratic confederation of Soviet republics. Such a system would rapidly lead to a further integration of Soviet and Western countries into the global economic system. This is certainly the aim of Leonid Abalkin, deputy prime minister, and Gorbachev's top economic adviser. Abalkin, highly respected in Soviet liberal circles, is quoted as saying that unless the Soviet Union carries out drastic reforms leading to a regulated market economy, it will deprive 'the country, ourselves and our children of the opportunity to live in a developed, efficient economy' (*The Guardian*, 10 April, 1990). In any case, in the long run, that is exactly what is going to happen. With a bit of luck, the process will be well on its way by the turn of the century. In the meantime, the Soviet people will have to tighten their belts, and restrain their passions.

WHAT THE WEST CAN DO TO HELP

First, Western governments must understand the situation. Any improvement in the economy — making *perestroika* work — favours the democratic forces and a furthering of globalization of the economy. On the other hand, a breakdown of the economy will inevitably lead to authoritarianism which could easily lead to a resumption of East-West rivalries. The former presages a period of peace and profitable trade, the latter, more conflict and economic waste. Western governments must therefore do all they can to help the Soviet Union move smoothly and rapidly through this transition phase.

Second, Western businessmen must organize Soviet private enterprises. An excellent model is provided by the McDonald hamburger chain — the largest McDonald hamburger restaurant in the world was opened in Moscow in January of 1990. It seats about 2,000 customers, and the queues outside were estimated at 5,000. It is expected to be the biggest and most profitable of all the McDonald restaurants in the world. However, the money cannot be taken out directly. The establishment of this particular unit represents the best in free market enterprise, and enlightened managerial and organizational skills. To assure the quality and reliability of their supplies, the company has leased land in the Soviet Union on which to raise selected beef and dairy herds, and grow their own potatoes, wheat and other supplies. In addition, the company has organized its own transportation and other service systems. An agreement with the Soviet authorities allows McDonald's to pay all its employees standard wages — but 20% in US dollars. Needless to say, jobs with the company are highly sought after, allowing the company to select highly qualified employees. Even though the profits cannot be taken out of the country as cash at this point, McDonald's has the opportunity of building up large assets for future production when, at some point in the future, the Soviet economy has become integrated into the global economy and, currently, for the purchase of goods and commodities exportable to the West.

Multinationals can play an enormous, positive role in the recovery of the economy. As with McDonald's, three categories of benefits can accrue to the Soviets: The injection of foreign capital, the creation of a new productive enterprise, and the transfer of technical and managerial skills. Properly organized, joint ventures should yield substantial benefits to all parties concerned.

THE CHANGING AXIS OF INTERNATIONAL CONFRONTATION

OVERVIEW

In due course the political liberalization of the Soviet Union will lead to a mixed economy, the normalizing of relations with the West and an integration into the community of free trading nations. In the meantime the continued instability of many Third World countries, and, in particular, the militant nationalism of many Moslem countries, could lead to a new confrontation. Early in the next century the centre of economic gravity may also have shifted significantly from the North Atlantic to the Western Pacific.

THE FUTURE OF EAST-WEST RELATIONS

As stated above, one of the major foreign policy objectives of a democratized Soviet Union is the normalization of relations with the West. Assuming an improved economic performance, as well as a substantial privatization of much of the Soviet economy, the possibilities for trade become enormous. Such developments also presage a diminution in the Cold War, which will wither away. This will not mean a total disarmament of the superpowers, but defence expenditures will be cut substantially. This, in turn, will release huge financial resources as well as managerial and technical personnel (40% of the world's scientists are engaged in defence research). It is not clear how much public money will be diverted into cuts in taxes, expanding education, rebuilding the decaying inner cities of the West, expanding welfare programmes, providing aid for developing countries, expanding space exploration or engaging in other programmes. A great part of current defence spending is purely consumption, involving outlays of funds which yield no economic return. Therefore almost any movement of financial resources to other sectors of the economy is likely to provide a significant stimulus to the economy, yet be less inflationary.

This will be even more pronounced for the Soviet economy. Thus within ten to fifteen years the Soviet bloc countries are likely to present a high technology economy with a rising consumer market. These countries will pose both a challenge and an opportunity for Western economies.

THE NEW THREAT

European history has shown that, in a pre-communicative society, economic adversity or backwardness coupled to rising expectations results in political instability. Political instability tends to favour the rise of fanatical or tyrannical leaders.

Before the end of the century, the major threat to world peace will shift from an East-West confrontation to a North-South split. The most aggressive, and potentially the greatest, threat will result from the militant nationalism of Moslem countries. Whether this force will manifest itself in its present form, which sets one country off against another, or whether there emerges a leader able to unit a pan-Arab, or even a pan-Moslem, movement is not clear.

For the moment, the most immediate threats are military dictatorships such as that of Iraq. President Saddam Hussein runs one of the most brutal states in the world. He has been building up its nuclear capability since 1975 when he obtained enriched uranium for a reactor from the French. A 1976 agreement with Italy enabled Iraq to produce weapons-grade plutonium. In June of 1981, shortly before the reactor was to go hot, the Israelis sent fighter bombers to destroy the Osiik nuclear installation north of Baghdad. It was a serious setback to President Saddam. However, the Iraqis were able to salvage 25 pounds of enriched uranium after the bombing.

The project has continued since then and has been expanded to develop nuclear missiles. A joint project with Egypt — known as Badr-2000 — and with Argentina, known as Condor-2, is to develop medium-range surface-to-surface missiles. It was at the Iraqi military area south of Baghdad at All-Hillah, that the Observer reporter Farsad Bazoft was arrested for taking soil samples. Bazoft was executed and was never allowed diplomatic contact. Although no reports appeared in the Western press other than the outrage of executing a reporter, there can be little doubt that Bazoft uncovered something which could have been a great embarrassment to the Iraqi government. On 28 March 1990, customs officials at London's Heathrow airport arrested a number of people who were involved in smuggling nuclear triggers to Iraq.

It must be clear from the preceding paragraphs that Iraq is rapidly developing a nuclear capability and will be, with Pakistan, a major military power with nuclear capability. What is so disturbing about the Iraqi situation is that the government did not hesitate to use poison gas against Iran and, worse, against its own Kurdish citizens when it felt it was to its advantage to do so.

In those Muslim countries which are making substantial economic progress, there will arise a middle class which will act as a buffer against both tyranny and strident fundamentalism. We have seen a more moderate democratic government emerge in Pakistan. It is probable, though not certain (particularly if Pakistan gets sucked into ethnic conflicts to its east, west, or north), that Pakistan will continue its economic progress and maintain political stability. Sudan, on the other hand, became a fundamentalist republic in the late 1980s. The fundamentalist National Islamic Alliance led by Hassan Turabi masterminded a coup which put General Bashir in power. It is an Ayatollah-type regime intent on imposing a strict Moslem code on the north of Sudan and trying to conquer and subdue the non-Moslem south. The regime finds little favour with business groups, the intelligentsia and other members of upper middle class society, some of whom, in fact, believe that General Bashir's regime is installing a new *jahiliyah* — the age of ignorance which preceded

Islam. This is clearly not a regime which will last for ever, but insofar as it controls the tanks it can severely impede further progress and may well represent that trend in the Muslim world most to be feared by the West.

Thus, over the next two decades there could emerge the awesome spectacle of a Moslem fundamentalism coupled to nuclear weapons with a global crescent of religious fervour stretching from West Africa to Indonesia. The only thing which would prevent a super-Ayatollah from launching his primitive nuclear arsenal in a holy war against the infidels would be the superpowers' more sophisticated micro-electronic weaponry which would be able to neutralize such a strike in-flight, or perhaps even pre-flight at the launch pad, rather than in retaliation alone.

In general, however, Arab power, both political and economic, will decline as oil declines in importance. The imponderable factor at this point is the rate of cultural change in Arab and other Mid-Eastern countries. If economic conditions continue to improve, and education levels with them, there is hope for a peaceful transition. If not, the turbulence which has characterized the last two decades will continue. The Western country under greatest threat, of course, is Israel. However the situation could easily escalate into a North-South conflict.

Authoritarian, and in particular, fanatical fundamentalist regimes are likely to push nuclear buttons when things go sufficiently against them. This possibility constitutes a grave threat to the future, not only of the Middle-East, but to the world as a whole. At a minimum, the rest of us would catch the fall-out. An enlightened joint East-West policy, aimed at enforcing peace, could avoid such a nuclear disaster. However, such an East-West peace plan must not merely look at the military aspects — involving an arms embargo, and possibly even a direct military peace keeping intervention — but must also concentrate on building up the region's economy and, in particular, upgrading its education infrastructure.

THE DECLINE OF OPEC

OVERVIEW

The political and economic power of the Organization of Petroleum Exporting Countries (OPEC) is based on the value of oil. That value will decline as alternative energy sources continue to exert strong competitive pressures. Coal and gas have made significant inroads. In the 1990s, the price of photovoltaic devices will continue to come down to alter the global energy picture. What will save OPEC countries from economic chaos is a shift in production from crude oil to advanced petrochemicals. This process has begun and presages an adjustment of the petrochemical industry in the West. The second economic strategy for most OPEC countries under threat is to develop photovoltaic systems to make the deserts bloom — a matter which will be discussed later.

THE PRICE OF OIL

During the post-war period, from the late 1940s onwards, modern industry relied increasingly on oil. Oil became economically the most desirable way to provide the increasing energy demands of industry, transportation and for electricity generation. It was plentiful, relatively clean, easy to handle and easy to store; it was also cheap. By the late 1960s, however, the rate at which oil consumption was increasing was clearly outstripping the rate at which new oil sources were being discovered. The economics of oil was shifting from a buyer's market to a seller's market. By the 1970s the matter became increasingly critical as oil consumption continued to increase.

Then came the oil price shocks of 1973-1974 and 1979-1980. The responses to these price rises manifested themselves in several different ways.

(1) The rising cost of oil drove up the prices of numerous products and services. This reduced consumption, or at least decelerated growth, bringing about a general decline in economic activity — the recession which reduced oil consumption. This represents the cyclic component of the price of oil.

(2) Sources of oil, previously unprofitable, began to be explored and tapped. North Sea oil wells, whose production costs were several hundred per cent higher than those of Saudi Arabia or the Gulf States, made no sense in the mid-1960s. However by the mid-1970s they made so much sense that, as the oil began to flow, the pound rose in value, almost by half against the dollar in four years.

(3) Energy conservation represented the third response. Governments provided grants and other incentives to industry and householder alike. Some governments passed laws that no new houses were to be built without double glazing. A new host of energy consultants appeared. By the early 1980s electricity consumption was actually declining in some countries.

(4) Alternative energy sources became increasingly important. Brazil experimented with running automobiles on alcohol. Many countries reintroduced coal for electricity generation, often in a new form which was environmentally more acceptable. Those that were lucky to have access to it used natural gas.

All of these responses combined so that by early 1983 the glut of oil caused the market to shift once again in favour of the buyer. OPEC, almost in disarray, was forced to drop the price of oil. Since then the price of oil has stabilized. This trend will continue until sufficient potential customers are persuaded that the price is right and the long-term supply is sufficiently reliable to warrant becoming, once again, increasingly reliant on oil. At that point the price of oil might start moving upwards again.

There are, however, technological alternatives which could put further pressure on oil prices.

THE RISE OF PHOTOVOLTAIC CELLS

Photovoltaic cells are devices which convert light (photons) into electricity (volts). The development of photovoltaic cells is closely linked to both fundamental solid-state physics and the semiconductor technology which produced the silicon chip. In 1954 Bell Telephone Laboratories, originator of the transistor, devised the modern photovoltaic solar cell. The new cells were made from single crystals of silicon, doped to give them the right electronic properties. A solar energy conversion efficiency of about 10% was achieved although the theoretical maximum is closer to 25%.

The first international conference on solar energy was held in 1956. The new solar cells generated considerable excitement, but their economics were terrible — it would have cost $200 to generate 1 watt of electricity in full sunlight.

The launching of the first Sputnik in 1957 saved the solar cells from temporary extinction. When the United States entered the space race, costs became no more important than in the arms race. Solar photovoltaic cells were ideal for providing the small amounts of power needed for the early satellites. The learning curve was beginning. NASA and the United States Department of Defense began spending about $2m a year on photovoltaic power supplies. By 1968 about $25m had been spent (peanuts compared to the $500m spent by that time on trying to create a nuclear power pack for space vehicles). An advisory committee, on which nuclear power specialists outnumbered the solar power specialists by about eight to one, recommended that NASA abandon the space nuclear programme and shift to photovoltaics. NASA did; as a result Skylab took to orbit and, once there, generated 25,000 watts by means of solar cells.

In the meantime the Arab countries threatened to cut oil supplies and the world found that it was beginning to run out of cheap oil. Solar energy was beginning to look more attractive, although the vast majority of power engineers still had their heads in the sand. Now power projections to the year 2000 take solar energy seriously. A programme for developing terrestrial photovoltaic power systems had been launched in 1972, but with only a trivial $2m per year support. That support increased substantially as oil became more expensive. The 1978 Solar Photovoltaic Act encouraged the United States Department of Energy to undertake a ten-year $1.5bn programme to develop various solar cell systems. According to one estimate, the world's total photovoltaic sales in 1976 amounted to less than $8m. By 1981 total sales had reached the $100m mark. Louis Rosenblum and co-workers from the Lewis Research Centre of the United States National Aeronautics and Space Administration observed that the cost of solar cells dropped from $35 to $13 per peak watt in three years.

During the 1980s a number of companies became involved: Westinghouse, Chevron, Boeing Aerospace, Radio Corporation of America (RCA) and Standard Oil of Ohio (SOHIO) in the United States, Sanyo Electric and Fuji Electric in Japan, AEG-Telefunken in Germany, ENI (Italy's state-owned oil company), to mention only a few. SOHIO signed a joint venture agreement with Energy Conversion Devices which hoped to produce cells for 33 cents per peak watt.

In the Soviet Union, the Ioffe Physical Engineering Institute of the Academy of Sciences has been experimenting with 'heterophotocells' made up of gallium, aluminium, and arsenide with an efficiency of 25 to 27%. 40 to 50% efficiencies are theoretically possible with these systems — far exceeding those of the traditional silicon-based photocells.

In addition to direct work on the photovoltaic cell itself, another approach involves the use of cheap plastic lenses to focus more sunlight onto the photovoltaics. Covering material developed at the Hebrew University in Jerusalem converts the sunlight into wavelengths more suitable to the photocell, thereby increasing the efficiency still further. A third approach, and one of the most promising, involves the transfer of technology developed for producing the silicon chip to producing more sophisticated and efficient photovoltaic devices. There is a whole new class of solar cells called conductor-insulator-semi-conductor (CIS).

At present, it is almost impossible to make a reliable forecast. Photovoltaic development depends on further advances in technology. These, to a large extent, will be determined by levels of funding — both in the private and in the public sectors. The amount of funding appears to be directly related to the price of oil. When oil is cheap, there is little interest in funding solar energy programmes.

It would be surprising if there were no further developments, so that during the 1990s the price of electricity from solar photovoltaics could drop sufficiently to become cheaper than either fossil fuel or nuclear energy for those countries with an ample supply of sunshine. Certainly, solar cells would become the least expensive source for all decentralized forms of electrical generation, particularly in underdeveloped countries.

The impact of this technology will be dramatic. The first impact is likely to be in the United States and other affluent countries which have plenty of sunshine. One of the largest single uses of electricity in the United States is for air-conditioning, and solar energy is perfectly matched to that demand; a lot of sunshine and a need for air-conditioning go hand in hand. Other uses will follow. These will range from general power generation to transport. Already we have seen the flight of a photovoltaic powered aeroplane, the *Solar Challenger*, across the English Channel on a clear July day. Its inventor, Paul MacCready, was quoted as saying: 'It's actually the most ridiculous use I can think of for solar cells ..... We just wanted to point out dramatically how much solar power can do.' That may be true for 1981. But what happens when photovoltaics get very cheap? Can an aeroplane designer of a trans-Atlantic jetliner afford not to coat the upper surfaces of the place with photovoltaics to provide power once the plane has climbed above the clouds? Some of the most successful locomotives rely on a hybrid power system, namely diesel-electric. Why not photovoltaic-jets? Once the technology has advanced to the point where the cost of installing the solar cells becomes sufficiently cheap to be justified by the saving in fuel costs, photovoltaic-jets will become a reality.

Most important, however, will be the impact on the Third World countries. One thing most of them have is a lot of sunshine. It has been the Third World economies which have been hit the hardest by rises in the price of oil. For example, in 1974 the rise in oil prices wiped out India's hard-won trade surplus. To understand what cheap photovoltaics will mean to the poorer parts of the world, let us examine the world's first village to be powered by solar cells, on the western edge of the Papago

Indian Reservation in south-western Arizona. The village, consisting of ninety-five people in fifteen families, was about 17 miles from the nearest electric facility. The villagers' traditional diet consisted of beans, tortillas, chilies and commercially available, non-perishable vegetable and tinned foods. Wild game and cattle provided an occasional supplement. The food pattern reflected, in part, the absence of refrigeration. Water was provided by a diesel-powered pump while lighting was by kerosene lamps and candles.

The experiment began on 16 December 1978. The photovoltaics provided electricity not only for pumping water and supplying lights in the homes and community buildings, but also for family refrigerators, a communal washing machine and a sewing machine. Life became easier, nutrition better.

Similarly the village of Tangaye, 120 miles east of Ougadougou, the capital of Upper Volta, found life a lot easier after a solar photovoltaic powered grain mill and water pump were installed. The mill was particularly welcomed by the women who used to have to pound the grain (sorghum and millet) with a large wooden mortar and pestle into coarse flour, and to stone grind by hand to obtain the fine flour. This arduous task generally took about two hours per day.

In October 1981 the world's largest photovoltaic power plant came online to provide electricity for two isolated Saudi-Arabian villages. As part of the $100m 'Soleras' agreement, signed in 1977 between the Saudi-Arabian National Centre for Science and Technology and the United States Departments of Energy and Treasury, supplying the power plant was part of a programme designed to explore several aspects of solar energy. Although producing only a very modest 350kw at that time (since then upgraded to 1,000kw) the plant provided a great deal of practical engineering experience under desert conditions. The Soleras projects are training a core of Saudi engineers and technicians so that the second generation of solar devices will evolve out of a national solar science programme.

The main impact of solar-powered photovoltaics will not be on family comforts but on agriculture and small industry. Most farms in developing countries have water available at less than 10 metres below the ground. The pumps, therefore, need only 1kw or less. Such pumps are being developed and tested under the auspices of the United Nations Development Programme. Pumps powered by the heat of the sun are also being developed, particularly in India. Cheap, reliable electricity for irrigation pumps and farm machinery, as well as for food processing industries, will greatly increase the productivity of the poorer parts of the world. The second silicon revolution, the development of cheap photovoltaics, will become a classic example of technology creating wealth by developing a non-resource — sunshine — into a major resource, useful energy.

THE IMPROVEMENT OF GLOBAL PRODUCTIVITY

OVERVIEW

Photovoltaic cells are but one example of technology altering the international economic order. Others will make the deserts bloom and the oceans yield.

NEW ECONOMIC STRATEGIES FOR OPEC COUNTRIES

As photovoltaic cells become economically viable, the international economic order will begin to change. First, oil as a vital resource will continue to decline in importance. This will have a significant impact on major oil exporters such as the United Kingdom, the Soviet Union, Mexico, Venezuela, Nigeria, Libya and the oil producers of the Arabian subcontinent. For some, the decline in global oil consumption and price could lead to economic chaos and, in due course, to political and military turmoil.

All countries whose wealth creation depends significantly on oil must begin to restructure their economies. In part this is already happening. Most major oil producers in the Arabian subcontinent are adding value to crude oil by refining it and converting it to a wide range of petrochemicals. Billions of dollars were spent erecting such plant. As the Arabian petrochemicals industry started to produce in bulk, much of the western petrochemicals industry was forced to develop new high-technology products and to seek new markets. However, both the proximity to markets, and the political stability of western countries continued to provide the industry with a certain comparative advantage.

More significantly for the OPEC countries of the Middle East, Africa and Latin America is the availability of sunshine and the possibility of using technology to make the deserts bloom.

MAKING THE DESERTS BLOOM

About a fifth of the land area of the world is classed as desert. In addition to outright desert there are vast territories of semi-arid land characterized by marginal productivity and periodic droughts followed by famine. About one out of eight people on this planet lives on desert or semi-arid lands — lands which are the source of so much human misery. The proper application of technical and managerial knowhow could convert the regions from low to high productivity, making such areas major exporters of energy, food and chemicals. Such a transformation calls for:

(1) the utilizing of three-dimensional agriculture at the perimeter of the desert areas where there is some water;
(2) the use of solar energy for pumping sub-surface water or water from other sources, including sea water, into the drier areas, and the use of crop plants particularly adapted to such conditions;
(3) using the hard-core desert areas for a high technology transformation, at the heart of which is the use of solar energy, first to produce cheap glasshouses from desert materials, and second to pump in sea water which is then converted to fresh water and valuable chemicals.

MAKING THE OCEANS YIELD

There is not sufficient space to examine these technical details further; this has been done elsewhere (*The Wealth of Information*, Chapter 5, see the bibliography at the end of this chapter). Nor is it necessary to describe in detail other technologies on the horizon, which are also described in the same book. It might be useful, however, to point out that mussel culture and other forms of coastal fish farming (such as 'salmon ranching' in the United States and Scotland), deep ocean mining (for example for manganese nodules), wave power and numerous other technologies are currently maturing so that not only the deserts but also the oceans will add greatly to global productivity. This will be a great stimulus to economic activity and alter patterns of wealth creation. As Arab oil money recedes in importance in international finance, other sources of wealth and new investment opportunities will arise.

THE CHINA FACTOR

Within the next two decades, among the greatest new sources of wealth and finance will be China. Events in 1989, culminating in the Tianamen Square massacre, have distracted both the Chinese, and the rest of the world, from the steady progress China had been making. Following the excesses of the Cultural Revolution in the 1960s, the Chinese government instituted a series of new economic measures in 1979. The formalization of this new policy occurred at the Twelfth Plenary Session of the Central Committee in October of 1984. The spirit of these reforms was widely proclaimed in a front-page editorial in *People's Daily* in December (1984), which declared obsolete the thinking of the old communist ideologues: 'Marx passed away 101 years ago ... there are many things that Marx, Engels and Lenin never experienced or had contact with. We cannot depend on the works of Marx and Lenin to solve our modern-day questions.' The editorial was aimed at the old guard who, it said, religiously clung to nineteenth century Marxist economic theories with no regard for present realities: '... There are many questions that are not written in books ... questions [which] require us to investigate reality to find solutions.'

The following points were announced in *China Daily* (22 October 1984) after a six-day meeting of the 12th Plenary Session of the Central Committee:

(1) *Planning.* Mandatory planning to apply only to major products with a main bearing on the nation's economy. Other operations to be subject either to general guidance, or left to market forces.
(2) *Management.* State control of enterprises to be relaxed. Businesses to be responsible for organizing themselves and for profits and losses. Managers to take full control and responsibility. Training for thousands of new managers.
(3) *Pricing.* The key to the nation's economic reform. 'Irrational' prices to be readjusted as real incomes are guaranteed.
(4) *Wages.* Pay to be linked to work rate, with bonuses for better production. Wage differentials between various professions to be widened to encourage incentive. Non-manual staff to be upgraded.

The announcement also said that, in the past, the state had equated the concept of ownership of enterprises by the people, with a concept of direct operation by the state. This had led to a rigid economic structure. Instead, enterprises should become independent producers responsible for profits and losses and capable of transforming themselves. Measures would be taken to link wages and bonuses to improved performance. The enterprises would decide themselves how to divide the excess earnings as bonuses or investment.

The author spent several weeks in China in the Autumn of 1984 as a guest of the government, travelling about two thousand miles by train, many hundreds of miles by car, visiting major cities (Peking, Shanghai and Canton), cities in the interior (Xi'an and Chengdu), smaller cities, country towns, and villages. The author's main interests centred on advances in technology and their impact on the economy and on society. Among these he was particularly interested in the use of computers. He also spent time studying the education system, especially the world's largest university, the Chinese Radio and Television University. The Chinese government was extremely obliging and as a result the author was able to visit schools, universities, research institutes, mills and factories, irrigation projects and a farm and factory commune, as well as numerous cultural and tourist activities.

In the previous (1988) edition of this work, the author presented his conclusions, at that time based on personal contacts and observations, coupled to published material, as follows:

(1) China has developed a strong technological base which allows it to move successfully from an agrarian to an industrial society. Although the bulk of the population is still rural, it is no longer engaged in mere subsistence farming. Not only did the author fail to observe a single case of malnutrition, but China is becoming a major grain exporter to such countries as the Soviet Union and Korea.

(2) China's light industry, although still largely antiquated, will become increasingly a global force. Most dramatic is the free enterprise zone adjacent to Hong Kong. Shenzhen, a former fishing village, is now a high-rise metropolis. One can no longer ascertain which side of the border one is except by looking at the flags and uniforms.

(3) At the same time, Chinese overseas investments also increased dramatically. Until 1982, Hong Kong banks were net lenders to China. The opposite is now the case. Hong Kong and China are merging into a single gigantic economic unit.

(4) China still has many problems. The transportation infrastructure is inadequate; the communications infrastructure perhaps even worse. Only now is housing being attended to adequately. However, in the author's view, the real limiting factors for the moment are education and technology. In spite of a high literacy rate, there is a desperate shortage of trained managers and professionals.

(5) However, the Chinese are working overtime to correct all these deficiencies. China's economy is no longer waiting to take off. Under the new economic policy it has taken off. Essentially one billion people are working overtime

> under the new incentive schemes. China will achieve in the 1990s what Japan achieved in the 1960s. It is moving at an incredible pace, acquiring information technology, education, and expertise by many and ingenious methods.

The new policies reflect the outlook and leadership of Deng Xiaoping. By the end of the 1980s, the problems for the Chinese leadership had become parallel to those of the Soviet leaders: once the economy and the political structure have been decentralized, the centre will have lost substantial power. Although China is ethnically much more homogeneous than the Soviet Union — Chinese minorities comprise only about 10% of the population — it is a much larger country, and its developmental stage lags behind the Soviet Union by at least a decade; it is twenty years away from becoming truly a communicative society. This means that, for now, there is much greater pressure on the Chinese leadership to maintain an authoritarian stance. All it took were a few entrepreneurial excesses and some overzealous students, and a nervous government clamped down. Nevertheless, just as in the Soviet Union, history is on the side of the technocrats while the partocrats are a dying species.

Thus, although the progressive Hu Yaobang lost his post as General Secretary and certain other liberals were downgraded during the late 1980s, the party will continue to purge itself of old-style militants, encourage consensus decision making, and allow factory and commune workers to elect their own managers. In the post-Deng era, in general, Deng's policies appear to have support within the higher echelons of the party, and also to have immense popular support. For these reasons it would look as though China is moving forward on a steady course, mixing a highly pragmatic form of socialism with a strong dose of capitalism. Only another Cultural Revolution or a major war could stop the rapid progress now being made. In the author's opinion, some time early in the next century China will have surpassed both the Soviet Union and the United States as the world's greatest economic power.

The author's visit to China in early May 1989 (shortly before the Tianamen Square incident) did not suggest any modification of the above analysis, formulated in 1987. Since then we have seen the premature rebellion of democratic forces representing the 'communicative era' portion of Chinese society. Keep in mind that at the end of the 1980s, China, in the author's view, was still two decades away from becoming a truly Communicative Society. There is no way that the Chinese technological, socio-political infrastructure of the late 1980s could support an orderly, democratic political system. It is a pity that the students, in their altruism and heroism, did not understand this. A pre-communicative society always prefers dictatorship to chaos and, as in the Soviet Union, the transition from a centrally planned to a free market economy is bound to create chaos.

Of interest is the emergence of He Xin as a prominent writer and intellectual. Mr He has written more than a dozen books and numerous essays criticising *rapid* economic liberalization. He also deplores certain trends in modern literature, including the tendency to blame a country's problems on traditional culture. Mr He believes that it takes decades or centuries to develop an educational and cultural base which permits democracy to flourish. He is quoted as saying: '..... if we had American-style personal freedom, then China would fall into terrible chaos' (*International Herald Tribune*, 21 March 1990). Needless to say, He Xin's writings are popular with Deng Xiaoping, and most unpopular with the vast majority of students and intellectuals.

The present author agrees with He's basic thesis, but disagrees with the time scale. If a country as relatively isolated and remote as the Kingdom of Nepal can show democratic stirrings in 1990, it will take China less than one generation to move into the Communicative Era. The *premature* revolution of 1989, although it undoubtedly raised the political consciousness of some ordinary Chinese, could not reach enough. The authorities, if they were unable to control the flows of information to the *outside* world, were able to control *internal* flows of information. Government propaganda carried the day. The chief impact of the rebellion, therefore, was to produce a reaction by the Chinese authorities which will delay further progress by three to five years. The significant net retardation of democratization will be caused not so much by future political repression, but by the economic chaos brought about by erratic, stop-start policies emanating from a shaken up central government. The most important contribution the West can make to democratization is to help the Chinese modernize their economy.

Hong Kong's absorption into the People's Republic should act as a further catalyst. One hopes that the citizens of Hong Kong will retain their traditional pragmatic stance and exercise political restraint after 1997. If they keep their heads down and do what they do best — organize commerce with, and within, China — they will greatly aid the democratizing processes. On the other hand, if they engage in counter-productive demonstrations and rebellions, they will leave the Beijing authorities no choice but to clamp down — brutally, if need be — thereby impeding further progress.

In the long run, it will have been Hong Kong which will have taken over China, rather than the other way round. If Hong Kong, as is likely, plays the role of an *effective* catalyst, one would expect China to democratize towards the end of the first decade of the 21st Century — that is within about ten years after 1997.

SUB-SAHARA AFRICA — THE GLOBAL BLACK SPOT

Over the next few decades the most serious problem for global society will be sub-Sahara Africa. It is ironic that in the 1960s, when looking at the global picture of poverty and growing population, Africa appeared to be one of the few bright spots. For example, the economies of the Far East (with the exception of Japan) seemed to be backward, and population growth almost hopeless. On the other hand, sub-Sahara Africa, at that time, was characterized by a richness of natural resources which could match its population. But, with some minor exceptions, its educational infrastructure was appalling. In contrast, the more sophisticated education infrastructure in much of eastern Asia (including India) allowed the human resources to manage more effectively their natural resources.

Any financial assessment of a country or a region must first and foremost look at the education level of the population. If education is valued, and is taken seriously, the prospects for economic growth are bright. This is true even when a country has virtually no natural resources whatsoever, as was the case of Singapore. Huge resources may be of little value if, in the absence of a proper education system, they cannot be utilized effectively. In such a situation, only the most extraordinary economic luck — as seen on the Arabian sub-continent — allows extensive economic development to take place. However, most of that development is largely physical, therefore superficial and spurious. Once the revenues from oil disappear it remains to be seen whether those Arab countries which have failed to develop a proper education system are going to be able to survive economically for any length of time.

The great tragedy for sub-Sahara Africa is that, on top of a lack of educated leadership and technical infrastructure, it is now subjected to what is perhaps the worst pandemic since the Black Death of the Middle Ages. The human immunodeficiency virus (HIV), the cause of AIDS, is threatening to cripple the economy. For many parts of Africa the health resources will be totally overwhelmed. The public health sector in many of those countries is so small that, if their entire health budget were devoted to screening, they could only cover a small portion of the population. Unless the outside world provides effective assistance, other problems endemic to the region — including kwashiorkor, malaria, typhoid and cholera — will spring up again with great force. This means foreign investors will be reluctant to invest, multinational companies will have great difficulty in finding Western managers or technicians to go to these countries, tourism — an important foreign exchange earner — will decline and the African economy will continue its downward spiral. Ultimately, of course, it will level off.

South Africa is in a state of transition. That there will be profound changes before the turn of the century is apparent. Several scenarios are possible. The least desirable is a white right-wing reaction to the progress currently being made. Such a reaction would, ultimately, lead to an explosion and a blood bath. The most desirable would be an orderly transition to a peaceful democracy. The likelihood is that the future of South Africa lies between those two extremes. The determining factor will be the effectiveness of the South African education system, the health of the economy, and the rise of a successful black middle class. Anything which favours any of these three factors will tend to favour orderly progress.

THE INTEGRATION OF THE GLOBAL ECONOMY

OVERVIEW

The global economy continues to expand and integrate. In post-industrial economies, the production of high technology goods requires not only the input of imported raw materials but of imported high technology components as well.

Ricardo's principle of comparative advantage becomes more powerful in global terms as transportation and communications technology continue to develop. This accounts for the rise and growth of multinational corporations, and an increasing multinational interdependence. TheEuropean Community is the first dramatic political product of this economic interdependence.

WORLD TRADE

World sea trade doubled between the mid-1960s and the mid-1970s, then continued to increase until the early 1980s when the full impact of the world recession caused a temporary halt. The increasing economic interactions of various political units reflect the decreasing costs of transport which, in turn, reflect advancing technology.

A dramatic example of the reduction of transportation costs is illustrated by the Port of New York (*Annual Report*, Waterfront Commission, New York Harbor, 1978-1979). Between 1966 and 1978, as containerization came to New York, the number of registered dockers was cut in half, even though the volume of goods handled more than doubled. Containerization set the stage for the introduction of automated container systems in which cranes load and unload containers from ships, railcars, lorries and storage depots (silos). Microelectronics is automating warehouses and all forms of transportation. The creation of a network of communication and navigation satellites will set the stage for pilotless aeroplanes and a new class of flying saucer type, lighter-than-air, craft, as well as crewless, fully-automated ocean freighters. These will match robotized transport systems on land which, in a sense, have existed for some time if one considers the transport of electrical energy and, in particular, the transport of gas or fluids in pipelines.

TRANS-EUROPEAN ENERGY SUPPLIES

As the sun rises over the Urals, moves across Europe, then sets in the Atlantic beyond the Irish shores, various groups of people, at various times, switch their electricity on, or off. The economics of electricity generation have always been plagued by the fact that electricity consumption is not a steady 24-hour activity but one which peaks in the morning and again late in the afternoon. Whatever capital costs are incurred, they are directed towards peak consumption. During most of the 24-hour day, much plant stands idle or is utilized at only a fraction of its capacity.

It is natural, therefore, that slowly, and without much publicity, the European electricity system has been integrating, even across the East-West political barrier. The housewife in Athens turning on her lights may well be using electricity generated in Russia. The development of extensive electricity grids is dependent on delicate phasing and control systems, as well as allocation regimes, all of which could not function without sophisticated electronic devices including computers. It has become increasingly simple to extend technologies developed for national grids to transnational ones. If there are political barriers to moving across national or regional boundaries, there are even greater economic pressures to overcome such barriers. The transnational sharing of electric power constitutes another example of the increasing economic irrelevance of political boundaries in the late twentieth century. It is also another example of microelectronic technology affecting a major industry.

Trans-European electricity is matched by trans-European gas pipelines. A network of gas pipelines stretching from central Algeria to Scandinavia, and from Russian Asia to the Atlantic, has been in existence for some time. The same considerations apply to gas grids as to the electricity grids discussed above; microelectronics made possible monitoring, control and allocation processes on a scale previously unthinkable. As it becomes cheaper and more efficient to pipe gas and oil for thousands of miles, the economic pressures to integrate consumer and supplier mount.

GLOBAL COMMUNICATIONS SYSTEMS

All forms of traditional electronic devices such as radios, television sets and telephones have been made more reliable, easier to maintain and operate, more durable, less breakable, less power consuming, faster to operate, more precise, more efficient, lighter and cheaper by the introduction of solid state microelectronics. The upshot has been a profusion of electronic devices all over the world: television aerials protruding from thatched Thai houses on stilts; transistor radios blaring from Nepalese hamlets in the Himalayas; video tapes sold in corner shops in virtually every major city.

The global telephone network is growing by leaps and bounds — almost doubling every decade. The system's capacity continues to grow as a result of a whole series of microelectronic improvements ranging from electronic switches (replacing electromechanical ones) to optical fibres and communication satellites. Global television emerged in the 1980s under the impact of cheaper and better video recording systems, cable TV and satellites, with increasingly cheap antennae for picking up satellite signals.

The driving force behind the rapid expansion of communications systems is threefold. There are first the requirements of the military. In the United States it was the potential for huge Defense Department contracts which spurred the development of the transistor. For the Soviet Union it is the requirements of their military which will pull that country irresistibly into the communicative era. The second factor which favours the expansion of existing communications systems involves a deliberate government policy to do so. The military junta taking power in Greece in the late 1960s is an example. The colonels engaged in a policy of encouraging the Greek telephone system to modernize and expand. By 1973 the Greek telephone system had expanded to surpass the European average. In France, following a report by Simon Nora and Alain Minc, the government began a conscious policy of expanding and developing *télématique* at all levels. In Britain the appointment of Kenneth Baker as Minister of Information Technology represented such a step; 1982 became 'IT Year' for Britain, with an energetic campaign including conferences, exhibits, spot commercials, seminars and posters, helping to create a public consciousness. In the 1990s, much will be accomplished by the various projects of the European Community.

The third force, the most global and the most persistent, is the straightforward market pull exercised by commerce. Services such as finance, transport and distribution are being automated even more rapidly than the manufacturing sector. The exponential increase of all forms of banking activity reflects, in part, that banks no longer physically transport money in any great quantity; rather they communicate credit information. The enormous increase in transport productivity associated with containerization could not have been possible without computers coupled to an extensive global communications network. In retailing, the appearance of the universal product code and other bar codes on food and other items sold in supermarkets will require increasingly sophisticated computers, robots and communications systems to optimise the automation of warehouses, stock control, market research and other aspects of the distributive system.

INFORMATION TECHNOLOGY

The office, in both commerce and manufacturing, is the primary locus of information work. It is this kind of work which has come to dominate post-industrial economies. The shift from paperwork to electronic systems greatly improves productivity. It usually brings about improved services to customers, and it can, if properly planned, improve job satisfaction. The few examples cited above should help to explain why telecommunications has become one of the fastest growing industries in the world.

One other important point to keep in mind when assessing the impact of microelectronics on society is that the next great boom in Western consumerism will be in the home electronic information/communication field. Within a decade the majority of homes in many post-industrial countries will have at least one home computer. Coupled to this information device will be a large range of peripherals including memory extensions, such as CD-ROMs, printers, modems, videodiscs and teletext, which greatly extend the capacity of individuals to acquire, store, process and communicate information. The widespread use of information and communications technology in the home will revolutionize the education system, work patterns and even patterns of thinking.

THE GLOBALIZATION OF THE ECONOMY

One of the biggest changes in the world economy over the last two decades has been that flows of money have replaced trade in goods as the force that drives exchange rates. The City of London's Big Bang represents one dramatic example of the impact of technology on the further integration of the world's financial markets. It comprises one of the best examples of how the barriers between domestic and international markets were obliterated. Transfer of financial assets from one country to another have come to swamp the flows of trade revenue in their effects on exchange rates. This has created an unstable situation which will increasingly damage the conduct of business in all countries. An editorial in *The Economist* (9 January 1988) calls for a world currency ('the phoenix') which, according to the author, should appear in about thirty years' time. The world phoenix supply would be fixed by a new world central bank — a descendant, perhaps, of the IMF.

One of the characteristics of a post-industrial economy is the transnational nature of the modes of production. Complex products involve combinations of high-tech inputs from many countries. This overwhelming trade will force the establishment of a stable world fiscal system, including a world currency.

The process has a historical parallel. With the rise of mercantilism during Europe's Middle Ages, there came a point when the traditional European feudal state was no longer viable, either in military or in economic terms. By the middle of the seventeenth century the outlines of a modern Europe, made up of nation states rather than feudal states, had begun to emerge. Similarly today, the traditional European nation state is rapidly becoming irrelevant, both in military and economic terms. Hence the rise of the European Community and the Council of Europe. At the time of writing, Austria and Turkey have applied for Community membership. In the 1990s one will see a number of Eastern European states, perhaps even the Soviet Union, join the Council of Europe, and from there evolve to join the European Community. German unification, and the entry of Czechoslovakia and Hungary into the European Community, are likely during the 1990s. By the turn of the century the European economy will have substantially outstripped both its North American and Japanese counterparts, as it expands further to integrate the revamped Comecon countries. Simultaneously, there will be further integration along the rim of the Western Pacific, comprising Japan, Korea, Taiwan, Hong Kong, Singapore and the other South East Asia Treaty Organization countries, Australia, New Zealand and, of course, China and other socialist countries. If one totals up the human and other resources of the area they are impressive indeed. The Western Pacific bloc will outpace Europe, just as the European Community has overtaken the United States as the world's largest economic unit. This process is to be viewed not as a threat but as an opportunity. Even though the European Community has outstripped the United States, and in spite of occasional differences and problems between the two, there has been a coming together of trading interests. The United States and Europe are trading partners far more often than they are trading adversaries. In a post-industrial economy, co-operative interactions tend to predominate over the competitive ones.

Around the turn of the century the world's economy will be dominated by four major blocs: North America, Europe, Comecon and the Western Pacific. By virtue of the fact that all four will be well along the evolutionary path into an information economy, all four regions will be integrating within each other, with each other and with the rest of the world. This in turn, as with the shift in Europe from feudal states to nation states, will bring about an integration of the political systems from nation states to region states, and to a further integration of global societies, ultimately leading to a global legal system.

Economic integration precedes political integration, and the financial community leads. Our grandchildren will be grateful.

POSTSCRIPT

Because we live in a rapidly changing world, education becomes crucial to providing people with the intellectual tools required for survival. Human capital is the most valuable asset a company (or a country) possesses. Physical assets, though helpful, are no guarantee of a company's future. A series of wrong decisions can cause a company which relies only on its physical assets to end up in oblivion. There was nothing more powerful a hundred years ago than American railways. Fifty years ago it was steel; twenty years ago, automobiles; ten years ago, oil. It is the quality of its human capital, the skills and education of its workforce, in particular its managerial workforce, which determines the long-term success of a company. In an uncertain world, the best single investment any organisation can make is in upgrading its own intellectual infrastructure.

T. STONIER

ACKNOWLEDGEMENTS

The author wishes to thank Marlene Ellison for help in the preparation of this chapter.

Some of the material presented here has appeared in previous works by the author (as listed in the bibliography).

BIBLIOGRAPHY

BELL, D., *The Coming of Post-Industrial Society*, Basic Books, 1973.

DIZARD, W.P. and SWENSRUD, S.B., *Gorbachev's Information Revolution*, Center for Strategic and International Studies, Washington (Significant Issues Series, IX:8), 1987.

GORBACHEV, M., *Perestroika*, Collins, London, 1987.

KHORUNZHIY, L., 'Essence and perspectives of individual supplementary farming', *Reports of the Academy of Sciences* (USSR), 2 (translated by A. Shtromas), 1979.

MACHLUP, F., *The Production and Distribution of Knowledge in the United States*, Princeton University Press, 1962.

MARKOV, C., 'The contribution of individual farming', *National Economy*, 6, 1982.

McHALE, J., *The Changing Information Environment*, Westview Press, 1976.

NORA, S. and MINC, A., *The Computerization of Society*, MIT Press, 1981.

PORAT, M., *The Information Economy*, Centre for Interdisciplinary Research, Stanford University, 1976.

SHTROMAS, A., *Political Change and Social Development: The Case of the Soviet Union*, Verlag Peter Lang, Frankfurt FRG, 1981.

STONIER, T., *The Natural History of Humanity: Past, Present and Future*, Inaugural Lecture, University of Bradford, 17th February, 1976.

STONIER, T., 'Changes in Western Society: educational implications', in SCHULLER, T. and MEGARRY, J. (eds), *World Yearbook of Education 1979: Recurrent Education and Lifelong Learning*, Kogan Page, London, 1979.

STONIER, T., 'Technological change and the future', in MAXWELL GASKIN (ed.), *The Political Economy of Tolerable Survival*, Croom Helm, 1981.

GASKIN (ed.), *The Political Economy of Tolerable Survival*, Croom Helm, 1981.

STONIER, T., *The Wealth of Information: A Profile of the Post-Industrial Economy*, Methuen/Thames, 1983.

STONIER, T., 'The microelectronic revolution, Soviet political structure, and the future of East/West relations', *Political Quarterly*, May, 1983.

STONIER, T., *The Communicative Society: a new era in human history*, International Public Relations Association (Foundation for Public Relations Research and Education), Gold Paper No.5, London, 1985.

STONIER, T., 'Technology and Third World productivity', *Technology Strategies* (Zurich), 1985, pp. 18-19.

STONIER, T., 'Coping with the post-industrial era', *The Treasurer*, 1988, pp. 21, 23.

TOURAINE, A., *The Post-Industrial Society*, Wildwood House, 1974.

1.3 Controversy and co-operation: political and legal influences on the investment decision

The international investor has become well acquainted with controversy, but finds it no less bewildering for all that. The critics often seem to be living in a different world, especially to the hard-pressed executive who knows too well that his career will be ruined if he becomes embroiled in a conflict with his local government. Part of the bewilderment arises from the knowledge that he is attacked for his investment policies, but will be attacked even more fiercely if the investment is withdrawn. 'We don't want you, we want you' appears to be the attitude of governments.

But the same executive also knows that there is another point of view to his. He represents a company that invests in several countries, but ultimately has to pay dividends to shareholders in its country of origin. However optimistic one may be, it is difficult to imagine that policies designed to produce those dividends, let alone the growth and survival of the company on a world scene, can always be in the interests of all the countries in which business is conducted. It is easy to rebut criticisms with remarks like — 'do you think we really intend to damage our own markets?' — but there are serious and perplexing issues at stake, made more perplexing by the frequently contradictory nature of the pressures. The following notes are designed to establish a few landmarks in the jungle of company-government relations and to propose methods of making the bargaining process more effective. The chapter is divided into four parts: major controversies; other issues; international organizations; and the corporate response.

MAJOR CONTROVERSIES

This section considers the five issues — finance, pricing, trade, employment and information — over which most of the controversies arise. The first four, at least, share a common characteristic: there are benefits and costs to both sides. This means that cooperation is as possible as conflict.

FINANCE

For the home country government the movement of funds out of a country in the form of equity or loans for foreign subsidiaries may be a severe setback if it comes at a time when balance of payments difficulties are being encountered. In the longer term the country will benefit from dividends, interest and other forms of remittance from the foreign subsidiary. From the country's point of view the balance of cost and benefit depends on the timing. If, for instance, the funds are moved out of the country at a particularly difficult time for the national economy, the government may find it necessary to curb spending (or even to impose import controls) to stem the outflow of funds. The results can produce a more lasting setback to the economy than any benefits a particular investment is likely to bring; yet it is at just such times that companies are apt to feel that investing in other economies is needed to boost their own income base.

This is an inescapable dilemma, one of many; but individual companies are likely to be able to justify the capital movements, if called upon to do so, on a number of grounds in addition to that of long-term income. Short term income may, for instance, be derived from the sale of goods or services to the foreign subsidiaries. The growing realization that it is both possible and desirable to charge for items like management services and technology transfer has altered the cost-benefit analysis from the national as well as from the corporate view. For the company, there is additional income, frequently at lower tax rates than dividends; for the country the calculation is more complex. At least those companies that do sell goods or services to their subsidiaries cannot be accused of exporting jobs; they may, indeed, be creating them.

For the host country there are a number of controversial issues including the following.

(1) Movement of funds. In the case of the host country, funds will normally be moved in the form of dividends, fees, royalties and interest. The country's priorities will be reflected in the varying levels of withholding tax and sometimes in direct prohibition of the movement of funds. While the measures will partly reflect the political complexion of the government, changes can usually be anticipated by watching the state of the economy, especially the balance of payments and the availability of foreign currency. Whatever the state of a nation's economy, remittances will have to be justified. Excessive dividends will be queried, and dividends over a certain percentage are illegal in some countries. Other forms of payment that incur lower withholding taxes, or none at all, will be particularly closely monitored. It has been noted, for instance, that where fees or royalties are free of tax, to encourage the development of management and technical skills, severe penalties are imposed if abuses are detected — and sometimes when they are suspected and while the company is attempting to produce justification. These occasionally include the imprisonment of executives. Funds are also moved in the form of loans. When these are repaid, there may be a serious effect on the nation's balance of payments —

another controversial issue. Companies needing to move money out of a country in the form of loan repayment are advised to do this at an early stage in an economic downturn rather than later. Such a policy is likely, in any case, to benefit the company as the downturn may well be accompanied by a weakening of the currency.

(2) Capital structure. A wholly owned subsidiary is typically highly geared (leveraged), and in some cases parent company equity may be only 10% of total capital, with substantial long-term loans negotiated in the host country. Short-term bank loans will also be at favourable rates of interest as a result of the parent company's credit-worthiness. This is the subject of considerable criticism in countries where foreign companies establish themselves relatively cheaply and absorb a considerable proportion of local savings. 'They are buying us with our own money' is a powerful plea for control over the foreign investor — especially when the demand is for local equity participation. This demand is not likely to grow weaker. 100% ownership is unpopular for another reason — the impact it has on the local money market, when attractive investments are not available to local interests. In developing countries there are measures of indigenization designed to ensure that there is a proportion of local equity in foreign enterprises. These measures apply in many parts of the world, particularly in the wealthier developing countries. There seems to be a certain wealth band (roughly between $1,000 and $4,000 per head per year) within which indigenization measures are likely; they are phased out as a country grows wealthier and begins to breed its own foreign investors. The measures stipulate various proportions of local equity according to the priority rating of the industry (high technology sectors are usually permitted a higher proportion of foreign shares) and the availability of local capital — sectors like retailing that are popular with local entrepreneurs may not be permitted any foreign equity.

(3) Prohibited or restricted sectors. There are a number of situations in which foreign direct investment is restricted or prohibited. These include the following. (a) Where no private sector ownership is allowed because of state ownership. This includes the postal services in most countries, railways in many as well as airlines and telecommunications in several. There are also a number of sectors which are nationalized in particular countries, like tobacco and matches in France. (b) Where foreign ownership is restricted as with insurance in Switzerland or radio and television in the United States. (c) Where foreign ownership is impossible because of private monopolies such as the Satellite Communications Corporation in the United States. In that country, some individual states prohibit or restrict the ownership of agricultural land by non-resident foreigners or foreign companies. (d) Where all investment is subject to restrictions, whether by foreign or local investors, as with insurance and banking in most countries.

(4) Incentives. Most countries offer incentives for investment as well as restrictions. Details of incentives available in European Community countries are

given in the next chapter. In general countries everywhere provide incentives, sometimes for all investors and sometimes for foreign investors only. These are often criticized within the country and in international organizations as being a misuse of national resources. Some incentives apply only to foreign investors. Others are offered as inducements to invest in areas of unemployment; there may be constraints in other areas. Foreign companies are frequently more responsive to inducements and constraints than domestic ones. Some countries, which do not normally have general incentives, are yet willing to negotiate concessions for important foreign investments. The State of South Carolina, for instance, offered to build a new highway and railroad as well as dredging a waterway to encourage BASF to site a new plant in the state; the Province of Ontario passed a law restricting trade union activity in Michelin plants in the province.

There is always scope for negotiation when a new facility is being considered. However there are a number of problems that need to be watched.

(a) Incentives change, sometimes frequently and often unexpectedly. In Britain, for instance, investment incentives changed seventeen times in one period of thirty years, and that included five major alterations in the system. Some changes are caused by shifts in political outlooks and priorities, others by variations in local economic conditions. For instance incentives are sometimes reduced or phased out when an economy improves. In developing countries, concessions are usually directed towards industry sectors which the country needs, and away from those it already possesses. To take advantage of concessions, it may be necessary to invest before competitors do so.

(b) There is a trap in being over-influenced by incentives. Allowing them to influence the investment decision can prove a mistake. Companies find themselves steered away from more profitable options and locked into uncommercial situations. The incentives are designed to compensate for a cost. A country or region of a country is trying to lure investors because they would otherwise decide to go elsewhere. The assistance may look attractive in the short term but may fail to compensate for the extra costs that the company will incur in the longer term. For instance one firm was persuaded to go to a remote region of another industrialized country, only to find in the first three years of operation that costs were well above estimate. Transport, supply and distribution were slower and more expensive than expected. Recruitment of adequate staff — skilled operators as well as managers — was also difficult. The area was one of high unemployment, but suitable labour was unavailable and this caused delays and expense. In the end the grants nowhere near met the costs, but their provision made withdrawal or relocation difficult. The parent company, in this case, was nearly forced into liquidation when the banks called in the guarantees that had been given against loans to the subsidiary. The calling in of guarantees against a subsidiary has been the occasion of actual bankruptcy for a parent company in other instances.

Experienced international operators make decisions in the light of market considerations and justify them on the returns expected without the incentives. These are then negotiated and form an extra income which, at least, compensates for over-optimistic figures in the calculations. Chapters 4.1 to 4.4 outline a basic policy for investment, control and remittance. In the terms of 4.2, incentives are a useful way of meeting losses that often occur in the early years of a new investment; this consideration obviously does not apply to tax concessions whose benefits are more apparent than real if they apply to years when there are no profits. Before negotiating concessions, a manager needs to have an eye on the additional costs they are designed to offset. These costs are frequently higher than the allowances and it is dangerous to allow the decision-making to be over-influenced by promises of assistance that can prove illusory.

PRICING

The issue of transfer pricing is a long-standing controversy which has become no less perplexing after the exposure it has received. The reason for transfer pricing is clear and simple — goods and services are transferred, so prices have to be determined. Finding a method of determination leads to complex problems, and proposed solutions have a way of turning sour.

There are several policy guidelines used by companies for charging between two units of a company and these include:

(1) charging a price that is normal in the market,
(2) charging a price that is based on costs,
(3) charging a price that will support other objectives like the transfer of funds or the minimizing of taxes,
(4) reaching a price as a result of a bargaining process between the units involved.

The problem for government is to know which guideline is being used and what are the implications for tax officials and for customs authorities — whose interests may be in conflict. For products that attract an import duty on the basis of their value a higher price will bring in more revenue, while the profits will be simultaneously reduced and bring in less tax. The following is the current position.

(1) A market price: most products and services do not have a *market price* since they have at least some measure of uniqueness; while there may be resemblances, neither companies nor tax administrations can rely on the market as a guideline.
(2) A cost-based price: surveys in the 1970s showed that the cost plus measurement was then the most common; this is certainly the easiest for the authorities

to appraise, but it was anomalous then and is less common now; the price is mainly determined by competitive and other conditions and so the relationship to costs will vary.

(3) A price that will support other objectives: the scope for fixing prices to serve other purposes is limited and is likely to cause considerable argument within the company, nevertheless it is frequently practised — as much for the purpose of moving funds, which can be done by altering credit terms as well as by pricing, as for tax reasons.

(4) A negotiated price: the internal bargaining method is widely considered the most satisfactory for company purposes. It creates as far as possible market conditions within the company and enables unit purchasing managers to compare internal prices with those obtainable outside. This does not necessarily make it acceptable to outsiders like tax inspectors who will not be easily convinced that the bargaining is unbiased.

A problem for governments is to know which method is being followed and what are the tax implications. Where a number of subsidiaries of companies based in a country with low corporate taxes are showing poor profits but not withdrawing, a manipulation of the transfer prices to save tax seems likely. Even so the facts are difficult to prove. A result of the difficulty is a growing demand, backed by international treaty organizations, for more openness in company accounts. The theory of *arms length*, the usual criterion for tax purposes, is most easily satisfied by a cost plus figure.

TRADE

Another issue which is simple in itself but gives rise to intractable problems is that of allocating trading areas.

The limitation of a subsidiary's markets appears commonsense to a company. There are many circumstances in which competition between subsidiaries is damaging, especially where a large customer finds himself approached by rival salesmen from the same firm offering different terms, or where different affiliates are operating in different segments of the market. On the other hand, countries find it intolerable that foreign instructions can restrict the export effort of local companies, especially after a take-over, and will take steps to prevent this. In the bargaining between companies and governments, the right to restrict the trade of the subsidiary may be more important than financial or fiscal incentives.

In fact subsidiaries are often more effective exporters than local companies, even with restrictions on their markets. The worldwide contacts and facilities of multinational companies make trade easier, and researches over many years have demonstrated that their export records can be three or four percentage points better than local companies even in the industrialized countries.

A different subject that comes under the same heading is that of the world product mandate. The phrase is used when a company moves a whole product division to another country, including research and development as well as production and marketing. The move of Philips' domestic equipment division from the Netherlands to Italy was a case in point. There are a number of examples in Canada where the government, faced with an exceptionally high degree of foreign ownership, has brought pressures to bear in this direction. Black and Decker, Westinghouse, Garrett Manufacturing and Litton Industries have all at various times moved world responsibility for a product to a Canadian subsidiary. Less is heard of world product mandates now than a few years ago, but it is likely that the concept will be revived; several governments can be expected to promote it.

EMPLOYMENT

The influence of a foreign company on a nation's employment policies is an example of the mixture of controversy and cooperation which is a theme of this chapter. Even governments most prone to intervene in business affairs are inhibited from restricting the employment opportunities that companies bring — often desirable employment in emerging industry sectors with high quality jobs. Further, companies have been enabled to grow internationally with the help of management development programmes and staff selection and training schemes whose introduction has brought benefits to the host country.

As against these advantages, reservations arise from a number of considerations such as the following.

(1) The appointment of foreign nationals and failure to promote locals. This is keenly felt in developing countries where indigenization laws have been introduced for labour as well as capital; in industrial countries also work permits may not be granted if local nationals are available.

(2) Style of management. There are complaints about alien styles and lack of respect for local culture and traditions; these complaints are partly offset by the recognition that foreign companies often bring high standards of management and superior techniques. The relationship between management styles and local cultures is an issue which goes beyond the scope of this book. Some companies are finding it worthwhile to employ specialists who can aid the adaptation of their methods to foreign countries without losing strengths which are of general application; these strengths may be the more valid if suitably adopted.

(3) Labour relations. This is another subject of controversy. American companies, in particular, are accused of disregarding labour practices in Europe including union recognition. They are sometimes able to reply that their employees benefit from their different practices in higher pay or improved conditions of service.

(4) National employment policies. Companies must expect to encounter a variety of policies which differ from country to country and may therefore be unfamiliar. All European countries, and many elsewhere, have laws providing protection against dismissal; these vary from compensation subject to a number of conditions to reinstatement in certain circumstances. Usually — but not

always — the law makes no distinction between foreign and national firms, and controversy has arisen over situations where foreign firms are alleged to be evading the law.

INFORMATION

The other issue around which major controversies have gathered is that of information. In some ways this is the key to the other controversies. It is felt that international companies are too secretive about their affairs — however open their public relations departments succeed in appearing — and this makes them difficult to deal with. As with the other issues, the problem is not straightforward. Companies are justified in maintaining that some of the demands would involve them in expenses out of proportion to the benefits brought by a comparatively small amount of extra information; at the same time they breed suspicion by refusing to discuss pricing policies or by making difficulties for union negotiators by appeals to decision-makers outside the country. Part of the problem, however, lies with governments. Some have higher national standards of disclosure than others, and there is no evidence that foreign companies prefer those with lower disclosure rules. Hence national aspirations could be met by rules that would apply to all companies.

In general policies follow problems, and to understand the problems that governments are facing is to understand how the law will be applied. The official is also interested in reliability; this applies to the government as purchaser as well as to the government as regulator. The company which has its own plans clearly defined and a reputation for stability should have the least problems.

OTHER ISSUES

There are a number of other issues on which laws and government pressures influence company policies. These are mainly to be found under the following headings.

Agents. In some countries there are laws protecting agent companies which provide a range of services against dismissal by foreign principals. The basis is that the agent has acquired a share in the goodwill of the company through developing a market. The force of such laws is often overlooked when negotiating agency agreements especially by companies based in countries which do not have such laws (such as Britain, Belgium and the United States). Many Latin American countries protect agents in this way as do most European; and it is likely that protection will eventually be extended to the whole of the European Community. Currently compensation is awarded of between three and ten years' anticipated profits.

Competition. Governments legislate to enforce competition and restrain companies from dominating a market. This aim proves difficult to achieve outside the United States because a company may be dominant within its national market but small in relation to world competition. As a result governments tend to support regional organizations, like the European Community, to restrain anti-competition policies.

Competition legislation, it should be noted, is not only applied against large multinationals. It is frequently directed against agency and licensing agreements held to be in restraint of trade.

Education. This links up with the question of employment. The employment of expatriates and the transfer of research and development to the home country can harm a country's educational progress by limiting the scope for research and employment in science and technology. On the other hand foreign companies are demanding employers and this may well help to raise educational standards especially in management. They may also provide funds for research in the host country.

Environment. Firms are accused of using their power to flaunt anti-pollution legislation or to move to countries which have lenient regulations. Against this, companies can claim that their resources and their research enable them to afford devices to overcome pollution.

Technology. One subject on which companies and countries would appear to have a common interest is the transfer of technology. Countries obtain the benefits of the knowhow and companies derive additional income from the results of expensive research. However the situation is not always so satisfactory in practice. From the national point of view it frequently appears that the wrong kind of technology is being transferred, and at an exorbitant price. From the company point of view the problems of transfer are compounded by national attitudes to change and the difficulty of ensuring that new methods are used effectively and that new products are not promoted before the market is ready for them.

INTERNATIONAL ORGANIZATIONS

A feature of the last forty years has been the gradual and laborious construction of a framework of international regulation for trade, exchange and investment. Some elements in the framework are backed by sanctions like expulsion from the organization or a withdrawal of reciprocal rights, while other elements are voluntary.

The framework includes regulations concerning trade and investment with attempts to reestablish some control over currency exchange fluctuations; an example is the European Community's regulations (the so-called 'currency snake').

The institutions, set up under treaty, that make up this framework include international organizations to which membership is open *on principle* (although not always in practice) to all countries, and other international and regional organisations with more limited membership. Some have more influence on corporate policies than others.

The United Nations and its subsidiary and affiliated organizations. All the organizations under the umbrella of the United Nations have some commercial implications, but those that especially affect company policies are listed below.

The General Agreement on Tariffs and Trade (GATT) was established to limit the growth of protectionism between member countries, which now include most of those with free market economies. GATT has established a series of agreements not to increase duties, except in exceptional circumstances which are carefully designated. There are also rules against subsidising exports, but which allow a number of exceptions. For instance export credit insurance is permissible and value added tax can be rebated on exports and levied on imports. In the latter case the rate must be the same as for home-produced goods. There are also rules against import quotas and non-tariff barriers. GATT has held a series of meetings, usually known as Rounds — the Uruguay Round is the latest — aimed at progressively reducing the obstacles to trade. However the world slump, the growth of economic unions and the increasing articulateness of poorer countries have between them slowed progress towards the organization's objectives.

In the view of the less developed nations, GATT has been biased from its inception towards the interests of the industrialized countries. For example the higher tariffs permitted on manufactured goods compared to those on raw materials have been seen as a discouragement to primary producers in their attempt to develop manufacture. This view has not diminished during the present Uruguay Round which has been taking up, for the first time, the question of trade in services — a move represented by some developing countries as an attack on their attempts to give birth to a service sector.

Although GATT is mainly known for its efforts towards freer trade, regulations that also affect companies are those that concern dumping. The regulations are complex and uncertain in their application; the appearance of flagrant under-pricing may well produce legal action — prices at 25% to 40% below costs are sometimes claimed.

The United Nations Conference on Trade and Development (UNCTAD) has been regarded by the developing countries as less biased than GATT towards the interests of the industrialized nations. The reason for this is a different voting system (one member one vote); but, as a result, this organization finds it even harder to reach decisions and to make them stick. It is also more geared to specific than to general principles, working through four main committees — for commodities, manufactured goods, invisible trade and shipping. In spite of slow progress, as a result of which press reports describe each fresh UNCTAD meeting as a failure, progress is made and the corporate planner would be unwise to write the organization off as of little importance. It represents the influence of growing markets, especially towards greater protection for commodities and freer trade in manufactured goods, but also in a range of measures designed to foster commerce.

UNCTAD has also established guidelines designed to constrain abuses of market power, including the limiting of access to markets and other restraints on competition between affiliates of a multinational firm as well as between independent companies. Technical assistance is offered to countries in dealing with problems that arise from dealing with restrictive practices as well as trying to protect the benefits of trade liberalization, to attain greater efficiency in trade and development, to promote social welfare and to eliminate restraints on trade.

Yet another aim of UNCTAD is to promote the more effective transfer of knowhow — especially technical expertise and especially to developing countries — and to establish machinery to improve communications on this subject.

The United Nations Centre on Transnationals was established to collect information on the activities of international companies and to advise member countries on their dealings with them. The Centre has produced a series of reports on subjects as diverse as the pharmaceutical industry, management contracts and much else. The Centre has also been involved in drafting a code of conduct much of which has now been accepted by the General Assembly. The following are the main clauses.

(1) The code is designed to assist in the control of international ('transnational') firms and to ensure that their activities contribute positively to international development.
(2) Companies must respect the sovereignty, laws and policies of the countries in which they operate, and the right of those countries to regulate their activities. Respect for socio-cultural values and traditions is demanded, as is active opposition to policies of apartheid.

The second clause proscribes political interference and corrupt practices, while a series of clauses concerns ownership and control. The subsidiary is to be structured in a way that will allow it to play a full part in local development and economic plans; personnel and training policies are to give priority to the benefit of local nationals. Exports from the subsidiary are to be promoted. Financial policies must conform with the laws of the country and not conflict with its economic policies; in particular the repatriation of capital, the transfer of profits and other cash transactions are to be timed to minimize the damage to the balance of payments. The subsidiary is also expected to avoid practices that may harm the local capital markets, to consult with the government when engaged in share issues or long-term borrowing, and to co-operate in efforts to establish local equity participation.

Transfer prices should be based on an arm's length principle. Restrictive practices, the transfer of technology, consumer protection and the physical environment are all considered in detail. Companies are called upon to disclose full information about their operations both for the company as a whole, for the country concerned and (as far as possible) by regions and products under the following headings:

(a) balance sheet;
(b) income statement;
(c) allocation of net profits;
(d) sources and uses of funds;
(e) new long-term investments;

(f) research and development expenditures;
(g) the structure of the enterprise (parent and subsidiary);
(h) ownership distribution;
(i) operations;
(j) employment;
(k) accounting practices; and
(l) transfer pricing.

The provision of information is subject to safeguards where confidentiality is important; otherwise representatives of labour are to be kept fully informed of developments and plans likely to affect the future of the employees.

(3) The third part concerns relationships between companies and governments. There are clauses on the role of foreign companies and the rights of countries to prohibit their entry into certain sectors, their treatment by governments, including their acceptance on an equal footing with domestic companies, the safeguarding of the confidentiality of the information that they do supply, and their rights in the face of nationalization, and in disputes over compensation and jurisdiction.
(4) Bilateral and multilateral agreements between states on issues arising out of the code are provided for, and governments agree not to use companies to further their policies in other countries but, on the contrary, to try to prevent companies interfering in internal affairs of host nations.
(5) The code is to be publicized by member countries and to be administered by the United Nations Commission on Transnationals.

The final clauses provide for reconsideration and revision.

The question readers will be asking themselves is what are the implications of this policy for company planning? The answer is made up of the following considerations.

(1) At present the code carries no legal consequences, but does represent the results of prolonged discussions on the part of a large number of experts and decision-makers. Corporate as well as government interests have been represented in the discussions, and the results will carry considerable prestige.
(2) The clauses include safeguards for companies as well as countries, and are designed to produce guidelines that are of benefit to both.
(3) While some companies may ignore the code with impunity, it is bound to be considered a basis for minimum acceptable practices.
(4) Some companies will find the clauses on disclosure of information costly to comply with when the demands cover data which are not usually kept or operations whose monitoring is not considered necessary. However an escape clause has been provided for such occasions.

(5) More difficult is how companies ensure that their subsidiaries observe the code. It often looks as if their critics are making inconsistent demands upon them — requiring that they grant a high degree of autonomy to foreign affiliates while at the same time holding head office responsible for any misdemeanours. The case of Nestlé is relevant here in the long-running controversy over the sale of formula milk in developing countries. The controversy started as a result of marketing policies adopted in one subsidiary that brought problems to other operations throughout much of the world. One upshot was a strong reassertion of central authority — subsidiaries were forbidden to adopt practices which might harm the company's reputation. Another consequence of the controversy was the establishment of a code of conduct by another offshoot of the United Nations.

The Food and Agricultural Organization has established a code of conduct on the marketing of breast milk substitutes. This is mainly designed to ensure that these products are properly used by restricting high pressure salesmanship and ensuring adequate labelling and consumer education.

The International Labour Office is another body which has promulgated a code; this concerns the social and labour policies of multinationals. It covers six main objectives.

(1) That international companies, whether in public or private ownership, should make a positive contribution to the economies in which they operate and reduce any damage that might result from their policies.
(2) That companies are encouraged to respect the sovereignty of states with national laws and practices. In particular they are asked to support existing conventions on freedom of association, collective bargaining, non-discrimination in employment and other social policies.
(3) That companies give priority to increasing opportunities and standards in host countries, to developing local nationals and to adopting non-discriminatory policies.
(4) That relevant training is provided for all employees.
(5) That wages, benefits and conditions of work should not be less favourable than those offered by comparable local companies. There should also be high standards of health and safety.
(6) That the best existing practices in industrial relations, including freedom of association and the right to organize are observed. Governments are asked not to offer incentives to foreign companies in the form of anti-labour measures. Procedures for regular consultation and the settling of disputes are included.

Organizations designed for a regional membership. There are about 25 organizations designed to promote growing unity and common policies among groups of countries. Many of these have aspirations to complete economic and other forms of integration. Others have more modest aims. The most advanced is the European Community (EC). Others include the Andean Common Market (ANCOM), the Latin American Integration Association (ALADI), the Caribbean Common Market (CARICOM), the Association of South East Asian Nations (ASEAN), and the Economic Community of West African States (ECOWAS). Most of them suffer frustrations of slow development because of the need to reconcile conflicting interests. In particular the poorer members of a regional organization perceive themselves at a disadvantage. Right or wrong, the view is that the interests of the wealthier members have priority. This view was responsible for the break up of two organizations, while others have built in safeguards for the poorer members.

Other common features which affect business planning include:

(1) moves towards common tariffs, although seldom towards the abolition of non-tariff barriers;
(2) constraints on foreign investment;
(3) measures for the free movement of people (often prevented in practice because of fears of mass emigrations);
(4) limited numbers of common projects which provide excellent markets; also national projects are supported by regional banks set up by the organizations.

Other institutions that influence trading patterns. The two most important are the Organization for Petroleum Exporting Countries (OPEC) and the Organisation for Economic Cooperation and Development (OECD). This latter body has 26 members, including all the most industrialized nations, but provides services to client nations as well. Its role is primarily consultative and advisory, with export staff servicing committees in most areas of primary production, manufacturing and service industries. OECD has also produced a code of conduct for multinationals, the first to be promulgated and become operational. This was agreed by governments and representatives of employers (through the related Business and Industry Advisory Committee to OECD) and trade unions (through the Trade Union Advisory Committee to OECD), and has been shown to be effective in a number of cases. For instance pressure has been brought to bear successfully on companies to pay compensation to employees where national subsidiaries have gone out of business.

THE CORPORATE RESPONSE

The response of companies to the difficulties encountered in dealing with governments has taken a number of forms.

(1) To establish a special department concerned with what is loosely called the 'non-commercial environment.' These external affairs departments exist to establish relations with governments and non-governmental bodies and pressure groups and ensure that corporate policies are relevant to local needs. Naturally only large companies can afford such departments, how large is

likely to depend on how sensitive the business is to social and political influences.

(2) To improve intelligence. A policy that is acceptable in one country may be controversial in another.

(3) To reconsider objectives. If a country is expected to provide a profitable and growing market, then establishing a satisfactory relationship both between head office and the subsidiary and between the subsidiary and the country is part of the marketing cost. Expenditure on promoting both the image and the reality of good citizenship is worthwhile. If the market is peripheral, controversies may not be worth the time and cost, nor may incentives. The need is to identify and give priority to objectives in such a way that corporate bargaining power is increased.

(4) Where the company is exposed to controversy and especially skilled negotiating ability is required, this is frequently provided from head office. One of the ironies of the company-government interface is that there is often pressure for greater autonomy for the local subsidiary; but when the going becomes rough, the corporate response is to move authority back to head office.

(5) Maintaining a relationship. It is too much to expect that corporate and national interests will always coincide. A foreign company, it has been said, cannot expect to be liked but it can be respected and worthy of respect. This means treating foreign investment as a long-term commitment and not using the limited liability of the subsidiary to evade responsibilities.

MICHAEL Z. BROOKE

Managing Director, Brooke Associates (Manchester) Ltd.

1.4
Corporate financial strategies

Strategy has come to be recognized as crucial to success in international operations. The ability to outthink the competition and to position the company in an advantageous place in world markets is vital. The need to maximize strengths and to minimize weaknesses has become a cliche, but that does not take away its significance. This chapter summarizes the strategic and tactical thinking which finance managers have at their disposal in the following series of checklists.

(1) Routes to diversification
(2) Appraising foreign markets
(3) Reading the commercial signs
(4) Export policies
(5) Foreign agent
(6) Sale of knowledge
(7) Motives for foreign investment
(8) Decisions to be taken once a new investment has been agreed
(9) The formulation of international strategies

The strategies available to the foreign operator, which the international finance manager will match in formulating his policies, are the subject of this chapter. It deals with internal, corporate policies and the pressures that help to determine them. The economic trends and national regulations, which also have to be taken into account, are considered in other chapters. The criteria for determining financial policies vary according to the business options employed; export, for instance, has different groundrules from investment. The principal options are considered in this chapter beginning with a general approach to international strategy.

STRATEGIES OF DIVERSIFICATION

A company enters the international scene for a number of reasons usually connected with the search for new markets. Sometimes the search is undertaken after deciding that geographical expansion is likely to be a more profitable use of resources than diversifying into new products. At other times new products are acquired by buying companies that are already international. The further stages of expansion abroad follow the well-known patterns which are outlined later in this chapter. Meanwhile each stage requires an ability to read the messages in the market and other aspects of the business environment. The checklists are designed to assist companies to reappraise their progress.

CHECKLIST 1 THE ROUTES TO DIVERSIFICATION

The following list sets out the options for diversification with comments. Naturally any combination is possible and many companies have taken the geographical route by accident; a firm has been bought as part of a policy of taking over suppliers, for instance, which already has subsidiaries abroad.

1. *Geographical.* To meet the requirements of a company conducting business across frontiers is, of course, the main purpose of this book. The advantages of operating internationally will not be new to our readers, nor will the disadvantages. The problem is to take advantage of the former while minimizing the latter. Profits are made abroad when a firm operates in economies which are diverse but in which its resources are not overstrained. Since different countries enter the depths and heights of their economic cycle at different times, any company which is especially subject to the effects of recession needs to look at international diversification. So, to a similar end, do those which are affected by seasonal variations. Many companies reduce their marginal production costs by entering foreign markets, and sometimes offset extra distribution by operating with wider margins (although these are subject to fluctuations in the exchange rate outside their control). The present author *used* to say that almost every type of business except the local bus company and the corner shop could justify a move abroad — until it was brought home to him that many small shopkeepers supplement their earnings with import-export businesses and that transport undertakings have been trying to reduce their deficits by running package tours.

Geographical diversification is unlikely to be a route to short-term profits or to the solving of problems at home; but provided the home base is secure, the ground is properly prepared (the market research has not been skimped) and the organization suitably restructured, taking business strengths into foreign markets can be the most profitable option in the longer-term. Finance managers will not need to be reminded that a useful by-product of a move abroad is an increasing ability to operate on foreign money markets. In general the larger companies concentrate on the industrialized nations. They are wary of countries at an early stage of development unless they are mining firms or commodity traders. Smaller companies are also wary of developing markets but they may well be advised to acquire experience in regions where margins are higher and competition less severe, at least if adequate insurance cover is available.

2. *Horizontal.* Expansion into related businesses in the same industry sector is a common strategy. Surveys have shown this to be the most profitable, at least in the short-term. Industries like chemicals and electrical components have adopted this route. It has been shown, in fact, that larger companies in both those sectors have expanded along remarkably similar lines, and that their 'horizontal' expansion (into electric light bulbs, domestic equipment, radio and television and professional equipment, as well as products like cables and generators in the case of the electrical components industry) has been accompanied by growth across frontiers as well. Head on competition in a wide diversity of national markets has been undertaken. Smaller firms are likely (and advised) to take abroad the policies adopted at home, rather than seek horizontal expansion internationally.

3. *Vertical.* Expansion into businesses which are either suppliers or customers is another option. Oil companies, for instance, have sometimes adopted vertical strategies taking them from oil exploration (necessarily international) to retailing which has caused problems for some of them and has become a less relevant strategy under modern oil market conditions. Some branches of manufacturing have also expanded vertically, a policy which has not always produced satisfactory results when it has extended as far as the retail outlet. Vertical expansion into suppliers is likely to lead a company abroad by definition since the affiliate must be where the materials or components are to be found. This strategy is used to ensure supplies but does have disadvantages. Purchasing officers find their scope limited if there is pressure to buy within the organization, and surveys have found the method to be less profitable than the horizontal. It is not recommended for small companies tempted to purchase a supplier with a view to controlling the quality of their supplies. Many have found this an expensive way to achieve their objectives.

4. *Marketing.* Some companies follow a diversification route that enables them to transfer marketing skills from one industry sector to another when operating in similar markets. This is seldom a direct route to international operations, although the marketing skills may well include export.

5. *Technology.* Some companies adopt a strategy of moving into businesses that use related technologies either in the product or the production process. Again this may take the firm abroad but only by chance.

6. *Finance.* Financial considerations produce the conglomerate, a company which is not tied to any particular industry sector but seeks to build up a balanced portfolio of investments which have different rates of return over different periods so that a steady income is assured. The fact that this method has been shown to be the least profitable route masks some outstanding successes. In fact the effect of averaging is that failures have put this strategy in an unfavourable light. It would seem that a long-term operation is necessary for success. Most substantial conglomerates find themselves operating internationally and many, like long-established trading com-

panies of Britain and other former colonial powers, have found themselves diversifying back home — partly because of changed commercial conditions and partly for tax reasons.

Whatever strategy is adopted for trade or investment, one of the secrets of success in operating abroad is the ability to interpret the non-commercial (political and social) as well as the commercial environment in foreign markets. The next checklist is a reminder about how this can be done.

INTERPRETING THE BUSINESS ENVIRONMENT

Numerous systems for appraising foreign environments and calculating risks and other factors are on offer. One that can be adapted to many purposes — from making more systematic the simplest back of the envelope calculations to clearing the path for highly sophisticated market or investment appraisals — can be found in a companion handbook *The Handbook of International Trade*, Macmillan 1988, ch. 5.1). This uses 8 headings, each with 10 subheadings of which the 10th always provides for industry specific items, to assess the suitability of any particular market. The main headings (with a summary of the subheadings in brackets) form the next checklist.

CHECKLIST 2 APPRAISING FOREIGN MARKETS

1. *The national economy.* (Wealth, savings, inflation, energy consumption, national budget priorities and credit position, balance of payments and wealth distribution).

2. *The social facts.* (Population statistics, medical services, potential for civil unrest, availability of managers, problems for foreign staff and the literacy rate).

3. *The political conditions.* (Membership of international, regional or development organizations or bilateral treaties, stability of government and civil service, options available for company formation and availability of local partners).

4. *The economic policies.* (National ambitions, nationalization, indigenization and other policies related to foreign ownership, tariffs, local content required, taxation and the possibility of corruption).

5. *Geographical and cultural.* (Position on trade routes, communications, land area, climate, local religions and cultural conditions).

6. *Production and supply.* (Potential as supply and distribution centre, availability of raw materials, legal constraints including patent laws, degree of industrialization, conditions for technology transfer and research and development).

7. *Marketing factors.* (How well established the local industry is, the strength of the competition, the position of the customer and the protection of the consumer, the advertising regulations, the acceptability of the product, the distribution channels and the availability of research services).

8. *Company factors.* (Existing markets and relationships with agents and licensees, capital available, return on investment forecasts, staff available, match with other projects and possibility of servicing other markets).

Another approach to understanding the environment in which the international trader and investor operates is to consider the landmarks of change which are apparent at a given time. Naturally some so-called 'landmarks' will be passing fashions, others will represent permanent shifts in the groundrules. Naturally, also, there will be a gap between the technical and commercial opportunities and the political adjustments that make it possible to realize the opportunities internationally. The importance of timing is not to be under-estimated. For instance up to now as many problems have been caused by premature assumptions about a unified market within the European Community as by overlooking opportunities. Changes in the business environment may be permanent but, notoriously, they do not work at the speed of business. Nor, of course, do changes of outlook on the part of employees or customers. The same is true of technical developments like on-line links and electronic funds transfer; nevertheless technical change must dominate any list of significant changes. The following topics are arranged in alphabetical order for ease of reference; they do not claim to be all-inclusive.

CHECKLIST 3 READING THE COMMERCIAL SIGNS

1. *Communications.* Communications gaps are narrowing physically but not necessarily mentally. An increasing speed of technical change is now commonplace; so is the consequence that foreign subsidiaries and representatives can be in closer contact with head office. No doubt this process is destined to go much further, with international conferences being held without any of the participants leaving home. The danger is that the immediacy provided by the new communications will lead to people underestimating the mental, legal and commercial distances, while the possibility of closer oversight will lead to the stifling of initiative. The fact that more rapid monitoring of foreign operations can lead to greater autonomy does not mean that this autonomy will happen; the reverse has to be guarded against. Over control that frustrates the local operations is too easy to impose.

2. *Competition.* A move from a negotiated to a competitive environment has been caused by a number of factors — legal, political and economic — coming together. Additionally companies are tending to face competitors in international markets rather than avoid them and are thus influencing the emergence of new centres of trade and finance.

3. *Exchange rates.* There has been a move from fixed to floating exchanges and slowly back again. While the financial community have come to terms with floating exchange rates, other industry sectors still find them a problem and the pressure to regulation (like the European Monetary System) is likely to increase; it may well become a reality as part of a package of international measures.

4. *Export related investment.* This kind of vertical expansion, the owning of customers, has already been seen as likely to increase. It is a feature of investment abroad on the part of companies based in developing countries (for example textile firms buying into clothing manufacturers abroad and food processors into restaurants).

5. *Government incentives and constraints.* These are likely to become more subtle as governments become more experienced and to include measures that influence the foreign investor in location, export, import, social and other policies. Most of the regulations exist at the moment, but they are likely to be brought together into packages designed to ensure their effectiveness. Freedom to conduct business in a country will be granted in return for an agreement when the capital is imported not to restrict exports, to keep down imports and to site facilities in accordance with national priorities.

6. *Growth.* There is a trend away from uncontrolled growth and towards social policies. This is particularly bewildering for companies because the criteria vary greatly from country to country and are more subject to political change than policies pursued on purely economic grounds. Nevertheless the trend, even if to a limited extent, accompanies growing wealth and sometimes precedes it. The emphasis on growth itself is a sign of another transition which is still continuing in some developing countries — away from policies of accepting established conditions (being bound by traditions) towards the attempt to manage development and thus grow.

7. *Investing near to the source of knowledge.* The traditional company kept a rigid distinction between research and development and production departments. This distinction included physical separation as well as different terms of employment. The abolition of the dividing line is an increasing necessity of high technology in many companies and plants are increasingly being placed near to research departments or to outside sources of knowledge. One symptom of this is the growth of science parks. A consequence is the introduction of a new criterion into location decisions. In some instances a multi-stage manufacture emerges with the high technology components or ingredients made in one country. Sometimes the assembly may be elsewhere again.

8. *National policies and international coordination.* The hazard of national commercial policies that are reinforced by international agreements has been creeping

up on companies for many years. In the past these agreements have often been helpful like the removal of trade restrictions (helpful, that is except to firms looking to protection). The modern trend is to use treaties to promote trade but also to provide common restrictions on international concerns, and to conduct negotiations on an inter-country basis. The European Community is an example, but there are now 64 organisations exercising or planning to exercise controls apart from innumerable bilateral treaties.

9. *Reconstruction.* War and civil strife are endemic in the world today, which means that at any given time there are countries in a period of post-war reconstruction. Such a period offers opportunities for the sale of a wide variety of goods and services.

10. *Trade.* There are three areas of transition in international trade that merit special attention.

(a) The transition from free trade and free movement of funds to economic management reinforced, as already explained, by international agreements.
(b) The transition from trade between two independent organizations to trade between two units of the same company (in most industrialized countries this change has already gone a long way, to well over half of all exports in the case of the United States).
(c) The emergence of new centres of manufacture and of finance, especially in the Far East and Latin America.

MARKET ENTRY AND OPERATION — THE OPTIONS

That there are three major groups of options for foreign expansion — through direct export, through the sale of knowledge and through investment — is universally recognized. More difficult is to determine the circumstances under which one or the other will be the most profitable. Checklist 2 can be used for this purpose; the subheadings can be scored to help determine the relative benefits of each method in a particular market.

Certain key issues will, naturally, determine the decision whether or not to export; these include the opportunities in the market, the nature of the competition, the suitability of the product and the impediments to imports. If export is impossible, the choice between licensing or some other knowledge agreement and direct investment will be decided on the resources available to the company, the potential income and the risks.

EXPORT

The overwhelming majority of firms with products or services that can be exported at all begin this way. Direct investment by a non-exporter is expensive because a whole series of business contacts has to be built up, as well as market research conducted, in an unknown environment. On the other hand, a firm that is not keeping all three options continually in the planning process is likely to be missing opportunities. The following checklists provide reminders of the main issues in the decision-making. Most are directly relevant to the finance manager since the methods of operation will limit the funding options.

CHECKLIST 4 EXPORT POLICIES

1. *Preliminaries* the answers to the following questions:

(a) What is the market research telling us about the adaptation of the product as well as the size and growth potential of the market?
(b) Do the promotion and selling policies need rethinking as well as the product policies?
(c) Is the image and market segment correct?
(d) Has the customer been correctly identified? Do local customs, regulations or distribution channels mean that the foreign customer is a different type of company from the domestic?

2. *The route.* The choice needs to be made and remade frequently. Among the possibilities are:

(a) direct sales from the home base to the foreign customer,
(b) sales to an exporter at home,
(c) sales to an agent abroad,
(d) sales through an experienced exporter in a different line of business (the so-called 'piggyback' option for the smaller exporter which has never developed greatly in Britain, but is more used in the States),
(e) sales through an office or subsidiary abroad.

Most companies use option c, an agent, at least until the growth of the business justifies their own presence in the market; the handling of agents merits a separate checklist.

CHECKLIST 5 THE FOREIGN AGENT
The first two items on the following list concern selection, where errors cause most of the recorded problems, but maintenance of the relationship is also important; a finance officer will be particularly concerned to monitor proposals to invest in the agent company.

1. *Selecting the type of agent.* There are about 30 different kinds of agency agreement available in various countries. In France, for instance, there are 27 defined by law. The agreements vary from the freelance salesman to the del credere agent who

provides a full range of marketing and financial services together with maintenance, stock-holding and perhaps some assembly. Questions about the kind of agent required for a particular market are accompanied by the recognition that answers may change. Stockholding and maintenance facilities are among those that are likely to be required once the sales grow. It also has to be remembered that some forms of agent (those that provide the fuller range of services) are protected by law in many countries — at present all the members of the European Community except Britain and Belgium). In these cases, it can be very expensive to dismiss an agent whatever the contract says.

2. *Selecting the agent.* A growing record of disasters, many of them with experienced exporters, bears witness to the importance of careful selection; casual acquaintances do not make good agents. Compatibility in every aspect is crucial along with the resources to grow with the business. There are many organizations, including government departments in most countries, able to help with a selection. Checks for credit worthiness and reputation should always be carried out.

3. *Servicing the agent.* The inability to keep the agent adequately supplied is another major cause of problems; an important issue is the degree of mutual involvement in one another's businesses. There is scope for a sub-checklist covering items like coordinated promotions, mutual reconsideration of product design and reconsideration of transport and distribution arrangements. The question of whether or not to invest in the agent company will also come on the agenda at some stage.

4. *Monitoring the agent.* The most successful practice is where the fullest possible amount of information is exchanged. The agent is, in effect, providing as much information as a subsidiary while the principal keeps the agent up-to-date on the progress of his business. Naturally such an arrangement cannot always be achieved but its achievement can be a target and where secrecy is required, this can at least be a conscious decision.

5. *Dismissing the agent.* One problem of dismissal has already been mentioned, some countries enforce high compensation; in all cases the need for a fallback scheme if the agent is unsuccessful is obvious. Not always so obvious are the problems caused by success and, if the agent is a small company without the resources to expand, the growth of the business may make a change necessary. A common route to foreign investment is where a company decides to buy, or buy into, an agent as a result of growth as an alternative to hiring a new agent.

THE SALE OF KNOWLEDGE

The sale of knowledge covers a wide variety of options which are as fast growing as they are numerous. Nevertheless currently only just over 10% of the money passing in world trade passes as payment for one of these options which include: licensing agreements, franchising agreements, technical assistance, management contracts, contract manufacture, and numerous other similar arrangements.

In many countries knowledge agreements are favoured by such measures as lower withholding taxes when payment is made and greater ease of remittance where exchange controls operate (note: this does not apply to all countries, some take the opposite line and apply higher withholding taxes to royalties).

The agreements cover the sale of different kinds of knowledge — technical in licensing, commercial in franchising and a total administrative package in management contracts. They all have in common that the principal is profiting from a specialised expertise which can be sold abroad with a minimum of investment in the market. Extra investment at home may be necessary to ensure that the stock of saleable knowledge is ahead of competitors. Intensive research at home is also needed to ensure that the foreign client does not become a competitor, an objection to knowledge sales mainly voiced by companies that do not use them. The following list is a reminder of the main issues to be considered in managing these sales.

CHECKLIST 6 THE SALE OF KNOWLEDGE

1. *The priority.* Sales of knowledge can be one off or regular, producers of small additional income or major sources of revenue. Companies have sometimes regarded such sales as low priority projects providing extra income when there were problems about exporting or direct investment; but there have always been exceptions in which licensing or franchising has been part of the core business, particularly in service industries like fast foods, car rental and hotels. Recent enquiries have shown that an increasing number of companies are giving a higher priority to these methods of operating abroad; a survey of management contracts, for instance, showed that a number of companies were intending to use them as major sources of business in the future; the contract method had only been employed in the past to provide a small additional income.

2. *Selecting the collaborator.* Knowledge agreements are almost always for a fixed term. Sometimes the principal is looking for a long-term contract to ensure repayment of the initial expenses which may be considerable and to prevent the collaborator setting up in competition. The latter will frequently argue for a shorter term arrangement in the expectation that his bargaining power will increase as his experience grows. Sometimes a longer term contract can be combined with periodical renegotiations to satisfy both parties. Competence, compatibility and credit-worthiness need checking and, as with agents, there are numerous organizations offering assistance. The difference is that the principal is usually able to obtain less outside help in a method of business where the selection is most critical, just because the arrangement is designed to last longer. A systematic evaluation plan is needed.

3. *Characteristics of the agreement.* The principal's main purpose will be to ensure that the licence or franchise is used effectively to promote his goods and services

and without damaging his reputation or restricting other parts of his business. Common stipulations are:

(a) for training (usually obligatory in franchises);
(b) restricted sales areas;
(c) arrangements for the transfer of expertise and knowhow;
(d) arrangements for the exchange of information either on all aspects of the business or on those to which the agreement applies;
(e) agreements about sources of supply;
(f) agreements about the use of patents, trade marks and other property of the contractor;
(g) to preserve confidentiality;
(h) arrangements about the transfer of staff where required.

Note that competition law in the United States and in the European Community prevents many restrictions in licensing and similar agreements.

4. *Forms of payment.* One advantage of the knowledge agreement, which is not always understood, is that funds can be transferred in a number of different ways. There can be:

(a) a lump sum payment in return for the sale of a patent, for instance, or the establishment of a management system;
(b) royalties for technical services or fees for franchising or management systems based on:
production,
sales,
value added,
profits;
(c) sale of supplies;
(d) interest or dividends where the principal puts in some capital;
(e) payments, based on costs or on man-days, for expatriate personnel;
(f) payments for training and other services.

Note: there is usually a minimum payment.

5. *Monitoring.* Except in the case of outright sales or exchanges between partners of similar sophistication, the principal will usually wish to monitor the progress of the relevant parts of the collaborator's business. As with agents, the collection of information on similar lines to that required of a subsidiary is valuable but not always practical.

INVESTMENT

There are many arrangements for international business which shade into one another, the distinctions are not as water-tight as the words suggest. Those already discussed — exporting, licensing and the rest — apply when the investment is primarily at home, although the placing of capital abroad in support of the business is always an issue. When facilities are built abroad, or companies owned, there comes a time when investment becomes a priority. The exact stage at which this is reached is a matter of debate. Selling subsidiaries are usually considered under export, although the issues involved in establishing them are the same as those for manufacturing and services outlined in checklist 7.

One distinction is between direct investment, where foreign equity is bought in order to manage a company as a subsidiary, and portfolio investment when the foreign shares are held for income and capital gains in the same way as shares in a domestic company. Again the distinction is blurred, particularly when motives are considered; the following checklists apply mainly to investment which is combined with management.

A number of surveys have shown that, in keeping with the step-by-step approach, most direct investments start as a defensive measure — usually to support markets that are under threat, but sometimes to ensure sources of supply. The main reasons for direct investment are listed in checklist 7.

CHECKLIST 7 THE MOTIVES FOR FOREIGN DIRECT INVESTMENT

1. *To defend a market* when it is under threat from such causes as:

(a) tariff barriers or import controls;
(b) demands for local manufacture;
(c) transport costs or delays;
(d) competition.

2. *To support a market* when it has grown beyond the capacity of agents, licensees or other collaborators.

3. *To support a market* where a local presence is required for other purposes like a more efficient spares and maintenance service.

4. *To protect shareholders* by spreading investment into different economies.

5. *To ensure that raw materials and components are available* when required and at an acceptable level of quality.

6. *To deploy resources and planning skills* on a global scale and, in particular, to make profitable use of under-employed resources in cash, expertise, staff or other forms.

7. *To reduce costs* (and increase availability) of capital, labour and supplies.

8. *To gain access to foreign knowhow and methods.*

9. *To respond to opportunities* offered by companies or governments or highlighted by intelligence reports within a company. These opportunities include off-shore production, where this is possible, and the use of tax havens.

If any of these motives applies to a particular market, there is a case for activating the procedures of investment appraisal. Once a need and an opportunity have been determined, a number of decisions have to be taken; these are listed in checklist 8.

CHECKLIST 8 DECISIONS TO BE TAKEN ONCE A NEW INVESTMENT HAS BEEN AGREED

The following decisions have to be taken although some will be pre-empted by circumstances if, for instance, local regulations do not permit 100% ownership or if a local company makes the first approach. Flexible guidelines are required, not decisions that impose a stranglehold.

1. *Ownership.* The proportion of ownership — minority, 50-50, majority or 100%. Most companies still prefer not to have partners where sole ownership is permitted, but practices are less rigid than they were 10 years ago and many have found that the disadvantages of sharing the equity are not as great as anticipated — while the expertise, risk-sharing and other contributions are worth having.

2. *The partners.* If the holding is to be less than 100%, a decision has to be made about who the partners are to be. There may be one or more other companies, in which case prolonged investigations are required and procedures for high level consultation worked out; or the shares may be sold on the local money market. In either case there will be some limitations on the freedom of choice on the capital structure and the methods used to transfer funds.

3. *The origins of a subsidiary* — whether it should be brought into existence by buying a going concern or by starting from scratch. The former method has many advantages — it brings with it, for example, an existing order book — but many companies prefer the latter because there are fewer problems to be inherited.

4. *Location.* This is a point at which incentives and other factors like communications and labour availability are taken into account. The model outlined in checklist 3 can also be used to determine the most suitable location; in this case items are weighted to fit the priorities of the company.

5. *Staffing.* Expatriates will frequently be used to staff a new venture, especially if it is started from scratch. Even if expatriates are soon withdrawn, they may be used to establish a management system. Many companies employ a finance manager from

head office for this purpose. A wider range of staffing policies, including an international grade of executives who will serve in any country, is available to established subsidiaries.

6. *Control and communications.* A clear system which provides adequate mutual information without snarling up the subsidiary with needless and frustrating procedures, is required from the start.

7. *Organization.* There are five main methods of organizing international companies, and priorities in the decision-making should decide which is the most appropriate. The five are:

(a) functional, when general managers abroad report to general managers at home (a director or corporate vice-president) while departments report to their opposite numbers;
(b) geographical, when foreign subsidiaries report to international or regional divisions or holding companies at home;
(c) product group, when foreign subsidiaries report to product divisions at home;
(d) matrix, when foreign subsidiaries report to both geographical and product divisions at home;
(e) project, when there is a flexible international organization with ad hoc arrangements for each activity, a structure that changes with the changing needs of the subsidiary as with project management.

8. *Profitability.* The purpose of the exercise is not so much to make profits for the subsidiary as to make money for the parent company and this is achieved by manipulating a complex of factors, some national and some international. Included are costs, prices (internal as well as to outside customers), the state of the markets, the ease of the transfer of goods and services and the problems of transferring funds.

CONCLUSION

This selective review of the issues that are considered in formulating international corporate strategies illustrates the kind of undertakings for which finance will be needed and from which income will be derived. The checklists can be used as reminders in reexamining existing markets or for looking at new ones. They are summarised in the final list (9).

CHECKLIST 9 THE FORMULATION OF INTERNATIONAL STRATEGIES

1. *The diversification route.* International business is seen as one of a number of international strategies which include diversification into competitors, suppliers, customers or companies where marketing, technical or financial expertise can be

used. These interact with one another and any one of them can lead to operations abroad which can also be undertaken in their own right.

2. *Interpreting the environment.* Identifying and understanding the opportunities and constraints in which the foreign business has to operate is worthy of greater attention than it often receives — especially the commercial consequences of non-commercial factors like politics, culture and local tastes and customs.

3. *A step by step approach.* Where practical market entry is through export or, less often, through licensing. Investment follows into a market that has already been prepared.

4. *The options.* Export, knowledge sales or investment are available for most circumstances. The purpose of regular reappraisal is to consider which method will contribute most to the central funds of the company and its long-term growth without incurring unacceptable risks.

MICHAEL Z. BROOKE

BIBLIOGRAPHY

BRITISH OVERSEAS TRADE BOARD, *Help for exporters* and numerous other pamphlets.
BROOKE, M.Z. and BUCKLEY, P.J., *The Handbook of International Trade*, Macmillan 1988.
BROOKE, M.Z. and VAN BEUSEKOM, M., *International Corporate Planning*, Pitman 1979.
International Directory of Published Market Research, Arlington, 1984.
TERPSTRA, V., *International Marketing* (3rd ed), Dryden Press, 1983.
WALSH, E., *International Marketing* (2nd ed), Macdonald and Evans, 1981.

1.5
International portfolio management

In a 1985 survey, it was estimated that over £185 billion worth of assets were either managed or advised by investment management companies based in the United Kingdom. Despite the October 1987 crash, the investment management business had grown to a multiple of this figure by mid-1989. According to W B S Phillips & Drew estimates the total of money managed in London amounted to £615bn by mid-1989. The size of the industry for investment services is clearly large and is a significant contributor to Britain's 'invisible' earnings.

This chapter presents an analysis of the industry and its 'products' and provides a guide to those wishing to make use of its services. It is slanted towards the investor investing overseas from Britain.

LONDON — THE INTERNATIONAL MARKETPLACE

Two strands of development have contributed to London's preeminence as a world centre for international portfolio management.

Its long history as a financial centre has been a major factor in commanding a significant proportion of the portfolio management business. The market's expertise in overseas investment has been complemented with the advantages of geographical and time zone location. From being a centre for capital exports and the home of an international reserve currency, London has become the lynch pin of the euro-currency markets. In doing so the City's relationships with overseas governments, public and private institutions and individuals, have borne fruit in attracting funds from overseas for portfolio management.

British institutions, which command the bulk of British private savings, have had a long and varied history of overseas investment. The ending of exchange controls, the North Sea oil boom and a more powerful currency have seen a substantial flow of funds overseas, giving the United Kingdom one of the world's largest overseas portfolios after Japan, Germany and Saudi Arabia.

The international portfolio management business evolved through a combination of factors. In the seventies the international business developed as an add-on to either the merchant banking or stockbroking functions. The growth of the domestic business came from a mixture of sources with areas of speciality apparent. For the merchant banks the business was a natural adjunct to their corporate finance activities. The rapid growth and diversification of international capital flows, however, has continuously enhanced the management role in international investment, to the extent that portfolio management has become a primary rather than an add-on business. Furthermore, the economies of scale in fund management operations suggested substantial rewards from emphasizing an independent business. Among the most recent stages in the development of the City of London as a whole, and the investment management industry in particular, is the demand for increased regulation. The Securities Investment Board supervises the City through a number of self-regulatory organisations, including IMRO (Investment Management Regulatory Organisation). As a corollary the development of fund management as an independent activity has been encouraged by the implementation of the Financial Services Act.

A SKILL INTENSIVE BUSINESS

The investment management industry is characterised by significant economies of scale and a relatively small work-force. The respondent firms to the Bank of England survey indicated that only 6,700 staff (an acknowledged underestimate) are employed in the industry. High profits can be earned per head. The critical factor in the labour equation is the high proportion of management with very specific investment skills. It is this workforce which is an essential resource supporting London as a centre for international portfolio management.

Perceiving London as the natural centre for fund management many large international groups have bought into or taken over United Kingdom fund management groups:

United Kingdom Fund Management Acquisitions post 1987

Acquirer	Acquired
Dresdner Bank	Thornton
Société Générale	Touche Remnant
Bank in Liechtenstein	G T Management
Deutsche Bank	Morgan Grenfell (sizeable fund business)
OCF	Framlington
Banque Indosuez	Gartmore
Hypobank 50% of	Foreign & Colonial Management

THE MECHANICS OF INVESTMENT

Investment management typically concentrates on the three major categories of financial assets: cash (currency), bonds and equities, and their derivatives (notably futures and options). Other important categories of managed assets include commodities and property, though to a lesser extent than the major categories. The investment management company, controlling one or several of these categories, generally performs the following functions:

ADMINISTRATION

It prepares valuations and transactions records, reinvests coupons or dividends, arranges cash flows, safekeeps cash and occasionally maintains tax records and accounts.

INVESTMENT PLANNING

It selects investments to meet specified objectives, typically associated with a client's liabilities. These objectives may include yield or income requirements, a preferred risk profile or a future expenditure pattern, perhaps associated with a pension plan.

DIVERSIFICATION

A diversified portfolio can raise returns for a given degree of risk. Hence managers will aim to invest funds in a spread of assets and markets.

CONTROL

It will carry out a continuous monitoring of account guidelines to ensure a client's objectives are being achieved. It is important to determine the appropriate yardstick with which to measure the performance of the portfolio.

MANAGEMENT

Management has to be both strategic and tactical: strategic management emphasises choice of markets, tactical management concerns securities in a single market. In both instances the aim of management is to outperform the yardsticks of performance indicated by a client's investment planning.

MARKETING

The growth and diversity of specialized managed products under a wide variety of brand names necessitates a strong marketing operation to both retail and institutional investors.

ACCOUNT STRUCTURE

The investment management function is usually carried out through two principal routes: either the individual account or the pooled fund. The pooled fund offers a number of advantages. For the smaller client the fund reduces the management transaction charges he would otherwise incur on an 'individual basis', but at the expense of losing some of his ideal investment requirements. The industry has, however, reached a state of development where a pooled fund exists to meet most people's needs. A pooled fund is also an ideal method for the large investor investing in specialist markets as this route ensures that the investor secures a specialist rather than a generalist fund manager.

Pooled funds. The United Kingdom boasts a wide variety of pooled funds. As can be seen from Table 1.5.1 pooled funds, whether investment trusts, unit trusts or offshore funds (shown under 'Other' on the table) are a major component of the industry.

Investment trusts. These are closed end funds and the oldest form of British pooled fund. A closed end fund does not stand ready to redeem shares representing investors' claims on the assets. Shares can stand at a premium or a discount to the net asset value, usually the latter.

Unit Trusts. These are open ended investment companies so shares may be redeemed at the shareholder's discretion. Shares stand at the net asset value of the fund.

Table 1.5.2 shows a comparison of investment and unit trusts.

Offshore funds. These are usually open ended and set up in offshore locations to enjoy tax advantages. They have appeal for investors wishing to earn income gross before tax. Offshore funds, being tax free at source, are ideal for attracting overseas investors wishing to buy United Kingdom investment expertise in international investment.

Under the Financial Services Act 1986 offshore funds are not eligible for marketing to domestic investors unless they conform to sections 86, 87 and 88 of the Act. Funds will qualify by being UCITs (Undertakings in Collective Investment in Transferable Securities) approved in a European Community domicile or having equivalent status in a recognised territory such as Jersey, Channel Islands, or winning individual approval from the Securities Investment Board.

TYPES OF INVESTMENT

CASH

The management of cash, or short-term liquid assets, has become more fashionable in recent years. At the end of 1984, 4.6% of the managed assets of British residents were cash and money-market instruments (sterling and foreign currency) while 11.7% of funds managed for overseas residents fell into this category. A significant proportion of the latter represents central band and international bank portfolios with a requirement for short maturity, high quality and liquid assets.

Table 1.5.1: Importance of the investment trust business for investment managers

	Investment trusts				Unit trusts				Pension funds				Other				Total	
	1.3.88		1.3.87		1.3.88		1.3.87		1.3.88		1.3.87		1.3.88		1.3.87		1.3.88	1.3.88
Management group	£m	% of total	£m	% of total	£m	% of total	£m	% of total	£m	% of total	£m	% of total	£m	% of total	£m	% of total	£m	£m
Investment																		
Alliance Trust	482	100	557	100	—	—	—	—	—	—	—	—	—	—	—	—	482	557
General Consolidated	82	100	84	100	—	—	—	—	—	—	—	—	—	—	—	—	82	84
Globe	930	100	993	100	—	—	—	—	—	—	—	—	—	—	—	—	930	993
Mezzanine Capital & Income	29	100	18	100	—	—	—	—	—	—	—	—	—	—	—	—	29	18
Moorgate	30	100	28	100	—	—	—	—	—	—	—	—	—	—	—	—	30	28
Scottish Investment Trust	484	100	536	100	—	—	—	—	—	—	—	—	—	—	—	—	484	536
Second Alliance	166	100	191	100	—	—	—	—	—	—	—	—	—	—	—	—	166	191
Updown	13	100	15	100	—	—	—	—	—	—	—	—	—	—	—	—	13	15
Independent management company																		
Foreign & Colonial	1165	57	1302	59	182	9	234	11	175	9	144	7	517	25	518	23	2039	2198
Grahams Bintoul & Co	37	100	(1)	(1)	—	—	—	—	—	—	—	—	—	—	—	—	37	(1)
John Govett	882	57	1024	63	220	14	254	16	420	27	320	20	16	1	18	1	1538	1616
Murray Johnstone	647	18	710	18	572	15	490	13	1894	51	1905	48	579	16	829	21	3692	3934
MIM Britannia	800	13	820	14	1100	18	920	15	2500	40	2350	39	1800	29	1910	32	6200	6000
River & Mercantile	124	100	136	100	—	—	—	—	—	—	—	—	—	—	—	—	—	—
Robert Fleming	1608	7	1689	8	3439	15	3443	15	9686	43	9754	44	7970	35	7500	31	22,703	22,386
Stewart Ivory	240	44	259	46	39	7	42	8	145	26	139	25	126	23	125	22	550	565
TAI Securities	156	100	151	100	—	—	—	—	—	—	—	—	—	—	—	—	—	—
Throgmorton	453	78	438	81	—	—	—	—	130	22	100	19	—	—	—	—	583	538
Touche Remnant	1956	57	2280	54	222	7	191	5	768	22	1096	26	483	14	676	16	3429	4243
Investment house																		
Discretionary Unit Fund Managers	7	34	n/a	n/a	14	66	n/a	n/a	—	—	—	—	—	—	—	—	21	—
Guinness Mahon Investment	162	28	147	27	107	19	99	18	273	48	258	47	31	5	44	8	573	548
Henderson Administration	759	10	873	13	1649	22	2035	30	4528	57	3150	47	738	10	634	10	7673	6692
Martin Currie	688	33	740	39	69	3	65	3	1328	63	1115	58	7	1	—	—	2092	1920
NM Rothschild	30	1	n/a	n/a	124	2	n/a	n/a	6800	97	n/a	n/a	—	—	n/a	n/a	6954	n/a
Plc companies																		
EFM	366	44	381	43	194	23	234	26	282	33	273	31	—	—	—	—	842	888
Other																		
British Investment Trust	395	66	430	67	—	—	—	—	196	34	212	33	—	—	—	—	581	642
Laurwood Ltd	60	75	63	100	—	—	—	—	—	—	—	—	20	25	—	—	80	63
Lazard Investors	264	8	299	8	412	12	420	12	1453	42	1560	12	1358	39	1370	38	3857	3649
Top Technology Ltd	37	96	n/a	n/a	—	—	—	—	—	—	—	—	2	4	n/a	n/a	39	n/a
Partnerships																		
Baillie Gifford	878	40	985	53	122	6	90	5	1206	55	796	42	—	—	—	—	2206	1871

Note: All figures supplied by respective management groups. Groups surveyed comprise the table. Although Dunedin Gartmore, GT, Baring and Hambros all responded to the survey, the above details were not provided by them. Classifications given are not mutually exclusive, n/a denotes figures not available. (1) Denotes figures not comparable.

Source: Money Management

Table 1.5.2: Comparison of investment and unit trusts

Investment Trust	*Unit Trust*
— is a company quoted on the Stock Exchange	— is a trust set up under the supervision of the Securities Investment Board
— has a fixed number of shares which are bought and sold through a stockbroker	— has units which are issued and redeemed by the Unit Trust management company
— has shares whose price is determined like those of any other quoted company by supply and demand	— has units whose price is determined by the net asset value of the fund
— has shares which, therefore, may stand at a premium or, more usually, at a discount to the net asset value	— has units which stand, within minor limits, at the net asset value
— being a company, cannot advertise to promote the sale of its shares	— can, through its management company, advertise to promote the sale of its units
— can take a long-term view as it has a permanent capital structure	— must have regard to the possibility of redemptions by unit holders and, therefore, must be cautious in difficult markets and when investing in unlisted or less marketable investments
— is relatively cheap to run and administer	— has more complex and hence more costly administration
— can borrow to provide gearing and invest more money on behalf of shareholders. The interest on these borrowings is allowed for tax	— cannot borrow to provide gearing
— can invest in a very wide range of securities, both listed and unlisted, and can hedge all currency risks	— is strictly controlled when investing outside the stock exchanges and cannot hedge sterling
— is suitable for both small and large investors	— is suitable for anyone who is not prepared to accept the risks and opportunities inherent in the discount usually pertaining to investment trust shares

Source: Foreign and Colonial Investment Trust Annual Report 1988

A combination of factors has contributed to the growing popularity of cash management. First, a legacy of the inflationary era of the seventies was the strong performance of cash relative to other assets. Over the period 1971-1984 cash outperformed both equities and bonds in the United States, a surprising result given the lower risk associated with cash. This result does not apply over the long run. Equities, in compensation for their higher risk, outperform cash and bonds. Second, cash, for the tax-free investor (typically holding assets offshore), currently enjoys high real interest rates. Third, many international banks have replaced many of their international loans with generally lower risk 'securitized' assets. The management of these assets is often approached from an investment management standpoint rather than from the traditional banking framework of asset-liability management.

A typical cash portfolio of money market instruments would comprise bank deposits, negotiable certificates of deposit (CDs), floating and variable rate notes and certificates, bankers acceptances, commercial paper, local authority bills, euronotes, medium-term notes and short maturity bonds. The investment manager's function is to use these instruments to achieve the twin objectives of high returns and excellent liquidity. By name, instrument and maturity selection the professional manager will typically exceed the return available from time deposits. This liquidity ensures good funds to meet clients' unforeseen requirements, and avoids the penalties from breaking bank deposits.

To be managed successfully, cash portfolios generally need to be in excess of £10m. Modern practice in liquid asset portfolios now includes futures and option instruments, traded on recognized exchanges, which broaden the scope of the manager's function and facilitate the achievement of target objectives.

CURRENCY

A related issue to cash management, the recognition of the importance of currency management is also a relatively recent phenomenon. Currency management is usually regarded as integral to international cash, bond or equity management, yet can also be viewed quite separately.

Currencies have become exceptionally volatile since exchange rates were allowed to float in the early seventies. Subsequent managed-floating arrangements, such as the European Monetary System, have reduced, not removed, the volatility between some bilateral and unilateral exchange rates. The degree of volatility is so high that it can often exceed that seen in equity investments. Currency management is essential for achieving the potential improvement in return available in the international market place, as well as limiting the considerable risks associated with currency exposure.

Currency management is essential for institutions with an international spread of business. Provided the current spread of assets and liabilities can be identified the mismatch whether potential or actual can involve a significant exposure.

There are a range of instruments available to the currency manager including spot, forward, futures and options. The spot, forward and futures markets provide a device for taking views on a particular currency for a time extending many months into the future.

The currency option market provides insurance against adverse market movements. Table 1.5.3 illustrates the relative merits of the various currency strategies available and shows the advantages of the asymmetrical profile of returns available from using currency options.

Objective: Hedge US$15,250 into Pounds Sterling on 2 November 1984 with $/£1.35 call options expiring on June 1985. [This Option gives an investor the right, but not the obligation, to buy £12,500 at $/£1.25 in June 1985]

Action: The option was bought at a cost of 4.2c and the exchange rate at the time was $/£1.22.

Table 1.5.3: Currency management — alternative strategies

Exchange Rate (£ :$) June1985	*No hedge*	*% Sale*	*Forward hedge*	*%*	*Option*	*%*
1.00	15,150	+21.0	14,820	0	14,820	+18.6
1.10	13,864	+10.9	12,500	0	13,434	+7.5
1.20	12,708	+1.7	12,500	0	12,278	−1.8
1.22	12,500	0	12,500	0	12,070	−3.4
1.30	11,763	-6.2	12,500	0	11,857	−5.1
1.40	10,893	-13.9	12,500	0	11,895	−4.9
1.50	10,167	-18.6	12,500	0	11,895	−4.8

Further strategies include dynamic currency hedging through option replicating programmes. These programmes have evolved from dynamic hedging in the United States equity market which, from its roots in the early 1980s, evolved into a US$100bn portfolio insurance business prior to the October 1987 crash.

BOND MANAGEMENT

According to the 1985 survey, management of fixed interest assets (other than cash) accounts for only 18.4% of funds managed for United Kingdom residents, but 45.8% of funds managed for overseas residents. The bulk of the latter category comprises investment in bonds issued by foreign governments, companies and supranational institutions, the principal issuers in the Euro and foreign bond markets.

Traditionally bond management has been passive in nature. The modern fixed interest markets are, however, radically different from their predecessors. Since 1979 real interest rates on fixed interest securities have risen dramatically throughout the world. Investors have become more confident of earning a real return on their capital.

Furthermore, fixed interest markets have become increasingly international, subservient to currency movements and hence volatile. Continuing current account disequilibria, for example, the Organization for Petroleum Exporting Countries and Japanese surpluses and the United States and less developed countries' deficits, have generated substantial capital flows. These flows have increasingly been channelled through the international bond markets. The most significant contribution to active management has come from the rapid expansion of the international bond markets relative to their domestic equivalents.

In addition, a multiplicity of new techniques are able to create a wide variety of pay-off patterns with different profiles. These techniques include integrating futures, options, innovative banking products, and dynamic strategies with equity related products.

EQUITIES

Equity investments dominate the British resident fund management market, accounting for 77% of funds managed. The picture is quite different for the overseas resident with equities accounting for 42.5% of funds managed. The emphasis on equities for British residents reflects the impact of the British tax system, though the 1988 Budget reform of income and capital gains tax is likely to change the equity and bond mix. International equity management is a response to very different movements in stock markets around the world, areas of dynamism rewarding the investor prepared to take a global view. Equities are of higher risk than cash or bond investments and, in theory, generally yield higher returns, whether on a domestic or an international comparison. Equity markets are so heterogeneous that correct equity selection has the potential for yielding higher returns than would be available from a hypothetical investment in the stock market indices. The debate between the relative merits of stock selection and market indexation continues to rage.

DERIVATIVES: FUTURES AND OPTIONS

The use of futures and options in fund management has been steadily increasing in recent years. By end 1989 over US$8bn of United States public funds were invested in leveraged futures funds. In the United Kingdom the tax liberalization proposed in the 1990 budget and the more rapid progress to the SIB authorization of retail futures funds is likely to develop an onshore market for the United Kingdom.

Futures funds are managed by modern investment systems which are considered one of the most effective means of implementing sophisticated asset choices. While employing diverse methods they usually use computer models to forecast and exploit the movement of currencies, interest rates, stock indices and commodities.

METHODS OF MANAGEMENT

For all categories of assets there are a variety of methods of management. These can be grouped under the two general headings of macro and micro — or, more commonly, the asset allocation and the stock selection approaches. It should be noted that each approach incorporates the other, the classification determines the emphasis. The contrast in these styles tends to be most pronounced for equity management. The macro approach places emphasis on the assessment of market movements using macroeconomic analysis. Analysis of individual securities or instruments under this methodology is considered to be of secondary importance. The bottom up method assumes that more added value is available from individual security selection than from predicting market movements.

The differences in style between investment houses largely reflect their preferences for either approach. There is usually some combination of the two methods but the emphasis will be declared in the company's management philosophy.

INTERNATIONAL FIXED INTEREST MANAGEMENT

A typical philosophy statement for fixed interest management reflects the bias towards the top down approach:

(1) Currency selection is critical for ensuring the successful performance of the international portfolio. Currency exposure is treated as a separate decision from the bond market allocation. When appropriate the forward and option markets in currencies are used to hedge the bond exposure. Fifty per cent of management effort is devoted to currency selection.
(2) Approximately 30% of management effort is concerned with the continuous assessment of risk and reward from the yield curve in each bond market. The duration of the portfolio is constantly modified according to these assessments.
(3) Individual security selection concentrates on credit quality, liquidity and volatility. Advantage is taken of the many anomalies that arise in the international bond markets. Fifteen per cent of the management effort is devoted to this task.
(4) Attention is also given to yield differentials between the international and domestic bond markets in individual currencies. Switching between markets is made in response to currency changes and capital flows.

Currency. International bond investment can earn significantly higher returns through currency selection. Foreign exchange markets are traditionally more volatile than bond markets, however, and as a result currency analysis warrants considerable management time.

Our model for currency projections uses a fundamental approach in analysing foreign exchange. The model assesses the demand for, and the supply of, individual currencies. At times of excess demand (supply) for a currency, the exchange rate will rise (fall). This framework incorporates, on the demand side, the transactions (a function of economic growth), precautionary (a function of crisis), and portfolio demand for the currency. The international supply of a currency includes the domestic money supply plus increases or decreases through the international banking system. We have found that, for portfolio demand, an emphasis on interest rate differentials and forward currency rates provides the best guide to relative value in the foreign exchange market. Besides straightforward use of spot and forward markets, extensive use is made of currency options to acquire and to hedge currency exposure. The range of strike prices on options is used to reflect strength of views and degree of hedging. At all times the managers are aware of currency volatility and its impact on options premiums.

The alternative uses of the currency markets are shown by the disposition of a typical fixed interest portfolio in early 1985. The majority of funds were invested in United States dollar bonds. However, sales of United States dollars in the three months forward market, and through six month call options, ensured exposure to the appreciating currencies — pounds sterling, Deutschmarks and Japanese yen.

Duration. The fixed interest team is continuously monitoring and adjusting the duration of bond portfolios. The parameters of the management task are: (a) duration is modified according to the outlook for interest rates and the risk-return choices presented by the shape of the yield curve; (b) the use of a number of methods and instruments to adjust duration.

(1) The outlook for interest rates is determined from a fundamental assessment of the prospects for the economy and, in particular, the outlook for inflation. In a majority of cases the broader economic issues are widely known and usually discounted in the market place; but at times government policy, sentiment, and lags in responding to new information can leave markets at levels different from true economic value. The degree of risk of interest rate changes is continuously changing, and therefore duration should be modified in accordance with these changes, in order to take advantage of inefficient pricing of the bond market.

(2) A variety of methods and instruments can be used to adjust the overall duration of a portfolio. The simplest case for reducing duration is the sale of securities to raise cash. Other methods to reduce duration would include shortening maturities, increasing coupons, selling Treasury note and bond features and purchasing put options on Treasury notes and bonds. The converse operations would be used to extend duration. In the non-US dollar bond market there are fewer available instruments to modify duration and fine-tune the portfolio. The degree of duration adjustment depends upon the shape of the yield curve and the managers' judgement of the risk of the outlook.

Security selection. The bonds purchased must satisfy the portfolio's requirements for credit quality, duration and liquidity. Considerable emphasis is also placed on international bonds for their yield advantage and tax-free characteristics. In addition management time is devoted to anomaly switching and new issue arbitrage.

(1) *Credit quality.* The international markets display a much wider variety of names and credit risks than are available within individual domestic markets. Unless portfolio guidelines permit, bonds must be rated at least AA by the leading rating agencies, or deemed the equivalent by the managers.
The market's assessment of these credit risks is, at times, inefficient and therefore taking advantage of mispriced credit risks should be considered as an important goal of instrument selection.

(2) *Anomaly switching.* This involves taking advantage of price discrepancies for similar quality bonds. Mispricing can be a function of market overreaction to a short-term deterioration in the fundamentals underlying the security, the circumstances of the particular issue or an unusual excess supply of paper.

(3) *New issue arbitrage.* The almost continuous supply of new issues in the international markets can provide opportunities for yield improvement. These opportunities can arise from a new borrower in the market, from innovatory deals, difficult market conditions or the large size of an issue.

(4) *Market selection.* While considerable progress has been made towards global bond markets there is still a differentiation between the international and domestic sectors in any particular currency: for example, between the United States domestic, yankee and eurodollar bond markets. Yield spread differentials can vary according to a variety of factors including currency changes, international capital flows and capital controls or taxes. The fixed interest team continuously monitors these market movements to take advantage of changing yield spreads.

INTERNATIONAL EQUITY MANAGEMENT.

Asset allocation. Investment companies emphasising asset allocation recognize the greater added value from market than from security selection.

The key to the asset allocation process is the specification of market forecasts. From forecasts are derived comparative expected returns for each market which are combined with currency projections. These are not binding but are necessary for developing a framework in which optimization techniques can be applied to the portfolio. Expected returns are combined with the risk or volatility parameters, determined historically or by forecaster estimates, to provide an optimal frontier for risk and return across markets.

This frontier of risk and return enables the construction of efficient portfolios with different risk and return preferences. The process covers portfolios moving internationally from any currency base.

While the above discipline is generally quantitatively driven it is open to qualitative judgement. Most quantitative methods are flexible enough to satisfy the subjective requirements of individual managers who may have strong views on individual markets and may want to weight their portfolios accordingly. The yardstick for an international equity portfolio is the Morgan Stanley Capital International Index (see Table 1.5.4).

Table 1.5.4: The composition (on 30 April 1990) of the Capital International Index

	%	%
North America	36.8	
of which USA		34.1
Europe	27.1	
of which UK		8.7
Germany		4.6
France		3.9
Switzerland		1.9
Pacific Basin	35.8	
of which Japan		32.7

Source: Morgan Stanley Capital International Perspective, Geneva

MARKET FORECASTING

The approach to equity market forecasting lays great stress on the different dynamics and characteristics driving individual equity markets. In addition, given the extreme difficulty of achieving perfect equity market foresight, as much weight is given to the testing of the variables which go to make up the forecast as to the bottom line number. It is our belief that the discipline of a set format and forecasting process has the benefits of focusing on all the relevant issues driving equity markets and at the same time tests the strength and conviction of the analysis of the various market specialists. The main variables used in equity market forecasting are set out below.

(1) ECONOMIC AND POLICY BACKGROUND

Based on the work carried out to set the global economic backdrop:

(a) an assessment of the growth of gross national product, industrial production, inflation and trade position;
(b) monetary and fiscal policy and interest rate structure.

(2) CORPORATE PROFITABILITY

An appraisal of both historic and prospective profit and earnings outlook both in an absolute sense and in a relative sense.

(3) CORPORATE DIVIDENDS

Dividend growth and cover is monitored by market with regard to the trend of pay out ratios and their cyclicality.

(4) LIQUIDITY ANALYSIS

An assessment of current and prospective supply of stock on the one hand, and an analysis of institutional cashflow (both domestic and international) on the other.

(5) Sentiment or Investor Confidence Indications

Analysis and comment on the likely determinants of investor confidence whether economic, political or technical.

(6) Valuation

An analysis of various valuation data, principally price earnings ratio, price to cash flow, dividend yield and most particularly the bond to equity relationship not merely in absolute terms but crucially in comparison with medium and long term history within the individual markets concerned.

STOCK SELECTION

Stock selection criteria vary by company and investment manager. The following description attempts to compare the flavour of the stock selection process and should not be considered to be definitive.

BUYING

The stocks purchased should satisfy the following requirements (except in Japan where different considerations apply): either (a) they sell at a significant discount to asset value, or (b) (the larger category) they are capable of sustained earnings growth at a rate which by our method of assessment will exceed the growth discounted in the current market price.

The characteristic of shares in the first category is the ownership of under-utilized assets; this indicates a low return on capital employed, which discourages competitors or makes it cheaper for them to acquire such a company than to start a new one. Selection therefore focuses on companies where it is believed that management changes will result in the assets being used more effectively in future, or where a takeover should otherwise be likely. Balance sheets must be strong enough to ensure that the company will not be forced to raise capital on unfavourable terms or to sell assets at distress prices.

The growth stocks purchased have the opposite characteristic — namely the ability to earn a high post-tax return on equity which must materially exceed the long-term bond yield. Only thereby can a company produce a consistent increase in earnings per share and combine immediate returns to shareholders in the form of dividends with future returns in the form of growth. These may be selling at a premium multiple to the market. The size of premium paid will depend on the excess rate of earnings growth over the market average and in particular on its visibility and likely duration.

A typical profile by a management company may read as follows. 'We stress the need to maintain contact, either directly or through brokers, with the management of the companies in which we invest. Using industry as well as company sources, we must be convinced that the company either operates in a rapidly expanding market or, if it is in a more stable market, enjoys a proprietary position backed by strong new product flows and sound marketing. We attach importance to management's own stake in any company and to its commitment to run the business for the benefit of shareholders. In particular, growth targets must be set in relation to earnings per share rather than to expansion for its own sake; and we expect that when new capital is raised, whether by issues or for takeovers, it will be done only on terms which do not dilute the interest of existing shareholders.'

In Japan the stock market has particular characteristics, prompted by the widespread involvement of the private investor and this has led to great volatility. We therefore follow a different discipline. We place greater emphasis on sector analysis and buy stocks which have one or more of the following attributes.

(1) Companies which have a comparative advantage over the rest of the world in technology or manufacturing ability.
(2) Companies operating in the area where they are likely to achieve a dominant position in the future.
(3) Growth sectors of the domestic economy.

In selecting all stocks we use a time horizon of about three years believing that our ability to achieve a better understanding than the market of a company's prospects is more likely to be achieved in the relatively long run. We always aim to have sufficient confidence in the stocks we hold that, should the share price fall, we are happy to add to the existing position.

SELLING

Stocks are usually sold for one of two main reasons.

(1) Because the stock market has become over-enthusiastic about a particular stock and has driven the price considerably higher than is justified by the valuation criteria.

(2) Stocks are also sold when it is perceived that the earnings prospects or other fundamentals of a particular company or sector are deteriorating. Sales only take place when the adverse factors are not already reflected in the price, and when they are likely to be more than temporary.

Currency allocation. See above under International Fixed Interest Management.

Cash allocation. The normal position is to be fully invested, the main exception being when the manager is unable to find enough shares which meet the investment criteria described above. A stock index future can be used to maintain market exposure. The occasion when a strategic decision to go liquid is made usually arises when credit markets are under stress and money rates are expected to rise sharply. Even then it is unlikely that the proportion invested in equities would fall below 75%.

Country weightings. Country weightings are determined by the asset allocation process. Mainly for reasons of liquidity, the major investment positions are in the larger capitalized stock markets namely the United States, Japan, the United Kingdom, Germany, Holland and Switzerland. Smaller markets are used if they have particularly attractive stocks, but these will necessarily form a minor part of the portfolio.

THE IMPORTANCE OF DIVERSIFICATION

A cardinal rule of investment is the benefit available from diversification. In general, the greater the number of securities held the lower the risk for a similar return. This applies to international investment as much as it does to an individual market.

A well-known result in individual equity markets is that the holding of about twenty-five securities achieves most of the benefits of diversification. Further additions to a portfolio achieve only marginal reductions in risk. In the international market place, a much larger number of assets will be required to eliminate as much risk as is possible. For British investors, the relatively poor — though improving — performance of the British economy makes overseas investment imperative. For the last fourteen years, the era of free floating exchange rates, home equity markets have benefited from the country's oil endowment with its positive impact on the pound sterling and the sharp increase in profitability of British companies associated with improved productivity and the shedding of labour. Even so, over the last five years the United Kingdom equity market has underperformed the rest of the world.

The dynamism of the Japanese economy, and the economies of the Pacific rim, have been reflected in a strong bond and stock market performance. Over the last ten years Japanese equities, as represented by the Tokyo Dow Jones index, would have shown a return to British investors of 27.1% per annum, 6.0% per annum more than that available from British equities and 14.6% more than that available from British bank deposits (see Table 1.5.5).

Table 1.5.5: Annual returns — sterling (1980-1989)

% pa	Money markets	Bonds	Equities
USA	13.9	16.2	21.4
Japan	15.7	17.5	32.1
Germany	10.5	11.3	22.0
France	11.1	12.5	22.7
United Kingdom	12.7	14.7	23.8
Canada	15.5	15.7	15.3
Australia	13.6	10.3	17.6
Netherlands	10.7	12.7	25.4
Italy	14.2	13.3	26.9
Switzerland	7.1	6.5	15.8
HongKong	-	-	17.5
Singapore	-	-	16.7

Source: Phillips & Drew

The variation in returns from markets is reflected in the performance of the United Kingdom unit trust industry (see Table 1.5.6).

SELECTION OF A FUND MANAGEMENT GROUP

A large array of fund management groups present themselves to the investor wishing to invest overseas. This industry shows segmentation by both type of client and by manager, whether specialist or generalist. A recent Bank of England survey categorises the industry by British client and manager type (see Table 1.5.7). The most important source of clients are the pension schemes which, according to the Bank of England survey, account for 60% of total funds managed. The investment management for this sector is dominated by the merchant banks although the

Table 1.5.6: Long-term investment returns. Offer to offer with net income reinvested. Current value of £100 over period indicated to 1st May 1990

Sector	UK general			UK growth			UK equity income			International growth		
Investment . . . months ago	12	60	120	12	60	120	12	60	120	12	60	120
Median Fund	94.6	194.7	584.2	89.1	183.9	515.1	93.4	217.5	601.6	106.0	180.0	491.7
No. of funds in sector	101	76	58	203	106	63	123	77	51	152	76	44
Sector	**Japan**			**Australasia**			**Far East (incl. Japan)**			**North America**		
Investment . . . months ago	12	60	120	12	60	120	12	60	120	12	60	120
Median Fund	93.5	268.2	899.7	100.1	135.4	173.0	102.3	233.5	630.2	109.9	136.3	434.9
No. of funds in sector	70	43	8	13	10	3	59	29	10	126	77	27
Sector	**Europe**			**Financial & Property**			**Commodity & Energy**			**Investment trust units**		
Investment . . . months ago	12	60	120	12	60	120	12	60	120	12	60	120
Median Fund	137.7	303.7	814.0	88.0	168.9	436.5	106.6	133.4	229.3	100.5	195.6	896.0
No. of funds in sector	111	31	5	20	12	11	28	21	7	10	7	5
Indexes												
Months ago	12	60	120									
FT Ordinary	97.5	199.7	533.4									
FT All Share	12	60	120									
	98.5	195.0	585.0									

Source: MBC Information Services

Table 1.5.7: Funds managed for UK residents

	Accepting houses		*Clearing banks*		*Insurance companies*		*Stockbrokers*		*Other*		*UK offices of foreign managers*		*All managers*	
Analysis by client	*£b*	*%*	*£b*	*%*	*£b*	*%*	*£b*	*%*	*£b*	*%*	*£b*	*%*	*£b*	*%*
Government and public sector	2.2	5.0	0.1	0.6	0.4	2.8	1.1	9.9	0.5	—	0.1	3.6	3.8	3.6
Private clients	2.2	5.0	2.9	18.2	—	—	2.7	24.3	6.8	2.4	0.1	9.1	8.4	7.8
Pension schemes	28.0	63.2	8.6	54.1	13.6	95.8	6.2	55.9	11.4	32.2	0.6	54.5	63.8	59.2
Unit and investment trusts	8.5	19.2	2.5	15.7	0.1	0.7	0.3	2.7	1.5	54.0	0.4	36.4	23.2	21.5
Insurance companies	0.8	1.8	0.3	2.0	—	—	—	—	—	7.1	—	—	2.6	2.4
Industrial and commercial companies	0.7	1.5	0.8	5.0	—	—	0.1	0.9	0.4	1.9	—	—	2.0	1.9
Other	1.9	4.3	0.7	4.4	0.7	0.7	0.7	6.3	0.5	2.4	—	—	3.9	3.6
Total	44.3	100.0	15.9	100.0	14.2	100.0	11.1	100.0	21.1	100.0	1.1	100.0	107.7	100.0

insurance companies, clearing banks and the independent fund management groups have a significant proportion of the market.

Traditional relationships are, however, coming under increasing scrutiny as the City revolution gathers momentum. The insurance companies and the independent fund management groups may well secure a larger market share in future as clients become more concerned about conflicts of interest between the corporate finance, market-making and fund management divisions of the merchant and clearing banks.

While traditional relationships and market niches determine which fund management group to choose, modern practice has increasingly focused on investment performance as the principal criterion by which to select managers. Most publicly quoted investment, unit trust and offshore funds are subject to extensive scrutiny and appear in widely publicised league tables of performance. The *Financial Times* magazines *Money Management* and *Pensions Management*, provide the most comprehensive assessment of publicly quoted funds' performance.

Good results over the long term will usually indicate the better investment management companies. Top of the table performance in the short term may merely indicate high return, high risk investment strategies which can deteriorate extremely quickly. In any performance universe of fund management companies, those managers that regularly achieve positions in the top quartile should be preferred.

A network of consultants has developed to assist individuals and institutions in selecting a management group most appropriate for the investors' requirements. The consultants build up substantial dossiers on the fund managers, their performance record and management histories. In doing so, the consultants perform a valuable service in the introduction of clients to the investment management groups. This function frees the specialist fund managers from some of the burdens of marketing their services and leaves them more time and resources to concentrate on the business they know best — portfolio management.

ADAM PARKIN
John Govett and Co. Ltd., Investment Managers

REFERENCES

Bank of England *Quarterly Bulletin*, June 1985. The survey points out that there is no way of telling what proportion of the total UK fund management industry has been captured by the returned data. The survey captures only the business in the competitive market place. A vast volume of funds are also managed within pension funds and insurance companies which do not actively solicit external business. The definition of investments in the survey included United Kingdom and foreign securities (including eurobonds), money market assets, and bank deposits, commodity and financial futures, options, participations in collective investment undertakings (such as unit trusts) and property.

The first investment trust, the Foreign and Colonial Investment Trust, was set up in 1868 with an initial subscribed capital of £1m. By the middle of 1985, its gross assets approached £1bn.

PARKIN, ADAM, 'Where diversification pays'. *Euromoney Magazine*, September 1984.

APPENDIX:

LIST OF THE BETTER KNOWN FUND MANAGEMENT CONSULTANTS

Bacon & Woodrow,
Investment Services Ltd,
Empire House,
St. Martins-le-Grand,
London,
EC1A 4ED.

Clay & Partners,
61 Brook Street,
London,
W1Y 2HN.

Frank Russell International,
75 Wimpole Street,
London,
W1M 7DD.

Noble Lowndes,
PO Box 144,
Norfolk House,
Wellesley Road,
Croydon,
Surrey,
CR9 3EB.

Towers Perrin,
Castlewood House,
77-91 New Oxford Street,
London,
WC1A 1PX.

William M. Mercer Fraser,
Burwood House,
16 Caxton Street,
London,
SW1H 0QU.

Watson & Sons Ltd,
Watson House,
London Road,
Reigate,
Surrey,
RH2 9PG.

The Wyatt Company,
Park Gate,
21 Tothill Street,
London,
SW1H 9LL.

2
CAPITAL STRUCTURES AND RELATED FINANCING ISSUES

Part 2 begins with a review of capital structure decisions and how they are taken. This is followed by two chapters on international banking, one from a supplier's and the other from a user's viewpoint. This is followed by a chapter on debt finance and one on the raising of equity on the major money markets. The sixth chapter details the work of international lending agencies by whom much international business is financed, while a final chapter provides a guide to mergers and acquisitions across frontiers.

2.4 Raising funded debt finance in major capital markets

Background
Some reasons for raising debt finance
Types of debt finance
Major capital markets

2.5 Procedures and costs associated with raising equity finance

United States
United Kingdom
Japan

2.6 Sources of funds from international lending agencies

The international lending agencies
The World Bank Group
The African Development Bank
The Asian Development Bank
The Inter-American Development Bank
The Nordic Investment Bank
The Caribbean Development Bank (CDB)
The European Bank for Reconstruction and Development
Summary of terms, conditions and qualifications of lending agencies' financing
Approaching the international leading agencies
Appendix 1: commercial co-financing: a case study
Appendix 2: World Bank guidelines for procurement

2.7 International Mergers and Acquisitions

Strategies
Reasons for cross border acquisitions
A strategy for international mergers
Conclusions
Financing
Key financial considerations
Criteria for financing international acquisitions
Sources of finance for international acquisitions
Conclusion

2.1
Capital structure decisions in an international context

Capital structure decisions in an international group usually fall into two categories:

(1) decisions on the optimal financial structure for the consolidated group;
(2) applications of capital structure policy within the group.

It is, of course, inevitable that there is considerable overlap between the two; however it is appropriate to determine the group's objectives on the one hand and the method of applying them on the other. Usually it is necessary to aim at an optimal solution rather than at a theoretical best capital structure.

The importance of managing the capital structure of a group must be stressed. It is essential that it is reviewed regularly and that decisions on objectives and applications are taken on a consistent basis.

CAPITAL STRUCTURE POLICY

Capital structure policy covers a number of areas. The most significant topics which require decision-making include the following:

Total amount of funding. There will be occasions when spending plans exceed the ability of a group to fund prudently; potential contingencies and the capacity of the group to fund at a rate commensurate with the group's actual or projected return on assets have to be taken into account.

This is a subject worthy of detailed discussion on its own. It is important to bear in mind that a group's capital structure ultimately depends upon its ability to generate earnings at a rate which will satisfy lenders and investors.

Nature of funding. The proportion of a group's requirements to be funded by borrowing as opposed to equity.

Types of equity. Decisions on the proportion of ordinary, preference or convertible capital together with related decisions on dividend policy and the retention of earnings.

Types of debt. The proportion of the group's funding programme to be funded by long-, medium- or short-term borrowings, together with related decisions on the proportion of fixed- and floating-rate liabilities.

Currency of funding. In an international group the currency of debt is an important decision which requires consideration of cost, availability, taxation, exchange controls and the group's policy towards the management of currency risk.

Location of funding. Both debt and equity can be raised at parent, subsidiary and associate level. Decisions on location can often raise complex issues which require detailed consideration.

Cost of capital. Equity, debt and the taxation effects of their respective location have an important impact upon a group's cost of capital and, by extension, upon investment decisions.

SOURCES OF FUNDS

There are three main methods of funding a group:

(1) conserving cash generated from operations;
(2) calling upon shareholders or others to contribute new equity;
(3) raising debt in whatever form from external sources.

Because the last source is indirectly interrelated with self-generated or shareholder-derived funds it is sensible to start any review of capital structure decision-making by considering the role of equity and its relationship to debt.

DEBT-EQUITY RELATIONSHIP — PRUDENT BORROWING LEVELS

This relationship is often oversimplified by using some target or maximum debt-equity ratio. Many companies and banks have developed concepts of prudent maximum borrowing limits which they usually express in terms of ratios. It is questionable if these ratios are particularly helpful in the crudest terms. They are often applied using historical figures; they take little account of the volatility or stability of a company's earnings, or the cost of the debt which needs to be serviced. In simple terms a prudent borrowing level is the amount of debt which a company can service in terms of meeting interest and principal payments out of future operational cash flows. If the borrowing is forecast to be met from other sources, such as from future sales of assets, raising new debt or from new external equity it is difficult to argue that such a borrowing is prudent.

It is necessary to reject the conventional wisdom that a certain level of borrowing may always, one way or another, be capable of refinancing. It is particularly dangerous to rely on being able to raise equity to restore health to a stretched balance sheet.

For many reasons it must also be accepted that capital is not a limitless commodity. The very fact that its nominal and real price has, in the 1980s and in most countries, made a quantum leap is an indicator of its scarcity. Moreover, it would be unwise to assume that outside shareholders will always be an available source of funds. One indication of this has been the significant gyrations experienced in most major stock markets. When markets are susceptible to these levels of change it will be a brave man who will bank on raising new equity with any certainty unless his company has a very strong track record and a valid need to justify a call on its shareholders.

Therefore, while a substantial equity base represents comfort to the lender and security to the borrower, its relationship to borrowing should not be the dominant measure in today's turbulent times. A level of borrowing thought sensible when interest rates were 7% may well look hazardous when they are 21% especially when those high rates may be hitting the company's customer base and thereby reducing its volume. Conversely a level of borrowing designed to accommodate exposure to fluctuating short-term rates may be unduly cautious if the company's debt is predominantly fixed rate and long-term. There is moreover a significant variance between the typical relationship of debt to equity in different countries. Although the evidence is not fully comparable, the very existence of the differences, apparent or real, demonstrates that any objective ratio cannot be particularly valid in itself.

It is therefore important to take at least as much note of the forecast cost of borrowing, and its relation to forecast cash generation, as of the debt-equity ratio. In the current environment of a decreasing nominal, but high real, cost of debt borrowers should frequently review their guidelines and determine carefully their exposure to fluctuating debt service costs. Bankers go some way towards this when analyzing a borrower's interest cover — the number of times net and gross interest is covered by pre-tax trading profits. This analysis inevitably tends to be a backward-looking process and is no clear guide to the prudence of any particular level of debt.

Cash flow is ultimately the key to corporate health. The borrower has a very clear interest in being able accurately to forecast, measure and compare cash flows. When horizons narrow and borrowers are forced into shorter and shorter maturities, cash-flow management becomes a key element, not only in funding strategy, but in managing the business as a whole.

EQUITY

Equity can arise in a variety of forms. The simplest and often the most valuable is the addition to reserves of retained earnings. An increasing net profit level is the surest platform for a continuing healthy capital structure.

In this context it is, at the very least, debatable whether shareholders' interests are best served by successful and growing companies paying out a substantial proportion of net profits by way of dividend, rather than by conserving them for reinvestment in the business for the ultimate benefit of their shareholders. For those shareholders who suffer taxation, it is usually inefficient to receive taxable dividends rather than to earn capital profits which are usually taxed at a more favourable rate. The logic of this viewpoint is particularly reinforced when companies call upon their shareholders to subscribe new capital out of what amounts to previously taxed income. Dividends have tended to become signals of corporate virility. It is quite tenable to maintain that a corporate policy to retain earnings, accompanied by excellent shareholder and public relations, would work to the ultimate benefit of shareholders.

Companies should also give serious consideration to the effect on the balance sheets of revaluing their fixed or other non-current assets. Some national accounting principles, notably United States accounting regulations, rule out regular revaluations.

However, in most countries such revaluations are possible and, provided they are consistently and professionally applied, should enable lenders to recognise the true worth of a borrower's assets. It must be recognised that revaluing assets does not of itself create extra value. The key issue will always remain the ability of the borrower to generate operational cash flow.

NEW EQUITY

New equity should normally be required only at a time when capital expenditure is planned which is not capable of being financed out of depreciation or operational cash flow.

Equity is often a valid option in the event of an acquisition. It can be used either in a paper-for-paper deal, by raising cash by way of rights for the purpose of funding an acquisition or a series of acquisitions, by using the vendor-placing technique, or by issuing new shares by way of a public offering in another capital market, such as the United States. The vendor-placing option amounts to the placing by, or on behalf of, the vendor of the acquiring company's shares of an amount equal to the purchase consideration. The placing is usually made to major institutions and can be a relatively easy and cost-effective method of financing a medium sized acquisition.

A strong growing company can justifiably finance growth by raising equity when otherwise expansion might be impractical. It will certainly find that pursuing consistent reporting and investor relations policies will contribute greatly towards the achievement of this goal.

In all cases it is difficult to over-emphasize the importance of raising equity, if it is needed, prior to closing an acquisition or committing major capital expenditure. Strategy dependent on a future equity issue can in uncertain conditions be extremely misguided.

There are more exotic forms of raising equity, such as liquidating investment trusts, but these are outside the scope of this chapter.

QUASI-EQUITY

Apart from the issue of ordinary capital, either by the parent or by a subsidiary or associate, it is sensible to consider other forms of issue which qualify for full or at least partial equity status. The use of an equity linked instrument can be viewed as a way of sharing risks and rewards between an issuer and an investor. Essentially the issuer accepts potential equity dilution in the future for identifiable interest saving costs in the short term. These instruments can be evaluated in relation to their position on the sources of capital scale ranging from long-term debt to equity.

Preference, redeemable preference and participating preference shares are usually closer to debt and are raised for specific purposes. Convertibles are different in nature and offer a useful vehicle to the issuing company.

Typically, convertible loan stock or convertible preference shares can be an attractive option if the trade-off between coupon and conversion factor is skilfully arranged, in the prevailing market, to satisfy both issuer and investor. For an international company there can be a major attraction in tapping individual markets for local currency finance, on a convertible loan stock basis, or by offering warrants to subscribe for equity in the parent or other listed group companies. This option can allow the borrower to tap local term debt markets which might be inaccessible on any other basis; it can also have the additional attraction of introducing the issuer to an entirely new body of investors.

Normally the convertible gives the stockholder an option to convert or to hold his stock to redemption. We are also seeing more convertibles where the stockholder has an obligation to convert. This will be attractive to borrowers or issuers who can afford a fairly high coupon as an inducement to stockholders to accept the obligation to convert at an applicable premium.

Debt issues with equity warrants can on occasions prove attractive to issuers. Their relative attractiveness, however, tends to be governed by fashions in the eurobond markets.

In general these quasi-equity instruments offer an extremely attractive and flexible option since their pricing and terms are often differently viewed by investor and issuer and to the satisfaction of both.

QUANTUM OF DEBT

Among the most important and difficult decisions is to arrive at the appropriate levels of gross and net debt. For companies liable to taxation the net cost of debt has usually been the cheapest form of funding and there has therefore been an incentive to maximize debt levels to take advantage of the tax benefit.

For many years in many, if not most, countries it used to be possible to finance operations with borrowed money at negative net costs. This was mainly due to the absence of real interest costs in most countries and currencies over many years. Real interest costs in this context meant the absence of any premium in prevailing gross interest rates over generally accepted measures of price inflation. For tax-paying borrowing corporations the net after tax cost of borrowing represented a real bargain and usually an erosion in purchasing power to the ultimate lender or depositor.

When set in the context of a generation of real economic growth and of an environment of greater or lesser inflation, this situation undoubtedly encouraged corporate funding strategies based on maximizing debt. Moreover, in spite of the insidious effects of inflation, fixed-rate debt was in fairly good supply. Corporate borrowers have therefore been able to fund their operations with debt at terms and at rates which have been, in retrospect, very attractive.

Unfortunately for borrowers, this era ended several years ago. Monetarist administrators in many parts of the western world instituted policies designed to return us all to the era of sound money (or in some cases have been reluctantly forced to follow the example of nations to which their economies or currencies are linked). The immediate sign was high interest rates in the name of controlling the money supply. The immediate effect was to return the world, in some cases for the first time in forty years, to real interest costs. When this situation was aggravated by considerable uncertainty as to what the future might bring, by the reduction of many companies' profitability and the consequent gearing up of corporate tax burdens, the result was a fundamental rethinking of corporate funding strategies.

Figures 2.1.1. and 2.1.2 illustrate the relationship between interest and inflation rates for two very different currencies (United States dollar and Australian dollar). It will be seen that in the late 1970s and 1980s real interest rates varying between 5% and 10% obtained — something previously unknown in more than a generation. Moreover there is little evidence, as yet, of real rates declining significantly, showing that a major change in the value of capital has occurred and is being sustained. This phenomenon is not peculiar to the currencies illustrated; virtually all currencies, major and minor alike, have experienced the same turnround, although to varying degrees.

The combination of exceptionally high real and nominal interest rates, coupled with inflation and the fact or prospect of recession, created a most difficult and challenging situation for borrowers and lenders alike. A major rethink of funding strategy was also opportune for other fundamental reasons. Many traditionally accepted relationships between competitiveness, purchasing power and exchange rates have been overturned by extraneous factors, be they interest rates, determined primarily by political considerations, or major changes in the actual or perceived values of nations' natural resources. Over the last few years we have experienced major fluctuations in currencies.

It is unlikely that many companies have been able to plan their funding strategies with these fluctuations in mind. There is also another broad factor to consider. Although it is not unusual to record shifts in economic balance of power or in the evolution of major industries, the speed and scale of these changes has created an additional element of insecurity. Largely as a result of a major change in the balance of power between depositor and lender, together with the other changes in relationships, the very rate at which currencies, interest rates, stock markets and indeed just about every financial indicator are moving, adds to the difficulty of operating in

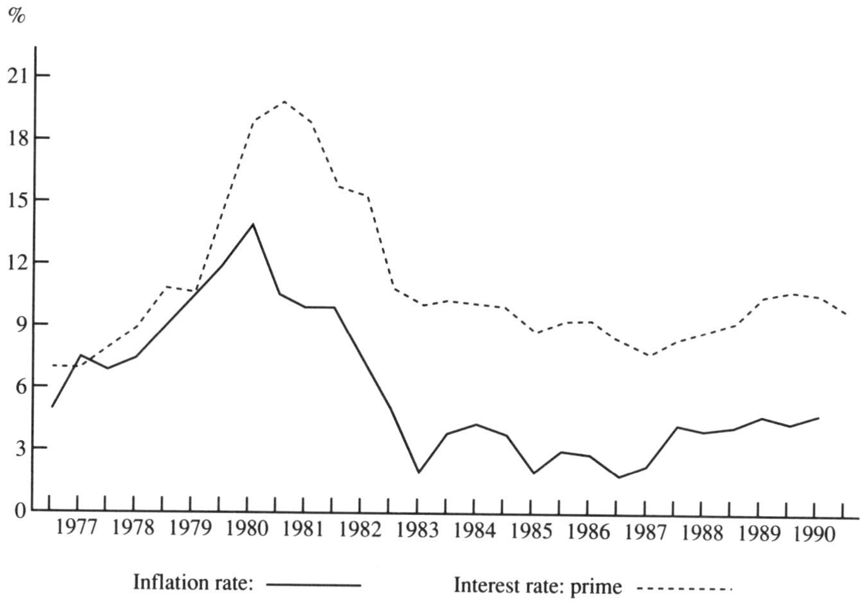

Figure 2.1.1 The relationship between interest and inflation rates for the United States dollar

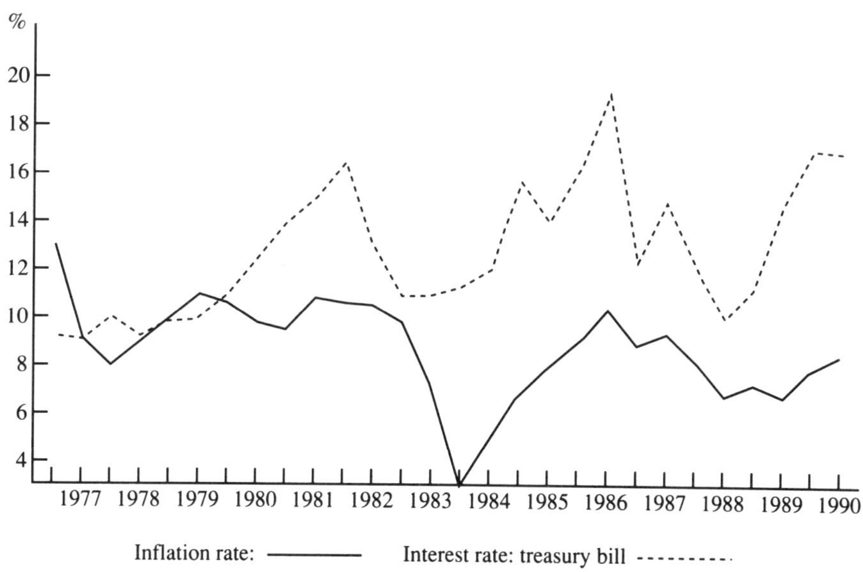

Figure 2.1.2 The relationship between interest and inflation rates for the Australian dollar

today's environment. In the context of this insecure environment it will normally be appropriate for international groups to follow cautious broad strategies. This will usually mean pursuing a relatively more modest debt programme when deciding upon their funding strategy compared with that which may have been appropriate in times of lower or negative net of tax debt costs.

However, as tax rates reduce in certain countries, the balance between debt and equity may be moving away from debt purely for this reason.

DEBT MATURITIES

Current uncertainty as to the future, together with volatile interest rate structures, make it more important than ever to plan debt maturities. Most companies, by reference to their forecasts of future cash flow, plan for a spread of maturities — short, medium and long — which match their perceived cash flows and allow some margin of security.

This approach, however, has to be reconciled with the potentially high risks associated with going along at what may prove to be high rates and with the problem of availability. For a combination of reasons long-term fixed-rate funding can become relatively difficult to arrange at a time when investors' appetites rapidly became exhausted after a number of fixed-rate issues. To some extent we are now facing a further problem arising from an unstable environment. Investors have become used to investing relatively short and at floating rates, and have less enthusiasm than traditionally was the case for a diet of fixed-rate paper. The end result can be that companies may have to pay a relatively higher margin over traditional benchmarks (for example, government bond yields) to launch a fixed-rate issue.

Some companies have projects which can stand these rates, but others question their basic assumptions and borrow either shorter than they would like to take bank offered floating-rate debt. The net result is that, regardless of availability, companies have narrowed their debt maturities and have come to rely on short- or medium-term debt, usually at floating rates. This concentration of short-term debt adds a further element of volatility to an already unstable situation.

AVAILABILITY OF DEBT FINANCE

From the supply side availability is a major issue. Restrictions take many and varied forms and cover the full range of maturities. Sometimes they occur when governments or central banks seek to impose lending restrictions or maximum lending rates upon lending institutions.

Normally some form of secondary market develops to provide availability, albeit at a cost; lack of local capacity can be a serious irritant detracting from the orderly funding of an international group. Companies are accordingly usually well advised to secure local borrowing lines even at the expense, on occasions, of paying what may seem unreasonable commitment fees for undrawn lines of credit.

During the early to mid-eighties, one particularly worrying issue facing British companies was the drying up of the availability of long-term fixed-rate sterling finance, especially as debentures used to be available in amounts of relatively small sizes. The domestic market was, and to some extent still is, characterized by unusually long maturities dictated more by institutional investor preference than by any natural inclination on the part of corporate borrowers to borrow for such periods. A gap had therefore arisen between the relatively short periods offered by fixed-rate bank loans or sterling eurobond issues and the long maturities demanded by debenture investors.

There have been developments which have resulted in a partial bridging of this gap. The development of the sterling eurobond market and the rapid growth in the availability of interest rate swaps (another subject in its own right) have created relatively attractive methods of borrowing fixed-rate sterling up to ten years. Investors are coming to appreciate that issuers cannot be expected to issue for periods entirely to their convenience, while on the issuers' part there have been changes to accommodate some investor-driven requirements on documentation. In the United States something similar has occurred. The long-term bond market has not died but has on occasions been in serious disarray. Corporate borrowers are frequently unable to tap it freely even if they are prepared to pay the going rate. The eurobond market has also proved to be an uncertain source of funds as market pressures and central banks have combined to reduce significantly the volume of issues in most of the major currencies. We have therefore witnessed instances of markets drying up and, in the process, contributing to volatility and instability as maturities are forced shorter and shorter.

Borrowers therefore face a real dilemma; they probably wish to maintain or increase their average maturity lengths but find fewer opportunities to do so and if they are successful it is at rates they can barely afford.

They have accordingly been progressively forced into shorter-term debt (at volatile rates) or into using a greater proportion of equity (if they can conserve or raise it) or into funding their operations by using new techniques discussed later in this chapter.

INTEREST RATE EXPOSURE

At times of high and volatile interest rates, exposure to fluctuating interest rates becomes a major consideration for borrowers. In many respects it is the opposite side of the coin to currency exposure, which is treated separately.

There is no magic method of minimizing interest rates; fortunately the borrower's objectives are often set in less stark terms. Even if interest rates cannot be reduced the mere introduction of a degree of certainty is often a major bonus to general management provided that rate is compatible with the returns generated from assets.

Certainty may be introduced by a combination of maximizing fixed-rate debt, hedging, for instance by using the financial futures markets, or by entering into currency or interest exchange agreements. Certainly over the last few years there has been an enormous increase in the application of interest rate hedging instruments as such techniques continue to become more and more refined to meet specific requirements. Management and awareness of interest rate exposure is fundamental to capital structure decisions; a sensible capital structure will minimize the risk inherent in having a significant element of uncovered floating-rate debt.

TYPE OF DEBT

It is appropriate to cover at this stage the main types of sources of debt finance.

Long- and medium-term debt. Reference has already been made to the uncertain nature of today's capital markets. Therefore although the following are in principle available to eligible corporate borrowers, in practice they may be difficult or impossible to tap, at least at the desired moment.

(1) Debentures, usually secured on assets and subject to relatively strict trust deeds, used to be a major source of funds to corporate names in the United Kingdom and hopefully will become so again. Similar instruments exist in most other major capital markets, and have major attributes in that they offer genuinely long-term fixed-rate money, even though restrictions imposed by the relevant trust deeds have frequently proved irksome.
Eurobond issues offer an alternative and rather more flexible source of long-term money. However it is a market which ebbs and flows according to currency and interest rate fluctuations, and is linked to a fairly narrow range of major currencies. Even within this range certain major currencies may not be available for extended periods. It is therefore an important source of funds but not a market to be relied upon at any particular time. Eurobond agreements are typically less strict than for equivalent bank loan or debenture borrowings. However the entry qualifications are high; only strong and relatively well-known corporations are able to raise funds in this way.

(2) The banking sector is another source of long- and particularly medium-term money. Usually this will be on a floating-rate basis and the borrower will be obliged to accept a fairly comprehensive and strict loan agreement. This may or may not prove to be a relevant factor in deciding upon the merits of this source of funds.

(3) In all cases it is possible to consider matching a term borrowing (bond or bank borrowing) with a currency exchange agreement. Such agreements, which can take various forms, can offer the possibility effectively to borrow another currency — one which may not be readily available in the normal course of business. Currency exchange agreements are not easy to arrange outside the major currencies but are worth pursuing if the borrower has a specific need for a term commitment in another currency. They also offer an opportunity to change currency course during the lifetime of an existing borrowing.
A different form of currency swap can be a useful method of permanently mobilizing surplus funds within a group. A group company in one country will lend an amount of domestic currency to another company, while simultaneously another group company will receive a loan of an equivalent amount,

usually from a company within the same group as the first depositor. After an agreed period the loans or deposits are reversed. This can be a valuable alternative to borrowing the equivalent sum from external sources and can sometimes have a most beneficial effect upon a group's structure — especially when gross borrowing is a limiting factor.

(4) Leasing is also a generally available source of term borrowing and should not be ignored on this count alone. In certain countries it can be tax based, where a form of initial capital allowance or tax credit is available in lieu of commercial depreciation rates. The company paying little or no tax on corporate profits can thereby benefit from relatively cheap finance which incorporates the tax incentive.

Occasionally this can be made to work in reverse; a company paying the current corporation tax may seek to accelerate its allowances by leasing assets over a fairly short period and thereby recover its tax allowances more rapidly than would otherwise be possible.

Disregarding any tax advantages a pure financial lease may offer a rare opportunity to obtain fixed-rate term finance on acceptable terms, particularly to smaller companies not able to secure such funds in other markets.

(5) Another source of term funds is to borrow in a short-term market while having a long-term back-up facility provided by a bank or group of underwriters. By accounting convention it is generally agreed that such debt should be treated as long-term. This technique, allied to an interest rate swap, can additionally generate long-term fixed-rate funds.

Short-term debt. It is not the purpose of this section to detail all the numerous sources of short-term finance; it is important to consider the major forms by which short-term money can be raised.

(1) Bank finance may come in various forms. Short-term loans, discounting of bills or overdrafts are among the most typical.

(2) Finance from outside the banking sector may come in the form of company-to-company loans (common for example in Australia) or by borrowing in one of the commercial paper markets. Both types of borrowing can be attractive. However, the former can offer no assurance as to continual availability, while of the latter the United States domestic market is now so large a source of funds that any well-rated issuer can normally expect to be able to rely on the market for most amounts and maturities. The more recent commercial paper markets are less reliable, due to their lack of size and maturity; they are becoming important sources of funding for creditworthy (and not necessarily rated) issuers, although these markets are generally investor driven.

Recognizing the fact that long-term funding is difficult, it may accordingly be justifiable to make increasing use of non-bank related short-term funds. So long as the providers of these funds are averse to investing long- or medium-term they will seek a spread of short-term investments. The strong corporate name should therefore logically find a market for its paper which is likely to be available for so long as conditions inducing squeezed maturities obtain.

Those companies who are able to avail themselves of this option should encourage the development of orderly structured commercial paper markets as one method of creating a valid alternative source of funds. Given the existence of the markets it will be in most eligible companies' interests to keep their names regularly in front of the investing public.

(3) Companies should of course not ignore any potential they have within their own groups to mobilize funds — this will usually be on a short-term basis. Within domestic markets it is usually fairly straightforward to arrange for group companies to lend to each other. (There can be exceptions where exchange control regulations prohibit foreign controlled companies from doing just that.)

Across national borders mobilization of surplus funds is not always possible. Exchange controls or withholding taxes may forbid or discourage intercompany lending. However, some opportunities usually exist. Intracompany trading usually gives a wholly-owned group's subsidiaries some opportunity to reduce surplus cash while, for the longer term dividend, remittances are a further means of mobilizing surpluses.

Specialized techniques. Given the difficulties faced by borrowers in funding their operations by traditional means, specialized forms of finance are likely to become increasingly important not only as solutions to particular problems but as a generic form of additional external finance.

The range of techniques constantly changes. The following is intended to give some guide.

(1) *Property finance.* Most companies own fixed assets and can, if they wish, avail themselves of the wide variety of property finance options, such as sale and lease-back. This type of finance provides a scarce source of long-term fixed-rate finance, albeit at rates which may prove very expensive.

One of the major considerations for the company is to determine the optimum value of fixed assets to retain. A company ought, in principle, to concentrate on its main business and not to hold valuable assets. However it would be unwise to reduce its fixed assets below a sensible minimum or be forced to dispose of assets in a hurry on unreasonable or poor historic yields.

(2) *Export finance.* Those companies involved in the purchase of capital goods from overseas suppliers can often obtain most attractive terms from suppliers who have access to term funding on subsidized terms. It is important for the borrowers to be aware of the incentives provided in the major countries which could be sources of supply.

(3) *Sale and re-purchase.* This technique can be an attractive method of financing

stocks — typically major imports of raw materials. Effective financing costs can be as low as any other form of short-term finance. The technique can additionally have genuine balance sheet advantages.

(4) *Tax-based term finance.* Several countries more or less deliberately promote term finance schemes, usually to encourage investment in a particular country or region. In the United States, industrial development or revenue bonds are a highly attractive method of financing certain capital assets. In Ireland, term loans under the Irish section 84 present another attractive option for obtaining a tax benefit when corporation tax is not payable.

(5) *Project finance and limited recourse financing.* Medium to long-term finance can be available for projects where the resultant cash flow can be shown to easily meet attendant debt service obligations. Characteristics of such finance arrangements can include a significant amount of risks being assumed by the lender.

CURRENCY OF DEBT

No consideration of capital structure would be complete without taking account of the effect of currency upon borrowings. This is not the place for any major exposition of policy in this area. It is a major topic and requires detailed consideration. So far as capital structure is concerned any decision on borrowing must include the currency option. Careful consideration will need to be given to cost, availability, taxation treatment of any gains or losses, and the accounting treatment to be applied to realized or potential gains or losses on exchange. Importantly the borrower will also wish to retain the comfort that he has some way out of a particular currency should his initial evaluation prove unfounded. He will also need to give most careful thought to his group's currency debt structure to ensure that it matches the particular policy the group wishes to apply to both the transaction and balance sheet exposures.

COST OF CAPITAL

Capital structure decisions must take due note of the group's perceived or actual cost of capital and the effect this may have upon investment decisions.

Cost of capital is not an exact science; it is possible to make numerous assumptions about the cost of debt to apply (historic, current or forecast) and perhaps even more about the cost of equity. Dividend policy and the incidence of taxation will both be additional important issues.

Typically, however, the borrowing company is likely to reduce its average net cost of capital by maximizing debt; this is sometimes advanced as an argument for aiming at what may be dangerously high levels of debt.Conversely a highly-rated company's earnings per share (EPS) may benefit, at a certain point, from maximizing equity. A sensible capital structure is likely to be arrived at taking note of the possible impact of debt levels on cost of capital, and earnings per share, but not allowing them to become dominant factors.

APPLICATION OF CAPITAL STRUCTURE POLICY WITHIN AN INTERNATIONAL GROUP

To date a number of factors influencing capital structure decisions for a group as a whole have been considered. In practice, at least as much consideration requires to be given to the application of policy. Frequently practical considerations require the amendment of any general policy as solutions are sought to specific problems.

It would be impractical to attempt to consider every form of practical issue that arises when managing the capital structure of an international group. The intention of this section is to highlight areas which require particular attention.

NATURE AND PROPORTION OF GROUP SHAREHOLDINGS IN SUBSIDIARIES AND ASSOCIATES

The proportion held, particularly in overseas companies, will frequently be a determining factor. A group with wholly-owned subsidiaries is likely to approach its funding and capital structure in a manner quite different to that of a group which comprises a variety of subsidiaries and associates with minority interests.

The existence of minority shareholders will require detailed consideration of their interests which may or may not be in concert with those of the shareholders of the parent company. Minority shareholders, for example, may not be willing or able to support the borrowings of the subsidiary company, leaving this liability to the parent. Dividend policy, at subsidiary level, and intercompany lending or borrowing are topics where minority shareholders will have particular interests.

So long as the parent has a potential interest in raising additional equity from minority shareholders it is unlikely that there will be a serious conflict of interests. However where this is unlikely, or when the payment of a dividend imposes a penalty upon the parent, such as withholding tax, a more difficult situation is liable to arise.

On the other hand, the existence of outside shareholders may in some cases be a distinct asset to the funding of a group. The shareholders may be willing to subscribe to additional equity in the subsidiary or associate, thus providing additional equity to the group and enhancing its capacity for further borrowing. Either a publicly listed company or a partnership with a limited number of external shareholders could provide this option. The parent company will need to consider these factors along with other broad commercial factors when determining its capital structure in any particular area.

The parent will also wish to take due note of the balance sheet effects of various structures. Whereas a subsidiary (50.1% or more owned) will normally be fully consolidated, a 50/50 joint venture may well be treated as one net item. Such treatment may reduce the impact of any debt in the parent's balance sheet.

EXCHANGE CONTROLS

Exchange controls, in one form or another, exist in most countries, although within the European Community these are slowly being withdrawn to meet the 1992 timetable. Countries where exchange controls are absent, such as the United States, Germany, Canada, the United Kingdom and Hong Kong, are the exception.

Exchange controls may take various forms:

(1) restrictions on inward and outward capital investment;
(2) timing restrictions on current trading (usually in the form of limiting the time within which export receipts must be repatriated);
(3) limiting domestic currency borrowing by foreign controlled companies;
(4) restrictions on remittance of dividends, royalties and other payments.

The existence or potential existence of exchange controls will inevitably have a major impact upon capital structures. Where exchange controls exist within the parent's own country the problems will be further compounded.

Exchange controls, or indeed the risk of their introduction, may therefore affect the location of particular investments, the working capital and borrowing capacity of particular companies, and decisions on equity when this is a factor determining remittability.

GOVERNMENT RESTRICTIONS

An increasing number of governments seek to influence foreign investment in various directions. This may take various forms.

(1) Governments may prohibit foreign majority held companies, allowing a maximum of perhaps a 40% direct equity stake.
(2) Other governments may seek to promote national ownership of certain industries or limit foreign investment within them (Australia and Canada have been recent examples of this approach). Accordingly any investment decision may be subject to the review of a foreign investment review authority which may require a proportion of national ownership.
(3) Legislation in certain countries, applying to local and foreign controlled companies, may impose certain restrictions on capital structure. Debt to equity ratios may be imposed or taxation allowances restricted.

These various restrictions may create significant problems when planing a new investment. When borrowings require support and external shareholders are unable to provide their share, an effective limit may be imposed upon total borrowing.

POLITICAL RISK

Investments in certain countries are undertaken with the implicit acceptance of a high level of political risk. Where this is the case, an investor will probably prefer to introduce a limited amount of equity and seek to borrow locally. His capital structure in such a case may well be determined more by risk criteria than by other factors.

AVAILABILITY OF LOCAL FUNDING

In certain countries access to local borrowing may be limited or local markets may not provide the full range of instruments available elsewhere.

Where availability is a major consideration it may be necessary to secure funds on a basis which is not ideal, such as short instead of medium or long. Occasionally local funds may not be available at all in the amounts required, due either to the limitations of the market or official restrictions. In such a case the parent may be obliged to inject either equity or intercompany debt as an alternative to restricting his activity in that territory.

TAXATION

Tax is inevitably a major factor when establishing or reviewing corporate structures.

Ideally a group will aim to borrow where it can obtain the greatest measure of relief, and earn profits where it can enjoy the lowest effective tax charge, and above all avoid making losses where relief is unavailable.

Structuring or restructuring decisions will usually have regard to:

(1) corporate tax levels in the host and home country;
(2) withholding taxes on dividends, interest and other payments, to the extent that these impose additional costs on remitting funds;
(3) the past, current and future tax position in various companies or countries;
(4) the availability of taxation relief for expenses and interest paid;
(5) the avoidance of structures liable to attack by fiscal jurisdictions.

The impact of taxation upon corporate and capital structures is often complex and profound. Lack of detailed consideration at the time of a particular investment and regular review thereafter can be very expensive.

CORPORATE STRUCTURE

Closely linked to decisions on taxation are those of corporate structure. The structure of corporate shareholdings has a significant impact upon the group's capital structure. The various factors to be taken into account are as follows.

(1) *Taxation.* This is often a major consideration and the raison d'être for many structures.
(2) *General management or commercial factors.* Often a group's management structure is quite separate from its fiscal structure. It is important that the two are not confused. Fiscal considerations should rarely detract from good commercial management.
(3) *Practical management.* Occasionally complex corporate structures impose burdens in terms of administration. These must be recognized at the outset and accepted as part of the overall cost of managing the group.

RESTRICTIONS IMPOSED BY LENDERS

In the section on capital structure policy, consideration was given to the various forms of funding open to a group. In spite of the cautious attitude to debt recommended it is inevitable that potential lenders will seek to impose their own restrictions upon a group's borrowing policy and practice. The nature of these restrictions will vary depending upon the strength of the borrowing company and the nature and term of the possible borrowings.

When lending to a parent most lenders will seek, but not necessarily obtain, some or all of the following:

(1) restrictions on total debt;
(2) equal treatment with other lenders;
(3) assurances by the borrower that the company is in sound financial health and that its major assets will not disappear.

When lending to a subsidiary of a group lenders may look alternatively for some measure of support from the parent, either in the form of a guarantee or of a letter of comfort.

Banking practice varies from place to place, but it is prudent to assume that restrictions will become stricter as the term of any loan increases. Only individual borrowers can assess whether they are likely to be influenced in their funding policy by the restrictions that bankers might seek to impose.

RESTRICTIONS IMPOSED INTERNALLY

In order to give effect to the group's capital structure policy it will be necessary to impose certain restrictions upon subsidiaries, and to require certain information to be provided on a regular basis.
Procedures will normally cover:

(1) the amount and term of any external borrowing undertaken by subsidiaries;
(2) the nature and source of borrowing;
(3) the support, if any, given by the parent;
(4) forecasts, short- and long-term, of borrowing needs;
(5) changes in corporate structure.

The object on the part of the parent will be to ensure, among other things:

(1) that group borrowings do not exceed any internal prudent limit or any externally imposed restriction;
(2) that decisions on maturities and currency taken centrally can be taken on the basis of acceptably complete and accurate information;
(3) that interest rate exposures can be monitored regularly;
(4) that the group does not become unduly dependent on any one lender;

(5) that the balance between equity, long-, medium- and short-term debt is kept under constant review.

In practice other advantages, not immediately related to capital structure, accrue from a degree of central control over borrowing. The degree to which it is necessary or appropriate to go will depend upon each group; it is however fundamental that control over borrowings and corporate structures is exercised.

J. J. A. HOWARTH

European Leisure plc

2.2 International banking facilities available to the multinational firm: a supplier's view

International banking is as old as international commerce and its development has closely paralleled the growth in international trade over a period of several centuries. The post-World War II period has been one of particularly dramatic growth in international trade accompanied in the last fifteen years or so by a liberalization of capital movements. De-regulation and re-regulation of financial systems and the replacement of a dollar based international monetary arrangement by a multi-currency system with the dollar, the deutschmark and the yen and, to a small extent, also the pound sterling as its pivotal points. This has been reflected in a dynamic expansion in the range and volume of financial services provided by the banking community. As part of this process, the banking community itself has undergone a dramatic transformation, leading to the development of multi-product institutions spanning large geographical areas and specific functions and followed in recent years by a restructuring of financial institutions — the process still under way. On the one side specialized institutions have sprung up to meet the demands of both public and private sector entities with worldwide activities while, on the other, some existing banks have positioned themselves to become providers of all financial services on a large scale. It is difficult to determine whether institutional development has in itself fostered this variety of banking services or whether banks have merely responded to the demands of industry and government for more sophisticated and complex finance and related services. Innovation of financial techniques has been very striking in recent years, but this has not been prompted only by diversification in the banking sector nor by client needs. The particularly complex monetary and economic environment of the last few decades and rapid technological advance in calculations, information and communication (the information technology as well as changes in the regulatory framework) have provided an ideal framework for financial innovation.

Banking services can be divided into two broad categories: those relating to the needs of the individual; and those associated with corporate entities and other substantial users of financial services. The first area is referred to as retail or consumer banking and, although this category of banking services has also undergone dynamic expansion, it is not strictly relevant to our subject, except in so far as a substantial part of banking liabilities are still provided by the retail depositor. It is in the area of wholesale banking services that the more publicized innovations have taken place. Wholesale banking involves the supply of financial services, including lending, foreign exchange, trade related transactions, corporate finance, capital market transactions, leasing, institutional investment management, factoring, export finance, project finance, multinational cash management, interest and exchange rate swaps, various lending facilities, and so on. Users of these services are from both the private and the public sector but, as we shall see in succeeding paragraphs, the growth in the use of wholesale banking services by the public sector has been particularly marked in recent decades. This is because of the balance of payments disequilibria which have dominated international monetary affairs following the breakdown of the Bretton Woods system and the oil price shocks of the 1970s.

A wide range of financial institutions provide wholesale banking services either as part of their overall mix of business or as institutions active solely in wholesale banking. These institutions include the major commercial banks in the Western industrialized countries, as well as large Japanese commercial banks. The leading commercial banks on the continent of Europe are often referred to as universal banks, reflecting the comprehensiveness of their range of services. In addition to the commercial banks, wholesale banking is practised by merchant and investment banks, specialist joint-venture banks, various consortia banks and a number of other financial institutions such as savings banks and organizations which tend to specialize in certain segments internationally, regionally or domestically. All these institutions tend to participate in large financial transactions through a process of syndication which is now a highly developed aspect of international financing. The scale of banking requirements is now such that no single banking institution is able to satisfy entirely on its own all the financial requirements of its most important wholesale customers.

One of the important steps in this process was the development of the eurocurrency market in the 1960s and 1970s. This has served as the corner-stone for a substantial development in international banking, affecting banks in several different centres and producing a new expansion in international finance unprecedented in scale since the nineteenth century. The development of this eurocurrency market is a phenomenon which has been the subject of a great deal of comment, some of it not entirely positive. For many economists the eurocurrency market has been responsible for a breakdown in the control of world capital flows and money supply, leaving the monetary authorities frustrated and unable to carry out their responsibilities with respect to their own domestic economies. Inflation, which has plagued the world economy since the end of the post-war boom immediately following the cessation of hostilities in the mid-1940s is blamed by some on the eurocurrency market and the fact that it has facilitated an uncontrolled increase in world monetary supply. This is not the place to continue the debate on whether the eurocurrency market has been of benefit to the world economy or whether, on the other hand, it represents an engine of inflation. For our purpose, its significance is that the international banking community has prospered and extended itself, both functionally and geographically, as a result of banking opportunities created by the growth of the euromarkets.

It is said that the origin of the eurocurrency markets lies in the Cold War. Some of the stories relating to the first eurocurrency transactions are no doubt apocryphal and have now taken on a legendary character. Nevertheless, it is true that in the late 1950s, Cold War tensions influenced the policies of the East European banks, who found themselves handling increased amounts of convertible currency as a result of the development of East-West trade. The official Soviet banks, with operations in London and Paris, were reluctant to deposit their surplus dollars in banks located in the United States. They felt that the American authorities might freeze those deposits as part of their Cold War tactics. Indeed, it is ironic to observe that many years later the eurocurrency market was to sustain a major shock following the American action to sequester Iranian assets deposited in the United States. As an alternative to leaving balances in New York, Eastern bloc banks offered them to other banks located in the principal European centres, notably the City of London, which was already emerging as the most important financial centre outside New York. These banks were happy to pay a market rate of interest for these dollar funds, since they could deploy them in making loans available to the major American multinational companies who had built up large investments in Europe and were in the habit of borrowing dollars for working capital purposes. In this way the interbank market for eurocurrency deposits was created — largely denominated in the American currency but, as years went on, also utilizing the other principal convertible currencies, such as Swiss francs, deutschmarks, Dutch gilders and even eventually pounds sterling. The growth in this interbank market for eurocurrency deposits, which quickly spread through the major financial centres of the world, forms the basis for all other eurocurrency activities which have developed since. The second important and notable step in the evolution of multinational banks was the gradual replacement of the dollar as the dominant transatlantic and reserve currency by the deutschmark and the yen. This process still under way was reinforced by a liberalization of capital movements and the emergence of Japan and Germany as the largest net capital exporters and a change in the status of the United States from a creditor to a debtor nation.

Reinforcing this development in the last five years or so was the 1992 programme of the European Community. Among other aims it has that of the creation of a single financial market. A Banking Directive and Investment Service Directive set out basic principles, including those relating to the working of banks and other financial institutions.

THE DEVELOPMENT OF MULTINATIONAL BANKING

One of the outstanding features of the development of multinational banks has been the re-emergence of the City of London after World War II as a major financial centre. This was based on a number of factors. In the first instance, there existed in the City a long tradition of international banking dating back to the nineteenth century when sterling had been the predominant currency used to finance international trade and investment. Although the War and consequent restrictions did limit the use of sterling, following the imposition of exchange control, the tradition and expertise still to be found in City institutions in dealing with international financial matters was still unrivalled by other centres.

Part of this tradition was bound up in the fact that a larger number of foreign banks were represented in the City than in other major centres. This strong overseas presence was not only due to the City's history, but also reflected a particularly benign and enlightened attitude on the part of the Bank of England and the British banking community. Other financial centres on the Continent were more restrictive, due to concern by the regulatory authorities that their internal monetary control and other arrangements might be prejudiced if they were to allow foreign banks to establish themselves in large numbers. Until recently most continental financial centres still operated cartel arrangements which made it more difficult for overseas banks to enjoy the necessary mix of domestic and foreign business that would justify opening a branch or subsidiary. However, with the publication of the Banking Directive — it will come into operation on 1 January, 1993 together with the Investment Services Directive — aimed at establishing a level playing field for all participants, the position is changing. As in many other developments in international finance, North American banks were pioneers in the development of a financial services industry, based largely in the City of London, that specialized in the international needs of the major corporations as well as sovereign nations. American banks pursued a policy of overseas expansion in the 1950s and 1960s, prompted by competitive pressures at home and the need to follow their major corporate clients, who were themselves engaged in overseas expansion. Short-term lending to these corporate clients in order to provide working capital and trade finance facilities was then, and to a large extent remains, the basic international banking service. Alongside the provision of short-term facilities, substantially in eurocurrencies but also in local currencies, the international banks also provide a variety of ancillary services such as the execution of foreign exchange transactions, documentary facilities connected with trade finance and other services of a short-term nature. Multinational corporations, which until fifteen years or so ago were dominated by American owned companies, found it convenient to deal with the local branches or subsidiaries of the same banks with which their head offices maintain their working relationships. The local subsidiary of a multinational believes that it receives a more intensive service, despite the fact that its local needs may be modest, due to the importance of the overall banking relationship which the parent group will enjoy with one or more banks. Intercompany transfers and other transactions requiring some uniformity of processing are also likely to be best handled under a single banking roof. In recent years the services provided to multinational companies by banks who make a virtue of their large number of geographical locations have become increasingly sophisticated, and operate in such esoteric areas as computerized cash management programmes. Major banks have sought to structure their international divisions in such a way as to serve the needs of multi-location clients as efficiently as possible. Most organizations of this type operate on a functional basis according to industry or commercial groups. These are in turn juxtaposed with areas of geographical responsibility. The system is seen as working perfectly if an international oil company, operating in a disjointed variety of locations such as Venezuela, Nigeria, the north-west shelf of Australia, the North Sea and California, can rely on a single bank to provide international banking services on the corporate level to all of its operating divisions. In fact, this paragon of comprehensive banking services has still to be achieved and most multinational corporations have moved away from the concept of concentrating their banking business with one major bank advertising a variety of geographical locations.

Just as banking in general can be separated between the retail function, which serves private individuals, and the wholesale functions designed to meet the needs of industry, commerce and governments, so the wholesale range of services can be separated into two main categories. The first of these categories of services can best be described as applying to self-liquidating transactions. Such services range from normal working capital facilities to foreign exchange, trade finance, letters of credit, other forms of documentary credit, export finance, and so on. The most basic service rendered by the international banking community to multinational corporations operating in several jurisdictions is the provision of short-term credit for working capital purposes. Although the bulk of such credit is undoubtedly provided in the form of facilities denominated in the currency of whatever country the operations are sited in, over recent years an increasing proportion of such short-term credit has been extended in the main eurocurrencies, allowing the corporate treasurer to make use of the fluctuations in exchange rates and interest rates, to achieve the most economical short-term financing. Short-term credits provided for working capital purposes are normally on an overdraft basis, or some other method which permits the borrower to draw down under a pre-negotiated facility up to certain limits and under certain conditions. The facility can be repaid when the corporate borrower is flush with cash and then drawn down again as requirements dictate. A commitment commission is almost always payable by the borrower to reimburse the bank for the cost in balance sheet terms of maintaining the availability of the facility.

Another typical service provided by the international banking community is foreign exchange. International banks fall broadly into two categories insofar as their foreign exchange activities are concerned. Most banks transact foreign exchange business primarily for the benefit of their commercial and industrial clients. They will deal in most of the currencies transacted in the market, some banks specializing in particular currencies, including the more difficult currencies such as the Scandinavian, Far Eastern and others that are less widely traded. Other banks deal in foreign exchange as jobbers, maintaining the liquidity of the market by quoting two-way prices in the major currencies, but quoting these prices primarily to other banks. In this sense the foreign exchange market can be compared with a stock exchange, where brokers transact orders on behalf of their clients and jobbers maintain positions and quote prices on which the brokers can execute orders. Since 1971, when the present era of relative floating exchange rates commenced, the volume of foreign exchange business has grown; so have the problems associated with foreign exchange exposure for companies operating in various parts of the world or actively engaged in exporting. Export and import decisions, capital goods procurement and overseas investment are rendered immensely complicated by the fact that exchange rates now fluctuate widely and unpredictably, altering the economics of any particular transaction from one day to the next and sometimes eliminating the profit margin on a particular activity.

A number of devices are available for the corporate treasurer wishing to protect his business against possible ravages created by foreign exchange movements. The most typical of these devices is the forward exchange contract to buy or sell a particular currency for a future delivery date. By this means the corporate treasurer has effectively locked in the cost of a particular transaction, assuming of course that the transaction is one which will be completed within the length of time accommodated in the forward exchange market. Although it is possible to make highly specialized transactions for longer periods, generally speaking the forward exchange market for most of the major currencies operates only as far forward as twelve months and most volume is transacted in the one to six month range. Forward markets exist in all the principal trading currencies and virtually all international banks are able to quote rates in these currencies. More sophisticated market-places such as the futures market, now exist which permit both professional foreign exchange dealers, speculators and corporate treasurers to enter into foreign exchange hedge positions either by trading in futures contracts or through the purchase and sale of options.

The increased sophistication of the foreign exchange market is the product of the era of international monetary tension that now exists following the breakdown of the Bretton Woods system. Although a good many currencies are still managed to some extent by their respective central banks, and certain trading blocs such as the European Community have put in place mechanisms designed to limit currency fluctuations, nevertheless the foreign exchange market represents a major financial and economic uncertainty which was not in existence during the lengthy period after World War II when world trade and investment expanded so dramatically. That the volatility of foreign exchange markets has increased significantly is now well recognised. This is reflected in a large turnover amounting — according to a survey conducted in the summer of 1989 — to $511bn a year.

Assisting the corporate treasurer to cope with foreign exchange problems is a major service provided by the international banking community. The aspect of that service just discussed dealing with so-called self-liquidating transactions has now been expanded to provide a service described as International Cash Management and International Hedging Service. These are intended to minimize the (net) cost of short term funds by using the cheapest sources of funds, and by obtaining a maximum return on those funds, and to reduce foreign exchange exposure — both transaction and translation — to the very minimum. However, as we will see later when discussing long-term banking functions, hedging foreign exchange positions on long-term capital or project investments is also an important service provided by a great many international banks.

Trade finance, primarily through letters of credit, is another staple of the international banking system. Despite a rise in multi-branch systems operating in a variety of centres, the most substantial portion of international trade remains financed through letters of credit. Letter-of-credit finance may indeed be the oldest form of international banking. It relies essentially on the availability of correspondent banks throughout the world. Other forms of trade financing have been developed over the years; many of these involve the acceptance of commercial bills. Indeed the Bill on London is considered one of the most traditional financial services available in the City of London. In the nineteenth century, with sterling as the predominant trade currency, an enormous proportion of world trade, including trade which did not specifically involve transactions originating in or terminating in the United Kingdom, was financed through the Bill on London. Even with the advent of exchange control after World War II, sterling was widely used for the financing of third country transactions. Only recently has this activity to a large extent come to an end, the dollar replacing sterling as the principal currency in use for financing international transactions, with the deutschmark and the yen in turn coming to be used in place of the dollar. In recent times the use of sterling acceptances in London has developed, with a number of transactions being carried out for overseas borrowers that are not strictly limited to specific trade deals. Marked volatility of financial markets associated with the demise of the dollar (a single currency) standard has also led to the rapid expansion of swap transactions. The two basic forms of swap transactions are foreign exchange and interest rate swaps. Such transactions enable corporations to reduce the cost of short-term funds by effectively exchanging existing liabilities with those whose cost of funds is lower and to hedge the Foreign Exchange exposure by trading it to other parties.

In providing an increasingly sophisticated range of banking services, aimed at financing self-liquidating transactions, international banks have had to keep pace not only with the growth in international trade but also with changes in trade patterns. This has meant, in particular, keeping up with the emerging trade between Eastern and Western Europe and between the developing world and the industrialized nations. The extension to branch networks of the major Western banking systems has been prompted to a large extent by an increased diversity in geographical patterns of trade. It is now possible for treasurers of multinational companies to identify banks headquartered in their own countries of origin which also operate branches in almost every country in which the company's business is transacted, either by direct operations or via their trade relationships. International banks may have followed their principal customers in establishing branch networks overseas, but they have also found that indigenous banking systems in many developing countries are at an insufficient level of development, permitting international banks to make major inroads into the home market as well as in that market pertaining to multinational trade.

Although the day-to-day bread and butter business of international banks remains fundamental to their prosperity and ability to carry out international activity on a large scale, it is the longer-term financial activities of these banks which has received the most attention in recent years. In particular the growth of the eurocurrency market has been to a large extent responsible for a massive increase in medium to long-term indebtedness on the part of both private and public sector borrowers throughout the industrialized countries, as well as newly industrialized countries such as Mexico and Brazil and a host of less developed countries. The expansion of this international debt, and its consequences for the economies of developing countries, is now a serious cause of international economic and financial tension. A prolonged period of high interest rates and an economic recession, accompanied by a fall in primary product prices and the persistently high cost of importing energy, has placed many sovereign countries on the brink of bankruptcy, or at least in serious difficulty in maintaining interest and principal payments on their external debts. To help resolve this problem bankers have created a number of different ways of reducing the burden of debt of the developing countries. In addition to creating a market where such debts can be traded (at a discount) it is now possible — if the debtor country agrees — to swap existing debt for equity in industrial companies or exchange it for other securities generating different interest rates, but with different maturities and partial cash payment.

DEVELOPMENT OF THE EUROCURRENCY MARKET

As already pointed out, eurocurrency activity began essentially as short-term finance provided to multinational companies seeking to finance their overseas investment and commercial requirements through banking facilities supplied in a highly flexible manner by international banks. It is probable that the first medium-term eurocurrency credit syndicated by several banks and organized on behalf of an international borrower was a credit put together for the benefit of IBM World Trade in the early 1960s. Term lending on a syndicated basis was already fairly well established in the United States' market. An important distinction must be made, however, between this first commercial operation and others which followed it, and sovereign borrowing activity as it developed, particularly after the first oil price increase in 1973. IBM World Trade and other multinational companies were at the time engaged in important investment activities in Europe and the rest of the world. Increasing success in these new markets produced working capital requirements which could not always be easily satisfied by the local banking community. They were thus ideal candidates for medium-term eurocurrency facilities provided by international banks, including their home banks and the banks in the various countries in which they were operating. These facilities were provided on a so-called roll-over basis, their cost was based on a negotiated margin over the cost of funds to the participating banks — funds which had been acquired in the interbank market for eurocurrency deposits.

It is important, however, to recognize a major distinction which characterized this sort of credit in the early days of the development of the market for eurocurrency loans. In almost every case the borrower was supplementing existing sources of finance with a facility constructed in a particularly flexible manner. Since these facilities were provided on the understanding that funds would continue to be available to the participating banks, if conditions developed in the eurocurrency market which made it impossible to secure the necessary deposits, the facility would lapse or would have to be repaid and, in any case, would not continue on the same basis. This need not cause embarrassment to either the borrower or the participating banks since the borrower would merely fall back on banking facilities available to him in his home market, or would consolidate the short-term debt represented by the facility through some other operation. In recent times, however, medium-term eurocurrency facilities, particularly those provided to governments and governmental agencies, have become the sole source of finance available to those borrowers, thereby placing considerable pressure on the system should anything happen to interrupt the smooth flow of funds on which banks participating in such credit depend for their deposits.

Although use of the eurocurrency market by governments and governmental agencies was already growing, even before the oil price increases, the phenomenon now known as recycling began as a result of the massive disequilibria in international payments balances which was a direct consequence of the huge increase in oil prices engineered by the principal oil exporting nations in 1973. At the time, considerable concern was expressed about how these deficits would be financed — the resources of the multinational institutions such as the World Bank and the International Monetary Fund were clearly going to be strained as a result of new demands from countries faced with massive oil import bills. The international banking system came to the rescue, amidst serious doubts as to its capacity to perform the role of intermediary between the oil exporting nations, suddenly enjoying huge balance of payments surpluses, and other nations, primarily those in the early stages of development, faced with significant borrowing requirements as a result of the oil price increase. The existence of the eurocurrency market and a smoothly functioning machinery for the transfer of liquidity from one banking centre to another permitted the international banking community to engage in the enormous amount of recycling necessary. This was accomplished without apparent undue strain; it was evidenced by a huge increase in the volume and diversity of medium-term loans provided by international banks of all types to a growing number of borrowers throughout the world.

In view of the importance of this aspect of international banking, it is worth dwelling on the technical features which have characterized medium-term eurocurrency loans. Although a great many such loans are actually contracted on an individual basis by banks, the more important transactions — and those generally receiving the most publicity — are loans which are syndicated amongst a variety of banks using different techniques. In a classic syndication, major banks act as the leaders, negotiate the terms of the credit, organize its documentation and then invite a number of other banks, usually including smaller banks, to participate in the loan on conditions that have already been generally agreed with the borrower.

The level of participation in any particular loan will vary not only according to the size of the participating bank, but also according to the position the bank enjoys within the syndicate. In some large transactions participants are invited at a variety of levels. Each of these levels will involve a different size of individual commitment and, although the margin fixed over the cost of funds to the participating bank will be common to all participants, there will be a variety of front-end commissions which reflect the particular position of the bank in the syndicate. Obviously the largest front-end commission is enjoyed by the so-called lead bank, for example that institution which has been responsible for initiating and negotiating the transaction and which enjoys the pride of place within the syndicate.

Variations on the syndication method have been developed. One of importance is the so-called club loan, whereby a group of banks operate together, having usually been pre-selected by the borrower. Although one bank will be named the agent bank and will be responsible for the documentation and for co-ordinating subsequent communications to the group, the banks will actually operate on an equal basis.

Syndicated transactions can also include other refinements. In some cases the entire loan will be initially underwritten by a group of banks who have agreed to work together on the understanding that, having secured the mandate from the borrower on the conditions offered, they will then subsequently seek participants. Should they be unsuccessful in attracting the interest of other participants, the original underwriting banks are committed to subscribing the entire loan for their own accounts. In other cases syndicated loans are offered for general participation to a number of banks before they have been actually fully underwritten, and banks may have an opportunity to comment on the conditions initially indicated by the organizing banks. Activity in this market has reached such a degree of sophistication and depth that it can truly be said to constitute a market in the sense that conditions are influenced by factors of supply and demand, with types of instruments still increasing and extending from simple debt to floating rate notes of various types.

One of the outstanding features of the evolution of this market in the last few years has been a rise in the relative importance of the dollar denominated instruments and a fall in other currency denominated instruments. Thus, in 1989, only 23% of the total comprised the non-dollar denominated paper as compared with 33% in 1986.

While the Euro-currency market has expanded very rapidly, its growth came almost to a standstill in the last few years. This has been due to securitization, that is an increasing preference on the part of corporations to borrow through capital markets rather than from banks.

THE EUROBOND MARKET

The eurobond market in its various forms represents another major service provided by the international banking community. It is a service in which London-based institutions have gained particular prominence in recent years. Indeed, the bulk of the activity in the eurobond market is now headquartered in London, even though many of the participants are foreign houses. The activity itself incorporates the initiation, or lead management, of eurobond issues, their underwriting and distribution and finally their trading in the secondary market.

Eurobond issues are similar in construction to debt instruments common in the major domestic capital markets, with the United States markets supplying the largest share of technical features. The most important distinguishing characteristics of eurobonds are their bearer form and the fact that interest payments, which are effected through the use of coupons attached to the main bond, are always made without deduction at source of withholding taxes. These two features, in general present in domestic capital markets, allow for the free circulation of eurobonds across national borders and make them ideal investment vehicles for individuals and institutions whose investment strategy is international. As mentioned previously, the distribution period and the fact that distribution is assured through an international underwriting syndicate makes it difficult for individuals and institutions, as end investors, to engage in complicated credit assessment procedures prior to subscribing to a new issue. For this reason use of the eurobond market is generally confined to well-known international corporations, transnational agencies such as the World Bank and the European Community, sovereign governments and municipalities, or agencies from the industrialized world. These borrowers are regularly contacted by the hundred or so issuing houses active in the organization of international capital market transactions.

Significant competition between the issuing houses exists and most corporate treasurers and finance officials or other qualified borrowers will maintain active relationships with several issuing houses. Prominent amongst these houses will be the international divisions of the major American investment banks, the traditional London-based merchant banks, merchant banking subsidiaries of the large American, European and Japanese commercial banks, specialized consortium banks and other private banks engaged in the securities business. The houses concerned will be skilled in designing the type of issue best suited to the objectives of the borrower. They will judge prevailing market conditions and the receptivity of investors to particular terms. They will then organize underwriting syndicates according to the nature of the issue and prepare the documentation, including those documents necessary to obtain a stock exchange quotation in London or Luxembourg.

Underwriting methods vary, as does the size of an underwriting group required to ensure the placement of different sizes and types of issue. The strength of a lead manager includes judgment as to the market, ability to organize and manage underwriting syndicates, ability to place a substantial portion of the issue with its own clients and the means of following the issue in the after-market by ensuring that a secondary market is maintained. Although issues are invariably listed at stock exchanges, secondary dealings in fact take place directly between the banks and other finance houses specializing in eurobond activities. All such houses will be members of the Association of International Bond Dealers, which provides self-regulatory services to the market.

The eurobond market has grown significantly in the last ten years. It is now far more than an offshore market and rivals in size and depth the two largest domestic capital markets in the United States and the United Kingdom. It represents a major facet of the business of international banking which is carried on in the world's principal finance centres. Eurobond business tends to provide the longest term of finance available from the international banking system. It represents a non-funded service provided by international banks, since these banks essentially act as intermediaries between borrowers and different classes of investor.

As in the case of Euro-currency markets, an increasing proportion of issues has been denominated in recent years in currencies other than the dollar. Thus, in 1989, no less than 58% comprised non-dollar securities as compared with 46% in 1986. The market has become more sophisticated. In addition to various types of debt its business now covers convertibles and debt with gilt warrants, thus competing increasingly with domestic gilt markets.

The question now being asked is whether the development of a direct European Financial Market is likely to affect the Euro-bond and Euro-currency market especially if the European Community moves to irrevocably fix exchange rates and reduce withholding taxes.

That such a development would affect the Euro-markets is beyond doubt. What cannot be answered at present is the timing and the severity of the impact of it.

EXPORT FINANCE

Concern about the deterioration in international credit quality has focused attention on the lending activities of international banks directed to the governments and public agencies of the developing world. Much of this medium-term lending is prompted by the export finance needs of the major industrial and commercial customers of the banking system in the industrialized countries. Indeed, export finance represents a major service provided by international banks to national and multinational corporations.

The export finance systems in the industrialized world are all government subsidized to varying degrees. The element of state subsidy in every case is the subject of elaborate international agreements under the umbrella of the General Agreement on Tariffs and Trade (GATT). The Berne Convention, supplemented by other agreements, seeks to regulate that portion of international competition for external trade which is provided by government subsidized financing arrangements. This international regulation is rendered extremely difficult due to the diversity of export finance systems in operation in the main industrialized countries. The systems fall into two main categories and, in some countries, both types of official intervention in export finance exist. Either a guarantee institute provides support for loans made by the banking system to finance exports, or a specialist government controlled bank or agency provides direct lending on soft terms in conjunction with credit facilities provided by the banking system. Whether through direct loans or via guarantees, the government subsidy provides credit either to suppliers or to overseas importers on terms which are usually substantially more favourable than market conditions in terms of interest rate and maturity.

The portion of an export order which will be susceptible to subsidized export finance varies from country to country, but tends to be in the region of 80%. Any further financing is supplied by commercial banks on commercial terms. International banks, especially merchant banks, are specialized in arranging and negotiating export finance packages, particularly for large exports involving capital goods being delivered over a period of time. In addition to exploiting to the maximum the different government subsidies made available to promote exports, bankers active in this area assist in structuring an order in the most competitive manner and include in their packaging a number of other financial elements which have a bearing on transactions of this type such as insurance, performance bonding and so on.

While most day-to-day exports are financed through supplier credits, very large orders tend to be financed on the basis of a buyer credit. Banks are expected to provide an up-to-date credit assessment of the importing agency and the country in which it is located. Normally large medium-term loans are specifically linked to a particular export or series of exports. However, given the degree of international competition which exists among the principal industrialized countries for large export orders, particularly those assuring employment in the home market, importing nations have learnt to exploit the desire of banks to assist their national customers. Requests to grant additional medium-term loans for balance of payments purposes are frequently made at the same time as discussions are being pursued with respect to export transactions. Few bankers have been able to resist this less than subtle pressure when it is exercised by governments having in their gift large export orders being competed for by several national industries.

The international agreements governing export finance have been interpreted very liberally by many industrialized countries. Export promotion schemes have become highly complex as each country seeks to gain some advantage over its competitors for export markets. The international banks are expected to be highly knowledgeable on the subject and be able to design the most advantageous packages to enhance the competitive position of their industrial customers. Multinational corporations frequently provide goods and services from more than one jurisdiction within which they operate. This prompts them to exploit the export finance possibilities in more than one country, to the extent that they ensure sufficient local content for any portion of a project or order being supplied by their group. This offers further opportunities for international banks to exercise their imagination in the field of international export finance. Many large projects in the developing world rely on capital goods and engineering services supplied by a variety of countries. Given the diversity of export finance systems, a major challenge for international banks financing such projects is to ensure maximum co-ordination in the structuring and documentation of a variety of export transactions destined for the same project.

TERM LENDING

The growth in term lending, as opposed to the financing of self-liquidating transactions, is of relatively recent origin in the international capital markets; term lending has its origins in the United States. Although the United States benefits from securities markets of unusual depth and diversity, the practice of extending medium to long-term credit facilities to the corporate sector developed in the post-war years, largely to cater for project financing which was not open to financing through the issues of debt securities. Another considerable advantage offered to industry by term finance, provided through the banking system, is that of flexibility. Although long-term finance is traditionally available in the United States, through the private placement of long-term fixed rate obligations with institutional investors such as insurance companies and pension funds, these normally have stringent requirements as to documentation and security arrangements. The covenants insisted upon by such lenders cause difficulties for companies whose basic situation may alter during the life of the loan without their relative credit standing being adversely affected. In such cases, complicated and sometimes protracted negotiations with the institutional lenders are needed to make the necessary adjustments. Furthermore, institutional lenders who are planning the structure of their investment portfolios over a long period of time normally preclude the possibility of a borrower prepaying its obligations in advance. Again, this removes valuable flexibility from the borrower, who may find more attractive financing sources during the life of his initial loan.

In contrast, term facilities provided by banks allow for very considerable flexibility. These are generally granted on the basis of a variable rate of interest, giving the borrower comparability of interest cost on a continuing basis. Since the rate of interest is varying and is fixed at a margin over the lending banks' own cost of money, there are frequent break periods during the life of a loan when an interest rate is being reviewed and when a borrower, giving relatively short notice, can prepay the loan if he has an alternative funding opportunity which is more attractive, either in terms of cost or in terms of maturity. Although the loan agreements entered into by borrowers taking term funds from the commercial banking system are strict and comprehensive, they can be fairly easily altered or amended to reflect a change in the borrower's circumstances. If a syndicate of lenders is involved, these amendments are usually negotiated with the agent bank, who then canvasses and seeks the approval of such changes from the members of the lending syndicate. Although more individual consents are needed in the case of a syndicate (at a minimum a two-thirds majority of the lenders must normally give their consent to any changes in the loan agreement), lending banks are traditionally somewhat more flexible than institutions such as insurance companies and pension funds, and are able to work with fairly sophisticated arrangements designed to suit the peculiarities of a specific case.

The term lending techniques developed in the United States banking market form the basis for eurocurrency term lending as it is now practised by international banks. Such loans increasingly benefit from imaginative arrangements designed to cater for the precise circumstances of a borrower or the circumstances of the investment which is being financed through medium-term facilities. Project financing is the most obvious example of specialized term lending practised by the international banking community, and is increasingly mentioned in the range of services which international banks now advertise to their prospective clients. As with many other euromarket activities, project finance has become fashionable and the term is very often somewhat loosely used by both bankers and commercial clients alike.

In its broadest sense, project finance covers all financing arrangements which are directed specifically at a project of a commercial, industrial or extractive nature. Many bankers speak of project financing as a broad category of finance, distinguished from general financing of the corporate sector, which is taken to mean working capital finance or other facilities provided for non-specific purposes. In fact project finance in the true sense of the term refers only to financing arrangements where the source of repayment of the loan is the cash-flow of a particular project and where (within a variety of limitations) the terms and conditions of the loan allow the lender only very limited recourse to the project sponsor should the cash-flow from the project prove insufficient to service interest and principal repayments of the loan. The element of recourse to the underlying borrower is a key factor in assessing the risk in project lending. For this reason, project loans are sometimes referred to as limited recourse loans.

Project lending involves a wide variety of financial techniques and incorporates a large selection of types of term loan. It is a fundamental characteristic of this international banking service that it can only be practised by institutions which have considerable internal skills and expertise in the field of project analysis. The lenders in a typical project are in a real sense partners with the project sponsor. Although their financial support is in the form of loans rather than equity, since they are normally substantially dependent on the success of the project in commercial terms for the recovery of their loans, their involvement in a project can be said to be of a quasi-equity nature. Generally speaking the security for a project loan will include a charge on all of the assets represented by the project, but should the project be a commercial failure it is unlikely that the liquidating value of these assets will be sufficient to cover the advance made by the bankers. Therefore the lenders are totally involved in the economics of the project and the commercial circumstances which determine its eventual success. Such circumstances revolve around the ability of the project sponsors to control initial and continuing costs and the prices which will be received for the project's output.

International project finance has been focused largely on the extractive industries and in particular the development of oil and gas fields, both onshore and offshore. The exploitation of mineral deposits, excluding hydrocarbons, is also an area in which project finance techniques are highly developed. In an oil and gas project loan the bankers must be satisfied with the estimation of productive reserves, this being an area of initial analysis critical to the overall analysis of the financial risks involved in the project as a whole. Project lending is introduced at the development stage of an oil or gas field and the risk is clearly that of cost control and ultimate price structure. In many cases the price of the output is guaranteed, at least during a period, by the availability of oil or gas purchase contracts with creditworthy purchasers. These contracts can then be assigned to the lenders thus giving them the assurance that the product will be sold at a fixed price. Most mineral development project financing also involves long-term contracts for the output.

International banks active in the project finance field will employ a variety of expert consultants in such matters as reservoir engineering. However, to interpret correctly the reports of such consultants, project banks must have individuals on their staff with specific technical training in the relevant areas. Since engineers with a financial grounding are not readily found within the banking system, only twenty or so major international banks have a sufficiently powerful project finance team to lead and structure a project loan. However the availability of projects which can be financed internationally on a limited recourse basis is highly dependent on the economic circumstances prevailing in the international market as a whole. Project financing is traditionally associated with long maturities, since most projects require several years to reach a mature stage at which cash flow is generated in sufficient quantities to ensure the servicing of the finance and profit for the sponsor. Ideally, project finance should be on a fixed rate basis in order to limit the number of variable costs and unknown factors facing the project. The only source of fixed rate finance available in the international credit markets is represented by the issue of eurobonds. Unfortunately eurobond investors are not attracted tocomplex credits, since they rarely have the opportunity and resources to perform their own evaluation and assessment of a project and its attendant risks. For this reason, project finance has been supplied largely through term loans provided by syndicates of international banks. (For further discussion on project financing, see chapter 3.1)

OTHER SERVICES

Other non-funded services provided by international banks are focused on various forms of advice. Although financial advice is traditionally a merchant banking activity, major commercial banks now also have specialists able to advise corporate and individual customers on financial problems of various kinds. In the light of the growing volume of international indebtedness, particularly by sovereign nations, a new advisory activity has emerged, consisting of assisting borrowers with the management and often the re-structuring of their external debt. Advice is also given on problems associated with exports, trade finance, foreign exchange and treasury management, and even the procurement of capital goods from the contracting of international services.

The qualification needed in order to be able to provide financial advisory services is one of broadly-based experience. International banks are exposed to a wider variety of problems than is generally the case with purely domestic institutions. Solutions generated for these problems in one case are often readily adaptable to similar but different cases arising in different countries. In fact the business of international banking is based to a large extent on the transfer and adaptation of domestic banking techniques to an international context. In all of the services provided by international banks there will be elements of technique which are characteristic of certain specific markets, currency blocs and other economic subdivisions of the world market. Experience with these elements will be found within an international banking house and represents the main service which commercial, industrial, governmental or individual clients can obtain.

International banking facilities available to multinational firms have been and are continuing to increase and change in scope and character. They now include a large and powerful number of financial instruments of both on-balance and off-balance sheet varieties. Denominated in various national and man-made composite currencies, covering funds needed for working and long-term capital as well as instruments providing hedging facilities against the exchange and interest rate risk and those enabling firms to reduce the cost of funds through a variety of techniques.

Propelled by rapid technological change and the internationalization of financial markets this process is likely to continue, calling for first class knowledge of finance and its various segments especially in the international context.

This chapter, originally drafted by S. YASSUKOVITCH, has been rewritten and updated by Professor T. M. RYBCZYNSKI.

2.3 International banking facilities available to the multinational firm: a user's view

The user of international banking services is today presented with a bewildering choice of possible banks; it is the aim of this chapter to present a series of points for consideration by corporate officers when directing banking business and to describe some of the facilities offered. Since, in practice, the availability of non-funding services from a particular bank often influences the user's final selection of a credit institution, all aspects of international banking services are discussed, in addition to sources of finance.

This chapter is also not restricted to consideration of the services offered solely by the international banks. Domestic banks have in the past offered a wide range of international services and continue to do so. In terms of, say, an international money transfer, a precise instruction is capable of being followed by the humblest of domestic banks. However, the increasingly complicated capital market related services are generally offered only by the more internationally oriented banks.

THE DEVELOPMENT OF INTERNATIONAL BANKING SERVICES

Some banks have a wide range of international interests, enabling them to conduct banking business overseas through their own branches. This type of organization started perhaps with the overseas British banks who operated in what was then the British Empire. Banks like Standard Chartered and Grindlays developed branch networks which were an integral part of a country's banking scene. The trend was continued in a slightly different fashion, with big, mainly American, banks opening overseas branches around the world. These branches avoided purely domestic business, and concentrated instead on providing international services. Initially these services were aimed at home-country multinationals but their new approach to banking was soon being offered to all large corporations in the country. This new approach which, in effect, split large corporate business away from other business, produced a minor revolution in bank service levels.

The account officer concept, the reduction of bureaucracy and the streamlining of procedures that this approach brought, caused domestic rivals to re-assess their own systems and reconsider corporate client needs. Of course the banks who had introduced new concepts in corporate banking to (say) London, were the same banks who were later forced to react to competitive pressures in their home country. Recently, a number of banks, particularly but not exclusively, European banks have established cross-border co-operation agreements — enabling each bank to benefit from the domestic strength of the other bank. One of the main driving forces behind this move has been the initiatives associated with 1992 and the need for banks to turn themselves into European operations.

Investment banks and other deal-oriented institutions previously found no need for permanent establishments around the globe. Typically they would be represented in London, New York and Tokyo, to cover Europe, the Americas and Asia respectively. However, as the capital markets in other locations such as Paris, Frankfurt and Sydney have grown, the investment banks have felt the need to establish offices in such centres.

Notwithstanding the restrictions imposed domestically by United States law, most major banks are now able to offer some degree of investment banking expertise. Indeed, recent developments have seen moves towards dismantling altogether the laws that separate commercial and investment banking activity in the United States and Japan. Here also there are continuing developments and we have seen, both in the United States and the United Kingdom, investment banks and merchant banks actively seeking deposits via the money markets.

In the United Kingdom, the impetus provided by the Big Bang resulted in the development of a new breed of financial institutions, the conglomerates. It is now possible to approach one group of companies for the services previously provided separately by Stockbrokers, International Banks, Merchant Bankers, Discount Houses and Estate Agents

However, recently we have seen a reduction in the number of institutions which can properly call themselves conglomerates with a number of banks going back to offering these specialized services in defined market areas.

This concentration of services will enable some very big institutions to compete with each other in the market place. The user is likely to find a bewildering choice in both the service quality offered and the cost of those services.

THE RANGE OF INTERNATIONAL BANKING SERVICES

The major international banking services fall under nine main headings:

(1) export services;
(2) import services;

(3) foreign exchange;
(4) short-term finance;
(5) cash management services;
(6) bid bonds and performance bonds;
(7) project finance and venture capital;
(8) advisory services;
(9) longer-term finance and capital.

There are over 400 banks in London. While many of them will offer all of the above services, there are often marked differences in performance when a particular service is considered. As in any market, certain banks will develop a specialist expertise both in terms of the products in which they deal and in terms of the geographic location of the markets. However, in certain cases this expertise can be transitory — a bank that performs a service particularly well one year may not perform so well the next year. Consequently it is necessary to monitor constantly the performance of a bank to ensure that it does not deteriorate.

When considering any one banking service it is, therefore, important to choose a bank on the twin aspects of charges and service levels. One must also consider how the choice of a bank for a specific service can be included in a co-ordinated approach to bank relationship objectives. It is also important that the development of a relationship should not be overly emphasized, since this could conflict with the principle of obtaining the lowest cost and best service deal. In too many cases the relationship can be used as an excuse to obscure the search for better solutions. It allows corporations, through inertia, to keep business with a bank which is unable to handle it efficiently.

EXPORT SERVICES

Fully international banks will encourage the belief that in all aspects of international trade they have significant advantages over their domestic brethren. If this is true, this comparative advantage should be of most interest to an exporting company. This is because an exporter has more control as far as payment terms and conditions are concerned, while an importer will usually be reacting to an exporter's directions.

In practice the simple distinction between international and domestic banks is misleading and it is necessary to consider the individual export services required when selecting a particular bank.

The main categories of export services provided by banks are:

(1) cash collection on open account;
(2) documentary collections;
(3) bills of exchange;
(4) countertrade and barter;
(5) foreign currency bank accounts;

(6) market intelligence;
(7) Export Credits Guarantee Department services.

CASH COLLECTION ON OPEN ACCOUNT

The procedures involved in operating an effective open account cash collection system are all in the domain of the exporter rather than the bank. A corporation should primarily look to instruct its customer on the exact routing of any payment by clearly stating these details on invoices and statements. Thus, if it is invoicing in United States dollars, instructions should be given to pay funds to New York for the account of the company's United Kingdom bankers for the order of the company itself. Similar delivery instructions are appropriate to all foreign currency. Delay can only result from non-sterling funds being transmitted to London. A bank's input in this system is to provide timely advice of the funds received and details of the payment. In addition, a bank will advise on the most efficient routing of funds and will help establish the bank accounts necessary to achieve this routing as discussed later.

DOCUMENTARY COLLECTIONS

When documentary credit services are considered, very different service levels become apparent. For example, some banks have been known (before proper control was exercised) to take up to seven days to review documents before remitting funds against a confirmed letter of credit.

Most large companies are now able to insist on same day settlement under letters of credit, allowing the bank say twenty-four hours to reclaim if the documents are not in order. Smaller companies, with a lower credit rating, may not be able to obtain this concession generally, but should be in a position to seek it from their main bankers. Certainly any longer than two days to consider documents could be considered excessive.

The relationship factor will also apply where documents do not totally conform to the terms of the credit. Too many banks will insist that the documents must be sent to the buyer for payment on a collection basis, thus considerably delaying the receipt of funds. A good relationship with the paying bank, together with an indemnity, can usually avoid this problem, although the indemnity itself should not be taken lightly.

Many companies are happy to allow the buyer to nominate a bank for letter of credit payments. Thus the exporter is forced to deal with banks with which he does not have an established relationship.

International banks can have a distinct advantage when it comes to the collection of foreign bills. They should usually have more contact with their overseas branch which will be processing the collection than a bank dealing through correspondents. To obtain the best service, therefore, it will be necessary to choose banks which have a significant presence in the centre where collection is to be made.

In addition, certain banks devote more attention to their documentary collections services than others. If a bank is undertaking a large volume of documentary credits then it is likely to have a better system for ensuring an efficient collection of funds than if its documentary collection department is small. This has become increasingly important in recent years as some banks, viewing their documentary collections service as too manually intensive, have directed the emphasis of their business away from this area reducing the size of their departments.

BILLS OF EXCHANGE

The provision of services in relation to bills of exchange is likely to depend on the credit lines offered and the rates of discount applied by the bank when discounting or negotiating bills. This would generally be a matter of negotiation.

COUNTERTRADE AND BARTER

Difficulties in paying for goods and services have led to the redevelopment of countertrade. In its widest sense, this includes all forms of compensatory trading arrangements from full barter to counterpurchase agreements where only a small proportion of any deal might be in the form of exchange of goods.

The depth of countertrade is difficult to establish but recent estimates vary between 5% and 30% of total international trade. Many countries are involved but the principal participants would include:

(1) Comecon countries;
(2) lesser developed countries;
(3) Middle East countries.

When a multinational is faced with the prospect of becoming involved in countertrade, the major banks can provide a variety of assistance:

(1) provision of finance and advice on forms of finance;
(2) acting as broker, identifying parties to a deal;
(3) determining the creditworthiness of counterparties;
(4) drafting documentation;
(5) preparing market studies;
(6) negotiation with counterparties and central supervisor authorities.

A number of major international banks now dominate the countertrade market and most are specialists with expertise gained before the 1983-1984 boom. Most have either set up their own in-house unit or have developed a joint venture with another bank.

FOREIGN CURRENCY BANK ACCOUNTS

Almost all banks in the United Kingdom will offer their customers foreign currency bank accounts. These can aid collections considerably but, without timely information, can result in both idle balances and the chasing of customers who have already paid. Advances in electronic banking have alleviated some of these problems for many companies, certainly in respect of the operation of United States dollar accounts.

The major United States banks are the leaders in new electronic systems and can offer various currency accounts utilising electronic data transmission techniques (as discussed further under Cash Management Services below). Despite these advances, however, there may not be instant funds available in many overseas locations where the domestic banking system is far less developed than those of the United Kingdom or the United States.

MARKET INTELLIGENCE

Several of the international banks in London produce regularly updated market information briefs on conditions abroad. These can be very useful to both treasurers and commercial managers. In addition, the bank should be able to offer advice on exporting to new markets and organizations within the United Kingdom that can aid exporters with regard to customs regulations, import duties and documentation.

EXPORT CREDITS GUARANTEE DEPARTMENT SERVICES

Lastly in this section it is appropriate to mention the provision of buyer or supplier credit under Export Credits Guarantee Department auspices. These services can only be offered by a recognized bank or licensed deposit-taking institution. In some cases foreign banks have established United Kingdom subsidiaries which specialize in export-related services, although Export Credits Guarantee Department credits may also be offered directly by the United Kingdom branch of a recognised overseas bank.

IMPORT SERVICES

As stated above, as an importer an organization will usually be reacting to the seller's wishes and therefore has less scope in choosing a bank to process payments. Notwithstanding this restriction there are three main considerations when choosing a bank to process import transactions:

(1) the cost of documentary services;
(2) the efficiency of payment systems;
(3) the expertise available to capitalise on foreign export promotion schemes.

DOCUMENTARY SERVICES COSTS

The cost of opening credits can vary considerably between banks, and the corporate treasurer will seek the bank or banks who can offer a good service at reasonable cost. The bank for its part will be concerned that the issuing of a letter of credit does not take an organization over an approved credit limit. In the United Kingdom the practice of debiting a company's account with the full value of a letter of credit on issue is now only seen with very small companies, although in many countries abroad this is normal procedure. Indeed it may even be required by law as a way of controlling imports (this can be relevant when, as an exporter, a company demands the security of a letter of credit).

EFFICIENT PAYMENT SYSTEMS

If an importer wants to deal on a regular basis on the finest terms with a supplier, it is important to maintain credibility by arranging timely payments. In arranging transfers to a value date, a payer needs to ensure that same-day value is obtained. Any loss of value will, in one way or another, fall on the importer, who will therefore be concerned that his bank should be capable of remitting payment at the latest possible opportunity while still complying with the exporter's payment terms. Too many banks have in the past put forward their payment systems (often citing their SWIFT connections) and said when pressed that their responsibility ends with the telexed payment instruction to their overseas correspondent. An unambiguous value-dated payment instruction is a contract for which a bank must be held accountable, and its duty is to ensure that good funds are received, in time, by the beneficiary.

EXPORT PROMOTION SCHEMES

Most companies are familiar with the assistance which can be given by the Export Credits Guarantee Department to encourage United Kingdom exports. This assistance takes two forms. An exporter can obtain comprehensive insurance against buyer default and can also obtain loans at subsidized rates. Other countries have their equivalent of Export Credits Guarantee Department, and it would obviously be beneficial to a United Kingdom company to take advantage of the appropriate scheme to reduce import costs.

Banks can provide a useful service by, for example, advising on the availability of any overseas export promotion scheme, and often perform a co-ordinating role via their overseas offices.

FOREIGN EXCHANGE

The art of foreign exchange dealing in corporations has developed strongly in the last decade. The factor that contributed most to this trend was the introduction of first Reuter's and later Telerate's information service. The development of these systems has allowed the treasurer to read the market better and it has therefore reduced the scope for banks to quote wide prices. However, it must be realized that the rates quoted are only indication rates and are not necessarily the actual rates at which the bank will deal.

Having become more sophisticated, and with the help of these information systems, the treasurer is in a position to choose the best bank for a particular deal. This choice will be based on both his experience of the bank's general competitiveness and the known capabilities in a particular currency.

The foreign exchange market is split in each currency between those banks which are market-makers and those which are not. Which type of bank one should approach is the subject of contrary arguments.

(1) From the market-maker you should obtain a fine market price, although he may have a book that 'looks the wrong way'.

(2) The non-market-maker will test a selection of market-makers for you and pass on the best price available between them, although he will need to add his profit margin.

It is often considered better to approach a market-maker and judge the price offered with the help of a monitor. Whichever is chosen, the need to deal quickly before the rates change must be considered.

A particular problem for treasurers can arise when dealing in currencies other than the United States dollar. If one wants to buy Finnish marks against the pound, then while there will be several Finnish mark/dollar market-makers, they might not be strong in dollar/pound. These deals therefore might call for the use of two banks — one for Fmk/$ and the other for $/£ — to get the best possible deal. Splitting the deal this way into its constituent parts has the added advantage of maintaining relationships with two banks.

Other factors when considering a bank for foreign exchange dealing include:

(1) whether commissions will be levied;
(2) whether delivery charges will be levied;
(3) the level of contact with the bank.

There is still a widespread practice among banks to try to levy a separate commission on foreign exchange transactions. For very small deals one can accept that a commission would be needed to remunerate the bank. On larger deals, however, the turn should provide adequate potential profit. When very large deals are concerned the turn alone will represent a significant profit to the bank (on converting $10m into sterling it is worth over $2,000 for five pips) so prices can be negotiated inside the market.

In addition to any commission charges banks may also charge for delivery of foreign currency (usually a telex charge plus a transmission fee). There appears to be little justification for these fees; if the bank is not in a position to complete its side of a contract (by delivery) it should not be offering to trade.

A further consideration is the range of associated contracts that a bank can provide such as foreign exchange options, range forward contracts, and break forward contracts. Sometimes one of these types of contract may be more appropriate than a straight spot or forward contract and some banks will offer advice on the best contracts to use.

By far the most important factor in considering a bank for foreign exchange services is whether personal contact can be established with dealers. Most large companies would not be willing to negotiate with an intermediate bank official who has the only contact with the banks' dealers. A company will always want the best prices, while a bank dealer will want to improve his book profits. The dealers may infer that any client dealing in foreign exchange either via a branch (for a clearer) or via an account officer (for other banks) is not monitoring prices closely. The price quoted may therefore reflect the dealers' perception of the client's sophistication.

Not being in direct contact with a bank's dealing staff also prevents a company from obtaining any feel for a market. It will therefore, not, for example, be able to take advantage of a dealer's view of short-term movements.

SHORT-TERM FINANCE

Many years ago a company needing non-equity finance used a combination of overdrafts, bill discounting and loan stock issues. The foreign banks in London found it difficult to compete with the domestic banks in these cases because:

(1) they did not have a large number of current accounts and were effectively unable to offer overdrafts;
(2) they were not eligible and therefore their bill discounting rates were expensive; and
(3) they had no source of long-term fixed rate deposits and were therefore unable to offer long-term loans.

In response to this apparent weakness the foreign banks began to offer Libor-linked credit lines. In developing this source of finance they successfully captured a significant percentage of the corporate finance market amongst the larger corporations. With the prohibitive long-term interest rates that prevailed until recently, many corporations found themselves more and more reliant on these funding sources.

COMMERCIAL PAPER

An increasingly popular form of finance available to major institutions is the commercial paper facility. This is a medium-term facility which can be drawn down through the issue of a series of short-term promissory notes whose maturities are usually one, three or six months. Each tranche of notes issued is offered for sale to an investor base so that the providers of finance may change every few months even though, from the company's perspective, the finance remains in place for the medium term.

Euronotes were formerly distinguished from commercial paper in that most dealers classified the former as underwritten facilities distributed by tender panel and the latter as non-underwritten paper placed by dealers. This distinction is now less important and no longer tends to be made. This form of short-term paper has been seen as attractive to corporates because of:

(1) low cost;
(2) flexibility;
(3) high availability of funds;
(4) simplicity in setting up a programme;
(5) enhanced investor awareness.

When assessing a dealer, apart from cost, corporate customers would normally focus on distribution capability and the advice and expertise available to help set up a programme. International banks have a particular advantage due to their wide ranging contacts.

MULTIPLE OPTION FACILITIES (MOFS)

With the increasing variety of short term funding sources now available, a number of banks have introduced a facility which makes it possible for a corporate to change its funding sources from time to time without the need to negotiate and maintain numerous different facilities. A multiple option facility is basically an agreement whereby a bank will arrange one facility, and hence one credit line, for a corporate which the company can draw down in a number of different forms.

For example, a total multiple option facility may be for say £50m. However, the corporate can then choose whether to borrow via overdraft, term loan, Commercial paper, bill discounting or other fund means. Perhaps also the corporate has the choice of a number of different currencies.

While the total that can be borrowed from each individual financing source under the multiple option facility may be less than £50m, the aggregate of all of the different facilities contained in the multiple option facility will typically exceed £50m — the total amount of the facility. However, the corporate must restrict the total amount borrowed at any one point in time under the multiple option facility to £50m.

The advantage of such a scheme is that the corporate customer has a number of different financing sources available within the same facility; as a result he only needs to pay a commitment fee on the multiple option facility total. The alternative would be to negotiate each facility separately which is not only more cumbersome but would also involve the payment of a much higher commitment fee in total due to the fact that the aggregate of the individual facilities is greater than the multiple option facility total as noted above.

Typically, a multiple option facility involves a syndicate of banks providing the funds. Different banks within the syndicate will commit to provide the different types of finance. Thus, depending on which form of finance a corporate customer chooses under a multiple option facility, a different group of banks will provide the funds. For example, the group of banks providing United States dollar funds may be different than the group of banks providing sterling funds.

A key role in a multiple option facility is that of the arranging bank who is responsible for putting together the syndicate of banks with the multiple option facility. An international bank will invariably undertake this role due to its contacts in the international banking markets.

HEDGING TECHNIQUES

Corporate treasurers are increasingly involved in taking an active rather than a passive role in the management of corporate assets and liabilities. Banks are, therefore, becoming more involved in the provision of instruments to facilitate hedging.

The corporate customer is looking increasingly at not only the instruments on offer but the advice available and the expertise of the bank. In particular, banks may be asked to provide financial futures, effectively acting as an intermediary or to write Forward Rate Agreements or options. They will also be requested to advise on the best instruments to use in a particular instance and the most cost effective method.

CASH MANAGEMENT SERVICES

ELECTRONIC BANKING

An area of rapidly developing importance for banks and major corporate customers is the provision of electronic banking services (EB). First, a corporate treasurer must decide whether to operate a cash management system or a treasury workstation.

A cash management system essentially provides users with balance information on accounts and a transfer of funds capability. A balance reporting system will provide information which enables treasurers to minimize the existence of idle non-interest bearing balances or to move balances from lower to higher interest accounts. Mismatches of currency flows can be more easily identified and cash receipts and payments can be effected on the account which gives most efficient use of funds.

Fund transfers can be effected electronically by one of the banking networks. This would be SWIFT for international payments or CHAPS (Clearing House Automated Payments System) for sterling payments. Although these systems require greater control than existing manual methods they dramatically improve cash management capabilities.

A treasury workstation is generally more sophisticated than a straightforward cash management system and would include a modelling capability to support treasury decision-making.

At present, the majority of software for treasury workstations is supplied from outside the banking community. However, most cash management systems are linked to one particular institution. The corporate treasurer must assess a number of factors in deciding which cash management system to adopt; the following questions need to be answered:

(1) are balances given current or for the previous day?
(2) how are value dated transactions dealt with?
(3) is the system real time? If not, how frequently is information updated?
(4) can funds be transmitted?
(5) how far ahead can clearing items be identified?
(6) are security arrangements adequate?
(7) which hardware does the system run on?

A major criticism of early balance reporting systems was their inability to supply information from third party banks. Most systems are now able to obtain such information through SWIFT networks.

GLOBAL MATCHING AND NETTING

Another increasingly popular treasury management tool is the matching and netting of currency payments and receipts. Setting up such a banking arrangement can help to reduce significantly the cost of managing international collections and payments and of managing global corporate exposure to foreign currencies. Bank accounts can be held abroad by a corporation for the purpose of processing collections or payments locally and then, if required, one remittance can be made to the domestic bank. The use of a lock-box overseas has become more attractive with the advent of electronic banking facilitating the management of a foreign currency float.

CENTRALIZED TREASURY REPORTING

Major corporate treasurers are increasingly gearing up their treasury functions to provide global centralized information to enable the most efficient management of funds and exposures. An important consideration when deciding on the form of a treasury system is the potential for upgrading any cash management system or treasury workstation.

BID BONDS AND PERFORMANCE BONDS

When bidding for overseas contracts companies are often asked to post bid bonds, which guarantee the integrity of the bid. On being awarded a contract a performance bond, to guarantee performance, will then be substituted.

These bonds usually have to be issued by a locally registered bank. They will be unconditional and although they may have a time limit will often be extended under threat, the threat being that if no extension is given, the bond will be called. These bonds are a source of concern to corporate treasurers largely because of unfair calling. However, it is accepted that without them a number of significant business opportunities would be lost.

Typically the bonds are, as stated above, issued by a local bank. The issue is made under guarantee from a London bank who in turn would have a counter-indemnity from the company concerned.

As a treasurer will have little or no contact with the local bank ultimately issuing the bonds, it is important to choose a London bank with whom a relationship has been developed. The London bank would then be expected to handle the overseas relationship.

PROJECT FINANCE AND VENTURE CAPITAL

Pure project finance, that is the financing on a non-recourse basis of particular ventures, is a concept that is more talked about than achieved. For a pure project finance deal many banks will feel that they are being asked to provide what amounts to equity finance and this, of course, is not their business. In order to convert a project into a more bankable proposition, even without recourse to investors, agreements may be required to guarantee both suppliers and offtake.

The nature of these agreements (particularly a take-or-pay agreement) will provide security for the borrowings. A take-or-pay agreement is an agreement whereby a customer will guarantee to take product from a project, at a price fixed in advance. It therefore guarantees a cash-flow to the project owners which will cover debt service costs.

The scale of many projects and the limited security offered in project finance have encouraged the formation of bank lending syndicates under a lead manager. These syndicates will often use government subsidized finance to reduce the costs to the project sponsors. Sources of finance for projects are not limited to commercial banks, however, but include the World Bank and other similar institutions.

If the planned venture cannot be financed by borrowings, then a corporation which does not wish to risk its own credit can look to sources of equity funds. These sources include:

(1) other corporations, who may be invited to participate as joint venture partners;
(2) the venture capital subsidiaries of both commercial and merchant banks;
(3) venture capital funds.

ADVISORY SERVICES

Over the past fifteen years some banks have seen their value to corporations in terms of the high quality advice they are able to give. They have seen margins on their core loans business falling and have therefore looked to stand back from this competitive environment. Offering advisory services has enabled them either to take fees, or to earn better margins on the banking business resulting from the companies they advise.

Merchant banks will suggest that they have always been able to offer advisory services to their clients. However, merchant banks offer practical advice mainly in the field of public stock issues and mergers and acquisitions. Their input on, for example, banking strategy or syndications is not generally at a level that would interest corporate treasurers. The advice provided by the banks falls under two main headings:

(1) cash management advice;
(2) foreign currency.

CASH MANAGEMENT ADVICE

Banks were the first organizations to offer a cash management consulting service to their clients. Many banks have now withdrawn from this field and have allowed other organizations to develop a significant market presence. A full cash management consultation will assist a corporation in optimizing its cash movements and positions to generate the maximum usable cash. The user should expect cash management advice to lead to savings in operating expenses and either a reduction in borrowings or an increase in deposits.

FOREIGN CURRENCY

In the foreign currency field the banks offer two main services:

(1) currency advisory services;
(2) foreign exchange exposure advice.

These two services are closely related. The bank will measure the client's exposure in order to assess the potential risk from doing nothing, and then demonstrate how the risk may be eliminated by a long-term swap or forward deal, arranged by the bank.

LONGER-TERM FINANCE

EUROCURRENCY MARKET

The removal of exchange control restrictions in the United Kingdom has both opened up the United Kingdom capital markets to overseas borrowers and, by encouraging overseas investment, turned more United Kingdom eyes to the Euromarkets as a whole. Before exchange controls were abolished overseas investment was conditional on finance from non-United Kingdom sources being available. Thus the only way to finance an overseas investment satisfactorily was through the Eurobond market. The removal of these restrictions encouraged many United Kingdom companies to repay existing foreign currency borrowings with sterling, and thus usage declined. This decline was, however, only transitory and non-sterling borrowings are now being made by companies to hedge foreign currency asset positions. The issue of Statement of Standard Accounting Practice number 20, and the provision it contains to allow matching foreign currency movements to be taken to reserves, has given further impetus to this trend.

The Eurocurrency market has three distinct advantages for the corporate fund raiser:

(1) in United States dollars at least, funds are freely available;
(2) documentation is simple;
(3) there are competitive pressures on issuing houses.

While in some currencies the central bank will organize a queuing system to keep an orderly market, and will expect a local bank to be lead manager, this is not true in either case for United States dollars. The market has over its life had difficult times for borrowers but these have not lasted long.

Documentation is simple and is closer to a bank loan agreement with covenants than to the trust deed familiar to United Kingdom companies with market borrowings.

The market place for mandates is fiercely competitive. A treasurer who habitually gives a mandate to his main bankers may be costing his company dearly.

In deciding to enter the bond market it is sensible to consider several banks and discuss issue prices and fees (all fees) before coming to a final decision. Perusing back issues of the financial press will assist the treasurer by allowing him to remove from his list any banks who do not have lead management experience.

SWAPS

A relatively recent development, normally associated with long-term finance, is that of the swap. In its broadest sense, a swap is the exchange of one flow of periodic payments or receipts for another. Two of the most popular forms of swap are the interest rate swap and the currency swap. An interest rate swap is an agreement by which two parties undertake to pay each other over a defined period amounts representing interest on an agreed sum but calculated on different interest rate bases.

A currency swap is an agreement between two parties to sell their respective currencies to each other on a future date (or dates) at the exchange rate established at the outset. In the intervening period, the parties pay each other amounts representing interest on the other's currency calculated on the same interest rate basis. Using swaps, separately or in combinations, has enabled treasurers to:

(1) manage existing debit, for instance, switching floating rate debt into fixed;
(2) diversify funding sources by raising funds in an alternative currency;
(3) widen techniques available in managing bond portfolios;
(4) hedge foreign currency cash flows.

Most major banks have in-house swap units. The most important factors when considering which bank to approach are cost and innovative ability. The innovative ability is important because this effectively drives the swap market and the possibilities for using swaps are limited only by the participants' ability to create new products.

CONCLUSION

It should be emphasized that the bank that is most successful in obtaining business is likely to be the one that can provide all services related to a particular programme and can demonstrate its expertise whilst offering competitive rates. Corporates would be unlikely to be happy dealing with a number of banks when they could deal with one bank which is able to create a whole package.

This chapter has been revised and updated by CHRISTOPHER TAYLOR of Price Waterhouse.

2.4
Raising funded debt finance in major capital markets

Companies have five principal types of funding for their short, medium and long term assets and trading activities. These are: shareholders' capital; bank finance; grants; credit extended by trading associations; and debt finance from the capital markets. This chapter looks at the reasons for raising debt finance, the types of such finance that are available and, briefly, the major sources. Debt finance is taken to mean money borrowed from individuals and institutions other than banks, on an agreed set of conditions and for a defined period, and represented by securities of some sort.

The capital markets are a source for equity capital and debt financing. The American, Japanese, German, French, Swiss and British markets are the largest sources of such funds in the world. In addition an international market exists outside the territorial boundaries of its constituent currencies, the eurobond market, which is of similar size to the German, Swiss and British but has achieved a higher volume of new business each year during the 1980s.

BACKGROUND

Debt financing probably predates bank funding in antiquity. Long before the first banks, as we now know them, kings borrowed money from rich merchants to finance their wars and profligate nobles borrowed to maintain their life-style. Banks came into existence because of the tendency of both classes of borrower to reschedule or default. The banks placed themselves between borrower and investor simplifying the fund raising for the former and giving assurance to the latter. The continuation of non-bank debt financing was in part a function of the willingness of investors to accept a higher risk in return for a higher rate of interest. It also reflected the ability of some borrowers of superior quality (such as governments) to appear as better credit risks even than banks and therefore raise funds directly from private investors.

The arrival of capital intensive industry and of the railways in the eighteenth and nineteenth centuries led to a major revival of the capital markets which provided fixed interest and multiple currency loans for maturities of up to 100 years and for a wide variety of countries. These ambitious financings funded the creation of the nineteenth century empires and, following numerous defaults, provided the basis for the twentieth century hobby of scripophily. More important, they laid the foundation of the major international capital markets.

During the post-war years London continued to be a major centre in spite of the weakened financial condition of Great Britain. In addition, European capitals and the United States gained increasing importance. Japan's claim to pre-eminence is much more recent, given by the strength of their domestic economy and the need to invest accumulated current account surpluses. There is an economic domino effect that has spread throughout the Asia Pacific region with rapidly growing reserves in other countries such as South Korea and Taiwan. The other important new departure was the emergence in the 1960s of the eurobond market, a capital market based in London but truly international in both its sources and its users of funds.

SOME REASONS FOR RAISING DEBT FINANCE

Companies raise debt finance for several distinct uses. These might be categorised as capital investment for organic growth, capital investment through acquisition, funding current business and funding consumer receivables.

ORGANIC GROWTH

Debt finance can be used for investment in plant and equipment because the incremental income generated by the new equipment can be shown to meet or exceed the cost of funds. The cash flow projected from the new investment can be measured with some degree of certainty and consequently wholly flexible funding is not required for most of the cost. Debt finance can be structured to match the projected life of the new investment, even where this involves a longer borrowing term than would normally be available from banks, which struggle to balance the longer term demands of their creditors (borrowers) with the short term availability of funds from their debtors (depositors).

Investments in property are especially well suited to funding with debt finance. This applies whether the property is intended to be rented out or used by the company itself. Debt finance can on occasion be raised against the security of the property for long periods and with interest and capital payments structured to match the anticipated cash flows from the property in question. Such finance resembles the mortgaging of residential property save that it can be separated from the estimation of the other cash flows of the borrower.

In this way, the financing of an investment can be isolated from the financing of the remainder of the company's business, leaving existing banking lines free for working capital demands. In these circumstances debt finance can frequently be less expensive than bank funding because the investor is exposed to a marketable item of real estate while the bank would see itself as further exposed to the credit of a company.

GROWTH BY ACQUISITION

Debt finance is frequently used as one of the methods of funding acquisitions. An acquiring company must weigh the cost of funding against the effect which an acquisition will have on its own existing shareholders. The consideration paid for an acquired company can be shares, other securities, cash or a combination of all three. Other securities include debt finance and convertible debt securities. Such funding is frequently attractive because it provides a stable base of debt capital for the enlarged group. This new debt finance can be subordinated to the demands of other creditors and can give tax advantages to some nationalities of investor in the target company in jurisdictions where capital gains tax arising from the acquisition is deferred by investors continuing to hold an interest in the securities of the successor company. This is particularly true in the United States and the United Kingdom.

The acquiring company will project the repayment and servicing of debt finance to provide an adequate additional return for its existing shareholders. The repayment can be achieved by the disposal of newly acquired assets or by the cash flow generated by those assets, and debt finance can be structured to provide flexibility to enable the acquiring company to operate in several ways. A high level of debt finance is sometimes used in relation to the equity base of the acquiring company to make possible the retention of control of the enlarged group. Such situations give rise to an increased risk that investors in the debt securities will not be repaid in full.

There has been a highly publicized growth in the United States of debt financed corporate acquisition. Leveraged buy-outs and the numerous progeny of this technique have existed for a considerable time. The recent publicity surrounds the introduction of debt finance which is deliberately below investment grade. Rating agencies exist which provide an evaluation of rating of the degree of credit risk involved in companies and in the classes of debt which they issue. Standard & Poors Corporation and Moody's Investor Services Incorporated are two such agencies, and credits rated by them as better than a certain level of risk are deemed to be of investment grade. Certain United States institutional investors, which acquire a high proportion of all debt instruments issued there, are stringently regulated for the protection of their ultimate investors — pensioners and fiduciary clients. Such institutions are legally prohibited from investing in paper rated below investment grade. High yielding bonds have been used extensively in the context of United States corporate acquisitions and the market now has outstanding issues to the nominal value of over US$200bn. However, an increasing number of well-publicized defaults, bankruptcies and criminal proceedings relating to the sudden ballooning of this market has hindered the successful export of such techniques to most other markets.

400

WORKING CAPITAL

Debt finance is also used by companies to finance the shortfall of current liabilities over current assets. Where there is a continuing requirement then medium-term debt finance should prove cheaper than bank finance, although lacking the flexibility. Companies that customarily extend credit for a longer period than they receive would find such funding appropriate.

Where seasonal cash flows lead to variations in working capital requirements short-term financing is required. In Europe this is most frequently provided by banks but increasingly companies use debt finance in the form of commercial paper. In the United States the commercial paper market has outstanding obligations for substantially over US$300bn. Smaller markets exist in Europe for eurodollars, sterling, French francs, Dutch guilders, Spanish pesetas and European currency units. Commercial paper is a short-term unsecured promissory note issued by a company and sold, directly or through an intermediary, to investors with short-term cash surpluses or an expectation that interest rates will change. The method benefits from almost all of the flexibility of short-term bank funding, and theoretically should be cheaper for creditworthy borrowers because there is no need to compensate the banks' capital for acting as a source of protection against loss by investors.

ASSET FINANCING

Debt finance can be used to fund existing assets of a company or assets which are themselves transferable. In particular, such funding is used by finance houses, specialist property lenders and the consumer credit subsidiaries of manufacturers and retailers of consumer goods. Such companies are able to match the maturities of assets and liabilities more precisely and more cheaply than by using bank finance. Medium-term notes, debt finance issued in less than issue size and for maturities not normally available in the public markets, help these issuers to achieve competitive funding as well as making it possible to fund assets off balance sheet.

Companies can isolate a group of assets, such as a portfolio of residential mortgage loans or a pool of receivables from autocar sales, and finance those without the debt investor having any recourse to the credit of the parent company. Ultimate recourse is available only by reclaiming the assets in question and disposing of them. Insurance against a part of any loss, an attractive return, confidence in the continuation of low historical levels of consumer default, and the belief that the mortgages or receivables can be resold all help make such investments interesting to purchasers of debt finance.

ADVANTAGES

Debt finance:

- can achieve longer maturities than bank funding;
- can be obtained over a range of maturities from seven days to forty-five years or more;
- can be structured to match anticipated cash flows;

provides assured funding once drawn;
provides a cheaper form of funding than banks or equity;
provides a different source of funding;
can be used to obtain subordinated funding;
is tax efficient where interest payments are deductible.

DISADVANTAGES

Debt finance:

is inflexible once negotiated;
can be time consuming and costly to arrange;
can bring about restrictions by way of covenants by which the borrower agrees to accept limitations on certain business decisions such as levels of gearing and other ratios.

TYPES OF DEBT FINANCE

COMMERCIAL PAPER

Commercial paper comprises short-dated negotiable promissory notes, usually unlisted, in bearer form and widely distributed to non-bank investors. It is issued for maturities of between one week and one year, varying slightly in differing markets according to local regulation and practice.

Commercial paper competes with government treasury bills, bank deposits and certificates of deposit for investor demand, and pricing is therefore dependent on investor perceptions of the credit and liquidity of alternative investments. It is usually distributed through dealers who buy notes as principals and resell or trade commercial paper. Liquidity, the facility with which a negotiable security can be traded or resold within reasonable price limits, increases with the strength of dealers, the frequency of issue by a particular borrower and the perception of credit. In the United States, where the market exceeds US$530bn of outstanding paper, some of the most frequent issuers take responsibility for the initial distribution and trading of their own paper.

Commercial paper is strictly regulated in the jurisdictions in which it can be issued (including France, the Netherlands, Spain, the United Kingdom and the United States). In the United States rating agencies provide a different estimate of the long and short-term credit risks affecting companies and commercial paper is bought or traded by reference to these short-term ratings. Companies of less than prime quality will frequently obtain a bank letter of credit to support their commitment to repay and thus obtain finer rates. Rating is being introduced to European markets by United States agencies and by newly established domestic agencies. It is not yet of paramount importance in domestic markets but is becoming essential for the successful issue of eurocommercial paper.

Commercial paper is not a committed source of funds and in the United States a degree of bank standby financing is required. In the United Kingdom this is not required, although many companies choose to support term borrowings in this way if it would normally be their intention to refinance each issue of commercial paper at maturity. The market is of great importance to companies with short-term or seasonal financing requirements seeking the benefits of debt finance from beyond the banking sector. It is cheaper than bank finance and provides an alternative or additional source of funds.

MEDIUM-TERM NOTES

Medium-term notes are traded securities issued for amounts or maturities that are not usually available in either the commercial paper or the bond markets. They account for less than US$120bn in the United States and for a smaller amount in the European markets and more than other sectors are dominated by direct issues of government securities competing for investors' funds. They are frequently issued by companies financing consumer receivables and thus requiring maturities of two to four years and amounts of US$10 to US$50 million from each issue. The maturities are shorter than most investors seek while the amounts preclude the liquidity sought by investors as a compensation for lower yields on other forms of debt finance. Medium-term notes thus form a highly specialized type of debt finance, with a relatively narrow market at present, but with significant potential for growth especially as the trends towards fiscal rectitude and reduced government borrowing continue.

PRIVATE PLACEMENTS

Unlisted issues that are not widely distributed, and for which no provision is made for secondary market trading, are called private placements. This market is an important source of debt finance for companies and has certain distinct advantages over public debt finance or bank funding. Private placements are a major feature of United States corporate debt financing with over US$130bn of new issues placed in 1989. Japan and Switzerland are other important sources internationally, although the term is applied differently in Switzerland.

In the United States, and to a lesser degree in the capital markets of the European Community, the private placement market provides a means by which small groups of institutional investors can match their complex future financial liabilities with high yielding assets. Such investors seek liquidity for the bulk of their holdings but recognise that liquidity is illusory and undesirable for a complete portfolio because such institutions form too large a part of the market. Also the public markets do not always provide sufficient securities of the quality and maturity necessary to match projected requirements. Placements structured to match the institutions' needs can appeal to borrowers for several reasons. Medium-sized and smaller companies do not necessarily have access to long dated public debt finance. Bank finance will cease to be an adequate alternative as requirements grow and longer maturities are sought. By contrast a private placement can be for a small amount (from a few million dollars up to several hundred million), does not involve publicity, does not require formal registration or Stock Exchange listing and requires no credit rating. The conditions of placement are a matter for negotiation between the parties enabling each to obtain terms, covenants and protections that might differ from public market practice. The maturity range is extensive (from two to three to over forty years) and can exceed that available from banks. The credit risk acceptable to investors, given the additional covenants that can be negotiated, means that subordinated debt finance can be raised enabling borrowers to strengthen their balance sheet without having recourse to raising new equity capital.

Private placements are also an important source of funds in the Japanese debt finance market where strict controls on domestic and international capital issues lead to anomalies and queues. The private placement provides a means by which investing institutions can effectively bypass such rigidity in supply. It is also a means by which financial institutions can achieve rapid balance sheet growth by lending or investing on more generous terms than the public market might accept. During 1987 and 1988 European and American banks found resistance in the public markets to the issue of subordinated debt finance which could be used as a substitute for raising further equity capital. The need was made greater by bank losses on Third World debt and calls from regulatory authorities to increase capital. In particular these have been co-ordinated worldwide and are popularly called the Cooke Ratios, after the man whose committee recommended their adoption. Japanese institutions however, faced with difficulties in placing massive surpluses of new income and with significant new availability of credit, chose to lend on terms which would not have been possible publicly.

In Switzerland there has long been an important market for the issue of unlisted securities that are more liberally regulated and more cost efficient for all but the most frequent and important borrowers. Although called private placements, such issues are traded and widely sold and are in reality public but unlisted issues.

HIGH YIELD BONDS

Junk bonds, as they have become colloquially called, have been developed in the United States as a means of financing highly geared operations. Most frequently used in the growing market for leveraged buy-outs and management buy-outs, junk bonds now account for over US$200bn of outstanding debt finance. Mostly placed privately with savings and loans institutions and groups of rich individuals, these securities offer income yields several percentage points above investment grade issues of similar maturity. The issues also impose tight limitations on the financial freedom of the borrower thus providing some degree of protection for investors. Purchasers of such bonds usually look only to future cash flows to finance the high interest payments and eventual capital repayment in the absence of an adequate asset base.

The market for bonds that are issued below investment grade is an American phenomenon which contributed to the bankruptcy of Drexel Burnham Lambert, the company that pioneered it. The market has not been repeated elsewhere. Investment funds were raised in London during 1988 with a view to being invested in leveraged buy-outs at above market fixed interest rates, but non-American investors and borrowers both appeared reluctant to engage in the level of risk perceived. The banking and financial services sectors have, however, been willing investors of quasi-equity capital and non-recourse debt reducing the need for junk bonds in a market where leveraged buy-outs are comparatively small, infrequent and too often unsuccessful.

UNSECURED BONDS

The unsecured bond issue is the principal instrument of domestic and international finance. A bond, or unsecured loan stock in the United Kingdom, is generally a certificate representing an obligation to pay an amount or amounts in respect of interest (fixed in absolute terms or by reference to another rate) and capital, stating the dates upon which and circumstances in which such payments shall be made.

A public issue of bonds is usually listed on a stock exchange and freely transferable and is capable of being traded at a price reflecting its interest yield in relation to current market rates and to its redemption date. Bonds may take physical form as printed certificates, representing entries in a register, or as bearer bonds, entitling the holder to ownership. Bonds can have a fixed, variable or undisclosed market rate. In the case of no rate being disclosed the yield is computed only from the difference between the price at which the bond is sold and its redemption price. Such securities are called zero-coupon bonds.

Investors in unsecured bonds do not have a lien over the assets of the issuer. In most cases their interests are protected by covenants governing some of the issuer's activities, specifically in the form of financial covenants stating ratios and borrowing limits. Restrictions include hindering the issuer's management from radically altering the nature of the business and an embargo on offering assets as security for future borrowings without similar protection for the bondholders. The interests of investors are frequently represented by a body of trustees or agents appointed at the issue date. Trustees are empowered to interpret aspects of the agreements governing the issue of bonds but would not normally choose to act on matters of importance and substance without first calling a meeting of the bondholders.

Unsecured bonds represent by far the highest proportion of all corporate debt as well as virtually all government sponsored debt. The instrument represents a larger proportion of all finance than shareholders' equity. Characteristics of bonds vary in different jurisdictions and each market needs to be examined separately.

SECURED DEBENTURES

Companies owning identifiable and transferable assets (such as real estate, stock receivables and securities) can mortgage these to bondholders as a means of reducing the investors' risk and thus lowering the interest rate payable. Providing security is also a means by which companies can raise debt finance despite an inadequate credit standing. Secured debt tends to be favoured in domestic markets but has little cross border application. The exceptions to this have occurred where primary commodities such as oil and gold have been mortgaged or where the security offered consists of a portfolio of listed equities.

The secured bond has developed from a means of enhancing credit or reducing cost to a means of funding financial assets with minimal commitment of capital. The rapid growth of specialist mortgage lenders in the United States and the United Kingdom has been supported by the ability of these entities to operate with a small capital base, refinancing pools of mortgages by the issue of collateralized mortgage obligations or mortgage backed note issues. The cash flows on such issues are serviced directly by the cash receipts from mortgagors. Repayment of the notes is directly dependent on repayment of mortgages although the originators arrange insurance to minimise the risk of loss. In the United States some such issues receive additional governmental guarantees and the market has grown to generate almost US$300bn of new issues each year.

MAJOR CAPITAL MARKETS

In this final section there is an introduction to the major capital markets, describing the size, characteristics and accessibility of each.

EUROBONDS

The eurobond market dates back to the mid-1960s when international investors sought a means of purchasing dollar-denominated securities without being subject to withholding tax imposed on interest payments from the United States. The success of the first issue (for an Italian motorway company) led to the evolution of one of the largest capital markets in the world and one of the most innovative.

A eurobond may be described as a security issued by a resident of one country and sold, through an international syndicate of banks, principally outside the country of the currency in which the bond is denominated. Eurobonds are issued in bearer form, preserving the anonymity of the investor, and interest is paid gross without deductions for tax. Interest is collected against the surrender of a coupon cut off the bearer certificate. Tax-free payment of interest is of such importance that bonds usually carry a clause obliging issuers themselves to bear the effect of any future withholding by grossing up payments — with this goes the right to redeem early in the same circumstance.

Eurobonds are traded over-the-counter in a telephone-based market centred on the City of London. Securities are electronically traded using two clearing systems to effect settlement. These two, Euro-clear and CEDEL, provide secure custody for some 95% of all bonds issued and provide a coupon cutting service to investors as well as facilitating the calling of bondholders' meetings. Ironically, therefore, the overwhelming majority of such securities are effectively held through a registrar.

The market has over US$900bn of outstanding debt securities. New issues were brought to market for almost US$200bn in 1989 with only just over half of all issues denominated in US dollars. The other important currencies were yen, deutschmarks and then European currency units, Canadian, Australian and New Zealand dollars, French francs and lire. Eurobond issues were also offered in a variety of other currencies. Many issues — including most of those in Canadian, Australian and New Zealand dollars — are transformed for the borrowers into obligations in another currency, normally dollars, using the swap market.

A swap is the term given to a financial contract by which two parties change the form but not the substance of a financial liability. The most common form of swap involves a borrower of fixed interest US dollar debt and a borrower of variable rate US dollar debt. The first undertakes to meet the interest payments of the second and the second those of the first. Each remains wholly responsible for his own capital repayments. The main advantage of such an interest rate swap is that borrowers with access to fixed rate funds can use them to obtain cheaper floating rate funds, while those without access to conventional fixed rate debt finance at reasonable cost can overcome that barrier.

Eurobond issues are normally for amounts of US$100m and more (less in minor currencies) and are for maturities of three to twenty years. The market is used by sovereign and parastatal, corporate and bank borrowers. Borrowers are usually of high credit standing and the market has an exceptionally good history of few defaults. Issues are structured as fixed or floating rate bonds, bonds convertible into equity or with warrant options to subscribe equity, and a variety of highly innovative alternatives (commodity linking, interest rate options, payments dependent upon outside events such as movements in the world's stock markets). The innovations are frequently introduced to take advantage of short-term anomalies in domestic or international markets or in tax treatment.

THE UNITED STATES

The United States is the largest capital market in the world both in terms of the aggregate sum outstanding and in respect of gross funds raised annually. In 1989 the sum of all capital markets instruments outstanding in the United States market was over US$16,000bn. Of this total (which includes equities valued at over US$4,300bn) government debt accounted for 21%.

The United States capital market is sustained by high domestic investment and a massive inflow of foreign capital which is necessary both to fund the federal budget deficit and to balance the record levels of international trade shortfall. Foreign holdings of United States Treasury debt amount to almost US$600bn.

The United States market is, through the requirements of the Securities and Exchange Commission (SEC), one of the most stringently regulated of the major capital markets. The market requires exhaustive disclosure and explanation which has in the past meant that timing of issues was adversely affected by the need to submit such information at launch. In 1982 Rule 415 of the Securities Act was adopted entitling borrowers to file issue documentation in advance against a possible future issue. Rule 415 'shelf' registrations have been important in the evolution of the medium-term note market where timing is critical. In an attempt to open the

United States market a move has been made in 1990 to improve access for overseas issuers through the introduction of exemptions contained in Regulation 144a.

The United States domestic market is also dominated by the rating of debt securities given by various established rating agencies. An acceptable rating is essential for the success of an issue by a foreign company in the United States and is important in achieving the finest terms for any borrower in the eurodollar market. The United States market provides all forms and maturities of issue referred to in this chapter and, together with the eurodollar market, is the most flexible source of debt funding. The US dollar is also the hub currency for the swap market providing an important reference point for most currency swaps.

THE UNITED KINGDOM

Since the 1940s the capital markets for debt finance have been dominated by the borrowing requirements of the British government. Until the late 1980s gross official sales of gilts (the name given to government debt securities) were in excess of £10bn each year. This position has been reversed, and since 1988, the British government has made significant repayments of the national debt. During this period the British government has used interest rate management as the principal device to arrest inflation within the British economy, resulting in almost consistently the highest real interest rates of any major currency. For this reason British companies have been reluctant borrowers.

The British market has an aggregate value of approximately £460bn of which less than £125bn is accounted for by government debt. The largest proportion of the total represents equity in United Kingdom companies. During the six years ending in 1989 the total of debt finance raised in sterling, other than by the British government, has risen from under £9bn in 1984 to almost £18bn in 1989. This comes from five sectors of the debt finance market, fixed rate eurosterling issues, floating rate eurosterling issues, convertible bond issues, domestic corporate bonds and issues in sterling by overseas governments and companies which are placed with British investors (called 'bulldog' or foreign bond issues). The bulldog market re-opened in 1979 following the ending of exchange controls. The market has been inactive since 1986-1987 because of concern by borrowers about high sterling interest rates and a volatile currency. The main attraction of the bulldog market, long initial maturities, is now found in many other markets.

The principal investors in sterling differ from instrument to instrument. The eurosterling market has traditionally appealed to German, Swiss and other European investors who are attracted by the high level of interest rates. British investors are becoming increasingly attracted but are reluctant investors when eurosterling bonds yield less than gilts, which occurs when continental European demand is at its highest based on short-term currency considerations. Amounts of £50 million to £100 million are normal and maturities range from five to twenty years. Maturities longer than ten years are predominantly aimed at domestic institutions. The sector is only open to borrowers of undoubted credit or for equity related issues (of which over £1.1bn were issued in 1989). The domestic market is dominated by pension funds and insurance companies which have a continuous demand for long-dated investments. This significant capacity to absorb long-dated issues is the most important and distinguishing characteristic of the British market. Domestic issues for the best corporate credits are issued on an unsecured basis for amounts ranging from £10m to £200m. Issues are normally for maturities of twenty years or longer and pricing is calculated by reference to the total yield of a gilt of comparable maturity. A wide range of other corporate borrowers is acceptable where security is used to underwrite the credit risk — secured borrowing is the preferred route for most investments beyond ten years.

JAPAN

The Japanese capital market is approximately the same size as the United States market and has developed into an important source of debt financing for American and European companies, banks and state agencies as well as for the principal international agencies. The sources of funding open to non-Japanese borrowers are the Samurai market (investment by Japanese investors in fixed interest yen securities issued by non-Japanese entities), the euroyen market and the extensive market for private placements. Briefly a market existed for foreign currency bonds issued in Japan (the Shogun market) but this ceased to be active in 1987 as market liquidity evaporated and tension between arrangers could not be resolved.

The Samurai market is tightly controlled by the Capital Markets Committee under the umbrella of the Ministry of Finance. In addition to the regulations which exist to control the size, maturity and documentation of issues, the capital markets committee determines the timing of issues and allocates queue positions several months in advance. Documentation can take two to three months or more to meet the requirements of the Tokyo Stock Exchange. AAA borrowers (undoubted credits as rated by the Japanese or United States agencies) have no restriction on the amounts that can be raised — others are restricted from Y30bn (AA borrowers) to Y10bn (unrated borrowers but still of good credit standing). Issues are for five to ten years although international agencies of which Japan is a treaty signatory, such as the World Bank, have privileged access to longer-dated Samurai issues. Samurai bonds are placed with Japanese institutional (and some private) investors.

The euroyen market is far less heavily regulated although timing approval is still required from the Ministry of Finance. Listing on the Stock Exchange in London or Luxembourg results in documentation and the time involved in preparation is in line with other eurobond issues (two to three weeks sometimes falling between the announcement of an issue and the signature of all underwriting and distribution contracts). There is no restriction on the amount of any issue, although the market depends heavily on the international investors' perception of the yen exchange rate which leads to volatile demand. Issues are for five years or longer and frequently corporate borrowers will issue euroyen bonds as a means of incurring a liability in another currency through the medium of a swap. The euroyen market has, since 1986, established itself as the second largest of the eurobond currency markets after the US dollar.

Private placements are the most important Japanese source of debt finance for most non-Japanese borrowers. Because the structure of the Japanese capital markets allows privileged funding for certain classes of investor and because of a drive for asset growth among these and other investor groups, banks and companies have been able to raise several hundred million dollars of funds for maturities of up to fifteen years and amounts frequently of over US$100m. Placements are denominated in yen or foreign currencies. Yen placements are usually swapped into dollar or other obligations; during 1988 opportunities have existed for exceptionally cheap funding to be obtained in this way. Placements have also frequently been subordinated and on terms that have enabled major international banks to count the funds as capital which could not have been raised in this form from any other capital market.

SWITZERLAND

The Swiss bond market is one of the world's largest sources of capital for international borrowers because of both the high level of domestic savings and the inflow of foreign capital for reinvestment and custody. The market is divided almost equally in amount between public and private issues although the vast majority by number are private placements. In addition to the availability of funds (caused by the historic perception of the Swiss franc as a strong currency) companies have been attracted by the low interest rates prevalent in Switzerland.

Listed public bond issues are stringently regulated by the Swiss National Bank (SNB) and the Securities Admission Board of the Swiss Stock Exchanges. Although there is no formal queue arrangement borrowers must approach the SNB through a mandated arranging bank (the lead manager) to receive approval. This procedure involves the submission of full details concerning both borrower and issue and can take one or more weeks. The lead manager is a member of one of the issuing syndicates and must be a Swiss bank. A lead manager is supported in underwriting by all of the members of its own syndicate according to an established formula. During the 1970s many foreign banks opened subsidiary offices in Switzerland to become members of these syndicates alongside domestic banks. Sixty-five per cent of all new issues are handled by the largest syndicate which comprises the three major Swiss universal banks and has recently been enlarged to include several Swiss subsidiaries of leading non-Swiss banks. Public issues are restricted to sums of above SFr250m and are charged high commissions and stamp duties. However, for larger borrowers and longer maturities, they tend to be the cheapest form of Swiss franc funding.

Private placement is the term applied in Switzerland to unlisted public issues. This sector first came to prominence in the late 1960s and is no longer restricted, as it was before 1986, to smaller issues and shorter maturities than the listed market. The issuing syndicate of an arranging bank does not automatically underwrite a lead manager's issue. However managers if any must still be Swiss banks. Expenses and fees are lower and this market has proved popular particularly for Japanese issuers of equity-related debt which accounted for approximately 30% of all funds raised in 1987 and more than half of all issues launched.

GERMANY

The total outstanding amount of deutschmark denominated securities is in excess of DM1,400bn of which almost two-thirds are debt issues raised by the financial sector on behalf of local municipalities and mortgage lenders as well as for their own funding. Foreign bonds account for only about 12% of the total outstanding.

During 1987 approximately 40% of all DM fixed interest securities were purchased at issue by non-resident investors. Sixty per cent, being domestic investors, was evenly divided between bank investors (for their own accounts and for managed funds) and others (principally private households and insurance companies). New issues of DM denominated securities have been consistent in volume at about DM100bn each year since 1983. Marginally greater activity occurred in 1985 and 1986 following the effective deregulation of the market by which innovative structures become acceptable and previous timing constraints (imposed by the Central Capital Markets Committee) were lifted. The German subsidiaries of foreign banks were also allowed to arrange issues for the first time.

The foreign deutschmark market is the principal source of DM debt finance for foreign and domestic companies alike. Registration requirements for German companies issuing domestically are so onerous that most choose to issue overseas through offshore subsidiaries. The arrangers of almost three quarters of all new issues are the three major German banks (Deutsche, Commerz and Dresdner). The lead managers confidentially notify the Bundesbank two days before launching an issue. Documentation will have been prepared by the launch date along similar lines to that required for any other eurobond or international bond issue (prospectus, containing terms of bonds and description of issuer, subscription agreement and paying agency agreement). Listing is usually arranged on the Frankfurt Stock Exchange and the prospectus is usually available in English and German languages. Issues range in size from DM50m to DM300m (DM500m for exceptional borrowers). Maturities are restricted by market demand to between five and twelve years with few exceptions. The market is open to a broad range of corporate borrowers including many with Third World links that would find it difficult to raise debt finance elsewhere.

JULIAN STURDY-MORTON
CL Alexanders Laing and Cruikshank

2.5
Procedures and costs associated with raising equity finance

The raising of equity funds by companies outside their domestic markets has historically been one of the less frequently used methods of financing international operations. The reasons for this are many and varied; on the one hand the demand by companies for new equity from overseas sources has been limited, for example, by the ready availability of debt finance on what are seen to be more favourable terms, and on the other the supply of such funds has been restrained by currency considerations and local investment regulations. Moreover, both sides of the equation have been influenced by exchange controls.

In recent years, however, as the worldwide investment community has become more internationally sophisticated, and in conjunction with the gradual progress towards a greater freedom of movement of capital, the possibilities for companies to raise fresh equity in a foreign country have increased.

Although companies may not have been raising new capital overseas they have, for some time, seen the merits of arranging for their shares to be listed on overseas stock exchanges. The advantages of an overseas listing include the following:

(1) it leads to greater awareness of the company and its products among the local investment community;
(2) it increases the marketability of the company's shares (note that in many countries certain institutions are allowed only to invest in listed equities); and, above all,
(3) it is a valuable prelude to any subsequent capital raising exercise, whether of debt or equity, in that country.

In this context it is important to distinguish between the primary markets for new equity and the secondary markets. Stock exchanges are secondary markets, providing facilities for the purchase and sale of shares which have already been issued to investors. The primary market for new capital is made up of the institutions, companies and individuals who make the initial subscription for the new shares — either by applying in response to a prospectus or by underwriting the issue. The listing of a company's shares on the local stock exchange is an important adjunct to a public issue; investors will be more willing to subscribe for shares for which they know there will be a ready market.

The purpose of this chapter is to examine the practical aspects of raising equity capital internationally and of obtaining a listing on overseas stock exchanges. The following pages give an outline of the procedures and costs involved in these countries. It is essential, however, for any company considering any of these moves to realize the importance of obtaining competent professional advice at an early stage. This will primarily involve seeking advice from a merchant bank or investment bank in the country considered; it will also, as any transaction progresses, require the involvement of lawyers, accountants and stockbrokers.

The United States, Japan and the United Kingdom are the most developed markets in the world where procedures for international equity raising are well established. A feature of both these capital markets is a substantial flow of funds into savings institutions including pension funds, insurance companies and mutual funds, which are then available for investment. In other countries, notably in Europe, the structure of the savings industry is centred much more closely around the banks, which channel the funds directly to their client companies, largely by way of loans or other non-equity securities. Switzerland, which has traditionally attracted foreign funds, also has a capital market with a substantial pool of foreign investment, but Swiss investors and investment managers tend to rely on the bond markets, rather than the equity markets, to satisfy their demand. A result of this predominance of the three countries discussed in this chapter has been that the substantial investment funds of the Middle East have to a large extent been attracted to these markets, although other Far East markets like Singapore and Hong Kong have also been among those to benefit.

The following notes relate primarily to public issues of capital; reference is also made, where relevant, to the possibilities of issuing shares on a private basis.

UNITED STATES

LEGAL BACKGROUND

The legal framework within which any examination of equity capital raising in the United States must take place is provided by two Federal Acts, the Securities Act of 1933 ('the 1933 Act') and the Securities Exchange Act of 1934 ('the 1934 Act'). The 1933 Act is the more important of the two since it regulates the primary sale of securities while the 1934 Act regulates the trading of securities following their initial distribution. Both Acts have two basic objectives: to ensure that potential investors can base their investment decisions on adequate information; and to prevent any misrepresentation or other fraudulent act in the issue or trading of securities. Both these laws are administered by the Securities and Exchange Commission (SEC) which is an independent federal agency established by the 1934 Act; its headquarters are in Washington DC and it is directed by five commissioners, no more than three of whom may be from the same political party. In addition to the federal security laws, issues in the United States must also comply where relevant with each state's own security regulations, known as the 'blue sky laws'; broadly speaking such compliance is not onerous once the information required by the Securities and Exchange Commission has been prepared. The Commission also administers the Foreign Corrupt Practices Act of 1977, which is interpreted to cover foreign issues, and certain other laws.

In relation to primary offerings, the 1933 Act achieves its objectives by requiring that an issuer file a registration statement with the Commission for its examination prior to any offer of securities. This registration statement is discussed further below. Suffice it to say at this point that the time, effort, expense and degree of disclosure required by this statement has in practice deterred many companies from making public issues in the United States. Nevertheless by its very size, the United States capital market will remain attractive to certain issuers. Furthermore, at the end of 1982, the Securities and Exchange Commission introduced new requirements for foreign companies registering under the 1933 Act and 1934 Act with the aim of simplifying disclosure and reporting requirements without prejudicing the ability of the United States investors to obtain appropriate information.

The Commission requires that any company whose securities are to be traded on any of the national stock exchanges, or on the over-the-counter market, files a registration statement; this statement is similar to that required under the 1933 Act. In addition, the company must file periodic reports giving financial and other information. The Securities and Exchange Commission's second objective — to prevent misrepresentation, manipulation and fraud — is attained by making an issuer and, in the case of a public issue, the underwriter liable: in civil law for materially false or misleading statements; and in criminal law for fraudulent manipulative acts and practices.

1933 ACT REGISTRATION

Although sales of securities in the United States are generally subject to the registration requirements of the 1933 Act, it is possible in certain instances to make a private offering which avoids the need to comply with the Act (but does not diminish the liability imposed by it). Such private offerings have to be made to a limited number of investors who are deemed to be financially aware and who do not intend to redistribute the securities to the public without going through the registration process. The procedures for both private and public offerings are described more fully below.

In a public offering the most important part of the registration statement to be filed with the Securities and Exchange Commission is a prospectus which must also be made available to all prospective investors. The prospectus forms Part I of the registration statement and in broad terms discloses the following information:

(1) a description of the issuer's business and properties, including a discussion by management of the company's financial condition and its results;

(2) a description of the shares to be issued and their relationship to the company's other securities;
(3) information on the company's management;
(4) financial statements and other selected financial information. The financial statements required would in most cases include three years' income statements and two years' balance sheets as well as three years' sources and applications of funds statements and statements of changes in shareholders' equity. In all cases the financial statements should be audited and consolidated.

Part II of the registration statement contains other information such as details of marketing and distribution arrangements, estimates of expenses and a list of exhibits being filed.

It is important to note that all financial information submitted to the Securities and Exchange Commission must either be compiled in accordance with United States generally accepted accounting principles (GAAP) or reconciled to these principles. In most cases foreign issuers prepare their financial statements under their own accounting principles and provide a reconciliation of them with generally accepted accounting principles. This may involve a considerable administrative burden, particularly at the outset.

In general, however, the Securities and Exchange Commission tries to maintain a flexible approach to the registration and reporting requirements for foreign companies. In instances where compliance with a particular rule is too difficult for a particular company, it is often possible for the company to obtain a waiver of the rule after a pre-filing conference with Commission staff. These pre-filing conferences are in practice a frequent occurrence in the case of foreign issues where a number of questions are bound to arise in relation to the Commission's rules.

Once the issuing company has completed its registration statement in conjunction with its professional advisers, the statement is submitted to the Securities and Exchange Commission. The Commission will then review it and may request the filing of additional information. Once the Securities and Exchange Commission has declared the registration statement to be effective, the issue of the securities may proceed. The time taken for a foreign issuer to register with the Securities and Exchange Commission may take several months and professional fees therefore tend to accumulate. In addition, on filing a registration statement, the applicant must pay a fee of 0.02% of the maximum aggregate price at which the shares are proposed to be offered.

In the case of an issue by a foreign company there are a number of specific SEC forms, which are really information checklists rather than blank forms for completion, which have to be submitted in certain circumstances and at various times. Those most commonly encountered are:

(1) form S-1 — the form for the initial registration of shares;
(2) form S-12 — the form for the initial registration of American depository receipts (ADRs) (see below);

(3) form 20-F — the form for annual reports of most foreign issuers;
(4) form 19-K — the form for annual reports of foreign companies which have issued ADRs;
(5) form 6-K — the form for periodic reports distributed to shareholders or for information made public in the company's home country.

The first two of these forms relate to 1933 Act registrations, the last three to 1934 Act ones.

All information filed with the Securities and Exchange Commission becomes public and is available for inspection.

1934 ACT REGISTRATION

Registration under the 1934 Act is distinct from 1933 Act registration since it applies to the registration of an entire class of securities with no amount specified, whereas under the 1933 Act a specific security of a specific amount is registered. Nonetheless the registration procedures, requirements and degree of disclosure are in all material respects identical and there is little need to discuss the 1934 Act registration here any further except to add that it is the 1934 Act which imposes certain continuous reporting requirements, including the publication of quarterly reports. Many companies find compliance with these requirements to be unduly onerous. Nevertheless, any company wishing to have its shares traded or listed in the United States must register under the 1934 Act.

SHARE LISTINGS IN THE UNITED STATES

There are two major stock exchanges in the United States, the New York Stock Exchange (NYSE) and the American Stock Exchange (ASE). Generally speaking the NYSE is for the bigger companies (as the figures shown below will illustrate) and the ASE for the smaller. There is, in addition, a popular over-the-counter market in the United States where the reporting requirements are more relaxed than those of the two major exchanges; this market tends to be used by smaller companies that do not qualify for listing on any exchange or that need a stepping-stone to a full quotation. The over-the-counter market has no fixed address; it is simply a network of dealers to which the public has indirect access through brokers.

The United States stock exchanges usually require that foreign shares are listed in the form of American depositary receipts. An American depository receipt (ADR) is a form of negotiable receipt issued by a United States bank or trust company ('the ADR agent') representing a stated number of shares in the foreign company. American depository receipts are registered in the name of their holders. The purpose of the depository receipt mechanism is to provide a United States investor with a security which has all the principal characteristics to which he is accustomed. They are as follows.

(1) American depository receipts are always in registered form. In many countries stock certificates are issued in bearer form with dividend coupons attached. On

the other hand United States share certificates are invariably issued in registered form so that dividends are paid directly to stockholders of record.

(2) The depository receipt mechanism enhances transferability. In many countries the transfer of a security requires the execution and witnessing of a deed, whereas a depository receipt is transferred by a simple endorsement.

(3) The depository receipt mechanism makes it much easier for a foreign company to comply with the United States regular way system for the delivery and settlement of securities transactions.

(4) Depository receipts may be issued in any ratio to the underlying foreign securities. This can be advantageous when the price of a single foreign share in its home market is lower than is customary in the United States, in which case each depository receipt may represent, say, five or ten underlying foreign shares. This is frequently the case with United Kingdom shares whose market price is often less than £1; United States shares tend to have market prices in the tens of dollars.

The procedure for creating depository receipts is straightforward. A United States trust company is selected as the ADR agent by the foreign company. The agent company receives and holds the underlying foreign shares through its foreign representative (a foreign bank) and in turn issues to the United States shareholder a corresponding number of depository receipts. Dividends on the underlying foreign shares are collected by the foreign representative and paid, in turn, by the agent in United States dollars (minus a small fee) to the registered holders of the depository receipts. It is the foreign company's responsibility to inform its agent in the United States of any material change affecting its shares for dissemination to United States shareholders. The agent will, furthermore, provide the necessary services for the transfer of the depository receipts. The agent will charge a fee for its services, usually payable by the foreign company, which is normally calculated on the basis of each 100 shares deposited.

The agent will also charge the foreign company a transfer fee which is generally in line with the transfer fee for United States company securities. It is a requirement of listing on the New York Stock Exchange and the American Stock Exchange that the foreign company sponsors its American depository receipts in this manner by entering into the requisite agreement with the agent for the provision of the services described above.

American depository receipts are in general treated like other securities for the purposes of registration under the 1933 and 1934 Acts.

Both the Exchanges have two categories of listing, domestic and alternate. The alternate listing standards are generally those applicable to non-United States companies which do not have a substantial following in the United States. The relevant qualifications for listing on both exchanges are summarized in Table 2.5.1.

The listing procedure for each exchange is similar. The first step in either case is a confidential and informal review of eligibility to which the applicant company will submit a certain amount of information about itself and its shareholders. This review carries no fee and implies no commitment to list. On the satisfactory completion of the review the applicant company will file its formal listing application. The information to be contained in a formal listing application duplicates closely the information required in the prospectus to be filed with the Securities and Exchange Commission. Once the listing application is granted the company signs a listing agreement which sets out its duties as a listed company. These duties relate to such matters as:

(1) timely disclosure and related notices;
(2) dividends and scrip issues;
(3) annual and periodic reports;
(4) shareholders' meetings and voting;
(5) treasury shares, redemption and tender offers.

The total time taken from the decision to seek a listing to the commencement of trading would, very roughly, be about twelve weeks. The fees involved are initial listing fees and an annual fee, both based on the number of shares or American depository receipts (ADRs) listed. On the New York Stock Exchange the initial fees comprise a one-time fee of $29,350 and a fee which is on a sliding scale from $11,750 per million shares for the first two million shares issued, falling to $1,500 per million shares issued in excess of 300 million. Foreign companies whose securities are trading in depository receipts pay an initial fee based on the greater of the number of depository receipts issued and outstanding or 10% of the depository receipt equivalent of shares issued and outstanding. The annual fee amounts to $1,175 per million shares for the first two million shares issued and $590 per million shares issued beyond the first two million, with the same calculation being made for depository receipts as for the initial fee. However, there is a scale of minimum annual fees, ranging from $11,750 for up to ten million shares issued to $58,700 for over 200 million shares issued. On the American Stock Exchange the one-time fee is $15,000 and the initial fee is on a scale from 1 cent per share for the first two million shares to $\frac{1}{8}$ cent per share for over ten million shares. The American Stock Exchange annual fee rises from a minimum of $3,500 for one million or less shares to a $10,000 maximum for over eleven million shares.

RAISING NEW EQUITY IN THE UNITED STATES

Private placements. As mentioned earlier, it is technically possible in the United States to sell shares on a private basis and thus to avoid all the registration requirements of the 1933 and 1934 Acts. This is done through the so-called 'private placement exemption'. The 1933 Act is designed to prevent the offer and sale of securities *to the public* without full disclosure about the issuer. If an issue is deemed not to be made to the public, it is considered a private issue. What constitutes a private issue is not set down in black and white and is, in each case, a question that should be answered by legal advisers. However, Security and Exchange Commission rules and interpretive decisions and court rulings have over the years outlined

Table 2.5.1: Qualifications for listing on the two major United States stock exchanges

	NYSE		ASE	
	Domestic	*Alternate*	*Domestic*	*Alternate*
No. of shares publicly held	1,100,000		500,000 of which 150,000 must be in 100 to 1,000 share lots	
No. of shares publicly held worldwide		2,500,000		1,000,000
No. of US shareholders	2,000 (holding 100 or more shares)		1,000 (of which 800 holding 100 or more shares)	
Alternative qualifications	2,200 total shareholders in conjunction with trading volume of 100,000 shares in latest six months			
No. of shareholders world-wide		5,000 (holding 100 or more shares)		2,000 (holding 100 or more shares)
For bearer shares, a statement of liquidity from a broker may be all that is required				
Market value of publicly held shares	$18m	$100m	$3m	$20m
Net tangible assets	$18m	$100m	$4m	$25m

	NYSE		ASE	
	Domestic	*Alternate*	*Domestic*	*Alternate*
Pre-tax income:				
Latest year	$2.5m	$100m cumulative for last three years	$0.75m	$30m cumulative for last three years
Two previous years	$2.0m	$25m minimum for any one of the last three years		$7.5m minimum for any one of the last three years
Alternative qualifications	$6.5m cumulative for three years, with $4.5m minimum in most recent year and all three years profitable			

the contours of what is a private placement. In summary, for an issue to be able to take advantage of the 'private placement exemption' it must:

(1) be offered to a limited number of offerees (no specific number is stated in law);
(2) the offerees must, by reason of their relationship to the issuer, have access to the same kind of information as would be provided in a registration statement;
(3) the offerees must be capable of appreciating and bearing the market risks, and
(4) the offerees must buy the shares for investment and undertake not to redistribute them to the public.

Although private placements of debt are much more common than of equity, the same institutional investors — banks, insurance companies and pension funds — form the usual market for such placements.

A private placement would be carried out, with the detailed assistance of an investment banker, on the basis of a private placement memorandum which would in general follow the lines of a prospectus under the 1933 Act.

The expenses of a private placement would in general be lower than for a public issue but with a private placement there are greater practical restrictions on the amount of funds that may be raised and, because of the reduced marketability of a private placement, the return that would need to be offered to attract demand would tend to be higher than for a public issue.

Public issues. The registration and reporting requirements that are involved in a public issue have been outlined above, as has information on the listing of foreign shares. A public issue in the United States would be handled by a firm of investment bankers who would be closely involved with the United States counsel of the foreign company in the preparation of the Securities and Exchange Commission's registration statement and the application for a share listing — if such a listing were sought — and would also act as underwriter for the issue. In the case of a large issue the underwriting will be syndicated among a group of underwriters. The level of underwriting fees charged in the United States is considerably higher than in the United Kingdom and can be as much as 7% of the money raised depending on the perceived risks attaining to the issue. When Tricentrol plc, a United Kingdom listed public company, made a new equity issue in the United States and Canada in 1980, the total expenses of the issue, including underwriting discounts and commissions but excluding United Kingdom capital duty, were estimated to be 11% of the gross issue proceeds.

In view of the complexities of a public issue the time taken to arrange one is considerably longer than for a private placement; a private placement may take about three months to complete whereas a public issue could take as long as six months.

Credit rating. A key element in both a private placement and a public offering is the obtaining of a credit rating. While not in any way obligatory, the path of any issue is eased considerably if a favourable rating is obtained from one or both of the two major credit rating agencies in the United States, Standard and Poors Inc. and Moody's Investors Service. A satisfactory rating will not only broaden the spectrum of potential investors — certain United States institutions are not allowed to invest in securities that do not have a certain level of rating — but will also enable the terms of the issue to be fined down. Therefore once the private placement of memorandum or, as the case may be, the registration statement is all but finalized, an approach would be made to one of the agencies with a request for a rating. The rating agencies carry out a detailed examination of the company's financial status, with particular reference to a range of key performance ratios. As a consequence their fees are substantial and, for a medium-sized company, could be as much as $100,000.

OTHER INFORMATION

There are currently 92 foreign companies whose shares are listed on the New York Stock Exchange, 25 of which are Canadian, nine Japanese and 23 incorporated in the United Kingdom. Seven years ago (in 1983) there were 46 companies with a total market value of $62bn.

Both the New York Stock Exchange and the American Stock Exchange publish useful booklets describing their listing standards and procedures. These books, along with other information, may be obtained from:

(1) New York Exchange Inc.
20 Broad Street
17th floor
New York
New York 10005;

(2) American Stock Exchange Inc.
86 Trinity Place
New York
New York 10006

In addition there are a number of useful private publications prepared by firms of lawyers and accountants in the United States and the United Kingdom which give more detailed information on the technical requirements relating to foreign equity issues in the United States.

UNITED KINGDOM

LEGAL BACKGROUND

The legal background to the raising of equity capital in the United Kingdom is provided by the Financial Services Act 1986, the most comprehensive overhaul of securities legislation for fifty years. The Act prohibits, with certain exceptions, the issue of an advertisement offering unlisted shares unless a prospectus has been produced, the contents of which are prescribed in the Act. These provisions replace the prospectus and public offer provisions of the Companies Act 1985 and of the Prevention of Fraud (Investments) Act 1958. This section assumes that the Financial Services Act 1986 has been brought fully into force although, as at February 1990, the provisions of Part V (Offers of Unlisted Securities) had not been, with the result that unlisted offers were still governed by the 1985 Companies Act.

The 1986 Act imposes liability in civil law on those responsible for misstatements in a prospectus and, in certain cases, criminal liability as well. The contents of the document which has to be published to obtain a listing (known as 'listing particulars') are set out in the Stock Exchange's handbook *Admission of Securities to Listing* (the so-called 'yellow book'). In the case of an unlisted offer, the required contents of a prospectus are set out in regulations made pursuant to the Act.

The remainder of this section deals primarily with the raising of new equity capital by a foreign company linked to the obtaining of a Stock Exchange listing, but it should also be made clear that the United Kingdom investing institutions are increasingly prepared to purchase foreign shares on a private basis. The way in which the United Kingdom market is developing in this respect is discussed briefly in the following paragraph.

PRIVATE PLACEMENTS

Since the dismantling of United Kingdom exchange controls in October 1979 the investing institutions have had greater scope for the deployment of their funds and the United Kingdom merchant banks have been quick to explore the new avenues that have been opened up. The availability of the private placement route for unlisted securities under the 1986 Act will depend on regulations to be made by the Secretary of State specifying the categories of persons to which such an offer can be made without a prospectus having to be published. As at February 1990, Part V of the Financial Services Act 1986 was not yet in force and accordingly no such regulations had been published. In a private placement of any kind in the United Kingdom the documentary requirements are not extensive compared with those of the Securities and Exchange Commission, and the additional costs are low, particularly in cases where the placement is carried out in conjunction with a capital raising exercise in the company's home country which has involved the preparation of a prospectus or equivalent. Moreover, once the documents have been prepared, the placing procedure itself is generally accomplished within a short period of time. In the case of a straightforward private placement, the foreign company would enter into a placing agreement with its merchant bank which would set out the terms on which the placing was to be carried out. If appropriate, the merchant bank would also underwrite the issue. The placement would be carried out at a price related to the price of the foreign company's shares on its local stock exchange. This form of issue by a foreign company is welcomed by the United Kingdom institutions, provided that the company is well enough known, since there are no longer any restrictions on dealing on a foreign stock exchange. As a variation on the direct placement of new shares, United Kingdom merchant banks have increasingly been acting as underwriters or sub-underwriters of issues made overseas. To the extent that they have to fulfil their underwriting commitments they are then able to place the foreign shares with United Kingdom investors.

CONVERTIBLE ISSUES

Although this chapter is primarily concerned with the raising of new equity capital by foreign companies, it is worthwhile at this stage to comment on the very successful market in the United Kingdom and, indeed, in the United States for convertible issues of foreign companies. A convertible loan stock is neither straight debt nor straight equity but a hybrid of the two. Broadly speaking, the attractions of a convertible to the investor are the greater security and the higher income compared with the purchase of shares, supported by the possibility of conversion in due course into the shares of the issuer when capital and dividend growth make it worthwhile. For the issuer, a convertible can be seen as a cheaper way of raising debt and an opportunity to increase its equity base in the future. Over time the terms and provisions that may be applied to convertible issues have become highly developed and there is now a wide range of possibilities open to an issuer. As with all issues the pricing and the setting of the terms is a matter of skill and experience, dependent largely on market conditions at the time of the issue, which must be left to the company's merchant banking advisers.

SHARE LISTINGS ON THE STOCK EXCHANGE, LONDON

There are, in principle, four major ways in which a foreign company's shares may be brought to the London market:

(1) an introduction,
(2) a placing,
(3) an offer for sale, and
(4) an offer for subscription.

A listing by way of *introduction* is the most commonly encountered form for a foreign company. It covers the situation where the shares to be listed are already of such a number and so widely held that no marketing arrangements are required. Shares are prima facie presumed to be so held if they are already quoted on another major stock exchange. Obtaining a listing by way of introduction is not therefore a method of raising new capital, whereas the following methods may involve either the issue of new shares to raise money for the company or the sale of existing shares to raise cash for the vendor shareholders.

A *placing* is allowed by the Stock Exchange only in certain circumstances. In a placing the issuing house subscribes for or purchases the shares by means of a placing agreement and then immediately places them through the stock market or with its own clients. The most common set of circumstances in which a placing is allowed is when there is unlikely to be significant public demand for the relevant shares.

For United Kingdom companies there is a limit of £15m imposed by the Stock Exchange on issues by way of a placing made by companies seeking a listing for the first time. Such a limit would not normally apply to a foreign company whose shares are already listed on a recognized overseas stock exchange.

An *offer for sale* describes the process whereby an issuing house subscribes for new shares, or purchases existing shares, which are then on-sold to the public on the basis of a published prospectus.

An *offer for subscription* is a less commonly encountered form of equity raising. It describes an issue of new shares by a company which are offered directly to the public by the company through a prospectus. Such an issue would not be underwritten.

Although the precise documentary requirements for each method of obtaining a listing are different, the information required by the Stock Exchange in each case is the same and is set out in section 8 of the 'yellow book' — and in section 3 which sets out the detailed contents of listing particulars.

The London Stock Exchange has fewer requirements as to the size of the company for whose shares quotation is sought than do the United States exchanges. The expected market value of the securities to be listed should generally be at least £700,000 and at least 25% of the shares to be listed should be in the hands of the public, for example, people not associated with the directors of the company or its major shareholders. In practice, however, a listing for a company with a market capitalization of as little as £700,000 would be exceptional not least because of the lack of marketability of the shares thereafter.

LISTING BY WAY OF INTRODUCTION

In the case of a company whose shares are to be listed by way of an introduction, the listing is handled by a sponsor which is, in most cases, a merchant bank. The sponsor will act as overall co-ordinator of the listing operation; the company's chosen stockbrokers will handle directly all the necessary dealings with the Stock Exchange. In addition it will be necessary, as it is in the case of any exercise to raise new equity, for the company to seek the advice of lawyers and accountants.

The required information on the foreign company is submitted to the Quotations Department of the Stock Exchange for approval. This information is incorporated in a listing document which normally takes the form of a printed circular available to potential investors. The listing document will as a general rule contain the same information as that required by the Stock Exchange for placing and offer for sale prospectuses; it will include the following details.

GENERAL

(1) A review of the history of the company and a detailed description of its business, together with an analysis by sales and trading profits of its more important activities.
(2) Details of all significant subsidiaries, associated companies and premises held by the company.
(3) A description of the company's organization and management, together with details of directors' shareholdings, emoluments, service contracts and interests in significant contracts.
(4) Details of the company's share capital, material contracts and outstanding litigation.
(5) A summary of the key provisions of the company's articles of association or bye-laws.
(6) The consent of any expert, including, for instance, the accountants, whose name and opinion are mentioned in the document

FINANCIAL

(1) A report by a recognized international firm of accountants showing the consolidated profits and losses, sources and applications of funds and the con-

solidated balance sheet for the last three years. The accountants must confirm that their report gives a true and fair view of the company's state of affairs at the relevant dates. In exceptional cases, the Stock Exchange may accept a shorter period if that is desirable in the interests of the company or of investors and the Stock Exchange is satisfied that investors will have the necessary information available to arrive at an informal judgment on the company. It is not essential that the accounts be presented in accordance with United Kingdom standard accounting practices, but the Stock Exchange expects the accounts to conform to the international accounting standards published by the International Accounting Standards Committee.

(2) A statement as to the financial and trading prospects of the company. Where a profit forecast is made, the principal assumptions on which it is based must be set out and the forecast must be supported by the accountants and the sponsoring bank.

(3) A statement by the directors of the company that, in their opinion, it has sufficient working capital for its present requirements, or, if not, how it is proposed to provide the additional working capital required. The phrase 'present requirements' is interpreted to cover the succeeding twelve months. That statement should be supported by a confirmatory letter to the Stock Exchange from the sponsoring bank, which will also need to be made available for public inspection.

(4) A statement of the company's indebtedness at the latest practicable date (which should not be more than one month from the date of the listing document). This last requirement may be relaxed in the case of major foreign multinational companies which are eligible for concessionary treatment. In such a case a statement should be given summarizing any material change in the borrowing position of the company since the date of its latest published information.

The Stock Exchange will consider requests from foreign companies for derogations from the items required to be included in listing particulars in the light of the regulatory standards and controls to which the company is subject, if it is listed on a major overseas stock exchange and if it conducts its business and makes disclosure according to the highest internationally accepted standards. In particular, consideration will be given to the necessity for an accountants' report and statement as to the sufficiency of working capital. However, the Stock Exchange's power to grant such derogations is limited to cases where the information is of minor importance or disclosure would be contrary to the public interest or seriously detrimental to the company and, in this latter case, the omission of the information would not be likely to mislead investors.

In addition foreign companies which are subject to public reporting and filing obligations in their country of incorporation (or listing, if different) or which the Stock Exchange is satisfied may properly be regarded as a company of international standing and repute may be permitted to publish, subject to certain additional infor-

150

mation, in place of listing particulars a document approved by the competent authority of another member state. Such documents must be in English, or accompanied by a certified translation.

Once a company has obtained a listing on the Stock Exchange it will be required to observe certain obligations on a continuing basis. The principal object of these is to secure the immediate release of information which might reasonably be expected to have a material effect on market activity in, and prices of, listed securities, whether it be information about regularly recurring matters or exceptional matters. The Stock Exchange will consider requests from foreign companies for derogations from the continuing obligations, using the same criteria as used to decide on derogations from the items required to be included in the listing particulars. Obligations relating to pre-emption rights, the purchase of one's own shares, disclosure levels and class tests may be subject to derogation if requested.

The Stock Exchange charges an initial fee for listing which is based on the *market* value of the shares to be listed; this ranges from £110, for a market value not exceeding £100,000, through £16,800 for a market value not exceeding £100m, to £75,720 for a market value in excess of £2bn. In addition there is an annual charge based on the *nominal* value of the shares listed. This charge ranges from £1,120 for a nominal value of £1m or less, through £8,760 for a nominal value not exceeding £100m, to £19,760 for a nominal value of over £2bn. These charges, which are levied for overseas companies at half the above rates, are subject to amendment from time to time. Other expenses will include the costs of printing and publicity, the fees of the sponsoring bank, along with brokers', accountants' and lawyers' fees. The overall costs of obtaining a London listing by way of introduction will vary considerably from case to case, but it is estimated that they are likely to amount to at least £200,000.

The time taken to obtain a listing will depend to a large extent on the time taken to prepare the accountants' report, but a total of three months would not be an unreasonable estimate.

RAISING NEW EQUITY IN THE UNITED KINGDOM BY WAY OF INITIAL PUBLIC OFFERING

The foregoing paragraphs set out the procedures for obtaining a United Kingdom listing by way of introduction. The listing procedures are similar when a placing or an offer for sale is being considered, but the most important element of such exercises for the company concerned is clearly the raising of the fresh equity capital. In either case the operation would be handled for the company by a merchant bank or issuing house which would work closely with the company's stockbrokers.

In the case of an offer for sale, the issue would be carried out on the basis of an agreement between the company and the issuing house in which the issuing house would agree to underwrite the issue. The agreement would be signed and the necessary listing particulars would be published some days in advance of the opening to the public of the subscription lists, during which time public applications for the shares on offer in the issue will be received. It is the custom that the subscription lists are closed one minute after they open, whatever the level of subscriptions received by that time. The time taken to arrange an offer for sale, including the application for listing, would be in the region of at least three months.

Underwriting commissions are considerably lower than in the United States and are usually around 2%, which includes sub-underwriting commissions and brokers' fees. Total costs of an offer for sale vary as a proportion of gross proceeds, depending on the size of the issue, but in general should not exceed 5%; for smaller issues this figure might rise towards nearer 10%.

In a placing the issuing house enters into a placing agreement with the company under which it agrees to subscribe or procure subscribers for the shares to be issued. The agreement is signed and the issue priced on the morning of the day on which the placing takes place; by the afternoon of that day the issuing house and the brokers will have completed the placing. A proportion of any issue in excess of £2m would, under Stock Exchange rules, be offered to the general public either by involving a second stockbroker or by offering 25% of the issue. The following day the necessary listing particulars would be circulated in the statistical services. Sub-underwriting is not required in a placing and therefore placing commissions are lower than underwriting commissions, generally 0.75%. Marketing costs are also lower in a placing than in an offer for sale (where Stock Exchange requirements involve the considerable cost of publication of the full prospectus in two national newspapers). The other expenses of a placing are to all intents and purposes the same as those in an offer for sale and so the overall expense ratio tends to be slightly less. The time taken to organize a placing, including the application for listing, would be determined largely by the time taken by the accountants to complete their work, but should not exceed two to three months.

UNLISTED SECURITIES MARKET

Since November 1980 a second-tier market has been operating in London under the auspices of the Stock Exchange, its name being the Unlisted Securities Market (USM). This market originally arose because the Stock Exchange felt that it should have closer control over those companies whose shares were increasingly being bought and sold under special rules, but which did not officially have a Stock Exchange listing. It has since developed into a flourishing market in the shares of those smaller companies which are deterred from seeking a full listing because of the time and expense involved or are unable to obtain a listing because, for example, they do not have an adequate trading record.

The main differences between the entry requirements to the two markets are:

(1) the percentage of the company's capital that has to be in the hands of the public for a full listing to be granted is 25%, whereas in the Unlisted Securities Market it is 10%; and
(2) to obtain a full listing a company normally has to have traded for the past three years, whereas in the Unlisted Securities Market the required period is two years.

Companies which wish their shares to be traded on the Unlisted Securities Market but which do not have sufficient of their equity in the hands of the public will need to enter the Market in conjunction with a marketing operation which may take the form either of a placing or of an offer for sale.

The Stock Exchange expects most companies to follow the placing route. The monetary limits applicable to United Kingdom companies do not apply to foreign companies but if the amount to be placed exceeds £5m the Quotations Department of the Stock Exchange should be consulted. The procedures for obtaining entry to the Market are in most aspects similar to those applying to a full listing. Accordingly, the costs involved are unlikely to be substantially less. To the extent that the raising of new equity is carried out by means of a placing there is a considerable saving of underwriting costs.

OTHER INFORMATION

As at the end of December 1989 the shares of 547 foreign companies from thirty-five countries with a market value of £1,471.1bn were listed on the Stock Exchange, 185 of them from the United States and 100 from South Africa. At the same date, there were 20 non-United Kingdom and non-Irish companies whose shares were traded on the Unlisted Securities Market. The Stock Exchange's 'yellow book' contains details on the requirements for listing shares in the United Kingdom. Copies are obtainable from:

The Primary Markets Division
Company Information Group
The Stock Exchange
46 Finsbury Square
London EC2A 1DD

The Stock Exchange also publishes a booklet on the Unlisted Securities Market.

JAPAN

LEGAL BACKGROUND

For thirty years after the last war all external transactions relating to Japan were governed by the Foreign Exchange Law of 1949 and the 1950 Law Concerning Foreign Investment, both of which laws enacted the concept of the prohibition — in principle — of all external transactions. Over the years those laws were gradually liberalized as Japan's economic status improved, until in 1979 the number of exemptions had become so unwieldy that the two laws were replaced by the Foreign Exchange and Foreign Trade Control Law, known as the Foreign Exchange Law, which came into effect in December 1980. Under this law all external transactions are allowed in principle unless they fall within certain defined categories, in which case prior notice to the Ministry of Finance or a licence is required. In certain cases the Ministry has powers to prevent a transaction from proceeding. The raising of equity finance in Japan by a non-Japanese company is one of the transactions that requires twenty days' prior notice.

The law which regulates the registration of foreign securities is the Japanese Securities and Exchange Law of 1948. This requires the filing of a registration statement with the Ministry of Finance before securities may be sold. In addition, certain forms to be completed in connection with a listing on the Tokyo Stock Exchange (TSE) are prescribed by certain ministerial ordinances.

PRIVATE PLACEMENTS

To all intents and purposes there is no market in Japan for the private placement of foreign shares. Virtually no new foreign equity has ever been sold in this way, although some companies have in the past swapped small amounts of stock, generally less than 1% of each other's capital, as evidence of good faith in various joint ventures or technological links. Moreover, if a company is listed on the Tokyo Stock Exchange, the private placement of its shares is not allowed unless the value of the placement is less than Y1m and the number of places is less than fifty.

PUBLIC OFFERINGS

A public offering would be managed by one of the Japanese securities houses. The major documents involved would be as follows.

Japanese registration statement. This statement gives background information on the company whose shares are to be sold. Part I of the statement is equivalent to a prospectus for these shares. This statement normally becomes effective thirty-one days after its filing with the Japanese Ministry of Finance.

Underwriting agreement. An issue of foreign shares in Japan would be underwritten by an underwriting syndicate consisting of a number of Japanese securities houses. The agreement would be between the issuing company and the lead manager of the underwriting syndicate.

Selling group management. This agreement would be concluded between the lead manager and the selling group members.

It can thus be seen that an issue of shares in Japan follows in many respects the methods employed in the euromarkets for the sale of debt securities.

Underwriting commissions in Japan are variable but are usually charged at around the 3.5% level. There is a tendency for brokers to be charging lower commissions now with a quotation for each individual deal. Ancillary costs involved for the issuing company would be the fees of Japanese counsel and a Japanese chartered accountant, both of which would be closely involved in the preparation of the registration statement, as well as advertising and printing costs. However, since January 1984, the financial statements have not needed to be audited by a Japanese chartered accountant and consequently these costs may be relatively small.

LISTING ON THE TOKYO STOCK EXCHANGE (TSE)

In order to obtain a listing on the Tokyo Stock Exchange the first criterion with which the foreign company must comply is to have more than 1,000 Japanese shareholders. This is achieved either by first making a public issue along the lines described above or by what is known as the 'introduction' method whereby, with the help of the company's chosen securities house, the requisite number of shareholders are obtained by day-to-day transactions on the company's domestic stock exchange.

In addition the Tokyo Stock Exchange imposes the following major requirements.

(1) *Number of shares issued.* The Exchange divides the company's issued capital into trading units, whose size depends on the average price of the applicant company's shares on its domestic stock exchange prior to the listing application, as follows:

Price per share	*Trading unit*
Less than Y3,000	1,000 shares
Y3,000 to Y6,000	100 shares
Y6,000 to Y20,000	50 shares
Y20,000 to Y100,000	10 shares
Above Y100,000	1 share

Having determined the trading unit the following are the numbers of shares required to be issued:

Trading unit	*No of shares issued*
1,000 shares	20,000,000 +
100 shares	2,000,000 +
20 shares	1,000,000 +
10 shares	200,000 +
1 share	20,000

(2) *Years of operation.* The applicant company must have been incorporated and in continuous operation for at least five full years before the listing is sought.
(3) *Net assets.* Y10bn plus.
(4) *Pre-tax income.* Y2bn plus for each of the last three business years.
(5) *Dividends.* Must have been paid in respect of each of the three previous years.

The documentation for listing will be compiled with the aid of the securities house; it consists principally of a listing application and a security report for listing application. In addition the applicant company must file with the Tokyo Stock Exchange copies of its stock administration agreement and dividend paying agreement (see below). It must also provide evidence that it can continue to pay dividends after listing.

Once the decision has been taken to seek a listing on the Exchange, in addition to the sponsoring securities house, the applicant company must also appoint the following representatives.

(1) Stock administration agent. This will be a bank which is entrusted by the Japanese Securities Clearing Corporation with the distribution of notices to the company's Japanese shareholders.
(2) Dividend paying agents. These will be the banks which the Japanese Securities Clearing Corporation, as official payee of dividends, entrusts with the onward distribution to the company's Japanese shareholders.
(3) Custodian banks. On the recommendation of the applicant company the Japanese Securities Clearing Corporation will appoint banks in Japan, and in the country of the applicant, as custodian banks. The share certificates for the shares held by Japanese shareholders will be kept in the custodian bank in the applicant's country and the Japanese custodian bank will act as liaison between that bank and the Japanese Securities Clearing Corporation.

The Japanese clearing system for transactions in foreign shares works as follows. A Japanese investor who wishes to buy foreign shares has to open a foreign securities transaction account with a securities house which issues the investor a receipt in lieu of the foreign share certificate. All accounts of the securities houses which buy and sell foreign shares on behalf of the clients are settled through the Japanese Securities Clearing Corporation.

Once listing has been granted, the foreign company is obliged to submit certain reports to the Ministry of Finance and certain documents to the Tokyo Stock Exchange on a regular basis. The listing fees payable to the Exchange consist of a fixed fee of Y2.5m and a variable fee, based on the nominal value of the issued shares, which varies with the percentage of the company's share capital in Japanese hands — the higher the percentage the higher the fee. Total additional expenses depend on the size and complications of the issue, but are in the region of Y40m to Y60m. There are also annual listing fees payable, as well as the annual fees due to the stock administration agents, dividend paying agents and custodian banks.

The total time likely to be needed to obtain a listing on the Tokyo Stock Exchange would be seven or eight weeks.

PRACTICAL DATA

As at May 1990, there were 120 foreign companies listed on the Exchange, 70 of them American and 19 British. The first issue that was made on the Exchange to raise new capital was by Bankamerica in 1976 when it raised $9.75m there, concurrently with an offering in the United States market.

This chapter was originally drafted by H. G. ASTON. The United Kingdom section has been revised by DAVID CHALLEN of J. Henry Schroder Wagg and Co Ltd; the rest of the chapter has been revised by MARK BURGES WATSON of Barclays de Zoete Wedd International Equities Ltd.

2.6
Sources of funds from international lending agencies

This chapter examines the provision of finance and related support that the international lending and development agencies can offer to the private sector. The chapter also considers the terms and conditions of available finance and the criteria which the private sector must satisfy to become eligible for this finance and support.

The role of the private sector in development has been the subject of increasing attention in recent years from both the international lending agencies, and the governments of their developing country members. As the latest *Annual Report* of the World Bank observes:

> 'Many developing countries are re-examining the role of the State in their economies, and showing interest in enhancing both public and private sector efficiency.'

The encouragement of private investment from abroad is now a major priority in those developing countries which have undertaken structural adjustment programmes. These programmes are intended to create modern market-orientated economies by correcting distorted patterns of incentive and promoting more efficient allocation of resources.

THE INTERNATIONAL LENDING AGENCIES

In theory a large number of institutions provide development finance to private sector borrowers. However in many cases statutory provision for private sector financing does not imply a significant channelling of funds to private enterprise. This chapter concentrates on those agencies which are international, multilateral or regional in character and which are a significant source of funds to the international private sector.

The analysis covers (1) multilateral agencies: the World Bank (IBRD) and its affiliates — the International Finance Corporation (IFC) and the Multilateral

Investment Guarantee Agency (MIGA) (but not the bank's soft loans affiliate, the International Development Association), and the European Investment Bank; (2) regional development banks: the African Development Bank, the Asian Development Bank and the Inter-American Development Bank; (3) a small selection of sub-regionals: the Nordic Investment Bank and the Caribbean Development Bank. Mention will also be made of the projected new European Bank for Reconstruction and Development.

In many cases the international lending agencies' assistance to the private sector is a statutory requirement. While this chapter outlines the relevant statutes, it concentrates on the levels of private sector financing undertaken in practice and indicated by recent allocations of funds. The increasingly popular methods of co-financing with commercial sources of finance are also considered, and an example is presented in the appendix. The terms, conditions and qualifications of private sector finance are summarized at the end of the chapter.

THE WORLD BANK GROUP

The World Bank Group consists of the International Bank for Reconstruction and Development (IBRD) — usually known simply as the World Bank — the International Finance Corporation (IFC) and the new Multilateral Investment Guarantee Agency (MIGA). The last two bodies have specific responsibilities to provide finance and related support for private sector involvement in developing countries. The IBRD itself has less direct contact with the private sector.

THE INTERNATIONAL BANK FOR RECONSTRUCTION AND DEVELOPMENT (IBRD)

The Bank was established in 1945 and is now owned by 152 countries; it exists to channel resources for development from its industrialized to its developing country members. The core of its activities remains the financing of development projects, principally in infrastructure. In the 1980s, the Bank began additional lending programmes in support of macroeconomic policy reform (structural adjustment), and institutional and sectoral reform such as: the Bank's lending is subject to certain rules laid down in its Charter; Bank lending must be for productive purposes only; there must be a reasonable expectation of repayment; all loans must be made to a government or guaranteed by the government concerned. While this last provision reflects the fundamentally public sector orientation of the Bank, due consideration to the private sector is offered in Article (ii) of the Bank's Articles of Agreement, whereby one of its purposes is:

> to promote private foreign investment by means of guarantees or participations in loans and other investments made by private investors; and when private capital is not available on reasonable terms, to supplement private investment by providing, on suitable conditions, finance for productive purposes out of its own capital, funds raised by it and its other resources.

In response to the perceived need for improved integration of private sector activity into development strategies, the Bank set up a Task Force in 1988 to examine the question and make recommendations, which now form the basis of an action plan for the World Bank Group as a whole. Here again, the Bank is less directly engaged with the private sector. Its role in the action plan is concentrated on supporting legal, administrative and fiscal reforms designed to create a more favourable environment for private investment. In particular, the Bank has supported the divestiture (privatization) of state enterprises, as well as the reform and restructuring of the financial sector on the grounds that: 'the ability of the financial sector to mobilize an adequate volume of savings and channel resources effectively to their most efficient uses is one of the most important ingredients for successful private sector development.'

The World Bank's involvement with the private sector is usually in an indirect role through a national intermediary, the local development finance company (DFC) or its equivalent. World Bank lending to the private sector, accompanied by a member government's guarantee of repayment, may also involve other sectors such as agriculture, energy, industry and small-scale enterprises. The terms and conditions of World Bank finance have a significant influence on the lending practices of the local development finance companies, which in some cases do little more than add to the World Bank finance a margin to reflect the administrative costs of their intermediary role.

At the same time the Bank has increased the amount of direct private sector co-financing of its projects, in line with its general policy of seeking to strengthen its operations by co-ordinating direct or parallel contributions from private and official sources. The latter predominate, mainly in the form of bilateral aid agencies, which committed nearly $10bn to co-financing operations in 1988-9, as opposed to a little over $1bn from the private sector. This relatively modest figure reflects the fact that the principal point of contact for private companies in the World Bank Group is the International Finance Corporation.

THE INTERNATIONAL FINANCE CORPORATION (IFC)

The International Finance Corporation was founded in 1956, with membership open to all members of the World Bank, and now has 133 member countries. Legally and financially the Bank and the Corporation are separate entities. The Corporation has its own operating and legal staff, but draws upon the Bank for administrative and other services. It is the only major international lending agency whose primary responsibility is to support private sector activity. Its role is formally defined as assisting the economic development of its developing member countries. It does this by financing private sector projects, mobilizing funds from other investors and lenders for projects, and providing technical assistance and advisory services to governments and to private enterprises.

The core International Finance Corporation activity of financing private sector projects from its own resources takes the form of loans and equity investments. In determining which investment opportunities to pursue, the Corporation applies three basic criteria. It invests only in those ventures which contribute to the development of the country involved, only those which can provide an adequate financial return and only those which, without its assistance, would not, as proposed, be able to attract adequate financing on reasonable terms and in a timely fashion.

Alongside these traditional activities, the operational aspects of the World Bank Group's new private sector action plan are largely entrusted to the International Finance Corporation. The action plan includes expanding the Foreign Investment Advisory Service (FIAS)[1] set up by the International Finance Corporation in 1986 to advise governments on the framework of policies and institutions necessary to attract direct foreign investment. The Corporation complements this advisory role with various types of direct support. An important subject is that of debt:equity conversions, which the Corporation encourages by making its own investments as well as through the promotion and underwriting of equity investment. The International Finance Corporation is also active in mobilizing finance and technological resources for private enterprises in developing countries. It has set up trust funds worth $4m in collaboration with five bilateral donor agencies to help such enterprises acquire modern technologies; and it has set up a new international securities group to sell their shares on the stock exchanges of London and Tokyo.

A related activity, also being expanded, is the underwriting of corporate securities issued by companies in developing countries. The growing importance of these activities is linked to the World Bank's policy of promoting privatization. Assisting this process is naturally a direct concern of the International Finance Corporation. It has recently established a unit on corporate financial services whose purpose is to work alongside the Corporation's investment departments to expand its privatization activities. These include the offer of advice to governments on preparing privatization deals, locating investors and conducting negotiations, as well as making investments in privatized firms. Future plans include assisting buyers to restructure newly privatized enterprises.

THE INTERNATIONAL FINANCE CORPORATION IN EASTERN EUROPEAN COUNTRIES

Hungary, Poland and Yugoslavia are members of the International Finance Corporation which is active in all three countries.

Yugoslavia: the Corporation's work in Yugoslavia is built on a long history of relationships. However, as the reform process moves forward, it expects the direction of its assistance to shift from being not only a lender to sound Yugoslav enterprises, but a facilitator of foreign investment, and a more activist role in the financial sector. With the help of the Foreign Investment Advisory Services, labour laws are being revised to remove some of the restrictions on management selection and behaviour.

Hungary: Hungary joined in 1985. The International Finance Corporation is expected to help in establishing joint ventures and in assisting in the financial sector.

In the various projects which it supports, the Corporation finds foreign partners, structures the transactions, helps to define and negotiate most of the transaction related documentation and facilitates discussions between foreign investors, domestic investors, the government and domestic financiers. The Corporation has been involved in the financial sector through its investments in a joint venture bank and the first Hungary Fund. In addition to this it advised Hungary how to develop markets for shares and bonds by assistance on technical and related institutional requirements. The International Finance Corporation expects that its activities in Hungary will accelerate as more foreign investors show interest in the reform process and as the drive towards a market economy enlarges the scope for both foreign and private domestic sector activity.

Poland: Poland joined in December 1987 with three objectives in mind. (1) The reform process underway was already moving in the direction of encouraging joint venture activity. Indeed there were already several hundred cases of investment by overseas Poles in private business. Most were small, in the trading or service sector, but there were several ventures of significant size in manufacturing. However, major investments by western firms were unknown. The Corporation's help was sought to facilitate this process. (2) Some elements of the co-operative sector were quite independent from state control and operated as independent enterprises. The Corporation was asked to support such enterprises. (3) The Corporation's experience and capability in the financial sector, be it on institution creation or advice, was sought as the development of the financial sector was considered key to the whole reform process. Following the change of government in Poland in September 1989, and meetings with senior government representatives during the Annual Meetings of the World Bank and the International Monetary Fund also in September, the Corporation agreed to undertake a more active role in assisting Poland and to provide advisory support in four areas: privatization, capital market development, private sector advisory services and the framework for allowing entry of foreign banks into Poland. The Foreign Investment Advisory Service is also active in legislating and in adapting regulations and procedures for the effective handling and promotion of foreign investment.

To conclude, the Corporation can help in substantive ways in the reform process taking place in Eastern Europe. The Corporation views its overall mandate of private sector development to be particularly relevant to the new situations arising in Eastern Europe.

THE MULTILATERAL INVESTMENT GUARANTEE AGENCY (MIGA)

The Multilateral Investment Guarantee Agency is the newest member of the World Bank Group. It was founded in 1985 by an international convention to advance the aim of promoting private sector investment in developing countries by providing specialized insurance services, principally insurance (Contracts of Guarantee) for would-be investors against certain kinds of non-commercial risk. These include war and civil disturbance, expropriation of assets by host governments, and the imposition of restrictions on currency transfers. By June 1989, 52 countries had ratified the Agency's Convention, and a further 21 countries had signed but not yet ratified.

To be eligible for guarantee, investments must not be made or irrevocably committed at the point of filing a preliminary application. The second step towards obtaining a guarantee is to complete a more detailed, definitive application. By June 1989, the Agency had received 69 preliminary applications for guarantee, covering potential investments in 24 member countries, and 15 definitive applications for investments in eleven countries. These applications came from a range of sectors including manufacturing, mining, agriculture, services, aquaculture, energy and forestry.

THE EUROPEAN INVESTMENT BANK (EIB)

According to Article 130 of the Treaty of Rome the task of the European Investment Bank is to 'contribute to the balanced and steady development of the Common Market in the interest of the European Community'. To this end the Bank, operating on a non-profit making basis, grants loans and gives guarantees for financing projects in all sectors of the economy, principally industry, energy and infrastructure, which further:

(1) balanced regional development;
(2) a common interest of several member countries or the Community as a whole; or
(3) industrial modernization and conversion.

In 1989, the Bank again played a major role in meeting long-term financing needs in the Community, particularly in anticipation of the Single Market in 1992. According to the Single European Act, notably in Articles 130 A to D, the task of the bank in connection with the Structural Funds (European Regional Development Fund, European Social Fund and the Guidance Section of the EAGGF) is primarily to promote the development of the Community and to reduce the disparities between the various regions. The Framework Regulation covers the five objectives of the Structural Fund:

(1) the development and structural adjustment of the regions whose development has lagged behind the rest of the Community (Portugal, Greece, Ireland, some regions of Spain and Italy, Northern Ireland, Corsica and the French Overseas Departments;
(2) the conversion of the regions seriously affected by industrial decline;
(3) the struggle against long-term unemployment;
(4) the integration of young people;
(5) the reform of the Common Agricultural Policy to accelerate the adjustment of agricultural structures and promote the development of rural areas.

Regional development has always had priority: 64% of lending from the Bank's own resources has gone to investment in less-favoured regions. Those regions also constitute the main target of the structural funds (objective 1). Finance is provided for investment mainly in industry but also in services and for all main branches of infrastructure — water, sewerage, irrigation, transport and telecommunications, improved gas or electricity supplies to serve industry, and much else. The protection of the environment and the improvement of quality of life are also a priority. In 1989, the World Bank and the European Investment Bank implemented their joint programme to improve the environment in the Mediterranean.

To help achieve the internal market, the Bank finances investment in transport and communications systems which, in turn, play an important role in industrial competitiveness and regional development. The Bank has increased its financing for a European transport infrastructure (the Channel Tunnel being a good example) and for air transport. The Bank also finances industrial projects involving co-operation between enterprises from different European Community countries and the development of European capacities in advanced technology fields. The Bank also makes loans for environmental protection, especially relevant as a response to the objectives of the Single Act (Art.130 R). Support for modernization and conversion may be either regional or sectoral. The Bank's operations, initially confined to the territories of European Community member countries, have since been extended to 12 Mediterranean countries and the 68 in Africa, the Caribbean and the Pacific (ACP) which are signatories to the fourth Lomé Convention. At the end of 1989, the Bank was allowed to extend financing facilities up to ECU1bn in Poland and Hungary. Most of the loan operations however continue to be concentrated inside the Community.

European Investment Bank lending is mainly financed from the Bank's own resources which are principally funds raised by normal borrowing operations on the capital markets. Outside the Community, various types of finance are provided on special terms from budgetary funds which the Bank manages under mandate from the Community or member states. Inside the Community, the Bank also grants loans from the resources of the New Community Instrument (NCI); the Commission of the European Communities has been authorized to borrow funds on the markets up to certain limits on behalf of the European Community. The Commission decides upon the eligibility of each project for a loan under directives laid down by the Council of the European Communities. The Bank, acting on behalf of the European Community, decides on the granting of loans and their terms and conditions; it also administers them in accordance with the procedures laid down in its statute and its usual criteria.

PROJECTS ELIGIBLE FOR EUROPEAN INVESTMENT BANK FINANCING

In pursuit of the aims already described, the Bank contributes towards financing the fixed investments and similar investments of fully specified projects aimed at a precise objective and capable of being carried through within a set period of time. It does not advance funds to meet the general liquidity requirements of companies or

Table 2.6.1: Financing provided (contracts signed) in 1988 and between 1984 and 1988. Lending in Spain and Portugal up to the end of 1985 is recorded under the operations outside the Community. Breakdown by origin of resources and location.

	1988		1984-1988	
	ECUm	%	ECUm	%
Loans from own resources and guarantees	9638.4	94.7	35694.4	90.2
within the Community	9118.3	89.6	33433.1	84.4
outside the Community	520.1	5.1	3361.3	5.7
Financing from other resources	536.6	5.3	3899.5	9.8
within the Community	356.5	3.5	3261.9	8.2
outside the Community	180.1	1.8	637.6	1.6
Grand Total	10175.0	100.0	39593.9	100.0
within the Community	9474.8	93.1	36695.0	92.7
outside the Community	700.2	6.9	2898.9	7.3

public authorities, nor for the acquisition of intangible assets or securities. Outside the Community the Bank may also contribute to financing feasibility studies and technical assistance. The Bank lends for projects making a direct or indirect contribution towards improving economic productivity in general. It always closely examines the economic benefits of projects and in particular their impact on employment. Where projects are mounted by firms operating in productive sectors, debt servicing payments must be met out of gross trading surpluses. With other types of projects, chiefly infrastructural works offering an indirect or long-term return, debt servicing may be covered by an undertaking from the government in whose territory the project is located, or by other means; in such cases the general economic benefits offered by the project are of overriding importance.

WHO CAN BORROW FROM THE EUROPEAN INVESTMENT BANK?

Private or public undertakings can obtain loans from the Bank, regardless of their legal status, provided that their projects conform with the criteria described. The Bank does not make the granting of loans conditional on the nationality of the borrower. Enterprises, or their subsidiaries in countries other than European Community member states, are eligible for loans. The Bank may also lend to states and financially autonomous public authorities such as German Lander, French departements and regions, British regional, county or district councils and Italian regions.

SMALL AND MEDIUM-SCALE VENTURES

The Bank places special emphasis on financing small and medium-sized ventures, which are particularly important in terms of job creation, by making global loans to regional or national financing bodies which use the funds to support investments chosen in agreement with the Bank. In operation since 1968, the global loan facility enables the Bank to channel credit to eligible small and medium scale ventures which, for material reasons, it is not in a position to finance through individual loans. The key objectives are strengthening the capacity of Community industry to compete internationally and pursuing its integration at European level — especially through the deployment of advanced technology and the maintenance of vigorous small and medium enterprises (SMEs). The Bank maintained its active support for investment by these enterprises, both within and outside assisted areas. It places special emphasis on financing capital projects mounted by such enterprises in industry, the service sector (tourism in particular), agriculture and fisheries. This support has been provided on a decentralized basis, through global loans furnished to financial institutions and commercial banks operating at national or regional level. The banks draw on the credit lines opened with them to advance global loan allocations for ventures approved by the European Investment Bank in line with its economic, financial and technical eligibility criteria.

Guarantees. The European Investment Bank can also help with the financing of projects which comply with its eligibility criteria by guaranteeing loans contracted directly by enterprises or public authorities with financing institutions or on the market. In return for its guarantee, the Bank requires that its risks be covered by customary security and a commission.

Development financing. Co-operation with other countries to help their development is a major Community policy and usually takes the form of grant aid. The European Investment Bank has, however, been entrusted with key responsibilities in providing investment finance for the twelve mediterranean countries and the 68 African, Caribbean and Pacific countries, signatories of the Lomé Convention. The importance of the private sector is fully recognized in the development of these countries. Its operations have, for the most part, taken the form of global loans — lines of credit advanced to intermediary institutions, largely development finance companies, or development banks established to provide long-term funding in support of small and medium-sized local enterprises.

Most of the finance is in the form of loans from the Bank's own resources on which an interest rate subsidy is normally paid from the Community budget. The rest is provided from budgetary funds which the Bank manages on the Community's behalf in making soft loans (particularly at long-term, minimal interest rates) or for risk capital operations.

The European Investment Bank is one of the best known, highest credit-standing borrowers (AAA) and its bonds are quoted on the world's major stock exchanges. Working on a non-profit basis, it passes on to its borrowers the benefits of the favourable terms and conditions which it is able to obtain.

THE AFRICAN DEVELOPMENT BANK

The African Development Bank (ADB) was established as an international institution to contribute to the economic and social progress of its members (as of 31 December 1988, the Bank had 75 members) by financing related investment projects and programmes in member states, either unilaterally or in co-operation with other development institutions of national and international status. For instance, in 1988 the Bank continued its co-operation with the World Bank (started in the mid 1980s) and participated in the implementation of structural adjustment programmes. The Bank also participated in the selection, study and preparation of projects contributing to economic development and, where necessary, it also provides technical assistance. In 1972, the African Development Fund (ADF) was established as an international institution (as of 1987 there were 26 participating countries) to assist the Bank and provide finance on concessional terms. Some special Funds also were created in order to assist member countries with particular problems like the Nigeria Trust Fund (NTF), which was established in 1976. The policies and procedures of the African Development Bank conform in large measures to those in force in other regional and international lending agencies. Nevertheless, the policies proposed by the Bank do in certain cases include innovations appropriate to African conditions. These include the general emphasis upon operations which will benefit several member countries at once — the multinational projects.

In 1988, loan approvals by the African Development Bank and the Nigerian Trust Fund amounted to $1,405.11m and $8.07m respectively, while African Development Fund loans and grants amounted to $763.04m (grants amounted to $25.20m.) Table 2.6.2 sets out the lending by sector.

The Bank finances specific projects which clearly contribute to economic development. Priority is given to those projects which are included in regional or national development programmes. Special preference is accorded to all projects which benefit two or more member countries and thus stimulate inter-African co-operation. Such projects may include transportation links, telecommunication links, irrigation and flood control, joint production or distribution of electric power and other forms of energy. A substantial proportion of the loans is directed to public utilities and projects such as the improvement of water supply; there are also projects in education, manpower and health. In some cases these are also agricultural projects which include developing access roads, setting up cost-effective organizational structures, providing research and extension facilities and financing imports and industrial projects; the Bank provides rehabilitation and industrial sector adjustment loans for financing inputs such as spare parts and raw materials. A high priority is also accorded to loans for development projects which demonstrate clear efforts towards self-help, mobilizing local resources or helping African countries attract additional foreign capital. For instance, in the agricultural sector the Bank's strategy emphasizes support for projects aimed at promoting food self-sufficiency and substituting food imports. Besides food production, assistance was

Table 2.6.2: African Development Bank Group Loan Approvals by Sector, 1967–1988 (in millions of US dollars)

Sector	*1967–1985*	*%*	*1986*	*%*	*1987*	*%*	*1988*	*%*	*Total*	*% share*
Agriculture, including agricultural lines of credit	1,973.013	29.00	607.352	37.03	889.593	41.57	419.400	19.27	3,889.358	30.48
Transport	1,679.930	24.69	130.015	7.93	273.486	12.78	376.043	17.28	2,459.474	19.27
Public Utilities	1,831.562	23.98	448.920	27.37	155.217	7.25	677.374	31.13	2,913.073	22.83
Industry, including industrial lines of credit	806.347	11.85	284.669	17.35	261.651	12.23	415.037	19.07	1,767.704	13.85
Education and health	681.684	10.02	158.103	9.64	141.127	6.59	66.683	3.06	1,047.597	8.21
Multisector	31.924	0.47	11.266	0.69	419.081	19.58	221.686	10.19	683.957	5.36
Total	6,804.460	100.00	1,640.325	100.00	2,140.155	100.00	2,176.223	100.00	12,761.163	100.0

provided to the export sector, to expand or regain capacity for generating foreign exchange. A loan or investment is not made in cases where the member government objects.

The equity capital of the bank is used to finance projects which satisfy sound banking criteria. As a result the Bank does not lend from its equity capital for special projects such as rural water supply and hospitals. The Bank encourages economic development through loans or suitable equity participation in new or expanding private and mixed enterprises. Private projects may include industrial, agricultural and other activities, but preference is given to those with substantial and broad indigenous ownership. In view of the need to increase the number of sound development projects presented to the Bank or other lending agencies for financing, the Bank considers loans to hire experts or consulting firms to carry out feasibility and engineering studies. The Bank has also, in 1987, organized a Round Table of Businessmen to advise its management on policies and strategies for developing the African private sector. In exceptional cases, the Bank considers a modest equity participation. Such participation can take the form of a direct investment in the common or preferred stock of the enterprises or the purchase of convertible debentures. Investment in industrial concerns, sub-regional or national development finance institutions, and possibly in autonomous enterprises providing public services, are examples of possible equity investments. The Bank aims to dispose of any shares it acquires to local purchasers as soon as such action is feasible.

THE ASIAN DEVELOPMENT BANK

The Asian Development Bank was established in 1966 and has 47 members. Its aim is to finance carefully prepared, appraised and supervised projects, to provide technical assistance to its developing country members in the Asia-Pacific region, and to promote investment and generally foster economic growth there. The Bank is owned by the governments of 32 countries from the region and fifteen countries from Europe and North America. According to its Article 2(i) the Bank's function includes the brief: 'to promote investment in the region of public and private capital for development purposes.' Bank lending in 1988 was made up of project and multiproject loans, programme and sector loans, credit lines through development finance institutions (DFIs) and agricultural credit. Including private sector loans, Bank lending in 1988 amounted to $3,145.6m. Loans from ordinary capital resources (OCR) totalled $2,062.2m. Loans from the Asian Development Fund (ADF) amounted to $1,083.4m. In addition, the Bank approved eight equity operations comprising six direct investments ($8.7m) and two lines of equity ($8m), totalling $16.7m. Two underwriting commitments for a total of $20m were also approved

Recognizing the important role of the private sector in economic development, the Bank assists private enterprises — especially small and medium scale industries — through its lending and technical assistance activities. It has made direct loans to

Table 2.6.3: Lending and Investment, 1988

	Number of projects	*Amount ($m)*
Lending		
Project Loans	34	1,797.2
Program Loans	6	660.0
Sector Loans	7	433.6
Credit Lines	2	245.5
Multiproject	2	9.3
Investment (a)		
Direct Investment	6	8.7
Lines of equity	2	8.0
Total	64	3,162.3

(a) Excluding equity underwriting operations.

private units in the industrial sector. In respect of direct loans to private sector units, the Bank requires the guarantee of the member government or another acceptable entity; but this year the Bank has substantially increased the loans without guarantee in order to allow more responsiveness to private sector needs and to enable it to play a more catalytic role. Also, there is now greater flexibility with regard to size of equity investments and loans.

Development finance institutions are considered the most effective conduit for Bank loans to the private sector. The Bank's first loan in 1968 was to the Industrial Finance Corporation of Thailand for lending to smaller enterprises. Co-financing of Bank-assisted projects provided by external sources rose to $774m in 1988. Co-financing from commercial sources fell to $94m from $212m in 1987, or 12% of the total compared with 43% the previous year. The Bank's co-financing arrangements with commercial sources vary in detail and format, and a typical example is difficult to present. A co-financing scenario is presented in the appendix, drawn from a variety of co-financed projects. Most such arrangements have been under parallel and joint financing formulas.

The Asian Development Fund (ADF) makes loans on highly concessional terms and almost exclusively to the poorest borrowing countries. There are also Special Funds — the Technical Assistance Special Fund (TASF) and since 1988, the Japan Special Fund designed to:

(1) finance or co-finance on a grant basis technical assistance projects, whether in the public or private sector, including project preparation, advisory services and regional activities;
(2) finance or co-finance private sector development projects through equity investments; and

(3) finance or co-finance, in special cases on a grant basis, technical assistance, components of public sector development projects financed under loans from the Bank. The loans are summarized in Table 2.6.4.

THE INTER-AMERICAN DEVELOPMENT BANK

The Inter-American Development Bank was founded in 1959, and is owned by its 44 member countries — 27 of these, known as regional members, are in the Western Hemisphere; since 1976 they have been joined by fifteen European countries plus Japan and Israel.
The Bank's functions are:

(1) to promote the investment of public and private capital in Latin America for development purposes;
(2) to use its own capital, funds raised in financial markets and other available resources for financing high priority economic and social projects in the region;
(3) to encourage private investment projects, enterprises and activities contributing to economic development and to supplement private investment when private capital is not available on reasonable terms and conditions. The Bank performs this function by making loans to local private firms for specific development projects in the region, by helping to finance industrial and agricultural credit programmes through local credit institutions that re-lend the loan proceeds to small and medium-sized manufacturing firms and to farmers. Loans are granted under terms mutually agreed with the Bank and, under its equity financing programme, by financing for the subscription of shares and capital participations in Latin American enterprises.

The Bank's assistance to private enterprises has been enhanced by the establishment in 1986 of the Inter-American Investment Corporation (IIC). Its status and function relative to the Bank are analogous to those of the International Finance Corporation and the International Bank for Reconstruction and Development. The mandate of the Inter-American Investment Corporation, therefore, is to foster the economic development of its regional developing member countries by encouraging the establishment, expansion and modernization of private enterprises especially small and medium-sized enterprises. It does this by investments (loans, direct equity and debt conversions), indirect investments through other financial institutions, and by mobilizing funds from other sources through co-financing, loan syndication and joint ventures. The Corporation had an initial paid-in capital stock of $200m.

The Bank's cumulative lending in the period 1962-1968 was $40bn which also served to mobilize additional resources for investment in projects and programmes involving a total cost of about $118bn. The Bank is well placed for continued growth, following its members' recent agreement on the seventh replenishment of its resources.

Table 2.6.4: Asian Development Bank Loan Approvals by Sector, 1987, 1988, 1968–1988[1] (amounts in $ millions)

	1987						
	Ordinary Capital Resources		*Asian Development Fund*			*TOTAL*	
	No	*Amount*	*No*	*Amount*	*No*[2]	*Amount*	%
Agriculture and Agro-industry	3	78.50	13	540.49	14	528.99	21.69
Energy	4	201.30	4	130.40	8	331.70	13.60
Industry and Non-Fuel Minerals	7	528.00	4	117.50	9	645.50	26.47
Transport and Communication	5	571.10	6	222.75	11	793.85	32.56
Social Infrastructure	3	102.00	2	33.70	5	135.70	5.57
Subsector	—	—	1	2.75	1	2.75	0.11
Total	22	1,480.90	30	957.59	48	2,438.49	100.00

	1988						
	Ordinary Capital Resources		*Asian Development Fund*			*TOTAL*	
	No	*Amount*	*No*	*Amount*	*No*[2]	*Amount*	%
Agriculture and Agro-industry	6	236.0	13	437.20	18	673.80	21.42
Energy	5	510.10	3	56.90	7	567.00	18.03
Industry and Non-Fuel Minerals	9	567.30	6	258.65	13	825.95	26.26
Transport and Communication	5	470.00	4	160.40	9	630.40	20.04
Social Infrastructure	4	278.20	5	166.96	8	445.16	14.15
Subsector	—	—	1	3.30	1	3.30	0.10
Total	29	2,062.15	32	1,083.41	56	3,145.61	100.00

Table 2.6.4: Asian Development Bank Loan Approvals by Sector, 1987, 1988, 1968–1988[1] (amounts in $ millions) continued

	1968–1988						
	Ordinary Capital Resources		*Asian Development Fund*		*TOTAL*		
	No	*Amount*	*No*	*Amount*	*No*[2]	*Amount*	*%*
Agriculture and Agro-industry	122	3,290.97	204	4,088.38	296	7,379.35	29.55
Energy	105	4,380.10	69	1,405.75	152	5,785.85	23.17
Industry and Non-Fuel Minerals	92	2,996.87	48	926.42	128	3,923.29	15.71
Transport and Communication	90	3,120.53	51	850.31	129	3,970.84	15.90
Social Infrastructure	90	2,864.64	47	845.42	128	3,710.06	14.86
Subsector	3	101.70	14	102.01	13	203.71	0.81
Total	502	16,754.81	433	8,218.29	846	24,973.10	100.00

(1) Includes loans to private sector without government guarantees
(2) A project which is financed from both sources is counted as one project

Over 40% of this lending has been committed to infrastructure projects (energy, transportation and communications), and this has helped establish foundations for private manufacturing and farm development throughout Latin America. Another third went for projects in productive sectors and a fifth for social infrastructure projects (such as health and education). This sectoral distribution is detailed in Table 2.6.5.

Table 2.6.5: Distribution of Inter-American Development Bank Lending (1962-1988).

Sector	%
Agriculture	21
Environmental and Public Health	11
Urban Development	4
Education	4
Energy	27
Transport and Communication	13
Industry and Mining	15
Other	5
	100

Co-financing. The Bank mobilizes additional resources alongside its own lending by a variety of co-financing mechanisms. In joint and parallel financing operations the Bank and the co-financing institutions make separate loans for the same project; in the case of joint financing, the Bank assumes responsibility for appraising and executing the project and administering both loans. In 1976, the Bank initiated its complementary financing programme for co-financing projects with private financing, in that the Bank makes two loans, funding one from its own resources and the other from the sale of participations to private commercial banks. The Bank's high credit rating and default protection facility has attracted $839m worth of private lending to some of the world's most heavily-indebted countries.

Bank operation. Periodically the bank sends specialists from its staff on programming missions to the various Latin American and Caribbean member countries. Together with national government officials and experts, these missions review each borrowing country's development plans, propose investment programmes and identify priority projects which may be appropriate for Bank financing. Individual loan applications flow from this process of consultation and analysis, which now includes evaluation of proposed projects' environmental impact, and of the extent to which they will benefit the poorest segments of the local population. In addition, at the request of potential borrowers, the Inter-American Development Bank may provide technical co-operation for feasibility studies and for the preparation of loan projects and applications, as well as for personnel training and other institution-strengthening activities. Technical co-operation is the Bank's central non-lending activity. It is designed to strengthen the institutional base of its less-developed member countries, and so improve the quality and efficiency of their development efforts.

After a loan application is approved by the Bank's board of executive directors, a detailed loan contract is prepared and signed between the borrower and the Bank. Under the contract, the Bank normally disburses the loan over a number of years as the project is executed and actual expenses connected with its execution are incurred by the borrower. Each disbursement request must be properly documented and its purpose verified by Bank staff. The Bank's disbursements are made in a variety of ways, including payments to individual suppliers of goods and services in freely convertible currencies. These suppliers are primarily individuals and firms in the bank's member countries, including a significant number from the non-regional members, since development projects financed by the bank require a whole range of capital goods and technology. The Bank requires its borrowers to observe certain rules in awarding contracts for the supply of goods and services necessary for their projects. Current regulations require international competitive bidding for procurement in all projects exceeding $200,000. The supervision of project implementation and certification of the borrowers' disbursement requests are among the important functions performed by the Bank's field offices located in each of the borrowing member countries. This network of field offices constitutes a major difference between this and other international agencies; with the exception of the United Nations development programme, the Bank is the only multinational lending institution which maintains fully staffed offices in its borrowing member countries.

THE NORDIC INVESTMENT BANK

In December 1975 the governments of Denmark, Finland, Iceland, Norway and Sweden established the Nordic Investment Bank (NIB), whose ultimate purpose is to strengthen the economies of these member countries. According to the agreement establishing the NIB: 'the Bank is expected to become an important instrument in the future development of co-operation among enterprises in the different Nordic countries.' The emphasis is placed on loans for private projects, and: 'only in special cases will the Bank engage in projects normally financed with governmental or municipal funds.' Projects qualifying normally involve more than one Nordic country, though proprietary interests can be confined to a single country. Since the spring of 1981, the Bank has financed joint Nordic Investments outside the Nordic area. For the financing of export projects there should be a defined project that concerns at least two Nordic countries.

Loans granted during the year 1988 amounted to SDR599m or US$807m and disbursed amounted to SDR599m or US$585m. The figure for loans granted does not include an approved one billion Danish crown facility for the tunnel and bridge link between Denmark's two largest islands. The energy sector still accounts for the largest portion of the loan portfolio, with approximately 29%. The growth in 1988, however, was greatest in the manufacturing sector.

THE CARIBBEAN DEVELOPMENT BANK (CDB)

Article 1 of the charter of the Caribbean Development Bank states the purposes of the institution as: to contribute to the harmonious economic growth and development of the member countries in the Caribbean and to promote economic co-operation and integration among them, having special and urgent regard to the needs of the less developed members of the region. The regional members are: Antigua, Bahamas, Barbados, Belize, the British Virgin Islands, the Cayman islands, Dominica, Granada, Guyana, Jamaica, Montserrat, St. Kitts/Nevis/Anguilla, St. Lucia, St Vincent, Trinidad and Tobago, the Turks and Caicos Islands. In addition there are three non-borrowing regional members — Colombia, Mexico and Venezuela — and two non-regional members: Canada and the United Kingdom.

According to Article 2, among the functions which the Caribbean Development Bank should perform in order to achieve its purposes are: 'to promote public and private investment in development projects by, among other means, aiding financial institutions in the region and supporting the establishment of consortia.' The authority to acquire equity in enterprises was first exercised in 1977; it has proved to be useful in circumstances where the Bank has had to take on a primary role in promoting new investment, or where the gestation period of a project is expected to be long. Soft loans from the special funds' resources of the Bank constitute the principal means of supporting small-scale enterprises via loans to development finance corporations.

Bank loans can be made to non-nationals for enterprises which are not necessarily heavily oriented to extra-regional export markets in the following circumstances:

(1) where a share of the equity considered reasonable by the Bank is held by, or offered to, nationals of the Commonwealth Caribbean, and arrangements satisfactory to the banks are made for ensuring majority equity ownership and control localized on the basis of a phased programme within a period considered reasonable by the Bank; and
(2) when there is a substantial use of local raw materials or the transfer of technology and skills to the region to a significant extent.

THE EUROPEAN BANK FOR RECONSTRUCTION AND DEVELOPMENT

Negotiations are now taking place among the countries of the European Community, the Organisation for Economic Co-operation and Development and Eastern

Europe concerning the establishment of a major new international lending agency. Its function will be to promote the development of free-market economies in the newly democratized countries of Eastern Europe. The details of the European bank for Reconstruction and Development's size, structure, rules and operational plans are still not known. The Bank's charter is due to be approved at a meeting of ministers from the member countries in May 1990. At this meeting, the site of the new bank will also be decided. Initial indications are that the bank will have a capital of ECU10bn, of which 30% will be paid-in. The countries of the European Community, together with the European Commission and the European Investment Bank will jointly be the majority stockholders, although the largest share for a single country will be held by the United States. The extent of the participation of the Soviet Union, both as a subscribing member and as a potential borrower, remains uncertain at the time of writing: but the eventual decisions on this question will have a significant bearing on the character of the Bank. A consensus has emerged, however, that the Bank's lending operations will concentrate on financing private enterprises and privatization processes in Eastern European countries; there will also be support of the infrastructure development necessary to facilitate the process of a market-oriented reform of centrally-planned economies.

SUMMARY OF TERMS, CONDITIONS AND QUALIFICATIONS OF LENDING AGENCIES' FINANCING

THE WORLD BANK

Sectors. Infrastructure (including transportation, telecommunication, water supply), agriculture, mining, urban development, health.

Scope of private sector. Through development finance companies to small and medium-scale ventures.

Type of finance. Long term loans and credit lines to development finance companies, the International Bank for Reconstruction and Development does not make equity investments.

Size of financing. $1m absolute minimum.

Interest rates. According to costs of funds from a pool of borrowed monies.

Currency. Mix of currencies.

Term. Generally between 15 to twenty years.

Commitment Charge. 0.75% on undisbursed amount of loan.

Grace period. Generally three to five years.

Guarantees. Government guarantee essential.

Security. Usual banking requirements.

Management requirements. Close supervision by World Bank staff.

Expenditure covered. Includes technical assistance, supervision, implementation and engineering services. There is a project preparation facility.

THE INTERNATIONAL FINANCE CORPORATION

Sectors. Agribusiness, manufacturing, mining, tourism, services, utilities and capital market institutions.

Private sector restrictions. The Corporation can never be a major shareholder and eventual full local participation is necessary.

Type of finance. Equity and loans, if necessary will join in underwriting of shares, debentures and other corporate securities.

Financing/loan size. Loan's maximum size is up to 25% of total project cost; loans in the range $1m to $30m, usually over $5m but can be under $1m.

Interest rates. Vary according to the circumstances of various transactions but related to and reflect commercial rates.

Terms. Seven to twelve years.

Commitment fee. 1% of undisbursed funds.

Guarantees. The Corporation is prohibited from taking government guarantees.

Security. Appropriate arrangements must exist for repatriation of investment.

Management requirements. Will take a monitoring role.

Expenditure covered. Can cover local or foreign currency expenditure for fixed or working capital.

THE EUROPEAN INVESTMENT BANK

The European Investment Bank offers its borrowers a range of financing options carrying various loan and interest rate formulae.

The terms and conditions of its loans are tailored flexibly and practically to borrowers' requirements and closely reflect conditions obtaining on the capital markets in which the Bank raises the bulk of its resources.

Loans are disbursed at par in line with the borrower's preferences and the Bank's holdings:

(1) in a single currency, in particular that of Member State of the European Currency Union;
(2) in several currencies, either in standard cocktails, the term, composition and rate of which are predetermined, or in cocktails tailored to the availability of currencies at the Bank and borrower's preferences.

A specific rate of interest is established for each currency and each loan term. Where a loan is disbursed in several currencies, the rate obtaining for each is applied.

European Investment Bank financing can take several forms, including:

(1) individual loans for financing one or more items of investment by one promoter; these may be granted direct to the promoter or via an intermediary (another company or a financing company);
(2) global loans granted to regional or national financial institutions which use the proceeds to finance investment by small and medium-sized enterprises with the agreement of the Bank and in line with its criteria;
(3) guarantee operations designed to facilitate investment.

The rate of interest on loans may be fixed either when the contract is signed, or at the time of each disbursement (open rate contract).

Loans are for the most part granted at a fixed rate of interest. Within certain limits, they may be granted at a variable rate or, since 1988, at a revisable rate.

Fixed-rate loans: the rates applicable are those obtaining at the date of signature of the contract or the dates of disbursement; they are not open to revision during the term of the loan.

Revisable fixed-rate loans: the rates applicable are those for fixed-rate loans, established for a given period (generally 4 to 10 years), after which they are revised on the basis of the rates then obtaining and the extent to which the Bank is able to arrange refinancing in the currency desired out of those selected at the time of contract signature and for the remaining term of the loan.

Variable-rate loans: the rates applicable are determined quarterly on the basis of the effective average cost of all variable-rate resources raised by the Bank.

AFRICAN DEVELOPMENT BANK

Sectors. Agriculture, transport, public utilities and industry.

Scope of private sector. Preference given to 'multinational projects' in more than one African state.

Type of finance. Loan and equity financing.

Size of financing. Multinational projects, maximum size $8m. National projects, maximum size $3m to a maximum of 50% of the project cost.

Interest rates. Loans carry a 7% interest rate (except for lending to industry and development banks) plus commission of 1%. A higher interest rate applies to loans for industrial plants, public utilities, roads and other projects affording early and substantial income and with approximate market rates.

Currency. Repayments in currency of disbursement valued at date of disbursement.

Term. Five to twenty years.

Grace period. Related to the timetable for implementation of the project.

Disbursement. Not made until project costs are incurred.

Commitment fee. A fee of 0.75% on undisbursed balance.

Guarantees. If not borrowing government, can be supplied by a bank, insurance company, foreign investor or supplier, or a foreign government.

Management requirements. Bank assumes no responsibility in the management of an enterprise or institution to which it has made a loan.

Expenditure covered. Preference should be given to African goods. Some local expenditure will be covered if there are indirect balance of payments implications. Does not cover working capital.

ASIAN DEVELOPMENT BANK

Sectors. Broad sectoral strategy with priority to agriculture, agro-industry, energy and social infrastructure.

Scope of private sector. 13% of total bank lending and 84% of bank assistance to industrial sector has been through development finance institutions.

Type of finance. Loans. Considering equity participation.

Size of financing. Average size of loan was $29.4m in 1981. The biggest loan to date has been $87.7m. Direct bank financing has been 37.2% of project cost.

Interest rates. Fixed rate of 11% on ordinary capital resources.

Terms. Ten to thirty years. The Asian Development Fund lends up to forty years.

Grace period. Two to seven years.

Commitment fee. On undisbursed portions of the loan to cover the Bank's borrowing costs.

Expenditure covered. Preference is for foreign exchange costs. The Bank is prepared to lend to a maximum of 5% of local costs.

INTER-AMERICAN DEVELOPMENT BANK

Sectors. Emphasis on development projects.

Scope of private sectors. Local private firms.

Type of finance. Lending to small- and medium-scale private ventures through intermediaries. Equity participation in Latin American enterprises.

Size of financing. No more than 50% of a project. For least developed countries the Bank will extend up to 90% of costs using concessional sources (average loans have been 25% of project cost).

Interest rates. Since January 1982 ordinary loans have been fixed at 10.5% per annum. Concessional financing has been extended at 1%/4% per annum (includes Venezuelan Trust Fund). Commission of 1% on loans.

Currency. Currency of any member may be used by the Bank or borrower.

Term. Ordinary loans, fifteen to twenty-five years (average life twelve to thirteen years). Special funds, twenty to thirty years.

Grace period. One to four years.

Disbursement. Four to five years.

Guarantees. For loans to non-governmental entities the Bank may require a government or public institution guarantee.

Security. Guarantee fee at rate determined by Bank for Bank guarantees.

Expenditure covered. No restrictions to procurement within the region. Loans cover foreign exchange financing.

NORDIC INVESTMENT BANK

Sectors. Energy sector accounted for half of lending in 1981. Others include mining/metals and forestry. In 1981 engineering sector received largest quota of loans.

Scope of private sector. Private and government sectors eligible.

Type of finance. Typical banking loans and guarantees.

Size of financing. Average size of loans 44.7 million special drawing rights over the past three years.

Interest rates. Based on cost as an AAA borrower of funds from international capital markets and sufficient to give profitable return to the Bank.

CARIBBEAN DEVELOPMENT BANK

Sectors. All sectors, for the time being excluding health and education.

Private sector restrictions. Will lend when finance not available elsewhere.

Type of finance. Equity and loans.

Financing or loan size. Lending not greater than two-thirds of project cost, subject to an acceptable debt:equity ratio. Equity not more than one-third of enterprise's equity. From equity capital resources (hard) $50,000.

Interest rates. Soft loans, 4%; hard loans (includes 1% commission), 10.5%.

Term. Soft, fifteen to twenty years; hard, ten to eighteen years.

Grace period. Soft, five years.

Expenditure covered. Normally foreign exchange costs subject to above criteria. In exceptional circumstances covers local costs.

APPROACHING THE INTERNATIONAL LENDING AGENCIES

THE WORLD BANK

Contact:

The Chief Information Officer
World Bank
1818 H Street
Washington DC 20347
USA
Telephone (202) 477-1234
Cable: Intbafrad, Washington DC

THE INTERNATIONAL FINANCE CORPORATION

There is no standard form of application for IFC financing. However, the Corporation needs certain preliminary information to enable it to decide whether an investment proposal warrants serious consideration. This should include at least the following items to the extent that they are relevant to a particular application:

(1) a description of the enterprise;
(2) its legal status and financial history;
(3) its present and proposed operations;
(4) the amount of financing needed and the purpose for which it is required;
(5) financial forecasts of operating results;
(6) information of the cost and availability of raw materials and other inputs, together with a review of technical assistance or other agreements; and
(7) pertinent market information.

Headquarters:

1818 H Street NW
Washington DC 20433 USA
Telephone (202) 477-1234
Telex: ITT 440098
RCA 248423
WU 64145
Cable: Corintfin.

European office:

New Zealand House
Haymarket
London SW1Y 4TE
UK
Telephone: 071-930 8511
Telex: 851-919462
Cable: Corintfin.

THE EUROPEAN INVESTMENT BANK

Initial approaches may be quite informal.

Any undertaking authority or financing institution wishing to contact the European Investment Bank should approach the Bank directly by telephone, letter, telex or telecopier (in any of the Community languages) at its head office:

100, 80 Konrad Adenauer
L-2980 Luxembourg
Telephone: 4379-1
Telex: 4530 BNKEU LU
Telecopier: 43 77 04;
or at

Liaison Office for the United Kingdom
23 Queen Anne's Gate
Westminster
London SW1 9BU
Telephone: 071-222 2933
Telex: 919169 BANKEU G
Telecopier: 222 2935

THE AFRICAN DEVELOPMENT BANK

Contact:

Chief Information Division
African Development Bank
OI BP 1387
Abidjan 01
Ivory Coast
Telephone: 32 07 11
Telex: 3717
3263
3498

THE ASIAN DEVELOPMENT BANK

The Bank has no set application forms for loans. Prospective borrowers are expected to address preliminary enquiries to the bank. On receipt of these enquiries the Bank decides what additional information is required.

Contact:

Chief Information Officer
Asian Development Bank
2330 Roxas Boulevard
(PO Box 789)
Metropolitan Manila
Philippines 2800
Telephone:831 7211
831 7251
Cables: Asianbank Manila
Telex: 231-3 ADB PH RCA
405-71 ADB PH ITT
63587 ADB PN ETPI

THE INTER-AMERICAN DEVELOPMENT BANK

Washington office:
808 17th Street NW
Washington DC 20577
USA

European offices — Paris:
IADB Special Representative in Europe
17 Avenue Matignon
75008 Paris
Telephone: 256 03 82
Telex: 650052

London:
Morgan House
9th floor
1 Angel Court
London EC2R 7HJ
Telephone: 071-720 4389
Telex: 896616

THE NORDIC INVESTMENT BANK

Head office:

Nordic Investment Bank (Nordiska Investeringsbanken)
Unioninkatu 30
ST 00171 Helsinki 17
Finland
Telephone: (358-0) 18 001
Telex: 12 2121 NIB SF
Cable: Niba Helsinki

Enquiries should be directed according to whether loans are in or outside the Nordic countries.

THE CARIBBEAN DEVELOPMENT BANK

Prospective borrowers should address preliminary enquiries to the bank. On the basis of these enquiries, the Bank will decide what additional information is required and will provide the prospective borrower with an appropriate loan application form.

The Secretary
Caribbean Development Bank
Wildey
St Michael
Barbados
PO Box No 408
Cable: Caribank
Telex: WB 2287
Telephone: 809 42 61152 (headquarters)
809 42 78100 (projects department)

BRIGITTE GRANVILLE AND PHEDON NICHOLAIDES

Royal Institute of International Affairs

APPENDIX 1: COMMERCIAL CO-FINANCING: A CASE STUDY

(reproduced from '*ADB: co-financing with commercial and export credit sources*')

The Asian Development Bank's co-financing arrangements with commercial sources vary in detail and format, and a typical example is difficult to present. The following scenario is, therefore, drawn from a variety of co-financed projects.

A *hydropower* scheme is proposed by a middle-income developing member country during the course of a project identification mission by a Bank team. It is included in the Bank's pipeline of possible projects for the country, and appears for the first time in the monthly publication, *Operational Information on Proposed Projects (OIPP)*.

Shortly afterwards a Bank fact-finding team makes a rough estimate of the project cost of around $180m. The foreign exchange portion — the component to be financed by external sources — is estimated at about $100m.

Based on the Bank's lending programme for the country, however, only $50m is available from Bank resources. Other sources of finance must be found to co-finance the remaining $50m. At this stage, discussions commence with the borrower and the executing agency on structuring a financial package for the project. After sounding out official sources, the government of the potential borrower finds that only $20m is available from a bilateral development funding agency of an industrialized nation. It obtains an agreement in principle to secure this amount. No other funds from official sources appear to be available.

After consultation with the Bank, it is agreed that the Bank will consider a loan of $50m and the government will obtain commercial co-financing of $30m. A statement to this effect is added to the project entry in the *Operational Information on Proposed Projects*. Enquiries begin coming in, to the Bank as well as to the government and the executing agency, within weeks after this particular edition is mailed out to its 2,000 subscribers. Enquiries are also received from commercial banks which had maintained direct contact with the Bank, the borrowing government or the executing agency.

Meanwhile, the Bank proceeds to the next step of the project cycle. A team of five experts leaves the Bank's headquarters in Manila to carry out a detailed appraisal of the proposed project to ascertain its technical feasibility, economic viability and financial soundness.

When this is done it is found that a more accurate estimate has raised costs to $220m, the foreign exchange cost has increased to $120m and the local currency cost to $100m. After consultations with the development funding agency of the industrialized nation, however, the bilateral loan is increased to $30m. The Bank loan remains at $50m and the amount of the commercial loan to be raised is now increased to $40m in view of the active interest shown in the project by commercial banks.

Part of the appraisal task is to work out the type of co-financing needed. In this instance it is agreed that the parallel financing formula should apply and that separate project components will be financed by commercial sources as well as by the bilateral source.

At this stage, attempts are made to ascertain precisely *when* the $40m in commercial co-financing will be needed. In this case it is found that the funds will be required more or less at the same time as the Bank loan and that the arrangement of a commercial loan should be a condition of Bank loan effectiveness. During this process interested commercial banks are kept informed of these developments.

Soon after appraisal, officials from the Bank, the government and the executing agency jointly prepare a short-list of commercial banks to whom invitations to submit offers of co-financing will be sent. This list is mainly based on interest shown by banks earlier. A total of forty commercial banks receive invitations sent out by the executing agency. These invitations include information on the project, the amount of financing needed, the borrower or guarantor, the type of currencies needed, expected terms of co-financing and the Bank services involved. The banks are given thirty days to respond.

Meanwhile, the appraisal team works out final details of its report and drafts the Bank's loan documents. The proposed loan is submitted for approval to the Bank's board of directors. An optional cross-default clause is included in the Bank's loan agreement.

A total of thirty-five replies are received from banks interested in co-financing the project before the deadline expires. These are carefully evaluated by the government and the executing agency and a preliminary report of their findings is forwarded to the Bank. Typically, evaluation criteria include the offered currencies, interest rates and other expenses; also included are the repayment and grace periods and other conditions. The commercial bank with the best evaluated offer is awarded the mandate.

On receiving advice of the award, the commercial bank proceeds to arrange a syndication of the loan. Five other commercial banks are invited to take part and agree to put up $6m each. The mandated bank, now manager of the loan syndication, puts up $10m. The lead bank drafts the loan documents and sends these to the borrowing government, the executing agency and also the Bank for examination and comment. The borrowing government, the executing agency and the selected lead bank go through the required loan negotiations. The Bank may send an observer to these negotiations.

At this stage a draft memorandum of agreement between the Bank and the lead bank, setting out the Bank's role as billing agency, is prepared by the Bank and forwarded to the lead bank, the borrowing government and the executing agency for comment and concurrence.

The loan agreement between the borrower and the syndicate of commercial banks is then signed, followed by the signing of a memorandum of agreement between the Bank and the lead bank.

The co-financing arrangement for the hydropower project is concluded.

APPENDIX 2: WORLD BANK GUIDELINES FOR PROCUREMENT

PROCUREMENT UNDER WORLD BANK LOANS

The responsibility for executing a project rests with the country which receives a loan, not with the World Bank. Procurement is, therefore, the responsibility of the borrowing country — the government or its representative agency. The Bank, however, is concerned that loans are used to procure goods and services in the most economic manner and that all eligible bidders have an equal opportunity to compete for contracts.

These objectives can best be achieved by international competitive bidding through which bidding opportunities are internationally advertised. Bidding notices are published in the World Bank's *International Business Opportunities* — and in the United Nations publication *Development Business*.

Bidders cannot be required to offer financing as a condition of bidding. Bids are evaluated on a cash price basis, exclusive of any financing terms which may be offered. They must be opened publicly and contracts must be awarded to the bidder submitting the lowest evaluated responsive bid, which may not necessarily be the lowest price offer.

For projects which are financed only partly by the World Bank different procurement procedures may be used for other parts. Such procedures, however, should not adversely affect the project's overall timetable, quality and financial viability.

PROCUREMENT IN CO-FINANCED PROJECTS

The following guidelines apply to parallel financing arrangements. These arrangements are co-financing operations in which the World Bank and another lender (or lenders) finance different goods and services or different parts of a project under separate loan agreements. Parallel financing is most often used in co-financed projects because many national aid agencies, export credit institutions and regional development banks restrict the use of their funds to purchases of goods and services of particular national origin.

Eligible projects are those that can be readily divided into separate components so that the different procurement procedures can be applied to their respective parts of the project such as large hydroelectric dams. The World Bank, the borrowing country and the co-lenders agree in advance on the segments of the project to be financed by each.

The normal procedures apply to those project components funded by the World Bank. In addition, the Bank tries to ensure that the borrower considers the following:

(1) economy, efficiency and overall project soundness (such as reasonable prices, compatibility of goods, equipment quality, coordinated timing);
(2) obtaining the best combination of price and financing terms; making project organization as simple as possible.

The World Bank may also want to be involved in financing specific contracts which are considered critical to the success of the project irrespective of possible interest by other lenders.

Contract packaging and financing should be done in a way that maintains the technical integrity of the project. Single contracts should be used whenever compatibility needs make the choice of different pieces of equipment dependent on each other.

NOTE TO CHAPTER 2.6

1. FIAS run jointly by IFC and MIGA is mandated to help countries establish sound laws, regulations and procedures for foreign investment and the promotion thereof.

2.7 International Mergers and Acquisitions

This chapter considers the strategy or policy aspects of decisions taken by senior management to expand across frontiers by acquisition, participation or other strategic alliances. There are many variations on this broad theme but the issue of practical viability is fundamental. That it is not always treated with the necessary healthy scepticism is demonstrated by the evident wreckage of some ill-considered foreign corporate adventures. Some of the fatalities, involving both corporations and individuals, have occurred at corporate headquarters, thereby demonstrating that a disease contracted in foreign parts can prove lethal or at least infectious at home.

The title of this chapter refers to any merger, acquisition or similar move other than in the country of incorporation or home-base. This definition would, for example, cover the acquisition by subsidiaries located outside the parent company's country of incorporation either in their host countries or in third countries.

A complex network of bilateral and multilateral transactions obviously limits the amount of detail which can be provided in respect of any particular permutation within the network. The intention is to establish both broad principles and an outline methodology for approaching the problem.

In analyzing international corporate expansion difference is a key principle. It is perhaps in recognition of this principle which separates the successful from the unsuccessful strategies of international corporate development, whether these are based on acquisition, local manufacture, distribution or licensing agreements or other methods of developing new markets.

In some important respects and in certain market areas, a foreign country in the context of this chapter is a different and sometimes hostile environment. Recognizing and dealing with this reality is made particularly difficult by the superficial similarity of most modern developed societies. This false impression is often heightened by the essential sameness of the surroundings in which the international businessman finds himself in major cities around the world.

The international corporate executive often finds himself in an unenviable position. He is often not trained or supplied with any care but is launched into space with what is sometimes a virtually impossible task. Small wonder then that so many international expansion policies come to grief.

The literature on the subject is still fairly thin, largely because the time which has elapsed since the start of serious post-war overseas mergers and acquisitions is relatively short. Nevertheless one may suspect that, when it comes to be written, it will reveal an outcome not materially different from that demonstrated by most of the academic analyses of mergers or take-overs in the United States and the United Kingdom. By and large they have not been very successful when judged by their impact on shareholders or employees or even by that most nebulous of concepts, the good of the company or corporation. If international acquisitions demonstrate an even worse record in future years, a major cause will no doubt be the scarcity of training, experience and sometimes care shown by the board instructing the executives and in turn by the executives charged with carrying them out.

There have been examples of carefully prepared and skilfully executed foreign acquisitions which have proved to be of considerable long-term benefit to all concerned, but they are all too rare.

There is little doubt that one of the crucial factors in their success was the early recognition of difference and a determination to deal with the problem from that starting point.

STRATEGIES

DEFINITIONS

The beginning of any corporate expansion strategy is the identification of a need for change and an assessment of the practical courses of action open to an enterprise. In this section we are concentrating on acquisitions as opposed to other methods of international expansion. Even within this broad area, however, there are various methods of dealing with the problem. The following list is by no means exhaustive but highlights the variety of courses theoretically open to companies.

Mergers. This is a word which the acquiror prefers to use in almost any acquisition context. The implication is that two companies have agreed to join together for their mutual benefit, and one giving up its independence or identity. In practice, however, true mergers are few and far between. In the international context they are even rarer because of the complications of incorporation, residence, legal requirements, share listings, antitrust controls on national or supra-national (such as European Community) levels and so on.

Acquisitions. In this case there is no attempt, for psychological or other reasons, to obscure the reality of one company acquiring another, at least of more than 50% of the target.

Take-overs, friendly or hostile. This definition differs significantly from the above in that it describes an acquisition which is welcomed or not recommended by the board of the company being bid for. Hostile offers are in practice no longer unusual in cross-border acquisitions.

Joint ventures or strategic alliances. In the present context this means joint companies formed specifically for the purpose of developing markets or technologies either in the host country or additionally in third countries.

Partial acquisitions. This refers to the taking by a foreign company of a minority or possibly a majority stake in a company which may be listed on a stock exchange or unlisted. Nowadays the partial offer — often known as stakebuilding — is widely used for strategic reasons and not necessarily as a prelude to a takeover.

Special arrangements. This category is intended to cover a variety of forms of co-operation entered into usually by large international companies although in the context of the European Community-based privately held firms, it is today a very common feature. Two venerable and highly successful partnerships are the Anglo-Dutch arrangements entered into by Royal Dutch and Shell Transport and Trading and by Unilever NV and Unilever PLC. Less happy arrangements in recent years, both of which have now been unwound, were the linking of Dunlop in the United Kingdom with Pirelli in Italy and Hoesch in Germany with Hoogovens in Holland.

In the financial world in recent years there have been several examples of the formation of consortium banks by large institutions. For a variety of reasons most of these have proved to be unsuccessful and generally speaking one or other of the partners has bought out the rest. However, on European turf, this consortium concept is now again gaining ground. In industrial activities the force of competition has sometimes led to the creation of multinational groupings, as in the case of Iveco in commercial vehicles. An interesting example of international co-operation lies in the field of accountancy or law firms where some large partnerships have linked up in various ways on an international basis to provide a full range of services to clients around the world. This trend led to the consolidation on a more formal basis of the now surpassed Big Eight firms.

REASONS FOR CROSS BORDER ACQUISITIONS

At first sight it may appear blindingly obvious why companies expand overseas by acquisitions, but a rigorous analysis of strategic objectives does not always take place. Indeed, there are times when what should be a carefully thought out strategic move becomes almost a reflex reaction to short-term variations in market trends. The following outline, therefore, seeks to establish both an explanation and a framework for corporate strategy in this area.

Although some of the pitfalls of foreign acquisitions have been emphasized, it is not really surprising that many companies choose this route. At times the lure of an existing market share and an established production and distribution network prove to be irresistible for a management looking at a potentially lucrative market from the outside. If the target company is successful, it is usually evident that a significant premium will have to be paid for its market share and established name. If, on the other hand, the company is ailing and in need of capital injection, it is not difficult for the potential predator to persuade himself that the problems are specific, can be readily identified and rapidly solved. Sadly, this line of thought is often an exercise in self-delusion and may be followed sooner or later by the ominous sound of the corporate tumbrels rolling.

WHY DO COMPANIES GO OVERSEAS?

The short and simple answer ought to be that they do it to protect and enhance the long-term growth of their earnings per share. This definition encapsulates all other factors such as turnover, pre-tax profits and investment. In practice, the issues are seldom as clearcut as this and various reasons will sometimes be given different weights according to the period chosen.

One obvious explanation would be based on the need to protect the company's markets. But this in turn would require amplification in terms of such problems as import barriers, legal restrictions and requirements for local content. Equally, there may be a requirement for a proportion of such goods produced to be exported either to the parent country or to third markets. Apart from such regulations, however, and indeed in areas where they do not apply, business strategy may well require transnational expansion. In addition to protecting a market there is also the opportunity provided by an expanding market. Overseas expansion may also afford opportunities for vertical integration of production or marketing processes, access to low cost labour, and opportunity to transfer and develop technology, the creation of an export base and the building up of offshore assets.

The common thread running through all of these and related reasons is that there are believed to be greater opportunities to increase trade and profits outside the home market or in some cases within the home market by means of wholly or partly-produced foreign goods. Cross border corporate strategies are often the precondition for acquisitions or strategic alliances.

WHY DO COMPANIES CHOOSE THE ACQUISITION ROUTE?

The basic alternatives available for overseas expansion are acquisition, joint ventures, establishment from scratch or exporting to the markets concerned. In many cases these choices are not necessarily mutually exclusive and may vary from market to market depending on the opportunities.

The simplest explanation for the choice of acquisition is one of time. Sometimes it is the only sensible way to achieve an objective within a reasonable time. Other things being equal, exporting from a reasonably low-cost home base on a marginal cost or marginal revenue basis is the optimum method both economically and financially. Unfortunately, for many companies this simple solution is often ruled out by political, economic or, specifically, balance of payments reasons in the host country. The establishment of a manufacturing operation from scratch suffers from a number of difficulties. This is particularly true in the case of consumer goods where brand names and market shares may be of crucial importance. Even where this is not the case there is a major problem for any relatively large company in building up a level of production to worthwhile figures in relation to parent company turnover. There are, of course, many examples of the establishment by foreign companies of production units in a variety of countries to produce both for the host country and for third markets. In many cases, however, the establishment of such plants follows the success of the parent company in obtaining a significant and growing share of the markets concerned and when, either in response to market conditions or to political pressures, local manufacture seems prudent. The Japanese have taught us in Europe how to establish strong local industrial or trading positions by starting on greenfield sites.

WHY IS THE DISTINCTION BETWEEN PRODUCTS AND STRUCTURE IMPORTANT?

Today, with reduced protectionism and restraints on trade around the world, goods and services are still reasonably freely traded. They are in this very real sense transferable. This simple fact serves to emphasize the difference between the goods produced by corporations and the corporations themselves. The latter are by definition legal entities having a fixed base or several bases. The incubus of the mobile and irresponsible corporation derives essentially from the fevered imagination of the politically committed. This general conclusion is by no means invalidated by the existence of both corporate tax havens and flags of convenience.

In practice, an overwhelming proportion of the world's corporations which produce and trade goods and services have a clearly identifiable and stable entity and location. The same or similar products, whether branded or not, may be produced and marketed in different countries by wholly-owned subsidiaries of the originating company, or by joint ventures, or under licence, or through an outright purchase of rights. There are several other variations on this theme but they all serve to underline the essential distinction between products which are traded and the corporate structures and mechanisms which define production, marketing, control and profit.

HOW IS A HOME BASE DEFINED?

In spite of many post-war movements towards economic and political integration, we still live essentially in a world of nation states. This provides us with a convenient starting point for our definition. The basic political entity is that of a state or nation which in turn provides both a general legal system and in most cases a clearly defined system of company law.

Beyond this basic framework, however, there may be considerable variations, from almost perfect freedom of operation to a full panoply of exchange controls, dividend limitation and employment laws. In addition to national law there may well be other legal or quasi-legal constraints provided by treaty and international agreements. Well-known examples of these are the European Community, the General Agreement on Tariffs and Trade and the Organisation for Economic Co-operation and Development.

Beyond the question of legal entity and residence there are other fundamental factors, the most important of which are the ownership and control of the business concerned. The structure of the potential bidding company, its capital and debt, will be crucial to overseas expansion, as will be the ability of management, either by absolute shareholding control or influence on outside shareholders, to determine corporate policy. To the extent that the shareholders represent a different interest to that of management, their attitude may be pivotal. Their reactions would, for example, be of overriding importance in cases where the parent company's share capital was to be issued as part of any transaction. Even where shares were not involved, shareholders may well be concerned about additional borrowings necessary to buy an overseas business and the impact which such borrowings might have on the parent company's balance sheet and other activities needing finance.

In many cases, government consents will be required. Sometimes the consents will be necessary both from the home and from the host governments. The question of jurisdiction can become extremely complicated; in some cases governments may claim jurisdiction or at least apply pressure in situations where their interest and standing are far from clear. For instance a home government may seek to prevent a subsidiary in a host country from acquiring another company in a third country.

Many governments now have legislation empowering them to review or block international expansion not deemed to be in the national interest — although infringements are more and more the exception, at least in the European arena. Beyond any specific legal restrictions there are also unofficial pressures which can and sometimes are brought to bear. In most countries there are required bodies such as the Justice Department in the United States, the Office of Fair Trading in the United Kingdom and the Federal Cartel Office in West Germany to which acquisitions must be referred and by which they are sometimes blocked — although currently in less than 5% of cases. In some cases there are established bilateral agreements which have the effect of limiting freedom of action in certain areas or which provide priority to the nationals or corporations of the partners on a bilateral or multilateral base.

Finally, there are certain international agreements, either legal or quasilegal, which can restrain as well as sponsor international expansion by acquisition. Although at present the United Nations does not represent a serious obstacle to most cross-frontier deals, there is a danger that proposals being developed at present may have adverse effects. The regulations and constraints are dealt with in more detail later but it is appropriate to comment here on some of the more obvious and important implications of recent trends.

Most governments legitimately regard the corporate entities within their boundaries as important national assets. Their reactions to this simple proposition vary enormously from rigid, detailed and sometimes draconian measures to an almost laissez-faire attitude. It is easy to understand why the less liberal governments take a close interest in these matters because of their effects on the national economy and, in particular, on the balance of payments, employment, taxation and future technical development. These are matters on which the short-term success or failure of governments often depend and they will therefore be anxious to ensure that the corporate sector and its control are regulated in the national interest as they perceive it. It should be emphasized, however, that a very small minority of cross-border mergers are currently being affected by any agencies, governmental or intergovernmental. And this position trend is to continue. The soon realized integration of the old German Democratic Republic into the European Community as part of the united Germany is just a good demonstration of how things can be done fast and effectively on the European Community level.

A STRATEGY FOR INTERNATIONAL MERGERS

There is a well-known dictum of historians which may be summarized as follows: 'When rulers find domestic difficulties too pressing, they look for ways of diverting the attention of the populace'. There is at least a grain of truth in the application of this dictum to the corporate sector. There have been many international corporate adventures in the post-war period which owed more to fashion, boredom, diversionary tactics or managerial instability than to any more acceptable criteria. The following guidelines, therefore, have these dangers firmly in mind.

START AT HOME

A point of departure for this exercise would be the obvious but very important question, why expand outside the home territory? The answer may be obvious but it is possible that the implications have not been fully considered.

Before deciding on a major cross border acquisition, management should have reviewed the obvious opportunities, direct or related, in their home markets and the markets they know best. The question of whether these have been fully exploited must be considered. Equally, before management time and effort is expended overseas, the question of unresolved domestic problems must be answered. There are many examples of the diversion of scarce management resources to new, difficult and essentially unimportant or irrelevant areas while a centre or home base is allowed to deteriorate. Most managers are human and there is something exciting about new markets, new cities and new problems with which to wrestle. In pursuing the question of 'Why?' other factors must be considered and specifically the question of the resources which are available for overseas expansion in terms of products, management and capital. It is also essential to consider carefully the practical alternatives to foreign acquisition, the principal ones of which are:

(1) the direct establishment of a wholly-owned subsidiary in the country or countries concerned;
(2) the export of goods from the home base;
(3) licensing arrangements with foreign manufacturers;
(4) joint ventures either with host country companies or with other foreign partners;

(5) strategic alliances with one or several foreign partners.

Apart from anything else this turning inward of the corporate eye is a very good discipline. Once such an exercise has been carried out, the risk to reward ratio will be understood and the board, having been persuaded of the arguments, should be fully behind executive management in implementing the agreed strategy.

THE SELECTION OF COUNTRIES AND PRODUCTS

The important concept of difference in the context of international expansion has already been explored. This concept has a very material bearing on the choice of foreign or amicably related countries in which to operate and the type of product which may be manufactured or assembled. In this selection process the question of corporate culture should be given careful consideration. Culture in this context refers to the whole ethos of business, industry and individuals and encompasses such essential factors as language, religion, ritual, taboo and some other aspects normally considered to apply only to primitive societies. In practice, however, the superficial sameness already identified in international business often masks enormous psychological and practical differences in outlook. Language is sometimes only a bridge to greater misunderstanding, because although the ideas may appear to mean the same thing the concepts behind the words are interpreted in an entirely or materially different way.

Beyond these general cultural factors lies a host of specific factors such as legal systems, labour laws, tax implications, the availability of the banking system and restrictions on dividend remittances. In the product field there will clearly be certain goods which will be suitable for one country and not for another and even the same goods may have to be differently labelled, handled and distributed. All of these factors will have a bearing both on the choice of country and the type of company to be acquired.

THE DEFINITION OF ACQUISITION CRITERIA

This is an exercise which in principle seems very simple and straightforward but in practice requires very careful analysis. When adopted by a board of directors it usually remains group policy until modified or abandoned. It serves as a principal source of a company's intentions and requirements in the field and in the normal way would be given not only to the company's closest advisers but also possibly to various intermediaries such as the mergers and acquisitions experts of investment banks and other business brokers. The following is a model outline of acquisition criteria.

(1) *Product area(s).*
(2) *Market(s) served*: whether these should be industrial, commercial or retail and whether it is necessary for the markets to be enjoying high growth rates.
(3) *Strategic market position*: whether or not it is necessary for a company to be acquired to be one of the leading firms in its market.

(4) *Barriers to entry*: whether there should be barriers to entry of technology, scale or other.
(5) *Product type*: should the products be distinctive and proprietary or would a company manufacturing commodity products be of interest?
(6) *Location*: the countries and regions within countries in which an acquisition might be made.
(7) *Currency*: are there specific currency zones which are particularly attractive or unattractive?
(8) *Capital markets*: should the acquisition prospect be located in an area with developed capital markets where the equity might be listed, new long-term capital raised and where there is access to local bank facilities?
(9) *Management*: is it necessary for a company to be acquired to have good management, willing to stay on after the company has been acquired?
(10) *Number and location of employees, human resources, management qualification.*
(11) *Capital intensity*: indicate whether the capital intensity of a business is an important consideration and whether a company with large capital requirements could be of interest.
(12) *Shareholding*: is there a minimum level of shareholding acceptable to the potential acquiror and would it be possible for the existing owners to retain some shares if they remain active in the management?
(13) *Amount available to be spent on acquisitions*: is there a maximum for a single acquisition? How might the purchase be financed?
(14) *Size*: specify the range of turnover required.
(15) *Capitalization*: are there maximum or minimum limits in terms of assets, debt structure and overall gearing leverage?
(16) *Profitability*: is it necessary for the pre-tax or trading profit margins to exceed a minimum level such as 10%? Is it necessary for the company to have a good trading record? Would a company which needed to be turned round be acceptable?
(17) *Goodwill*: specify the limit, if any, on the proportion of the purchase price which can be represented by goodwill.
(18) *Legal and fiscal regimes*: must agreements be subject to a specified legal system, to a particular tax regime, or to freedom to remit profits and dividends and to depreciate goodwill?
(19) *Environment risks or obligations*: a point often undervalued.
(20) *Production facilities and quality standards*, including the need for capital investments after the mergers and acquisitions transaction.
(21) *Synergy*: finally — and to some the crucial criterion — is synergy with existing operations.

ANALYSIS OF THE OPPORTUNITIES

Following a board's decision in principle to make transnational acquisitions and the development of suitable acquisition criteria, the next stage will be to establish the extent to which practical opportunities exist in the fields identified. There will, of course, be many factors other than the mere existence of suitable companies to be taken into account. In order that no important factor should be overlooked it is necessary to obtain a wide variety of information and advice. Such advice will normally fall into several different categories. For example, professional advisers might include experts on the economy of the country concerned, its legal system and markets. More specialist advice of various types may be required, plus that provided by engineering consultants. In certain non-European countries it will be essential to understand the political environment and the relative importance of individual ministers, their staying power and their expectations. This raises the problem of the employment of a local political adviser for very large transactions. He may be no better than a fixer, or he may genuinely have his finger on the pulse of all-important trends relevant to the acquisition. In some cases it may be possible to obtain a more independent view from somebody not connected with a particular regime and who is not a national of the country concerned. Another alternative — which is relevant to a small number of cases — will be to obtain the necessary information from embassy or consular sources. This alternative does, of course, depend to a large extent both on the quality of the people concerned in the diplomatic service post and their ability to obtain the necessary information. In most developed countries much information is readily available and any devious and sometimes dangerous information-gathering exercise is happily unnecessary.

These references to unusual examples of industrial intelligence gathering should not be allowed to divert attention from more common and basic problems — to obtain as full an understanding of the economic, legal, fiscal and financial factors as possible and to supplement this background information with specialist advice about products and the company itself. There is no excuse, in most cases, for not doing a thorough job in these areas before important decisions are taken. If, on the other hand, material facts cannot be established then the degree of risk may become unacceptably high and the prospect accordingly declined.

PRIMARY SELECTION

When the board has come to a basic decision that it must expand internationally, and has taken the view that in order to make a material impact on turnover and profits it must expand by acquisition or other equity-related deal structure, then it is faced with difficult choices.

The first of these relates to the country or countries which it decides are relevant. An order of priorities must then be established because although country A may indeed be preferable, it may not be a serious possibility and countries B and C may be practical alternatives, although somewhat less attractive. Furthermore regional aspects of the target country chosen can play a decision role (infrastructures, qualified labour, tax incentives and others). Once markets have been established as real possibilities — and this means countries with given national frameworks and legal systems — the choice of company or companies within one or more markets must be made. In order that such a choice may be rationally based it is often necessary to determine which product or products from the parent company's range may be of interest and importance either to manufacture or to sell, or both, in the target country, or indeed to export from it. This type of analysis should produce a practical matrix and an order of priorities. It would be surprising, however, if for a typical company the permutations based on the three variables of country, company and products were particularly complex; certainly a large sheet of paper rather than a computer should suffice for primary selection. In the final analysis there will be some practical constraints which will tend to reduce the number of variables in all three categories. Indeed, it may well be that for many companies a major planning exercise will establish that given the criteria agreed by the board, there may be only one company in a single target country or region which both meets the criteria and is available for acquisition or partnership.

The importance of the primary selection exercise, therefore, is to save both executive and advisory time and money. Detailed theoretical exercises about the value of this or that acquisition may provide interesting and amusing work for corporate planning or acquisitions departments (together with valuable and educative opportunities for foreign travel). They may also provide sound bread and butter business for various advisers and consultants, but they will have little practical value for the company which actually pays all the bills. In this context, a well-informed local may repay what appears to be an expensive fee by cutting through all such expensive and time-wasting exercises to demonstrate clearly that whatever the statistics and other information may suggest, the particular company concerned will not be permitted or cannot be motivated to fall under foreign ownership for reasons which cannot and will not ever be fully or officially explained.

One other factor is the dynamic relationship between stalker and prey or amicable partner. In spite of the way change has become commonplace, there are still examples of long-term attempts at acquisition that have failed to take account of changes in the target company. The need for a continuing updating of information, if a sustained pursuit is to be undertaken, should be obvious; it is sometimes ignored and with results that can even be farcical.

ANALYSIS OF THE TARGET COMPANY

It follows from what has been said above about selection that unless the process has reduced the number of possibilities to a few or even only one, such an analysis will always be relative and will compare available companies and countries. Normally the process will be in two stages — choosing a country first and then one or more companies within that country. It may well be that a final analysis of two apparently equally interesting possibilities will arrive at a conclusion based on a comparative weighting of factors which are materially different as between the two companies. Clearly, in such an evaluation there would be a range of factors beyond the fundamental ones touched on above. Of the ones which spring to mind, however, the most obvious is that of comparative cost in relation to immediate and longer-term return. What, over a five-year period for example, are the likely effects on the earnings per share of the parent company comparing the two possible targets? Other factors to bear in mind are the impact on the company's gearing or leverage, the currency factors (does the acquisition require a mismatching of currencies?) and perhaps most important of all, what will the comparative impact be in terms of the management time required from the centre to monitor and control one of the businesses compared with the other? A model checklist for either individual or comparative analysis would run to several sheets of paper and would cover every sensible aspect of the target company's business and its impact on that of the parent company and any other subsidiaries. If a major foreign acquisition is in contemplation, however, there is no excuse for not adopting this due diligence approach or attempting to short-circuit it.

PLANNING THE APPROACH

From the foregoing it will be clear that considerable planning and preparation is necessary in order to identify potential and practical acquisition opportunities. Once this has been done, however, it is important to plan the approach to the company or its controlling shareholders with equal care. It is not uncommon for much painstaking and expensive analysis to be completely wasted by an ill-considered or careless approach. This danger can be avoided by some fairly uncomplicated forethought, including the best estimates available, about the likely reactions of the various interested parties to what is contemplated. At one extreme there will be companies where shareholders and managers will be expecting an approach from one or other foreign suitor, particularly where the company has been the object of speculation for some time. At the other extreme will be companies which not only are not listed on any stock exchange, but which are located in countries where the degree of disclosure is minimal. If, in addition, such companies are also highly secretive about their affairs, then it will be extremely difficult to make preliminary soundings.

In planning the approach every important element will have to be considered upfront. This is not simply a question of which are the relevant official bodies, if any, which need to be monitored, but also an appreciation of the general attitude in the country to acquisitions or mergers of the type proposed. Most countries have bodies specifically charged with considering acquisitions of domestic companies by foreign companies. In very large cases, the ministry of finance or economic affairs and the central bank will have a role to play. In countries with a developed stock market it is common and functional for either official or semi-official bodies to regulate the actual conduct of an acquisition.

Once again what is required for a successful approach is to establish a checklist and a list of priorities, thus ensuring that no material aspect is overlooked. One recent example of lack of planning occurred when a direct approach was made to the board of a target company at that most sensitive of periods between the closure of the year-end and the publication of the group's results. Even the most cursory reading of the company's financial calendar would have prevented an error which not only set matters off on the wrong foot but clearly indicated inefficiency and carelessness on the part of the potential acquiror. This examples demonstrates the important role to be played by qualified, experienced, international mergers and acquisitions advisors, most often found in financial institutions of the target country.

NEGOTIATING AND DEALING

Once initial contact has been made and not rejected out of hand, then the next critical phase commences. In this area, too, timing can be all important in maintaining the confidence of the potential vendors and management. Sometimes a tendency to rush things will result in the abrupt termination of negotiations by a sensitive or prickly management. The question of price will, of course be central to both potential buyer and potential seller although it is not always the overriding factor. Often, price should not be discussed in the early contact phase, unless the target wants it. It is essential for the acquiror to have a clear and early idea of how far he is prepared to go in price terms. One danger to guard against is that there is an inner momentum about negotiations (particularly if they are the apparent culmination of an expensive, tedious and long-drawn-out exercise) which may lead to false syllogism, justification on grounds of opportunity cost, machismo, or a fateful combination of all three. The serious and sensible negotiator will seldom allow himself to be placed in a position whereby the benefits of a painstaking approach are cast, like caution, to the winds in the sometimes heady, sometimes desperate, atmosphere of international negotiation. From time to time it may be acceptable to regard a contract, sometimes even a large one, as the stakes in a game of poker. Such a gambler's approach is never acceptable in large international acquisitions.

Again, it is important for corporate executives involved to appreciate that such an initiative is not a normal corporate move (unless, of course, buying and selling companies is familiar to the organization concerned). Equally, it is the duty of the main board to ensure that although reasonable flexibility is given to their negotiators, there is a clearly understood limit beyond which the project is either deferred or abandoned. It is particularly important that as this vital function of price changes, its impact on such matters as borrowing limitations, currency factors and alternative investment opportunities is fully appreciated.

Price, although crucial, is, as already noted, by no means the only important factor. On the assumption that a price can be agreed, it is essential for both parties to understand precisely what is being bought or sold. Are there, for example, any exclusions from the apparent package, such as subsidiaries or minority interests which are either excluded or which must be disposed of under the terms of existing agreements? Are there any royalty or licensing agreements or certain other contractual obligations (such as supply, purchasing and joint ventures) in either domestic or third markets which may be affected by a change of ownership, control or strategic alliance? In the case of the disposal of part of the business, have terms been clearly agreed and understood about how intercompany debt shall be dealt with? Tax optimization, especially in cross border deal making, is one of the most important and complex matters to be observed and to be resolved.

In a very few countries foreign controlled companies, even where registered in the host country, may have no access or only restricted access to the domestic banking system. Even where this is not the case the local lenders, both those providing bank facilities and those providing medium or long-term debt, may wish to review their facilities in the event of a change of control. It may, of course, be possible to renegotiate or replace such facilities. The important thing is to appreciate that they are matters to be considered and dealt with in advance. In most cases continuity of management represents a crucial factor and it will therefore be essential to have a clear understanding of who will stay and who will go following completion, and the terms and conditions upon which both will happen.

There are other important factors which may have a particular bearing on cross-frontier acquisitions. I have already referred to the question of management, but in the broader context the whole subject of employees must arise and this in turn may involve negotiations with trade unions about continuity of employment, redundancies and related matters. Increasingly pension payments, and in particular, whether or not the provisions made by the company being acquired are adequate as compared with those of the bidding company, have become a major factor.

In recent years there have been some nasty shocks when this matter has been overlooked until after the event; to discover, for example, that the under-funding of pensions must be corrected and that this will cost, say, 10% or more in excess of the purchase consideration may cause unpleasant surprises back at corporate headquarters. Similar considerations may apply to the whole field of insurance. Different companies and countries have varying attitudes to this vital area, and the application of best international practice to a newly-acquired subsidiary may prove very costly.

The importance of individual contracts and longer-term contractual relationships will vary from industry to industry and from company to company. Nevertheless, in almost every business it will be essential to maintain the goodwill of important customers on the one hand and to ensure there are no major contractual (or environmental) time-bombs on the other. The ability of a potential buyer to satisfy himself on these matters will, of course, depend essentially on the degree of willingness of the vendors. In the case of an unrecommended bid, the risks will be very great because little, if any, co-operation will be obtained from the victim. Even in cases of recommended offers, however, the need to maintain confidentiality for stock market or other reasons may mean that it is extremely difficult to discuss the likely attitude of customers and suppliers with them. In such cases heavy reliance will inevitably be placed on the assurances given by the vendors and this will essentially require judgments on the part of the purchaser. However, representations and warranties are standard parts of contracts, this basically protecting the acquiror.

Apart from the examinations of specific large contracts, work in progress and stocks, there is a broad area normally requiring judgment on the part of the existing board; I refer, of course, to contingencies in both the broad and narrow senses. If there is a longer-term published record of a company's affairs, then it should be possible to see whether, historically, management has been prudent or otherwise in dealing with these matters. If not, and particularly where accounting standards do not require much in the way of disclosure, then commercial judgment will be increasingly important. This quality will also apply to such difficult but important matters as directors' valuations or investments, the undervaluation or otherwise of properties and other fixed assets, the adequacy or otherwise of replacement cost and management accounting, and the quality of research and development or product development in science-based or market-based companies.

Underlying all of these factors, by definition, in the international sphere are the questions of exchange rates, interest rates and stock market movements. These are all factors which can change materially during the processes leading to a bid or to an acquisition outlined above. Since the breakdown of Bretton Woods and its replacement by much looser international exchange rate agreements, a new element of volatility has been introduced into international financial transactions of every sort. This volatility has affected exchange rates, interest rates and stock markets to a degree unheard of. Value judgments about these changes are clearly inappropriate here; suffice it to say in the present context that they have introduced additional uncertainty but probably also greater opportunity for the shrewd and observant potential bidder and his mergers and acquisitions advisors.

CONTRACT AND COMPLETION

This section assumes that it has been possible to negotiate both a satisfactory price and other arrangements for the acquisition of all or part of the company concerned. It is by no means unique, however, for a deal to be announced, only to be followed some weeks or months later by an announcement of a failure to complete. Sometimes this is understandable if, for example, a regulatory authority in the target country is against the proposals. Sometimes, however, it is totally inexplicable to the independent observer and commentator in that failure has resulted from a lack of care and definition.

In order to ensure that careful preparation and skilful negotiation are not brought to nothing it is essential to have all the basic aspects of completion worked out and agreed prior to any announcement. Key elements in such arrangements will be the form of contract, the legal system under which it is established, provision for arbitration in the event of disputes, and the form and content of warranties and indemnities. Clear provisions for future transactions will be necessary in cases where less than full control is involved, as will termination or related provisions in joint venture or similar companies. One common major pitfall is that of taxation. It is usually essential, prior to completion, to provide for tax clearances from the relevant authorities, together with arrangements for dealing subsequently with any unresolved elements. Another crucial area is that of management continuity as evidenced by service agreements and related undertakings. Finally, in order to ensure that all these and other relevant matters are dealt with within the spirit of any agreement in principle, it is essential to establish a timetable, a list of documents required, a checklist of action to be taken and a clear definition of the party or parties responsible for the action concerned. Careful attention to these matters and procedures should avoid that merchant banker's nightmare, the completion meeting where either a cheque is missing or a bank facility is not in place or one of the essential signatories has not turned up.

FUTURE OPERATIONS, REPORTING AND MONITORING

The nearest one will get to a guarantee of success in this area of international acquisitions is when there is a sound economic and commercial basis for what is being done and genuine goodwill and a willingness to make it work on the part of both parties. Even in such circumstances, however, it is essential to ensure good mutual understanding. This is not merely a pious phrase but describes specific and vital procedures. In other words, before the transaction is completed those individuals who will be responsible after the event for the success or failure of the venture must clearly understand what their actual responsibilities are, to whom they will report and the method by which it will be done. Such an understanding will involve matters such as whether all existing products will continue to be manufactured, whether all plants will remain open, whether all subsidiaries will continue to remain under the control of the company acquired and whether, for example, the financial function will be controlled from outside the country or within it and, in such cases, within what limits. As in all corporate situations personal relationships will be the key to success. Where seniority, responsibility and reporting are clearly set out and accepted before the event, the possibility of misunderstanding, subsequent disillusionment and even failure will be much reduced.

The three areas touched on above which must be covered by agreement are the operation of the business, the reporting by management of its progress and the monitoring of this progress in relation to defined objectives by the parent company. If the acquisition has been carefully conceived, prepared and implemented, most of the key elements in these areas should be perfectly clear and straightforward. There should, however, always be a mechanism or clearing house where matters either not dealt with or particularly obscure can be resolved before they become serious problems. One such problem can result directly from the nature of the transaction itself; it is by definition international and therefore involves, directly or indirectly, currency movements over an extended period. In almost all cases local management bears no responsibility for the acquisition or the financing thereof. It is, therefore, both unfair and, in the long run, self-defeating to judge management on the basis of arbitrary and volatile currency movements when the fault (if any) may lie nearer home.

Even in the most successful acquisitions there are potential problems in the fields of reporting and monitoring. Most of these can be avoided by applying a little of that scarce commodity, commonsense. The biggest danger to avoid is the two-headed information explosion — requests for such volume and detail that on the one hand, they madden local management asked to provide them and, on the other, inundate those in the parent company who receive them (and who cannot possibly absorb them anyway). In order to avoid situations which are both absurd and dangerous, it is essential to identify the minimum level of key information compatible with responsible control but which neither alienates nor inundates local management.

There is, after all, little point in spending time and money in acquiring a business which loses its motivation either immediately or gradually.

Managers in a foreign subsidiary usually respond to autonomy, motivation and clearly understood operating and reporting procedures. International corporate headquarters have a legitimate interest in the progress of the foreign company and, indeed, a responsibility to the parent company board for reporting and monitoring its progress and, where necessary, taking corrective action. Again, this is something which should be accepted by both parties and clear cut procedures adopted. There is no need for these to be particularly formal so long as the necessary information is obtained and the required discussion takes place. Corporate styles inevitably differ depending on geographical, political and cultural factors. Nevertheless, from a longer-term point of view there is usually a strong case for making the relationship a two-way one and encouraging visits from the foreign subsidiary to corporate headquarters and, where practicable, to fellow subsidiaries around the world. In this way, not only does a corporate identity have chance to develop but there may even be genuine cases of that over-used phrase 'cross-fertilization of ideas' becoming a reality.

CONCLUSIONS

The principal conclusion which emerges from the above analysis is that international corporate expansion by acquisition, merger, joint venture or alliance is not easy. There are casualties and even fatalities, both corporate and personal. Many of these have resulted from a lack of preparation and, in particular, the failure on the part of management to think through both the concept and the detail in advance. Even where this is done, however, it is essential to realize that, because of a lack of information and the volatile nature of some of the variables, the eventual outcome may differ materially from the original plan. A sensibly defined policy can, however, always be adjusted or modified to accommodate important changes and consequential impacts on other parts of the programme. On the other hand, a vague plan will become even vaguer and more dangerous in a dynamic situation.

The stakes are high, the rewards great. This catalogue of dangers and failures is not intended to turn the reader away from international mergers and acquisitions, but to ensure that they are carefully planned — to achieve the rewards and avoid the disasters. Starting from an awareness of the national and corporate differences, the key point with which this chapter began, a number of activities are needed to overcome the obstacles. These include: careful study, an agreed plan, clear responsibilities, decisive action, sound management, sensitive monitoring, flexibility — and, of course, luck and good judgment.

Beyond these factors, however, there is a very important principle which applies to every business, whether internationally spread or not. The principle is particularly applicable to international acquisitions because, by definition, they have not grown organically and absorbed the culture of the parent company. This principle is that industry and commerce are, by their nature, dynamic. The significance of this for international mergers is that, in normal circumstances, the acquisition should be only the first step in a long-term corporate plan involving that particular acquisition or venture. There is an understandable tendency, because these deals often seem more like a major strategic war than a tactical skirmish, to breathe a sigh of relief at the end of a successful campaign and to regard the problem as having been resolved for all time. Such an attitude is likely not only to diminish the value of the investment just made, but also to store up for the future problems for both the parent company and its new child.

Finally, if a board is serious about international acquisitions, mergers or similar corporate developments it must be prepared to devote resources of both corporate staff and money to the exercise. It must recognize that the exercise may be expensive, budget accordingly and include the costs of the highest-quality advice available.

There are many examples of failure resulting directly from attempting to do a cut-price job. Cheap advice usually turns out to be expensive and nasty, and cleaning up the resultant mess even more so. First-class advice is seldom expensive in the long run if it is procured and used in the proper way. This should not be taken as an injunction to budget lavishly for corporate staff, extensive travel or expensive advisers. A defined budged and estimates of expenses can be established before the event in informal discussions with potential advisers. A clear understanding of what is required should also be established, together with their initial comments on the practicality of what is proposed. The laying down of a clear brief with agreed objectives and within defined timescales and budgets will save a lot of time, future arguments and recrimination. In the last analysis, if policy is sensibly adopted and implemented there is seldom a more effective way of expanding international business in many fields.

FINANCING

Central to the analysis in the previous section were the questions of relative value and finance. In this section, it is assumed that a practical proposal has been identified and that all the other necessary factors, apart from financing, have fallen or will fall into place. It is clear, however, that unless a viable method or methods of finance can be established there will be no final deal. Faced with the enormous complexities of a large international transaction of this sort one is tempted to indulge in nostalgia for that era of simplicity and innocence when a man with a bag of gold or a box of glass beads or, indeed, a few bold men, armed with muskets, could expand internationally by 'acquisition'. History, of course, indicates that this was not always the end of the story and that from time to time somebody arrived with bigger and better muskets to challenge the status quo.

Putting such yearnings for a golden age behind us and concentrating on the harsh reality of modern political, commercial and financial conditions, it is possible by careful analysis to find a way through the maze or to establish fairly quickly either that there is no sensible way or that it is simply not worth the effort.

KEY FINANCIAL CONSIDERATIONS

(1) *The financial position of the purchaser.*

This is an obvious starting point for any analysis and must include the latest published information, the up-to-date estimated situation as indicated by management accounts and internal projections and the longer-term estimates, including and excluding the target company, based on carefully thought out assumptions. This information should, in turn, indicate clearly what additional capital requirements will face the group either from the parent itself or from its existing subsidiaries and associates. This exercise will also lead to the highly relevant question: can we afford it without starving our other businesses of vital capital for expansion?

(2) *The availability and transferability of capital resources.*

A group's overall financial position should be established by analysis along the lines indicated above. Beyond the question of the absolute stock and flow of capital, however, more specific questions arise. These may be summarized briefly by the following questions. Are the resources in the right currency or currencies? If not, can they be freely exchanged into appropriate currencies? Are the resources in the right place in terms of international structure? Can the resources be freely transferred either back from a subsidiary to the parent or from the parent to a suitable finance vehicle?

There is nothing more frustrating for an international group wishing to expand overseas than having a huge theoretical financing capability but in practice being almost completely unable to shift resources from any part of the group to any other part. Such actual or potential frustration does tend to predispose companies to expand in areas where restrictions are few or non-existent. Unfortunately, however, some of the greatest potential opportunities for rapid market growth arise in areas with the greatest restrictions on commercial and financial freedom. Apart from the mass of government and central bank regulations there are other potential snares such as the (plausible) rights of minority investors or associated companies.

(3) *The financial position of the company being acquired.*

This is obviously a crucial factor, particularly if the acquisition is a large one in relation to the group as a whole. If the offer is not recommended then it is usually extremely difficult to establish the true underlying financial position of the company. As stated above, however, unrecommended acquisitions are still unusual in the international, specifically European field and the normal assumption is that financial information will be provided. Even in such a case, however, there is no guarantee that it will be sufficiently up-to-date and sufficiently detailed to provide a full picture.

Nevertheless, a view will have to be taken by the potential buyer after the maximum possible research has been done. In addition to any analysis of the target company's present and short-term financial situation, it will be necessary to consider what direct and indirect effects its acquisition by a foreign company may have. For example, will its bank facilities continue on the same terms and without the guarantee of its new owner?

(4) *Additional capital to develop the enlarged business.*

Foreign companies seldom acquire a business overseas without some idea of expansion beyond the level already contemplated by existing management. Normally they hope that by the introduction of products, new markets, new production expertise, management and capital they will be able to boost substantially the level of business and profit. Capital requirements should be quantifiable with reasonable accuracy and must obviously be built into the group's overall capital requirements involved in a foreign acquisition. Attention must be given to: the cost of acquisition; the replacement of existing facilities where required; development capital for the new acquisition; and overall group capital requirements.

CRITERIA FOR FINANCING INTERNATIONAL ACQUISITIONS

By this stage the basic decisions on the value of a business and the expected return on investment will have been taken. The practical application of possible financing routes may, however, modify matters significantly. There are several important variables in the equations and the evaluation of the relative risks of choosing one course or another or a mixture of courses should be based on the following criteria:

(1) the maximum level of acceptable debt (gearing or leverage) in both the parent and subsidiary;
(2) the use of equity capital as part of the financing package;
(3) the possible listing on the foreign and other international stock exchanges of the parent company's stock;
(4) the retention by the vendors of a minority of the share capital and the maintenance of a stock market listing for this;
(5) the estimated cost of using equity or equity-related capital;
(6) the cost of debt finance — long, medium or short-term;
(7) the availability and cost of hybrid financing instruments, such as preferred or preference shares, convertible stocks, bonds with warrants attached;

(8) the currency or currencies available;
(9) the regulations and general attitudes governing the remittance of profits and dividends;
(10) the scope for transfer pricing within the acquired company;
(11) matching currencies in terms of both capital and income in relation to the assets and earnings expected to be acquired;
(12) the tax position of both buyer and seller, domestically and internationally;
(13) the possibility of finding a way out should the merger fail, after all precautions have been taken.

SOURCES OF FINANCE FOR INTERNATIONAL ACQUISITIONS

INTRODUCTION

It is axiomatic that the form of consideration used by the buyer must be attractive to the seller. Beyond this fundamental principle, however, there are many other matters to be considered and in particular whether the various authorities in the two or more countries concerned will agree to a particular type of instrument or instruments. From the buyer's point of view, however, what may be thoroughly attractive to the seller may not suit the buyer because they may, for example, involve unacceptable costs associated with the particular instruments or unacceptable risks. There may be a major foreign exchange exposure which cannot be covered or hedged, or the issue of a debt instrument to the vendor may result in excessive borrowing ratios for the purchaser. These and other aspects will form part of the analysis of available sources of finance and in the last analysis, as in so many other areas, a compromise may have to be reached between conflicting interests and such a compromise may involve some creative financing. Other things being equal, the broader the range of practical options the better the prospects of a successful deal; a variety of options is likely to provide a more attractive and flexible package.

As noted above, the financial position of the company being acquired and the freedom to use its resources will be material factors in the calculations. In some cases, where such a company is not well managed or well advised, it will be possible for the foreign buyer to obtain a deal which is largely self-financing as a result of subsequent asset disposals or major cost-cutting exercises such as plant closures. In other cases, however, it will be clear that the financial position of the target company is weak and that in addition to the purchase consideration, substantial further capital will be required. It is, of course, a peculiar feature of international transactions of this sort that the foreign currency element is important, even critically so on rare occasions. The volatility and sharp movements in relative currency parities in recent years have created not only many difficulties for international executives, but also some golden opportunities. A weakening currency in the target country combined with a strengthening one in the potential bidder's is sometimes a powerful incentive so long as weakness is not a symptom of a deep malaise in the society and economy of the country concerned. In the immediate post-war period, for example, many United States corporations were able to acquire or establish businesses in Europe on the strength of a very favourable exchange rate. In recent years the boot has been on the other foot and exchange movements have opened up many favourable opportunities for German and Japanese companies to move into the United States. There is, of course, always a danger that opportunity will turn into opportunism which in this context implies seizing, sometimes without much thought or preparation, a chance to acquire a foreign business largely because exchange rate movements appear to make a transaction financially attractive. International wheeling and dealing of this sort can be even more dangerous than similar activities carried on in the home territory. In any case, what happens after the acquisition is made is what matters. Seldom is the exchange rate a determining corporate strategy factor.

Not all international acquisitions are based on favourable exchange rates. There are, in practice, many examples of companies moving defensively from a weak and depreciating currency base to one where both the currency is likely to appreciate further and the market itself grow at an above average rate. In such cases it is, of course, essential that the currency aspects of the transaction enable the purchasers to benefit from the appreciation or, at worst, not suffer from a continuing devaluation of their own currency. In principle, the payment for an acquisition is a simple matter involving cash, shares or other quoted or unquoted securities. In practice, however, there are many variations on these basic themes, dictated by such factors as gearing ratios, borrowing limitations and exchange control regulations.

One need only consider, for example, the case of the actual final payment being made in cash denominated in the vendor's currency. The funds thus used to finalize the transaction, however, may well have been borrowed by the purchaser in his own currency from his local capital market or the international market and then exchanged from one or more currencies into local currency. Equally, funds may have been raised by the placing of a line of the purchaser's own stock in his local market. The key point about these examples is that the vendor's requirement for cash does not, in most cases, limit the use by the purchaser of a wide variety of financing options. Some of these are considered further below.

(1) Cash in the form of local or foreign currency, emanating from existing treasury resources.
(2) The purchaser's ordinary shares or common stock. This option raises a number of questions including that of dilution of existing shareholders and the acceptability of such securities both to the vendors and to relevant authorities in both countries.
(3) The issue of shares in a locally formed subsidiary or offshore finance vehicle. This is often difficult or impossible to achieve because what is normally created is a security little different to those previously held by the vendors. The position may be different where the purchaser has other assets or businesses which may be included to form a larger and stronger entity.

(4) Enlarging the share capital of the target company by means of an issue of new shares subscribed by the purchaser and maintaining a listing for all the capital. This would permit partial or total realization by the vendors but suffers from the great disadvantage that control must pass without full realization by all existing shareholders.
(5) The issue by the purchaser of straight bonds or notes denominated in the purchaser's currency. In this case both the currency and the company will provide the ultimate security for the vendor; it may have sold a business in France for the United States dollar denominated notes of a United States corporation.
(6) The issue to the vendor of convertible bonds by the purchaser, denominated in the vendor's own currency. In this case the vendors will have to be satisfied that the security concerned is adequately covered as to both capital and income in the relevant currency.
(7) The issue of bonds or notes denominated in a currency other than that of the purchaser or vendor. Clearly the same comment applies here. Such a security will, in fact, be only as valuable as the issuer's ability to guarantee servicing and redemption of the obligation in due time, bearing in mind that his assets and income in that currency may be minimal.
(8) Issue of bonds with warrants or options attached. The latter would provide rights to convert or to acquire shares or other securities in the parent company. They would normally be denominated in the same currency because of the difficulties associated with options to convert from a security denominated in one currency into a security denominated in another.
(9) Performance related payments. These arise when part of the payment is deferred and becomes payable either after a specified period or upon the achievement of certain defined profit targets or both. The principal advantages of this method lie in the relationships between payment and profit and management continuity.
(10) Asset swaps or payment in the form of (assessed) assets transferred into the target company.

The above options are all essentially related to the company being acquired and the vendors directly. There is, however, a further series of options not related directly to the acquisition, although producing the necessary funds for it. In general, this series of options will require more explanation and probably more commonsense than in the case of linked transactions. Some of these options are listed below.

THE ISSUE OF SHARES OR COMMON STOCK

Such an issue may be specifically to finance an acquisition or may be a more general fund-raising exercise. Depending on the normal market practice or regulations, an issue may be by way of rights to existing shareholders or a placing to the market generally or, where possible, a so-called vendor consideration placing — where the shares are theoretically issued to the vendors of the foreign business but which are immediately and wholly placed with the market either in the purchaser's or vendor's stock exchange. To a degree this last choice will depend on whether or not the purchaser's shares are listed on the local market and there is adequate market capacity.

THE ISSUE OF CONVERTIBLE STOCK

This halfway house between equity and debt is sometimes attractive, particularly in uncertain market conditions. Key factors in its suitability will be the effect it has on overall borrowing ratios and the element of actual dilution implied by the conversion premium. Another factor of great importance will, of course, be the rate of interest.

THE ISSUE OF OTHER FORMS OF SHARE CAPITAL

In certain market conditions it may be difficult to issue ordinary share capital (common stock) but possible to find takers for other forms of share capital such as preference or preferred shares or stock. Such instruments often provide a degree of security of capital and of income or dividend flows not available on ordinary shares. Naturally such securities do not provide participation to the full extent in the benefits of a really successful enterprise because they do not share the full risk. In some cases, however, they do offer a degree of participation in rising profits by means of an increased coupon. Also there are attractions in the fact that the securities may be redeemable in certain circumstances.

DEBENTURES AND OTHER LONG-TERM INSTRUMENTS

A wide range of theoretical opportunities exists in this field but in practice there would be clear limitations imposed by such factors as overall borrowing ratios, existing charges on assets and currency exposure. Nevertheless, with the development of the eurobond and other international markets it is now possible for large companies of appropriate standing to issue long-term debt instruments in a variety of acceptable currencies.

The essential distinction in the long-term debt field is between secured and unsecured obligations. To the extent that it is possible to issue the latter the whole operation may become much less complicated because the impact on existing capital structures will be limited. This can be an extremely important factor for any large and complex international operation. The network of interconnected debt and security involved in an international debenture operation can make even the stoutest heart quail and it often becomes clear that the time and expense involved in the operation are not justified if there is any other conceivable way to finance the acquisition. If it is possible to issue an unsecured medium-to-long-term bond, then the additional interest cost which reflects the lack of specific security may be far outweighed by other savings in costs and time. Depending on market conditions and, in particular, the volatile movements of currency and interest rates, the capacity of the new markets is virtually limitless for an individual company of good standing. In addition, several of the major domestic markets provide great borrowing capacity if the corporation is prepared to pay the interest rates now prevailing. The structure of individual markets in terms of borrowers, lenders and investors means that different markets have appetites for different maturities. In the United Kingdom domestic market, for example, there is little call for medium-term debt instruments by investors because these are principally the life offices and pension funds with much longer actuarial requirements. Although by and large secured debt is not usually an attractive option for the buyer of a foreign business, there may be important exceptions. Where there is a clearly defined asset, for example, it may be possible for the buyer after the event to use that asset as specific security to refinance short-term borrowings on an attractive basis without interfering with the terms and conditions of existing debt in other parts of the group.

LOAN NOTES

Typically, a loan note issued to a vendor will be unquoted, or short duration (normally payable by annual instalments) and guaranteed or underwritten in some way by the purchaser. The note is likely to take the form of a very simple instrument and is effectively deferred cash. The principal reason for using an instrument of this type is usually the wish of a vendor to defer, and in some cases reduce, the taxation which is payable on capital disposals in several large markets. The instrument is in common use in the United States, for example, in particular where family sellers are disposing of a business to a larger corporation. Although the main reason for using loan notes is usually the requirements of the vendors, there may also be advantages to the buyer in deferring and staging his payments. There is often the additional advantage that the coupon carried by such notes is below market rates because the income is of lesser value to the vendor.

BANK LOANS

The growth of medium-term bank lending is a phenomenon of recent years in a number of important capital markets, although in others it has long been familiar. To some extent the actual definition of medium-term loans was no more than a recognition of reality. In other words, the so-called overdraft or until further notice facilities were accepted by both borrower and lender as hard core borrowings having the character of medium-term debt. The various crises affecting credit markets in recent years, however, caused some of these loose assumptions to be seriously questioned. In addition, a regime of rapid inflation and high interest rates resulted in the corporate sector as a whole in several important markets failing to maintain former levels of funded debt as the balance between long-term, medium term and short-term debt changed. Both central banks and lenders were concerned that the medium-term element should be put onto a proper footing. Sometimes this resulted in the production of loan agreements which differed little, if at all, from a full-blown bond prospectus. This was understandable in the sense that the banks had moved into a role of intermediary between the normal funding institutions and the ultimate borrower. The mismatching and capital base problems created by this longer-term trend must be considered elsewhere; suffice it to say here that these problems have not yet been fully resolved.

Assuming that the credit standing of the potential bidder is good and that regulations permit, there is normally a wide choice of bank loans and similar facilities available. Similar conditions apply in this field as in other funding areas. The most obvious of these is the overall borrowing capability of the company both before and after the proposed acquisition. Thereafter, the effects on other existing loans and loan limits must be considered, together with the question of maturity of the loans in relation to other outstanding debt, cash flow projections and additional funding requirements. Loan maturity is, of course, a fundamental principle in financial planning and nowhere more so than in the area of international acquisitions. There are, unfortunately, many examples where the principle has been ignored or taken far too casually and the result has been extremely adverse.

The acquisition of another business is usually conceived as a long-term investment and, save in wholly exceptional circumstances, should be funded accordingly. There are, of course, practical difficulties in using equity or raising equity finance to fund a purchase. Sometimes it is virtually impossible to issue long-term debt, or there may be a firm commitment for a future disposal of other assets to fund the purchase and a bridge is required. In such circumstances commonsense and the assessment of risk will usually provide an answer in the shape of a balanced financial package which takes account of market realities on the one hand and the need for safety on the other. In such a package medium and long-term bank debt may both have a part to play and even, in certain circumstances, short-term loans if they can be refinanced on a predetermined basis. Borrowing short and lending long may be necessary to enable the wheels of the world banking system to turn but borrowing short and investing long can be disastrous for companies, particularly where the additional risks of international acquisition are involved.

Once the suitable maturities have been established, other questions which arise are the rate of interest on the loans, whether the rate is fixed or floating, what currency or currencies are borrowed and what security, if any, will be asked for or offered.

OTHER MEANS OF FINANCING

The decision to make an international acquisition often follows from or stimulates a thorough reappraisal of a company's strategy. Such a review may well indicate that it would be sensible to dispose or swap certain subsidiaries, activities or assets. The net proceeds of such disposals may well then be available to finance, in whole or in part, the acquisition. Capital as a scarce resource in a company environment is not necessarily a bad thing, particularly where it forces difficult but important choices on management.

A relative assessment of investments in companies or countries can be a very good discipline. Many decisions will, of course, be of a lower order than ones involving the cessation of an activity or the disposal of a major investment or subsidiary. The process of appraisal may, for example, indicate clearly that far too much of the group's capital is tied up in inventory or stock or that substantial land and buildings assets are totally unnecessary for continuation of the main business.

This is, of course, just one method of accumulating cash at the centre for an acquisition. Cash or near cash assets may already be there as a result of a related or unrelated prior disposal and the reinvestment of such resources in overseas businesses which appear to have a higher long-term rate of return than an alternative investment in bank deposits, gilt-edged securities and so on, is a sensible utilization of such resources.

CONCLUSION

The main elements of capital resources available for foreign acquisition have been considered. The list is by no means exhaustive and deals with the principal categories rather than every type of facility available. New financial instruments are being developed continually be it along the lines of the probably already dismissed use of junk bonds, be it LBO or MBO financing concept. It is essential to consider the full range at the time an acquisition is being planned. Examples of particular facilities which may be of use but which have not been dealt with in detail here include leasing, mortgages, sale and lease-back and zero coupon bonds.

Consideration of the multiplicity of factors, instruments and their changing nature leads naturally to what is, in my view, a fundamental conclusion about capital resources for foreign acquisitions; this is that capital is one of the three basic elements in such a move (the others being commercial logic and management resources). Surprisingly, however, its availability and provision are not always considered as an integral part of the planning process. All too often the basic decisions have been taken and the finance function is then instructed to provide the means. This is an inefficient way of conducting business and can lead at best to reduced flexibility and increased costs, and at worst to failure to complete the transaction. The clear message is that consideration of the financial aspect should be both central to and contemporaneous with the other key elements. This means not only the full involvement of a corporation's financial management in the decision-taking process but also early consultation with financial advisers, bankers and others familiar with market conditions, new financial instruments and related foreign exchange, taxation and similar matters.

This chapter, originally drafted by JOHN McARTHUR, has been revised and rewritten by DR. HANS DAHM and ROBERT ARNOLD of the Westdeutsche Landesbank, Düsseldorf and London.

APPENDIX: CASE STUDY — GERMAN ACQUISITIONS AND MERGERS

Germany has been experiencing a steep increase in mergers and acquisitions which is expected to peak in 1991. Figure 2.7.1 shows the number of transactions in the past along with estimates for the future. It also shows that between thirteen and fourteen per cent of the transactions are international.

Number of Transactions Involving German Firms

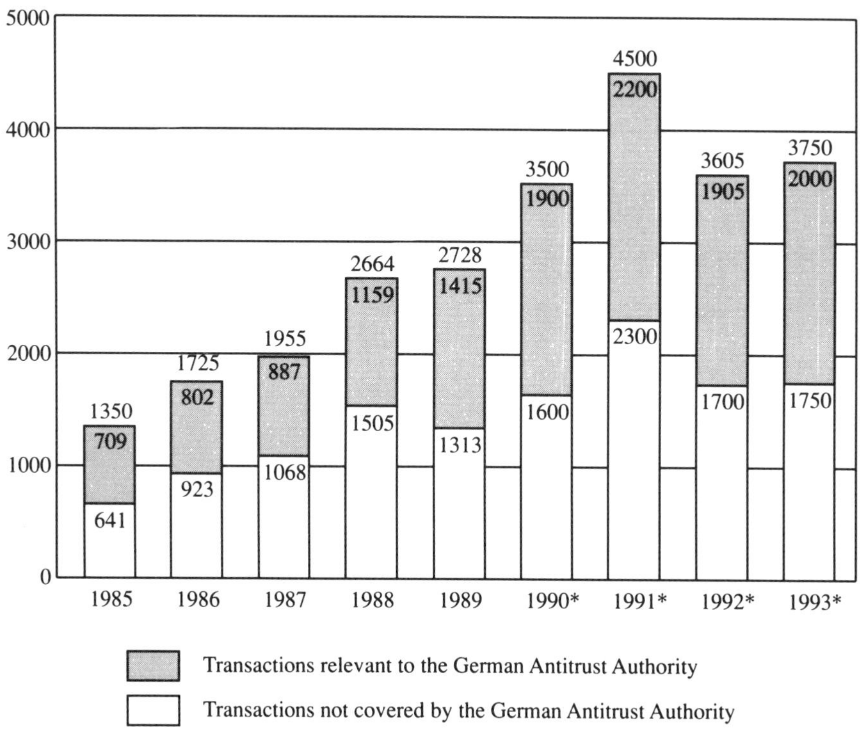

German target regions in 1989:

Germany (West)	87%
Europe	10%
U.S./Canada	2%
Japan	1%
other	1%

*Dr Dahm estimates

Sources: *WestLB Mergers & Aquisitions, German Antitrust Authority, Wupper-Report*

Figure 2.7.1 German M & A boom unbroken — with East/West potentials a reality

Figure 2.7.2 shows that a large majority of the transactions involved are minority holdings. German companies show an unusually high level of willingness to accept participation by third parties on a basis of less than 50% of the equity.

Level of participation quotas intended by industry type

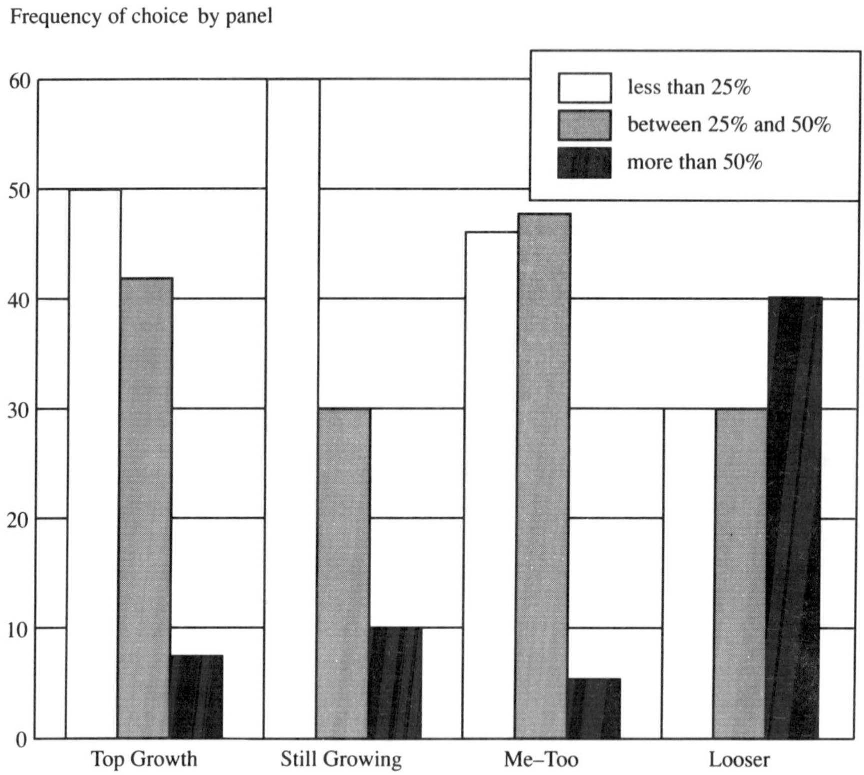

Source: *Dr.Wieselhuber and Partner — Survey, WestLB M&A*

Figure 2.7.2 German privately-held industry leaders are open to step into minority participations (and vice versa)

While the German merger boom has been strengthened by supportive attitudes of Supervisory or Advisory Boards, it was corporate managements who played a large part in initiating and above all implementing such increasingly complex and often transnational transactions. The advantages have been identified as:

(1) risk reduction — the merged company is better able to hedge against risks;
(2) greater potentials in market, technology and management terms;.
(3) greater flexibility, especially to improve competitive reactive energies;

(4) repositioning — the speeding up of a company's efforts to achieve a new position in the market in relation to the competition;
(5) optimizing distribution and logistics systems to improve customer service and to reduce cost;
(6) ability to pool resources — in research and development, production, purchasing and personnel for instance — and thus to reduce expensive facilities;
(7) ability to internationalize products, franchises, know-how and management.

Among the factors found to be pressuring German companies into alliances are:

(1) accelerated technology change, both domestic and globally;
(2) shorter production cycles;
(3) increased capital requirements;
(4) the discovery of existing or potential corporate weaknesses;
(5) tougher global competition, including the increasingly aggressive entries of enterprises from Eastern Europe and Asia-Pacific into world business;
(6) costly state regulation on subjects like the environment or expense redemption policies in pharmaceuticals, energy consumption and others;
(7) a need to import management skills and to upgrade corporate cultures.

Figures 2.7.3 and 2.7.4 illustrate how the advantages can be realized and the pressures operate in a merger, respectively strategic alliance between an American and a German pharmaceutical company.

Superdrug Inc
(USA)

Competitive strengths:

- R&D capacities
- new compounds
- global marketing
- financial strength

Corporate goals

- increase market share in Germany and EC
- merge existing sub

Specialpill GmbH
(FRG)

Competitive strengths:

- specialized products
- effective distribution
- modern production
- good management

Corporate goals

- add new compounds
- grow internationally
- position for Single European Market

Figure 2.7.3 Practicable cross-border strategic alliance model: Example in the pharmaceutical industry

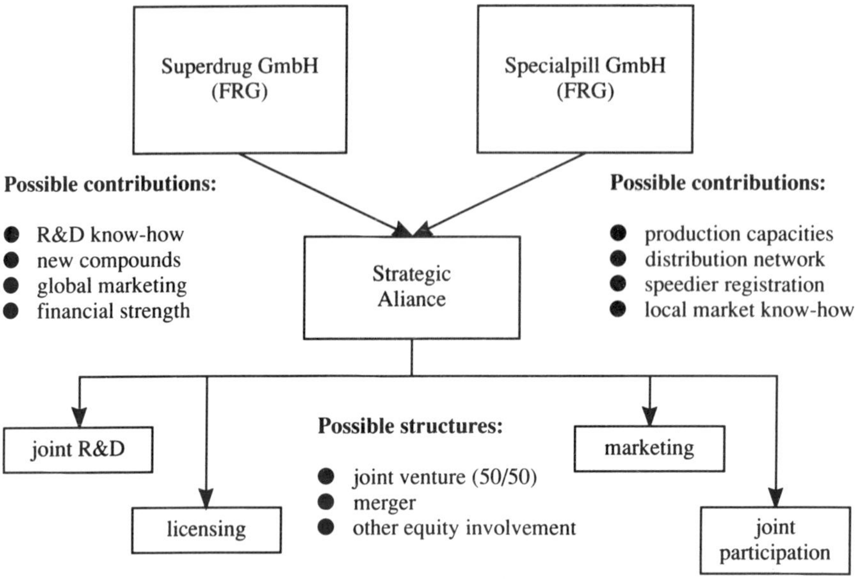

Figure 2.7.4 Practicable cross-border strategic alliance model: Example in the pharmaceutical industry

In spite of the small proportion (14%) of mergers that are currently international, German companies have found considerable advantages in cross-frontier alliances. The less international a company's targets, the more fragile and marginal the future is likely to prove. Figure 2.7.5 shows the merger preferences for companies based in France, Scandinavia, Italy, Spain, the Netherlands, Germany and Switzerland. Most countries seek alliances with United States companies first; German companies rank Japan second.

CHARACTERISTICS OF GERMAN ACQUISITIONS

(1) Approach preparation and execution are critical for the achievement of desired results (more than recorded in other countries). Key factors are:
   (a) clear and convincing communication of the entrepreneurial and multi-dimensional motives;
   (b) disclosures of long-term strategic aims, along with willingness to be flexible;
   (c) understanding and acceptance of the partner's corporate culture;
   (d) agreement — in quantifiable terms — on the expected benefits of the merger or of the participation or alliance;
   (e) anticipation of potential strains on the corporations involved, including the human factors;

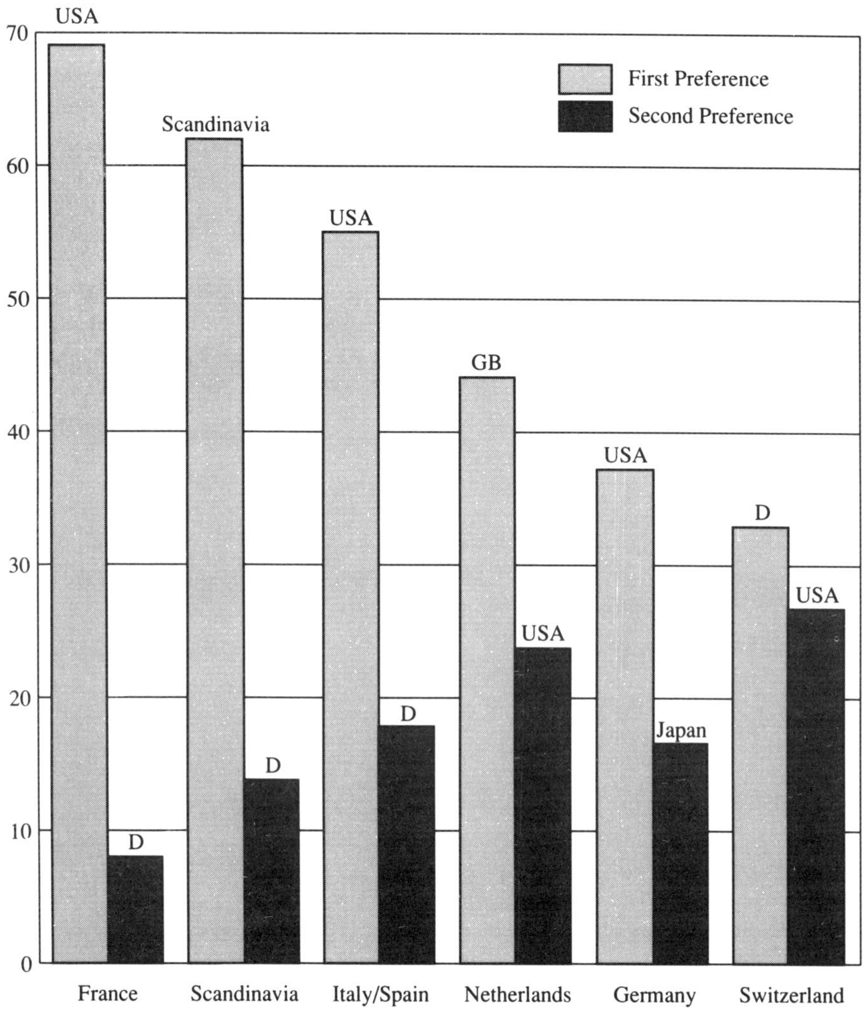

Source: *H. Werner, WestLB M&A*

Figure 2.7.5 Preference for potential corporate allies

(f) clear definition of management structures and competence at the interfaces between the old, the merged, or the allied companies.

(2) Certain problems have arisen from:

(a) *dogmatism* on the part of the acquiring company stifles initiative and inhibits the very factors on which the German partner has built its success;

(b) *new success criteria* set by the outside partner can cause confusion and demotivation;

(c) *role changes* occur that were not anticipated by the target company finally taken over;
(d) *status and place in location* are called in question with demotivating results.

(3) Value systems and corporate cultures have to be considered. These cover issues such as: communication, confidence, sensitivity, sense of humour, professional discipline, mobility, innovativeness; also included are the ability to think internationally, to accept risk, to retain an enquiring mind and not to be status conscious.

(4) Some contradictions in German thinking:
(a) do it now: wait until the time is ripe — timing is vital;
(b) love of an ordered society: need for less rules and guidelines in a changing world.

(5) Contrasts between German and British management styles. Incompatibility between managers in the two countries often causes problems. The following are some of the differences that lie behind this partial though not incurable incompatibility:
(a) German managers are often specialist by training (usually technical), accustomed to quick, individual decision-making; British managers are generalists (often trained on the job), accustomed to consensus decision-making;
(b) German managers are more internationally minded;
(c) German managers often do not integrate readily and can be volatile; British managers are more team-minded and pragmatic;
(d) German managers are more relationship-minded and democratic; British managers are more status conscious and authoritarian.

TAX IMPLICATIONS OF GERMAN CROSS-FRONTIER MERGERS

Both the purchase price and the financing required have tax implications, as do the types of purchase which can be assets, partnership shares, or equity shares in the so-called capital companies (GmbH, AG or KGaA).

The following are some tax-relevant considerations, which in any case need to be assessed by auditors as well as tax and legal experts.

(1) *Timing*. Correct timing of the transaction can avoid additional net asset taxes.
(2) *Contract*. Choose a foreign takeover or participation contract to reduce stock exchange sales tax, if the target is publicly listed.
(3) *Property*. Consider placing real estate in the hands of a GmbH or partnership to avoid real estate purchase taxes.

Figure 2.7.6 explains how the increase in assets acquired can guide the tax strategies of takeovers in Germany.

Tax Objectives	Aquisition/Participation Target Type Assets	Partnership Shares	GmbH/AG Shares
Step-up	YES (directly)	YES (supplementary balance required)	YES (German holding company required)
	Purchase price allocation strategy and accelerated depreciation to be used.		
Tax Deduction of Financing Cost	YES (German GmbH or KG)	YES (supplementary P&L statement required)	YES (German holding company required)
Tax Pooling of German Profits and losses		LIMITED (without municipal trade tax)	POSSIBLE (tax corporate pooling)

Figure 2.7.6 Step-up of assets acquired for depreciation, and tax deduction of financing costs should guide tax strategies of acquirors in Germany

TYPES OF BID

Hostile bids are feasible in spite of conventional wisdom to the contrary. The following have been identified as factors with heavy impact. Not all of them apply in any given circumstances and some may backfire.

(1) Ownership strategies and structures.
(2) Financing; in this the captive or house banks have an important role to play.
(3) Composition and authority of advisory or supervisory boards and of personalities.
(4) Vulnerability of the target company (its management skills, research, reputation, strategic market position).

It remains, however, that hostile bids are still extremely rare on German turf. The following explains why.

(1) Publicly quoted companies (AGs) have two-tier boards whose existence, composition and duration complicate takeovers.
(2) The number of quoted companies available to takeover bids is small. There are only around 470 quoted AGs and most of these have controlling shareholders or major shareholder blocs.
(3) About 60% of listed shares are administered by banks; this does not make for an active market or an easy purchase of a majority holding leading up to the really critical 75.01% barrier to change the statutes.
(4) Managers, directors and institutional investors do not favour hostile takeovers.
(5) Workers' representatives on supervisory boards are hostile to takeovers.
(6) Pension provisions do not provide spare cash for takeovers.
(7) There are just (so far) not many would-be predators around.

SOME EXAMPLES

The best known examples of strategic moves of well-known corporate names in Germany show that quality and selectivity are dominant motives rather than size or power. The following are some illustrations.

Degussa-Merck, segment leaders look without success for the benefits of a partial merger or reciprocal participations on asset transfers.

Siemens-Robotron-Nixdorf, implications of German unification or crisis management.

Asea-MTA, giant acquires dwarf with a strong niche position in its industry and technology.

Logsped AG, entrepreneurs create a main independent logistics player.

Against hostile — or semi-friendly — bids, the following defences are available: registered shares, share pooling, preferred non-voting shares, voting right limitations, creation of conditional equity, use of powers of supervisory and managing boards, use of qualifying majority powers (75.1%), spin-off options for shareholder groups, legal break up, going public, activitation of house bankers, relobbying of opinion makers, social pressure, bonuses for managers and shareholders, use of company statutes or articles of incorporation, use of previous owners' wills, licence call-backs or royalty payments, shareholder loans.

This appendix has been supplied by DR HANS DAHM, Westdeutsche Landesbank.

3
FINANCE AND CREDIT

Part 3 looks at a number of issues that concern the financing of investments, exports and projects internationally. Finance for long term projects and for trade are the themes of the first two chapters, followed by one on the fast-growing topic of leasing. Chapters 3.4 and 3.5 deal with the insuring of capital risks and with credit control (both have useful addresses of sources for further information). Investment incentives available in the European Community are explained in the sixth chapter; a final chapter deals with compensation trading in its many aspects.

3.1
Financing long term projects

INTERESTS INVOLVED

Major projects form the most exposed part of making and financing investments. Obviously the bigger a project the greater will be the effect on an owner of given size. But the exposure is not just financial; governments, potential suppliers, employees and the press all become interested and try to influence a project for their own reasons.

Government interest in a new project may be to boost a depressed area, to increase employment, to widen the tax base, to boost exports, or to provide supplies for a nationalized industry. Suppliers of both capital equipment and working materials are always looking for and encouraging new orders. Within a company the promoter of a new project gains importance and develops his career; in a sense, all its employees are suppliers to a project and have similar interests. The press are interested in a big project, not least if it fails dramatically; years of cost overrun and hundreds of millions of pounds lost always make a good story.

A press cutting from the *Financial Times* in February 1989 gives a recent example.

> The projected capital cost of a scheme to harness the tidal waters of the River Severn to generate electricity has risen sharply.
>
> A barrage across the estuary from Cardiff to Weston-Super-Mare would cost £8.5bn at 1988 prices compared with £5.54bn four years ago, according to an interim report of the latest feasibility study. Transmission reinforcement costs have risen from £392m four years ago to £850m.
>
> The £4.26m feasibility study has been commissioned jointly by the Severn Tidal Power Group consortium, the Central Electricity Generating Board and the Department of Energy. The consortium comprises Sir Robert McAlpine & Sons, Balfour Beatty, Taylor Woodrow Construction, Wimpey Major Projects, Northern Engineering Industries and GEC Turbine Generators.
>
> The interim report says the barrage would take nine years to complete and would generate 7,200 MW of electricity during a 120 year lifetime.

> The report shows that at a nominal 5% rate of return on capital, the cost of generating electricity from the barrage is likely to be 3.79 pence per KwH (kilowatt hour), compared with an estimated 2.24 pence per KwH for the proposed 1,175MW Hinkley Point C nuclear power station.

The members of the Severn Tidal Power Group are contractors, and are understandably interested in working up a new project. But an owner is needed to counterbalance these interests, and to ensure that the design is feasible, the construction quick and economical, the operation efficient, the pricing of the tolls competitive, and that the yield justifies the sums spent. As with any big project the burden of failure falls primarily on the owner and it is for him to maintain the purpose of the project against the interests of the other parties involved.

It is sometimes claimed that the products of private industry will always be more expensive than those from public industry because the owner's profit is an extra cost. In practice, non-profit making organizations have no particular reputation for cheapness, and there can be heavy cost overruns in capital projects when an owner's influence is undermined or non-existent. For example, a local authority could purchase land for reasons of political policy, keep it during a public consultation exercise, and then develop it using its own direct labour organization. Although the asset would be passed between its various departments at carrying cost with no profit made, the result could be some very expensive council flats.

Banks acting as issuing houses, lenders and financial advisers to capital projects act partly as suppliers to the project, with the usual supplier's interest in it going ahead, particularly in the earning of front-end management and commitment fees. But as lenders or, most of all, subscribers to equity issues, their interest moves much closer to the owner's as their return will depend on the proposals proving to be a financial success. They are thus one of the most disinterested sources of advice available to a company considering a capital project, and usually they consider financial advice as part of their service in providing or finding the money.

Competition between banks, and their sales efforts, reduce this effect. Ideally, a bank's enthusiasm for making new loans should be balanced by its anxiety for their security. There is never an absolute point at which a company becomes over-borrowed, but as its borrowing increases it becomes more and more vulnerable to default or to being forced into an act of insolvency by some unexpected adversity. The only sign a company may get that it is venturing into dangerous ground is its bank's increasing hesitation to make new loans. If a company shops around too much for its borrowing, its bankers may get carried away by competition into over-lending, against their better judgment; they may forbear from giving salutary but unwelcome advice about over-borrowing for fear of losing a client; and no one banker may know the extent of a company's borrowing or feel much responsibility for its financial health.

An owner with a project in mind should therefore make a firm decision between his competing bankers if he wishes to appoint one as financial adviser. At an early stage he should compare his banks' costs and services, choose one of them and then normally stick to it. The constant threat of replacement may keep the bankers on their mettle, but it will also keep their own position in the front of their minds, and not get the best from them as partners in the promotion of the successful project. Appointing joint advisers is usually a mistake; it is more expensive, reduces the coherence of the advice and the bank's responsibility for it, and increases the proportion of sales talk in the advice given.

PREPARING DATA

The reasons why a corporation decides to embark on a project are usually not quite the same as the qualities which make it financeable. A private sector company will often start from a market opportunity — sometimes an approach from potential users or a possible new product thrown up by improvements in manufacturing techniques. A public corporation may start from changing demand for a statutory responsibility or from the needs of public policy. By deciding to consider the project in detail the owner will have judged that it is probably financially worthwhile, but considerable work may be necessary to translate this into terms which will be relevant to lenders and investors.

Small firms frequently complain of the difficulties of raising money for their own small investment projects, despite the large number of venture capital houses and the banks' alleged willingness to provide loans for business development. A profitable established company usually has no difficulties under this heading because its ordinary capital expenditure can be supported by its existing activity. However, a very large project may be too large for this activity, may need to be justified to its financiers on its own merits, and the company may come across similar problems to those of a small firm but on a larger scale. Despite appearances, banks and investing institutions are keen to support new projects; they can understand risks and long-term returns and need not be put off by initial losses, so long as a project can be shown to be properly profitable in the end and is sensibly capitalized.

The question put by investors and banks will usually come back to the return offered on risk capital, the cover for commitments to loans and other fixed outgoings, and the relevant skills and reputation of the management involved. The financial adviser will expect to cover this ground in some detail and to understand the economics of the project as follows:

(1) expected volume and pricing of the products or output in relation to any existing market and to the present prices of competitive products;
(2) the components of operating costs — supplies, staffing, subcontracting and overheads — any special exposures to commodity prices or important supply contracts;
(3) exposure to market entry by competitors and the vulnerability of prices once capital expenditure is committed;

(4) expected running-in time before full output is achieved;
(5) the contracts making up capital costs with currencies, payment terms, price escalation and any special credits;
(6) working capital requirements and how they build up;
(7) the management involved and its qualifications and previous experience.

The volatility of sales, profit and capital costs is almost as important as their expected values, and it is valuable to calculate the effect of, say, sales falling short by 10% or the construction period overrunning by one year. Most important of all is to bring out the assumptions taken in any projections and to compare the values with recent actual experience. This comparison with actuals goes for overall results of a project as well; investors and lenders will certainly compare the expected return from a new project with what has been achieved in comparable projects elsewhere, if any such exist, and will discount forecasts which seem too high by such comparisons. If apparent comparisons are not really valid it is worth taking the initiative in explaining the differences. The other major area of explanation should be the legal and contractual framework of a project. This will cover not only the ordinary suppliers, users and capital expenditure contracts, but can also involve:

(1) guarantees and warranties received from capital equipment;
(2) product liability;
(3) price regulation or control;
(4) patents and royalties payable;
(5) special terms of leases or concessions;
(6) profit sharing and other employee agreements.

In its final structure a project may involve several different companies, perhaps to act in different countries, to hold the assets and to act as managers or to obtain tax advantages. Initially, however, the project should be presented as a whole, starting from the market demand for the end product and working the return back to the overall capital requirements. For example, a dock installation may be built for lease to a port authority, and it would be tempting to look no further than the rent negotiated. However, unless the owner could see convincing demand for its use, he would become vulnerable to gaps in the lease contract, to poor reviews or even to requests to renegotiate. This is commonplace with property companies, who define a good asset as much in terms of suitability and alternative demand as in the covenant of the existing tenant.

In the early stage of seeking advice it is not necessary to work out the return beyond the level of operating profits and depreciation. Interest, loan repayments and tax charges can unduly complicate a presentation and will be subject to endless variation with different assumptions about capital structure. The first principle is to establish the operating return; if it is adequate, the financing will be worked out later as a secondary exercise and the advisers will expect to do so as part of their service. Special supplier credits, grants or tax concessions are an exception to this.

COMMON FACTORS

The financing of projects is somewhat different from the other purposes for which money is raised: working capital, acquisitions, or to fund losses. One advantage is that the borrower will have worked out his requirements in detail, probably with clearly set out estimates of capital expenditure and timed cash flows. Such an overall plan provides a better start for a money-raising exercise than the ebbs and flows of a large group's working capital requirements. The borrower is also more likely to have shown the overall picture to one lender or financial adviser rather than raise facilities here and there as he goes along.

Another advantage is that the working of a project as it proceeds encourages lenders and shareholders with a feeling of participation, even if progress is not as good as originally planned. Loans for the purchase of ships often provide for the ship's earnings and outgoings to pass through a special earnings account. The account is charged as security for the loan, and the balance should build up if the ship trades profitably to meet interest and repayments. This encourages the lender, even if unexpectedly poor trading means that loan servicing has to be stretched or deferred; he is kept informed automatically of up-to-date trading results and can be confident that, if profits are made, they will be available to meet any backlog.

A company involved in a project and funding it with borrowing may find this borrowing becoming large in relation to its overall resources. Even though such project lending may have full recourse to its total assets, the matching of this borrowing to the project gives some comfort to other general-purpose lenders and increases the level of borrowing which can be considered reasonably safe. For example, supplier credits to exporters under official schemes are usually ignored in overall borrowing calculations, even though there is recourse to the borrower when the export credit insurance does not apply. Special lending to finance valuable stocks, of copper or whisky, for instance, partly falls into the same pattern.

This matching can prove an illusion, particularly for capital projects, when the assets involved can be specialized and have little real security value. The other aspects of lending for projects also have corresponding disadvantages. It is rare for any project to proceed exactly on schedule, and a perfectly reasonable time lag or cost overrun may unduly alarm project lenders, even though it can be catered for within the resources of the project as a whole. Many projects also require a longer payback period than fits comfortably into bank lending. Although the corporate bond market can sometimes be tapped to allow some matching of a project's funding, it is usually available only to the very best covenants, and the repayment period is often shorter than a project's payback period.

PROJECT FINANCE: GOOD AND BAD

In ordinary corporate financing, whether for a project or for other purposes, the borrower undertakes to service and repay the loan unconditionally, without reference to the success or otherwise of its particular purpose, and all the borrower's assets are in theory available to help towards repayments. This does not apply to project finance in its specialized financial sense. Only the project itself is available to support the financing, and lenders must look for repayments to flows of income from the project and the intrinsic value of the assets involved. The same effect can apply to equity investment. Normally a company raising equity capital will offer its own ordinary shares, which will participate in its profits from all sources. An equity project financing would offer an interest in a specialized subsidiary company whose results would entirely depend on the project in hand. The same approach could be used for a joint project with several sponsors or parents.

All loans must have borrowers who promise to repay them, but for project financings the borrowers are usually dummy companies with no other assets than those involved with the project. Occasionally the same effect is achieved by restrictions in the loan agreements waiving the right to repayment other than out of certain restricted assets or income.

The best reason for this approach is that a project is too big for the strength of its promoters or participants and the amounts involved would therefore swamp their balance sheets or market capitalizations. If so, their present interests may become partly irrelevant and the lenders or shareholders will have no choice but to look to the project itself for their return. The same reasons can apply to a smaller project if its promoter has a weak covenant so that the project is again out of proportion on a smaller scale. Here the promoter has the alternative of finding a larger company which can fund the proposal out of its own resources; although this involves loss of control it can sometimes prove the better alternative. The reason is that many projects are better developed within a large organization:

(1) immediate use can be made of accelerated tax allowances;
(2) losses in the early years can be absorbed;
(3) there may be long lead times before any return is generated, and most external financing caters for this rather uneasily;
(4) a large company may have the spare manpower and physical resources for the project in the early years.

When several different interested parties are involved, the various risks of a project can be separated out and covered by appropriate trading agreements. This is how the Channel link is being financed by Eurotunnel. The project is too large, and its construction takes too long for the financing to depend on a promoter's covenant. Instead it is owned by project companies and financed without recourse to the promoters or (financially) to the British or French governments. The risks are split up as follows:

(1) the construction consortium accepts certain penalties for time and cost overrun;
(2) part of the revenue, from vehicular traffic, can be estimated with some confidence;

(3) the railways have agreed a minimum level of throughput and thus part of sales is assured;
(4) part of the risk is covered by the stand-by loan facilities and by the subscribed equity capital;
(5) the governments are responsible for road access and provide the necessary statutory background and concessions.

In this way, lenders should be assured of a limit to their outgoings to pay for capital expenditure, and of a stream of income to meet interest and repayments. For Eurotunnel, the limits to the penalties for overruns were set fairly low, and the financing is being renegotiated. Successful financings of this type are, however, relatively rare. If the project is at all complicated there are likely to be too many holes in the logical net by which the repayment of the funding is reasonably assured. Alternatively, the assurances given by some of the participants may have to be so much strengthened that effective guarantees of the whole financing are given.

Lenders may get a good press for it at the time, but project financing always conflicts with their basic preference for a good responsible covenant. In personal lending the best customer is the respectable borrower with the intention of honouring his commitment, even when times are difficult: security is traditionally a secondary matter in corporate lending; the concepts of respectability and honour are not quite the same, but the covenant of a well-established public company, even if unsecured, can have considerable value. In project lending there is always the danger that some unforeseen change in the ownership of one of the companies involved or in the pattern of trade may leave the lenders exposed with no one whose duty it is to repay them. Thus project financing is always more risky, and correspondingly expensive in the margins and commissions of the loans involved, quite apart from the incidental costs.

Sometimes a promoter merely wishes to dissociate himself from a project, rather than being forced to by necessity. A small strongly growing company with aggressive management may be concerned to maintain an unbroken record of profits growth. A large mature company may want to show a strong balance sheet in its published accounts. Such companies may invite their bankers to provide leases of operating assets with short break clauses; or to lend for new projects to an associated company without recourse, or on terms where the recourse is not obvious. In this way a commitment or a project's early losses are kept out of the company's results, and the good record remains unimpaired, at least for a time.

The same devices are used for opposite reasons if a company is getting into difficulties, particularly if it is in danger of a breach of covenant to maintain certain levels of borrowing cover. Such covenants are usually drafted mechanically on the basis of the last audited results. If some of the company's borrowing and the assets it finances can be left out of the consolidation, cover for the remainder will be improved. Lenders should be suspicious of such financings; good quality borrowers should not have to resort to them. But if the company offers attractive fees and its best assets as security the mixture of risk and reward may be better than direct lending to an undoubted company at thin margins.

These types of project financing are much more common than the genuine big project financing, with its risks separated and allocated between its participants. They go beyond the proper matching of resources and assets and the allocation of risk, into the realms of creative accounting. Accountants are attempting more forcefully to bring such commitments back into their promoters' balance sheets, for example through the proposals for 'controlled non-subsidiaries' in Exposure Draft 42 of the Accounting Standards Committee: Accounting for special purpose transactions. But the inventiveness of finance directors seems likely to stay ahead of accounting standards, particularly when the occasional genuine project financing creates precedents for the counterfeit.

PROJECT FINANCE WITH PUBLIC BODIES

Governments often become involved in project financing for rather different reasons, apart from the obvious point that very big projects will often be promoted by governments or need government involvement to become possible at all. Direct government involvement in a project may bring many unwished-for side-effects:

(1) too easy credit on the back of an implied government guarantee;
(2) pressures from employees for public sector terms of service;
(3) government responsibility for, or exposure to, day-to-day aspects of the project's management.

If government participation is not part of its policy but merely arises as a byproduct of investment incentives, these effects can be minimized by limiting the government's support in the ways described above. Otherwise the wish for project lending not to qualify as public sector borrowing is very similar to a company's wish to keep project lending from being consolidated.

Government can create opportunities for project finance by cultivating private involvement in infrastructure projects. This has been British government policy for some time, and was confirmed in the Green Paper: *New Road by New Means*; but the transactions achieved so far have been few. The time required to negotiate a complicated contract with a government department makes it likely that someone will change their mind, or the financial markets will change, during the process. Also, government support for a project through Parliament or the planning procedures can very easily expand into general support, and therefore an implied financial guarantee. To guard against this, government has to seem very unforthcoming and meticulous in its contractual requirements.

The prospects for successful joint deals between the public and private sectors have undoubtedly been damaged by a number of recent examples where governments have repudiated the borrowings or commitments of subsidiaries which had apparently been entitled to government support — Irish Shipping, the International Tin Council, Kongsburg Vaapenfabrikk and MMC Metals, for instance. After these examples there may be little margin between the minimum government support required by private participators and the maximum beyond which government considers it has guaranteed a project.

SOURCES OF FUNDS

Even the largest banks and investment institutions have a quite small capacity for new, imaginative instruments; they have their own auditors and regulatory authorities, who usually discount loans and securities which do not conform to standard patterns. Quite apart from this, a bank will wish to maintain a wide spread of interests in its loan portfolio and not use up too much of its fire-power in a single commitment. It follows that a large project, of say $100m or more, should be funded through simple securities which can be marketed — and explained — to large numbers of participators. The end result of a financing must be equity or preference capital, or lending in the usual patterns. The development of junior lending, often with options or conversion rights, has been a valuable new facility for project financings. It is too soon to judge whether its supply will survive the collapses of management buyouts, for which it is often used. There is scope for considerable variety in the contracts and in the companies involved in the project, using these relatively few different types of building bricks to make up a suitable structure.

Occasionally a project is so big that it exceeds the capacity of the market. If a big issue is a sale of an existing holding, such as a privatization issue, it can be broken into several issues without damaging the company concerned. Even so, the issues should be well spaced, or the first can be blighted if investors become convinced that the second will provide an opportunity to invest more cheaply later on. This is why partial sales often contain assurances that the vendor has no intention of selling his remaining holding. If the money is raised for a new project it is essential that the whole sum required is committed at once. Sometimes this can be achieved by issuing partly-paid shares; sometimes by tapping several markets simultaneously, or combining an equity issue with a banking syndication or a bond issue. Leaving part of the cost uncommitted runs the risk that a deteriorating market or bad early experience would make it impossible to raise it at all later on. It is much easier to fund a big scheme if it can be broken up into manageable phases, each justifying its own capital cost independently.

It seems to be in the nature of project financing to over-gear a project, with too much borrowing and too little equity capital. This may be partly because all projects have projections showing the development of capital expenditure and subsequent profits, and these create an illusion of certainty. Equity capital is also frequently more expensive than lending, both in the rating on which shares can be issued and in the tax treatment of the income to remunerate it. Nevertheless, a proper proportion of equity capital is of the greatest value. Very few projects are so mechanical that their requirements for money can be accurately forecast, even when the source of income is a fixed amount due under a contract. Changes in short-term interest rates, time overruns during the construction period, even the incidence of leap years, can all throw out the forecasts of capital requirements, and a line of risk-bearing equity money to meet these variations can be invaluable for the smooth development of the project. Otherwise management can be distracted from its principal task with the project into negotiating relatively small extra loan facilities, reorganizing security and explaining small overruns to disenchanted lenders.

A proper amount of equity capital also limits the exposure of participants. A project set up on the basis of a £100 company with massive loan facilities will have to rely on its parentage or on specific guarantees for every sort of supply; even the landlord of its offices will ask for parent company guarantees. If the same project had an issued and paid up capital of several hundred thousand pounds its ratings with the credit agencies would be quite different and requests for guarantees would be kept back to really major commitments, which the participants might wish to control anyway. A proper equity capital also encourages the managers of the project, who will feel that they have been entrusted with talents to trade with rather than merely being puppets of the parent companies involved.

There are some special points which arise in setting up the structure and in finding subscribers. The first for project financings is that the industrial companies participating in a project will all have their own bankers, to whom they may well be valued high-quality customers. These banks will provide a natural first port of call in funding a project. They will perhaps be more confident in the project because of their contacts with a participator and their knowledge of his competence. They will also be more vulnerable to pressure if they express scepticism about the strength of their security or of letters of comfort.

In a very big project the right geographic spread of lenders can help to improve the marketing of the debt and also the strength of the security. On the one hand local banks always have an extra interest in participating in a project in their area. If they do so, their participation will encourage others from further afield — banks on the spot may know of possible dangers which are not apparent further away, and it is always suspicious if a funding does not include any local partners. On the other hand, it is useful to have high-quality overseas banks in a syndicate if the project has a major government involvement. Local sources of money may be unable to complain if the project is nationalized, if new taxes are introduced, or if a public participator in a project takes a lenient view of its own obligations. When important foreign banks are involved such an action can become an international incident.

DOCUMENTATION

Legal documentation has been one of the major growth areas of the last twenty years and project financing has been one of the particular growth points. As an example of how documents can multiply, the following is a list of the thirty different documents required for a recent ship financing.

Summary of the transaction: at the request of the guarantor the owner orders a ship from the builder and enters into a long-term bareboat charter with the charterer; the charterer supervises the building; the owner arranges for the financing.

(1) Building contract between the builder and the owner.
(2) Supervision agreement between the owner and the charter.
(3) Charter party between the owner and the charterer.
(4) Temporary indemnity between the guarantor and the owner (pending completion of the financing).
(5) Agreement between the owner and the charterer covering lapsing of the charter if the financing is not completed.
(6) Acknowledgement by the builder of the appointment of the charterer as supervisor.
(7) Agreement between owner and charterer on payment of supervision fee.
(8) Certificate of incumbency of officers of charterer.
(9) Power of attorney granted by charterer.
(10) Authorities from charterer.
(11) First addendum to building contract between the owner and builder.
(12) Provision for settlement of extra reserve asset costs between owner and charterer.
(13) Loan agreement between owner and bankers for concessionary building loan.
(14) Bond and assignation in security.
(15) Delivery order.
(16) Deed of assignment of charter party.
(17) Notice of assignment of guarantee.
(18) Deed of assignment of guarantee.
(19) Notice of assignment of guarantee.
[(14) to (19) are security documents for the concessionary loan.]
(20) Shipowner's agreement.
(21) Commercial loan agreement between owner and bankers (to provide the remainder of the money).
(22) Bond and assignation in security.
(23) Construction security deed.
(24) Deed of assignment of guarantee.
(25) Notice of assignment of guarantee.
[(22) to (25) are security documents for the commercial loan.]
(26) Guarantee between owner and guarantor.
(27) Certificate of authority of guarantor.
(28) Deed regulating priorities (between the two sets of security).
(29) Letter of intimation between the two sets of bankers.
(30) Letter of undertaking to bankers on insurance arrangements.

There are several reasons for the way in which paperwork has got out of hand. One is that word processing has made it too easy for commercial lawyers to handle long documents. Each time an old agreement goes wrong, they can now simply draft a new clause to cover the point and add it to their standard. Another cause is the instinct for secrecy, whereby none of the parties to a project are supposed to see any details which do not actually concern them directly. Instead of one agreement with five parties, therefore, there will be five or six agreements between sets of two or three parties out of the five, and then other parties indirectly involved will have to have formal notice of the agreements in their turn. All this can make a bible of documents in which the same text can appear five or six times, once substantively and otherwise as an appendix to other agreements.

Even for a simple project, therefore, it is quite possible for the documents to get out of hand and get past the comprehension even of those whose concept the project was. The result is certainly not any greater effectiveness when it comes to exercising one's rights but merely an obscuring of what those rights are supposed to be. It is commonplace when something has gone wrong to trace back through a bulky loan document or subscription agreement and find that the agreement is quite silent on the point in hand. Even if the point is covered, loopholes are likely to become more numerous as a document gets longer; a short and simple agreement is much more likely to be effective if it ever goes to court. In the long run the variety of events which can happen in the real world is infinitely greater than the number of legal agreements, which are finite sequences of a finite number of characters, and the attempt to cover every contingency is bound to end in failure.

If a project is at all complicated it is therefore most important to keep the documentation under strict control, even though there will be every temptation for it to get out of hand. One of the greatest safeguards is to insist that no money is advanced, no orders given to suppliers and no commitment undertaken until all of the documents are completed in every respect. This means that the wish to get started will cut short discussions of niceties which could otherwise continue interminably.

D. C. CROSS

Hambros Bank Ltd

3.2
Sources of trade finance and their costs

INTRODUCTION

The sources of international trade finance are as varied as the requirements of those exporters and importers who seek such finance. International trading may be categorized into three types in respect of the period that finance is required; sources may also be categorized into the availability of finance — up to two years (short-term) up to five years (medium-term) and over five years (long-term).

In the following overview of the services of the financial organizations that provide all types of finance for exporters and importers, particular reference is made to the base on which costs are calculated and to the form of security that may be sought for the degree of finance provided. Throughout this chapter the particular customs of any one financial centre or country are not examined in depth except where, for the purpose of illustration, a full example is given. Specific mention however is made of such international trading documents as bills of exchange, promissory notes, invoices and shipping, air freight, post and trucking documents, which either singly or together form and are accepted universally as documents of title and confirmation of debts owed or to be received.

For international trade in general, standardization of such documentation has and continues to take place. Similarly, guidelines to which most trading nations adhere have been drawn up by the International Chamber of Commerce to bring about uniformity of customs in the issue and, for example, use of documentary credits, collections and contract guarantees. As it is not proposed to reproduce the detail of these publications here, their content is strongly recommended to the reader as are the rules and regulations of governmental and other export credit schemes.

Mention should also be made of foreign exchange and the benefits and risks that can occur through financing trade internationally by the use of foreign currencies. Many countries have stringent exchange control regulations which it is not feasible to list here, but which limit or prohibit the use of other currencies by their nationals. All international traders are therefore advised to make the fullest enquiries as to the effect such regulations could have on their trading activities, and especially on their cash flow position should the settlement of debts be unduly delayed by the non-release of foreign exchange abroad. To the question of exchange control regulations must be added the problems that may surround the charging of interest, and its remittability, in respect of exports to certain countries and the various taxes that may be levied and withheld from allowable interest. Examples illustrating these points are given in the text that follows; but it should be remembered that countries often change their controls and regulations without warning so that frequent enquiry on these points is of the essence.

SOURCES

The principle sources of international trade finance are:

(1) banks;
(2) factoring and forfaiting;
(3) discount and money markets;
(4) leasing and hire purchase.

The method of finance chosen will depend in the main on:

(1) the trading record between exporter and importer;
(2) the degree of trust the exporter has in the importer;
(3) the amount of the transaction and the period for which finance is required;
(4) the import and export and exchange control regulations of the respective countries;
(5) whether government assistance is available;
(6) the customs of the trade.

Those engaged in international trade may be simultaneously exporters and importers; in order to examine the total financial facilities available the following discussion is divided into two parts: firstly facilities available to exporters; secondly, those available to importers. As a conclusion reference is made to merchanting (or third country trade) which involves many of the aspects of both exporting and importing.

TRADE FINANCE FOR EXPORTERS

The following are the principal financial facilities usually available to exporters. They take account of the time factor, amount, currency, security for monies borrowed, trust between the parties involved and costs.

(1) From banks:
  (a) overdrafts and loans, unsecured and secured;

  - (b) negotiation of outward collections;
  - (c) documentary letters of credit;
  - (d) acceptance and discount;
  - (e) governmental export credit schemes.

(2) From banks and other financial institutions:
  - (a) factoring;
  - (b) forfaiting;
  - (c) leasing and hire purchase;

(3) Confirming and export houses.

(4) Foreign currency and eurocurrency finance.

OVERDRAFTS AND LOANS, UNSECURED AND SECURED

All lending banks will normally raise the question of security. For international trading transactions the most readily available, and normally the most acceptable, form of security would be the documents of title to the goods, which provide evidence that shipment has taken place, rather than the goods themselves. Modern transportation methods have to an extent imposed certain limitations on this maxim in that the movement of goods by rail, air or road does not generally involve the issue of document of title but evidence that goods have been consigned to, or to the order of, a bank abroad will usually be acceptable security. Similarly, short sea journeys often make the submission to the exporter's bank of the bill of lading as a document of title impractical but, if the release of the underlying goods at their destination is subject to bank control there, the exporter should be able to obtain the required finance. Here it is pertinent to mention that — before exporters decide to supply goods (and banks agree to lend) against trade documents to be drawn on a potential importer — it is imperative that the fullest enquiries are made as to the importer's ability to pay, in a reasonable time, for the goods ordered. Banks will normally undertake to perform this task on behalf of exporters (and will in any case make the fullest enquiries for their own satisfaction) but it is to be recorded that until a sound relationship has been established bankers will, in the event of default by an importer, look first to the exporter and any credit insurance that has been assigned.

Similarly, all parties engaged in international trade should be permanently on guard against fraudulent or forged documents, bills of lading, orders for goods, letters of credit and others. It is also not uncommon for favourable drawee status reports to have been issued fraudulently overseas. One safeguard against such happenings continues to be the employment of a well-established, energetic and reliable agent in the importer's centre, especially if the area or country has already gained a certain reputation. Collecting banks in such areas may not be prompt in advising an exporter's bank of serious problems so that drawees could vanish, goods arrive before documents of title and further instructions be necessary, all of which will go unheeded. The resultant non-payment for imports could cause serious loss to an exporter.

UNSECURED OVERDRAFTS

To obtain an unsecured overdraft of a significant amount an exporter will need to be of substance and backed by records of favourable trading. Normally facilities of this nature will be required and granted for working capital needs. It is not a method encouraged by banks for the financing of international trade as it is often difficult for a bank, and an exporter, to differentiate between working capital needs and trading finance requirements. Where, however, an exporter's international operations are covered by export credit insurance an approach for unsecured facilities is likely to be more favourably received.

SECURED OVERDRAFTS

Apart from any other form of security normally associated with borrowing money from a bank, documents relating to the export of goods can be offered as security in the following manner.

(1) By means of documentary collections whereby the documents are sent by the exporter's bank to a bank in the importer's country for presentation on an acceptance or payment basis. In such cases the exporter's bank will expect the face value of the documents that form their security to be in excess of any overdraft granted. They will also look to all collections being in support of a current trading position with a fluctuating turnover. Where documents are to be released to importers against payment only, the bank will wish to maintain control of the documents of title and to have the express authority of the exporter to enable it to take possession of and dispose of the goods should a default in payment by the importer or non-recovery of overdrafts to the exporter occur.

Where documents (and thereby, in practice, the goods also) are to be released against acceptance for later payment, the exporter's bank will require full recourse to the exporter to cover possible default and a full knowledge of the financial viability of the importer (the drawee where bills of exchange are being used to support the export). Here the general attitude of banks to drawees is worthy of note and further explanation. When scrutinising export bills a bank will look, in an ideal situation, for a spread of activity with no particular concentration on any one importer as to amount, time given by the exporter to the importer for payment, or type of merchandise. The principal reason for seeking what is termed well-spread bills by banks is the question of non-payment. Many exporters seek trade finance in support of cash flow and, as in theory overdrafts are repayable on demand, a succession of unpaid bills could find a bank reluctant to continue an overdraft line supported by such security. Export insurance and, in particular insurance credit risk, is covered elsewhere in this volume, but mention here is relevant as even claims under government schemes take time to settle.

(2) Documents may also be sent to the importer direct by the exporter. Usually termed open account trading, this method is normally used between trading

partners in countries of close proximity which have few, if any, export, import or exchange control regulations. The offering of evidence of an established trading pattern under such a method could induce banks to make available finance by way of overdraft, any approach being enhanced if export credit insurance is held. It should be remembered, however, that where stringent export, import or exchange controls do exist it is often not possible to consider the financing of international trade in this manner.

From a cost point of view overdrafts can be a relatively inexpensive form of borrowing as the amount drawn down should not exceed that which is required. Major (medium- or long-term) borrowings are normally arranged for specific purposes on specific conditions so that overdrafts could be termed marginal borrowing.

This having been said, unsecured overdrafts usually attract a higher rate of interest than those that are secured, though both will be geared to base rate or the cost of funds to the bank on a fluctuating basis plus a lending margin. When documents for collection are handled additional charges are levied and exchange costs will be incurred in respect of foreign currency transactions. For all forms of overdraft an arrangement fee may be payable to the bank for setting up the facility and, if this is substantial in relation to turnover, it could be decisive when computing overall costs.

LOANS

Normally bankers expect that overdrawn accounts will show fully fluctuating balances on regular turnover. However, there are often cases where the nature of the exports or the payment characteristics of the importing country demand that finance for a set period is raised. Here, and providing the drawee risk is acceptable, a loan for a definitive time would be more appropriate. Bankers would expect to judge each case on its merits, the more so the longer the period of the loan sought and the possible delays in obtaining eventual payment from the importing country. The cost of such finance would normally be either aligned to the cost of funds to the lending banker on a fixed or fluctuating basis or to base rate plus a lending margin.

Such margins in turn vary with the risk insurance and other security held and the past general pattern of payments by the importing country. Loans are usually granted either on a fixed interest basis or a floating (fluctuating) rate basis. For the former, a loan is fixed for a definite period and at an agreed rate. Any changes in market rate do not affect such arrangements once concluded. On a floating rate basis the rate changes as market rates change. However, for both types once the agreed period of a loan has expired the borrower normally has the option, if repayment cannot be made immediately, of continuing for a further period at a fixed rate or of rolling the loan on — either for short periods or on a daily basis until repayment is made. In either case the extension of loans incurs additional charges by way of interest that can fluctuate considerably over what was originally allowed for in a trading transaction.

In the event of loans falling due for which no extensions are possible and export bills which support such advances remaining unpaid, serious effects on cash flow and profitability can occur.

NEGOTIATION OF BILLS OF EXCHANGE OR INVOICES

By the word negotiation is meant the financing by a bank of export documents (including bills of exchange and documents of title as appropriate) or funding the payee of a cheque or draft drawn and payable abroad. When a bank negotiates it is buying an exporter's shipping documents at the time such documents are sent abroad for payment. The result is that the exporter receives payment against the bank, looking to the overseas buyer for repayment, normally on the understanding that the transaction is with recourse to the exporter in the event of a default. In considering such finance a bank would be concerned with the following:

(1) The ability of the exporter to repay monies against an unpaid bill or documents when it is necessary for a bank to exercise its right of recourse. To this end, wherever possible, bankers will seek a general form of irrevocable authorization enabling them to dispose of goods and retain the sale proceeds, but without prejudice to any rights against an unpaid bill of exchange (where these are in use).
(2) The period that has been allowed to the importer before payment is due.
(3) The security in the goods. Where documents are to be released to an importer against acceptance and an undertaking to pay at a future date, a banker will be concerned not only with the financial standing of the exporter but equally with that of the importer and all export, import and exchange control regulations in force.
(4) Is export, import and insurance held, and is an assignment to the bank possible? Here the banker will be aware that where finance is to be granted to an exporter against an assignment, the bank's rights and benefits become no more than the rights and benefits of the exporter.

Where finance is sought on a non-recourse basis the lending banker must be totally concerned with the financial standing of the drawee and the benefits of any assigned export credit guarantees. Such arrangements are ideal in many ways as finance can be raised by an exporter without liability or contingent liability being reflected in the books of the exporter. Costs, by the very nature of the transaction, would normally exceed those for finance with recourse.

The costs of raising negotiation finance with recourse would be governed by the period for which it is required and are, therefore, normally related to base rate or the cost of funds on a fixed or fluctuating basis to the lender, plus margins as appropriate. The cost to the exporter depends largely upon the prior financial arrangements that have been made with the importer and, in particular, if those arrangements allow bills of exchange to be claused at not less than the interest charged by the lending bank. For interest in general most bills of exchange drawn are claused. For example, in the United Kingdom exporters rarely draw trade bills of exchange without interest payable by overseas buyers. However, as an example of bills without an interest clause, exporters to, say, the United Kingdom may by trade custom draw an unclaused bill in sterling which their bankers will negotiate at the current sterling bill rate for the particular usance. Such rates are normally laid down by the central bank or by the local association of banks and are usually calculated on the spot rate in London, plus interest at a margin above the fine trade bill rate in London for the usance of the bill, plus transit time to the United Kingdom, local stamp duty and bank charges. It is therefore the rate of exchange that embraces all factors.

If the bill or documents are promptly paid and proceeds plus full interest can be freely remitted immediately, the interest cost to the exporter should be nil or negligible. It is essential that prior agreement has been reached between the exporter regarding liability for interest, documentation and other charges; in its absence the exporter tends to be the loser while belated agreement is being reached during the period that bank finance is outstanding.

Here, as an example, it is relevant to add that when entering new markets in certain emerging countries exporters should, among other things, fully investigate potential delays and interest shortfalls that may arise from conditions and regulations in the buying country. A lack of immediate foreign exchange availability will often cause central banks to delay the remittance of the proceeds of goods imported, notwithstanding that the importer will have paid the local currency value of the bill on its due date. Even providing that the drawee submits the correct exchange control documentation with an application for foreign currency to be made available on the date of local payment (in other words the proceeds are in the pipeline), the period of delay between that date and the release of the foreign exchange by the importer's central bank is indeterminate and can often increase or decrease without notice.

In order to overcome the problems sometimes posed by exchange rate fluctuations, and where bills of exchange are customarily used, it is often possible to operate the exchange as per endorsement system. These bills are for negotiation by banks which have a subsidiary or branch in the drawee's country. The negotiating bank pays away the face amount of the bill which is drawn in the currency of the domicile of the drawer, calculates the equivalent foreign currency amount due on maturity from the drawees, that is in the latter's local currency, including the negotiation charges and interest due, and endorses these details on the bill of exchange. The drawee is then liable for the local currency amount so endorsed.

Thus the drawer receives and the drawee pays in their respective local currencies, avoiding exchange risk. Should, however, the bill be unaccepted, or unpaid, the negotiating bank has recourse to the drawer in the amount of the currency endorsed.

DOCUMENTARY LETTERS OF CREDIT

Documentary letters of credit are issued in most countries in accordance with guidelines instituted by the International Chamber of Commerce and known as the *Uniform Customs and Practice for Documentary Credits*. One of the effects of this publication has been to encourage the use of standard terminology, and the definitions of the parties to documentary letters of credit — along with their responsibilities and benefits as described in this publication — are recommended for further detailed study as a prerequisite for what follows here.

For the beneficiary (exporter) documentary letters of credit (credits), and especially those that are irrevocable and confirmed, are able to provide a secure method of immediate domestic payment for exports; in some cases they do make provision for preshipment finance. Because credits are used extensively for the payment of goods in general they are normally of a short-term nature. However, where individual country regulations permit, they can be issued for medium-term periods or extended to cover such periods.

By inserting a 'red clause' in a credit a beneficiary is able to receive an advance payment in amounts and on terms as stated in the credit, with which to put together goods (usually specific commodities such as wool, wood, meat) for shipment. When the produce has been shipped the documents called for in the credit are presented to the advising bank (who will also be the bank which made the advance payment) for negotiation. The 'red clause' advance, plus interest and any exchange or other charges as applicable to the beneficiary, is then repaid from the proceeds of the negotiation.

In the case of other credits, their terms will entitle the exporter, provided all terms and conditions are complied with, either to payment at sight or after a stated usance or — if a documentary acceptance credit — to discount the acceptance of the advising bank. An acceptance credit calling for drafts on the advising bank is only practicable if there is an active local bill market in that bank's centre in which their acceptances will attract bank bill rates.

Where a credit calls for drafts on the issuing bank or applicant, drawn at sight, the exporter still receives payment at sight. Where usance drafts are called for, the normal practice is for the credit to contain terms to the effect that the drafts are to be negotiated on a sight basis for account of the beneficiary. This may possibly include interest, but will not always do so. The arrangement enables the exporter (beneficiary) to obtain payment as if the usance drafts were at sight. Should, however, the credit not have been confirmed by the negotiating bank a right of recourse remains against the beneficiary (exporter) until the documents have been taken up by the issuing bank.

Other forms of credits can also assist exporters financially.

Transferable credits. Transferable credits are those that may be passed on by the beneficiary, through the advising bank, to a second beneficiary. This can be of great assistance to those who act on behalf of the ultimate buyer (or importer) but who either do not know who the exporter will be at the time the sales contract is agreed or do not wish the importer to have knowledge of the exporter.

Revolving credits. Revolving credits are credits in which the amount of any drawing, normally within a time span, is reinstated when certain conditions, such as shipment, have been met. Such credits can materially assist the cash flow of exporters provided the basis on which they are to be reinstated is totally clear.

Back-to-back credits. Back-to-back credit is the term used to describe a credit which is issued by a bank on behalf of a customer against the backing of another credit received in favour of the customer. Such credits are of most benefit to those who are not supplying goods but are looking for financial gain by arranging a transaction. Where the actual supplier of the goods requires the comfort of a credit, the customer will seek such a credit against a similar incoming credit already received. The second credit, backed against the first, is normally sought for a lesser amount. This type of credit is often used in those areas of the world with an active entrepôt trade.

Revocable credits. Revocable credits are those which, although issued by banks, do not carry an irrevocable undertaking by the advising bank to pay. Such credits may be cancelled (or amended) at any time up to the point where the advising bank has negotiated, paid or accepted documents. They therefore do not provide the same degree of financial security to an exporter as an irrevocable credit.

When credits are used, exporters (beneficiaries) will be charged an advising and confirmation (where applicable) commission by the advising bank and will also be charged for the negotiation or acceptance of documents presented in terms of the credit, unless the credit states that all charges are for account of the applicant. Where usance bills are called for interest is also payable in accordance with the terms of the credit, but exporters will need to pay particular attention to exchange risks where credits in their favour are expressed in foreign currency.

Stand-by credits. Stand-by credits are by nature similar to a guarantee covering a specific contingency or a default by an applicant in performance of this commitment. The credit will therefore only be drawn or claimed on by a beneficiary in the event of such contingency or default occurring. This type of credit is perhaps more commonly used by banks in some areas where local laws prevent them issuing a guarantee. An example of this can be found in the United States where banks which require to guarantee overdrafts of United States residents in other countries need to use stand-by credits. In relation to foreign trading transactions, an exporter who makes frequent shipments to a particular buyer for settlement by, say, open account may call for a documentary stand-by credit in his favour; he can draw on this should the buyer default at any time.

Acceptance and discount facilities

A normal documentary export bill of exchange is sent on a collection basis — exporter on importer — with a second clean bill being drawn by the exporter on the exporter's bank or through an acceptance house in those centres where such organizations exist, at a usance expected to coincide with the date the remittance in settlement of the commercial bill is due to be received. A bank will accept the second bill in order to ensure that the bill is discountable. If the exporter's bank then discounts the bill it becomes the lending banker as well, though the exporter may well wish to use another vehicle for discounting bank accepted paper. In any event, at the maturity of the discounted bill the exporter will need to ensure that the commercial export bill has been paid and the proceeds received to meet the maturing discount. Here it is necessary to emphasize the necessity of dealing only with sound drawees (importers) who are domiciled in countries without complex exchange control regulations which could delay the remittance of import payments. Acceptance and discount charges are payable to provide finance by this method, together with collection charges on the documentary export bills. Exchange rate fluctuations must be guarded against where foreign currencies are used.

In most important finance centres of the world there is a discount market (normally comprising discount houses) which deals in the prime short-term money market, government and commercial bills, short-dated stock and certificates of deposit. Trading usually takes place with central banks, commercial and merchant banks, and commercial, industrial and insurance companies. This affords the opportunity for banks to rediscount trade bills, other banks' bills or their own acceptances. Likewise, banks purchase bills from the discount market and it is the nature of the type of bill that, first, determines the rate at which it is purchased from sellers, including exporters, and, second, determines its standing in money markets in general.
Here, taking the London money market as an example, there are four main categories of bills:

(1) eligible bills, those bills accepted by specified banks which, therefore, command the finest bank bill rates;
(2) ineligible bills, being those bills accepted by other banks and attracting a slightly higher rate;
(3) fine trade bills, which require the acceptors to be first class company names and enjoy fine rates; and
(4) trade bills, which support general trading and attract normal market interest or discount rates.

GOVERNMENT ASSISTANCE TO EXPORTERS

The type of assistance will vary from country to country, but usually takes the form of credit insurance, preferential interest rates, additional lines of lending or a combination of these.

Credit insurance. Internationally this is the most common method. Sellers may consider that exporting to a particular country carries greater risk than is considered reasonable, usually because of political or economic instability. Where the government of the exporter's country wishes to encourage exports it may, for a fee, underwrite such risks. Therefore — should the importer default for reasons beyond control — the exporter will be reimbursed through the governmental credit insurance scheme. Such schemes often cover simple default as well and benefits thereunder are usually assignable, providing lending banks with additional security or forms of comfort. Transactions usually covered range from exports of consumables and durables to light and heavy capital goods where payment terms range from sight to five years and beyond. In certain countries government schemes will assist foreign buyers to raise finance (buyer credits) to purchase the exports of that government's country, and often such credit insurance schemes are offered by private insurance companies alongside those of their governments.

Preferential interest rates. Either separately or in combination with credit insurance, governments may institute schemes whereby exports are encouraged by ensuring that approved borrowers receive preferential interest rates to finance their exports. This may be achieved by the central bank lending to the commercial banks the necessary funds at subsidized rates, by (occasionally) a national export bank being set up for the purpose, or by the commercial banks' lending being underwritten by a government credit insurance department enabling the banks to lend at a lower rate due to the lessened risk.

Additional lending lines. In countries where credit is short, either through government controls or for economic reasons, lending lines in respect of exports may be given priority as government policy.

FACTORING

This is a method of finance arranged not only by some banks but also, and in many countries more commonly, by finance houses.

For both types of lenders however it is normal to agree to purchase, without recourse, either sets of documents covering the export of goods, or book debts covering the shipment of goods where the importer (or buyer) is known to be of acceptable financial standing and the operations are of an established and continuing nature. Provided the export documents are in order and the requirements (often rigorous) of the lenders are met, the exporter receives immediate unencumbered funds. Recourse to the exporter is often available, though, should the goods be of sub-standard quality or if political or economic factors make payment by the importer impossible.

As the main benefit to an exporter is a reduction in administrative and collection cost and the elimination of bad debts and the need for credit insurance, the lender's interest in the transaction (as the owner of the debt) is normally disclosed to the importer. However, where this is not acceptable, undisclosed non-recourse finance is sometimes available. By this method the exporter sells to the lender but remains as agent for the delivery of the goods and subsequent collection of payment overseas. As above, recourse to the exporter is held in respect of quality.

Costs will depend on the nature of the debts purchased and, in particular, on the country risk of the importer; they are usually calculated as a discount of the debt either to the full face value or to a percentage leaving a margin which, when the debt is fully recovered, will be subsequently paid to the exporter. Exchange risks to the exporter are normally eliminated as debts are purchased for local currency. Factoring is used most frequently to provide finance of a short-term nature.

FORFAITING

Where exporters wish to assist buyers of their goods — normally items of a capital nature — by arranging finance up to and including the long term, but without recourse to the exporter(manufacturer), forfaiting is often the most viable system.

Buyers (importers) will need to signify their indebtedness to the exporter either by promissory notes, bills of exchange or book debts; all of these are normally required to be avalised, that is guaranteed by a third, acceptable party, usually a bank. These future undertakings, often spread over a period, may then be offered by an exporter or manufacturer to a bank or finance house for negotiation, without recourse. In purchasing such guaranteed debts the financial organization assumes complete responsibility, including that of country risk.

Rates of interest in forfaiting are on a fixed basis, affording the exporter definitive unencumbered funds without question for future adjustment claims. Once finance is provided the exporter no longer has to account for such items as receivables or carry a contingent or any other form of liability. All risks from the exporter's viewpoint have been eliminated though, by the nature of non-recourse finance, searching enquiry may have been made into the underlying transaction both by the avalising and the forfaiting financial organization. An arrangement, commitment or other form of fee is payable for setting up such finance which for a manufacturer has definite advantages in respect of cash flow and forward projections.

LEASING AND HIRE PURCHASE

Brief mention is made here of the use that both leasing and hire purchase companies can be to exporters, in that they are often able to provide importers with finance and thereby ensure good payment to exporters. Banks generally have taken a financial interest in such organizations, though it should be emphasized that it is normally a combination of the financial standing of the importer, the nature of the goods and the taxation and depreciation positions of the financial organizations providing the finance that govern viability. In practice it is often usual for an exporter to approach a bank to set the wheels in motion for financial arrangements to be raised for an importer.

CONFIRMING AND EXPORT HOUSES

Confirming houses provide a source of finance for exporters and importers alike. Their function is to act as an intermediary between seller and buyer, confirming to the exporter that payment will be made and to the importer that delivery will be effected in accordance with the underlying contract. Confirming houses are normally known and trusted names to both parties to a transaction and, by adding their confirmation, eliminate much of the risk element inherent in open account trading.

In becoming a party to a trading transaction the confirming house guarantees that payment will be made to the exporter and can, if required, provide immediate payment against shipping documents. For the importer short-term credit (normally up to 180 days) is available to allow goods to be sold and import bills met. In such a manner any cash flow problems of both exporters and importers are eased.

The use of confirming houses provides an alternative (though not always a more expensive) source of finance for international traders when perhaps existing bank credit lines are fully utilized. They also enable exporters to quote cash prices to end buyers which might not otherwise be possible if the exporter needed to extend credit to achieve a sale.

Export houses also carry out the same functions as a confirming house but can act simply as an agent for the exporter, or indeed as an export trader.

FOREIGN CURRENCY FINANCE

For all forms of foreign trade finance an exporter may have an opportunity to contain costs by the judicious use of foreign currencies. Subject to any exchange control regulations extant in an exporter's country, borrowings could be in either the national currency, the currency of the importer (buyer) or a third foreign currency where available.

The major currencies of the world are normally available in most financial centres at varying interest rates. In international trade it is preferable to borrow in the currency in which eventual payment for exports is to be received, thus avoiding any exchange risk on the transference of funds. Should, however, an exporter wish to borrow in an alternative currency because it is cheaper in interest terms, it must be recognized that an exchange risk is being taken when it comes to translating export proceeds into the currency borrowed. A change in foreign exchange rates could not only readily absorb the interest differential but also eat into the trading profit of the exporter. Here insurance can be taken out by covering forward (buying for future delivery in the currency borrowed), but the cost of this exercise often equals the difference in interest rates and still leaves the export proceeds (should they be in a currency other than the national currency of the exporter) to bear the cost of translating them into the national currency of the exporter.

A recent development of the foreign exchange market has been the introduction of Foreign Exchange currency options. Currency options which are available for major currencies, first appeared in London in the mid-1980s with increasing use now being made of these instruments. Options permit customers and counterparts to buy and sell the right to exchange one currency for another without putting them under any obligation to do so. A currency option is like an insurance policy in that the option buyer pays a single premium in return for receiving certain rights. Whereas the foreign exchange forward contract (covering forward) requires the customer to deliver on or between specified dates an agreed amount of currency sold by him and receive an agreed amount of a different currency, the currency option is a means of hedging against currency movements. Since there is no obligation to exercise the option, the buyer is able to take advantage of favourable movements in the price of the underlying currencies; his loss, should such movements prove adverse, is restricted to the premium paid. Currency options are usually currently dealt in units of £100,000 sterling or equivalent for currencies.

Where any doubt exists and speculation is to be avoided, the receipt of foreign currency funds — for which there is no immediate use in the same currency and which are not required to be retained in that currency for future use — should be covered; they should be sold forward, in order that a fluctuation in foreign exchange rates is guarded against.

EUROCURRENCY FINANCE

Over the last thirty years a pool of funds has become available to finance international trade which is not tied to the financial system of any one country. These funds are termed eurocurrencies as they are funds owned *outside* national boundaries and include most of the major world currencies, with a market existing in the world's financial centres. The main characteristic of this market is that eurocurrencies cannot be bought or sold, only borrowed or lent. Interest rates for eurocurrency borrowing are often lower than the borrowing rate for the same domestic currency and loans in eurocurrencies are available for all periods, though they are usually granted in sizeable or large amounts only. It should be borne in mind that an exchange risk will exist if the currency borrowed is not that of the underlying transaction, as the borrowing must be repaid in the same currency.

TRADE FINANCE FOR IMPORTERS

The principal financial facilities usually available to importers are as follows.

(1) From banks:
   (a) overdrafts and loans, unsecured and secured;
   (b) loans against goods or documents as security;
   (c) clean acceptance and discount facilities;
   (d) supplier credit;
   (e) documentary letters of credit and refinance credits.
(2) From banks and other financial organizations:
   (a) discount of local trade bills;
   (b) hire purchase.

OVERDRAFT AND LOANS, UNSECURED AND SECURED

Finance of this nature would normally be available to borrowers of undoubted standing on an unsecured basis, would be of a short-term nature and would, in the case of overdrafts, need to be fully fluctuating. Under such arrangements payments can be made in respect of imports (subject to any exchange control regulations that may be in force) and usually the domestic sale proceeds of such imports would be paid to the bank in repayment of loans or reduction of overdrafts.

The cost of finance would be linked to base rate or the cost of funds to the bank of a fluctuating base (overdrafts) and to the cost of funds to the bank on a fixed or fluctuating basis (loans), plus an agreed lending margin.

Where collateral security is available finer interest margins should be possible.

LOANS AGAINST GOODS OR DOCUMENTS AS SECURITY

Such loans against goods (which are often termed produce loans) are available to finance the import of basic commodities and raw materials; they may also be granted in support of the import of finished goods. They are usually of a short-term nature and are designed to support an importer from the time the goods are exported up to the time the importer disposes of the goods, either by sale or by feeding them into the manufacturing process. They are given as single loans or against revolving limit covering a regular turnover.

The following are the principal criteria a lending banker will normally apply to such propositions.

(1) A thorough knowledge of the borrower who will need to be of proven integrity, known business judgment and good past trading record.
(2) An allowance by way of a margin between the value of the goods and the loan granted is fairly commonplace, with the cost of finance being linked to base rate or the cost of funds — on a fixed or fluctuating basis — plus an agreed margin.
(3) For how long is finance required? Bankers do not wish to lend against stock which does not turn over regularly.
(4) Does a firm contract of onward sale exist or has the banker to rely on the borrower's expertise to find a satisfactory buyer to take up the goods? If the latter, lending interest margins could be higher than if firm on-sales contracts are held.
(5) Sound knowledge of the type of goods involved. Are they perishable and is the basic price liable to fluctuation, either locally or internationally?
(6) Are special handling or storage facilities required and do only special markets exist for the disposal of the goods in question? These factors could be decisive should the goods subsequently have to be sold by the bank at a forced sale value.

Where normally accepted security is not available or is not sufficient to cover the size of the loan sought (as could happen where an exporter is able to meet all other criteria but is also of modest means), then the underlying goods or title thereto will be the only security to which a banker looks. In such cases the following sequence usually occurs.

(1) While goods are in transit the bank will require control of the shipping documents. These will need to comprise complete documents of title to the goods, for instance full sets of endorsed bills of lading.
(2) When goods have reached their destination the bank will require that they are warehoused and insured to their order. Here all costs will be for the importer's or borrower's account.
(3) When goods are to be released prior to repayment of borrowings, the bank will require that they are held by the borrower in trust on the understanding that

payment will be made to the bank immediately after receipt of the sale proceeds by the borrower (or within an agreed and stated period of time).

(4) In addition, banks will seek from a borrower the right (by pledge or hypothecation) to sell the goods in the event of a loan default. This normally includes the right of the bank either to dispose of the goods once a loan repayment demand has not been fulfilled or to dispose of the goods without first demanding loan repayment. Both are operative only whilst the bank holds the goods or the documents of title thereto.

CLEAN ACCEPTANCES AND DISCOUNT FACILITIES

Where an importer has to pay for goods immediately on arrival, but will not receive payment for goods sold until sometime afterwards, banks will often agree that a usance bill of exchange (often termed 'an accommodation bill') may be drawn by the importer on them for acceptance. Once accepted, such bills may be discounted by the importer, perhaps with the bank who accepted the bill or in the discount market in general.

The proceeds from the discount would be used to pay for the underlying imports which are normally released to the importer in trust by the bank (acceptor) concerned so that sale proceeds may be received in time to meet the maturing acceptance.

The provision of such finance would attract an acceptance commission together with discount charges based on the cost of funds in the discounting area. Money markets are a source of finance to importers, mainly as a result of the involvement of discount houses in those markets, and fuller comment follows in this section on this involvement.

SUPPLIER CREDIT ON DOCUMENTS AGAINST ACCEPTANCE (D/A) OR PAYMENT (D/P) BASIS

Supplier credit on documents against acceptance. An exporter can assist an importer by dealing on an open account basis covered by term drawings, that is by allowing the importer to receive goods (or documents relating thereto) in trust and then waiting for a prior agreed period for payment. Similar assistance can also be provided by the exporter drawing usance bills of exchange or documents and routing them through a bank, provided such bills or documents may be released against acceptance by the importer. Interest on such arrangements is usually for the importer's (drawee) account at the rate applicable in the exporter's (drawer) country of domicile.

Importers making use of such arrangements would need to be aware of the need to cover any foreign currency exchange risk where applicable and to make full enquiries on a regular basis about interest rates in the exporter's country to ensure the continued viability of this type of import finance.

Supplier credit on documents against payment. Some exporters (and certain trades) draw on importers on a documents-against-payment basis, instructing the bank through whom the documents pass to clear, store and insure the goods if they are not taken up on arrival. In such instances the importer may be able to arrange bank finance under which usance documents against payment or landed goods are released in trust, provided that any documents against payment bill of exchange have already been accepted.

In granting such finance a bank is virtually guaranteeing payment to the exporter as, at maturity, it is most unlikely that it could recover the documents or goods from the importer in the event of default. For this reason the cost of releasing documents or goods in trust under such arrangements is normally higher than finance arranged on a D/A basis.

DOCUMENTARY LETTERS OF CREDIT AND REFINANCE CREDITS

Often importers are able to agree credit terms with suppliers whereby the importer arranges for a documentary letter of credit to be issued which calls, for example, for 180 days sight drawings on the importer. Providing the issuing bank is willing to release documents against acceptance, the importer will be able to utilize sale proceeds of the goods to meet acceptances at maturity.

Where an issuing bank is in a centre with an active bill discount market, the importer may be able to arrange for a documentary acceptance credit which would allow for payment to the exporter on a sight basis but calling for usance drafts on the issuing bank. Such drafts are then accepted and discounted by that bank at the bank bill rate, the proceeds being used to reimburse the advising bank claim.

If, however, there is an active discount market in the exporter's centre, finance for the importer could be provided in that centre where a documentary letter of credit calls for drawings on the advising bank. In such cases the advising bank would accept and discount the exporter's drawings at the bank bill rate of discount, the importer receiving the goods on arrival. The face amount of acceptance is claimed from the issuing bank at maturity who in turn looks to the importer for payment.

In both the above-mentioned systems it is essential that agreement is reached between importers and exporters as to where acceptance and discount charges are to be paid and by whom. Responsibility for charges is normally included in the terms of the documentary letter of credit.

Under refinance credits an importer may receive finance overseas from an advising or confirming bank. The importer's bank issues a sight documentary credit accompanied by usance bills but incomplete as to date and amount drawn by the importer on the advising bank. The advising bank advises the credit (but not usually the refinance terms so that an exporter could be unaware of the arrangement) and retains the incomplete usance bills until presentation of the beneficiary's (exporter) documents for payment. Provided all else is in order, the beneficiary receives immediate payment, the advising bank at the same time completes the usance bills and accepts and discounts them at the bank bill rate in that centre. Simultaneously the advising bank will negotiate the sight documentary credit claiming payment from the issuing bank but funding the same bank with the proceeds of the discounted usance bills (the refinance acceptances). Thus the issuing bank will not approach the importer for funds until maturity of the acceptances, though the funding of the acceptance and discount charges may have been sought at the time they were incurred. The importer in deciding on the viability of this type of finance will need to pay close attention to the cost of bank funds in the centre of the advising bank, against the cost locally, and the cost of covering any forward exchange risk.

Variations, internationally, in the modus operandi between banks often occur on the provision of this type of finance, but it is the cost of funds in an alternate centre that determines viability.

DISCOUNT OF LOCAL TRADE BILLS

Where importers are not willing to supply local end buyers on an open account but prefer to hold an acceptance of the buyer, the parties to such acceptances may be of sufficient financial standing for an importer's bank or a discount house to grant discount facilities. Such arrangements, where they are in support of trade transactions, would attract trade bill discount rates plus an agreed margin, and banks or discount houses themselves may in turn rediscount the bills in the appropriate financial centre. Where the drawer of a discounted bill subsequently asks for it to be withdrawn, the discounting organization may impose a penalty in the same manner as in the case of early repayment of a fixed loan.

HIRE PURCHASE

As mentioned above under **Trade finance for exporters**, an importer may be able to arrange finance by hire purchase and perhaps in conjunction with the exporter. In such instances repayment would normally be on a scheduled basis, and the cost of hire purchase finance is usually greater than that available elsewhere.

MERCHANTING OR THIRD COUNTRY TRADE

For those merchants who wish to trade with exporters and importers, both of whom are operating in countries apart from the place of business of the merchant — for instance an importer in Hong Kong who buys goods from Germany through the medium of a United Kingdom merchant house — there are various forms of international trade finance available. The granting of a particular form has significant effects on the exporters or importers who trade through such merchant houses. Normally merchanting or third country trade is ideally brought about by the merchant (or middleman) receiving payment for goods before they are actually bought and dispatched to the importer. Here the merchant would be able to pay an exporter immediately, but it is the importer who would need to raise advance payment finance.

Where finance needs to be carried by the merchant, bank overdrafts or loans in the most appropriate currency to minimize exchange risks could be sought, with the judicious use made of currencies to contain costs. Here both exporter and importer could benefit either by receiving payment for goods immediately they are shipped or by not having to pay for goods until they are either received or received and sold.

There are undoubtedly charges at both ends of such a transaction. However, market conditions could well be such that the merchant is not prepared to bear the cost of overdrafts or loans and seeks that the exporter (supplier) draws a trade bill of exchange on the merchanting house. By accepting such a bill the merchant could discount it and pay the exporter immediately for the goods, provided that the exporter is prepared to recognize that a bill drawn and discounted remains a contingent liability until it is finally paid. Such bills are trade bills for discounting and attract lesser rates than bank bills.

The merchant could draw a bill of exchange on the importer covering goods shipped, which is then offered to the merchant's bank for negotiation. Here the proceeds may be used to pay the exporter (supplier) but care needs to be taken over the use of foreign currencies, their cost and which party to the transaction is finally to bear costs and risks in the event of default.

Merchants may also raise funds through accommodation bill acceptances, and discount in order to pay exporters (suppliers) and thereby finance importers where both exporters and importers do not wish to show contingent or other liabilities.

The full use of documentary acceptance credits is also advocated for this type of international trade finance, and charges will be proportionate for the risks accepted by banks in undertaking to honour documents correctly presented and in order — documents which provide definitive assurances for the supplier.

Merchant houses may also be forfaiting to cover transactions where long-term finance is required.

JOHN A. LEDGER

Standard Chartered Bank

This chapter was originally drafted by P. Burfoot.

3.3
International leasing

Equipment leasing now plays a large part in corporate finance throughout the western world. No business enterprise can afford to ignore this option when it comes to expanding plant capacity, or renewing any type of equipment.

Leasing offers a number of clear advantages against most other forms of finance. It allows the lessee to bring new assets into use, usually with only one rental to be paid in advance. This frees financial resources for deployment elsewhere in the business.

Leasing represents an assured form of credit, in contrast with options such as bank overdrafts. It cannot be withdrawn as part of a general squeeze on credit. The pattern of rentals over the life of a lease can often be tailored to give flexibility, matching anticipated variations in the lessee's cash flow. The leasing company's continuing title to the goods under a lease agreement allows it to offer highly competitive credit terms.

In most countries leasing has grown to its present level from small beginnings around 1970. The United Kingdom experience is a good example of the long run trend of growth in leasing business in recent years. The following table tracks the continuing increase over the 10 years to 1989 in the United Kingdom leasing penetration ratio — that is the proportion of all fixed investment in equipment (as opposed to real estate) which is financed by leasing.

THE STRUCTURE OF LEASES

Leases can be structured with great flexibility to meet the requirements of the lessee customer. The length of a lease period will depend largely on the type of equipment: a period of 2-3 years would be typical for motor vehicles, 4-5 years for industrial plant, or up to 10 years for aircraft and ships.

Leasing terms may also vary in other respects. For example, interest variation clauses, providing for rentals to move up or down in line with a specified base lending rate or financial market rate, are commonly inserted by lessors in the longer and larger leasing deals — though fixed rates are available on shorter leases.

Leasing of equipment as % of all United Kingdom investment in equipment, 1980 to 1989*

Year	*(a) cash amount (£ million)*	*(b) as % of total investment*
1980	2,175	11.1%
1981	2,102	11.1%
1982	2,740	13.3%
1983	2,894	12.9%
1984	3,958	15.3%
1985	5,612	18.5%
1986	5,054	16.4%
1987	5,887	17.0%
1988	7,569	18.0%
1989	9,290	19.0%

* If in addition to pure leasing, account is taken of leases with purchase options (see below), then Equipment Leasing Association members financed as much as 27% of all United Kingdom plant and equipment investment in 1989.

Leasing agreements fall broadly into two categories. Firstly there is the *finance* or *full payout* lease. In this case, the lease period covers most of the expected useful life of the asset; and the rentals over the agreed primary lease period will give the lessor a full return on his investment in the asset. If the lessee wishes to continue using the asset after the end of this period, the lessor will usually agree to a secondary lease at a peppercorn rental. Otherwise, the lessee may be permitted to arrange the second hand sale of the goods, as the lessor's agent, with the bulk of the sale proceeds returning to the lessee by way of rental rebate.

If the lessee wishes to cease using the equipment and terminate the agreement before the end of the primary period, it may be possible to arrange this by negotiation with the lessor, subject to a termination payment to compensate the lessor for the loss of the remaining lease rentals, less any rental rebate arising from the sale proceeds. It is not advisable, however, for the customer to enter into a finance lease if he does not expect to use the equipment for the full term, since the termination arrangements offered by the lessor may appear unattractive.

In economic terms a finance lease is close to a hire purchase agreement — except that title in the assets never passes to the lessee. Yet for tax reasons, the lessor may have to structure all arrangements in such a way that the lease does not turn into a deferred purchase arrangement, even though the lessee's financial commitments might be similar to those under a hire purchase structure.

For a lessee in the business sector, a finance lease may be readily substitutable for a hire purchase facility — which is sometimes known as lease purchase or purchase option leasing. Under the latter structure, title to the goods passes to the customer at the end of a hire period on payment of a nominal option fee, following a series of instalment repayments similar to lease rentals, over the hire period. Fixing an option fee at a nominal level guarantees that the customer will complete the purchase by taking title if he has kept up the payments throughout the term of the agreement; but also ensures that legal title remains with the financier up to that time, giving him greater security than on an unsecured loan agreement.

In many cases the choice of financing arrangements, between lease and hire purchase, will depend on the tax positions of the respective parties to the agreement (see below).

The other type of lease is the *operating lease*, which covers a substantially shorter period than the expected useful life of the plant, and where the leased asset has a substantial residual value at the end of the lease period. Under this structure the lessee is thus relieved of the residual value risk which arises either from outright purchase or on a finance lease. This risk may be assumed instead by the leasing company, or by the manufacturer or an unconnected supplier or dealer, if such a party has a buyback agreement with the lessor.

In the United Kingdom market, an important variant of the operating lease is contract hire in vehicle leasing. The business car tends to be a significant part of the remuneration package at certain levels of employment in the United Kingdom. Around one third of all company cars are financed by leasing, and contract hire — which now accounts for most leasing in this sector, and plays an important part also in commercial vehicle leasing — offers a variable range of fleet management services, provided in conjunction with the capital financing under an operating lease structure.

The operating lease is widely available for the types of assets for which a freely accessible second hand market exists — notably in aircraft, vehicles and computers; and (increasingly) for certain types of printing machinery. For all other plant types, the finance lease is more prevalent in the United Kingdom.

Leases are introduced to leasing companies in a variety of ways. For large and medium ticket capital goods, it is normal for the customer — having selected his goods from a supplier — to approach a leasing company, either directly or through a lease broker, to negotiate a lease agreement whereby the leading company will acquire the asset from the supplier and set up the lease agreement with the lessee. In the small ticket sector, the device of sales aid leasing is more common. The equipment dealer will have a standing facility with one or more leasing companies, allowing him to offer leasing finance to the customer as part of the sales service.

TAXATION FACTORS

The tax system in most countries has an important influence on the choice as between leasing and other options in equipment financing. In the taxation of corporate income, most countries are in line with the United Kingdom where the legal ownership approach applies to leased assets. The leasing company is recognized as being in the trade of leasing, and so claims capital allowances (in respect of depreciation) on assets acquired for leasing. In the United Kingdom the lessee claims a full deduction against his own taxable income on his expenditure on lease rentals (except in the case of expensive cars, where special restrictions apply) — and these rentals are of course treated as taxable income of the lessor.

A few countries, however, apply the economic ownership principle. In this case it is the lessee — at any rate on a finance lease — who depreciates the assets for tax purposes.

Under the legal ownership principle, the use of leasing is particularly advantageous where the leasing company is better able to make maximum use of capital allowances than the lessee would be if, instead of using the taxation option, he acquired the asset and claimed the allowance himself. If in any year a company is not in a taxpaying position, for example because of poor profitability, the claiming of additional capital allowances on any newly acquired equipment will be of no immediate benefit. In the United Kingdom the structure of the leasing industry — and the pre-eminence within it of banks, who tend to be consistently in a taxpaying position from year to year — has been largely shaped by this taxable capacity aspect.

The most favourable fiscal environment for the development of leasing in the United Kingdom was in the period from 1972 to 1984, when — as a deliberate incentive to favour fixed investment generally — all taxpayers were entitled to claim 100% first year allowances, for most types of plant in the year of acquisition. Many United Kingdom industrial and commercial companies were tax exhausted in this period, having no liability to tax on undistributed income. Consequently they tended to lease in growing numbers.

In countries such as the United Kingdom and the United States, where the leasing market is long established and highly competitive, conditions in the market place ensure that the benefit of tax depreciation allowances to lessors is fully passed on to lessees in the terms of lease rentals. The level of leasing business was therefore very much boosted by the pre-1984 United Kingdom tax regime, though all taxpayers acquiring plant — whether for their own use or for leasing to end-users — were treated in principle in exactly the same way by the tax system.

In the 1984-86 period, however, the United Kingdom corporate tax system underwent a fundamental change, with a move to less generous capital allowances concurrently with a reduction in the corporation tax rate. In place of 100% first year allowances, capital plant now qualifies for 25% writing down allowances on the reducing balance basis: taxpayers can claim 25% of the cost against taxable income in the first year, $18\frac{3}{4}$% (i.e. 25% of the outstanding 75% tax-written-down value) in the second year, and so on. The United Kingdom tax changes coincided with a general recovery in profitability in British industry, leaving fewer companies tax exhausted. The United Kingdom tax system is thus no longer so favourable to leasing as it was pre-1984, and leasing now has to trade much more on its underlying commercial attractions.

Similar tax changes to those adopted in the United Kingdom — involving the removal of accelerated depreciation — were made a little later in the United States, with broadly the same implications for leasing businesses.

Apart from corporate income tax, the indirect tax system also helps to shape the leasing industry. In European countries, value added tax (VAT) is charged in full on lease rentals. In most of these countries the VAT treatment of hire purchase is quite different from that of leasing, with the financing charges under HP (the excess of loan repayments over initial capital cost) being treated as a VAT-exempt finance charge, in the nature of interest. In these circumstances, private consumers (who cannot of course reclaim the VAT paid on their expenditure) find it more advantageous to use the HP structure rather than the pure lease, because of the lower VAT burden. VAT-registered businesses, whose own sales are wholly or partially VAT-exempt — so that they cannot fully recover VAT paid on imputs such as lease rentals — also have a VAT incentive to avoid the use of leasing. Most businesses, however, whose own sales are fully subject to VAT — whether at a positive or zero rate — can fully recover the VAT which they incur on lease rentals, and are therefore not inhibited by the VAT system from using leasing.

In the United States, which has no VAT system, a variety of sales tax regimes are imposed by most individual states. Some such states subject lease rentals to a sales tax at up to 5%, which is not recoverable by lessee businesses against the sales tax due on their own output. This can give rise to a tax penalty against leasing.

ACCOUNTING RULES

The accounting regulations which govern financial reporting by companies, as applied to leases, are similarly subject to much international variation. The most significant of these variable factors are the rules for accounting by lessees, rather than lessors. In the United States and the United Kingdom, lessee companies are now required to capitalize finance leases, and treat them for accounting purposes in much the same way as if they had acquired legal title to the assets. The leased equipment must appear on the lessee's balance sheet — while the lessor's balance sheet will at the same time report the latter's financial investment in the lease, which in practice will come to a similar amount though technically it is a different item — and depreciation on the leased assets must be charged to the lessee's profit and loss account (with an accruals adjustment to reconcile the notional depreciation with the actual rentals paid).

For the lessee, there can be both advantages and disadvantages in inflating his balance sheet with additional assets and corresponding liabilities. The principle effect of having to capitalize an item which might otherwise be kept off the balance sheet, is likely to be some diminution of financial flexibility. If the lessee is a publicly quoted company, many of the latter's key financial ratios will be adversely affected by the capitalization of any additional item; and the lessee's credit lines from potential lenders could also be influenced by the gearing effect of the size of the balance sheet.

In the United Kingdom the lessee capitalization rule was introduced through the SSAP 21 accounting standard on leasing and hire purchase transactions, which was adopted by the Accounting Standards Committee in 1984 and became effective in 1987. The corresponding rule in the United States is laid down in the FASB 13 accounting standard, which was adopted earlier and on which the United Kingdom rules were based. In most other countries, however, including Japan, West Germany and France, no such rule is yet in force.

The International Accounting Standards Committee, which represents the accountancy profession throughout the Organisation for Economic Cooperation and Development countries, has produced its own accounting standard on leasing (IAS 17), which favours capitalization by lessees. This international standard, however, has only advisory status. It does not have direct force in any country, and has little influence in countries such as West Germany, where the professional accountancy bodies are not involved in formulating the statutory accounting rules. The European Commission is currently giving consideration to possible harmonization of rules on this and other accounting matters, to apply to all 12 member states of the European Community. This initiative is still in its early stages, and there are no imminent moves to extend the lessee capitalization rule beyond those countries presently applying it.

One complicating factor is that, in many countries, the same rules apply to the definition of profit for financial reporting and for tax purposes — in contrast with the British and American position, where there are a number of differences between the two, particularly in the case of depreciation rules which are critical to leasing. In the former countries, lessee capitalization for accounting purposes could bring with it a move to economic ownership rules for capital allowances (see under Taxation above).

Lessee capitalization is never applied to operating leases which, for accounting purposes, are treated in the same way as short term plant hire — no balance sheet entries for the leases, with only the rentals being charged to profit and loss account. Wherever the capitalization rule is applied for finance leases, the effect has been to increase interest among potential lessees in the operating lease structure which allows the lease to be kept off-balance-sheet.

OTHER FORMS OF REGULATION

Aside from taxation and accounting rules, there are some other forms of public regulation of leasing, of which lessors and lessees in some countries will need to be mindful. Leasing is conceived here as essentially a financial service to the business sector; in some countries legislation devised to protect private consumers in credit transactions can impinge also on certain types of leasing.

Thus in the United Kingdom the Consumer Credit Act 1974, and secondary legislation enacted thereunder, applies to leases with a capital value of less than £15,000, to those lessees who are defined as consumers under the Act; and this includes unincorporated businesses, as partnerships or sole traders. For leasing agreements which are so regulated, extensive additional documentation is required beyond that used for unregulated agreements; and the Act regulates certain commercial terms of leasing, particularly in respect of early terminations.

Banking legislation, in the form of prudential supervision by the authorities of the capital adequacy of banking institutions, also impinges on the lessor's part in a leasing transaction, though it is not a factor of which lessees will need to be aware. Where leasing companies are themselves banks, or are subsidiaries of banking institutions, their commercial exposures on leases will be subject to the same sort of risk asset weightings as applied to bank loans, for the purposes of regulating their free capital in relation to credit commitments. In most countries, only those lessors who are — or are part of — retail deposit taking institutions are subject to this form of supervision, though in some countries such as France, certain forms of leasing are themselves subject to banking supervision, however the lessors fund themselves. These regulations have some bearing on the type of commercial terms which leasing companies can offer; their investments in leases have to pass the tests of governmental regulation of capital adequacy (as well as the internal appraisal of rates of return and so on), which would in any event be applied.

THE LEASING INDUSTRY

There are many different types of company in the leasing business. In the United Kingdom the major finance houses, which belong to the Big Four clearing banks, account for the greater part of the market by value of business. They tend to dominate the large ticket leasing market. One of the largest industrial projects ever undertaken in Britain — the Essochem Olefins Fife Ethylene Plant at Mossmorran near Grangemouth — was financed mainly by leasing, through a consortium of financial lessors.

Some of the larger merchant banks, and the minor clearing banks, are also key players in the market for medium ticket finance leases. In the sales aid sector of small ticket leasing, there are a number of specialist lessors, mainly outside the banking sector. Vehicle leasing constitutes another distinct sector, in which a number of specialist leasing companies (some very small) compete with contract hire subsidiaries of the major finance houses. In computer leasing, there are several specialist companies which act both as dealers and lessors in mainframes and other equipment, offering operating leases on the strength of their expertise in the second hand market.

Finally, there are some significant captive lessors, particularly in the computer and office equipment sectors, who lease goods manufactured by their parent companies, as part of the latters' strategies for influencing the second hand market in their branded products.

Most other countries in which leasing is well established present a similar picture to the United Kingdom, with a variety of leasing companies specializing in distinct niches in the market place, all in fierce competition for customers' business.

LEASING ACROSS BORDERS

Because of the variable taxation rules as noted above, and different systems of commercial law in each country, leasing tends to be segmented into national markets though it is a major activity worldwide. The larger leasing companies tend to be in multinational groups, but with separate subsidiaries in each country where they do business. Direct cross-border leasing, where the lessors are incorporated in a different country from that in which the lessee is based, are uncommon except in the leasing of ships and aircraft.

In the United Kingdom, the tax rules provide very restrictive capital allowances on equipment leased to non-resident lessees. The relevant legislation was first introduced in 1982, in part to address the phenomenon of double dip, where capital allowance claims might effectively be duplicated, by a lessor based in a country with legal ownership rules, and a lessee in another country where economic ownership rules apply. It remains to be seen whether the United Kingdom restrictions on outward leasing to any other country are compatible with the principles of the European Single Market, when this comes into effect after 31 December 1992. The European Commission has made some preliminary moves towards a Directive on corporate tax harmonization, attempting to address at least those aspects of the tax system which impinge directly on international business transactions. It seems very unlikely, however, that the fiscal barriers to free trade in financial services, even within the European Community, will be removed by the 1992 deadline.

Tax considerations also inhibit inward cross-border leasing to a country such as the United Kingdom. In order to take advantage of capital allowances in the United Kingdom, a company needs a stream of taxable income in the same country. A solution to this problem is sometimes available through various forms of collaboration between leasing companies based in different countries. Back-to-back structures are a common feature, whereby some Japanese and other foreign banks in the United Kingdom can earn a small margin on United Kingdom leasing business in partnership with an established United Kingdom leasing company. The latter company, which may have taxable capacity but no funds immediately available to match an investment opportunity in leasing, can act as the lessor, claiming capital allowances, while a foreign bank, seeking opportunities for international financial investment, provides the funding on hire purchase terms.

In some countries, such as the United States and Australia, both in domestic leasing and in international corporate relationships, other structures can be used, based on the securitization principle, splitting the relevant financial investment into the entitlement to the rental income stream on the one hand, and legal ownership with entitlement to capital allowances on the other. These arrangements, known as leveraged leases or non-recourse funding transactions, have not — largely because of uncertainties in the tax treatment — taken hold in the United Kingdom, where the back-to-back structure is more prevalent in vertical partnerships.

CONCLUSION

Whether through sophisticated transactions on very fine margins in the large ticket sector, or through the bread-and-butter domestic leasing of the more traditional type, it is clear that equipment leasing is very much part of the future on the world financial scene. The United Kingdom experience, where the real volume of leasing business more than doubled between 1983 and 1989, in spite of moves towards less favourable regimes in both the tax legislation and the accounting requirements, demonstrates the fundamental resilience of leasing in the current commercial environment.

A. THOMPSON

Equipment Leasing Association

3.4
Insuring the credit risks associated with trade

PART 1 GOVERNMENT SCHEMES

BACKGROUND

Export credit insurance is available to exporters in all major countries (the names and addresses of the official export credit insurers in forty-two countries are listed later in the chapter). The elements of cover available differ from country to country in several respects, but the underlying motive of all governments is to encourage competitive exporting.

Exporters are trading in a complex world marketplace. They are not only competing against foreign sellers operating under different terms and conditions, but selling into countries with varying abilities to generate hard currency payments and granting credit to buyers often with uncertain creditworthiness.

The many credit risks in exporting can be commonly defined as the events which may prevent payments being made by the intended due date, whether caused by government or buyer default.

The worldwide economic situation at any one time has a fundamental effect on risk. During a boom customers can overtrade without adequate capital and exporters often miss or overlook the warning signs of inability to pay. During any trading conditions the foreign exchange rates between the exporters' and the buyers' currencies can fluctuate, causing a loss to either party — in any export transaction there is a foreign currency risk for one of the parties.

It is not only in the less developed countries that exporters experience credit losses. The European Community and the United States are suffering high rates of business insolvency, with many importers amongst them. Insolvencies are only the tip of the iceberg, however, since the bulk of the problem causing expense and loss to exporters lies below the surface and is felt in terms of payment delays, usually without interest cover and often with a foreign currency shortfall. The transfer delay markets are increasing annually with a considerable number of countries declaring their inability to meet commitments. The spate of countries applying for

International Monetary Fund support or international rescheduling of external bank borrowings all indicate warnings for exporters, even if individual buyers in those markets are creditworthy and pay on time. Experienced exporters look first at the country risk before even considering the creditworthiness of individual buyers.

Clearly the first requirement for exporters is to apply sound credit management to export sales and marketing so that the risks can be identified and minimized. Even so, because of the risk of unexpected events between order date and payment due date, it is prudent to consider credit insurance cover in addition to modern management techniques. The cost of export credit insurance can be established in advance and costed into export pricing whereas the cost of a serious payment or a complete bad debt write off cannot be foreseen. As a vital tool in the exporter's armoury, a credit insurance policy can be regarded as a budgeted expense to avoid unbudgeted losses.

Credit insurance should not be seen as a substitute for credit management but rather as underpinning the cash-flow and profits. Besides the payment of claims when losses occur, credit insurance also carries other major advantages. It provides a view on customers and countries so that the exporter can avoid significantly high risks. It can support exporters entering new markets. More adventurous use can be made of credit terms within the cover available. However, probably the most widely advertised ancillary benefit of cover is the access given to export finance, often at preferential interest rates.

THE CREDIT RISKS

The credit risk loss most commonly encountered by exporters can be divided between commercial and political causes.

(1) default by the customer at due date;
(2) insolvency of the customer;
(3) failure or refusal of the customer to accept goods properly delivered under the contract.

Political or economic risks can be grouped into the following:

(1) a moratorium on external payments decreed by the buyer's government, or that of the paying country if not the buyer's;
(2) action by the buyer's government that prevents completion of the contract;
(3) events outside the exporter's country which delay or prevent payments being made;
(4) full local payment resulting in a shortfall in the exporter's currency when transferred;
(5) war and events not insured commercially which prevent the contract being completed;
(6) cancellation or non-renewal of export licences or the banning of certain exports after the contract is signed.

INSURANCE AGAINST CREDIT RISK

Almost all the credit and collection risks faced by United Kingdom exporters can be insured with the Export Credits Guarantee Department (ECGD). Similar cover to that of the Department is provided for their own exporters by government departments or agencies of most major exporting nations. A later section deals with some of the differences in the cover provided in various countries.

Cover for export credit risks is also provided by private, non-governmental, insurance companies in many countries. The private insurance market provides a mixture of commercial and political risk covers. These schemes are fully discussed at the end of the chapter.

A basic justification for any government's credit insurance scheme is the need to support and encourage the export efforts of that country's industry in competing against other countries.

EXPORT CREDITS GUARANTEE DEPARTMENT INSURANCE COVER

The Department was formed in 1919. It is an institution of the British government, now related to the Department of Trade and Industry, with headquarters in London and Cardiff and regional offices around the United Kingdom serving local exporters.

It operates under the Export Guarantees and Overseas Investment Act 1978. Section 1 of the Act deals with normal credit insurance activity, section 2 covers business which does not meet normal criteria but is deemed necessary in the national interest. Section 3 authorizes the preferential rate export finance schemes, and section 4 deals with foreign aid loans. Section 5, covering cost escalation cover for capital goods, was discontinued in December 1983.

The Export Credits Guarantee Department is a government department which does not cost the taxpayer anything; it is charged with balancing its operating expenses and claims against its premium income.

Cover for standard repetitive business is given on a comprehensive, whole turnover, basis on which all exports, including good risks, must usually be insured for at least one year at a time. Premiums for short-term business, up to six months' credit, range across a wide spectrum according to circumstances.

Cover for non-repetitive business, in the form of large value contracts on terms of payment between two and five years, is provided by specific policies with individual premium rates. The Export Credits Guarantee Department covers both exporters granting supplier credit and British banks making buyer credit loans direct to overseas borrowers to enable the exporters to be paid by cash by shipment date. The Department also provides guarantees to British banks providing export finance on supplier credit at special interest rates.

EXPORT CREDIT GUARANTEE DEPARTMENT STATUS

In 1991, however, the Export Credit Guarantee Department's status and structure will be radically altered. The intention is to run the Cardiff-based Insurances Services (covering exports on short term credit) and the London-based Project

Group (handling exports of projects for capital goods on medium term credit) as separate organizations. The Insurance Services Group will be converted into a company with the aim of privatization as soon as possible. The Project Group will retain its status as a Government agency.

COMPREHENSIVE SHORT-TERM POLICY (CST)

Around 20% of United Kingdom exports are insured under this type of policy, the standard arrangement for exporters selling on terms of up to six months. The Export Credits Guarantee Department requires an acceptable spread of risks, usually on a whole-turnover basis, with a flat premium rate charged as a percentage of insured sales regardless of payment terms. It is possible to exclude whole markets and individual customers, mainly associated subsidiary companies. If the exclusions are substantial a premium loading may be applied.

The comprehensive short-term policy may be renewed annually and is available to any type of exporter whose goods or services are sold from the United Kingdom to a buyer outside the United Kingdom.

Exporters can choose to have cover for shipments only or to add pre-shipment risk cover where the goods are to be exported within twelve months of date of contract, for an additional flat premium on total turnover. Pre-shipment risk cover is attractive to exporters of non-standard goods that cannot be easily resold.

RISKS COVERED

The risks covered by the Department are:

(1) insolvency of the buyer;
(2) the buyer's failure to pay within six months of due date for goods he has accepted;
(3) the buyer's failure to accept goods despatched to him (where such action is not due to the exporter's actions and where the Department decides against legal enforcement);
(4) a general moratorium on external debt decreed by the government of a buyer's country or of a third country through which payment will be made;
(5) any other action by the government of the buyer's country which prevents performance of the contract;
(6) political events, economic difficulties, legislative or administrative measures outside the United Kingdom which prevent or delay the transfer of payments or deposits;
(7) legal discharge of a debt in a foreign currency which results in a shortfall at the date of transfer;
(8) war and certain other events preventing performance of the contract, provided that the event is not normally insurable with commercial insurers;
(9) cancellation or non-renewal of a United Kingdom export licence or the prohibition or restriction on the export of goods from the United Kingdom by law (only applies to pre-shipment risk cover).

The Export Credits Guarantee Department also cover the failure of public buyers — in central, regional, provincial and local government — to perform the contract, provided the default was not caused by the exporter.

PERCENTAGE OF LOSS COVERED

Exporters must bear a self-retention or a portion of any loss, to encourage prudent credit granting and the need to supervise any difficult situations.

For the insolvency and failure to pay risks the Department pays 90% of any loss. For the failure to accept risk, 20% of the original sales value is deducted from the loss, the Department then paying 90% of the balance. For the other risks, classed as political, it pays 95% of any loss except where losses occur before shipment under pre-shipment risk cover, when only 90% is paid.

PAYMENT OF CLAIMS

Insolvency claims are paid immediately on proof of insolvency. Default claims are paid six months after due date. Claims for failure to accept goods are paid one month after resale or disposal by other means. Claims for delays in transfer or shortfall in local currency payments are paid four months after due date or after completion of transfer formalities, whichever is later. Claims for all other political risks are paid four months after the event causing loss, or the loss itself, whichever is later. However, payment of claims can be deferred for certain markets as circumstances dictate.

PREMIUM PAYMENT

Exporters pay the premium on comprehensive short-term policies in two parts. A non-refundable amount is paid each year, fixed according to the volume of exports and the use of credit limits. Premium is then paid monthly on shipments and contracts (where pre-shipment risk is held) at the agreed rate per £100. In these days of high claims, an increasing number of markets attract additional levels of premium (market rate surcharges). There is no need to declare individual transactions to the Export Credits Guarantee Department, who therefore only get to know about individual customers and contracts in the event of difficulties leading to a claim.

CREDIT LIMITS

All insured customers must have a credit limit which represents the Department's maximum liability. The credit limit is either agreed direct by the Department or allowed by the policy's in-built discretion.

Exporters have a great deal of discretionary power; they are allowed to deal up to a specified limit, usually £5,000, without reference to the Department provided satisfactory information is held on file. If trading experience is satisfactory the discretion can be increased to at least £20,000. Above the discretionary limit a specific credit limit is issued by the Department after checking the buyer's creditworthiness.

PAYMENT TERMS

Comprehensive short-term policies normally cover terms up to six months, although payment terms are restricted for some markets either as a matter of prudence or by local decree. Exporters receive details of markets where maximum payment terms are restricted. Under the credit limit system it follows that the shorter the terms the more insured sales are possible within a limit.

NON-UNITED KINGDOM GOODS

The Export Credits Guarantee Department, via a comprehensive short-term policy, will cover goods imported into the United Kingdom and then re-exported, provided that they do not compete directly with goods available from United Kingdom manufacturers. Cover is also available to manufacturers and merchants for goods delivered from a third country to the buyer without coming into the United Kingdom by specific endorsement to the comprehensive short-term policy. The existence of such cover (previously in part covered under the now defunct external trade policy) recognizes the increasing importance of multi-sourcing in today's trading conditions around the world.

NON-STERLING EXPORTS

The standard range of hard currencies is automatically included in the policy and full cover applied to insured sales. Unusual currencies can normally be accommodated as required. The Department will also issue a Foreign Currency Contracts Endorsement subject to additional premium, to pay up to 15% extra on a valid claim for the normal risks, where the exporter proves an extra loss through selling the currency forward or through borrowing in currency.

ADDITIONAL COVER

The standard comprehensive short-term policy can also apply to export contracts made with a British merchant or confirming house, to sales to subsidiaries and associates, to sales ex-stock and following demonstrations and trade exhibitions, and to royalty payments.

SUBSIDIARIES POLICY

Separately from the comprehensive short-term policy, it is possible to insure sales made by a foreign subsidiary (and associate companies in certain circumstances). It is not always necessary for the goods concerned to have been originally supplied from the United Kingdom, provided that there is an identifiable return to the United Kingdom from the foreign subsidiary (or associate company if applicable).

EXTENDED RISK ENDORSEMENT

The extended risk endorsement (ERE) replaces, in part, the extended terms policy (CXT) and extends the cover given to exporters under the CST policy to sales where credit terms of between six months and two years are appropriate. It is also utilized for sales on short term credit where the delivery period exceeds twelve months and pre-shipment cover is needed.

EXTENDED TERMS POLICY

The extended terms policy (CXT) is now only given to exporters of capital and semi-capital goods involving credit terms between two and five years where delivery is not more than two years from contract date. In April 1991 the extended terms policy will be replaced by the Supplier Credit financing (SCF) Facility (mentioned later in this chapter).

MEDIUM-TERM CREDIT

The comprehensive kind of whole turnover insurance is not appropriate to the medium-term credit which is normally granted on capital goods where the productive usefulness will not begin for a long time after delivery by the exporter.

SPECIFIC POLICY

For this type of export the Export Credits Guarantee Department issues specific policies for single contracts. Cover usually commences from contract date in view of the risks in the longer manufacturing period. Risks covered are the same as for comprehensive short-term policy excluding cover for private buyers' non-acceptance of goods shipped. Cover is limited to 90% for all risks. Credit up to five years can be covered, and this can be increased if it can be proved that foreign competitors are offering longer credit. Premium rates are higher on specific policies, reflecting the longer-term risk.

The Export Credits Guarantee Department always stress the need to refer to them early in the negotiation for an indication of cover, so that cover conditions can be established and the premium calculated into the costings.

A modified policy is available for aerospace and shipping, recognizing the special needs of those industries, especially regarding airworthiness certificates and construction periods.

CONSTRUCTIONAL WORKS POLICY

This policy recognizes the essential elements of construction projects: the execution of specific works; the customer known as the employer; the combination of supply goods and performance of services; and payment normally authorized by an engineer's certificate of work done. During the period awaiting the certification of contract invoice, cover relates to the contractor's costs incurred. Thereafter cover is for sums owed by the employer. Extra cover is given by the Department for the contingencies of extra works and escalation of pricing in a contract within defined limits. Part of the extra premium for this is paid when cover is taken out, and the main balance paid only when the extra cover is used.

FOREIGN SUBCONTRACTING

Major capital contracts increasingly require multi-contracting by exporters in different countries, the foreign buyer making a single main contract with one supplier who then manages the required subcontracting arrangements. There are reciprocal arrangements in the European Community for the credit insurance of the main contractor to include up to 40% by value in subcontracts from other member countries and 30% from certain non-members (Austria,Japan, Norway, Sweden and Switzerland).

SERVICES POLICIES

The Export Credits Guarantee Department will provide cover for a variety of services — technical and professional assistance, refits, conversions, overhauls and repair work, leasing and hiring contracts and supply of know-how under licence — on the same basis as a comprehensive short-term policy.

The Department will cover earnings for these services either under a comprehensive services policy, where there is a regular pattern of business on short-term credit and the whole turnover is insured, or under a specific services policy, for single contracts such as a consultant's services in a major construction.

If leasing or hiring contracts are the operational type, designed to produce revenue on a capital asset, the earnings can be insured under the services policies. Special policies are available for financial or pay out leases where the leasing is really a substitute for a sale.

PERFORMANCE AND OTHER BONDS — UNFAIR CALLING COVER

The Export Credits Guarantee Department's support against the unfair calling of bonds is available to exporters where contracts carry normal cover, including pre-shipment risk, and where the Department approve the buyer's country for this kind of cover. On comprehensive short-term and supplemental extended-term policies only public sector buyers are included and tender bonds are excluded. The Export Credits Guarantee Department reimburse 100% of a loss provided the exporter was not defective in performance. On the comprehensive short-term, premium is charged by an additional 0.01% on the pre-shipment risk premium. Where the underlying contract falls within the scope of the Extended Risk Endorsement premium is individually assessed on the basis of the length of the pre-shipment period involved. On the supplemental extended-term 0.02% per month is added to the premium. On the specific policies the premium is charged at an additional 0.5%.

PROJECT PARTICIPANTS INSOLVENCY COVER

The Export Credits Guarantee Department will insure United Kingdom members of major consortia with foreign contracts against the losses incurred when a consortium member becomes insolvent. Cover of 90% is given, and the contracts must be for £20m or more, either on a joint venture or subcontract basis. A mix of United Kingdom and non-United Kingdom exporters is acceptable.

Premium is charged at 1.5% per annum on the amount and period required and the amount of loss is taken to be the additional costs to the insured of taking on work obligations of the insolvent member. Paid claims are lodged with any liquidator to qualify for salvage.

TENDER TO CONTRACT COVER

This is a particularly useful facility for exporters at the tendering stage of major capital contracts in excess of £10m (United Kingdom content) quoted in foreign currency, covering them against exchange rate fluctuations between tendering and contract date. Without this cover exporters have to make a significant assumption of the sterling value of their currency quotation at the future date of the contract award. The risk can be covered in the forward market, but if the exporter does not get the order he has to close the forward exchange deal with the consequent risk of loss. Without covering forward, a successful tender could face a lower sterling value on a currency bid.

The Export Credits Guarantee Department TTC cover requires the exporter to estimate his sterling receipts and the period involved. The Department supplies guaranteed exchange rates to enable the exporters to quote in currency. Thus the unsuccessful bidder has only incurred the Export Credits Guarantee Department premium. The successful bidder tells the Export Credits Guarantee Department his intended sterling values and is paid up to 25% of any subsequent shortfall. Any exchange gains are paid over to the Export Credits Guarantee Department.

In the event that the exporter finds it impossible to enter into forward contracts to sell all the currency sums involved, then additional cover is possible under the forward exchange supplement. For an additional sum of £5,000, the Department will maintain its guaranteed forward exchange rates until it becomes possible.

GUARANTEES TO BANKS FOR EXPORT FINANCE

Significant support is provided to exporters by the Export Credits Guarantee Department in that it will guarantee banks providing export funds at special subsidised interest rates, thus reducing costs for the exporter and also increasing the supply of funds available over and above normal borrowing limits.

The Export Credits Guarantee Department does not provide funds, contrary to popular belief. All guaranteed finance is provided by banks in return for fees from the exporter or borrower and interest make-up from the government.

SPECIFIC GUARANTEES TO BANKS

For financing exports of capital goods and services on terms of over two years, insured by the exporter under specific policies or by supplemental extended terms policy, the Department will provide an unconditional guarantee to the banks for 100% of any bill or note against which payment has not been received three months after due date, and will take recourse to the exporter for any uninsured amounts. Interest is fixed for the whole credit period at ranges agreed by the Organisation for Economic Co-operation and Development international consensus according to category of buyer's market. Premium is charged according to length of credit risk period.

SUPPLIER CREDIT FINANCE FACILITY

In 1991 the Export Credit Guarantee Department intend to introduce a new supplier credit facility, provisionally known as the Bills and Notes Purchase Facility (NBP), to provide exporters with a simple and flexible guarantee for supporting supplier credit financing on credit terms of two years or more. The intention of this new facility is to replace both the extended terms credit insurance policy and the Department's specific bank guarantees.

The Bills and Notes Purchase Facility will be on the basis of 100% unconditional guarantee given to the banks, structured to enable a bank to purchase Bills and Notes in respect of supplier credit transactions the Department approved. It will cover non-payment of Bills or Promissory Notes which have been purchased by the bank from the exporter without recourse on a transaction by transaction basis.

GUARANTEES FOR BUYER CREDIT FINANCING

For export contracts involving substantial credit it is sometimes more convenient for the foreign borrower to borrow the funds from a British bank and to pay the exporter on cash terms. The Export Credits Guarantee Department, in common with the government insurance agencies of most developed countries, are able to guarantee national banks providing this kind of substantial finance.

The advantages over supplier credit are:

(1) the exporter receives virtual cash settlements;
(2) the buyer can take advantage of longer credit terms;
(3) pre-delivery payments can be arranged for work stages;
(4) capital goods exporters with limited recourse-worthiness can take on worthwhile contracts.

There are many variations of buyer credit deals and it is possible only to quote some theoretical standards.

The international consensus guidelines put markets into three categories which decide maximum credit, minimum interest rates and minimum down payments. Subject to these guidelines, buyers have to pay 15% to 20% contract values direct to the exporter by the date of contract. The balance of 80% to 85% is paid to the exporter by a United Kingdom bank out of a loan made by that bank to the overseas buyer, and that loan is guaranteed 100% by the Department for principal and interest.

Contracts must be of at least £1m (usually £5m is more suitable) and can include foreign goods or services, which cannot normally be financed in the buyer credit. The buyer thus pays the contract down payment and the non-United Kingdom element direct to the exporter; the bank pays the United Kingdom element less its down payment; the exporter is therefore fully paid, almost without a recourse risk, by delivery date or soon after.

The four key legal documents involved are:

(1) supply contract between the exporter and the buyer;
(2) loan agreement between the United Kingdom bank and the foreign borrower or buyer;
(3) the Export Credits Guarantee Department guarantee to the United Kingdom bank;
(4) premium agreement between the Export Credits Guarantee Department and the exporter.

From this it will be seen that the bank's relationship is with the borrower, not the exporter. The Export Credits Guarantee Department's only link with the exporter is via the premium agreement, whereby recourse may be taken. The only recourse risk for the exporter is if he is in default in performance at the time that the borrower defaults in repayments. Premium costs are based on market and length of credit involved.

A recent development in Export Credits Guarantee Department is to produce a scheme to reduce significantly the legal delays in checking the documentation in buyer credits. The conditional form allows the United Kingdom bank to satisfy itself that the loan agreement is enforceable in both countries. This speeds up loan completion but leaves the bank vulnerable if a subsequent default by the borrower cannot be remedied legally. Premium costs are the same as for standard buyer credits.

LINES OF CREDIT

The Department also guarantees United Kingdom banks for lines of credit made available to foreign banks for use in importing United Kingdom capital goods. Fairly small individual contract values can be financed from any number of different exporters, subject to the agreement of the borrower, the United Kingdom bank and the Department. Whereas the delays are considerable in arranging a line of credit, there is usually little delay or difficulty in financing a contract once the foreign authority has approved its inclusion.

The three kinds of line of credit are:

(1) project line of credit, where several United Kingdom contracts might be approved to supply or service a major project;
(2) general purpose line of credit, also known as a shopping basket credit, whereby unconnected contracts can be financed for the supply or service to any number of end-buyers in the borrowing country;
(3) Financing Contracts (Overseas Banks) Endorsements (FINCOBE) and Associated Borrower Endorsement (ABE) lines of credit; these are restricted to British export finance houses lending to first-class overseas borrowers (usually banks) where repayments of loans are not dependent on performance under supply contracts. The Export Credits Guarantee Department insures a

British export finance house against non-repayment of a loan it makes to an overseas borrower. Financing Contracts (Overseas Banks) Endorsements and Associated Borrower Endorsements eliminate the need for the Export Credits Guarantee Department to become involved in the time-consuming scrutiny of supply contracts and loan agreements, as the cover is given within the framework of a comprehensive policy.

FINANCING IN FOREIGN CURRENCIES

Outside the comprehensive short-term and extended terms fields (mentioned earlier in this chapter) the Export Credits Guarantee Department is prepared to support financing across a minimum range of twenty-six major currencies.

EUROPEAN HARMONIZATION

European Community members have agreed to work together to eliminate the differences in national credit insurance schemes which distort competition between them. As a basic step towards harmonization, Community insurers do not apply the preferential fixed rate interest to export on two years' credit or more to other member countries.

The advent of the European Market in 1992 is likely to accelerate the existing trend by Community insurers to provide cross-border credit insurance support to exporters in foreign territories.

The Dutch, French and German credit insurers, for example, are already particularly active in the United Kingdom market.

BERNE UNION AND ORGANISATION FOR ECONOMIC CO-OPERATION AND DEVELOPMENT CONSENSUS GUIDELINES

The Export Credits Guarantee Department was a founder member in 1934 of the Berne Union, correctly known as the International Union of Credit and Investment Insurers. Since 1974 the Union has been an international forum to enable collaboration in avoiding a credit race between major countries and to expand and improve credit insurance techniques. The Union consists of forty members from thirty-two countries, including private insurers and various kinds of government bodies.

Since governments themselves are not members, any agreements are subject to subsequent direction from individual governments. Under Organisation for Economic Co-operation and Development (OECD) auspices, government representatives meet to control international export credits and arrange the swap of information on credit over five years. In recent years this group has established the international consensus guidelines, which categorize countries into three groups according to per capita income, and set minimum down-payments, interest rates and maximum credit periods for each group. In July 1988 these guidelines were amended to introduce a commercial rate element for the first time and currently stand thus:

	Rich	Intermediate	Poor
Minimum payments by delivery	15%	15%	15%
Minimum interest rates for:			
2 to 5 years	Commercial	9.15%	8.3%
over 5 years	rates	9.65%	8.3%
Maximum credit	5 years	8.5 years	10 years

DIFFERENCES BETWEEN THE EXPORT CREDITS GUARANTEE DEPARTMENT AND FOREIGN INSURERS

There have been many allegations that the Organisation for Economic Co-operation and Development guidelines have been exceeded by some countries, and that due collaboration has been avoided in a bid to secure competitive orders. It is worth looking at some of the ways other countries help their exporters, since there are many aspects of trade and finance which are not subject to consensus guidelines.

ORGANIZATIONS

Some countries such as the United States and Canada have state organizations which provide both insurance and finance. Most, however, have separate bodies, with government influence much stronger in insurance than in finance, although state facilities for refinancing in some countries make the provision of funds much easier.

INSURANCE BODY DIFFERENCES

The key distinctions appear to rest on whether the bodies are government departments, such as Export Credits Guarantee Department and New Zealand's EXGO, or agencies such as Eximbank in the United States, Coface of France and Norway's GIEK. The relative power of the agencies varies widely.

The forthcoming privatization of the short term sector of the Export Credit Guarantee Department's business is likely to have a significant impact on its operations.

Eximbank is described as an independent corporate agency of the United States, with a government representative on the board with no voting power, yet Eximbank's lending is limited by Congress.

Denmark's EKR is run by a government appointed council which includes government, bank and business members, as does Canada's EDC. In Germany, Hermes is a private company which acts on behalf of the government. Its commitments are limited in total by the economic ministry.

In Italy, SACE's liabilities are limited by law, whilst in Japan ceilings are fixed annually by parliament.

Eximbank works with a private organisation, FCIA, which is a representative company for some fifty insurance companies and covers the buyer risks, with Eximbank taking the political ones. FCIA reinsures the larger policies with Eximbank.

Most countries set limits on annual or total commitments without seeming to inhibit official support to exporters, except perhaps in the United States and Italy. The lack of any official limits on Coface in France is said to give it more scope to act faster and allocate cover better by country than most countries.

EXPORT FINANCE BODY DIFFERENCES

In the United Kingdom the major banks provide export finance, backed by guarantees from the Export Credits Guarantee Department, the latter now also being available to all authorized banks. Short-term finance is available in most countries at market rates with insurance cover on the exports a prerequisite in some cases, such as the United Kingdom.

It is for medium-term credit that differences appear significant and affect availability of finance and thus competitiveness. Whereas the banks in the United Kingdom compete vigorously to finance medium-term credits, Eximbank is almost the only source in the United States. In Germany the official KFW competes with commercial banks in lending. In Japan commercial banks finance 30% of major contracts, with Eximbank providing the other 70%. France has a sophisticated refinancing system as well as a state body, BFCE, for longer maturities.

CREDIT INSURANCE FACILITY DIFFERENCES

The whole turnover principle for short-term cover in the United Kingdom, the United States, Canada and Australia is not followed in Germany or Sweden, where individual markets or even buyers can be selected. Whereas the whole market concept may spread the premium cost between high- and low-risk markets, experience shows that even with higher premiums for selected markets, exporters in Germany and Sweden prefer that option.

Most organizations cover both commercial and political risks in the same policy. Some, such as France, offer a choice. For medium-term credit, all countries offer specific policies for single contracts. For buyer credits, however, Germany's Hermes does not cover lines of credit.

The percentage of cover varies between 80% and 100%. Eximbank in the United States covers political rather than commercial risks. France covers 90% on supplier credit and 95% on buyer credits. Not all countries provide support for performance bonds comparable to that of Canada, Germany and Sweden. On the other hand, a number of countries do provide cost escalation cover on major contracts. The minimum size of eligible contracts varies widely. Countries with low rates of inflation have no such cover and have criticised the providing countries.

Exchange risks cover varies widely. Apart from tender to contract cover, the United Kingdom does not provide this form of support, and nor does the United States. However France insures the risk for exporters in United States dollars with no forward exchange cover, and Germany limits the cover to certain currencies.

OVERALL DIFFERENCES

An Eximbank report to Congress in 1979 described the United Kingdom, France,

Italy and Japan as the most competitive, with the United States and Canada the least competitive.

France's system of credits mixes (finance plus soft loans) is highly effective and outside the consensus guidelines, with the United Kingdom hardly using this technique at all.

Countries such as Canada, with only one body providing both insurance and finance, are said to be quicker to make offers to buyers than the United Kingdom, where banks and the Export Credits Guarantee Department have to work together to devise mutually acceptable export credits.

Table 3.4.1 shows the main features of export credit systems in eleven major countries.

Appendix: Export credit insurers of major countries

Argentina	CASC	Compania Argentina de Serguros de Credito a la Exportacion SA, Sarmiento 400 4°Piso, 1347 Buenos Aires
Australia	EFIC	Export finance and Insurance Corporation, 9th & 10th floors, Export House, 22 Pitt Street, Sydney, NSW 2000 (Postal address: PO Box R65, Royal Exchange, Sydney, NSW 2000)
	EPIC	Export Payments Insurance Corporation, PO Box 2595, 2 Castlereagh Street, Sydney, New South Wales
Austria	Grant	'Garant' Versicherungs AG, Wohllebengasse 4, Vienna 4
	OKB	Oesterreichische Kontrollbank AG, Export Guarantee Dept., Strauchgasse 1 A-1010, Vienna
Belgium	CBAC	Cie Belge d'Assurance-Crédit SA, 15 Rue Montoyer, Bruxelles 4

Table 3.4.1: Main features of major export credit systems

Country	*Credit insurance*	*Export finance*		*Cover/guarantees, etc.*	
		Short-term	*Medium & long-term*	*Short-term*	*Medium- & long-term*
Australia	EFIC—Govt corp.	Commercial banks ABERC	Commercial banks, EFIC or official marketing boards	Comprehensive; whole turnover or agreed group of countries	Supplier and buyer credits. Guarantees to banks
Canada	EDC—Crown corp.; some private sector, independently	Commercial banks	Commercial banks or EDC or both jointly	Comprehensive guarantees; whole turnover of acceptable risk	Supplier and buyer credits. Guarantees to banks
Denmark	EKR—govt appointed representative council	Commercial banks	Central bank organisation in co-operative with commercial banks	Comprehensive, whole turnover and specific type guarantees	Supplier and buyer credits
Finland	VTL—govt agency	Commercial banks	FEC, with bank backing	Comprehensive or specific	Specific policies
France	Coface—nationalised company	Commercial banks	Commercial banks; BFCE (state agency) for maturities over 7 years	Comprehensive	Supplier and buyer credits
New Zealand	EXGO—govt dept	Commercial banks	Commercial banks; also Export–Import Corp. and govt credits via reserve bank	Political and commercial risks. Bank guarantees	Supplier and buyer credits. Bank guarantees

Norway	GIEK—govt agency	Commercial banks	FFE (owned by commercial banks)	Comprehensive or selective	Supplier and buyer credits
Sweden	EKN—state agency	Commercial banks	SEK govt. commercial banks organisation (50/50)	Choice of political risks only or combined with commercial risks. Whole turnover, or single transaction country or buyer	Same as for short-term
United Kingdom	ECGD—govt dept; some private sector, independently	Commercial banks	Commercial banks	Comprehensive guarantees; whole turnover	Extended terms, specific (supplier credits) Buyer credits
United States	Eximbank—govt agency jointly with private sector	Commercial banks	Eximbank, or Eximbank/banks jointly; also Private Export Funding Corporation (PEFCO)	Comprehensive guarantees; whole turnover or acceptable spread	Supplier and buyer credits
West Germany	HERMES—private co. acting for govt with Treuarbeit AG	Commercial banks	Commercial banks or KFW (state agency) or both jointly	Comprehensive; whole turnover not compulsory—single transaction cover widely used	Supplier and buyer credit

(cont.)

Table 3.4.1 (cont.)

Cost escalation	*Performance bonds*	*Other facilities*				*Re-financing*	*Country*
		Pre-shipment cover	*Local costs cover*	*Exchange risk cover*	*Investment insurance*		
No	Yes	Yes	Yes	Partial	Yes	Yes, by ABERC	Australia
No	Yes	Yes	Finance only	No	Yes	No	Canada
No	Yes	Possible	Yes	Yes	No	No	Denmark
Yes	Yes	Yes	Yes	No	Yes	No details available	Finland
Yes	Yes	Yes	Yes	Yes	Yes	Extensive facilities	France
No	Yes	Yes	Yes	No	Yes	No	New Zealand

No	Yes	Yes	Yes	Yes	Yes	No details available	Norway
No	Yes	Yes	Yes	Yes	Yes	Yes, by SEK	Sweden
No	Yes	Yes	Yes	No	Yes	No (but contingent liability on foreign currency loans)	United Kingdom
No	No	Yes	Yes	No	No	Limited to pre-agreed supplier credits	United States
No	Yes	Yes	Yes	Yes	Yes (via Treuarbeit AG)	Provided by AKA—bankers consortium—with some Bundesbank backing	West Germany

Appendix: Export credit insurers of major countries (cont.)

Belgium (cont.)	AC	Les Assurances du Crédit SA, Avenue Prince de Liège, Jambes-Namur
	OND	Office National du Ducroire, 40 Square de Meeus, Bruxelles 1040
Brazil	IRB	Instituto de Resseguros do Brasil, Avenida Marechal Camara, 171 ZC-00, 20,000 Rio de Janeiro, RJ Brazil. PO Box 1440
Canada	ECIC	Export Credits Insurance Corporation, PO Box 655, 151 O'Connor St., Ottawa K1P 579
	EDC	Export Development Corporation, 151 O'Connor St., Ottawa K1P 579, Ontario
Cyprus	ECIS	Export Credit Insurance Service, Ministry of Commerce and Industry, Nicosia
Czechoslovakia	Statni	Ceska Statni Pojistovna, Nove Mesto, Spalena, PO Box 841, 113-04, Prague 1
Denmark	EKR	Eksportkreditradet (Export Credit Council) Codanhus, GL Kongevej 60, 1850, Frederiksburg, Copenhagen V
Finland	VTL	Vientikakuulaitos (Export Guarantee Board) Eterleranta 6, PO Box 187, SF 00131 Helsinki 13
France	Coface	Compagnie Française d'Assurance pour le Commerce Exterieur, 12 Cours Michelet, La Defense 10, 92800 Puteux (Postal address: Cedex 51, 92065 Paris La Defense)

West Germany	Hermes	Hermes Kreditversicherungs AG, PO Box 500740, Friedensallee 254, 2000 Hamburg 50
	GKS	Gerling-Konzern Speziale Kredit-versicherungs AG, Gerling-Hochhaus, 5000 Köln
Greece	ECIF	Bank of Greece, Export Credit Insurance Fund, 21 E Venizelos Ave, Athens
Hong Kong	HKECIC	Hong Kong Export Credit Insurance Corporation, South Seas Centre, Tower 1, 2nd floor, 75 Moy Road, Timshatsui East, Kowloon (Postal address: Box 98548 TST, Post Office, Hong Kong)
Hungary	ALLAMI	Allami Biztosito (Insurance Enterprise of the State), 1813 Budapest, Ulloi ut 1
India	ECGC	Export Credit & Guarantee Corporation Ltd, PO Box 373, Bombay 400221, Express Towers, 10th floor, Nariman Point, Bombay
Indonesia	Askrindo	P:T Asuransi Indonesia (Indonesia Export Credit Insurance Co Ltd), Darnareska Building, 17th floor, Jalan Medan Merdeka Selatan No 13, Jakarta 10001
Ireland		The Insurance Corporation of Ireland Ltd, Burlington House, Burlington Road, Dublin 4 The Hibernian Insurance Co Ltd, Hawkins House, Hawkins Street, Dublin 2

Israel	IFTRIC	The Israel Foreign Trade Risks Insurance Corporation Ltd, Mayo Building, 74 Petah Tivkah Road, PO Box 20215, Tel-Aviv 61201
Italy	INA	Instituto Nazionale delle Assicurazioni, Via Sallustriana 51, 00100 Roma
	SACE	Sezione Speziale per Assicurazione dei Crediti all'Esportazione, Piazza Poli 37, Roma
	SIAC	Societa Italiana Assicurazione Credito Spa, Via Rafaello, 00139 Rome, Matarazzo 19 (Postal address: Casella Postale 2446 AD, 1-00108 Rome)
	SIC	Societa-Italiana Cauzioni (Cia. di Assicurazioni e Riassicurazioni), Via Crescenzio 12, 00193 Roma
Jamaica	JECIC	Jamaica Export Credit Insurance Corporation Ltd, Bank of Jamaica Building, Nethersole Place, Kingston
Japan	MITI	Export Insurance Section, International Trade Bureau, Ministry of International Trade & Industry, 1-3-1 Chome Kasumigaseki, Chiyoda-ku, Tokyo
Korea		Export Import Bank of Korea, 16-1, Yoido-Dong, Youngdungpo-GU, Seoul 150
Luxembourg	ODL	Office du Ducroire Luxembourgeois, 8 Avenue de l'Arsenal, Luxembourg

	SNCI	Société Nationale de Crédit et d'Investissement, c/o Ministère des finances, 3 Rue de la Congregation, Luxembourg
Malaysia	MECIB	Malaysia Export Credit Insurance Berhad, 2nd floor, Wisma Damansara, Jalan Sewantan, PO Box 11048, Kuala Lumpur
Mexico	Fondo	Banco Nacional de Comercio Exterior SA, Via Caranza No 32 –4° Piso Centro, Degacion Cuailhtamoc 0600, Mexico DF
	FOMEX	Fonda Para El Fomento de Las Exportaciones de Productos Manufacturados (Fund for the Promotion of Exports of Manufactured Goods) Camino A Santa Teresa No 1679, Colonia Jardines del Pedregal, Delegacion Alvaro Obregion, PO Box No APP 389, CP 01900, Mexico DF
	COMESEC	Compagnia Mexicande Seguros de Credito, Insurgentes Sur No 587, CP 03810 Mexico DF
Netherlands	NCM	Nederlandsche Credietverzekering Maatschappij NV, Keizersgracht 271-287 PO Box 473, 1000 AL Amsterdam-C
New Zealand	Exgo	Export Guarantee Office, State Insurance Building, Lambton Quay, PO Box 5037, Wellington CI
Norway	GIEK	Garanti-Instituttet for Eksportkreditt (Export Credit Guarantee Institute) Postboks 1756 Vika, Oslo 1

Pakistan	ECGS	Pakistan Insurance Corporation, Export Credit Guarantee Scheme, M.J. Jinnah Road, PO Box 4777, Karachi 2
Philippines		Philippines Export Credit Insurance and Guarantee Corporation, Room 520, Central Bank, Main Building, Vito Cruz Street, Manila
Poland	WARTA	Warta Insurance and Reinsurance Co Ltd, 00-916 Warszawa Si u'Traugulta 5a, Warsaw
Portugal	COSEC	Compania de Seguros de Creditos, EP Avenida de Republica 58-13° 1094 Lisbon
Singapore	ECICS	Export Credit Insurance Corporation of Singapore Ltd, 10 Shenton Way, 17-03/09 MAS Building, Singapore 0207
South Africa	CGIC	Credit Guarantee Insurance Corporation of Africa Ltd, 31 Dover Street, Randburg, 2194 Johannesburg 2000 (Postal address: PO Box 9244, Johannesburg 2000)
Spain	CESCC	Cia Espanola de Seguros de Credito y Caucion SA, 3 Raimunda Fernandes Villaverde, E-28003 Madrid (Postal address: Apartado Correos 524 Madrid 3)
	CESCE	Compania Espanola de Seguros de Credito a la Exportacon SA, c/Velazquez 74,2800 1 Madrid
	CCS	Corsorcio de Compensacion de Seguros, Ministeriod de Hacienda, Serrano 69, Madrid 1

Sri Lanka	SLECIC	278/5 Union Place, Colombo 2 (Postal address: PO Box 2213 Colombo 2)
Sweden	EKN	Exportkreditnamnden (Export Credits Guarantee Board), Norrlandsgatan 15, PO Box 7334, S-10390 Stockholm
	Svenska-kredit	Svenska Kreditforsakrings AB, Box 7073, S-10382 Stockholm 7
Switzerland	Federal	The Federal Insurance Co Ltd (Eidgenoessische Versicherungs AG) Flossergasse 3, 8039, Zeurich Geschaeftsstelle fuer die Exportriskogarantie, Kirchenweg 8-CH 8032, Zurich
United Kingdom	ECGD	Export Credits Guarantee Department, PO Box 272, Export House, 50 Ludgate Hill, London EC4M 7AY
United States	Eximbank	Export-Import Bank of the US, 811 Vermont Avenue, NW, Washington DC 20571
	FCIA	Foreign Credit Insurance Association, 40 Rector Street, 11th floor, New York, NY 10006
Zimbabwe	ZCIC	Zimbabwe Credit Insurance Corporation of Rhodesia Ltd, PO Box 1085, Harare

PART 2 PRIVATE INSURANCE MARKETS

BACKGROUND

The previous part has outlined the credit insurance facilities available through the Export Credits Guarantee Department (ECGD) and various other major government or government controlled bodies. While the Department still retains its dominant position in terms of credit insurance support, the past decade has seen the emergence of a number of alternative underwriting sources in the private sector offering a range of facilities which either complement or act as alternatives to those of the Department. In particular there has been a significant increase in the availability of insurance against the political risks through the private sector.

The London market dominates the private sector although similar credit insurance arrangements are available through, for example, European and United States companies. As mentioned in part one, the European influence is likely to increase with the advent of the European Market in 1992. The following pages describe the facilities offered by the major United Kingdom based companies involved (see the appendix for names and addresses).

TRADE INDEMNITY PLC

Trade Indemnity plc are the largest specialist credit insurers within the United Kingdom. Since their formation in 1918 they have traditionally sought to base their portfolio of business on United Kingdom domestic sales, with export cover only available on a limited basis as an adjunct to the domestic credit insurance policy. However, given the limitations of such arrangements with regard to the risks and markets which could be covered, Trade Indemnity have expanded direct into the export credit insurance field through the vehicle of their export cover policies.

EXPORT COVER POLICY WHOLE TURNOVER

The policy provides an annual cover for direct United Kingdom exports or third country transactions undertaken by British companies on specifically agreed payment terms (usually maximum 180 days). It can also provide similar cover to companies operating outside the United Kingdom, subject to local licensing arrangements.

Within the whole turnover concept, Trade Indemnity is usually prepared to consider insuring the whole of an export portfolio or a selection within that portfolio (such as one market or a group of markets). In addition various deductible arrangements are also available which provide for the exporter to take first losses and selected accounts cover as required. This can either be on the basis of aggregate first losses, 'each and every' first losses, or specific datum line and threshold arrangements. Cover normally commences from date of despatch of the goods, although work in progress (the manufacturing and pre-shipment risk) can also be included if required with the conditions applicable to each market identified at inception.

Risks covered. The risks covered by Trade Indemnity are commercial, and political by specific endorsement.

(1) Commercial:
   - (a) insolvency of the buyer;
   - (b) the buyer's failure to pay within six months of due date for goods he has accepted.

(2) Political:
   (a) non-transfer of local currencies properly deposited;
   (b) contract frustration caused by events outside the control of both the buyer and the exporter;
   (c) government, public sector buyer default.

The standard indemnity level for all risks is 85-90%, although this is subject to negotiation dependent upon the nature of the business insured.

Payment of claims. Insolvency claims are paid within thirty days of confirmation of debt by the liquidator, receiver, or equivalent. Default claims are paid six months from due date. Government buyer and other political causes of loss claims are paid from four months to fifteen months from the due date or event causing the loss, depending upon the market involved.

Premium payment. Premium rates are set at the inception of the policy according to the market and the terms of payment applicable to the business transacted. Premiums are usually payable quarterly in advance at a pre-set figure with an adjustment at the end of the year to reflect actual annual turnover levels.

Credit limits. Trade Indemnity require credit limits to be established on individual customers which are either agreed direct or are established on the basis of the exporter's own experience or information on the customer.

The discretionary limit is usually set at a minimum level of £10,000 and allows exporters to justify credit given up to that level based on information from bank or approved agency sources or trading experience, or a combination of both. Above the discretionary limit a specific credit limit is issued by Trade Indemnity based on their assessment of the buyer's creditworthiness.

Multi-market policy

The multi-market policy is a relatively new facility. The intention is to provide exporters with combined credit insurance facilities for both export and domestic sales on the basis described above.

Insurances of Credit Co (IOCC)

Insurances of Credit Co are the United Kingdom arm of Les Assurances du Crédit SA, the Belgian credit insurance company who have established bases in a number of European (mainly European Community) countries.

The cover, normally offered on a whole turnover basis, is similar to that provided by Trade Indemnity but is limited to the commercial risks of insolvency and default on payment by the buyer and is primarily concerned with trading within Europe.

The policy arrangements mirror those of Trade Indemnity in terms of claims waiting periods and payment of premiums. Insurances of Credit Co do however, place greater emphasis on their own specific vetting of credit limits on buyers and provide indemnity levels of 75% to 85% dependent on the market concerned.

AMERICAN INTERNATIONAL UNDERWRITERS (AIU)

American International Underwriters is a major American based company which has been providing various forms of credit insurance support in the United States and overseas for a number of years.

Its London-based operation provides a package of political risk covers ranging from one-off arrangements for specific countries to a form of blanket arrangement for total export turnovers or an acceptable range of markets.

In addition, the company now has whole turnover export credit policies which provide cover against both commercial and political risks.

POLITICAL RISKS

Under its political risk policies, American International Underwriters can provide for the following:

(1) Sales to public buyers;
(a) contract repudiation;
(b) import and export licence cancellation;
(c) currency inconvertibility or exchange transfer;
(d) wrongful calling of guarantees or bonds;
(e) expropriation of the buyer;
(f) any other act of government preventing the buyer from honouring his contract.

(2) Sales to private buyers:
(a) currency inconvertibility or exchange transfer;
(b) import and export licence cancellation;
(c) civil war, rebellion, revolution;
(d) expropriation of the buyer;
(e) any other act of government preventing the buyer from honouring his contract.

Indemnities. The normal indemnity level is 90%, although this may be varied according to the nature of the risks to be insured.

Payment of claims. Various waiting periods may be applied (for example from six months to two years) which again reflect the nature of the risks to be insured.

Premium payment. Premium rates are individually assessed and are based on the market concerned, the goods, the quality of the buyer and the experience of the exporter. Payment of total premiums due is usually required in advance.

Comprehensive export credit policy

Cover is available for sales of goods of both United Kingdom and foreign origin to private and public sector buyers, usually on an acceptable whole turnover basis which might mean one market or a group of markets. Occasionally transactions with single buyers may be covered. The policies are underwritten on a deductible basis whereby the exporter bears an agreed first loss with the insurers being liable for losses arising above that figure.

Risks covered. The risks insured under the export credit policy are the normal commercial and political risks through which the buyer fails to make payment of the gross invoice value of goods supplied. Cover can be extended to cover the pre-delivery risks with the exception of contract cancellation.

Indemnities. For the whole turnover policies the normal indemnity is a maximum of 90%. For single transactions the level of indemnity is 80%.

Payment of claims. Claims are payable for commercial risks at six months from due date and for political risks at nine months, unless specifically amended to reflect particular market conditions.

Premium payment. Premium rates are set at inception of the policy and premiums are payable in advance. Minimum premiums are a standard requirement (currently $50,000).

Credit limits. The operation of the policy including credit limits is essentially based on the exporter's own credit management functions. Credit limits are required on each buyer with whom the exporter trades and are normally set within an overall agreed discretionary authority on the basis of the exporter's own experience with the buyer. Where the discretionary authority is insufficient for proposed future trading then the insurer will issue a specific credit limit based on their own assessment of the buyer's creditworthiness.

PAN FINANCIAL INSURANCE CO LTD

Pan Financial Insurance Co Ltd (Panfinancial), originally established as a joint venture company between the United States, Swedish and Japanese Insurers is now owned by Scandia International. The cover offered to both United Kingdom and overseas companies was originally limited to the commercial risk of the insolvency of the buyer, but Panfinancial has now expanded its facilities through to a range of political risk covers.

INSOLVENCY CATASTROPHE INSURANCE

The policy offers cover on an annual aggregate first loss or excess loss basis and is intended to provide the exporter with catastrophe cover against major losses arising. The exporter carries all losses for his own account up to the agreed annual aggregate level. Cover is normally provided on a whole turnover basis with a maximum liability imposed and with the smaller, insignificant losses excluded from the scope of the policy.

Risks covered. Cover under the policy is limited to the commercial risk of the insolvency of the buyer.

Indemnity. Panfinancial provides a 100% indemnity for all qualifying losses above the annual aggregate up to the level of the agreed maximum liability.

Payment of claims. Claims are payable once the annual aggregate has been exceeded and within thirty days of confirmation of the debt by the liquidator, receiver or equivalent.

Premium payment. There is no premium rate as such, but a total premium outlay is called for at the inception of cover as a flat cost.

Credit limits. The operation of credit limits under the policy is based on the exporter's own credit management controls and knowledge of his buyers which allows considerable discretion and minimal referral to Panfinancial for specific vetting.

CONTRACT COMPLETION INSURANCE

The policy provides single contract insurance protection through political risks, subject to a normal maximum term of three years.

Risks covered. The risks for which the exporter can select cover are:

(1) public buyer default or repudiation;
(2) contract frustration;
(3) export or import licence cancellation;
(4) transfer delays;
(5) war;
(6) any other government actions which prevent the buyer from performing.

Indemnity. The normal indemnity levels are 90% to 95%, although these might be varied according to the nature of the risks insured.

Payment of claims. Waiting periods are imposed on all claims payments which reflect the nature of the market risks involved.

Premium payment. Premiums are assessed and payable in advance on the basis of the particular risks insured in the market concerned.

WRONGFUL CALLING OF GUARANTEES

Panfinancial will provide protection against the political risks causing the wrongful calling of on-demand bank guarantees, bonds, and other instruments with an indemnity level of 90% to 95%.

NON-HONOURING OF LETTERS OF CREDIT

Cover is available on a single contract basis against the political risk for the bank's failure to honour its obligations under a letter of credit with an indemnity level of 90% to 95%.

LLOYD'S OF LONDON

Lloyds' underwriters are not able to provide protection against the commercial risks of insolvency and default on payment by the buyer. However, certain Lloyd's syndicates will offer specific cover for a range of political risks which prevent performance of the contract. The cover itself can be provided through both the pre-delivery and post-delivery periods of a contract up to a maximum time scale of three years and is available to exporters in the United Kingdom or overseas.

Risks covered. There are a considerable number of variables available through Lloyds' which are at the exporter's option. Some of the most common are:

(1) contract termination (public buyers);
(2) import or export licensing restrictions;
(3) events of force majeure which frustrate the contract;
(4) public buyer default;
(5) exchange transfer or currency inconvertibility restrictions;
(6) unfair calling of bank guarantees.

Indemnities and payment claims. The normal indemnity level is 90% and claims waiting periods between four and thirty months are imposed to reflect the nature of the risks insured.

Premium payment. Premiums are assessed at inception of the cover and are usually payable in advance or can be phased against individual despatches.

SUN ALLIANCE INTERNATIONAL

Sun Alliance International is a fairly new addition to the credit insurance ranks. The company provides cover on either a whole turnover catastrophe or selected top account basis against risk of insolvency or protracted default for sales into Western Europe.

CREDIT AND GUARANTEE INSURANCE CO LTD

This company provides specialist credit insurance facilities in relation to business transacted in Denmark, Finland, France, the Netherlands, Norway, Sweden and the United States of America.

The policies are specific in that they cover individual contracts in excess of £100,000. Cover is provided against the insolvency risk with variable indemnity levels possible up to 100%. Premiums are set at inception and are payable in advance.

BLACK SEA AND BALTIC GENERAL INSURANCE CO LTD

Cover is provided against the political risks on a specific basis for contracts with buyers in the Comecon Bloc countries. Both United Kingdom and non-United Kingdom goods are acceptable, the cover can be applied to the pre-delivery and post-delivery risks, and extended credit terms up to a maximum of five years are possible.

Indemnity levels are normally 90%, and premiums are assessed and are payable at the inception of the cover on the nature of the risks and the market insured.

APPENDIX: MAJOR UNITED KINGDOM PRIVATE EXPORT CREDIT INSURERS

American International Underwriters (UK) Ltd,
120 Fenchurch Street,
London EC3M 5BP

Black Sea and Baltic General Insurance Co Ltd,
Black Sea and Baltic House,
65 Fenchurch Street,
London EC3M 4EY

Credit and Guarantee Insurance Co Ltd,
Surety House,
Lyons Crescent,
Tonbridge,
Kent TN9 1EN

Insurances of Credit Co,
Park House,
22 Park Street,
Croydon CR0 0YH

Lloyd's of London
(via accredited brokers only)

Pan Financial Insurance Co Ltd,
International House,
World Trade Centre,
1 St Katharine's Way,
London E1 9UN

Sun Alliance International,
Leadenhall Court,
1 Leadenhall Street,
London EC3V 1PP

Trade Indemnity plc,
Trade Indemnity House,
PO Box 228,
12/34 Great Easter Street,
London EC2A 3AX

BOB A. RAND

Bain Clarkson Credit and Political Risks Ltd

3.5
Credit control for difficult countries

The now familiar World Debt Crisis of the 1980s brought a new dimension to credit control. One after another, countries in Latin America, Africa and elsewhere found it necessary to borrow vast sums and reschedule their international debts. The problems of these, and other countries that may join them, will go on for many years but meanwhile they have in some way to go on trading internationally to help house, feed and clothe their populations. Nowadays the competent international credit controller is someone who can readily assess country as well as customer risk and can manage both, thereby promoting profitable sales and successful settlement even in the more difficult countries.

This chapter discusses the ways in which such risks can be assessed, how some of them may be wholly or partly laid off and how, for those which are acceptable, the danger of default or protracted delay on payment may be minimized. Credit control for direct exports to those countries and the special circumstances which may be encountered when operating through local subsidiaries are both covered. An order from a customer in a difficult overseas market immediately begs the question: will their country have the invoiced currency available and allow it to be remitted to the United Kingdom?

If the answer is clearly NO and there is absolutely no way of securing the debt outside the country of risk, then there will be little point in going on to assess the *customer's* ability to pay as the order ought to be rejected anyway. For most of these countries, however, the answer is never so emphatic and the credit controller's skill lies in identifying those to which, in some cases perhaps only temporarily, his company should be prepared to sell, provided of course the customer risk is manageable.

COUNTRY RISK ASSESSMENT

Assessment of country risk involves the gathering of pertinent information and its synthesis, creating the model explained below. This kind of modelling cannot claim to be scientific, but to do it really effectively requires dedicated resource. For this reason most exporters who take risk assessment seriously prefer to use some form of external information service, if not the full services of a professional forecasting agency.

An Appendix to this chapter lists a small but by no means exhaustive selection of forecasting agencies, some of which have arranged for their information to be computerized and made instantly available through a variety of on-line databases.

Before entering into any contract for regular information or forecasts, however, exporters should check the range of countries covered in depth by the agency, the relevance to their particular line of business and, most important, how frequently the agency's data is updated.

COUNTRY RISK EVALUATION METHODS

Professional forecasters gather a wide range of opinions and information to present a consolidated view of each country. Some use modelling techniques, assigning scores and weights to a broad range of economic and political factors, assessed both quantitatively and qualitatively. Those factors which can be quantified would include a country's liquidity, debt servicing ratio and earning capacity. The more imprecise qualitative judgements would focus on political, sociological and cultural conditions. Obviously one country cannot be assessed in this manner in isolation, and so would be measured against some ideal score using regression analysis. Comparison of the scores over a period establishes a trend indicating improvement or deterioration.

The financial ratios used in this methodology can be especially useful, but it must always be remembered that they are only indicative, never absolute; one ratio on its own can be virtually meaningless. For the export credit controller, assessing a particular country will normally involve gathering as much relevant information as possible from forecasters and other sources (see below), preferably visiting the country in person, and blending all the facts in the context of the particular line of business. The objective of this should be to manage, rather than necessarily eliminate, the risks identified.

COUNTRY RISK — SOURCES OF INFORMATION

The main sources of country risk information, some of which are detailed in the Appendix to this chapter, are the commercial agencies, official governmental bodies, credit institutes and associations, and the banks. Major banks issue free regular publications on key country trends as well as economic reviews and, as major creditors of the debtor countries, their information should by necessity be sound and reliable. All the countries of the world are classified by the Organisation for Economic Co-operation and Development (OECD) into three categories according to wealth, for the purpose of establishing consensus interest rates and for officially supported export finance (see also Chapter 3.4). This in itself can be a fair indication of a country's creditworthiness. For those exporters with other credit insurance policies, the special conditions which the underwriter applies to certain countries may provide finer reference and additional indicators. No matter how the exporter is represented in a market — by an agent, distributor or other representative — the people on the spot will always be invaluable sources of information; they have access to all the local statistics, publications and gossip; they understand the implications for an exporter's particular line of business.

Neither can the value of a personal visit to the country under scrutiny be overemphasised. Export salesmen's visit reports should offer as much relevant information as possible, but this should not inhibit credit controllers from visiting the market themselves. A visit taken from a deliberate credit management standpoint can provide enormous insight into a country's economic prospects and those business opportunities for which foreign exchange is reasonably assured.

EXPORT CUSTOMER RISK

Given that the levels of country risks (or the options for combating them) are acceptable, it is then necessary to assess the *customer's* ability to pay. As with domestic customers, this is all about solvency, liquidity and potential growth. Assessment should again start with the gathering of data from all available sources. These are detailed below.

(1) CREDIT REPORTING AGENCIES

The most fruitful ready made sources of customer information are normally the credit reporting agencies. Some of the better known agencies now have on-line databases available to those companies that can afford the subscription (see Appendix for details of a Database Directory). Their strengths tend to lie in reporting on customers in the more developed countries. For some of the more difficult countries there may not even be a local agency in the market itself.

(2) BANKS

Information obtained from banks may often do little more than marginally confirm hopes or suspicions. Written reports tend to be bland and non-committal but, on occasions, a foreign banker may be happy to provide considerably more information verbally.

(3) LOCAL REPRESENTATIVES AND EMBASSIES

Whatever their trading relationship to the exporter, local representatives will be a major source of customer information. In the case of agents, if (as should be the case) their commission depends upon successful payment from the customer, they will have a vested interest in keeping their ears to the ground, and acting as a first line of customer risk assessment.

Local embassies may also be able to provide useful information or point the exporter towards an appropriate source.

(4) THE EXPORT SALES LEDGER
For existing customers, the exporter's own sales ledger should contain a wealth of information, provided past and current performance can be summarized and processed to produce individual customer profiles.

(5) VISITS TO THE MARKET
As with country risk assessment, without denigrating the value of export salesmen's visits, separate visits by credit controllers can enable them to consider each customer from a totally different viewpoint. They can speak in more detail with bankers and financial institutions, and gain a wealth of risk assessment information from visiting a customers' factories, warehouses and other premises. During such visits it is often possible to obtain up-to-date financial statements which can be analyzed (see below) and cross-checked against the views of bankers and other interested parties. But the greatest benefit lies in on-the-spot evaluation of the calibre and integrity of management, organizational structure, levels and quality of stocks and the general strength of the customer's trading or manufacturing base.

ASSESSING A CUSTOMER BY REFERENCE TO FINANCIAL STATEMENTS

The legal financial requirements of company accounting vary considerably from country to country and in some of the more difficult ones it is often impossible to obtain up-to-date audited financial statements. In such cases, however, customers can often be persuaded to part with accounts that are not available to the public at large.

Given a reliable set of financial statements, conventional ratios and trends of liquidity, working capital and profitability can be constructed. (See Reading List in the Appendix).

It has to be remembered, however, that conventions acceptable in the United Kingdom will not necessarily apply abroad. Asset values in particular need to be treated with scepticism from the viewpoint of the exporter's ability to realise their value if they have to be taken over.

In the final analysis, ratios and other conclusions drawn from financial statements cannot be an end in themselves. They are just one of the tools to be used in overall customer risk assessment.

MANAGEMENT OF THE RISKS

Once the degree of risk is determined, exporters must decide whether they are going to take the risk, to try to offload all or part of it or to reject the business.

To assist this process as a regular activity, it is normal to classify customers and countries into several categories, from high to low risk, and to assign credit limits in terms of maximum exposure per customer and country.

Credit limits can be constructed at various levels, by reference to a variety of criteria, and normally represent a compromise between marketing and credit department considerations. The overriding factor for a difficult market might be the overall amount the exporter can afford to lose without catastrophic side-effects. At the customer level it is the amount which, having regard to their other commitments, the customer's earnings and general financial situation are going to enable them to pay and remit through their exchange control.

A technique favoured by some exporters is to treat certain risky customers (or indeed a difficult country) as marginal; these exporters pursue a deliberately suicidal policy by continuing to sell, while investing little marketing effort, knowing that some time the customers or country will be unable to pay their way. In the meantime, however, profits will have to be good and, while trade continues, credit limits will be constructed by reference to the profit made on sales to the customer or country over a previous period, such as the last six months.

However the categories and limits are determined, they must be kept constantly up-to-date; potential transgressions must be instantly reported for appropriate action. This particularly applies to any marginal customers whose debts should be rigorously pursued as soon as they become overdue.

LAYING OFF OR SHARING A RISK

When careful assessment shows a risk to be unacceptable, the credit controller has the choice of either rejecting the order or, if it is possible and cost effective to do so, of shifting all or part of the risk to someone else.

There are five main ways in which the risk may be shifted, all of them bringing additional opportunities for directly or indirectly financing the export.

DOCUMENTARY LETTERS OF CREDIT

Letters of credit are discussed in detail, along with other settlement methods, later in this chapter. It will be seen that guarantees of payment may be obtained from the issuing bank in the customer's country and additionally from a confirming bank outside the country of risk. This is subject to the type of letter of credit and provided that all documentation is properly prepared and presented.

CONFIRMING HOUSE FINANCE

Confirming houses grew up as trade with the Commonwealth countries developed; their role is to seek suppliers in the United Kingdom to satisfy order enquiries from customers in those countries. The customers pay the commissions. As time went by, it became common for an exporter to take the initiative by asking a confirming house to introduce buyers and to lend their guarantee of payment by way of a contract of confirmation.

In this way the buyer could enjoy a longer period of credit from the confirming house than the exporter would be prepared to grant. Naturally, for paying the exporter normally within thirty days and without recourse, the confirming house would charge a substantial fee. This was made up of the financing cost, normally competitive with overdraft rates, plus what was in effect a proportionate credit insurance premium, reflecting the cost of the confirming house's own credit insurance cover, surcharged to allow for the expense of administration of their policy.

These days most of the confirming houses have been taken over by the major banks in the form of a modern export finance bank service backed by credit insurance, evidenced by what are still known as confirming house policies. Many belong to the British Export Houses Association, which is incorporated in the British Exporters Association (see Appendix) and can advise exporters in which products and markets their members specialize.

FACTORING

Most factoring companies are subsidiaries of the major banks, offering a range of services, usually under an annual agreement. For basic factoring, the exporter passes all invoices to the factor for collection and normally receives 80% of the value at date of invoicing and the balance when the customers pay — or at an agreed average due date. The percentage advanced can be without recourse provided the exporter keeps within credit limits established by the factor. The financing element of the cost is usually competitive with overdraft rates. In addition, the factor can offer a full sales ledger and credit control service. The factor's separate fee for this service, however, can be 2% or more of sales value, which is usually more than it would cost the exporters to run their own operation. There may also be commercial objections to placing a third party between seller and buyer.

FORFAITING

In forfaiting operations, exporters forfeit their rights to debts to a forfaiting bank in return for payment without recourse.

The bank in its turn is looking for good quality country risk paper. Thus forfaiting normally includes the discounting of bills of exchange or promissory notes evidencing debts due from customers who are either State concerns or who can otherwise arrange for the bills or notes to be guaranteed or avalised by a State or major national bank. The risk in the bills or notes thus becomes a State risk, and there is a flourishing market for this type of paper.

Forfaiting operations are particularly prevalent in trade with the East European countries. They tend to favour medium to long term credit transactions, where a series of bills or notes maturing at intervals are involved, but there is a growing market for short term deals.

CREDIT INSURANCE

Insurance cover against non-payment or delayed payment of export debts through customers' or the more difficult countries' inability to pay has been traditionally obtained from either the Export Credits Guarantee Department (ECGD) or the private insurance market.

The development of the European Single Market will, from mid-1990, make it possible for any Community member to insure with any underwriter in any Community country; as part of the inevitable re-positioning of underwriters, the insurance services part of the Export Credit Guarantee Department is being sold to private investors.

The wide variety of facilities available from the insurers is described in Chapter 3.4.

In general terms it is always sensible to shop around for credit insurance using the services of a specialist broker. Companies with a wide export portfolio may also consider self insurance, which simply means not insuring the risk but taking it themselves. The decision can be monitored by examining performance over the last few years and comparing the credit insurance premia that *would* have been paid, with the losses that *were* incurred by way of bad debts or the financing cost of overdues. A strong argument against such a strategy, however, is the simple fact that past payment performance is no guide to the future, especially when dealing with the more volatile markets.

INTERNATIONAL METHODS OF SETTLEMENT

Settlement for exports is normally arranged by one of the methods described below, but may in any event be delayed through the operation of exchange controls, which are covered later in this chapter.

OPEN ACCOUNT

This means that the documents evidencing shipment or title are sent direct to the customer, who can thus withdraw the goods from Customs as soon as they arrive without any incentive to pay the exporter, apart from fear of a stop being put on further supplies or of legal action. Some exporters also elect to send the customers, via their bankers, a bill of exchange for acceptance (known as a 'clean bill'). Until the customer chooses to accept it, the exporter is totally at risk. Open Account terms are not recommended for the more difficult markets.

DOCUMENTARY COLLECTIONS AND DOCUMENTARY BILLS

This method involves the use of a third party, usually a local collecting bank, to act as honest intermediary, exchanging the documents evidencing shipment or title for the customer's payment or promise to pay. The customer's promise to pay arises when the exporter has agreed to grant a period of credit, say sixty days, before payment becomes due. The promise is normally made by the customer by accepting a usance bill of exchange (otherwise known as a tenor draft) and such collections are sometimes referred to as documentary bills.

Bills used in export documentary collection operations are designated foreign bills and, in order to bestow a reasonable level of payment security for the exporter, they must be protested for non-acceptance or non-payment. This procedure, which is not permitted in every country, involves instructing the collecting bank to the effect that, in the event of dishonour, they should call in a Notary Public to note the customer's default and formally protest the bill. The advantage of protesting a foreign bill is that it can then normally be sued upon in a court of law in its own right. Additionally, the mere instruction to protest in the event of dishonour acts as a notice of intent and an incentive to the customer to pay his debt on the due date.

The act of protest, however, is normally published in a local official gazette and may cause undue and undesirable concern amongst the customer's local creditors. In addition, at the time of protest, whatever the invoiced currency of the debt, it will normally be converted to local currency; the local value so determined will usually carry through to any subsequent legal action and any resulting judgment. Where weak, eroding local currencies are concerned, a substantial exchange loss can result.

Instructions to banks enclosing documents for collection need to be precise and the documents themselves as accurate as possible. The collections are usually arranged through the exporter's bank but certain very large multinationals, which are well represented abroad, may choose to deal direct with a collecting bank in the customer's market.

A set of Uniform Rules for Collections has been produced by the International Chamber of Commerce (Publication No 322) but banks in many of the more difficult countries decline to adhere to them.

Documentary Collections, whilst more secure than Open Account, do not of themselves offer any protection against country risk. The banks involved have no obligation to check the accuracy of the documents and give no guarantees of payment. This payment method should not be confused with documentary letters of credit, which are described below.

DOCUMENTARY LETTERS OF CREDIT

A documentary letter of credit is a written undertaking given by a bank at the request of a buyer to pay up to a stated sum of money *within a prescribed time against stipulated documents.* This method is the most likely one to be used for difficult countries. There are three main types of Letter of Credit.

(1) *Revocable.* The undertaking given by the issuing bank can be revoked by the bank, or by a customer on whose behalf it has been issued, at any time prior to payment. It thus offers very little security and in practice is rarely used.

(2) *Irrevocable.* Here the issuing bank's undertaking is given absolutely, subject to the documents presented conforming in every detail with the conditions of the letter of credit. The issuing bank, however, will be located in the same country as the customer and its ability to pay will be governed by its local exchange control authority's willingness to allow the invoiced currency to leave the country.

(3) *Irrevocable and confirmed by a bank outside the country of risk.* Here, in addition to the issuing bank's undertaking, there is a further guarantee from a bank in a different, economically stable, country. British bank confirmations offer most security simply because discrepancies can be sorted out quickly, but confirmations from the United States or West European countries are not uncommon. Once opened by the issuing banks, letters of credit are advised through their local correspondents, known as advising banks. For a confirmed letter of credit, the advising bank will normally also become the confirming bank, but this does not have to be the case. A letter of credit can be opened for immediate payment upon presentation of acceptable documents — termed a *Sight Credit* — or for deferred payment at a determinable future time after such presentation.

For deferred payment an *Acceptance Credit* is usually issued, requiring a usance bill of exchange (tenor draft) to be drawn on and accepted by the advising bank (or in certain cases by the issuing bank or the customer). The bills involved are normally readily discountable to provide export finance.

Alternatively, a bill of exchange may be avoided by the opening of a *Deferred Payment Letter of Credit*, which itself provides for a waiting period before payment. In this case any confirmation will be evidenced by the bank's written undertaking upon presentation of satisfactory documents.

Except where they emanate from the Chinese Peoples Republic, letters of credit should make reference to the International Chamber of Commerce's publication No.400, Uniform Customs and Practice for Documentary Credits (UCP). This is an established set of international rules officially accepted throughout the whole of the world except, at present, the Chinese Peoples Republic. The uniform customs and practice in effect defines the default conditions which apply to a letter of credit operation wherever the letter of credit itself is silent on a particular topic. It follows that, to override any standard rule, the letter of credit must, as appropriate, specifically allow or prohibit the particular condition. The whole essence of a letter of credit operation is that:

(1) the customer should arrange for it to be opened in such a way that the exporter can meet the conditions without difficulty;
(2) the exporter should be able to present, within the prescribed time limits, documents which conform absolutely with the letter of credit and with each other.

In those few words are synthesized much of what can go wrong with a letter of credit operation. Official measurements show that over 50% of the sets of documents presented against letters of credit fail upon first presentation. There is exquisite irony in the fact that in those very transactions where exporters are seeking to offload otherwise unacceptable risks, they prejudice their quest for security largely through their own shortcomings. It behoves exporters to devote as much resource as is necessary to ensure that credits are issued abroad with conditions they can adhere to and that documents — whether produced within their own organization or by external bodies such as shipping companies or inspection agencies — will conform accurately and be available for presentation within the specified timescales.

ADVANCE PAYMENT OR CASH WITH ORDER

World trade thrives on credit; payment of the invoiced currency before shipment is only likely to be encountered with small value orders, or totally unknown or uncreditworthy customers given their agreement.

COUNTERTRADE

Countertrade or compensation trading is a generic term encompassing a variety of ways of achieving full or part exchange of goods or services to eradicate or minimize the need for a foreign country to part with scarce foreign exchange. The topic is covered in detail in Chapter 3.7.

TRANSMISSION OF FUNDS

Funds can be transferred by cheque, bankers, draft, airmail transfer between banks, and electronic transfer between banks.

Electronic transfer, using the banks' SWIFT system and telegraphic, telex or cable transfer, is far and away the fastest medium and, to encourage customers and banks to use this method, exporters should stipulate it in their payment instructions and be prepared to pay for the modest cable or telex charge involved. The payment instructions should also be absolutely precise as to the bank (name, address, sort code) and account (name and number) to which the funds are to be sent. A transfer may be part of a much larger cash management operation whereby funds are routed to a particular bank account — perhaps one per currency — to optimize the flexible use of the money and to achieve the economy of large scale banking operations.

OVERSEAS EXCHANGE CONTROLS

Exporters should usually only be prepared to invoice customers abroad in preferred, convertible currencies if, for no other reason, than the simple fact that there is no foreign exchange market for non-convertible currencies. In any event invoicing in a weak currency would, because of creeping devaluation of that currency, give rise to a considerable exchange loss over the period of credit granted. An extreme example of this was the Bolivian peso which, when it gave way to the Boliviano in 1987, lost six zeros. Bolivia's inflation rate had been running at over 20,000% per annum. More recently, on 28 December 1989, it was reported in the *Financial Times* that the Argentinian currency — the Austral — had slumped 21% against the US Dollar in a period of just one day; in that part of the world such rapid devaluations are by no means uncommon.

Where, for the reasons explained above, the invoiced currency is not the customer's national currency, the customer must buy the invoiced currency in order to pay the exporter; this transaction is usually rigidly controlled by the local exchange control authorities especially in Africa, Latin America and the Middle East. In these and other countries exporters will encounter a variety of regulations, the more common of which are described below, together with the actions which the exporter should take to minimize their effect. The section concludes with a discussion of the extreme situation which arises when a moratorium is declared and debts are rescheduled.

DELAYS ON EXCHANGE

A shortage of the invoiced currency causes a delay between application for exchange and its allocation. Countries with a persistent deficit of hard currencies sometimes impose a statutory waiting period. Customers are normally required to deposit the requisite local funds with the collecting bank or the Central Bank when applying for exchange.

TWO-TIER RATES OF EXCHANGE

To reduce imports, a dual rate of exchange is imposed by the foreign government. The free-market rate operates for all transactions other than the import of specified goods, whilst a rate less favourable for the importer is applied when granting hard currency exchange for those imports.

In severe cases of exchange shortage, a rate of exchange more favourable than that applicable in the sparse free market may be guaranteed for postponed payment of outstanding debts, provided creditors are prepared to wait a considerable time for their money.

PROMPT PAYMENT BY CUSTOMER

Customers face heavy fines if they do not deposit local funds and apply for exchange immediately upon or soon after the arrival of the goods. A long waiting period for foreign exchange then invariably ensues.

STATUTORY SETTLEMENT METHODS

The local authority may insist that all imports are settled by bank collection or letter of credit. This enables all outgoing exchange to be monitored via the commercial banking network. Bills of exchange attached to the collections may bear a heavy stamp tax.

PRIOR IMPORT DEPOSIT

Customers are required to deposit a percentage of the value of their import licences with the Central Bank. The percentage varies according to the extent to which the goods being imported are essential to the country's economy and can range from 10% to 1,000%.

The funds so deposited remain with the Central Bank for a period, typically of six months, without earning interest. This obviously discourages the customer from importing at all but, in certain countries, continued business can be so important or profitable that the exporter might agree to loan the prior deposit to the customer. Repayment of such loans, as well as payment for the goods, could however be delayed through exchange shortages as indicated above.

DOCUMENTATION REQUIREMENTS

Many foreign governments control imports through the issue of import licences; they permit foreign exchange to be remitted to the supplier only on presentation of a licence and a variety of other documents including, for instance, the customer's tax clearance certificate. Any irregularity in documentation can delay payment for the import.

LOCAL SETTLEMENT OF AGENCY COMMISSIONS

In certain countries, when payment is collected through a documentary collection, the collecting bank must ensure that any agency commission is paid to the agent locally, out of the collection proceeds. The exporter accordingly receives a net remittance.

MINIMIZING THE EFFECTS OF OVERSEAS EXCHANGE CONTROLS

Exporters should keep abreast of exchange control regulations as part of their country risk assessment procedures. Wherever the kind of controls described above are prevalent or likely to arise, exporters should:

(1) ensure that their credit insurance and other risk-shedding strategies are adequate to meet the threats posed;
(2) obtain estimates of exchange delay trends and circularize such information to all interested parties, especially sales and marketing departments who may wish, if possible, to adjust their prices accordingly;
(3) ensure that all documentation leaves the United Kingdom in good order and that, where a particular settlement method or certification procedure is required, it is strictly followed;
(4) verify that customers deposit local currency at due date and present all required documents in good order to support their exchange applications;
(5) ensure that customers give a written undertaking to remain liable for the full currency value of each invoice and to make up any exchange shortfall which may occur during the period between their depositing local currency and being granted an allocation of the invoiced currency;
(6) monitor the fair allocation of exchange and ensure prompt follow-up by local representatives;

(7) in extreme exchange shortages consider any dual rate of exchange options; an exchange loss may be preferable to the debt going into a rescheduling process.

RESCHEDULING OF DEBTS

If a country reaches the point where it can no longer meet its international payment obligations, it may temporarily call a halt to all foreign exchange transactions while it aggregates its total commitments and devises a plan for discharging them.

This plan will normally provide for the debts to be repaid by instalments over a defined period with interest at an agreed rate.

As soon as such a moratorium is announced, exporters affected by it should ensure that a central bank exchange control authority and local representatives can be provided with comprehensive details of all outstanding debts. A central bank will normally lay down the manner in which debts are to be substantiated, and may even require claimants to have their listings audited and consularized. Local representatives should meanwhile ensure that all documentation is correct and available as required.

Exporters with the comfort of appropriate credit insurance will consider making their claims. For those without such comfort, if, as often happens, the rescheduling scheme includes the option of directly or indirectly investing in the country, this should be considered against the long-term and perhaps uncertain alternative of repayment by instalments. Exporters with a subsidiary in the market may be able to use the blocked debts as working capital or to reinvest them as equity, perhaps at a preferential exchange rate, in their own or some other company.

A third party may be interested in the blocked funds: rescheduling schemes often prompt a variety of offers from entrepreneurs willing to discount exporters' debts for immediate payment in the United Kingdom. Discount rates can be high — the going rate for certain African countries has been generally between 65% and 75%. So realizations could be as low as 25% of the invoiced currency in return for the transfer to the entrepreneur of the local currency blocked in the foreign country. In some countries the realization has been even lower. A further variation on the swap theme might be a countertrade deal, the exporter taking goods or services from the debtor country in liquidation of the debt, suitably discounted. Much of the blocked debt which arose during the so-called World Debt Crisis in the 1980s represented bank loans and, while some of these have been repaid, a good deal has been progressively rolled over and in part written off. Like the remainder of the bank debt those due to commercial organizations and credit insurance agencies have still to be repaid.

COLLECTING THROUGH SUBSIDIARIES

Having a subsidiary company in a difficult market bestows considerable advantages in credit control terms. If the subsidiary is manufacturing or importing and selling in its own name on domestic terms and conditions, it will have complete involvement in collecting its own ledger debts. The same may not be true, however, when it is playing the part of third party agent, receiving commissions on orders referred to its British parent for invoicing direct to customers.

RE-INVOICING

There will be a tendency for the subsidiary to put more effort into collecting its own ledger debts before those referred to it by the United Kingdom parent for collection, unless it can be made to feel the same sense of ownership of those debts. If local regulations allow, this can in some countries be achieved by a process of re-invoicing. Although this may sound administratively cumbersome, it is often well worth the additional effort which in any case can be minimized by the growing use of computers, automatic data transmission and local printing facilities. With re-invoicing, the British parent will still ship the goods to the customer, but will invoice them to the subsidiary at a transfer price and in a currency previously agreed. The subsidiary will then re-invoice the customer locally in the normal trading currency at the normal market price. The transfer price payable by the subsidiary will take account of their mark-up and any credit period differential. The transfer currency will depend upon the group's foreign currency management policy.

The advantage of re-invoicing is that external customer debts get fully into the ledger of the subsidiary, and are progressed alongside ex-stock sales. Meanwhile, the customers maintain a full business relationship with the local entity, using a language and currency which they understand. Efficient systems are necessary to avoid goods getting to their destination before the corresponding documents, thereby causing demurrage penalties and other problems. In certain countries it will also be necessary to demonstrate to the local authorities that tax, price control or other regulations are not being transgressed.

NETTING OF PAYMENTS

Where subsidiaries sell into one another's stocks on a large scale, further advantages can accrue by netting off cash flows either bilaterally or multi-laterally, if permitted by local exchange control authorities. If a British company has subsidiaries in two other countries and they all buy and sell to one another, there could regularly be six different flows of cash. These can be examined, translated into an agreed currency, and offset against each other to produce the minimum requirement of physical cash transfer. Book entries are, of course, necessary to give effect to the receipts and payments which would have occurred if netting had not taken place. The big advantages to the multinational are that most of the group's cash stays with the company rather than floating within and between banks, and bank charges are considerably reduced.

COLLECTING OVERDUE DEBTS

For the really difficult, high sovereign risk markets, good risk assessment should always indicate some secure payment method or guarantee by way of credit insurance or the like. Nevertheless, risks will be taken, markets will not seem to be all that bad and debts will go overdue without security.

In such circumstances the prerequisite of all good debt chasing is an efficient ledger system, always up to date and capable of highlighting debts as they get near to and pass their due date.

It is then equally important that staff be dedicated to the chasing function. Staff beset with considerations of ledger posting, cash allocation and other tasks will always feel they have no alternative but to leave the chasing job until last.

INITIAL PROGRESSING METHODS

When local agents or other representatives are employed, they should be kept posted with analyses of customers' accounts. They should fully earn their commission by ensuring that customers pay promptly on the due date in local currency and that the transmission of the full invoiced currency value is not unnecessarily delayed. In many difficult markets there is a prolonged exchange delay and eventual remittance will depend upon agents ensuring that accurate documentation is provided to the Central Bank at the right time. When debts become overdue without any information as to their payment status, these should be specifically referred to the agent by the fastest possible means — normally telex, fax or telephone. If a collecting bank is involved it should also be exerting pressure on the customer and keeping the exporter informed.

When there is no local third party to represent the exporter, communication is normally with the customer. It pays dividends to get to know and keep in touch with the person within the customer's organization who has the largest vested interest in seeing suppliers' invoices get paid. This may be the finance director, the accounts payable officer or a plant manager who relies upon repeat orders if the plant is to be kept running.

Communications should again be of the fast, electronic variety and using the customer's language will often lead to a more ready response. It is also advisable to give as much information as possible in the first communication to enable customers to identify which invoices they should be paying. This avoids subsequent time wasting replies of the 'What was our order number?' variety.

FOLLOW UP TECHNIQUES

If initial approaches produce no results, stronger action becomes necessary.

(1) Obviously exporters should communicate in a more determined manner, but they should never make threats they are not prepared to carry out.
(2) Local chambers of commerce, embassies or trade organizations may be worth approaching for assistance. Customers dislike bad publicity and the very suggestion that an official body, or indeed the customer's bankers, are going to be approached for help in debt recovery may be sufficient to encourage the customer to pay up.
(3) In extreme circumstances, consideration may have to be given to employing,

directly or indirectly, a local debt collection agency. In some countries, notably in Latin America, lawyers will act in this capacity and, like collection agencies, may operate on a no collection, no fee basis. Successful collection, however, will attract a considerable fee of perhaps 30% or more.

Before engaging a collector, therefore, fee tariffs need to be checked along with the following matters.

(a) Does the agency specialize in commercial rather than consumer collections?

(b) What is their success rate?

(c) Are their collection methods of a face-to-face variety or do they simply rely on sending letters to the customer?

(4) Alternatively, the credit controller might visit delinquent customers. Unless the amounts overdue are very large, this would probably be linked to a visit for other purposes.

The visitor must however go totally prepared and must:

research the facts about the customers;

research the facts about the country being visited;

go with an up-to-date picture of the accounts and, just prior to visiting the customer, obtain an update from head office;

go with a mandate to negotiate such matters as debt restructuring;

respect the customers' laws and traditions and try to speak their language.

Much good information is available from trade ministries and elsewhere (see Appendix) and, given such preparation, the value of a credit controller's visit to the market cannot be overstated. Quite apart from debt collection, country or customer risk assessment can be enhanced and valuable relationships established with banks, customers and agents. These contacts should facilitate the future control of credit.

(5) Legal action

Before embarking on legal action, careful research is necessary to establish the chances of obtaining a judgment for the total debt plus legal fees. There are good arguments both for and against legal action.

(a) Arguments for:

there is a moral issue involved — the exporters have kept their part of the bargain and supplied goods or services, the customers have not kept their part and paid their money;

failure to take strong action may gain the exporter a reputation as a soft touch in the market;

a successful action means the exporters get their money.

(b) Arguments against:

legal actions abroad are often protracted, subject to complex local law;

legal costs are high and not always included in the judgment for the defendant to pay;

the debt is normally translated into the local currency equivalent at the commencement of the law suit; if this local currency is weakening against the invoiced currency, at the end of a successful suit the sum awarded will be worth substantially less than the original invoiced value; a successful judgment may put the customers out of business with possible undesirable public relations overtones in terms of adding their work force to the unemployed and gaining the exporter an unwanted bad reputation;

On balance it is always worth exploring alternatives to legal action, such as the following.

(6) Restructuring the debt. This implies the establishment of a debt recovery programme, agreeing to go on supplying the customers, preferably on some secure basis with the support of their local bankers, and receiving payment of the old debt by instalments over an agreed period, perhaps with interest at an agreed rate. Much will depend on the circumstances of the case and the degree of overriding country risk but, provided the customer's management can be made sound and a ready market found for its products, such an arrangement may in the long run prove a more profitable alternative to a legal process. In certain cases a restructuring may be forced on the exporter by way of a statutory solution imposed by an automatic court procedure in an attempt to overcome a threatening insolvency and keep the customer in business.

(7) Doing a deal. If a customer is in financial difficulties and it appears obvious that there is very little to be gained from restructuring or legal action, it is sometimes worth seeing whether — in advance of a likely bankruptcy — a deal can be struck; this means accepting less than the value of the debt in full discharge of it, on the half a loaf is better than none principle.

APPENDIX

SOURCES OF COUNTRY RISK ASSESSMENT INFORMATION

A small selection of commercial agencies

S.J. Rundt & Associates Inc.,
130 East 63rd Street,
New York, NY 10021,
USA

Dun & Bradstreet Ltd,
Holmers Farm Way,
High Wycombe,
Bucks HP12 4UL,
England

Frost & Sullivan Inc.,
106 Fullerton Street,
New York, NY 10038,
USA

Sullivan House,
4 Grosvenor Gardens,
London SW1 W0DH,
England

OFFICIAL SOURCES

Department of Trade and Industry,
1 Victoria Street,
London SW1H 0ET
Publications and ad hoc advice

International Monetary Fund,
Washington DC,
USA
International financial statistics, yearbooks etc.

World Bank,
Washington DC,
USA
World debt tables and other information

United Nations,
New York,
USA
Monthly bulletin of statistics

European Community
Economic commentaries

INSTITUTES AND CREDIT ORGANIZATIONS

Institute of Export,
Export House,
64 Clifton Street,
London EC2A 4HB

Institute of Credit Management,
Easton House,
Easton on the Hill,
Stamford,
Lincolnshire PE9 3NH

FCIB (Finance, Credit and International Business) Corporation,
520 Eighth Avenue,
New York, NY 10018-6571
USA

OTHER USEFUL CONTACTS

British Exporters Association,
16 Dartmouth Street,
London SW1H 9BL

International Chamber of Commerce,
Centre Point,
103 New Oxford Street,
London WC1A 1QB

On-line Database Directory — all subjects — published by
Cuadra/Elsevier,
52 Vanderbilt Avenue,
New York, NY 10017

READING LIST

CLARKE, B. W., (ed) *The Handbook of International Credit Management*, Gower 1989. Detailed coverage of all aspects of international credit management written by eighteen experts from various countries.

EDWARDS, H., *Getting paid for exports*, Gower 1990. A sound basis for credit management procedures, including interpretation of accounts and ratios.

SCHMITTHOFF, C. M., *The Export Trade*, Stevens 1986. The definitive book on the Law and Practice of International Trade.

Croner's Reference Book for Exporters, Croner Publications Ltd. Well-known reference for export procedures, finance, documentation, exchange control requirements and much else. A loose-leaf book, updated monthly.

Uniform Customs and Practice for Documentary Credits (1983) and *Guide to Documentary Credit Operations* (1984), International Chamber of Commerce Publications Nos. 400 and 415. Essential for anyone handling Documentary Letters of Credit.

BRIAN CLARKE

Credit Training Associates

3.6 Investment incentives in European Community countries

The contents of this chapter are:

European Community research and development programmes;
Grants and loans available from the European Community:
  The European Regional Development Fund,
  The European Social Fund,
  The European Agricultural Guidance and Guarantee Fund,
  The European Investment Bank,
  The New Community Instrument for Borrowing and Lending,
  The European Coal and Steel Community;
National incentives in the European Community countries.

In this chapter the European Currency Unit (ECU) is equal to:
BF and LF 42.6157; DM 2.04592; Dfl 2.30515; £0.717522; DKR 7.86114; FF 6.92321; LIT 1511.93; IR £0.769240; DRA 193.240;
PTA 131.457; ESC 179.884; US$ 1.21364 (as on 28 February 1990).

AID GRANTED BY THE EUROPEAN COMMUNITY TO RESEARCH AND DEVELOPMENT

To strengthen the scientific and technical basis of European industry and to promote its international competitiveness, the Community is being given the task of supporting the efforts of firms — including small and medium-sized firms — research centres and universities in the field of research and technological development and of promoting cooperation.

There are essentially three levels at which Community research is conducted:

RESEARCH BY THE COMMUNITY'S JOINT RESEARCH CENTRE

In-house research is carried out at the Joint Research Centre (JRC). The JRC consists of four different establishments: Ispra in Italy, Geel in Belgium, Petten in the Netherlands and Karlsruhe in West Germany. The main area of research is nuclear energy research but research is also conducted in areas such as environment and remote sensing.

SHARED-COST OR CONTRACT RESEARCH

Contract research is carried out at universities, research centres or private companies on the basis of cost-sharing contracts with the Community. Because of the greater combined resources available, this type of research action enables certain projects to be launched which otherwise would not have been feasible. Projects usually involve a consortium of companies and institutions. The community generally finances 50% of the cost of these projects. Most of the specific research programmes are carried out in the form of shared-cost research.

CONCERTED-ACTION PROJECTS

In the case of concerted-action projects the priorities and workplans are determined at Community level but the research is funded by the Member States. The Community ensures close coordination of work done at national level and pays the costs of coordination (including: definition of objectives, exchange of information, publication). Part of the work on certain specific programmes, and the whole of the Community medical research programme, are carried out in this form.

SUMMARY OF COMMUNITY RESEARCH AND DEVELOPMENT PROGRAMMES

THE ESPRIT II PROGRAMME

European strategic programme for research and development in information technologies (ESPRIT).

Aim: to help provide the European information technology industry with the technology base it needs to meet the competitive requirements of the 1990s, to promote European industrial cooperation in IT and to contribute to the development of internationally accepted standards.
Programme: the following sectors are covered by the programme — microelectronics and peripherals, information processing systems, information technology application technologies.
Duration: 1988-1992.
Budget: ECU1,600m.
Contract: shared-cost contracts.

THE RACE PROGRAMME

Research and development in Advanced Communication in Europe (RACE).

Aim: RACE deals with integrated broadband communications (IBC) and aims at laying the foundations of the Community's communications infrastructure for the 1990s and the 21st century.

Programme: the programme covers integrated broadband communications, development and implementation strategies, technologies and prenormative functional integration.
Duration: June 1987-May 1992.
Budget: ECU550m.
Contract: shared-cost contracts.

THE BRITE/EURAM PROGRAMME

Basic Research in Industrial Technologies for Europe (BRITE)/European Research on Advanced Materials (EURAM).

Aim: to promote the application of new technologies in manufacturing industries.
Programme: the programme covers advanced materials technologies, design methodology, application of manufacturing technologies, development of a European aeronautical technology base.
Duration: 1989-1992.
Budget: ECU499.5m.
Contract: shared-cost contracts.

THE ENVIRONMENT PROGRAMMES STEP AND EPOCH

Science and Technology for Environment Protection (STEP).
European Programme On Climatology and natural Hazards (EPOCH)

Aim: The aim of the environment programmes is to protect the environment and to study the impact of human activity on the climate.
Programme: STEP comprises research into environment and human health, risks associated with chemicals, air and water quality, soil and ground water protection, ecosystems, protection of European cultural heritage, environmental protection technologies, major technological hazards and fire safety. EPOCH will comprise research into past climates and climate changes, climate processes and models, climatic impacts and climate-related and seismic hazards.
Duration: 1989-1992.
Budget: STEP — ECU75m, EPOCH — ECU40m.
Contract: shared-cost contracts, coordination activities, education and training activities, studies and assessments.

THE BRIDGE PROGRAMME

Biotechnology Research for Innovation, Development and Growth in Europe (BRIDGE).

Aim: to strengthen the scientific base of Europe's biotechnology and thus improve its international competitiveness.
Programme: the program will cover the following sectors — information infrastructures (including data processing), enabling technologies (such as protein design and

gene mapping), cellular biology, pre-normative research (including safety assessments of toxicity).
Duration: 1990-1994.
Budget: ECU100m.
Contract: shared-cost contracts, training awards and studies.

THE JOULE PROGRAMME
Joint Opportunities for Unconventional or Long-term Energy supply (JOULE).

Aim: to develop the use of non-nuclear energy in the Community.
Programme: the four sub-programmes of JOULE cover models for energy and environment, rational use of energy, energy from fossil sources, renewable and geothermal energy.
Duration: 1989-1992.
Budget: ECU122m.
Contract: shared-cost contracts, concerted actions and training or mobility grants.

OTHER RESEARCH AND DEVELOPMENT PROGRAMMES:
medical and health research programme (ECU65m, 1987-1991);
radiation protection programme (ECU21.2m, 1990-1991);
the DELTA programme — development of European learning through technological advance (ECU20m, 24 months starting March 1989);
the DRIVE programme — dedicated road infrastructure for vehicle safety in Europe (ECU60m, 36 months starting January 1989);
the AIM programme — advanced informatics in medicine (ECU20m, 24 months starting mid 1989);
the BCR programme — the Community Bureau of Reference (ECU59.2m, 1988-1992);
raw materials and recycling programme (ECU45m, 1990-1992);
the ECLAIR programme — European collaborative linkage of agriculture and industry through research (ECU80m, 1988-1993);
the FLAIR programme — foods linked to agro-industrial research (ECU25m, 1989-1993);
decommissioning of nuclear installations (ECU31.5m, 1989-1993);
the TELEMAN programme — remote handling in hazardous or disordered nuclear environments (ECU19m, 1989-1993);
controlled thermonuclear fusion (ECU795m, 1988-1992);
the STD programme — scientific cooperation between the European Community and developing countries (ECU80m, 1987-1991);
the MAST programme — marine science and technology (ECU50m, 1989-1992);
fisheries programme (ECU30m, 1988-1992);
the SCIENCE programme — stimulation of European scientific and technical cooperation and exchange (ECU167m, 1988-1992);

the SPES programme — stimulation plan for economic science ECU6m, 1989-1992);
large-scale scientific facilities (ECU30m, 1988-1992);
the MONITOR programme — improvement of the evaluation of research and development programmes (ECU22m, 1988-1992);
the DOSES programme — development of statistical expert systems (ECU4m, 1989-1992);
the VALUE programme — valorization and utilization for Europe (ECU38m, mid-1988-mid-1992);
EUROTRA programme — European Translation Programme (ECU27m, 1989-1990).

GRANTS AND LOANS FROM THE EUROPEAN COMMUNITY

The European Community's structural instruments help to fund measures that are carried out within the Community and that meet common objectives such as the economic development of regions, the promotion of employment, environmental protection, new sources of energy and the improvement of the infrastructure. These structural instruments can be divided into instruments making grants and instruments making loans.
Grants are given mainly by the three Structural Funds:

(1) the European Regional Development Fund (ERDF)
(2) the European Social Fund (ESF)
(3) the European Agricultural Guidance and Guarantee Fund (EAGGF)

Loans are granted mainly through:

(1) the European Investment Bank (EIB)
(2) the New Community Instrument (NCI)
(3) the European Coal and Steel Community (ECSC)

REFORM OF THE STRUCTURAL FUNDS

In June 1988 more precise rules were laid down for the tasks of the Structural Funds in order to make them more effective and to coordinate their operations both between themselves and with those of the European Investment Bank and the other financial instruments. The reform which came into force on 1 January 1989, had to be undertaken in order to promote economic and social cohesion with a view to completing the internal market by 31 December 1992. The most important elements of the reform are:

(1) doubling of the budget between 1987 and 1993 to bring the total from the three funds to ECU14.1bn in 1993;

(2) establishment of five priority objectives:
   (a) objective 1, promoting the development and structural adjustment of the regions whose development is lagging behind;
   (b) objective 2, converting the regions seriously affected by industrial decline;
   (c) objective 3, combating long-term unemployment;
   (d) objective 4, facilitating the occupational integration of young people;
   (e) objective 5, reforming the common agricultural policy with a view to speeding up the adjustment of agricultural structures and promoting the development of rural areas;
(3) close collaboration in the form of partnerships between the Commission and national or regional authorities in the planning and implementation stages;
(4) funds are to be funnelled into multi-annual integrated programmes instead of into individual projects;
(5) improved evaluation and control of the funds.

The Structural Funds contribute to the achievement of objectives 1 to 5 on the basis of the following breakdown:

objective 1: ERDF, ESF, EAGGF Guidance Section
objective 2: ERDF, ESF
objective 3: ESF
objective 4: ESF
objective 5a: EAGGF Guidance Section
objective 5b: EAGGF Guidance Section, ESF, ERDF

Financial assistance for objectives 1, 2 and 5b is given on a geographical basis. The Commission draws up lists of eligible regions per Member State. Financial assistance for objectives 3 and 4 is given on a functional basis, and the two objectives apply to all twelve Member States.

The other structural instruments can also contribute, each in accordance with its own rules, to measures supported by one or more of the Structural Funds in connection with one of the five objectives.

Community action with respect to the Structural Funds is undertaken in a three-stage process. First of all Member States submit plans explaining their policy and setting out their intentions, notably regarding the use of the Community structural instruments. The Commission then assesses these plans and, in consultation with the Member States and where necessary the regional or local authorities, determines the broad lines of the technical and financial assistance to be supplied by the Community. This Commission response to the national plans takes the form of a Community support framework. Thirdly, as regards the financial assistance itself, the Commission proposes that for each objective the emphasis should be on operational programmes but other forms of assistance are also possible: part-financing of national aid schemes; global grants; part-financing of suitable projects; support for technical assistance and preparatory studies.

The level of Community financial assistance depends on certain criteria such as the seriousness of the problems, the financial resources of the Member State concerned or the particular benefits of individual projects. The ceilings set for Community assistance are as follows:

(1) objective 1 regions will be granted a maximum of 75% of the total cost and, as a general rule, at least 50% of public expenditure;
(2) for other regions the maximum rate is 50% of the total cost, and as a general rule, at least 25% of public expenditure;
(3) by way of exception, preparatory studies and technical assistance measures carried out on the Commission's initiative may receive 100% financing.

In operational programmes that can be funded by more than one Structural Fund, individual projects may receive assistance from only one fund at any one time. It is, however, possible to combine Community grants and loans in order to provide the method of funding best suited to the type of measure in question. The rates of assistance from the funds to be applied to the individual measures within operational programmes may also be varied under the combination arrangements. The combined level of grants and loans must also be compatible with the rules concerning simultaneous application of different financial instruments. In the case of projects in which the European Investment Bank and other Community financial instruments are involved, the ceilings on Community assistance are generally fixed as a proportion of the total cost as follows:

50% of loans, whether these are loans granted by a single Community financial instrument or the sum of the loans provided by a number of those instruments;
70% in the case of the combination of Community loans and grants for the financing of a single project. This ceiling may be exceeded in justified cases, although the level of 90% must not be exceeded.

EUROPEAN REGIONAL DEVELOPMENT FUND (ERDF)

According to the Single Act, the European Regional Development Fund is intended to help redress the principal regional imbalances in the Community through participating in the development and structural adjustment of regions whose development is lagging behind and in the conversion of declining industrial regions. Regional assistance is thus directed towards objectives 1, 2 and 5b. In this context the Fund will help to strengthen the economic potential of the regions, support structural adjustment and growth and create permanent jobs.

In the regions covered by objective 1 — those whose per capita gross domestic product, on the basis of figures for the last three years, is less than 75% of the Community average — emphasis will be placed on developing the economic infrastructure including, where appropriate, the development of facilities to exploit any tourist potential. Financial assistance may also be given on an exceptional basis to general education establishments as well as hospitals and related facilities in cases where the regions concerned are seriously under-equipped. The following types of infrastructure could be financed.

Transport: a high priority for the objective 1 regions should be their integration into the basic Community networks for road, rail and inland waterways as well as the creation of modern port and airport infrastructures.

Telecommunications: the handicap of peripherality could be reduced by developing a modern telecommunications network.

Vocational Training: the provision of technical training establishments is of vital importance to the objective 1 regions in order to eliminate existing deficiencies in vocational training.

Research and technological development: the creation of science and technology facilities will be encouraged.

Environment: environmental infrastructures including basic services and, for example, sewage treatment and water supply.

Energy: the provision of infrastructure, the exploitation of local energy resources, alternative and renewable energy, energy saving and oil substitution.

Rural areas: measures will be encouraged in the field of roads, electricity, water supply and telecommunications in order to ensure a balanced distribution of economic activity between conurbations and rural areas.

In the regions covered by objective 2, which are regions with an average unemployment rate above the Community average and where employment in industry has declined since 1975, emphasis is placed on developing productive investment. The aim is to create new jobs to replace those lost in the declining industries. Objective 2 regions mostly have a high research and development potential but there is often a mismatch between the research base and the technological capacity of local firms. The Commission therefore encourages measures to improve the diffusion of the results of research and development activities and innovation and technology transfer towards local firms. Measures supporting infrastructure in objective 2 regions will be directed towards the regeneration of areas of industrial decline, including inner cities and infrastructure whose modernization provides the basis for the creation or development of economic activity.

In the regions covered by objective 5b, which are regions with a high proportion of agricultural employment in total employment, low farm incomes and a low level of socio-economic development, investment measures in production are encouraged which create or protect long term jobs. Importance is also given to infrastructure directly connected with economic activities creating non-agricultural jobs and to the development of the inherent potential of the regions by means of measures that stimulate the activities of small and medium-sized companies.

EUROPEAN SOCIAL FUND (ESF)

Eligible operations under the European Social Fund are to support vocational training operations, to subsidize recruitment into newly created stable jobs and to subsidize the creation of self-employed activities. These measures can be fitted into the various objectives of the reform of the Structural Funds.

Vocational training includes any measure designed to provide the right skills which will equip people to undertake one or more specific types of job on the labour market as well as any technical training adapted to technological change. In the regions covered by objectives 1, 2 and 5b, vocational training means any basic and further training which will equip trainees to use new production and management techniques.

The scope of the European Social Fund is as follows:

- With regard to the priority objectives 3 and 4, which are applicable throughout the Community, assistance will be granted to operations that intend to:
  - combat long-term unemployment by means of the occupational integration of persons over the age of 25 who have been unemployed for more than 12 months;
  - facilitate the occupational integration of persons under 25 from the age at which compulsory full-time schooling ends, however long they have been looking.
- In respect of objectives 1, 2 and 5b assistance will be granted to operations that intend to:
  - encourage job stability and develop new employment possibilities for persons who are unemployed, who are threatened with unemployment within the context of restructuring requiring technological modernization or changes in the production or management system and who are employed in small and medium-sized companies;
  - facilitate vocational training for any working person involved in an integrated programme.
- With regard to objective 1 in particular, assistance is given to persons who are on an apprenticeship contract, who are being trained within the framework of national vocational education systems or who are employed on Community work schemes.

European Social Fund assistance covers the following expenditure:

- the income of persons receiving vocational training;
- the cost of preparing, operating, managing and assessing vocational training operations, including the costs of training teaching staff;

- the cost of subsistence and travel costs of those covered by vocational training operations;
- the granting, for a maximum of one year, of subsidies towards recruitment into newly created stable jobs and towards the creation of self-employed activities.

THE EUROPEAN AGRICULTURAL GUIDANCE AND GUARANTEE FUND — GUIDANCE SECTION (EAGGF)

Measures taken under the Guidance Section of the European Agricultural Guidance and Guarantee Fund are designed to adjust, strengthen and reorganize agricultural structures, convert production to other types of farming and guarantee farmers a fair standard of living. This Fund provides financing under objectives 1, 5a and 5b.

Under objective 5a, which deals with speeding up the adjustment of agricultural structures with a view to the reform of the common agricultural policy, the Fund finances the following common measures:

- measures accompanying the market policy that help re-establish a balance between production and market capacity (set-aside schemes, afforestation, abandonment of certain types of production and so on);
- measures to assist the modernization and adjustment of production structures (such as reorganization of holdings, installation of young farmers, early retirement);
- measures to promote the improvement of the structures for processing and marketing agricultural and fishery products (investment projects, producers' associations and others);
- protection and preservation of the environment;
- measures to support farm incomes (income aid, compensatory allowances in less-favoured and mountain areas).

The Fund assistance for regions designated under objectives 1 and 5b mainly comprise measures intended to deal with the backwardness of agricultural structures. Financial assistance by the Fund may relate to the following:

- encouraging retirement from farming in order to restructure the agricultural sector and to make land available for young farmers;
- the conversion, diversification, re-allocation and adjustment of production potential;
- the improvement of rural infrastructure which is essential to the development of agriculture and forestry;
- the reparcelling of land including associated works;
- individual or collective land or pasture improvement;
- irrigation, including the renovation and improvement of irrigation networks, the creation of collective irrigation works from existing main channels, the creation of small irrigation systems not supplied from collective networks and the renovation and improvement of drainage systems;

the encouragement of investment in the tourist and craft industries, including the improvement of facilities in farmhouses;
protection of the environment and maintenance of the countryside;
the rehabilitation of agricultural production potential which has been destroyed by natural disasters;
afforestation and the improvement and reconstitution of woodland, including the associated works;
the development of agricultural and forestry advisory services, and improvement of facilities for agricultural and forestry vocational training.

THE EUROPEAN INVESTMENT BANK (EIB)

The European Investment Bank is an independent non-profit making Community institution. Its prime function is to promote the balanced development of the Community through financing capital investment. Investments which may be considered for financing by the Bank must contribute to one or more of the following objectives:

economic development of the Community's less privileged regions;
improved transport and telecommunications infrastructure serving the Community's interests;
protection of the environment and conservation of the Community's architectural and natural heritage;
urban development;
attainment of the Community's energy policy objectives;
strengthening the international competitive position of Community industry and furthering its integration on a European level;
supporting the activities of SMEs;
cooperation with a large number of developing countries.

The Bank raises most of its resources on capital markets within and outside the Community and on international markets.

The European Investment Bank advances medium and long-term loans. The term is determined by the type of project and its expected life and generally ranges from 7 to 12 years for industrial projects, extending to as much as 20 years for infrastructural schemes and projects in the energy sector. As the Bank works on a non-profit-making basis, the rates charged on its loans reflect the cost of its borrowings. Loans are generally concluded at a fixed rate, but it is possible to arrange variable-rate loans. Rates are the same for all countries and sectors. The loans are granted to public or private-sector borrowers who may be operating in any of the productive sectors such as infrastructure, energy, industry, services and agriculture.

In the case of large-scale investment schemes, individual loans are concluded either directly with the promoter or through a financial intermediary. Ventures promoted by SMEs and smaller-scale projects in infrastructure or those designed to make more efficient use of energy or to protect the environment are more often financed through the global loan device. Global loans are lines of credit made available to banks or financial institutions operating at national or regional level. They draw on the funds to support a wide range of investment schemes undertaken by SMEs or local authorities. The Bank will finance only part of the investment cost, the remainder being met from the borrower's own funds and other sources of credit. Under normal circumstances, a loan may not exceed 50% of the total investment cost.

Although it is an autonomous institution, the European Investment Bank helps in achieving Community-wide economic and social cohesion through its support for regional development, communications infrastructure and the corporate sector. In particular, it plays an active role in the operational procedures introduced by the reform of the Structural Funds and is involved in determining the loan and grant mix of the financial assistance provided for by the various financial instruments.

THE NEW COMMUNITY INSTRUMENT FOR BORROWING AND LENDING (NCI)

The New Community Instrument has the objective of financing, in the form of loans, investment projects which contribute to greater convergence and integration of the economic policies of the Member States. The prime purpose of this new loan facility, which is administered jointly by the European Investment Bank and the Commission, is to finance investment in accordance with Community priority objectives. These are energy, industrial investment and infrastructure. The principal beneficiaries are small and medium-sized enterprises and those companies that are concerned with the development of energy resources, energy conservation and infrastructure linked to productive activities contributing to regional development. With the introduction of the Instrument, the Community increased its borrowing capacity by widening its scope of raising resources.

The Instrument provides a broader and more diversified guarantee for Community lending because its borrowings are guaranteed by the general budget of the European Communities. The Bank grants and administers loans under the Instrument in the name, for the account and at the risk of the Community.

THE EUROPEAN COAL AND STEEL COMMUNITY (ECSC)

The financial instruments of the European Coal and Steel Community make up a cohesive system of loans and grants to facilitate and support development, modernization and the continuous adaptation of production apparatus in a sector where investment is costly and where decisions by producers in a market economy have considerable social and job consequences for workers.

The Community grants the following loans:

- industrial loans to coal and steel industries to facilitate their modernization and the marketing and consumption of coal and steel products;
- conversion loans to investors who, by creating new and economically sound activities, are capable of reabsorbing redundant coal and steel workers into productive employment.

These loans are granted, either directly or in the form of global loans, to firms (mainly small and medium-sized enterprises) or to public organizations. Conversion loans and some industrial loans may, subject to certain conditions, be eligible for interest subsidies. In the case of conversion loans, the interest subsidy is linked to the creation of permanent jobs.

The Community also contributes to the achievement of economic and social cohesion through its role in the operational procedures introduced by the reform of the Structural Funds. Just like the European Investment Bank, it is involved in determining the loan and grant mix of the financial assistance provided for by the various financial instruments.

NATIONAL INCENTIVES IN THE EUROPEAN COMMUNITY COUNTRIES

Governments use a variety of incentives to encourage investment in their countries. These include the following:

TAX-RELATED INCENTIVES

Accelerated depreciation. This covers any method of depreciation permitted by the tax authorities which enables firms to write down the value of fixed assets for tax purposes more quickly than their true decline in economic value, thus improving cash flow and reducing interest charges.

Depreciation at choice. This involves complete freedom to choose the spread of depreciation. Normally the firm gains the greatest advantage by taking 100% allowance in the first year, but there may be circumstances where it is better to carry it forward in full or in part.

Initial allowances. There are accelerated first-year allowances below 100%, which may be additional to normal writing down allowances.

Advanced depreciation. This is accelerated depreciation relating to any year, other than the first.

Diminishing balance depreciation. Permission by the tax authorities to use this method means in effect that a larger proportion of the cost of an asset is charged in the early part of its life than would be the case with straight line depreciation.

Favourable inventory valuation methods. Many countries now permit valuation methods or give allowances which reduce taxable profit below the level at which it would be assessed with the use of the first in first out principle.

Tax-free reserves. In some countries, the creation of tax-free replacement reserves are permitted and capital gains are tax free provided that the gain is used for replacement purposes.

NON-TAX INCENTIVES

Grants. The effect of investment grants is different from tax-related incentives in that grants benefit unprofitable as well as profitable companies. In fact, the unprofitable firm may benefit more if grants reduce the base for calculating depreciation allowances. If the investment proves unprofitable, grants mean in effect that the government bears part of the loss, whereas depreciation allowances bring less tax relief. Usually the cash benefit is obtained more quickly from grants than from tax reliefs.

Cheap loans and interest subsidies. This type of incentive may take the following forms:

public money may be lent at less than market rates of interest;
favourable repayment conditions may be granted on loans from public funds;
public bodies may guarantee private loans.

Price subsidies. Wage subsidies fall into this category. If investment in equipment and labour is complementary, that is if investment in equipment creates a greater need for labour, then wage subsidies encourage investment. If, on the other hand, investment in equipment is a substitute for labour — the installation of labour-saving machinery, for instance — wage subsidies discourage investment.

CONTROL OF AID GRANTED BY EUROPEAN COMMUNITY COUNTRIES

The Treaty of Rome stipulates that aid which has the effect of distorting or threatening to distort competition, insofar as it affects trade between Member States, is incompatible with the Common Market. However, certain aid is justified when it is granted for social and economic reasons. The Commission is vested with powers of control over aid granted by Member States.

With respect to regional aid, the Commission published a communication in February 1979 informing the Member States of the principles which it would apply to regional aid systems in force or to be established in the regions of the European Community. In this communication the Commission established a number of differentiated ceilings of aid intensity for various categories of regions in order to avoid the bidding up of aid levels in the wake of the removal of customs and trade barriers inside the common market. The very nature of regional aid requires that it be awarded selectively. Successive enlargements of the Community have broadened the range of its regional diversity and confirmed the need to develop new policy instruments for the control of regional aid. At the same time, the Single European Act gave new impetus to greater economic and social cohesion and provided that the Community shall aim at reducing disparities between various regions and the backwardness of the least favoured regions. In response to these needs the Commission decided in 1987 to adopt a systematic approach to the evaluation of aid in the least-developed regions of the Community. This approach was published by the Commission in August 1988 in the form of a Communication describing in detail the method for the application of Article 92(3)(a) and (c) of the Treaty of Rome to regional aid.

Article 92(3)(a) regions are those suffering from abnormally low living standards or serious underemployment where the per capita gross domestic product does not exceed 75% of the Community average in purchasing power parities. These regions lie mainly on the southern and western periphery of the Community. In the 92(3)(a) regions, the assessment is made relative to the Community average. Given particularly severe development problems faced in such regions, the Commission has decided that it may allow operating aids in certain circumstances.

Article 92(3)(c) regions are those with more general development problems in relation to the national as well as the Community situation. Often they suffer from the decline of traditional industries and are frequently located in the more central prosperous parts of the Community. In its Article 92(3)(c) method, the Commission has established a system which takes account of national regional problems and places them in a Community context. It uses two alternative primary indicators, income as measured by gross domestic product/gross value-added and structural unemployment. Both are assessed in a national context. The better the position of a Member State relative to the Community situation, the wider must be the disparity of a region in order to justify the award of aid. Unlike Article 92(3)(a) regions, the Commission does not in principle allow the award of operating aid in Article 92(3)(c) regions, and aid must be linked to initial investment and/or job creation.

SUMMARY OF NATIONAL INCENTIVES BY COUNTRY

BELGIUM

NON-TAX INCENTIVES

General incentives:
- interest rate rebates;
- delayed repayment of loans;
- subsidies.

TAX INCENTIVES

Regional incentives:
- reconversion zones: aid is available for investments made in development areas that contribute directly to the setting-up, development, adaptation or modernization of industrial or handicraft enterprises, public services or service-rendering enterprises;

employment zones: these areas, where unemployment is severe, benefit from exemptions such as corporate income tax exemptions on dividends and retained earnings, exemptions from real estate tax, withholding taxes and registration tax.

General incentives:

depreciation: industrial buildings, machinery and equipment situated in certain development areas may be depreciated at a rate equal to twice the normal straight-line depreciation. This method may be authorized for a maximum of three consecutive tax periods;

investment deduction: a deduction amounting to the percentage of the increase of the consumer prices in the previous year plus 2% (1.5% as from 1991) with a minimum of 4% (3.5% as from 1991) and a maximum of 11% (10.5% as from 1991) is granted on all qualifying investments. The percentage for 1990 should be 5%. The increase is 10% for investments in new products or technologies not damaging the environment or reducing the negative effects on the environment and for investments which rationalize the use of energy;

investment allowance: allowances for specified investments such as reinvestment of capital gains realized from shares;

incentives available to small and medium-sized enterprises encouraging economic expansion;

innovation companies: innovation companies dealing exclusively with the production and marketing of innovative high technology processes are granted tax incentives such as corporate income tax exemption of dividends up to 13% of the paid-up capital during ten years, increase of investment deduction, ten-year exemption from real estate tax if the investment is located in the Brussels area, and ten-year exemption from registration tax;

co-ordination centres: for ten years, co-ordination centres are taxed on a small national income determined on the basis of operational expenses, not including personnel and financial charges. Exemption from real estate tax, withholding tax on interest and dividends and registration tax is also provided.

DENMARK

NON-TAX INCENTIVES

Regional incentives. In order to promote the establishment of industrial and other business enterprises, the Danish state grants subventions for capital expenditures and offers loans. The subventions may be granted up to 25% of the capital expenditures (in certain cases up to 35%). The Danish state grants subventions for relocation when a firm moves to a development area. Loans cannot exceed 50% of the capital investment. The current interest rate is 8.25% per annum. The regulations of the Area Development Commission apply to enterprises that receive state loans or guarantees.

General incentives. The Technical and Industrial Development Fund grants loans, with favourable interest terms, to Danish enterprises for research and development projects aimed at new products or production methods. The Danish Government recently proposed to abolish the Act on the Technical and Industrial Development Fund and to replace it by a new scheme with general incentives.

TAX INCENTIVES

Regional incentives. There are no special regional tax incentives. However, the allocation to a special investment fund for tax purposes is a major advantage for capital intensive businesses as it allows for tax depreciation before assets are acquired. This scheme will, however, be abolished as from the income year 1990.

General incentives. In order to encourage efforts in the field of research and development, tax deductibility has been introduced for expenditure on basic research and on certain approved projects (tax deduction of 125% of expenditure in connection with Eureka, Esprit, Brite or Race research projects).

FRANCE

NON-TAX INCENTIVES

Regional incentives. In 1963 the French government set up the Territorial Planning and Regional Development Agency (Délégation à l'Aménagement du Territoire et à l'Action régionale — DATAR). Incentives are designed to promote the following objectives:

(1) to create new activities or expand existing activities in certain areas;
(2) to convert declining industries;
(3) to decentralize industrial activities outside Paris and Lyon.

The Development Agency has grants available, known as the PAT (prime d'aménagement du territoire), the amounts of which vary from FF35,000 to FF55,000 per job created, up to a maximum of 25% of the amount invested. These grants are available for industrial operations in development zones, provided there is a minimum investment of FF20m by a business with a turnover of at least FF300m or which is controlled (50%) by a business with at least this turnover, and provided at least 20 permanent jobs are created within three years. The PAT is also available for research and related activities.

General incentives. Development grants are available for manufacturing, scientific and technical research enterprises and for certain other activities, such as management, engineering, consulting and data processing.

TAX INCENTIVES

Regional incentives. Available tax incentives take the form of tax holidays (up to ten years in the three enterprise zones Dunkirk, Toulon-La-Seyne and Aubagne-La-Ciotat), exemptions from local business taxes, reduced transfer taxes, accelerated depreciation, and duty-free imports in the two free-trade zones Gex and Haute-Savoie.

General incentives. Qualifying research expenses may give rise to a tax credit which may be offset against corporate income tax.

FEDERAL REPUBLIC OF GERMANY

NON-TAX INCENTIVES

Regional incentives. As a consequence of the tax reform which is in force from the beginning of 1990, non-tax incentives on a regional basis are no longer granted.

General incentives. Investment grants of 7.5% are granted for certain assets connected with the production of energy. The tax-free investment grant for qualifying investments in the iron and steel industry is 20% of cost, unless a higher rate can be claimed under another regulation.

Tax incentives. Special West Berlin incentives:
Under the Berlin development law, West Berlin enterprises enjoy the following tax concessions:

(1) reduced corporation tax;
(2) lower trade tax on income;
(3) individual tax benefit;
(4) accelerated depreciation;
(5) subsidies.

Regional incentives. Enterprises located in the eastern border zone qualify for accelerated depreciation of up to 50% of the cost of investments in movable fixed assets and up to 40% of the cost of immovables. This depreciation can be claimed at any time and in any amounts at the taxpayer's option within the first five years of acquisition.

General incentives. Fixed assets acquired for research and development purposes qualify for accelerated depreciation of 40% if movable and of 10% to 15% if immovable. Accelerated depreciation is also granted for certain assets connected with energy production. Accelerated depreciation is furthermore claimable for a variety of fixed assets acquired for specific purposes:

(1) protection of the environment;
(2) coal and ore mining;
(3) insulation of buildings against noise and heat loss;
(4) energy-saving investments;
(5) ships and aircraft;
(6) investments in older buildings in city centres that are to be preserved.

GREECE

NON-TAX INCENTIVES

Regional incentives. Greece is divided into four territorial areas. The following incentives are available depending on the area.

(1) In order to promote productive investment, direct cash grants in the form of capital aid are available from the state. The size and availability of the grant depends on the area in which the enterprise concerned is operating.
(2) Cash grants for special investments concerning the protection of the environment; the substitution of oil or electrical energy by other sources of energy; the establishment or extension of laboratories for applied industrial, energy or mining research; and the establishment of highly advanced technology units.
(3) Government interest subsidies are granted in certain areas for a duration of six years.

General incentives. Government interest subsidies are granted to companies (three year duration).

TAX INCENTIVES

Regional incentives. Manufacturing, handicraft, mining, agricultural and other enterprises investing or relocated in certain areas are entitled to 40%, 55% and 70% (depending on the area) tax-deferred reserve on the cost of productive fixed assets acquired between 16 June 1982 and 31 December 1992.

General incentives. Foreign investments aiming at promotion of national production or otherwise contributing to the economic development of the country may obtain, with government approval, a freezing of income tax rates for a specified period not exceeding ten years. Companies which export may deduct from their taxable income the equivalent of 1% to 3% of total export sales, depending on the type of products exported. Commercial enterprises acting as agents of foreign companies who export Greek products in exchange for foreign products as well as manufacturing companies processing products for export on behalf of foreign companies are entitled to reduce service fees by 5% in computing taxable income.

REPUBLIC OF IRELAND

In Ireland there are a number of agencies responsible for handling different aspects of the Government's programme of aids to industry. However, the provision of information and services to companies considering an industrial investment is co-ordinated by the Industrial Development Authority (IDA). An extensive range of incentives is available for all manufacturing operations and for a wide range of international services.

NON-TAX INCENTIVES

Capital grants for buildings and equipment are available to industrialists to set up operations in Ireland. The following are also available to various sectors:

(1) training grants;
(2) research and development grants;
(3) interest subsidies;
(4) employment grants;
(5) feasibility study grants;
(6) rent subsidies;
(7) ready-built premises.

TAX INCENTIVES

The rate of corporation tax applicable to profits from goods manufactured in Ireland is 10%. The reduced rate also applies to profits from international financial service operations located in the International Financial Services Centre in Dublin and to offshore banking and certain other operations located in the Shannon Airport Zone. The relief is available only to corporations, but there is no requirement that the corporation should be resident in Ireland. Accelerated tax depreciation allowances of up to 50% are available on the net cost of new plant and machinery and industrial buildings purchased before 1 April 1991. Any capital grants received are deducted in arriving at the net cost for depreciation purposes. The normal annual tax depreciation rates for plant and machinery are 10%, 12.5% and 25%, depending on the useful life of the asset, and 40% for industrial buildings. Accelerated tax depreciation will be phased out from 1 April 1991 onwards, resulting in the normal annual rates only being available from 1 April 1992 onwards.

ITALY

NON-TAX INCENTIVES

Regional incentives. Since 1950, the government has attempted to attract new industrial enterprises to southern Italy. This area, known as the Mezzogiorno, comprises the provinces south of Rome, Sicily, Sardinia, certain small islands and designated zones in Tuscany and Marche. Non-tax incentives consist of the following:

(1) cash grants: between 15% and 40% depending on the total amount of the investment;
(2) low-interest loans: cannot exceed 40% of the investment;
(3) rebate of social contributions.

General incentives. Low-interest loans are granted to small and medium-sized enterprises for new investments in fixed assets. Grants and soft loans are available for research and technological development. All businesses carrying out research projects performed to the extent of at least 60% in Italy are eligible for incentives.

TAX INCENTIVES

Regional incentives. Tax benefits available for the Mezzogiorno are higher for companies formed after March 29, 1987 for the specific purpose of realizing new industrial initiatives in southern Italy. These companies are entitled to a ten-year 100% exemption from corporation income tax (IRPEG). All other companies are entitled to a 50% exemption from corporation tax for ten years from the date of incorporation. All companies are eligible for a ten-year 100% exemption from local income tax (ILOR) relating to profits earned from new investment, expansion, reopening, or modernization of existing plants in southern regions. Income earned by any company in any part of the country is exempt from local tax if it is reinvested in the Mezzogiorno areas. A value-added tax (VAT) rebate of 4% is given on investment in new machinery and equipment in southern Italy; the rebate is automatically credited against total value added tax liability.

LUXEMBOURG

NON-TAX INCENTIVES

Interest rate rebates on loans from subsidized credit institutions — the extent of the rebate on interest rates is usually not more than 3% and is for a limited period of time, normally five years. The rebates are granted for financing acquisition of tangible and intangible assets, for the cost of training workers and for the cost of investments undertaken for the protection of the environment.

In certain cases the government will provide up to 40% as guarantee for repayment of capital and interest on loans that qualify for interest rebates.

Cash grants are available for investments qualifying for interest rate rebates. The cash grant is limited to 15% of the total investment project.

A lump-sum cash grant is granted for organization, management and promotion studies.

The government and the communes may intervene in the acquisition of land for the construction of new industrial plants and also in the levelling and drainage of such land.

TAX INCENTIVES

Tax credits. An investment tax credit of 12% is allowed in respect of additional investments in fixed assets, other than land and buildings.

A further tax credit is allowed in respect of new investments in tangible depreciable assets, other than land, buildings and motor vehicles, of 6% up to LF6m, and 2% in excess of LF6m. These tax credits were temporarily introduced in 1977 to stimulate the economy. The expiration date was extended each year up to 1989 when this law became permanent by incorporation in the Company Income Tax Act.

Tax holidays. New businesses and business activities that are considered to be favourable to economic growth or to the structure of the national economy are granted a partial (25% of the profit) tax holiday for the first eight years, on condition that businesses not benefiting from such exemption are not put at a competitive disadvantage. There are special concessions for taxpayers who come from abroad and establish themselves in Luxembourg.

THE NETHERLANDS

NON-TAX INCENTIVES

Regional incentives. Investment premiums are granted to new and existing industries and service enterprises in certain regions and under certain conditions. The premium amounts to either 10% or 25% (the rate depending on the particular investment) of 90% of the capital expenditure on fixed assets. The total amount available for premiums each year is limited and fixed every year. It is therefore possible that once all funds have been distributed, an investment might not receive a premium although it fulfils the necessary conditions.

General incentives. An energy bonus encourages certain investments which contribute directly to energy conservation and investments for the development of new sources of energy. The bonus amounts to either 25% or 40% of the investment.

An environmental bonus amounts to between 5% and 15% (sliding scale depending upon the particular investment) of the amount of certain limited types of investments.

State guaranteed loans through the National Investeringsband N.V., whereby the state will only guarantee 90% of the amount of the loan.

Grants for expenses incurred for research and development work through the Innovation Incentive Subsidy Regulation of 1984.

TAX INCENTIVES

The principal investment incentive (the WIR) has largely been withdrawn. As of 1 January 1990 the small scale investment supplement has also been withdrawn and replaced by the Investment Deduction. This deduction is on a sliding scale from

18% of the amount of the investment (investments of Dfl3,000 to Dfl50,000) to 2% of the amount of the investment (investments of Dfl392,000 to Dfl448,000).

PORTUGAL

The code of tax benefits and incentives which forms part of the 1989 tax reform in Portugal was published in July 1989 with retroactive effect to 1 January 1989.

NON-TAX INCENTIVES

General incentives. The internationalization of the Portuguese economy has made it necessary for the State to assist with the modernization and the restructuring of existing industry and to promote initiatives with high growth potential and at satisfactory technological levels. Such assistance and promotion is currently mainly based on six programmes covering agriculture, energy, industry, regional development, telecommunications and tourism. Non-reimbursable subsidies are granted which represent a percentage of the total qualifying investment for each project submitted.

TAX INCENTIVES

General incentives. Capital gains — Net capital gains on the sale of shares are tax exempt during calendar years 1989 through 1992 if shares are held for more than twelve months.

Dividends — Only 80% of the dividend distributed by quoted companies is subject to tax.

Interest — Interest in respect of state bonds issued before 3 May 1989 (issued before 31 December 1988 for all other bonds) is tax exempt whereas 80% of the interest in respect of state bonds issued from 3 May 1989 through 31 December 1989 (issued during calendar year 1989 for all other bonds) is subject to tax. For state bonds and other bonds issued during calendar years 1989 through 1992, the interest is exempt from the 5% withholding inheritance tax.

Tax incentives will be tailored for holding companies, investment banks, investment funds, property investment and management companies, regional development companies, savings pension funds, securities dealers and stock brokers, venture capital companies and contractors for NATO infrastructures.

SPAIN

NON-TAX INCENTIVES

Regional incentives. Regional incentives are subject to the Law 50/1985 of 27 December 1985 and the Regulation 1535/1987 of 11 December 1987; modified by the 1988 reform of the European Community Structural Funds. This Decree distinguishes between three different zones:

(1) promotional areas;
(2) reindustrialization areas;
(3) special industry incentive areas.

Non-tax incentives can be subventions of a percentage of the approved investment, low-interest loans or preferential conditions for the repayment of loans. The amount of the grant oscillates between 20% and 50% depending on zones and regions.

TAX INCENTIVES

Regional incentives. In the above mentioned regional zones, a 50% reduction in the social security contribution payable by the employer is granted.

General incentives. A tax credit of 5% is granted for investments in new fixed assets (excluding land); higher credits are available for expenditure on research and development of new products or industrial processes. A tax credit of up to Pta500,000 for each man-year of increase in the annual average of personnel is granted.

UNITED KINGDOM

NON-TAX INCENTIVES

Regional incentives. Certain areas of Britain which suffer from high and persistent unemployment have been designated Assisted Areas. These fall into two categories: Development Areas and Intermediate Areas.

Regional Selective Assistance is available throughout the Assisted Areas. It may be claimed by both manufacturing and service sector firms. The amount awarded will be related to jobs created or preserved and capital expenditure costs. There is no formal minimum or maximum grant. A simplified application procedure applies for grants of £25,000 or less.

The Enterprise Initiative introduced two new grants, collectively called Regional Enterprise Grants, for firms which have no more than 24 employees and are located in a Development Area. They are investment grants of 15% of the cost of fixed assets, to a maximum grant of £15,000 and innovation grants of 50% of the cost of projects involving innovative products and processes, to a maximum grant of £25,000.

Grants are also available for development in certain inner urban areas suffering from long term economic decline and neglect.

General incentives. Assistance for Exceptional Projects provides £4m a year to support large-scale, innovative and high-risk projects which are likely to lead to exceptional national benefits. Both investment and research and development projects may qualify.

These non-tax incentives apply specifically to England, Wales and Scotland. In Northern Ireland there is a more generous, but broadly similar, grant regime.

TAX INCENTIVES

There are currently no specific tax incentives given for inward or outward investment in the United Kingdom.

Regional incentives. Enterprise zones are designated areas targeted for economic revitalization. Expenditure on the construction, extension or improvement of any commercial or industrial building in such an area attracts a 100% allowance. Such buildings enjoy exemption from local property taxes for up to 10 years.

General incentives. Before 1984 generous depreciation (capital) allowances permitted the whole or a large part of the capital cost of many business assets to be immediately deducted for tax purposes. This system is now virtually phased out.

IRA VATER

Price Waterhouse, Brussels

3.7
Countertrade

Countertrade is practised in at least one of its forms, by almost all countries whatever their political or economic status. It is to be found everywhere but because of its very nature, statistics are limited and often conflicting. In 1983 the International Monetary Fund [1], which is opposed to countertrade, estimated its share of global trade at 1%; this conflicted with Cohen and Truell [2] who, the previous year, estimated it at 30% and Euromoney [3] which said it had grown from 8% to 35% as well as the 10-15% suggested by the Department of Trade and Industry [4]. Certainly, taking the Third World alone, there is huge potential but a lack of convertible currency as evidenced by a collective debt of $1.2 trillion. Yet it is quite wrong to imagine that countertrade activity does not extend beyond the developing countries.

Euromoney estimates that more than 100 countries now engage in countertrade as opposed to only 15 a decade ago. There is opportunity and the clearing banks have responded. In the first six years of its existence, Lloyds Bank Countertrade Section claims to have been involved in $4bn worth of business. Multinational corporations are also involved and many now have their own countertrade divisions but it is not only the large multinationals — small and medium sized companies are involved as well. The one difference that can be drawn is that small and medium sized firms do not engage in all the forms of countertrade.

Countertrade is now a global phenomenon and so it is not restricted to, for example, cash-poor, resource-rich developing countries with poor marketing channels or isolationist political regimes who may see in countertrade a useful tool of central economic planning. Central planning is now discredited as an economic system, but countertrade is practised within the Western hemisphere between developed countries for high value-added items including civil jet aircraft and mainframe computers. Countertrade not only gets around currency restrictions but import trade barriers as well. Canada requires 50-100% offset for all military and civilian procurement valued over C$100m and this has no doubt helped maintain a Canadian trade surplus.

VARIOUS TYPES OF COUNTERTRADE

(1) Barter. Barter is not a generic term for countertrade but a specialist type of countertrade which is not very common as it involves cumbersome procedures and so is costly. With barter, full payment is made through an exchange of goods and services. No convertible currency is involved. Although attractive for developing countries, it is limited in its range as suitable trading partners have to be found. Developing countries, perhaps the most needy and most willing to trade to make up domestic shortfalls in resources or production, too often share the same characteristics of limited infrastructure and a limited range of goods and services.

(2) Switch Trading arises from bilateral agreements most commonly between nations with a similar economic infrastructure, who have difficulty maintaining an equilibrium in their trade. Although a joint clearing account is created whereby transfers are debited and credited in, for example, clearing roubles, these units have no convertible significance. Trade depends upon the exchange of goods and services to an equal degree avoiding both surpluses and deficits which, in practise, it is impossible to achieve. As a result of an impasse created when two partners are unable to trade effectively, a countertrade specialist may step in and use either certain of the goods, services or commodities on offer — or the wider access afforded by acquiring a sum of these clearing roubles at a discount — to introduce a new buyer willing to accept these goods but at the new price created by discounting the clearing unit of currency. Switch trading is a specialist activity which requires the professional expertise found in Vienna, London and New York.

(3) Compensation. This is an ironic title for a means of payment which frequently involves the acceptance of unwanted goods. In this type of contract, found quite commonly in the Soviet Union in the past, the buyer would seek to defray the total cost of a contract in scarce foreign exchange reserves by seeking a partial payment in goods. The problem that arises with compensation is that the list of goods available is limited and consists mainly of goods which the buyer for one reason or another was unable to sell himself on world markets. The price for goods taken under compensation requires to be negotiated and may involve heavy discounting.

Unless the party agreeing to compensation is familiar with these goods or, even better, is able to integrate them into his own production or sales network, compensation can only be considered if the contract allows for an intermediary, a countertrade specialist who will realise cash from these goods; he will require both a fee and a discount on these compensation goods known as disagio. Not all contracts allow for an intermediary to be introduced and, since the intermediary incurs costs, this point has to be dealt with at the contract negotiation stage. Another point is that the compensation may constitute a significant proportion of the contract price and there may be a penalty for non-completion.

(4) Counter-purchase (sometimes called parallel contracts) requires two contracts to be exchanged simultaneously, one is dependent upon the other although each is effected separately. Commonly found in high value industrial sectors such as electronics and electrical engineering, a state buyer from a country with a shortage of hard currency asks the seller to agree to a countertrade equivalent to a fixed percentage of the sales contract price. The original sales contract is fulfilled by exchanging the goods in question for a stipulated sum in convertible currency, effecting 100% payment. The next stage is for the supplier to fulfil his obligation under this second contract and spend a fixed percentage of the original sales contract price within the buyer's country. The percentage may vary but the important point to note is that the supplier receives full payment for his deliveries immediately or under credit arrangements; there are no restrictions on what goods or services may be taken in countertrade, and the second half of the deal can only be fulfilled once suitable goods have been found. An original supplier may find new lower cost sources of supply for raw materials, components or sub-assemblies. However, this open access is granted only when the original contracted goods may be regarded as national priority items for acquisition. For the supplier agreeing to this request, the risk is much reduced as the choice is greatest; there is every opportunity to select and so integrate the countertrade acquired within his own production at home, not only minimizing his costs in accepting countertrade but also perhaps reducing his total overall costs as well when new sources of supply are found.

(5) Buyback agreements. Usually long term agreements, extending over ten years or more, they are invariably connected with the granting of licensing and production rights. As a form of industrial co-operation, this represents a longer term investment by the supplier in a new production centre abroad which will produce goods according to his designs with his quality control, with or without his brand name as well. Payment for the license, commissioning of plant, training and consultancy will not be outright but will involve part of the total contract price to be spread over a number of years. Buyback may extend beyond the total contract price originally agreed and become a source of revenue to the investing buyer. For the buyer acquiring the technology, this arrangement spreads the costs and assures him that a fixed percentage of production each year will go to the technology supplier guaranteeing him a fixed level of production and exports. For the supplier of the technology, buyback which has the very specific meaning of accepting countertrade products manufactured under licence, has few of the risks attendant on other forms of countertrade. The supplier may find a new source of supply which has just been newly equipped with the latest machine tools, is cheaper than his other product centres, more modern, more flexible and eager to develop export business. For multinational corporations, buyback can offer the possibility of tapping into new geographical markets more readily sourced from this new production base. For the supplier there is no need for a countertrade specialist as he is acquiring fixed quantities of his own production over a fixed duration. For companies wishing to phase out production of a mature product, the sale of a licence with buyback at a fixed price would make sense to both buyer and seller alike.

ESCROW ACCOUNTS

These are used by firms of all sizes. Situations are commonly found worldwide where buyer and seller do not know each other and there is a known shortage of convertible currency within that particular economy. Given that a supplier for industrial equipment has to spend money on the various production inputs before the item in question can be completed, one can clearly see how expenditure may start 6-9 months before the due date of delivery. When delivery is accompanied by uncertainty over payment, an escrow account may be used. Here, an intermediary who is a countertrade specialist may sell goods on behalf of the buyer and then place the proceeds from that sale into a blocked or trust account. The supplier is notified that there are now convertible funds available for payment and the transaction is completed in the normal way without the supplier being involved personally in the countertrade which was fundamental to the successful completion of the deal.

EVIDENCE ACCOUNTS

In countries where countertrade is mandatory, it is important to ensure that any undertaken by a subsidiary with any particular country is properly accredited by that country to the parent group as well as to the subsidiary. For the government concerned evidence accounts are a means of monitoring compliance with countertrade regulations. For the parent group it may also uncover opportunities for subsidiaries within the group.

INDUSTRIAL OFFSETS

These, like counterpurchase, are found in high value-added areas, most commonly in defence and civil aircraft sales. Industrial offsets are a mechanism whereby the direct sale of defence equipment or aircraft becomes more affordable. There are two means by which this is achieved.

(1) Local sourcing. Wherever possible, an undertaking is given to use local sources of supply which may include anything from low value-added raw materials to high value-added navigational equipment. Local sourcing has two beneficial effects for the national buyer: it defrays the total cost in terms of foreign currency, encourages more to be spent within the local economy and therefore has economic and employment advantages. For the supplier it may be the price required to clinch a deal; it could also have serious side-effects in that supplying, for example, electronic systems to an airframe manufacturer to a fixed value may mean displacement of traditional suppliers to that particular airframe manufacturer.

(2) An undertaking that best efforts will be made in seeking areas of export potential overseas where the buyer may earn some convertible currency. In this type of

situation the airframe manufacturer may be acting as a consultant to nationalized industries advising them of what to produce and where to sell it. On occasion some companies have taken on the task of selling goods from the buyer's country abroad in the company's own international marketing network as the local economy has been so weak in terms of infrastructural base. A good illustration is provided by Rank Xerox which, in order to sell copiers and printers in Brazil, exports Brazilian steel to Europe and Venetian blinds to the United States in a trade worth $100m annually. Heinz is now moving into Third World countries. Kodak is in Poland retailing film and cameras in exchange for a frozen goods export countertrade to the United States.

GENERAL POINTS ON WHICH TO NEGOTIATE

(1) What is the value of the countertrade as a percentage of the total amount of the contract?
(2) Is there a penalty for non-performance of the countertrade element in the contract? If less than 10% many have chosen to forego the countertrade but the buyer may be asking more than 100%.
(3) Is there a clause equivalent to force majeure which would indemnify the supplier in case of non-completion of the countertrade if beyond his control? Note the case of Rolimpex FTe vs Czarnikow Ltd when, in the early 1980s, the Polish Government placed an export ban on sugar at a time when the world market price was extremely high because of a shortage in face of demand. Czarnikow argued that a Foreign Trade Enterprise was an arm of executive government and could not therefore renege on a contract. The issue at question was whether indeed a foreign trade enterprise was an arm of executive government or a parastatal body similar to a British nationalized industry, owned by the State but quite detached from government. The High Court and Appeal Court rulings found in favour of the latter.
(4) May obligations be transferred to a third party? Remember someone has to pay the costs of a countertrade specialist.
(5) Over what time period is this countertrade obligation to last? What quantities will be exchanged over this period in total and within each year?
(6) What range of goods may be included within the countertrade? Do they currently meet any existing international standards?
(7) When dealing with centrally planned economies, is it possible to acquire countertrade goods normally handled by another state foreign trade enterprise? Traditionally, the Soviet Union might allow this, but Poland did not.
(8) Are there any geographical limits to indicate where these goods may be sold?

RESPONSES TO COUNTERTRADE

Politically countertrade is not liked. It is seen as a threat to the development of international trade by the General Agreement on Tariffs and Trade and the International

Monetary Fund. Although banks have frowned upon this development as well, many have since decided that if it was here to stay they may as well secure a share for themselves. All the major clearing banks now have departments dealing with this specialist activity which used to be the exclusive territory of merchant banks and countertrade houses. Multinational corporations likewise have developed autonomous specialist countertrade divisions as independent profit centres to deal with the demands of countertrade, not just for the immediate future but planning also over the next 10-15 years and viewing the potential of countries such as India and Indonesia. Countertrade is growing as an activity and is becoming increasingly innovative. Despite this, a word of caution has to be voiced and that is that only a small percentage of countertrade transactions are successfully completed. There is still a lack of understanding of the potential offered but information both on the potential to be offered by countertrade and how countertrade actually works, is provided by private sector initiatives such as the following in Europe.

AUSTRIA

The Liaison Office for Foreign Trade (Evidenzburo Wien) — a non-profit making body founded in 1968 offering expertise particularly on Eastern Europe — has representation in Bucharest, Sofia and Warsaw. Chiefly now involved in resolving countertrade problems.

FRANCE

ACECO (Association pour le Compensation des Echanges Commerciaux) was founded in 1977 as a non-profit organization with 230 members. Membership has tripled since 1983 reflecting a global increase in the use of countertrade. Presently 45% of its membership consists of small and medium sized companies, dispelling the myth that countertrade is only used by very large concerns. Created by banks, companies now make up 60% of the membership, and trading houses now form the largest group. Organized as a club it arranges local seminars in nine regions of France. In mid-1987 ACECO made its database available in French and English to subscribers worldwide; but in early 1988 the costs of updating 60 country files in two languages and making them available on-line proved too great and this service was reduced to 15 country files, available henceforth only to ACECO members and staff.

WEST GERMANY

The Compensation Office of the Foreign and Wholesale Trade Association of Hamburg is a non-profit organization, serving mainly Hamburg, which acts as an intermediary in locating partners for countertrade transactions. It also answers questions, acts as an information exchange between buyers and sellers of countertrade goods and advises on sources of know how for countertrade transactions; the office does not act as a broker.

HOLLAND

The Office for Countertrade BV (OCT) was established in 1984 by the Rotterdam Chamber of Commerce as a private company to provide mediation services and advice to Dutch companies concerning countertrade. OCT endorses pro-active countertrade where the exporter takes the initiative. OCT estimates that only 1 in 20 proposed countertrade deals in the Netherlands is actually consummated. By charging low fees, OCT attracts the small and medium size firms which account for three quarters of its activities. Unlike the national associations reported above, OCT is a profit-making organisation but remains small.

All the evidence points to countertrade accounting for a sizeable and growing share of world trade. The response to industry by government has been piecemeal, and the failure of international bodies such as the United Nations to provide guidance on countertrade because of opposition from the International Monetary Fund and the General Agreement on Tariffs and Trade has done nothing to help the situation. Countertrade will not go away because the demand for it to remain is too strong. The British Government has failed to take any initiative which would help British exporters or the City of London to maintain a competitive advantage in the area of financial services, presumably because the Department of Trade and Industry estimates for countertrade in global trade on which policy is based are lower than any others.

NOTES

1. International Monetary Fund Annual Survey of Exchange Agreements and Exchange Restrictions, International Monetary Fund 1983.
2. COHEN, R. and TRUELL, P., 'Brazil considers central controls over currency: design to guard reserves measures could delay its interest repayments', *Wall Street Journal*, 25 October, p.3.
3. ROWE, MICHAEL, 'Moving up Market', *Euromoney, Trade Finance Supplement*, February 1989, pp.2-4. See also AGGARWAL, RAJ (1989) 'International Business through Barter and Countertrade', *Long Range Planning*, Vol.22, No.3, p.75.
No reliable papers as to its overall volume are available as there is much secrecy in this business. Estimates are unreliable especially since it is estimated that only one in twenty deals which are discussed actually go through. The US Department of Commerce estimates that countertrade involves over 20% of world trade, while others have estimated it to be 30%; some companies specializing in countertrade estimate it to be as much as 40% of world trade.
4. *The Banker*, May 1989, p.93.

BIBLIOGRAPHY

ACECO, *Practical Guide to Countertrade*, Metal Bulletin Books 1988 (translated from the French). The main French banks were among the 11 founders of ACECO.

AGGARWAL, R. 'International Business through Barter and Countertrade', *Long Range Planning*, Vol.22, No.3, 1989, pp.75-81.

ASIWAJU, G., *Countertrade as a Strategy for International Marketing and Payments*, unpublished PhD Thesis, UMIST, Manchester, 1990.

Countertrade and Barter, Metal Bulletin, various issues.

Countertrade Outlook, Weekly, Alexandria, Virginia, USA.

FRASER, C. and ROBERT E. H., 'Competition as an Alternative to Ownership in Developing Markets: Beliefs, Attitudes and Uses', *Journal of World Trade*, Vol.22 No.6, December 1988, pp.95-106.

KASSAYE, W. W., 'Countertrade Prospects and Dilemmas for Small Businesses', *American Journal of Small Business*, Vol. IX No. 3, Winter 1985, pp.17-25.

LECRAW, D.J., 'The Management of Countertrade: Factors Influencing Success', *Journal of International Business Studies*, Vol. 20 No.1, 1989, pp.41-59.

McMILLAN, R., 'Swopshop Tactics Come of Age in Asia', *Asian Business*, Vol.25 No.10, 1989, pp.56-58.

PALIWODA, S. J., 'Countertrade', in THOMAS, M. J., *Marketing Handbook*, Gower 1989, pp.711-731.

PALIWODA, S.J., *International Marketing*, 2nd ed, Heinemann 1990.

MICHAELS, P., 'Countertrade: A Powerful Global Competitive Strategy for US International Traders', *Advanced Management Journal*, Vol.54 No.3, Summer 1989, pp.8-14.

REISMAN, A. and others, 'Seeking out Profitable Countertrade Opportunities', *Industrial Marketing Management*, Vol.18 No.1, February 1989, pp.65-77.

UNECE, 'Special Meeting of Experts on the Impact of East-West Compensation Trade on Small and Medium-Sized Enterprises in the ECE Region', *TRADE/AC.24/R.1*, 22 February 1990.

UNECE, 'Compensation Trade as it Affects Small and Medium Sized Enterprises in the ECE Region — A review of Problems Encountered and Possible Solutions', *TRADE/R.536*, 5 October 1988.

UNECE, 'Private Sector Measures on Selected ECE Member States that Provide Assistance for Countertrade Transactions', *TRADE/R536/Add.6*, 29 August 1988.

STANLEY PALIWODA

University of Calgary

4
INVESTMENT APPRAISAL AND CONTROL ISSUES

Part 4 contains detailed advice on international investment appraisal, corporate financial policies, the measurement and control of performance, remittance and dividend policies and insurance. The last chapter is a more specialized analysis of the role of capture insurance companies.

4.4 Remittance and dividend policies in international groups

Intra-group relationships
Remittance policies
Remittances and corporate structure
Policy in countries with exchange controls
Remittances and country risk
Dividend policies
International financial policies
Host country environment and legislation
The corporate structure, size and maturity of subsidiary companies
The dividend considerations and financial position and requirements of the subsidiary company
Conclusions

4.5 Deciding on insurance programmes: the role of captive insurance companies

The concept of international insurance programmes
Risk management
The role of captive insurance companies
Feasibility study
Conclusion

4.1
International capital project appraisal methods

We shall consider two related methods of valuing the multi-currency cash flows of an international capital project. A comparison of the methods in their simplest form reveals how we can obtain the net present value of multi-currency cash flows without introducing bias due to different forecasts of foreign exchange gains or losses. This enables us to make a financial assessment on the basis purely of the commercial and fiscal merits of the project. The question as to what extent the project exposes the company to foreign exchange risk and whether the risk can or should be hedged can then be treated separately.

In our initial comparison between the two methods we assume that all foreign currency net cash flows are remitted to the parent company and therefore translated into the home currency. Subsequently, we show how to treat the unremitted cash flows of an international project and how to deal with interrelated taxation in more than one jurisdiction.

METHOD 1

First, forecast net incremental cash flows of the project in the foreign currencies. Then discount the foreign and home currency cash flows using the appropriate nominal discount rates for each currency, given the expected rate of inflation for the currency and the project's risk. Finally, translate the resulting foreign currency present values to the home currency using the current spot rates of exchange between the foreign currencies and the home currency. The net of the different present values, translated into the home currency, gives the home currency net present value of the project.

Table 4.1.1 demonstrates the application of method 1 to cash flows in a foreign currency subject to inflation at the rate of 50%. For the sake of simplicity, it is assumed initially that there are no taxes. The appropriate real discount rate for the project is assumed to be 8%.

Table 4.1.1: Valuation of expected incremental cash flow from foreign project with zero taxes. Method 1 (in thousands)

	End of year			
	0	1	2	3
CURRENCY B (50% INFLATION)				
Net incremental cash flow	−300	300	450	675
Net present value at 62%	215.4194			
Spot foreign exchange rate (A/B)	× 2.00			
CURRENCY A				
Net present value	430.839			

Thus the expected nominal discount rate R is given according to Fisher's proposition,

$$\begin{array}{l}\text{Nominal} \qquad\qquad\quad \text{Real} \\ (1+\text{Discount Rate} = (1+\text{Required Rate} \times (1+\text{Expected Rate} \\ \qquad\qquad\qquad\qquad\qquad \text{of Return}) \qquad\qquad \text{of Inflation})\end{array}$$

$$(1 + R) = (1 + 0.08) \times (1 + 0.50)$$

$$R = 0.62$$

The net incremental cash flow in row 1 of the table discounted at 62% gives a net present value of $215,4194 denominated in currency present values into the home currency A (dollars). If the present spot rate of exchange is two units of A for each unit of B as indicated in the table, the present value of the foreign currency cash flow translated to currency A is

$$(A2.00/B1.00) \times B215{,}4194 = A430{,}839$$

In method 1 we simply translate present values denominated in foreign currencies to present values in the home currency using the current spot rate of exchange between the currencies. If a project involves cash flows in several different currencies, we can translate the present value of each foreign currency cash flow into the home currency and then compute the net of all the translated present values.

A variation on method 1 is to deflate the nominal foreign currency cash flows by using the appropriate foreign rate of inflation as the discount rate. The deflated cash flows are then discounted again using the sum of the foreign real rate of interest and the project's real risk premium as the discount rate.

The two versions of method 1 are mathematically equivalent. They will give the same net present value if the discount rates reflect the same assumed real rates of interest and the same expected rates of inflation.

METHOD 2

Forecast the foreign currency net incremental cash flows for the project. Translate each expected future cash flow into the home currency using forecast spot rates of exchange. Discount the resulting home currency cash flows at the appropriate home currency nominal required rate of return reflecting the project's risk. Alternatively, deflate the project's nominal home currency cash flows and then discount at the corresponding required real rate of return reflecting the sum of the real rate of interest plus the project's risk premium.

In Table 4.1.2 we show the application of method 2 to the foreign currency cash flows of the project. The rate of inflation in currency B is 50%, in currency A it is 20%, and we shall assume that the real rate of interest is zero. We assume initially that all the project's foreign currency cash flows will be remitted to the home country at the forecast exchange rates shown in line 3 of the table. If we use purchasing power parity as the basis of these forecast exchange rates, we obtain the same result as was obtained by method 1. Under purchasing power parity a future exchange rate at time *t* is given by:

$$S_t = S_o \frac{(1 + G_A)^t}{(1 + G_B)}$$

where S is measured in units of A per unit of B and G_A and G_B are the rates of inflation in currencies A and B, respectively. For example, the expected exchange rate of 1.28 at the end of year 2 in table 4.1.2 is obtained from,

$$S_2 = 2.00 \times \frac{(1.20)^2}{(1.50)}$$

$$= 1.28$$

The remitted cash flows are translated into currency A at the resulting forecast spot rates and then discounted at 29.6%. This discount rate was obtained from the Fisher effect by multiplying one plus the real discount rate (1 + 0.08) by one plus the rate of inflation (1 + 0.20) to obtain one plus the nominal discount rate (1 + 0.296). The net present value of $430,839 in currency A is exactly the same as the value obtained under method 1.

The fact that the two methods give the same answer has some useful implications. In method 1 we did not have to forecast changes in future spot exchange rates, so the

Table 4.1.2: Valuation of expected incremental cash flow from foreign project with zero taxes. Method 2 (in thousands)

	End of year			
	0	1	2	3
CURRENCY B (50% INFLATION)				
Net incremental cash flow	–300	300	450	675
Cash flow remitted to parent company	–300	300	450	675
Foreign exchange rate	×2.0	×1.6	×1.28	×1.024
CURRENCY A (20% INFLATION)				
Remittances received in home currency	–600	480	576	691.2
Present value at 29.6% = 430.839				

net present value obtained using that method did not reflect the effects of possible foreign exchange gains or losses. In method 2 we used purchasing power parity to forecast future spot rates of exchange. Method 2 gives the same answer and is, therefore, equivalent to method 1. It follows that the net present value obtained using method 2 does not reflect any net effects of possible foreign exchange gains or losses either. This is a very desirable property, for we want to be able to analyze an international capital project on the basis of its commercial merits without having its net present value biased by different forecasts of possible foreign exchange gains or losses. The question as to what extent the project exposes the company to foreign exchange risk, and whether such risk should be hedged, can be treated as a separate issue.

If the two methods give the same result, which should be used? In our example there were no taxes, and taxes may be payable in both the host country and the parent company's home country. If you look again at method 1 in Table 4.1.1, you will see that although it would be possible to use an after-tax cash flow in row 1, there is no way you can include home country taxes without altering the method. The alterations that are required are already included in method 2. That is, forecasts of future exchange rates are needed in order to be able to translate taxable income into the home currency so that expected home country tax liabilities and foreign tax credits can be estimated in each future period.

In Table 4.1.3 taxes are introduced into the example using method 2. In row 2 the estimated taxable income for each period is now shown, and in row 3 the estimated foreign income taxes at a 30% tax rate for country B. Thus is obtained the after-tax cash flow in row 4, which is assumed (for simplicity) to be remitted to the parent company. However, country B withholds taxes at 10% on all remittances abroad,

Table 4.1.3: Valuation of incremental cash flow from foreign project with differential inflation and remittance of all after-tax cash flows (in thousands)

	End of year			
	0	1	2	3
CURRENCY B (50% INFLATION)				
1. Net incremental cash flow	–300.0	300.0	450.0	675.0
2. Estimated taxable income		200.0	350.0	575.0
3. Country B corporate taxes at 30%		–60.0	–105.0	–172.5
4. Cash flows remitted to parent company		240.0	345.0	502.5
5. Withholding taxes at 10%		–24.0	–34.5	–50.3
6. Remittance after-tax		216.0	310.5	452.2
7. Foreign exchange rate	×2.0	×1.60	×1.28	×1.024
CURRENCY A (20% INFLATION)				
8. Remittances received	–600.0	345.6	397.4	463.1
9. Estimated taxable income		320.0	448.0	588.8
10. Corporate tax at 50%	–160.0	–224.0	–294.4	
11. Foreign tax credit		134.4	178.6	228.1
12. After-tax cash flow	–600.0	320.0	352.0	396.8
Net present value at 29.6% = 38.760				

leaving the after-tax remittances in row 6. The expected after-tax remittances then must be translated at the expected foreign exchange rates shown in row 7. These exchange rates are based upon the purchasing power parity formula given earlier. The home country A levies tax on all remittances of foreign taxable income but allows tax credits on foreign taxes paid. The estimated taxable income in row 9 was obtained by translating the currency B taxable income in row 2 into currency A taxable income using the foreign exchange rates in row 7. The resulting taxable income in row 9 is taxed in country A at 50% as indicated in row 10. However, tax credits for foreign taxes are allowed to be offset against these home country tax liabilities. The estimated foreign taxes paid are given in rows 3 and 5. The total foreign taxes paid in currency B have been translated at the rates given in row 7 and entered in row 11 as tax credits. Thus we can now obtain the net after-tax cash flow in row 12. The net present value at a discount rate of 29.6% is $38,760 (rounded) in the home currency after all taxes.

The distinction between estimated taxes in the foreign and home countries emphasized in method 2 can be important, if taxes payable in the home country on project earnings do not match the tax credits allowable on the project's foreign taxes. If taxes incurred in the home country on a project's foreign earnings exceed the available tax credits for foreign taxes paid, the after-tax incremental cash flow of the project must reflect the additional tax payable in the home country. On the other hand, if tax credits exceed home country taxes payable on the project and if the parent company is already in a non-taxpaying position, additional unused tax credits (if they are permitted to be carried forward) may extend the non-taxpaying period. In any such cases we require the framework of method 2 in order to evaluate the net incremental impact of the foreign project on the parent company's taxes.

UNREMITTED FUNDS

So far we have assumed that all after-tax incremental cash flows from the project are remitted to the parent company. It may be, though, that the parent company wants to retain cash in the foreign country for further investment. Also, many foreign countries restrict remittances to some proportion of reported profits earned in the country. If unremitted funds cannot be reinvested profitably in the foreign country, or if they are in danger of being expropriated, the profitability of a foreign project could be affected adversely by non-remittance.

Table 4.1.4 shows how to analyze a project's unremitted cash flows. The method is similar to that of the preceding table, except that some of the after-tax cash flow is not remitted until the end of year 3. For example, note that in year 1 the after-tax cash flow in row 4 is 240,000 but that only 140,000 is remitted in row 5. The remaining 100,000 of unremitted cash flow in row 6 is assumed to be reinvested at a rate of return equivalent to the project's 62% required rate of return (equal to 8% real) in currency B. Similarly, 100,000 of unremitted cash flow is retained and reinvested at the end of year 2. By the end of year 3, the reinvested unremitted cash from years 1 and 2 will have accumulated to 424,400 in row 7. If the cash is remitted at that time, a 10% withholding tax would be payable (row 8), and the after-tax remittance would then be translated at the year 3 exchange rate (1.024). In rows 12 and 13, the taxable income is the same as in the preceding table, but the foreign tax credits are less for years 1 and 2 (row 14) because foreign withholding taxes are lower owing to the smaller remittances in those years. In year 3, withholding taxes and tax credits are correspondingly higher when the postponed remittances eventually are paid. The net present value of 38,760 (rounded) in this example with deferred remittances is exactly the same (allowing for rounding errors) as in Table 4.1.3 where it was assumed that all after-tax foreign cash flows were remitted immediately.

The reason the net present value is unchanged is that we did not introduce any penalties for delayed remittances, there may be tax advantages to a particular remittance policy. It was assumed that unremitted cash flows were reinvested at the after-tax required rate of return until finally being remitted at the end of year 3. The compounded future value of the deferred remittances was then discounted, leaving the net present value unchanged. When the unremitted funds cannot be reinvested in the foreign country at the required rate of return for the risk involved, this reduces

Table 4.1.4: Valuation of incremental cash flow for foreign project with deferred remittances (in thousands)

	End of year			
	0	1	2	3
CURRENCY B (50% INFLATION)				
1. Net incremental cash flow	–300.0	300.0	450.0	675.0
2. Estimated taxable income		200.0	350.0	575.0
3. Country B corporate taxes at 30%		–60.0	–105.0	–172.5
4. After-tax cash flow		240.0	345.0	502.5
5. Remitted cash flows		140.0	245.0	502.53
6. Postponed remittances		100.00	100.0	
7. Future value of postponed cash flows (when remitted)			424.4	
8. Withholding taxes at 10%		–14.0	–24.5	–92.7
9. Remittances after-tax		126.0	220.5	834.2
10. Foreign exchange rate	×2.0	×1.60	×1.28	×1.02
CURRENCY A (20% INFLATION)				
11. Remittances received	–600.0	201.6	282.2	854.2
12. Estimated taxable income		320.0	448.0	588.8
13. Corporate tax at 50%		–160.0	–224.0	–294.4
14. Foreign tax credit		118.4	165.8	271.6
15. After-tax cash flow	–600.0	160.0	224.0	831.4
Net present value at 29.6% = 38.760				

their discounted value. The longer remittances are deferred and the longer unremitted funds are committed to unprofitable investments, the lower the resulting present value.

Even if unremitted funds are invested profitably abroad, they may risk being frozen, indefinitely blocked, or expropriated. Unless expected returns from the reinvestment of unremitted funds compensate for the probability that some portion of the funds may never be remitted, the present value is reduced. In any analysis, you can adjust the future value downward to reflect such adverse possibilities. For example, you can multiply the 424,440 future value in the example above by one minus the probability of expropriation.

A conservative way of analyzing foreign projects is to include only those cash flows that can be remitted through normal channels. The benefits of possible circumvention of restrictions (for example through prices that are charged in transactions between divisions that are in different countries) or offsetting of excess foreign tax credits can then be discounted separately. Other items that may merit separate treatment include the ability to reduce or defer taxes by combining profits from operations in countries with relatively low and high taxes, or to move expenses and revenues from one affiliated company to another and reinvest profits in low-tax countries.

These examples have assumed that the real rate of interest remains constant and equal for currencies A and B, and a real discount rate of 8% was used throughout. However changes in real rates of interest and differences in real rates of interest for different currencies could have been incorporated. This can be done by adjusting the real discount rate for different real rates of interest in the formula used above to calculate a nominal discount rate from the real required rate of return and the rate of inflation.

REQUIRED RATES OF RETURN FOR INTERNATIONAL PROJECTS

The capital asset pricing model (CAPM) provides a framework for estimating the required rates of return to be used as discount rates for each currency cash flow. The model estimates the required rate of return for a single period in terms of the risk free rate for that period plus a premium for the asset's non-diversifiable risk as measured by the beta factor. The value of the beta factor reflects the sensitivity of the asset's present value to changes in the value of the market portfolio, conventionally represented in the form of a broad stock market index. The risk free rate is defined as the rate of return expected on an asset if the returns on the asset are uncorrelated with the returns on the market portfolio. Yields on 90 day treasury bills are often suggested as a suitable surrogate for the risk free rate. Franks, Broyles and Carleton (1979) recommend that this rate be adjusted for personal taxes that would be paid by shareholders in tax jurisdictions such as the United Kingdom that employ an imputation tax system.

For international projects it is important to state the required rate of return for a future period initially in real (uninflated) terms using, for example, the CAPM and then to adjust the real required rate of return for the anticipated rate of inflation in the economy of the foreign currency, as was illustrated in the example above. In real terms the required rate of return for a given future period is given by:

$$\text{Future Real Required Rate of Return} = \text{Future Real Rate of Interest} + \text{Real Risk Premium}$$

where, approximately,

$$\text{Real Risk Premium} = 0.07 \times \text{Beta}$$

For example, if we are estimating the discount rate to be used for a foreign currency cash flow in year 5 of the project, the real rate of interest that is used above is a forecast of the real rate of interest on Treasury bills in that currency for the period in question. (If an imputation tax system operates in the home country for that currency, then their after personal tax real rate of interest is used.) Many multinational companies employ real risk premiums between 4 and 12% per annum depending on their perception of the project's risk. Franks and Broyles (1979) and Franks, Broyles and Carleton (1985) discuss in some detail how to estimate the beta factor for a capital project in order to estimate the appropriate risk premium.

Once the real required rate of return for the foreign currency cash flow is determined for the future period in this way, then it should be adjusted for the anticipated (foreign) inflation (the Fisher effect) as follows:

$$\text{Future Nominal Discount Rate} = (1+\text{Future Real Required Rate of Return}) \times (1+\text{Expected Future Rate of Inflation}) - 1$$

The future rate of inflation used above is the forecast for the foreign currency's economy and assumed to be the basis of the forecast of the foreign currency cash flow for the same future period.

While it is not always necessary to use a different discount rate for each future period in the life of the project, it is desirable to do so when significant changes in either or both the real rate of interest and the rate of inflation are expected in the economy of the foreign currency. The discount factor for a year 5 cash flow, for example, is simply the product of the one-period discount factors for each of the five years. The over-riding principle of consistency is that the discount rate used should be calculated on the basis of the same assumptions regarding the foreign rate of inflation and the real interest rate that were made when forecasting the foreign cash flow for the period.

Since international projects involve a degree of diversification for shareholders which it would not be possible to achieve through investment within their own country, we could question whether risk and therefore the risk premium in the discount rate for a foreign project should be different from that for a similar project in the home country. The answer to this question depends upon whether stockholders' portfolios are already internationally diversified. If they are, then there would be no net advantage to company diversification abroad for the purposes of risk reduction. Therefore, the risk premium for a project would not be altered by the fact that the project is to be located in a different country. Such questions do not have precise answers. Nonetheless, we know that for a variety of reasons, including information costs, shareholders still invest disproportionately in securities traded on domestic stock exchanges and that financial markets across the world are not yet fully integrated in this sense. From the point of view of shareholders who perceive risk in relation to their own domestic markets, a capital project has lower systematic risk to the extent that its performance does not relate to the domestic economy. Thus the Capital Asset Pricing Model implies that the discount rate for such a project is correspondingly lower.

SUMMARY

We have shown two equivalent methods for obtaining the net present value of a multi-currency international capital project. The first method does not require any forecasts of future foreign exchange rates and thus does not incorporate any anticipated foreign exchange gains or losses into the resulting net present value for the project. The first method, however, does not permit the computation of interrelated tax effects between jurisdictions over time. The second method facilitates analysis of interrelated taxation by introducing exchange rate forecasts of a form that maintains mathematical equivalence to the first method. Thus, the second method permits the financial analysis of a multi-currency project on the basis both of its commercial and of its fiscal merits without introducing bias from different forecasts of foreign exchange gains or losses. The question as to whether it is possible or desirable to hedge the project's multi-currency cash flows is a corporate treasury issue that should be taken seriously but now can be analyzed separately.

JACK BROYLES

Cranfield School of Management

(This chapter has been adapted, with permission, from Franks, J.R., Broyles, J.E. and Carleton, W.T., *Corporate Finance*, Kent 1985)

REFERENCES

FRANKS, J.R. and BROYLES, J.E., *Modern Managerial Finance*, John Wylie, 1979.
FRANKS, J.R., BROYLES, J.E. and CARLETON, W.T., *Corporate Finance*, Kent, 1985.

4.2
International corporate financial policy

There is no fundamental difference between establishing the corporate financial policy of a group of companies operating wholly in one country and establishing the corporate financial policy of a worldwide group — the same basic rules apply. Objectives are established for the holding company towards which the operating companies work; guidelines are provided; performance targets are set; budgets and company plans are agreed. Standards of performance are laid down by the parent company and adapted for each type of industry represented within the corporate body, while a modus operandi is created into which the operating units fit. Standardization is the norm and wherever possible reporting systems from all the individual companies or units need to be brought into line. The difference lies in coping with the problems of communication, of understanding (be it through language, or cultural attitudes), of accessibility and of risk, both political and economic. In addition international corporate strategy has to be built around a knowledge of the different practices that proliferate in worldwide business communities. It must conform to local legislation and regulations governing all manner of activities. It must cater, in the particular context of this chapter, for the effects of foreign investment regulations, exchange control and profits remittance regulations, involvement in international money markets, local taxation laws and so on.

Because of geographical distance and the importance of local knowledge in foreign markets, international corporate financial policy is more likely to work within the framework of a decentralized form of management than would be appropriate for operating units in the same country. It must also be sufficiently flexible to take into account the national interest and aspirations of the host country. Where there are local shareholders in the group company, their interests must also be taken into account.

Environmental factors have become an increasingly important part of business life, especially for foreign investment. This is especially true when that investment is in one of the developing countries.

In general terms, especially in the case of mature industries, investment in a developing country can be said to offer greater growth opportunities than in Britain or the other developed countries of Europe, North America and Australasia. However prospects tend to be limited by political and economic instability. Attitudes to foreign investment over the years have been variable, ranging from recognition of a national need to the rigidly doctrinaire. There has been a trend in developing countries towards regulating foreign investment in such a way that the commercial benefit is shared between the local economy and the investor. Some of these regulations have been somewhat onerous to the extent they have frightened, or forced, investors away. In a number of cases there are now signs that the pendulum is swinging back, as developing countries grapple with the burdens of foreign debt. Direct equity investment is being positively encouraged in certain countries. Nevertheless the risks arising from exceptional levels of inflation, price controls, and the problems of continuous devaluation of local currencies remain endemic.

The implications of all these issues will be examined below although, because of their diversity, no attempt is made to cover all the different types of legislation, regulation and practice which are likely to be encountered throughout the world. Instead an attempt has been made to illustrate the principal types of problem likely to be met in direct investment overseas. In addition an appendix is provided in which some of the main sources of business related information covering all parts of the world are listed.

STANDARDIZATION OF ACCOUNTING SYSTEMS

Before dealing with the practical details of establishing a corporate financial policy for an international company, it is necessary to identify clearly what one is striving for. A common approach and purpose in the worldwide development of the business and a means of directing and monitoring performance must be established.

In financial terms the group objective may be to seek a real growth in profits that will enable progressive dividends to be paid from a business that shows, in its balance sheet, increasing financial strength from a sound cash-flow. Standardization of both the statutory and management accounting systems is required. To the maximum extent possible the methods used by the operating companies and the parent company must be designed to satisfy the needs of both sets of management: individually to assist local management to run the group as a whole.

To a great extent accounting standards and the more recent Companies Acts, based on European Community directives, are helpful in achieving this standardization.

THE PROFIT AND LOSS ACCOUNT (HISTORIC)

In conformity with the consolidating Companies Act 1985, most British companies, including parent companies of international groups, will prepare consolidated profit and loss accounts for their ordinary activities along either of the general lines shown in Table 4.2.1.

Table 4.2.1: The profit and loss account (historic)

	Format 1			*Format 2*		
(a) I	Turnover	x		Turnover	x	
(a) II	Cost of sales	x		Changes in stocks of finished goods		
(a) III	Gross profit/loss		x	and in work in progress	x	
(a) IV	Distribution costs		x	Own work capitalised	x	
(a) V	Administrative expenses		x	Other operating income	x	
(a) VI	Other operating income		x	Raw materials and consumables		x
				Other external charges		x
				Staff costs		x
				Depreciation		x
				Write-offs — current assets		x
				Other operating charges		x

(a) VII	Trading profit	x		
(a) VIII	Share of associated companies profit	x		
(a) IX	Income from trade investments	x		
(a) X	Interest receivable	x		
(a) XI	Interest payable	x		
(a) XII	Profit/(loss) before taxation		x	
(a) XIII	Taxation		x	
(a) XIV	Profit/(loss) after taxation			x
(a) XV	Profit attributable to minority interests			x
(a) XVI	Extraordinary items			x
(a) XVII	Profit attributable to parent company			x
(a) XVIII	Dividends			x
(a) XIX	Earnings per share			x

Overseas operating companies, irrespective of any local statutory requirements, will need to return information to the United Kingdom on a similar basis. Their internal accounting systems must conform to these accounting headings and indeed to the more detailed information also required under the United Kingdom Companies Act.

Since the parent company performance is to be judged on results set out in this manner, the selected presentation should be adhered to as the ultimate in both the statutory and management accounting systems.

Certain elements of the format 1 profit and loss account will be dealt with in greater detail below, as particularly relevant to the establishment of corporate financial policy (this chapter) or in monitoring it (chapter 4.3). Although key elements of format 2 can also be identified for companies attracted to that alternative, for the sake of simplicity references in this chapter will be restricted to format 1.

THE BALANCE SHEET (HISTORIC)

It is likely that the most frequently used balance sheet layout conforms to format 1 of the Companies Act 1985. The alternative format 2 layout contains similar information in all respects except that it does not differentiate on the face of the balance sheet between creditors due to be paid within one year and creditors due to be paid after one year. The two formats provide for the substantiating data leading up to the main balance sheet headings to be given by the maximum use of notes. The standard balance sheet headings used by most British companies are along the lines shown in Table 4.2.2.

Standard instructions are usually issued to all operating companies to ensure that their accounting systems conform to these headings to the best extent possible. If they cannot conform special adjustments will need to be made to accounting returns in the parent company.

Certain elements of the balance sheet, as in the case of the profit and loss account, will be referred to again in this and the following chapter. In addition further information relevant to company borrowings also needs to be set apart.

THE CASH-FLOW

A uniform approach to the group cash-flow statements is required so that the content is useful and readily comprehensible for both local management and parent company purposes.

Cash-flow statements do not of course need to be consolidated. The important matter of establishing and monitoring cash-flow to the parent company is conducted as an exercise on its own, which is referred to later in this chapter. Nevertheless operating company cash-flows do need to be easily understood at the parent company level. They represent a vital element in controlling and monitoring individual company performances both at home and overseas.

FACTORS IN ESTABLISHING FINANCIAL POLICIES FOR OPERATING COMPANIES OVERSEAS

Since the ultimate objective in any group of companies must be to improve the performance of the parent company, corporate financial policy is concerned to ensure that, in the aggregate, the performances of the individual operating companies, at home and overseas, combine to meet this objective.

The fundamentals for the establishment of appropriate financial policies for constituent companies can be expected to be the same wherever they may be. What is different is that if company operations are established overseas it may neither be possible nor desirable to put these policies into practice. External factors have to be taken into account.

THE PARENT COMPANY SHAREHOLDING POSITION

In many countries it is essential that a foreign investment is properly registered; this means that any shares issued to shareholders resident externally must be registered as foreign capital by the appropriate company in the host country before remittances of any profit against that capital, or its eventual repatriation, will be allowed. The amount of the registration will be related to money or the value of goods, such as new plant or machinery, introduced into the country and will normally be expressed in hard currency — sterling or dollars — rather than in the local equivalent. In this

Table 4.2.2: Format 1 balance sheet

		Say	Say	Say
(b)	Fixed assets (net values)			
(b) I	Intangible assets	50		
(b) II	Tangible assets	350		
(b) III	Investments	100		500
(c)	Current assets			
(c) I	Stocks	500		
(c) II	Debtors	200		
(c) III	Investments	200		
(c) IV	Cash at bank and in hand	50		
(d)	Prepayments and accrued income	50	1,000	
(e)	Creditors: amounts falling due within one year			
(e) I	Short-term borrowings	(100)		
(e) II	Other creditors	(300)	(400)	
(f)	Net current assets (liabilities)			600
(g)	Total assets less current liabilities			1,100
(h)	Creditors: falling due after more than one year			
(h) I	Long-term borrowings	(150)		
(h) II	Other creditors	(100)	(250)	
(i)	Provision for liabilities and charges		(25)	
(j)	Accruals and deferred income		(25)	(300)
(k)	Net assets = capital + reserves + minority interests (if any)			800

Borrowings are the total of (e)I and (h)I, i.e. 100 + 150 = 250

Thus:

Net assets or shareholders' equity (k)	800
+ Borrowings ((e)I + (h)I)	250
+ Balance of creditors > one year (h)II	100
+ Provisions for liabilities and accruals (i) + (j)	50
is equal to funds employed, i.e. (g) + add back (e)I	1,200(*l*)

Any references to borrowings in this and the following chapter relate to the aggregate of (e)I and (h)I where the (e)I heading relates to short-term borrowings falling due in under one year and the (h)I heading to borrowings falling due in over one year.

Thus net assets or shareholders' equity	(k)
Plus borrowings	(e)I and (h)I
Balance of creditors (> 1 year)	(h)II
Provision for liabilities, charges, accruals and deferred income	(i) and (j)
is equal to funds employed	(l)
which in turn is equal to	
Total assets *less* current liabilities	(g)
with short-term borrowings added back	(e)I

way the value of the remittances is maintained where restrictions are expressed as a percentage of the registered foreign capital and exchange rate fluctuations are likely.

It is not always possible or desirable for the parent company to own all the shares in an overseas subsidiary.

(1) It may not be permissible under local foreign investment regulations. In most of the developing countries prospective foreign investors are encouraged to take local partners if they wish to set up operations. Many countries have policies with which potential investors are required, or advised, to comply.

(2) There are regulations in certain areas, such as the Andean Pact countries, which define different classes of company according to the proportion of foreign shareholding and set out the benefits (or otherwise) of each.

Proportion of foreign shareholding	*Classification*
Above 49%	Foreign
Above 20% and below 49%	Mixed
20% or less	National

Originally, in the Andean Pact countries, certain activities (such as public services) were reserved for national companies, other activities (such as retail sales) were reserved for mixed companies. New investors were required to start with, or to agree to phase down to, no more than a 49% shareholding. There were limits on remittance of dividends, on the re-investment of profits and on the payment of royalties and technical fees, especially to the parent company. However their recent bitter experience with foreign debt has caused some of these countries to revise their view of the benefits of foreign investment.

In Venezuela, for example, a new decree published in January 1990 has removed all restrictions on the remittance of dividends, and the re-investment of profits, and has considerably liberalized the payment of technical fees and royalties. Reserved activities have been greatly reduced in number, new and existing foreign investors can freely purchase existing national companies and phasing down is no longer a requirement.

(3) In a number of countries there is a perceptible benefit in having a local shareholding of up to, say, 25%. It takes the heat out of the discussion when business performance is subject to negotiation with local governments or institutions. The management can talk on behalf of local shareholders rather than just those overseas. Also 25% is a key percentage because of its frequent relevance in passing extraordinary or special resolutions where a 75% voting majority is required.

The politico-economic climate in many of the countries which have felt the need to lay down ground rules for foreign investment is unstable. Even if the foreign investor has a shareholding position already successfully established it is by no means certain that circumstances will not change. The position must be regularly reviewed.

FINANCIAL STRUCTURE — LOANS

The parent company may wish to establish a policy of maximum borrowings in the local currency for each of its overseas subsidiaries, but this is not always possible.

(1) In certain countries limits for short-term local currency borrowing by foreign owned companies are laid down. In Kenya, for example, dependent on the proportion of national or resident shareholders, local borrowing is restricted to the following percentages of Paid Up Capital, Foreign Loan Capital and Reserves:

40-50% Kenya nationals	40%
over 50% Kenya nationals	60%
over 50% Kenya residents	40%
all others	20%

(2) Restrictions on the remittance of profits can interfere with group strategy if a policy of high gearing is followed. The high yield benefit which provides the pay-off when the increased risk of substantial borrowing is accepted can be foiled if dividends are restricted to a proportion of share capital, which by definition is lower if borrowings are higher.

(3) Offshore borrowing may normally be resorted to, either by the investing company or by the local company. The latter may wish to borrow offshore because it is easier and cheaper, or it may be forced to by local borrowing restrictions. In each of these circumstances it is essential that care is taken to ensure that exchange and limited remittance of profits risks are properly taken into account.

EXCHANGE CONTROL

Exchange control can be a perpetual threat, or indeed a reality, in the less economically stable countries. Its impact can be severe or slight in a disconcertingly changeable way. It is not of course confined to the overseas country alone. Exchange control, limiting British investment overseas, was exercised in this country, under supervision of the Bank of England, from 1947 to 1979. It could well come back again if there was a change of government.

Overseas there are still inhibiting exchange control restrictions in some countries, remittances not being allowed except under quotas agreed by central banks on an annual basis.

There is a risk, in certain countries, that approved items can have been deposited with the Central Bank for remittance, in due course, at the ruling rate of exchange at the time of deposit. However, since no foreign exchange has been forthcoming, the payments have stayed in the pipeline, while the local currency has devalued substantially. How, when, and at what rate of exchange the items will eventually be remitted remains problematical.

There are also many instances when the repatriation of disinvestment proceeds has had to be delayed, or made in deferred instalments over a number of years. Among recent instances are the repatriation terms under the scheme to reduce foreign investment in India and the disinvestment rules laid down by the governments of Ghana and Trinidad.

TAXATION

The attractiveness or otherwise of overseas investment can also be strongly influenced by taxation.

Overseas corporation tax. There may be cases where underlying rates of corporation tax in overseas countries are lower than in the United Kingdom. However this is not such an attraction as it seems. Although the overall taxation on profits for the group may be potentially lower than that effective in the United Kingdom (35%), this is not the whole story. Once income from the lower taxed companies is actually remitted taxation at United Kingdom rates is applied to the relevant profits, and double tax relief (DTR) is limited to the lower rate paid overseas. A simple example illustrates this.

	Overseas subsidiary (wholly owned)	
Profit before tax	100	
Local tax at 25%	25	
Profit after tax	75	
Distribution (say) received in the United Kingdom	50	
Distribution grossed at 25% (the underlying rate)	67	
Overseas tax paid	17	
Net received	50	
United Kingdom tax payable (67 at 35%)	23	
Double tax relief (restricted to paid)	17	
Additional tax payable	6	
Tax payable is (overseas) 25 + (United Kingdom) 6		= 31
out of profit before tax		100 = 31%

In a number of cases overseas rates of corporation tax are now higher than in the United Kingdom. In which case no double tax relief is available for the excess over the basic United Kingdom corporation tax rate of 35% (see withholding tax illustration below).

Special tax arrangements in overseas countries. There are a number of countries in which special corporate tax arrangements are available, at the government's discretion. These include special incentives such as pioneer concession schemes whereby new investors are given tax holidays in the early years of an investment. Care has to be taken, however, because it is difficult to make profits (which would otherwise be taxable) in the carly years of such an investment.

In Brazil an interesting system is in force, known as the fiscal incentive investment scheme. Under this a proportion of tax otherwise payable (at present 24% of the basic 40% tax payable by large companies in Brazil) can be allocated for the creation or development of new business in the depressed areas of Brazil. Although there is a high risk attached to this investment, it can sometimes be successful.

The practical effect at home is to reduce the tax paid by the company, part of which can genuinely be treated as investment. However, for double tax relief purposes the utilized fiscal incentive proportion reduces the underlying rate in Brazil, and hence increases the liability to tax on profits remitted to the United Kingdom.

Withholding tax. In addition to corporate taxes there is a further tax payable on remittance of profit (or indeed other payments like royalties and commissions) in many countries. Because of this there are instances where corporation tax (which may be lower than in the United Kingdom) plus withholding tax on dividend remittances exceeds 35%. In this case there is no double tax relief on the excess. An example illustrates this.

	Overseas subsidiary (wholly owned)	
Profit before tax	100	
Local tax at 25%	25	
Profit after tax	75	
Distribution (say)	50	
Less withholding tax at 25%	12	
Received in the United Kingdom	38	
Distribution grossed at 25%	67	
Overseas tax paid (17 + 12)	29	
Net received	38	
United Kingdom tax payable (67 at 35%)	23	
Double tax relief (restricted to 35%)	23	
Tax payable is (overseas)		
25 + 12 + United Kingdom nil		=37
out of profit before tax		100 = 37%

Use of penal rates of withholding tax as a form of exchange control. It should be noted, as an example, that the Brazilian government effectively uses the tax system as a means of controlling cash outflow from the country through foreign investment. Withholding tax is applied on a graduated scale, with excess (or penalty) withholding tax being applied, in addition to the normal 25% rate, to any annual remittances of profit in excess of an average annual remittance over a three year period on the following scale.

Average remittance (net of 25% withholding tax)	*Rate of extra withholding tax*
12% to 15% of registered foreign capital	40%
15% to 25% of registered foreign capital	50%
Over 25% of registered foreign capital	60%

It will be seen that the foreign investor can quickly get up to a level of tax which is so high that he will, of necessity, restrict his remittance of profit to the lower level. In practice this is a form of exchange control on dividend remittance. The official position on remittance of profits on foreign capital, and the repatriation of such capital, is that the central bank in Brazil may impose restrictions for a limited period of time. The dividend restriction is currently specified as not more than 10% per annum in the case of necessary businesses and not more than 8% in the case of so-called luxury businesses. In fact these restrictions, introduced in the years 1964 and 1965, have never been exercised, although currently dividend remittances are subject to a few months delay. The Brazilian government's commitment to honouring its obligations to overseas investors, despite its foreign debt servicing problems, is to be commended.

Advance corporation tax (ACT). Another aspect of taxation that needs consideration is the effect of overseas earnings on the ability to recover advance corporation tax in Britain. In other words if a group of companies has a disproportionate amount of foreign income, to the extent that advance corporation tax payments on dividend distributions are not fully recoverable from tax actually payable in this country after the United Kingdom tax liability has been reduced by double taxation relief, then the group will be left with substantial advance corporation tax write-offs, or double taxation relief displacements.

This is a complex problem and suffice it to say in this chapter that it provides a strong incentive towards arranging international group activities in such a way that, where the problem is encountered, every effort is made to increase direct income from overseas. The objective is to try to ensure that as many remittable charges as possible are deductible for tax in overseas companies and thereby wholly assessed to tax in Britain. This subject is discussed under the following heading.

THE ESTABLISHMENT OF DIRECT SOURCES OF INCOME — PAYMENT FOR TRADEMARKS, PATENTS, KNOWHOW, CONSULTANCY AND ADVISORY SERVICES, AND INTEREST ON LOANS

In addition to seeking income from overseas investment by dividends, or interest on loans, parent companies should endeavour to increase their income from more direct sources. Clearly wherever trademarks, patents and knowhow are exported, royalties, fees or commissions should become payable. Whenever this can be achieved the parent company has the benefit of the following.

(1) Getting some form of compensation for the asset, especially where there is a less than 100% shareholding in the company to which the trademark or patent is assigned.

(2) Establishing a source of income which becomes payable (and indeed can be paid) even where the operating company is not in profit.
(3) Establishing a source of income which can become inflation adjustable. For example, royalties, together with commissions, can be made payable as a percentage on turnover rather than as a value per units sold; when prices go up with inflation parent company income goes up in equal proportion.
(4) The fact that, dependent on the overseas tax rate, this type of income is directly taxable in Britain rather than overseas can make arrangements potentially more tax efficient in group terms, especially where the group has a paucity of taxable income in this country.

In addition, wherever possible, when expertise is passed to an overseas subsidiary or associated company, a consultancy or advisory fee should be charged. This provides a single major shareholder with a means of specific compensation for work done which benefits the local company as a whole. Other shareholders would benefit disproportionately if the sole method of shareholder settlement were by way of dividend.

Unfortunately, in recent years a number of multinational companies have tended to exploit these possibilities to maximize remittances while reducing taxes. Remittances have been made in the guise of royalties or advisory fees which have not been supportable in commercial terms. As a consequence it is becoming more and more difficult to get the inland revenue departments of host countries to permit these charges as deductible for taxation purposes, or to allow them to be increased adequately even where there is a sound and proper basis for the charge. In some countries payments of this nature are simply not allowed to be made to parent companies, although they are permitted where the foreign investment shareholding is below 50% or some other established level. In Brazil, for example, royalties are payable in specifically approved circumstances from 1% to a maximum of 5% of the net income of the manufacturer or of the value of the product sold. Permissible payments are tax allowed but are subject to withholding tax. Technical and advisory fees can also be paid, again in approved circumstances, during an introductory period of five years which may be extended for a further five years. However the payment of royalties or advisory fees is not permitted between a Brazilian subsidiary and its holding company abroad.

Finance managers in the parent company of an international organization need to be familiar with all aspects of the subject-matter referred to above. There is a considerable bibliography available to provide up-to-date information. Details of some of the principal sources of information are provided in the appendix to this chapter. The essential point to remember is that only the latest information on regulations and rulings governing foreign investment will do. The rules are liable to change quickly.

What has been said and specifically illustrated by examples is characteristic of the type of problem international companies face in the world in which they operate. It is also representative of the general approach host countries are increasingly adopting in their desire to attract and accommodate the right kind of foreign investments and to take a larger share of the benefits provided by those investments.

FINANCIAL POLICY IN AN INTERNATIONAL GROUP

In the same way as policy is laid down in any association of businesses working towards a common purpose, group financial policy is laid down by the parent company.

Objectives are set which constituent companies are required to meet. Guidelines are provided which give an indication of what is expected and, in the better managed organizations, a two-way discussion between managers at the centre and in the operating companies is undertaken; in this the ways and means of achieving the objectives are examined and agreed.

The difference in an international organization is that the various points enumerated in this chapter will form a background to these discussions and need to be taken into account. In addition the ultimate objective has to be concerned with the performance of the group as it affects the parent company's position in the United Kingdom.

We can express the group objective in another way, as the achievement of a desired level of average growth per annum in income per share (over a specified period) which will be available for distribution to shareholders, such profit to be projected from an agreed base. It is then evident that we are essentially talking about the level of income which will be available to the shareholders in Britain ((a) XVII in the profit and loss account, Table 4.2.1 above), which will also need to have a substantial degree of cash backing.

Given this we can begin to see the form the guideline discussions should take. The parent company must indicate its position and expectations in answering the following questions.

STRUCTURE OF THE GROUP

Shareholding position

(1) Does it wish overseas companies to be wholly owned or is it prepared to accept a degree of local participation?

(2) What advantages or disadvantages are there in reducing foreign investment:
- (a) to less than 100% or 75% but above 50%?
- (b) to less than 50% but not less than 25%?
- (c) to less than 25%, or indeed 20% where associated company status is likely to be lost?

(3) Does it want to encourage a degree of local participation?

(4) If local participation is to be encouraged, what level of participation is sought?

(5) How is local participation to be introduced in an established company? (See below.)

(6) If there is no anxiety to reduce its shareholding but if local pressures developed to the extent that it would clearly be wise to do so, what would the position be then?
(7) Have contingency plans been prepared to deal with any immediate need to introduce a local shareholding?
(8) What steps need to be taken in the United Kingdom or abroad to obtain the necessary official approvals and consents to change the parent company shareholding?

Base financial policies

(1) How is the operating company overseas financed? Will the parent company be prepared to provide further finance by equity or loan capital? If so in what proportion?
(2) Are there any local restrictions on borrowing by a foreign owned company? If so what are they and how, if at all, can they be avoided?
(3) Are there any local restrictions on borrowing to be laid down by the parent company? The parent company should agree basic borrowing policies with local management — debt to equity ratios and interest cover among others. In addition it will be concerned to ensure that borrowings by all subsidiary companies, in aggregate, conform to any restrictions applied to the group as a whole and are consistent with borrowing policies expressed in group terms through the consolidated balance sheet and profit and loss account.
(4) What is the parent company's view on offshore borrowing? What is the relevant cost of borrowing and how does it relate to exchange risk? To what extent is the operating company covered for exchange risk by parallel deposits or earnings?
(5) What is the parent company's position on providing support for local company borrowings like loan guarantees, comfort letters, letters of knowledge and consent? What are the benefits of so doing?
(6) What is the parent company's position on intercompany lending or borrowing within the group?
(7) Is there a detailed knowledge of the exchange control ramifications and a grasp of any inherent exchange risks? Both of these are important.
(8) What is the parent company policy on the deployment of surplus funds in the short and long term?

PROFITS

Specific policies. Specific policies appropriate to each operating company will need to be agreed, dependent on the particular circumstances of each. These are likely to cover, in particular, aspects of the relationship between sales volume, production capacity, turnover and profit. Questions to be asked include the following.

(1) How is the operating company to maintain gross profit margins in the face of

inflation (or hyperinflation), over-capacity (under-capacity), price controls, national and international competition?

(2) What is the parent company's view on productivity? How are improvements to be achieved in developed and under-developed countries? What incentives or restrictions are there on the import of new technology? What restrictions are there on relocating or closing down inefficient and unprofitable plants?

(3) What is the parent company's view on pricing policy, with particular reference to intra-group transactions? In theory all companies in a group should work on an arms-length basis in dealing with each other. However sometimes there are cogent reasons for adopting a particular policy which may be seen to favour one company at the expense of another. In these instances the policy should be understood by and agreed with all the interested parties. It should be an accepted concept, subject to the guidelines promoted by the Organization for Economic Co-operation and Development for multinational enterprises and ensure that any minority interests are unharmed and that the interests of the group will supersede the interest of the individual companies.

(4) What is the parent company's view on overhead costs in relation to the relevant turnover and gross profit factors? Is there a standard cost and profit structure which can be usefully indicated?

General policies. Each company will require guidance from the parent company on its profit objective. This would normally take the form of a growth target provided it is projected from a base which is in itself satisfactory, or some form of return on capital employed.

(1) What is the parent company's profit expectation? This objective must be realistic and hence achievable. Ideally growth in profits should be linked to some operational figures such as sales volume so that, for example, growth in gross profit should be equal, at least, to inflation plus sales growth.

(2) What is the parent company's expectation on returns on capital employed? This would be expressed at a gross and net stage, for example, trading profit to funds employed — (a) VII to (1) — and profit after tax to shareholders' equity — (a) XIV to (k) (see Tables 4.2.1 and 4.2.2). The level of expectation needs to take cognizance of any local problems, such as the competitive situation, price control, borrowing factors, taxation rates.

CASH-FLOW

The parent company would normally expect operating companies to generate adequate cash-flow to finance working capital investment and dividend distributions, with adequate funds left over to provide a comfortable foundation for fixed asset investment (with or without augmentation by additional funding) and a reasonable degree of surplus to ensure continuing financial soundness. In an international group the parent company may also require to give guidance on more specific matters, including the following.

(1) Are there problems in routing cash either into or out of the country? If there are restrictions on the remittance of dividends to overseas investors, what should be done with the unremittable funds? Should, or can, dividends or other dues be paid out locally and temporarily invested outside the business? What is the withholding tax position then? What should happen to the income earned on such temporary investment?
(2) Guidance should be given as to the timing of dividend payments and indeed, any intra-group transactions. As with pricing policy, all items of a current account nature should be treated as normal commercial transactions. Due balances should be paid off at least monthly so that no element of free financing, which can of course be deliberately engineered, is allowed to creep in. Guidance should be given on the desirability of buying sterling forward where the value of dividend, or other remittances, is likely to be endangered by currency devaluations. If the value of sterling is in doubt the reverse should of course apply.
(3) What are the parent company's views on credit policy? In many overseas environments, the principle of extended credit to customers, particularly in consumer goods markets, is not so widespread as in this country. Clearly cash sales, or cash on delivery sales, are to be encouraged in the appropriate circumstances.
(4) Subsidiary company policy on extended credit, both in buying and selling should be determined. The role of credit insurance agencies, such as the Export Credits Guarantee Department, should be determined.
(5) What is the group position on stock durations? To what extent, if any, can they be safely reduced in one company if shortfall positions can be covered from another company in an adjacent country? Is there a case for stockpiling in certain countries? How easily can items be transferred from one location to another within the group as a whole?

DIVIDENDS AND OTHER UNITED KINGDOM INCOME FACTORS

Given that the parent company objective is to be able to achieve an adequate degree of growth in Britain from income made available to it from its operating companies overseas, backed up by dividend and other income remittances which will enable it to make payments to its own shareholders, it is clear some guidance on dividends and other income remittance is necessary. The fundamental policies to be agreed with overseas companies are as follows.

(1) What is the parent company position on direct income charges like royalties or commissions? Is this type of income preferred to dividends? Can it be paid to the principal shareholder overseas, or to any foreign investor, under the laws and regulations of the host country? Is there a tax advantage or disadvantage locally or in the United Kingdom?
(2) What proportion of profits should be paid in dividends? Is there any restriction or penalty on dividend distributions to foreign shareholders? If there are

restrictions what is the most appropriate policy to maintain the quantum of dividend remittances over a period of time? Are there advantages in not paying the maximum permissible in any one year?

(3) What is the parent company's position on these matters in companies which have local shareholders? It should be clearly understood that local shareholding interests must not be ignored. In such instances dividend and other United Kingdom remittance policies should be structured on an arms-length basis. Local shareholders should neither benefit from nor be at a commercial disadvantage as a result of the foreign investors' control.

(4) Dividend distribution should be on the basis of what would be expected in local circumstances, particularly where the subsidiary or associated company is a public company in its own right.

(5) It is possible that foreign investors may be at a disadvantage in that trademark and patent rights are given to overseas companies with local shareholders (with not infrequently substantial shareholdings) in the knowledge that they cannot be paid for other than through profits earned as dividends. Where this situation has to be accepted the circumstances must be carefully taken account of in investment appraisal.

SPECIAL FORMS OF EXPENDITURE

Finally the parent company needs to establish its position on special items of expenditure, namely major capital expenditures, substantial investments outside the classification of working capital, and any capital expenditure outside the group's established line of business.

(1) What is the parent company's view on expenditure limits for overseas companies?

(2) Are there any new investment areas, or diversification activities, which are to be particularly encouraged?

GENERAL FACTORS

In addition to, and arising from, the above there are a number of general policies which need to be established.

The need to establish how local shareholding participation might be increased in an overseas company has already been mentioned. There are two principal methods.

Disinvestment. The appropriate proportion of the parent company shareholding is sold. This is done either by an open offer in the local share market or by placement through a local bank with associates of the local company, such as suppliers, customers, employees, selected institutions or individuals or some combination of these. Care has to be taken over the taxation implications, particularly establishing the extent of any capital gains, and also to ensure that the repatriation of the proceeds is appropriately secured.

*Dilution.*The parent company's interest is reduced to an agreed proportion by an appropriately priced rights issue to which the parent company does not subscribe. This is in fact best done by ensuring that the parent company does not have the right to subscribe — the issue is made open to residents of the host country only. In this way any risk that the parent company is taxable on the value of the rights it failed to take up is avoided. The new shares which would otherwise have been allotted to foreign shareholders are then sold through the open market as described above. The overseas company then gets the benefit of the subscription capital.

British and overseas government consents. Finally care must be taken to ensure any necessary government or central bank consents are obtained. Although in this country Bank of England consent is currently not required, Treasury consent is required under section 765 of the Income and Corporation Taxes Act 1988 in cases where it is proposed that either:

(1) shares or debentures in an overseas subsidiary are to be issued; or
(2) shares in an overseas subsidiary are to be transferred, except to enable a person to be qualified to act as a director. Exemption from the need to make application is given if proposed transactions conform to certain circumstances covered by the Treasury's general consent. Although application is made in a prescribed form to the Treasury, the proposals are actually examined by the Inland Revenue. Guidance notes are issued by the Treasury.

FINANCIAL ADMINISTRATION IN AN INTERNATIONAL GROUP

Apart from the need to ensure that group financial policies are adhered to, it is essential to make sure that there is a network of financial management through which it is possible to control the group's finance activities. This means that local finance managers have to be able to communicate with the parent company in English, have some understanding of United Kingdom requirements, in addition to their own, and are able to conform to the management information flow timetable laid down for the control and measurement of their own company's performance (see chapter 4.3).

Communication is improved by personal contact. It is desirable, wherever it can be arranged, to ensure that finance managers in overseas companies have the chance to spend some time with the parent company, particularly before they take up a finance director appointment in a foreign subsidiary. It is always helpful for overseas managers to have had some experience of the parent company's problems and manner of working before they take up the most senior appointment in their function.

At the same time the management of the parent company must ensure that they also keep in touch with the overseas companies as much as possible. Visits should be frequent, and preferably on a regular basis. In addition the parent company can improve the degree of its understanding of and influence over overseas companies through internal audit. This is particularly important as a way of ensuring that local companies conform to and properly understand group systems and procedures. An internal management audit system provides a potential senior finance manager in the parent company with detailed knowledge of the practical problems of overseas operating companies.

Security of assets and personnel is an important feature of international company operations these days. Again the internal audit system can do much to keep matters under surveillance in these areas. Internal control systems must always be kept up to scratch in the international business environment.

CONCLUSION

It is essential in international financial management, and indeed in international management generally, to be as fair and reasonable towards local expectations and aspirations as to one's own, and to insist that host country and foreign investor interests share the benefits of industrial activity. The guidelines of the Organization for Economic Co-operation and Development, to which one is strongly recommended to adhere, underline the importance of this. These guidelines for multinational companies urge enterprises:

> . . . To manage their financial and commercial operations, especially liquid foreign assets and liabilities, in a way consistent with the balance of payments and credit policies of the countries in which they operate, and to refrain from using transfer pricing which does not conform to an arms length standard.

It is always worthwhile to attempt to see one's investment from the host country's point of view. Where there are foreign exchange earning problems in a country, a company is advised to attempt at least to balance the transactions of its subsidiary, if possible to encourage it to earn more foreign exchange than it pays out in dividends and other remittances to its parent, and to see that its standards of behaviour are of the best. In this way the group can be proud of its contribution to international business and happy in the knowledge that it is providing employment, commercial and industrial expertise, and other economic benefits to its host nation.

I. N. SPURGEON

APPENDIX: SOURCES OF BUSINESS-RELATED INFORMATION FOR ALL PARTS OF THE WORLD

The Department of Trade and Industry,
1 Victoria Street,
London, SW1H 0ET.
(Tel: 071-215 5000)

These offices house departments covering markets and projects in all parts of the world. However, for more general information under The Enterprise Initiatives, the Department of Trade and Industry's regional office for Greater London is at:

Bridge Place,
88/89 Ecclest[illegible] Square,
London,
SW1V 1PT.
(Tel: 071-215 0572)

There are also regional offices in Birmingham, Bristol, Cambridge, Cardiff, Glasgow, Leeds, Liverpool, Manchester, Newcastle-upon-Tyne, Nottingham, Reading, Reigate and Belfast.

The Export Market Information Centre,
1-19 Victoria Street,
London,
SW1H 0ET.
(Tel: 071-215 5444/5)

Contains commercial and trade statistics for most countries that issue them and market surveys, trade directories and economic development plans for many countries of the world. It also has a Product Data Store, a central bank of product and industry-based market information.

HINTS TO EXPORTERS

A series of booklets containing information on passport and entry formalities, local holidays, economic factors, currency and exchange control regulations, methods of doing business, social customs and many other matters. These booklets are updated regularly. They were previously known as *Hints to Businessmen* and provide a very useful background to over 100 different countries. They are obtainable from the regional offices of the Department of Trade and Industry, or directly from:

Hints to Exporters Unit,
The Department of Trade and Industry,
Lime Grove,
Eastcote,
Ruislip,
Middlesex,
HA4 8SG.
(Tel: 081-866 8771)

The Department of Trade and Industry also publishes a number of *Country Profiles* in selected instances.

AREA ADVISORY GROUPS

Also under the wing of the Department of Trade and Industry are the seventeen area advisory groups whose committees, made up principally of businessmen representing organizations with export or direct investment interests in the relevant parts of the world, meet regularly to further trading activities and associations. Currently these area advisory groups are:

European Trade Committee
East European Trade Council
North America Advisory Group
Latin American Trade Advisory Group
Caribbean Trade Advisory Group
British Overseas Trade Group for Israel
Committee for Middle East Trade
Tropical Africa Advisory Group
United Kingdom — South Africa Trade Association
Australia and New Zealand Trade Advisory Committee
South East Asia Trade Advisory Group
British and South Asian Trade Association
Japan Trade Advisory Group
Hong Kong Trade Advisory Group
Korea Trade Advisory Group
Sino-British Trade Council
Anglo-Taiwan Trade Committee

Although these groups are principally export-oriented they are also concerned with the development of direct investments in their particular areas. Names and addresses of members and the secretary and the secretarial offices are listed in the British Overseas Trade Board's Annual Report published by the Department of Trade and Industry.

FOREIGN AND COMMONWEALTH OFFICE, BRITISH EMBASSIES, HIGH COMMISSIONS, AND CONSULAR POSTS WITH COMMERCIAL DEPARTMENTS

There is a Foreign and Commonwealth Office department covering all parts of the world, in contact with embassies, high commissions and other posts overseas.

FOREIGN EMBASSIES — COMMERCIAL ATTACHÉS

The commercial liaison offices of most foreign embassies in London will provide guidance on regulations and principles affecting foreign investment in their countries. Where necessary they have publications available to guide and advise would-be investors.

INTERNATIONAL BUSINESS ORGANIZATIONS

As well as having considerable practical knowledge locally, a number of the major international banks publish frequent and regular reviews of commercial and economic interest on various countries of the world. In addition, there are useful publications on specific matters such as foreign investment regulations published by chambers of commerce. International firms of auditors also publish useful booklets — see, for example, the Price Waterhouse *Information guide for doing business in . . .* series, which covers a large number of countries all over the world, and the Ernst and Whinney *Doing business in . . .* series, covering the major countries of Europe.

4.3
Measurement and control of performance

The principal purpose of the preceding chapter has been to provide some background on the special types of problem experienced by finance managers involved in international business. This chapter deals with the organization of financial management and control in a group of subsidiary and associated companies overseas and with some of the particular difficulties that are likely to be encountered.

Again it has to be emphasized the concern is with the specific characteristics of international management rather than the basics of financial management generally. In practice the two are similar. The essential objective of financial management in an international group is to run the business in the same way as if all the group companies were in Britain while ensuring that: methods and systems are properly designed to accommodate the complexities of different commercial environments, the changes in the value of currencies, the implications of excessive rates of inflation, as well as the additional complications of communication and understanding over considerable distances, in different languages and against ever changing political and economic backgrounds.

The fundamentals of business style, which will be assumed throughout this chapter, are that it is very important to ensure a highly disciplined approach to business decision-making, followed by a full commitment to agreed objectives by those who have the responsibility to achieve results, and a continuous monitoring of performance against these objectives. In addition it will be assumed that English is the language of communication and that normal conditions prevail throughout the world, that there will be no insuperable obstacles to immediate and routine communication by airmail, telephone, telex or compatible computer systems.

PLANNING CYCLE, GUIDELINES, BUDGETS AND COMPANY PLANS

In the previous chapter the special factors that are likely to need attention in preparing guidelines for the financial management of overseas operating companies have been identified. Parent company financial policies for each overseas company should be brought into the open, discussed when necessary and agreed with the local finance director and general manager. The overseas management is then in a position to establish its operational plans, and to construct budgets and estimates of the financial outcome in appropriate detail. Such a system is the foundation stone of any approach to management accounting at the group level. The annual programme is as follows.

(1) At the operating company level
  (a) Receive guidelines from the parent company.
  (b) Discuss and agree guidelines with the parent company.
  (c) Outline the company plans for the next year. This to be supported by a brief summary of the principal financial consequences such as profit and loss account, cash flow and balance sheet projections for at least the immediate year (the budget) and, where appropriate, two or possibly more years to illustrate the longer-term implications of current business decisions.
  (d) Discuss and agree these outline plans with the parent company.
  (e) Prepare a firm and detailed budget for the immediate year which then becomes the committed profit and loss account and cash flow budget for that year, and firm up the projections for the additional years.

(2) At the group level
  (a) Discuss and agree guidelines.
  (b) Send out guidelines to the operating companies.
  (c) Discuss and agree outline plans with the operating companies.
  (d) Confirm the committed budgets and financial projections for the immediate and ensuing years.
  (e) Aggregate and consolidate all the operating companies' budgets and financial projections, together with the similarly agreed budgets and projections prepared for the parent company's own operations.
  (f) Examine and evaluate the consolidated budget and financial projections for the group as a whole, against the basic group objectives. From this study, guidelines for the following year will be established.

Each year the parent company will have a group profit and loss account in sterling for at least three years, together with projected group balance sheets for the same period. Both will be set out as proposed in chapter 4.2. The problem of aggregating the budgets and projections from the individual companies overseas, which will have been presented locally in a number of different currencies, is dealt with below.

THE LAYOUT OF BUDGETS AND FINANCIAL PROJECTIONS

The layout of the group profit and loss account presents no problem. It is simply a repetition of the basic profit and loss account headings over the appropriate number of years. It is usually desirable to maintain an initial link with results that have actually been achieved. The profit and loss coverage should therefore start from the previous year's actual figures, arranged as in Table 4.2.1. The layout of the group balance sheet should also conform to the essential headings set out in the previous chapter over the identical years (see Table 4.2.2).

In addition at the group level it is necessary to ensure that there are adequate estimates, budgets and projections of the income flow and cash flow expectations for the parent company. It is important to know that the group dividend projections are likely to be satisfactorily covered. Cover must come not only from profits but also from the flow of income projections, the net of tax dividend, royalties and other earnings of the parent company in Britain, from its subsidiaries and associates overseas, and from the cash flow projections for the domestic operation. The cash flow is, of course, based on the income flow but will differ, principally because of timing. Its sole concern is with the cash receipts and payments that will flow into and out of the parent company.

Detailed statements will need to be prepared at group level to ensure that the principal sources of available income and cash flow are identifiable so that the relative importance of each is understood and so that performance can be monitored. This is of particular importance where significantly changeable exchange rates are involved. In sterling terms, forecast and actual cash receipts may fluctuate considerably. It is essential to monitor the situation and to attempt to determine the most opportune times to remit, in instances where discretion can be exercised.

PREPARATION OF THE COMPANY PLAN DOCUMENTS

Each of these group statements will be built up by aggregation and consolidation from the basic documents prepared at the operating company level in local currencies.

PROFIT AND LOSS ACCOUNT

Although this will conform ultimately to the basic accounting headings in Table 4.2.1, it will be expanded at the operating company level. The headings need to be broken down into constituent parts to enable the essential elements of the business to be identified. The parts would include variable, fixed and semi-variable costs.

BALANCE SHEET AND CASH FLOW

The balance sheet and cash flow projections should be brought together for local management purposes in accordance with the layout in Table 4.3.1 which, in its turn, relates to Table 4.2.2. From this it is possible to extract the information required for the group balance sheet and at the same time, through the annual source and application of funds and movement in reserves analysis, readily identify the factors which influence the strengthening or weakening of each company's balance sheet and cash and borrowings position. Again, wherever necessary, each operating company will expand its headings to suit its own management needs and to assist in highlighting the principal issues. These will include the debt:equity ratio, the current ratio, fixed asset expenditure, investment in the major categories of stock, control of trade debtors, utilisation of trade credit and liquidity.

Table 4.3.1: Balance sheet and cash flow projections

		Say
(k) I	Share capital	
(k) II	Reserves	
(k) III	Profit and loss account	
(k)	Shareholders' equity*	800
(h) I	Long-term borrowings	150
(e) I	Short-term & OD borrowings	100
		250
(h) II	Balance of creditors (> 1 yr)	100
(i) & (j)	Provisions etc.	50
(l)	Total liabilities (or funds employed)	1,200
(b) I & II	Fixed assets less depreciation	400
(b) III	Investments	100
(b)		500
(c) I	Stocks	500
(c) II	Trade debtors	
		250
	Other debtors	
(c) III	Short-term investments	200
(c) IV	Cash	50
(c)	Current assets	1,000
	less balance of current liabilities i.e.	
(e) II	Trade creditors +	
	other creditors	300
		700
(l)	Total assets (or funds employed)	1,200

*Includes minority interests (if any)
Includes prepayments and accrued income (d).

AVAILABLE INCOME IN BRITAIN

Finally it is necessary for individual companies to identify separately in their various estimates, budgets and projections any dividends, royalties and other relevant remittance items, which have been included. These will be needed to construct the parent company income and cash flow statements.

MONITORING PERFORMANCE

As explained in the preceding section, the profit and loss account, balance sheet and cash flow budgets for the immediate ensuing year will have been established as part of the annual planning cycle. The figures to which each individual company and, in turn, the group will be committed are normally agreed in the last month of the year preceding the budget year.

At the operating company level the profit and loss account and cash flow budgets will also have been broken down by months, so that the business of monitoring actual performance against budget can commence with the first month of the new year.

The essential principle of financial control in an international group, and indeed in any group, is to build up the information flow in such a way that local management benefits from the more detailed information it needs and group management is provided with the less detailed information it needs, using either the same information sources or simple abstracts therefrom.

AT THE OPERATING COMPANY LEVEL

A detailed analysis of the profit and loss account, and the cash flow statement should be prepared for management on a monthly basis. All the headings will be compared to budget for the individual month and for the cumulative period of the year. In addition the cumulative profit and loss account figures should also be compared with the actual results for the same period in the previous year. Brief explanations of any significant variances will be required. For the operating company, of course, all financial reports will be presented in local currency.

This information should be sent to the parent company within a week or so of the month end. It should incorporate estimated figures if necessary, together with a short formal report from the general manager covering the political and economic scene and any other aspects of the business worthy of attention. In this way the parent company is kept adequately informed as a matter of routine. At the same time local management benefits from the simple discipline of explaining what has happened, what is happening and what it expects to happen.

At the end of each quarter actual results, not estimates, are reported. This report should be supplemented by a revised estimate of the profit and loss account and the cash flow for the full budget year. In practice the quarterly cash flow revision will be an update covering the next twelve months on each occasion, broken down by quarters so the year and cash and borrowings position can be established. Significant changes in the estimated profit or loss for the year and the cash flow revision must be explained adequately at the same time.

AT THE GROUP LEVEL

Apart from having sight of the monthly reports it is normally desirable to prepare some formal review of progress to date, and of the revised estimate for the year, on a group basis at least at quarterly intervals. This would take the form of a statement of consolidated group profits set out as in Table 4.2.1, with spaces across the page for cumulative months to date (actual, budget, difference), estimate for year (latest revision, budget, difference) and last year (actual, current year, difference).

Satisfactory explanations of the reason for significant differences between the cumulative actual and cumulative budget and latest revision for the year, annual budget, and the last year's actual figures should be provided. In this way the parent company board is able to follow progress against the official budget, in the cumulative figures, and have early warning of any change in the budgeted results for the year. The impact of differences in exchange rates is also a factor in the presentation (see below).

In addition to updating its position at the group profit and loss account level, on a quarterly basis, the parent company should also review the following items.

(1) The individual contributions from subsidiaries making up the sales volume (if appropriate) or turnover and the trading profit figures, as well as the relevant share of profit from the associated company figures. Again comparisons at the cumulative and revised estimate for the year stages should be supported with suitable explanations of the differences.

(2) The updated position on flow of income and cash flow for the parent company, comparing actual and revised estimates for the period to date and the full year with the budget and with the previous year's figures. Again suitable explanations of the differences are needed. Finally it is essential, where there is any form of doubt as to the group borrowing position, to ensure that there is no danger of contravening any restrictions or covenants built into any borrowing agreements at group level. Overall this position can be monitored from the budgeted or estimated balance sheets described in Table 4.3.1. If there is no risk there is no need to worry about the position through the year. However, if the margin between actual and estimated borrowings and equity cover is slender or is uncomfortably sensitive to fluctuations in relevant rates of exchange or other factors, then the debt:equity position must be carefully monitored.

(3) The debt:equity position — the actual and the revised estimate at the year end — can be monitored by aggregating borrowing details, which will form part of the basic cash flow statement provided by individual subsidiary companies, and individual company details of expected profits and retentions. Again, if necessary, the sensitivity to exchange rates or other changeable factors must be examined.

PROBLEMS WITH EXCHANGE RATES

With the exception of the hyperinflation countries, and certain other countries whose economies are especially unstable, there is no particular difficulty if converting budgets and forecasts in foreign currencies into sterling.

Initially figures are put together in the local currency concerned. For group purposes budgets and forecasts are then converted to sterling at the rates appropriate to the accounting policies used by the group, for instance, at the estimated year-end rate where that will be the ruling rate when the profit and loss account and balance sheet is prepared for the full year. In normal circumstances, in the quarterly up-date, it makes sense to convert all the cumulative actual results, the cumulative and year-end budgets and the revised estimates for the year to sterling, at the exchange rates ruling at the relevant quarter's end. In this way no distortions as a result of exchange differences in comparisons of the budget or estimates will arise.

Nevertheless, where it is recognized that there are factors affecting rates of exchange that will significantly alter expectations, there is every reason for working such assumptions into the exchange conversion rates used for the group revised estimate for the year. There is also a need to reflecι the impact of significant devaluation assumptions in the operating companies' own budget and forecasts, where their results are likely to be significantly affected; where a currency provision for loss on exchange in respect of off-shore debts is required, for example.

THE CALCULATION OF EXCHANGE DIFFERENCES

Additionally, it is desirable to indicate the effect of exchange differences when the latest estimates for the year are compared with the previous year's actuals.

Assume an overseas company achieved after-tax profits of US$1m for the year to 31st December 1988 (when the United States dollar was 1.809 to the pound sterling) and US$1.3m for the year to 31 December 1989 (when the United States dollar was 1.613 to the pound sterling), an increase of 30% in currency terms. In sterling the 1988 profit would be £552,791 and in 1989 £805,952, a gain of 45.8%. The 1989 profit eliminating exchange is:

$$\text{£}805{,}952 \times \frac{1.613}{1.809} = \text{£}718{,}629$$

This means that the 1989 sterling value is converted back to United States dollars (× 1.613) and reconverted to sterling at the 1988 rate (÷1.809). This gives a 30% increase over the 1988 value in sterling. Clearly the difference of £87,323 (£805,952 minus £718,629) represents the gain on exchange.

EXCHANGE RATE SENSITIVITY

The formula used in this example is:

Budgeted profit (in sterling) x last year's (budgeted)
exchange rate/anticipated exchange rate for the current year

This formula enables the effect on profit caused by a change in rates of exchange to be established for any currency. The sensitivity to exchange rate fluctuations can be identified for each individual company. However a short cut can usefully be taken when there is a large number of subsidiary companies and when there is a strong relationship between most of these currencies and the United States dollar. Thus a figure can be calculated which would reflect the effect of, say, a 10 cents change in the United States dollar rate of exchange on group profit after tax. For example the formula could be applied simply to the sum of the sterling profits after-tax figure derived from such currencies.

In the case of the above quoted figures a change in the United States dollar rate of exchange of [E±0]10 cents would have the following effect on 1990 group after-tax profits (assuming that was the budget year and local profits were budgeted to improve again by 30%):

1990 budgeted profit = £1,047,738
(£805,952 x 1.30) x 1.613 (the budget exchange rate) = US$1.69m
Converted at 1.713 = £986,573, a loss of £61,165
Converted at 1.513 = £1,116,986, a profit of £69,248

PROBLEM COUNTRIES

HYPERINFLATION COUNTRIES

In certain countries of Latin America, such as Argentina and Brazil and until recently Chile, one of the consequences of the prevailing levels of high inflation has been the acknowledgement by government of the need for constant devaluations of the currency. Hyperinflation, as an economic condition, is experienced where annual rates of inflation run consistently at levels of 20% to 30% or more. The rate of exchange adjustment process is known as crawling peg devaluation. Monthly devaluations are announced. Sometimes these are arbitrary and are based on a particular economic policy the government is pursuing. In other cases the rate of devaluation per annum bears some relationship to the difference between the rate of inflation experienced in the country concerned and the rate of inflation experienced in the hard currency country to which its local currency is naturally related, the United States in the case of Latin American countries.

The consequence is that the condition cannot be ignored in the context of reporting, budgeting and projecting results within an international group of companies.

The speed of change at this level has the following implications.

(1) Currency budgets and forecasts over just a few years become meaningless unless inflation assumptions are made and stated. Similarly, rates of exchange forecasts require to be calculated. These are best calculated on the basis of some relationship like the inflation differential, although it is wise to check this assumption to ensure it fits the experience of preceding years. Sometimes political factors weigh in and distort the pattern over a number of years and a certain element of inspired guesswork is required to adjust one's assumption to a more appropriate basis (see section on economically unstable countries, below).

(2) Forecasting values in currencies has to be done initially in constant (real) terms. It is then translated into inflated (money) terms. In this way:
   (a) strategy and performance expectations can be properly evaluated and understood and growth rates are not distorted by inflation factors;
   (b) the anticipated effect on profit and loss accounts and balance sheets (in

money terms) can be evaluated, while likely cash flow consequences and remittance to the parent company projections can be examined.

(3) The effect of currency devaluation to the United States dollar is an integral part of the risk of investing in the hyperinflation countries of Latin America. It should be considered as such in evaluating the impact of exchange rates on the conversion of currency results to sterling, since it reflects the prevailing decline in the purchasing power of those currencies. Thus the group exchange difference calculation should reflect only the sterling to dollar differential.

(4) All budget and forecast projections derived from currency projections should be converted to pounds sterling at the forecast conversion rates referred to above.

(5) Hyperinflation and government responses to it — involving price control, the indexation of loans, loan interest and other such factors — can create totally different business characteristics from those that prevail in Britain. Sound advice from local management is essential to trade successfully in such an environment. Care has to be taken if assumptions are made that prices, and hence profit margins, can be maintained in the face of inflated costs. It is not always possible to protect one's business in this way. Borrowing in hyperinflation countries is dangerous, especially where a particular industry is affected by price controls. Local currency loans will carry an exceptionally high rate of interest, or may be increased by a monetary correction factor linked to inflation. These may be automatic or obligatory adjustments. If prices cannot be increased to cover costs, cash problems will quickly follow.

ECONOMICALLY UNSTABLE COUNTRIES

There are other circumstances where adjustments to exchange rates, in budgets and other sterling value projections, need to be anticipated, which are not confined to the hyperinflation countries. Whenever adequate doubts as to the strength of a particular currency exist, and the effect is likely to be of significance in group terms, some attempt to forecast the consequences on currency conversion should be made.

There is, unfortunately, an increasing number of countries where economies are in such a parlous state that their currencies live under the constant threat of a major devaluation. In such circumstances either regular, but inadequate, mini-devaluations do take place, or the condition tends to remain totally untreated over an increasingly uncomfortable period of years. Eventually some really unpalatable action has to be taken and a major devaluation is conceded. The problem is the need to predict the time and scale of that major devaluation.

Apart, again, from the inflation differential route, one of the best indicators of what that devaluation should be is to be found in the parallel market rate. These unofficial market rates often provide a practical guide to the true value of a currency, though the timing factor remains extremely difficult to predict. Group finance managers would be well advised to take cognisance of these alternative exchange rates, at least for management sensitivity purposes, if not to be reflected more formally in group plans, or indeed accounts.

Local finance managers need to maintain an awareness of the state of the currency in which they trade, through the local or world press, their contacts with bankers and other financial institutions, and generally keep their ears to the ground. They must keep their parent company well informed of possible and probable developments. Finally it should be mentioned that, in the context of preparing forecasts, possible revaluations of currencies are not so important. As a matter of prudence they should generally be ignored except in sensitivity calculations.

INFLATION ACCOUNTING

One other important factor in controlling and managing business finances is inflation accounting; this is especially the case in the hyperinflation countries, but also in a number of other countries where double figure inflation is a continuous problem.

In Argentina, Brazil and Chile, for example, inflation accounting with a liberal use of indexation, is a statutory requirement. It is also essential in management accounting. Some form of replacement costing must be used as a means of identifying real profit margins and of maintaining a suitable pricing policy. The best approach is for any replacement costing system to be fully integrated with the inflation provision, being the difference between book cost and the replacement cost, retained in the business to help financing. At the operating company level such systems should be fully supported by cash flow projections on the usual monthly basis. This provides an extra safeguard to the financial position by highlighting the peaks and troughs of the annual cash flow cycle, and should be rolled forward for at least a twelve-month period continuously. In addition depreciation provisions must conform to local practice, where assets are indexed, or additional depreciation charged to cover the inflating cost of fixed asset replacement where they are not.

FINANCIAL CONTROL THROUGH THE PLANNING CYCLE — BUDGETS AND PROJECTIONS

We now have all the data that is needed to control the business, both at the group and operating company level, at home and overseas.

AT THE GROUP LEVEL

From the profit and loss account budget and projections we can identify trends and projected growth rates at the salient points from sales volume or turnover to profits attributable to the parent company, earnings, and dividends payable.

From the balance sheet projections we can identify evidence of emerging strengths and weaknesses. We can examine the projected trend in the debt:equity ratio in relation to any restrictions or limitations laid down under loan agreements and the like. We can calculate and consider trends in the various balance sheet ratios with particular reference to return on capital employed.

We have the means to examine details of the group's sources and application of funds.

From the parent company flow of income and cash flow projections we can examine trend projections and identify reasons for expected changes in the profit and cash position. The budget and projections will illustrate the extent to which dividend payment growth expectations are likely to be covered.

From the supporting data in sterling, summarized from the individual operating company information, sources of profit and cash remittances can be identified, as can the potential users of funds or of borrowing power. This enables the parent company management to get a feel for the relevance and effect of these projections on central group resources.

AT THE OPERATING COMPANY LEVEL

Operating company profit and loss accounts, initially in local currency, also enable us to identify trends. From the additional data provided, trends in cost and profit structures can be examined such as profit to turnover; productivity ratio trends can also be calculated. Income cover on interest costs, if any, can be examined as it is projected over the review period.

All of this is best done in local currency. However, in the case of the Latin American crawling peg devaluation currencies, conversion to United States dollars can give a better perspective to the local company's expected performance than the local currency values would give.

From the balance sheet and balance sheet movements budget and projections, in local currency or sterling (or United States dollar) equivalents, trends in balance sheet ratios and cash borrowings can be examined. Again a picture of the developing financial strengths and weaknesses of the business will have emerged.

CONTROLLING AND MONITORING FINANCE-ORIENTED DECISIONS

FIXED ASSETS

Fixed asset investment projections in the company plan for the budget and subsequent years will give parent company management the opportunity to consider and agree the outline proposals for any major expenditure programme. In addition it is essential, for the proper control of international group financial policies, to establish limits and procedures to govern and monitor the principal elements of the capital expenditure budget. Limits should be laid down.

(1) To govern what local management can commit themselves to, as a capital investment expressed as the local currency equivalent of, say, up to £10,000 or £50,000.

(2) To govern what must be referred to the parent company executive, or director, responsible for the subsidiary before any commitment is made, for example in excess of £10,000 or £50,000.

(3) To govern what must be referred to the board of the parent company before any commitment is made, for example in excess of £50,000 or £100,000.

Applications for approval of expenditure in the latter two categories should be written applications in which reasons for the investment are amplified and cost details provided. The application should also identify the anticipated financial return on the investment (preferably the discounted cash flow yield), explain how it will be financed and identify the expected impact on both the profit and loss account and balance sheet of the subsidiary. It should also identify the cash flow both on the local company and that company's dividend remittances to the parent.

Projects should be monitored. Once agreed, expenditure on projects which extend over a period of time must be monitored on a regular basis. Expenditure and timing must be compared to the original appraisal and commented on. In selected cases periodic reports should be sent to the parent company so that the discipline of proper accountability is maintained.

CURRENT ASSETS

Stocks. Stocks in the local company balance sheet projections must be considered against the background of expansion in sales volume, inflation, import problems, recommended durations and so on.

Debtors. Debtors should similarly be related to sales expectations, turnover, credit limits, inflation and other relevant factors.

Other current assets or liabilities. These can be similarly treated and considered through the budget and further year projections, sufficiently in advance to influence policies and attitudes.

Shareholders' funds—foreign capital registration. On the other side of the balance sheet the likely pattern of growth in shareholders' funds can be examined well in advance. The sensitivity of individual company situations can be examined so that the likely consequences of an unexpected reverse can be evaluated. The build up of retained profits is an important factor in considering both the items which follow, namely borrowing and dividend policy.

Additionally it is essential to examine the pattern of the development of shareholder's funds in the context of foreign capital registration. Separate projections are required where this is a factor in establishing the extent to which dividend remittances will be permissable.

Borrowings. The way in which each company's borrowing policy is likely to develop can be examined from the budget balance sheet and projections. The extent to which the debt:equity ratio is likely to conform to the guideline requirements will be evident from the individual company plan balance sheet projections.

Dividend policy. Dividend policy can be established or controlled through examination of the projected profit and loss account, cash flow and balance sheet details. Additionally projected inflation accounting requirements (current cost accounting adjustments) and the ongoing financing needs of the business will help to identify what can be paid.

FINANCIAL CONTROL THROUGH THE PLANNING CYCLE — MONITORING PERFORMANCE

Once the annual budgets for profit and loss account, cash flow and balance sheet have been agreed, and policies have been established, the monitoring task commences.

AT THE GROUP LEVEL

(1) By the preparation of cumulative profit and loss accounts (probably on a quarterly basis) for the group at the current rates of exchange. This group summary with its revised estimate for the year is supported by details of individual company sales volume, turnover and trading profit figures (also in sterling) where appropriate. In this way a simple analysis of performance to date (and of the revised annual estimate) is provided.

(2) By the preparation of cumulative and revised estimates for the year of income and cash flow statements to the parent company. These are converted from currency at current rates of exchange, or at actual sterling values in the case of cash already received.

(3) By control of the developing debt:equity situation with particular reference to the estimated changes affecting the year end position.

AT THE OPERATING COMPANY LEVEL

(1) By monthly reports from management, in local currency terms, detailing estimated profit and loss accounts and comparing estimated actuals with budget on a monthly and cumulative basis.

(2) By comments on important variances in the cash flow which are likely to have a significant bearing on the budgeted year end balance sheet.

(3) By comments on aspects of business generally, for example, sales or turnover (again with reported actuals against budget) production, outstanding orders, surplus capacities, labour relations, and so on.

(4) By quarterly reports, again in local currency terms, confirming the cumulative actual profit and loss position to date, and revising the estimated profit for the year on the basis of one, two and three quarters actual results respectively.

(5) By quarterly formal reviews of borrowing, current and estimated, for the year end and for twelve months ahead.

LIAISON WITH OVERSEAS SUBSIDIARIES — THE PROBLEM OF KEEPING IN TOUCH

As mentioned at the beginning of this chapter, one of the biggest differences between managing a group in this country compared to managing a group overseas is the difficulty of communication. Language and cultural barriers can also create unpredictable problems due to misunderstandings. In addition, the inherent differences in national character and behaviourial patterns can confuse relationships in even the most well ordered and soundly established businesses. There has been progress in improving international understanding in recent years, but there is still a problem. Local managers will not necessarily respond to parent company policies thought up in London and applied uniformly throughout the world. Management characteristics and performance potential in Europe and North America, Latin America, Asia and Africa will all be different. There is every sense in acknowledging this and making sure that management is only asked to do things it can reasonably be expected to do, and in an appropriate way.

Where indigenous local management capable of maintaining standards to the group's specification does not exist, special action has to be taken. This means that expatriates will need to be sent to develop and train local managers to the appropriate level. Fortunately, the finance area is one where, generally speaking, local nationals of the required standard of accounting and financial education can be found. They will nevertheless need to be trained in the group's ways, and developed to acceptable practical standards.

In certain countries work permit problems will be encountered if expatriate accountants are to be introduced, particularly where adequate numbers of apparently suitably qualified accountants are deemed to be available. In these circumstances the training and development role, for a limited period, may be enough to persuade the authorities to accept an application. Failing that, a straight exchange of two finance managers, between the territory and Britain will often do the trick; if not the temporary assignment of a competent expatriate manager on a consultancy basis may suffice. It is also desirable to ensure that senior managers in head office have also had some experience of working overseas. Only in this way can they get to know something of the practical problems which face managers outside this country, especially where operations in developing countries are involved.

REPRESENTATION AND THE PROBLEM OF ASSOCIATED COMPANY RELATIONSHIPS

It is no longer always possible, due to government restrictions in certain countries, for the parent company to have direct representation on subsidiary company boards. In most instances it is not necessary. The operating company board appointments are vetted by the parent company. The chief executive of the local company will be keenly aware that his position depends on a continuing satisfactory performance. Generally speaking there should not be conflicts of policy between subsidiary companies and their parent. If there are, or threaten to be, clearly the parent company has the voting power to overcome the difficulty. This is not necessarily the case in the relationship between associated companies and their principal minority shareholders.

In the context of this chapter, therefore, it must be admitted that it is not always easy to persuade an associated company to conform to group financial policies or practices. The sensible approach is to ensure that such policies and practices are sound, so that the persuasion element in having the associated company follow them is minimized. Since, in any event, group finance policies and management accounting methods should be constructed in such a way that they are firstly of value to local management and after that useful for group purposes, there does not need to be too great a difficulty. In this case liaison can be improved by insistence that there is a principal minority shareholder representative on the associated company board. At least in this way there is a formal and legally supportable reason for ensuring that the representative and hence the parent company has access to planning papers, management accounting reports, budgets and other relevant information.

As far as publication of results is concerned, one has to do the best one can with the information available from the associated company's statutory accounts. Particular care must be taken if the associate is itself a public company and is connected to a group which is also a public company. The share of the associated companies' profits or losses shown in the group profit and loss account should only be based on results published by these companies. Alternatively it should be sufficiently obscured in an amalgamation with other companies that individual results cannot be identified in advance of local publication.

THE IMPORTANCE OF REGULAR VISITS AND THE DESIRABILITY OF GROUP INTERNAL AUDIT

Finally, in addition to communication through the lines of responsibility delineated in the group organization chart, there is an important case to be made for personal representation through visits. It is essential for parent company finance managers, with specific responsibility for overseas companies, to ensure that they visit these companies on a regular basis. Indeed this should be a two-way affair. It is essential that parent company executives know the people and the physical environment, within the business and outside it, of each overseas company. They must also know something of the way of life of the country in which it operates. Equally it is important for senior managers, like the finance director of the overseas company, to know something about the parent company, its head office people, its environment and its culture. You cannot begin to relate effectively to any company, from the subsidiary up to the parent or vice versa, until a visit has been made and some feel for the internal and external environment has been established.

Additionally there is much to be said, in any international organization, for regular management audits to be carried out to the parent company's specification.

Ethical standards vary, but international companies are required to conform to home country standards. This is a demanding challenge which undoubtedly requires considerable attention if things are to be kept under control. Beyond that, it is essential for good housekeeping that adequate internal control systems are established in overseas companies. Again these systems are best kept intact and up to scratch through periodic visits by competent internal auditors. Policy on this must be firmly established by the parent company.

Finally the parent company's finance managers with overseas responsibilities should visit their companies at least once a year, preferably when company plans and budgets are being discussed. In this way they can influence decisions immediately from their knowledge of group policies and attitudes. In addition they have an opportunity to see things for themselves and to discuss generalities which are both important to the financial health of the business and to their understanding of it. Apart from plans and policies they should ensure there is time during their visit to discuss the following, and indeed any other matters of relevance to their fields of responsibility:

(1) staff — managers and potential managers in the finance and accounting function. They should examine and be familiar with local succession plans and be sure to find time to meet all potential senior managers in their working environment;
(2) internal control, the internal audit programme, the international audit report (if any), the local external auditor's report and management letter;
(3) general matters relevant to the finance and accounting function such as insurance, remittance problems (if any), consolidation problems (management and statutory accounts), international accounting standards, computer developments.

At the same time it is desirable for the visiting finance managers from the parent organization to meet as many outside businessmen, local and expatriate, as possible. This will help to broaden their outlook and experience. In particular they should meet the partner in charge of the local audit, managers of local banks (international and otherwise) and the commercial secretary at the British Embassy or High Commission. The more parent company executives can get to know the local business environment, and to share in the hopes and fears of their locally-based colleagues, the more likely it is that they will gain their respect as people with something to offer and establish their position as people who are truly able to help.

I. N. SPURGEON

4.4
Remittance and dividend policies in international groups

INTRA-GROUP RELATIONSHIPS

As a preamble, before discussing remittance and dividend policies in international groups, it is helpful to say something about the relationship between the companies in such groups. In fact these policies largely reflect that relationship and the management style that accompanies it. Two somewhat contradictory factors usually influence that relationship:

(1) on the one hand, maximization of the advantages obtainable from the existence of a group;
(2) on the other hand, recognition that individual companies of a group may operate in different legal and fiscal jurisdictions and may require a degree of local autonomy.

A typical arrangement is for all affiliated operating companies spread around the world to be linked with each other through a current accounts system, with clearing through a central shareholder company or through a service company of the group operating on behalf of all companies. Instead, then, of all companies settling debts to each other on an individual basis, involving many payments, this arrangement permits one net periodic payment in one direction between each operating company and the central company in order to settle all debts. This is an advantage of membership of a group.

Similarly, as a means of optimizing the cash flow of a group, it is usually advantageous to hold the surplus cash of all the operating companies in one central point. This facilitates the steering of cash into the most profitable investments from the viewpoint of the group as a whole; it ensures profitable and consistent investment of the surplus cash, particularly if held in a major financial centre such as London or New York, the size of the funds giving the investor bargaining muscle; and it imposes a discipline on the local company which hopefully is transmitted through to the market place so that the flow of cash into the group from outside is enhanced.

On the other hand, recognising that different jurisdictions may be involved, the relationship between affiliates is frequently an arm's-length one so that the operation is acceptable and defensible in the different countries. For example, supplies may be invoiced from one company to another on commercial terms that would apply to a third party, albeit recognising that the credit risk between affiliates is negligible, and settlement would also be at the going commercial credit period for the type of business. Also this dispersed holding of the surplus cash can be contained by exchange control regulations in various countries and by withholding taxes on interest payments.

Obviously the relative weight given to such factors varies from one international group to another, but they have significance for remittance and dividend policies.

REMITTANCE POLICIES

TYPES OF REMITTANCES

The main types of remittances are:

(1) from operating companies to the centre:
   - (a) surplus cash;
   - (b) dividends;
   - (c) service fees and royalties;
   - (d) training courses and publications;
   - (e) payments on behalf of expatriate staff;
   - (f) interest on loans from the group or shareholder;
   - (g) amortization of loans from the group or shareholder;
   - (h) payments for supplies;

(2) from the centre to the operating companies:
   - (a) share capital increases;
   - (b) loans;
   - (c) payments for supplies.

CASH FLOW EFFECT

An international group which seeks to maximize its cash flow by turning over its cash rapidly will aim at a flow of regular remittances from operating companies.

Operating companies would be expected to observe all contractual payment terms in their debts to other companies of the group and to settle them by due date, preferably by payment through the current account system cleared centrally. Whether the cheaper, more convenient, method of one monthly payment is used, or more frequent individual payments, depends on the strength of local fiscal and legal considerations. A one monthly payment which involves an element of pre-payment which is not recognized in the price may be unacceptable locally.

Exceptionally, remittances may be held up if it is in the overall group interest to finance short-term cash requirements of an operating company through delayed remittances, say for supplies to the rest of the group, in other words by allowing the operating company to run up its current account debt to the group. Long term, this is not a course to be recommended and even in the short term it may cause an erosion of financial disciplines. If this is done it should be closely monitored, and preferably the financing element be clearly identified as separate from the normal in-term credit elements in the current account. Ideally a separate, interest-bearing current account should be employed for this purpose.

Proper accounting records and practices are essential to a smooth flow of remittances. These involve agreement of monthly or quarterly transactions and balances between operating companies or the centre, prompt investigation into disputed items, analysis of balances and monitoring of overdue items.

REMITTANCES AND CORPORATE STRUCTURE

Reference has already been made to the possibility of financing short-term capital requirements through a current account; this is a flexible financing method.

In the interests of maximizing cash flow, it is important that the corporate structure of a company facilitates remittances of surplus cash to the shareholder or central service company. This is not the case if the company is entirely financed by share capital since it is probably that as it matures a positive cash generation would develop, exceeding its dividend declaration possibilities, for example because the cash flow exceeds net income or arises before the dividend can legally be declared and paid. Remittability of the cash is thus frustrated by the corporate structure.

It should be the policy to foresee this and structure the company appropriately with, say, shareholder loans to permit remittance of surplus cash through interest payments and amortization. If share capital is unavoidable, the use of redeemable shares is another aid to remittability. Local borrowing from banks should also be used to obtain an appropriate capital structure and also to maximize exchange exposure.

POLICY IN COUNTRIES WITH EXCHANGE CONTROLS

In order to reduce the impact on the cash flow of a group of companies, particularly the loss of flexibility caused by exchange controls, the policy should be to maximize and accelerate remittances out of the country. Borrowing in local currency to finance the remittances should be exploited, giving the added advantage of a currency hedge.

Good documentation of all foreign debts and timely applications to the foreign exchange authorities for the foreign currency allocation are essential, as are monitoring and follow-up.

Different types of remittance tend to be subject to different degrees of control; for example those at the bottom of the above list of types would generally be more likely to be authorized than those at the top. The authorities would tend to give preference to foreign exchange for supplies, particularly essentials, rather than for dividends. Therefore, if a choice of the type of remittance is possible, the local company should give preference to the types of remittance at the top of the list and work down. Freedom to repatriate profits may have been an important part of the deal whereby the investment was undertaken particularly if external funds have been invested.

Remittances into the country with exchange controls should be avoided. Any legal flexibility in the exchange control regulations permitting the non-repatriation or delayed repatriation of foreign currency earnings into the country with exchange controls should be fully utilized. Permission should be sought from the authorities for the maintaining of a foreign currency bank account outside the local country, into which any foreign currency earnings can be paid and used for settlement of foreign debts, outside the control of the local exchange authorities. A saving of conversion and bank charges is also achieved thereby, but the ability to do this will depend on the host country's need for the investment.

REMITTANCES AND COUNTRY RISK

A country's past record in permitting free remittability of funds, and a view on probable future performance, is a factor in assessing country risk against which decisions on major investments in that country are judged. In order to ensure remittance rights in respect of major investments, it is nowadays quite common for concession agreements or joint venture agreements signed with governments or government entities to include specific provisions; ratification by the central bank or parliament is also desirable.

For example, for an export-oriented project, the specific provisions should recognise that substantial initial investments would have to be financed mainly from foreign sources and that in the operational phase the company's or joint venture's proceeds and payments would also predominantly be in foreign currencies. The provisions should permit the company to operate offshore bank accounts and to credit such accounts with the foreign exchange proceeds of the exports in order to meet the company's foreign currency obligations. The provisions should explicitly guarantee that foreign currency would be made available to meet obligations to contractors and suppliers of materials, equipment and services, to make interest payments and loan repayments in respect of third party and shareholders' loans, to make dividend payments to shareholders and to make payments connected with the repatriation of the capital invested. Further non-discrimination or most favoured nation clauses should also be included to protect remittance rights. For instance, to ensure that the company would be treated no worse than any other company seeking remittance rights in the event of a major national disaster impinging on the balance of payments and foreign currency reserves.

DIVIDEND POLICIES

The dividend policies in an international group determine the portion of foreign affiliated or subsidiary companies' profits that should be remitted to the shareholder (or to the centre) of the group. They are closely related to and, therefore, find their objectives from the following general financial policies and considerations.

(1) The international financial management and, more specifically, money management policies which set the pattern for the transfer of funds between the corporate affiliates — the foreign companies and between operating companies and the centre.
(2) The dividend policies and requirements of the parent companies or holding companies of a group.
(3) Taxation and other cost considerations.
(4) Host country environment and legislation .
(5) The corporate structure, size and maturity of operating companies.
(6) The dividend considerations and financial position and requirements of the operating company.
(7) For a British parent the dividends from abroad may be essential to fund the parents' dividends and advance corporation tax.

INTERNATIONAL FINANCIAL POLICIES

In large international groups the size and the complexity of financial operations make it essential that they are centralized with regard to financial policies and financial planning. They may still leave the implementation of the financing and remittance programmes and operations to a large extent decentralized; in other words centralized planning and policy-making with, however, decentralized implementation of transactions. In terms of remittance policies, a generally accepted basic policy in large international groups is that no surplus funds should be maintained by operating companies and any funds surplus to operational requirements should be remitted to the centre.

This principle of central pooling of cash resources is being applied by a large number of international groups because it makes it possible to optimize the use of resources; surplus funds of strong cash-generating operating companies can be made available for cash-requiring companies elsewhere. However there are some exceptions; exchange control and the attitudes of workers' representatives in some countries are among them. As long as surplus cash is properly deployed, it is often questionable if remittance to the centre is necessary. Would a parent want to use surplus Spanish pesetas to invest in Australia? The level of the surpluses is very relevant as is the parent's borrowing capacity.

Dividend payments by operating companies to holding or parent companies are one way of remitting funds, in this case profits, to the centre. As such, dividend payments form part of a general remittance policy. However, the objectives of a dividend go further, since in a group of companies a dividend flow to the holding or parent company (or companies) is essential since it is the only way to provide for dividend payments to the public shareholders in the parent company at the end of the chain. This makes, in the totality of the remittance policies, intra-group dividend policies and the resulting intra-group dividend flow a more independent component which is determined by a number of its own particular considerations. These considerations can to some extent be deduced from the ones that influence the dividend policy of the publicly owned parent company (or companies) of a group.

THE DIVIDEND POLICIES AND REQUIREMENTS OF THE PARENT COMPANIES OR HOLDING COMPANIES OF A GROUP

In general there are a number of factors that determine the dividend policy and decisions in a company of substance with a large public shareholding and which is quoted on one or more of the important stock exchanges in the world. We confine ourselves here to the factors that apply in general as in this chapter there is no need to go into a greater number of special factors in specific cases.

The first factor which should be mentioned is what might be called the dividend tradition. Most large companies or groups of companies, whether national or international, prefer to follow a stable dividend policy. They prefer to avoid ups and downs in dividend payments and like to see a stable trend in their dividend records. This leads to a level of dividend payment that seeks to provide shareholders with a dividend that grows in line with the company's increasing investment and earnings.

A second factor, or rather combination of closely related factors, determining the level of dividend payments of a public parent company has to do with the financial performance and position. It requires that the distribution of earnings to shareholders has to be compatible with the financial results, the overall financial strength and the cash resources, including future demands thereon. In addition, and in this context since it is closely related to these factors, the current and anticipated business climate has to be taken into account.

A third separate factor is the rate of inflation. Many dividend policies aim at protecting the dividend, and thereby the shareholders, from the eroding effect of inflation. This factor follows logically from the fact that the company itself will aim at obtaining a real return on its investments and, if successful in this, will have no problem over the longer term to pay shareholders and increased dividend in real terms.

A fourth factor is the considerations regarding the financial public relations which are the expectations of shareholders and the financial community at large. It cannot be ignored either that the dividend payment conveys a message as to the degree of confidence about the company's prospects and its dividend-paying abilities. The dividend has, therefore, an important value as a signal which can make the financial public relations considerations important.

A company may also wish to distribute a proportion of its earnings which is in line with other companies in the same industry. Some companies may want 100% distribution from subsidiaries as a matter of principle.

The above summary of general factors influencing the dividend decision, together with sometimes special considerations, will determine the dividend requirements of the parent company in a group and thereby be a major factor to determine the required flow that has to come from the operating companies in a group.

TAXATION AND OTHER COST CONSIDERATIONS

Cost considerations are often relevant in deciding whether or not a subsidiary company in a group should pay a dividend to its parent.

The taxation cost of paying a dividend is normally the most important and most common cost item. The taxation cost can be incurred at the paying end by the subsidiary company in the form of withholding taxes, and in some countries various forms of additional levies if the dividend payment reaches certain levels. Supplementary taxation can also be incurred by the receiving, holding or parent company in the home country of a group, depending on the taxation laws in that country and the tax position of the receiving, holding or parent company.

Apart from the taxation cost, in an international group there can be cost items like remittance and transfer costs, but these items are normally of minor importance. In some countries there is a dual exchange rate system, imposing an unfavourable exchange rate on financial remittances like dividends.

Cost considerations can be decisive if the dividend-paying subsidiary company in a group is known to have a cash deficit which has to be funded again by its parent company. In those circumstances it is sometimes not considered advisable to propose a dividend payment if significant taxation or other costs are being incurred by so doing, but if this situation persists for a period of years, it must call into question whether the company should continue to operate in that overseas country.

HOST COUNTRY ENVIRONMENT AND LEGISLATION

There are a number of risks and exposures to which foreign subsidiaries are submitted which are related to the political and economic environment of the host countries in which they are operating.

The main risks are of a political, economic or financial nature, and the most common are uncertainties regarding political stability, risks of ownership, state of the economy, balance of payments, financial reserves, exchange controls and other restrictions on the use of funds and uncertainties regarding taxation. The exposures to these risks of subsidiary companies in this context are normally made subject to a careful assessment and regular review, and the degree of exposure existing at times is a factor that will have to be taken into account when determining the dividend policy and making the dividend decision for a subsidiary company.

It is important to realise that it is not only in exceptional or extreme cases that this is being done. In countries with the highest degree of political, financial and social maturity there might be the need to consider and access these risk areas. Many countries, including the major industrialized nations such as Japan, the United Kingdom, the United States, France and West Germany have, in the past, employed a variety of foreign exchange and capital controls which were designed to restrict the inflow or outflow of capital and financial remittances for the balance of payments or inflation control purposes, but the main difficulty in these countries now is taxation.

It appears, therefore, that the process of environmental risk assessment is a normal one and, apart from being done for other purposes, it has to be part of any decision on dividend policies and payments of a subsidiary company in an international group. Clearly, if there were, for example, risks of funds being closed in or regarding the ownership of a subsidiary company, or the threat of adverse changes in tax legislation, these would have an influence — probably an overriding one — on the dividend decision.

THE CORPORATE STRUCTURE, SIZE AND MATURITY OF SUBSIDIARY COMPANIES

There are between the subsidiaries in international groups large differences in size, financial strength and maturity. Furthermore, there are differences in corporate structures, and sometimes in a group there are companies in which there are substantial outside shareholdings. The outside shareholders can be the public in general or a government, or the subsidiary company can be a type of joint venture entity. It sometimes happens that government and business interests are shareholders in an operating subsidiary which is associated or affiliated to an international group.

For the purpose of this chapter it is sufficient to make the reader aware of the differences in size, financial strength and maturity. A foreign subsidiary or affiliated company with a substantial outside shareholding, a strong financial position and an established, far-reaching degree of maturity and autonomy will largely follow its own financial and dividend policies. In any type of joint venture, the dividend policy has to be agreed between the shareholders, and this takes away some of their freedom in the dividend decision. In international joint ventures, the shareholding companies can be of different nationalities, subject to different tax regimes, and a specific agreement on the dividend policy can in those circumstances be of prime importance.

THE DIVIDEND CONSIDERATIONS AND FINANCIAL POSITION AND REQUIREMENTS OF THE SUBSIDIARY COMPANY

Much of what has been said under the previous heading has to do with the dividend policy of the foreign subsidiary itself. The size, maturity and degree of financial strength determine the subsidiary's dividend policies and so does its corporate structure. What should be added under this heading are some more purely financial considerations which depend on the subsidiary's own financial requirements and its financial strength.

A subsidiary company which goes through a phase of rapid expansion of its investments and activities will have substantial financial requirements. It depends on its size and financial position as to whether it will be able to raise and maintain an outside borrowing level to finance any financial deficits resulting from its investment programme and activities. The ability to do so will determine the capacity it has to maintain a programme of dividend payments if this would be considered desirable by its parent or holding company. There are variations in this type of consideration, as even a foreign subsidiary company of less substance and maturity will still be able to borrow with support from its parent company and thereby be able to pay a dividend although it might have cash deficits for one or more years.

CONCLUSION

In any dividend policy in large international groups, a main objective is to maintain the maximum possible flexibility for general financial management purposes. Other objectives, as we have seen, are:

(1) to avoid unnecessary or substantial payments of taxes or the incurrence of other substantial costs;
(2) to avoid political and financial risks in host countries;
(3) to maintain financial strength and a strong local borrowing base in the larger companies in an international group to enable them to borrow on their own account when, for various reasons, this seems preferable to providing finance from the centre (or from the parent company).

The dividend decision might often call for a balancing of conflicting aims such as cost versus considerations of risk and financial discipline. In practice there is a continuous process of consultation between the parent and subsidiary companies in a group via the existing financial management and reporting procedures.

It is generally thought that, in addition to a specific profitability target, subsidiary companies are required to make a reasonable distribution of such profit by way of dividend, both as a sound business objective and as a measure of financial discipline. However, once the profitability requirement is established, the question of dividend falls into place as partly a financing matter, both for the group and the company, and partly a reinforcement, but a secondary one, of the primary financial discipline, the need to make profits. This is not to deny that subsidiary or affiliated companies in a group with large outside shareholdings and with an established, far-reaching degree of autonomy have to follow their own financial and dividend policies.

This chapter was originally drafted by J.H. Macdonald; it has been revised and updated by Brian Walsh, GKN plc.

4.5
Deciding on insurance programmes: the role of captive insurance companies

In order to ensure the protection of a group's assets and earnings, both human and material, a careful evaluation of risks will need to be made, followed by decisions as to the most cost-effective methods of financing those risks.

An insurance programme is just one of several methods of financing risk. The choice ranges from full commercial insurance, which is the most common medium, to total self-retention, which may be applied to small exposures or to non-insurable risks. In between these two extremes, partial insurance retention covers the range from a modest deductible under a conventional policy to the creation of a wholly-owned subsidiary insurance company (captive).

For small to medium-sized companies operating in only one territory, a conventional insurance programme is normally the most appropriate. However for larger international groups a number of different considerations apply, including:

(1) the desire to have uniform worldwide coverage;
(2) the differing standards of insurance practice in overseas territories;
(3) the scope of cover available in or for some parts of the world (this has become particularly pertinent in connection with products liability insurance where a shortage of market capacity could become a semi-permanent feature);
(4) the varying legislative requirements that affect insurance arrangements;
(5) the overall amount of premium expenditure and the benefits that may accrue from significant self-retention.

The aim of this chapter is to examine the potential benefits, limitations and main requirements of an international insurance programme and the methods by which suitable arrangements can be achieved. The role of risk management will be outlined and the captive insurance company as a risk financing option will be considered.

THE CONCEPT OF INTERNATIONAL INSURANCE PROGRAMMES

The purchase of insurance on the best possible terms is achieved by utilizing the bulk buying power of a group which is international in it operations. However, unlike other commodities, it is not always possible to purchase insurance for major risks internationally from one source at one place. A large number of countries insist that risks within their borders are insured with locally licensed or admitted insurers and certain risks are frequently directed to state organizations.

One method of complying with local legislation, yet still using corporate buying power to obtain the best possible terms, is known as the global plan. The objective of such a plan is that the international group can buy uniform cover, irrespective of territory, for a wide variety of risks. This may be achieved by a combination of underlying covers arranged with locally admitted insurers in the various territories, interlocking with centrally arranged master or differences in conditions policies. These latter policies are designed to achieve a consistent standard of cover internationally and thus to eliminate any gaps which may arise by virtue of deficiencies in local policy wordings as compared with the desired minimum standard of cover. Similar policies can also operate to provide cover in excess of that available locally to provide limits of cover (sometimes known as differences in limits policies) which will protect international groups on an adequate and consistent basis.

Thus these plans are designed to provide a wider range of cover than may be available in any one location and a uniform level of protection, whilst still complying with both the spirit and the letter of local legislation and proving good corporate citizenship in the host country.

BASIC PRINCIPLES

There are certain fundamental requirements which need to be considered carefully in formulating an international insurance programme and these are now examined.

Well defined international corporate insurance policy. Before an insurance programme can be carried into effect internationally, a well defined group policy on risk management and insurance must be agreed in a form which recognizes the need to harmonize corporate objectives with differing legislation and insurance markets in all the countries concerned. Sufficient flexibility must exist to cater for unique local situations without distorting the plan as a whole. Reasonable discretion should be given to local management to reflect their special needs within the overall framework. A group policy should be on risk management principles in order to deal with risks in a way which is to the best economic advantage of the corporation as a whole, utilizing conventional insurance, where it is most cost-effective, as one of the various risk-financing techniques available (see risk management below).

Effective central control. An international insurance programme cannot function without overall control on a group basis. In the absence of control, programmes will become disordered. Local interests, who may not comprehend the entire group picture, can make parochial decisions which are in conflict with corporate needs and objectives. If this is permitted, a corporation could find itself in a position of dangerous exposure arising from unco-ordinated arrangements. This control should also include a cohesive approach to the appointment of intermediaries, because their function may be varied by local regulation.

Selection of suitable insurers. The key to the utilization of corporate purchasing power for an international insurance programme is to select insurers who have the necessary representation in all countries concerned to underwrite the required insurance for local operations, and who offer a facility to negotiate centrally for the establishment of local policies whose terms reflect the size and spread of the total account.

For those corporate risks such as fire, business interruption and liability, which have a catastrophe potential and require large underwriting capacity, it is usually necessary to involve a number of insurers for each class of insurance in the various locations. Where one or more insurers are not represented in certain countries, although otherwise suitable, this difficulty can normally be overcome by arranging for another of those selected to front for the share required. This involves combining its own proportion of the local insurance with the share intended for the unrepresented insurer, to whom the premium and corresponding part of risk can then be reinsured.

An alternative arrangement, sometimes employed, is for one company to issue 100% of the local policies in every case, sharing the premium and risk to the others involved entirely by means of reinsurance.

In the co-insurance method of placing insurance internationally, one insurer is selected as the leader and negotiations take place primarily with this company, which traditionally carries out surveys and agrees wording and rates on behalf of the others. Normally the leading insurer selected offers the greatest underwriting capacity or local representation, or a balance of both features.

It is, however, very important to select a company which has sufficient *direct* representation in the countries concerned and does not rely heavily on reinsurance from other diverse local companies with whom it may have co-operative agreements but over which it cannot exercise direct underwriting authority. Similar care is needed if the co-insurance route is used, to ensure that the lead office has the necessary reputation to facilitate others accepting their proposals.

In the case of smaller corporate risks to be insured internationally, one insurer can frequently issue all the local policies 100%, thus simplifying the process involved.

A second major benefit arises from the technique of involving the same panel of reinsurers or co-insurers in all local insurances where important corporate risks are concerned. In the event of very bad losses in one territory, if insurance were to remain placed on a purely national fragmented basis, premiums would almost inevitably rise steeply and in extreme cases cover could be withdrawn at the first opportunity. However where all the major insurers concerned are participating in the insurances of all local operations to a similar extent, their own overall experience is ameliorated and the insured corporation retains much better bargaining power, supported by the weight of its total account.

Selection of suitable intermediaries or advisers. There are many aspects to be considered in the establishment of an international programme which requires professional assistance. Many of the major international insurers have departments specializing in the handling of business for multinationals and whose advice can be sought. Alternatively there are firms of international insurance brokers with wide expertise in the co-ordination and placement of insurance for international groups.

The most important consideration is that the professional adviser should be capable of acting as a single reference point in all negotiations, with the ability to implement instructions in all countries concerned.

In the event that, for historic or commercial reasons, local brokers are used, then an alternative mechanism must be employed to ensure common foundations and negotiations. These could be reflected in the appointment of an internal risk manager, or a lead broker.

FLEXIBILITY OF INTERNATIONAL INSURANCE PROGRAMMES

An international insurance programme which is properly controlled and co-ordinated in the manner described lends itself to considerable flexibility, particularly in conjunction with a corporate policy on self-insurance, with or without the use of a captive insurance company.

Self-insurance. Where a corporate decision is taken to self-insure either certain classes of risk in their entirety or, alternatively, losses to a predetermined level by means of deductibles, with the balance of risk insured on an excess of loss basis, a well-designed international programme facilitates implementation.

The ultimate decision as to the balance between the amount of risk to be insured and the amount to be retained will depend on a variety of factors, not the least of which will be the character and corporate philosophy of the organization concerned and its general attitude towards risk management. Other influencing factors will be:

(1) overall size of the exposures involved;
(2) size of individual exposures;
(3) nature of the risks;
(4) risk-bearing capability of the organization concerned;
(5) availability and cost of insurance cover.

In general the purchase of insurance protection is most appropriate where:

(1) there is a catastrophe hazard — where the risk exposure embraces loss potential which could result in financial embarrassment;

(2) it is obtainable at a cost which is relatively lower than any other available risk financing alternative;
(3) the insurer provides an essential cost-effective specialized service in addition to insurance cover — statutory inspection services for pressure plant, lifting tackle, or other dangerous activities;
(4) the insurer may provide a desirable independent interface in relation to the handling of claims;
(5) there is a statutory obligation to insure.

Even when insurance cover is arranged it may be cost-effective for the policy to be subject to a deductible so long as the premium discount allowed is sufficient to compensate for the risk accepted, taking into account the amount retained for any one loss and the possible accumulation in the event of an unusual and unexpected series of losses. Decisions in any particular case will represent a careful balancing of all the factors involved. Risks which have a profile of high loss incidence but low severity per loss are the most likely to be amenable to self-retention because the aggregate loss level within a given period can be more readily assessed with a reasonable degree of accuracy, given statistically valid historic loss data. The further the profile moves towards low incidence but high potential severity the less the inducement to self-retain. It is the true profile of the risk which must be utilized. This may not be reflected in its historic record.

Master policies. Master policies are an essential part of the programme for an international group if the objective of uniform cover worldwide is to be achieved. They provide the required degree of cover where policy wordings in certain territories are inadequate or where the cover is either unobtainable or unduly expensive. Each master policy is tailor-made to suit the particular requirements of the corporate buyer.

These requirements will principally be difference-in-conditions and differences-in-limits cover but they can, and frequently do, incorporate some primary cover where territorial regulations allow and there is a perceived benefit in arranging the cover centrally. They may also include repayment or indemnity agreements between the insurer and the insured for those circumstances where the local policy provides more cover than the corporate programme requires: where the regulations in a particular territory do not allow a premium credit for a deductible.

SUMMARY

A well-designed international insurance programme, backed by the necessary corporate authority, makes best use of insurance purchasing power and goes a long way towards ensuring that poor claims experience in any one territory does not result in the imposition of unacceptable terms or withdrawal of cover.

Whichever insurance strategy is adopted, some form of co-ordinated control will ensure that the best results are achieved.

RISK MANAGEMENT

Risk management is concerned with the maintenance of financial stability through cost-effective methods of protecting assets and earnings. Loss or damage to assets inflicts an often avoidable hardship upon individuals, the employer organization and the national economic and social interest.

Any organization is aware of normal trading risks but many are less certain of their capacity to withstand fortuitous loss. While insurance provides some protection, certain exposures are uninsurable and, even if full cover is thought to be purchased, the hidden costs of loss are substantial.

Risk management quantifies uncertainties. By recognizing risks and avoiding or controlling their consequences, a financial strategy is formulated which relates directly to the scale and scope of activities.

To be used effectively, risk management calls for a high degree of skill in a wide variety of specialities. In addition to the conventional fire, mechanical, security and safety engineers, specialists are needed in such technical subjects as chemical engineering, civil engineering, industrial hygiene, environmental science, crime prevention in the wider context of industrial espionage and computer security, accounting, asset appraisal, insurance and reinsurance. All these skills must be co-ordinated and applied properly if successful risk management is to be maintained and converted to the ultimate financial gain of the organization concerned.

Neither can they be applied solely to what we may term the external risks traditionally faced by a corporation. The growth of consumerism and the continuing advancement of standards for public safety require all of these skills and more to be addressed continuously to the improvement of all manufactured products or services.

The practice of risk management involves the identification and evaluation of all risks to which the organization is exposed. A number of alternative strategies are considered, independently or together.

RISK AVOIDANCE

Certain risks are so inherently hazardous that they should be completely avoided.

RISK REDUCTION AND CONTROL

Risk control is critical. A comprehensive accident prevention and loss control programme should be laid down. Although insurers provide expert risk control advice in some territories, the purchase of external technical services is often necessary.

RISK RETENTION

The spread of risk, incidence of loss and loss potential may be such that a strategy of partial or total self-insurance is suitable. Probably self-insurance will take the form of a deductible or first loss cover, but it may be that the formation of a captive insurance company would be a viable proposition.

RISK TRANSFER

The final strategy considers the transfer of residual financial risks to a third party, generally an insurance company. Sometimes it is possible to transfer risk by contract conditions, although this needs considerable legal knowledge and forethought.

THE ROLE OF CAPTIVE INSURANCE COMPANIES

INTRODUCTION

The practice of risk management, as has been explained, sets out to achieve improved financial control of risk, and one of the most important aspects is the efficient provision of risk finance.

The risk manager of any large corporation has at his disposal a number of risk financing methods, including the possibility of using a captive insurance company. The specific methods appropriate to a particular case will depend on the size, character, objectives and, frequently, the temperament of the organization concerned. Whether or not there is a role for a captive to play will be decided in the context of the overall risk management philosophy and risk financing objectives.

There may, additionally, be new needs within the organization which cannot be satisfied by the existing insurance market. These may include such things as directors' and officers' liability and kidnap. Insurance markets are not stable either in capacity terms, or in premium levels. Captive participation in a variety of ways can help to ease such difficulties as may be generated.

In general, consideration of captive possibilities is relevant only for an organization which can satisfy captive requirements as regards premium volume and spread of risk. Although a captive insurance company can take many forms, and there are numerous permutations in use, for the purpose of this chapter a captive is a wholly-owned subsidiary established by a non-insurance parent to participate in the risks of the parent and its other subsidiary and associated companies. Thus association or group captives and so-called rental captives are not brought into consideration as they have less application to large corporations. The principles involved, however, are similar in all cases.

The insurance capacity problems which have developed in the liability field have resulted in the formation of a number of association-type captives specifically aimed at providing high indemnity limits.

Risk management embraces a logical progression through the steps of risk identification, evaluation, avoidance or reduction as an essential preliminary to the choice of risk financing techniques to be employed. Ultimate choices will depend on the outcome of those steps and will reflect decisions made relating to risk retention. The problem which a risk manager often faces is not whether a risk should be wholly retained or fully insured but what amount should be retained and what is an appropriate level of insurance in the particular circumstances of his organization. Utilizing a captive can be a way of achieving the best of both worlds.

THE EMERGENCE AND DEVELOPMENT OF CAPTIVES

In considering the links between large corporations and captives, it is necessary first to identify what the large corporation seeks as regards the treatment of its risks and the related attitude of commercial insurers. Apart from the fundamental issues of security and service, which are requirements common to all buyers, the large corporation generally seeks high limits of indemnity and a broad cover, both in terms of perils and the geographical scope of their application. It also seeks keen pricing which reflects both the historic record of its business and the inherent economies of scale. Perhaps most importantly, it seeks individual treatment as regards desired cover, costs and services. Implied in these requirements are certain considerations which commercial insurers may wish to resist. Typical requirements could include the following.

(1) Broad cover for material damage, consequential losses and legal liabilities which may tax the underwriters' ability to assess the degree of hazard posed by certain perils, processes or territories.
(2) High deductibles or self-retentions which limit the insurers' prospective involvement to catastrophe losses only. This approach is essentially one of obtaining protection without traditional insurance company services and their associated costs. The random incidence of catastrophic events can often lead to sharply differing views regarding the cost of cover.
(3) A specific recognition of the financial implications of an insurance transaction in respect of cash flow, premium payment terms and interest income. Both the buyer and seller of insurance will recognize the importance of this issue, but the seller may see the investment return in some instances as his sole recompense.

The fundamental conflicts which can arise may seem irreconcilable but, as in most cases where there is a matching of need and service, there will be found methods which satisfy most of the requirements of the interested parties. Any gulf between the attitudes of large corporations and commercial insurers is usually a matter of price rather than principle.

Post-war business developments brought a new style of executive leadership to commerce and industry, with a questioning of, and resistance to, established practice. Large companies began to question the logic of buying ground-upwards insurance from organizations which were often of lesser financial substance than themselves. They sought broad cover, which often telescoped hitherto segregated lines of business, and convenient payment terms. Insurer resistance was gradually eroded and an increasing number of large corporations entered the insurance business, albeit on a modest scale, through participation in their own risks.

Captives are not, in fact, a totally modern phenomenon. They began to emerge in the early part of this century in the United Kingdom and the United States. The early captives were few in number and most often were subsidiaries of very large multinationals or of companies engaged in trades where their customers or other business connections constituted a ready case of insurance availability.

Contemporary captive developments which began in the United States during the 1950s and 1960s resulted from buyer dissatisfaction with the direct insurance market's attitude towards high level deductibles on property insurance and the premium reduction given when such deductibles were conceded. During the 1970s the direct insurers in the United States resolved their differences with large buyers on deductibles and, in fact, now co-operate actively with captives on a broad basis. This co-operation did not slow down captive developments or cause any return to the traditional market. There was a second surge in captive establishment by United States companies during the mid-1970s, induced by the United States liability explosion. Many of these latter captives were concerned primarily with professional and product liabilities.

In the United Kingdom, contemporary captive development gained momentum in the mid-1970s. After a slowing in the early 1980s, there has been further growth since 1985. United Kingdom thinking in most cases demonstrates a corporate desire to participate significantly in its risk and a dissatisfaction with the response of direct insurers to this aspiration. There is evidence that the gulf in attitudes between large buyers and direct insurers in the United Kingdom has been narrowed.

It seems unlikely that the United Kingdom will experience liability developments similar to those in the United States but there have been a number of cases recently where the primary or sole motive for a United Kingdom company establishing a captive has been the insurance of legal liabilities.

The mid-1980s have experienced a hardening of reinsurance markets and rising fronting fees from primary insurers. Such trends tend to reduce net premiums available to captives and thus threaten their viability. In general, however, the arguments leading to the establishment of captives remain valid. They continue to represent an alternative source of risk financing and provide valuable cover and capacity where it is not otherwise available. One of the consequential results has been a growth in the number of territories making themselves attractive as captive domiciles.

MOTIVATION FOR FORMING A CAPTIVE

There are numerous reasons given by companies as to why they form a captive. They may include:

(1) reduction in the net cost of insurance;
(2) greater flexibility of insurance protection;
(3) non-availability of market, or cost which is deemed prohibitively expensive for certain classes of risk, such as product liability, product recall, professional indemnity, political risk, strikes;
(4) higher credits for deductibles or self-insured retentions;
(5) a desire for individual rating which rewards good experience and risk management;
(6) improved cash-flow;
(7) centralization of risk;
(8) more positive attitudes to risk control.

Motivation varies widely. Some captives are established solely for the purpose of funding an elected or imposed deductible. Others only undertake risks to which the commercial insurance market is deemed unreceptive, either towards the cover sought or the premium rate. In some instances the buyer seeks to establish orderly access to the catastrophe coverage or reinsurance markets and in other cases to create a risk-bearing profit centre designed ultimately to engage in broad insuring activity. The underlying motivation is always a net cost saving. It is probable that the greatest single benefit for most captives, particularly in the United Kingdom, is that of access to the reinsurance or wholesale market. Reinsurers are the main providers of catastrophe protection. With regard to captives their unique blending of portfolio and risk underwriting skills and their lesser expense structure usually enables them to allow greater deductible or retention credits than direct insurers. Tax benefits which might accrue to a captive have not so far been mentioned. Sponsors of captives may profess that their motivation ignores taxation considerations alone but if this test is met it is prudent to recognize tax benefits and to avoid insurance underwriting or investment regulations which would complicate and increase the captive's cost. These are the main reasons why the great majority of captives are registered offshore. Tax deferment can enhance the captive's risk-bearing capability in its sensitive developing years, but in the longer term any funds which are surplus to insurance requirements are likely to be subject to parental demand for other areas of investment.

From this brief summary it becomes apparent that there are a variety of reasons for forming a captive and its ultimate role in the insurance programme of a particular company is likely, therefore, to depend as much on the overall philosophy of the company concerned, particularly as regards retention of risk, as on the nature of the risks involved.

Tax status. In recent years a number of developments affecting the tax status of captive insurance companies have taken place in both the United States and the United Kingdom.

Although the tax benefits of locating offshore have always been of secondary importance to the majority of captive owners, any moves which positively discriminate against captives, whether offshore or onshore, must be viewed with concern.

Legal developments in the United States have called in question the tax-effectiveness of captive subsidiaries of companies domiciled there. This may be reflected in non tax-deductibility of premiums and less favourable treatment of reserve building offshore. Premium payments made by United States' companies to captives owned by their non-United States parents may also fail to achieve tax-deductibility. The protection afforded by many captives, however, in terms of capacity and covers not otherwise available, is such that their continuation in the United States' market is not currently in doubt.

There is no evidence that tax authorities in other countries intend to adopt a similar stance over the fundamental issue of tax deductibility. However, other developments affecting captives have occurred. In the United Kingdom it might be argued that the Finance Act 1984 reduced the tax advantages for subsidiaries of United Kingdom parent companies registered in low tax areas, but otherwise has done nothing to deter the captive movement. Indeed, by regularizing the tax position, the 1984 Act may even have strengthened the status of captives in the insurance market by weeding out those few captives for whom the tax benefits rather than risk financing motives were the prime consideration.

The supervision of insurers by the state to provide consumer protection has little relevance to the captive insurer transacting only related business. Recognition of this is given in most offshore locations more readily than in the major territories. As regulations can be a significant administrative burden, selection of the right location continues to require careful consideration.

CAPTIVE CRITERIA

There are recognized criteria for the operation of a successful captive which require acceptance by the parent organization and should be used to judge risks proposed for captive participation and their subsequent treatment. In any assessment of projected captive operating results it is essential to recognize that insurance has to be viewed on a long-term basis and that potential results for any one particular year should not receive undue emphasis.

Commitment. The establishment of a viable captive calls for a positive commitment by the parent company for the captive to be operated in an efficient, professional manner similar to a conventional insurance company.

Risk control. For a captive operation to be successful, a high standard of risk control is vital. Success is often dependent on support from reinsurers, and a continuing good loss experience, backed by effective loss prevention measures, is likely to command reinsurance support on the most favourable terms.

Spread of risk. Good insurance practice demands that the portfolio of business written by a captive should be spread over a wide range of risk exposures without undue accumulation at, or dependence on any one location.

Premium volume. The amount of premium flowing into a captive, together with any investment income generated, needs to be enough to cater for:

(1) expected claims payments;
(2) management, legal and accounting expenses;
(3) cost of reinsurance protection;
(4) provision of technical reserves.

In addition there should be a reasonable expectation of sufficient surplus to enable general reserves to be accumulated in order to provide the financial strength necessary to meet occasional exceptional losses.

The assessment of premium levels assumes particular importance and calls for expert guidance when a captive undertakes direct insurance without the benefit of premium rating established by a commercial insurer.

Loss experience. Anticipated future losses arising out of risk exposures insured by a captive should be at a level which is well within its financial capacity if full advantage of a captive operation is to be obtained. Historical loss data alone does not necessarily present an accurate picture for the purpose of projection and the assessment of future loss levels must, in addition, pay due regard to likely internal and external developments, including the influence of a continuous risk improvement programme and the potential for significant loss.

Risk participation. A captive should participate to a meaningful extent in the risks which it accepts, choosing a risk retention limit commensurate with its financial capacity. This is one way of demonstrating to reinsurers, where such support is required, confidence in the quality of risks insured.
Risk will be assumed in either or both of the following ways:

(1) on a direct basis, the captive issuing policies for 100% of the cover required or participating with insurers operating in the commercial insurance market through a percentage share by way of co-insurance or through specific layers of cover;
(2) by way of reinsurance from an unrelated direct insurer who, in consideration of a fee, would act as a front for the captive and would issue policies, optionally provide risk engineering and claims handling services and agree to reinsure to the captive the whole, or a substantial part, of the risk.

Reinsurance. A captive reinsures that part of a risk assumed which is beyond its chosen retained limit.

Reinsurance of the excess amount above the captive's retention may be arranged either on a quota share basis or on an excess of loss basis or a mixture of both.

Quota share means that the captive retains an agreed percentage of the total risk and passes the balance to one or more reinsurers who each accept an agreed proportion. Claims are shared in the same proportions. Excess of loss reinsurance means that the captive retains the first part of each risk up to its chosen limit and the balance is ceded to reinsurers, either as a whole or in layers. In the event of a claim the captive bears the whole amount up to the limit of its retention, the balance being borne by the reinsurers.

In addition, to safeguard overall financial stability, the aggregate retained loss limit can be controlled, subject to availability of cover at reasonable cost, by arranging stop loss protection which reinsures the excess above an agreed annual accumulation of retained losses. This can be particularly important in the early years whilst reserve funds are being accumulated. The stop loss cover can be reviewed periodically and revised or discarded as financial capacity to bear loss develops.

Through a combination of these various methods a reinsurance programme can be structured which will protect a captive against excessive loss from any one occurrence and against an exceptional series of losses in any one year.

A captive has direct access to the established professional reinsurance market. It is therefore able to buy protection against losses in excess of its net retention at a cost generally more favourable than that which would be available from the direct insurance market.

FEASIBILITY STUDY

GENERAL

Before becoming committed to a captive operation it is highly desirable that a full objective feasibility study be undertaken in order to establish that the particular circumstances satisfy the fundamental captive criteria outlined above and that the contemplated captive will produce the desired result. Although such a study could be undertaken internally by using existing in-house capability, the greatest benefit is most likely to be derived from utilizing the services of an independent external organization with wide experience in this work.

The purpose of a feasibility study is to ensure that long-term far-reaching decisions are taken only on the basis of proper research and adequate information and to provide an informed view on the following major considerations.

(1) Whether a viable captive can be formed and operated.
(2) Where it should be established.
(3) How it should be operated.
(4) What return on investment can be expected.

Before embarking on the full study it is normal and desirable practice to carry out a preliminary examination of relevant facts to establish an initial view as to whether a captive is a realistic possibility. If the conclusion is reached at this stage that a captive is unlikely to be a viable proposition then other risk financing alternatives should be explored.

PRELIMINARY STUDY

The pre-feasibility examination focuses on the organizational structure, the nature of the risks and insurance, the premium and loss history over the preceding five to ten years segregated by class of risk and year, including specific details of any large losses incurred. Information regarding any circumstances which might inhibit a captive, such as debenture or lease requirements, needs to be considered, as well as more general background information such as the latest report and accounts and the nature of operational activities.

DETAILED STUDY

The full feasibility study is intended to produce an enduring and rewarding strategy.

It involves input from various disciplines which fall into the three major categories of scientific or technical, finance and insurance or reinsurance. The proper blending of these functional inputs is the key to an effective study, which should embrace:

(1) a careful examination of the risks which are considered to be appropriate for insurance by the captive;
(2) a review of the parent company's financial position, in order to determine its risk bearing capability;
(3) a determination of the quality of risk control exercised by the parent and its commitment to a risk improvement policy;
(4) an opinion regarding the viability of a captive;
(5) if formation of a captive is recommended, the details of location, capitalization, taxation and legal aspects, classes of risk for inclusion, net risk retention and reinsurance, risk control, fronting, if applicable, and management;
(6) financial projections based on the above considerations, including the relative net costs of alternative captive possibilities.

Risk analysis. Careful examination of all risk exposures is necessary in order to determine those which are considered to be appropriate for insurance by a captive. Generally the most favoured risks for inclusion are those which are measurable and thus predictable, those where there may be an insurance availability or affordability problem, or those where the risk is self-retained in whole or in part.

Material damage, consequential loss, marine cargo and personal accident insurance are normally suitable subjects for a captive. The most effective strategy for participating in these classes will vary greatly, from limited to total involvement on either a direct or reinsurance basis, with possible different levels of retention for each class and variable levels and methods of reinsurance protection for the captive. Liability insurances can also be undertaken by a captive, but participation will usually be via reinsurance since the services of an authorized insurer may be necessary to satisfy risk requirements or legislation. Since liability risks and insurances are subject to the vagaries of changing legislation or interpretation and are essentially long-term in character, great care must be taken in their evaluation and treatment. Certain special risks, for which insurers often require significant self-retention or co-insurance participation, may be appropriate for captive treatment. Examples of these could include political risks, strikes, riot, libel and slander, pollution, professional liabilities, flood, kidnap and ransom and product guarantee or recall.

The basic objective of risk evaluation in this context is to identify the various risks of a catastrophic or less predictable nature and those of a non-catastrophic or more predictable nature. When it is cost-effective and possible, the captive will retain and finance all or most of the non-catastrophic risks and the catastrophic risks will be transferred wholly or partly to insurers and reinsurers. Risk-identification is the cornerstone of a feasibility study and skilled engineering evaluation is vital to this aspect of the study. Surveys are usually made of a cross-section of the risk exposure and a determination of the estimated maximum loss (EML) is carried out as regards the major property risks in order to satisfy reinsurance requirements.

An integral part of risk evaluation is detailed analysis of as much information as can be obtained relating to losses incurred during preceding years, including historic loss and premium data in respect of insured risks. The objective is to:

(1) establish the cost effectiveness of any existing insurance arrangements;
(2) detect possible loss patterns over a statistically valid period;
(3) identify any developing trends which could have implications for the future.

The results of such analysis provide the basis for:

(1) assessing risk retention levels;
(2) establishing insurance needs;
(3) projections of captive trading results.

Risk bearing capability. The parent company's financial position is reviewed to determine its risk bearing capability. This evaluation will govern the ultimate capacity of the captive, even though its prime security is represented by capital employed plus the level of reinsurance protection arranged. Recommendations regarding the amount of risk to be retained and the extent of reinsurance required are designed to produce a meaningful captive participation in relation to its own resources and to avoid any harmful impact on the overall financial results of the parent organization. Nevertheless, in the last resort, if the captive is exposed to liabilities greater than its own financial resources and if, in consequence, losses are suffered which cannot be met, or which cause a shortfall in required solvency margins, then it is the parent organization which must ultimately bear the cost.

There are several different formulae which can be used to calculate risk bearing capability of a corporate group, but in the final analysis a judgment is often made which is based on a combination of financial assessment and the corporate temperament. A formula often found to be an acceptable guide is to regard the equivalent of between 1% and 5% of pre-tax profits as being a reasonable amount of risk for an organization to retain in any one year. On this basis, for example, the retention capacity of a company that produces a profit of £20m could be from £200,000 to £1m. The corporate tolerance for fluctuations in results will govern the level of retention chosen. This part of the study is but one of several important areas which require the application of experienced financial skills.

Risk control. It is important to determine the quality of risk control which is exercised by the parent and the operating subsidiaries in order to be aware of the attitude toward risk improvement policy. A company which has a strong commitment to risk control will optimize captive benefits.

Recognizing this, the feasibility study must lay considerable stress on the need to establish and maintain an effective risk control programme which is regularly monitored in order to measure actual achievement against intention. Site surveys are an important service provided by insurers within the terms of a conventional insurance programme. They fulfil the purpose not only of obtaining underwriting information but also of making risk improvement recommendations which ensure the maintenance of adequate risk control standards.

In the context of a captive operation, especially for risks in which a commercial insurer is not involved, the achievement of proper risk control standards is an important aspect of captive management in order to protect the interests of reinsurers and ensure continuing reinsurance protection on the best possible terms. Any risk control weaknesses and the need for improvement must be highlighted.

Captive viability. An opinion as to the viability of a potential captive must be formulated during the course of the study and this will be based on the outcome of the risk analysis and evaluation. It is essential to recognize that the captive structure should be such that the original capital cannot be impaired in the early years and the balance sheet is not subject to undue fluctuation thereafter. Therefore the captive premium income, together with any investment income earned, needs to be sufficient to provide for reinsurance, claims, administrations and other corporate costs.

CAPTIVE FORMATION CONSIDERATIONS

(1) *Location.* The study will review various captive domiciles and examine whether a particular one may be more appropriate than others. The areas explored in the course of the study will reveal whether the parent organization may, through an established company, expansion plans or otherwise, have a greater affinity for a specific territory. The particular aspects to be examined for the various territories which are most popular will include:
   (a) corporation profit tax rate;
   (b) capitalization fee or tax;
   (c) annual registration fee or tax;
   (d) insurance company requirements;
   (e) exchange control;
   (f) local legal requirements;
   (g) investment opportunities;
   (h) professional assistance available locally;
   (i) communications;
   (j) a view of the economic, social and political circumstances;
   (k) any restrictions on the format of business permitted — for example, only captive reinsurers can be established in Luxembourg;
   (l) any special relationship between the domicile of the parent and a particular captive location — for example, common currency such as in the United Kingdom, Gibraltar, Isle of Man, Guernsey or a United States' dollar area.

(2) *Capitalization.* Capitalization recommendations will reflect the need to demonstrate that the captive is a bonafide insurer, maintains a solvency margin which will be adequate for the risks undertaken and will satisfy authorities, reinsurers and other companies with whom it may wish to establish trading relations. The specific details of minimum capital requirements and solvency margin are incorporated in the study.

(3) *Taxation and legal aspects.* Captives must comply with the regulations relating to insurance companies in their country of residence, unless these have been superseded by rules specifically governing captives. The captive has to be considered to be a valid insurer by the various government authorities, including the tax authorities in the territories of the parent and associated companies, if premiums are to be allowed as a tax-deductible expense. The main requirements are that there must be a real transfer of risk and that all transactions must be conducted at arm's length in a similar way to those undertaken between unrelated parties. The tax and legal aspects of both the parent's country of residence and the proposed location for registration of the captive should be considered in consultation with the parent's accounting and tax advisers.

(4) *Classes of risk for captive participation.* The scope of the feasibility study includes careful examination of all identified risks and the detailed risk analysis and evaluation enables conclusions to be drawn as to the particular risks which are suitable for captive participation in the initial stages of development. Forecasts should also be made of areas for possible future expansion. These conclusions are used as a basis for preparing financial projections to illustrate expected trading results to be achieved from a variety of assumed possibilities.

(5) *Risk retention and reinsurance.* The net amount of risk to be retained by the captive will be decided by careful consideration of the risk profile of the various risk exposures to be protected, as related to captive financial resources. In most cases there will be two levels of risk retention:
   (a) the maximum amount of loss for which the captive will be liable in respect of any one occurrence;
   (b) the maximum aggregate liability in respect of all losses occurring in any one financial year.

   Reinsurance protection will be arranged for that part of the captive's exposure which is in excess of its selected retention. This is likely to involve a combination of excess of loss reinsurance above the selected limit for each loss occurrence and aggregate stop loss cover to avoid excessive accumulations of net losses. The reinsurance strategy selected should be designed to ensure that the captive's capital is not unduly exposed, particularly in the early stages of development.

(6) *Fronting.* Arrangements involving a fronting company may be desirable or necessary. Fronting is essential in any case where the captive wishes to participate in risks in those countries which prohibit the writing of insurance direct except by a locally licensed or admitted insurer. In those circumstances it becomes necessary to find a locally licensed insurer who will agree to provide the required cover and will cede an agreed proportion to the captive by way of reinsurance. Fronting may also be necessary where a loan agreement may stipulate a requirement for admitted insurance. Even when a non-admitted insurance is permitted, fronting may be considered desirable for the following reasons:
(a) the fronting company can often provide, through its branch office network, certain required facilities such as policy issue, claim services and general servicing;
(b) the fronting company will ensure that policies are written at market rates which may be important to satisfy reinsurers;
(c) fronting can assist in demonstrating to regulatory authorities that the relationship between the captive and its parent is established on arm's length principles;
(d) the fronting company may well be able to offer full risk engineering and risk containment services.
These matters must be weighed against the disadvantages of possible additional costs through duplication of services and the loss of revenue by reason of the fee usually required by the fronting company for the provision of its name and any other services required.

(7) *Investment.* Funds available for investment comprise capital, insurance technical reserves and short-term cash; examples are premiums held temporarily between receipt from an insured and payment to reinsurers. A captive may have to settle claims as they arise, so its investment plan needs to be structured with sufficient liquidity to meet all likely situations.

In the United Kingdom, the provisions of the Financial Services Act 1986 require that anybody giving financial advice needs to be registered. It is unlikely that this will directly affect offshore captives, but care should be taken to ensure that investment advisers are suitably qualified and registered.

(8) *Captive management.* Considerable knowledge of the technicalities of insurance is necessary. In some cases this can be provided by internal staff, but most often it has been found to be more practical and cost-effective to employ external specialist managers. The extent of management services required and the associated costs need to be assessed so that the operational implications for the captive can be appreciated. There is a need to define the manager's role and how it interfaces with the captive board and other advisers. Consideration must also be given to the board make-up and numbers and perhaps also the

remuneration of outside directors. The manager's function will normally include:

(a) compliance with all legal and technical requirements within the captive's territory of residence;
(b) general administration;
(c) underwriting and policy issuing;
(d) risk engineering and loss prevention;
(e) accounting and statistical services;
(f) claims control; and
(g) reinsurance administration.

It is important to ensure that the control of an offshore captive can be demonstrated as being independent of its parent. If revenue authorities deem the control not to be independent of the parent then it is possible that the captive will be assessed as resident in the territory of the parent.

In consequence, as much work as possible must be done, and be seen to be done, in the offshore location by the captive acting independently of its parent.

FINANCIAL PROJECTIONS

Specific examples will be included in the study of specimen profit and loss accounts illustrating the outcome of various captive possibilities examined. These would be based on alternative levels of:

(1) risk participation;
(2) risk retention;
(3) reinsurance cost;
(4) claims cost;
(5) investment yield.

Their purpose is to enable decisions to be made on the basis of informed judgments which are themselves based on detailed analysis of all the relevant facts.

CONCLUSION

A captive represents only one part of an overall risk management programme, as indicated in Figure 4.5.1, but in those cases which meet the fundamental criteria it can make a significant contribution to the risk financing arrangements of a large organisation.

The main benefits are to provide greater capacity for insuring the risks concerned and to reduce the net cost of insurance or the net cost of insurable losses which are retained. This is done without reducing the protection against catastrophic losses which is afforded by access to the insurance market. There are additionally the

Figure 4.5.1

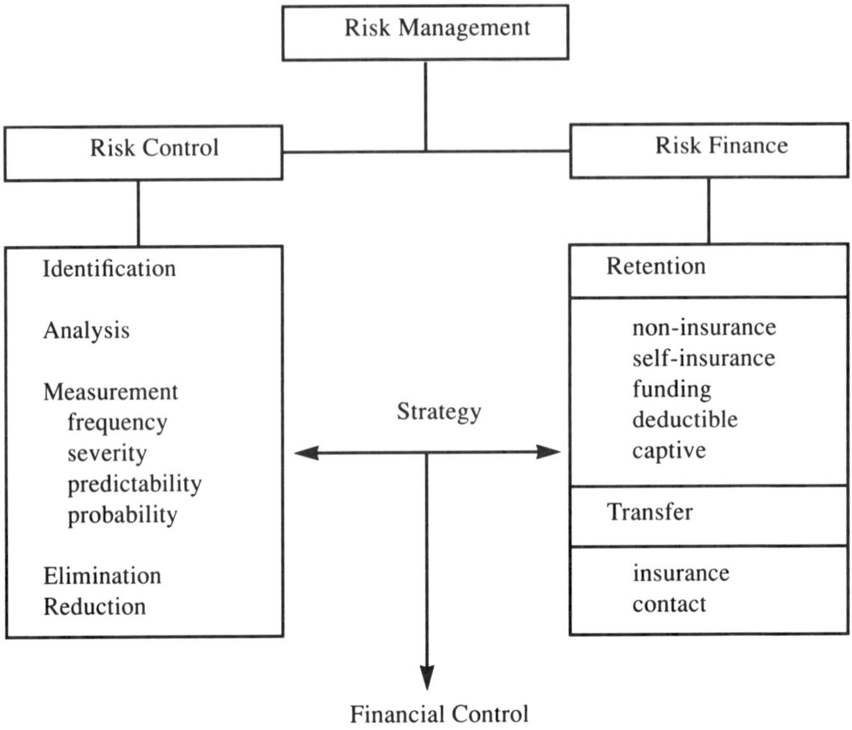

following benefits which may not be present in every case due to different circumstances:

(1) greater flexibility in scope of cover than might otherwise be obtainable while still recognizing the need for arm's length dealings;
(2) positive funding and segregation of reserves for self-borne risks;
(3) centralization of risk management administration;
(4) more positive attitude to risk control due to self-interest in insurance results; and
(5) investment freedom within the constraints of commercial prudence and arm's length considerations.

As an insurance company, a properly constituted captive receives certain benefits, a notable one being the acquiescence by the authorities in technical reserves being set against pre-tax earnings. The business also involves fiduciary responsibilities which must be observed if the accompanying financial benefits are to be retained. Establishing a captive usually requires a large financial commitment, systems reorganization and alterations of relations with the commercial insurance market. It should not be lightly undertaken. If, however, a captive is established it enables a large corporation to satisfy its desires for participation in its own insurable risks with probable financial advantage.

Originally drafted by Kenneth J.Duffy;
this edition checked and revised by
Miss T. McHugh, B.Sc.,
Commercial Union
Risk Management Ltd

5
RISK AND RISK REDUCTION

Part 5 is about risks — how to understand them and how to reduce them. The first five chapters are concerned with types of risk that a finance manager faces: currency, trading, balance sheet, exchange and political. These are followed by three chapters about instruments available for limiting risk and their uses — financial futures, swap financing and options and equity derivatives.

5.7 Swap financing

History
Principles
Role of the banks in the swap market
Credit Risk
Market Developments
Conclusion
Bibliography

5.8 Options and other derivative products

What are derivatives?
The tools of risk
The politics of risk
Customer-driven innovation

5.1
The various classes of currency risk

WHAT DO WE MEAN BY RISK?

The word risk is used in two different senses. The first is a dispersion of expected outcomes of an uncertain event. The outcomes can be both good and bad, and the risk itself is seen as neither good nor bad.

The other sense of the word is something undesirable. In this second sense a business risk is the possibility that the business may sustain a financial loss from an uncertain feared event. The word risk is variously used of the possibility, of the degree of probability of the feared event occurring, of the feared event itself and of the maximum amount of loss which it is feared may occur. If we fear that there is a 2% chance of an earthquake destroying our factory, causing a maximum loss of £10 million, then the word risk is used of our fear itself, of the earthquake (the feared event), of the 2% probability and of the £10m maximum loss.

Currency risks are about exchange rates going either up or down. They are two-way risks from which the business may either gain or lose. However, if the size of the potential loss passes a threshold beyond which it threatens the independent survival of the business, managers see it as a risk in the second sense, as something to be avoided. So whether currency risk is viewed in the first or the second sense depends on the size of the potential loss to which it exposes the business.

The management of business risks in the second sense goes through several stages:

(1) a conscious or inadvertent acceptance of vulnerability to the feared event,
(2) vulnerability,
(3) occurrence of feared event,
(4) crystallisation of consequent financial loss,
(5) effects of that loss.

Active management of a risk is always needed at stage (1), and may well be needed at all the other stages.

We have already noted that risks can be either one-way or two-way risks. Many of the latter are market risks. Earthquakes, like other natural disasters, are one-way risks: there is no such thing as a negative earthquake. On the other hand risks from financial and commodity markets, which include all exchange risks, are two-way risks: a currency can go either up or down, and currency fluctuations are capable of resulting in either gains or losses. What is uncertain about the fluctuations is their direction and amplitude, not whether or not they will occur.

VOLATILITY OF EXCHANGE RATES

Since 1973 the major currencies have been under a floating regime. Exchange rates have been much more volatile under this system than they were in the previous Bretton Woods era. The swings are much larger, and their direction is now generally unpredictable. The major currencies, which have been floating independently in this manner, include the US dollar, the German D-mark, the Japanese yen, the Swiss franc and the pound sterling. Some currencies are floating freely in the sense that their central banks do not normally intervene to maintain a particular parity, but they have a natural link with one of the four major currencies. For example, the Canadian dollar with the US dollar. The bulk of the other currencies are either in a managed float, with the central bank keeping the currency within some band of parity with a weighted average basket of currencies, or pegged by the central bank to another currency or to a similar basket. The European Monetary System currencies are widely regarded as pegged in this way to the D-Mark. These pegged currencies, too, are floating against all those currencies which are not part of their peg or basket. If and when sterling joins the exchange rate mechanism of the European Monetary System, it will no longer float independently, but it will still float against the dollar and the yen and other non-European currencies. No currency is stable against all other currencies.

This system of floating currencies has brought a change in the size and nature of the risks facing those who operate and trade across frontiers.

Volatility is in fact very high. Exchange rates have moved by as much as 5% in a day and by 10% in a month. In a year an exchange rate may on average move by nearly 20% between high and low, and 40% is within the range of observed swings. These are major shocks to the conduct of business. The risks need to be understood and defined.

COMPETITIVENESS AND FINANCIAL CURRENCY RISK

The most fundamental distinction is between competitiveness and financial risk. Competitiveness risk is caused by movements in the **real** exchange rate, which measures changes in the competitiveness of one currency against another. Other classifications have been used in financial theory, but for practical management, what matters is whether the risk is from movements in **real** or **nominal** rates of exchange, and what tools are available to manage the risks. Financial theory assumes that currency risk management is an independent, free-standing management problem. In practice, many companies treat marketing and competitive issues as primary means of maximising the value of the firm, and financial management issues like currency risk as secondary and ancillary to these marketing and competitive objectives.

ILLUSTRATION: COMPETITIVENESS RISK

Over a 12-month period sterling fell from DM3.80 to DM2.70, that is by 10%. Over that same year German prices rose by 4% and British by 9.2%. As 1.092/1.04 = 1.05, British prices therefore rose by 5% more than German prices, taking each price-level in its own currency. Allowing for the 10% fall of sterling against the deutsche mark, British prices became $5\frac{1}{2}$% more competitive against German prices in that period. The calculation is:

$$0.90\ (\text{£ drop}) \times 1.05\ (\text{inflation differential}) = 0.945$$

$$\text{and } 0.945 \text{ is } 5\tfrac{1}{2}\% \text{ less than } 1$$

Competitiveness risk evidently has two essential characteristics:

(1) it is caused by movements in the **real**, not the nominal exchange rate; the nominal exchange rate is the normal, familiar rate like £1 = $1.50;
(2) the threat is to the competitive **costs** of a business; if its costs become less competitive than the costs of its rivals, incurred in other currencies, then either its margins or its market share must suffer, or both; this is the risk from adverse changes in the real exchange rate.

Competitiveness risk is clearly a risk in the field of marketing rather than a financial phenomenon. Financial risk on the other hand is defined as the risk of adverse effects upon the financial outcomes of particular business transactions from adverse changes in **nominal** rates of exchange.

TRADING RISK

There are two types of financial currency risk: trading and position risk. Trading risk is caused by a mismatch between the currency of **sale** and the currency of **cost**. It is the risk of achieving less than the planned gross margin on a given sale if the exchange rate, at which the currency of the sale is ultimately converted into the currency of cost, is less favourable than the exchange rate used or assumed in the pricing decision.

EXAMPLE

We tender for a large contract. Our costs are in sterling and we wish to realise a price of £10m. However, the customer requires us to offer a price in US dollars. We find that the spot rate is \$1.50 = £1, so we quote a price of \$15m. Our tender is successful and two years later, when we receive the \$15m, we find that the best rate at which we can sell the \$15m for pounds is \$2.00 = £1. We therefore receive into our sterling bank account £7.5m instead of the planned £10m. Our trading currency loss is £2.5m, 25% of our desired price.

This loss is not absolute; it is incremental compared with the intended effect of **the rate of exchange used in the pricing decision**.

The loss is in fact:

$$\$15\text{m} \times (1/1.50 - 1/2.00) = -£2.5\text{m},$$

which is the price multiplied by the difference between the rate used in the pricing decision (\$1.50) and the rate at which the exchange deal was done (\$2.00). The pricing decision is at the heart of this definition.

POSITION RISK

Trading risk is caused by a mismatch between the currency of cost and the currency of the selling price. Position risk on the other hand is caused by a mismatch between **assets and liabilities** — or **future cash in- and outflows** — in a currency. It is the risk of loss from adverse movements in the exchange rate between our base currency and the currency in which we have the mismatch.

EXAMPLE

Our company has only a single asset, a British Government gilt-edged security bought at par for £1m and redeemable two years later at par. It finances this as follows:

	£
Share capital	500,000
Loan of SF2m sold for £ at SF4=£1	500,000
	1,000,000

If over the two years to maturity the Swiss franc moves from SF4 to SF3 = £1, then repayment of the loan will cost us £2,000,000/3 = £666,667, and we realise an exchange loss of £166,667. This is the simplest form of position risk. We have financed a sterling asset with a Swiss franc liability, causing an imbalance of minus SF2m in that currency. Position risk is the subject of 5.3.

NOTES ON CLASSIFICATION OF CURRENCY RISKS

The classification adopted in this chapter differs from the usual one. We are not, for example, using the categories of transaction and translation risk.

Transaction risk is seen as a risk leading to a cash gain or loss, whereas translation risk is a risk occurring only when we restate assets and liabilities in our reporting currency in annual financial statements: it is therefore sometimes also called accounting risk. However, if a trading risk begins with a pricing decision in January, is a receivable on our annual reporting date of 31 March and becomes a cash collection and spot currency deal in July, then that same risk or mismatch is a translation risk if **our focus** is on the effect on 31 March, and a transaction risk if it is on the cash outcome in July! It seems more helpful to use the translation and transaction concepts as different **ways of looking** at each risk, not as different risks. The distinction is important, but it is in the eye of the beholder.

The distinctions used here have been chosen for their relevance to practical management. Trading risk centres on the pricing decision, and the exchange rate used in that decision. Position risk focuses on the financing decision and on the general business issues arising from changes in nominal exchange rates. Competitiveness risk, in our terminology, is concerned with the threat to **competitiveness** from movements in **real** exchange rates. Real and nominal exchange rates pose threats which are different in kind and have different management implications.

The usual classifications imply that currency risk is a free-standing management issue, which can be managed by the financial manager without reference to other business functions. This is seldom how managers see it. Position risk can often be managed by financial managers in isolation, but trading risk can only be managed in conjunction with commercial managers, and competitiveness risk is primarily managed by such functions as purchasing, facilities planning and marketing, all of them closer to line than to financial management.

ALFRED KENYON

Vindale Ltd

5.2 Competitiveness and Trading Currency Risks

COMPETITIVENESS CURRENCY RISK

THE REAL EXCHANGE RATE

Competitiveness currency risk has been defined in 5.1 as a risk caused by movements in the real (inflation-adjusted) exchange rate and as a threat to the competitiveness of our costs. Figure 5.2.1 illustrates the concept of the real exchange rate. It shows how sterling and the D-mark have moved in real terms against the weighted average of the currencies of their respective trading partners. Each is plotted against a horizontal equilibrium line calculated in the London Business School. The horizontal lines are not important to managers.

What matters is that each currency gets relatively more competitive when the graph moves downward and less competitive when it moves upward. Whenever a business takes commercial decisions, it takes those decisions in the light of its recent or current experience of its competitiveness. If we can predict the future trend in the real exchange rate, then we can assess whether, in this respect, we are likely to gain or lose competitive edge.

The diagrams show that during 1979 sterling began a major movement towards greater uncompetitiveness whereas the D-mark began one in the direction of greater competitiveness.

BUSINESS IMPACT

These particular movements were steep and sustained for a number of years. In fact, real exchange rates tend to stay relatively competitive for months or years at a time, and then relatively uncompetitive for significant periods. This pattern is not invariable, but not uncommon either. The implications for business can be quite dramatic. In the United Kingdom it is quite evident that after 1979 many manufacturing companies with sterling facilities and wage costs became very uncompetitive in world markets, not least in their United Kingdom home market. Automobile manufacturers are the best known example of this. Not only did they find it harder to compete in export markets, but increasingly they found their domestic market penetrated by

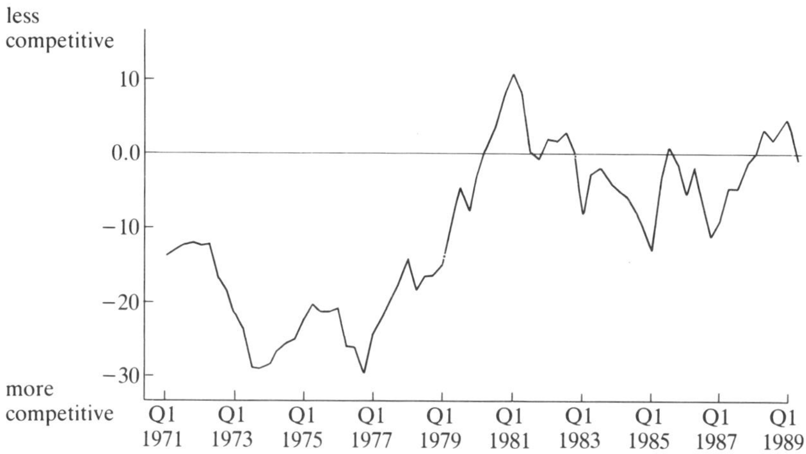

Figure 5.2.1 UK Competitiveness
(% deviation from Purchasing Power Parity)

Germany Competitiveness
(% deviation from Purchasing Power Parity)

imported cars. Nor is the significance of these changes confined to trades which are obviously involved in imports and exports. In the United Kingdom, catering establishments and public houses in places frequented by foreign tourists found trade very buoyant in the mid-1970s, when sterling was weak in real terms, and very poor in the early 1980s when it was strong.

These examples clearly illustrate how competitiveness currency risk threatens the market share of a business and thus its ability to earn good margins. If the business incurs its principal costs in an uncompetitive currency, it may experience shrinking sales or margins or a mixture of both: the outcome depends on how far it lets its margins take the strain, rather than lose sales.

Few businesses can easily change the currency of their principal costs. As currencies tend to stay uncompetitive for some years, the harmful effect on such a business is usually of long duration.

MANAGING COMPETITIVENESS CURRENCY RISK

The management of competitiveness currency risk concerns such functions as marketing, facilities planning and buying. An important contribution of finance managers who are constantly aware of the currency markets, is to recognise this risk and to bring trends in real exchange rates to the attention of their marketing, planning and buying colleagues.

PLANNING DECISIONS

Most management actions in this field concern longer-term decisions about the location of facilities. With hindsight it is clear that 1972 would have been a good year to expand capacity in the United Kingdom rather than in Germany; the converse is evidently true of 1979. Investment or acquisition decisions of this kind are not made every day. But when we do make them, it must pay to take the prospective course of the real exchange rate into account. Fortunately the real exchange rate tends to be less difficult to predict than the nominal. Its movements are often slower and more sustained, as figure 5.2.1 illustrates.

MARKETING

Long-term marketing decisions are even more fundamental. A decision to enter a certain country or to devote fresh resources to expansion in a country, will be better informed if we take note of likely changes in the future competitiveness of our currency of cost. We may be willing to sell at a loss for a while in order to capture a certain market, but we could be in difficulties if we badly underestimated the size of that loss. 1979 would not have been the best year for a motor vehicle maker with component and assembly plants in the United Kingdom to start a major sales drive in Germany.

BUYING

The element of cost over which we usually have the greatest degree of control in the shorter term is that of bought-out materials, components and subcontracts. The point is, of course, inapplicable to those homogeneous raw materials and commodities for which there is a single world price like oil, gold or sugar. Buying is one of the most professional activities in business. Nevertheless buyers are often better at comparing costs today at today's spot exchange rates than at identifying the most economic longer-term source. Specifically they may not always recognise the need to watch the likely course of future real exchange rates.

Still more critical is a decision to place a subcontract for a major contract of sale. If in 1980 we had to select a subcontractor for a compressor in a large petrochemical complex, would it have occurred to us to look around for a supplier in Germany rather than in the United Kingdom? It used to be thought unpatriotic not to buy British, but what if our decision to buy a British compressor lost the entire contract to a non-British competitor?

TRADING RISK

In 5.1 trading risk was explained as the risk arising from a mismatch between the currency of the selling price and the currency of cost. The losses or gains from this risk were found to be the amount of the mismatch multiplied by the difference between two exchange rates used in:

(1) a pricing decision;
(2) the actual exchange deal, which sells the receipt from the customer for the currency of cost, or conversely buys the supplier's currency in exchange for the currency in which we are selling.

FORWARD AND SPOT EXCHANGE DEALS

If we want to go on holiday in Italy and go to the bank at the airport to buy lire for sterling, we are doing a spot exchange deal. However, if we need to pay 90 days from now for a machine which an Italian supplier has sold us for Lire110m, we can ask our bank for a different kind of exchange deal and at a different exchange rate: the forward rate. This forward exchange contract will not be implemented by either side until day 90 from now.

Some people look upon a forward deal as a kind of insurance against risk, but the analogy is not close. The difference between the spot and forward rates is called the forward premium or discount. This premium differs sharply from an insurance premium in that it can be negative. The forward rate can be cheaper than the spot rate. It is merely today's market exchange rate for day 90. **No risk is transferred to the bank.**

When people talk of the cost of covering forward, they mean one of two concepts: an **absolute** cost — the transaction costs which are: (a) the bank's very small bid-offer spread or dealing margin; and (b) the greater internal clerical costs of the hedger: recording, confirming and diarising the deal; an **opportunity** cost — the more important cost of foregoing the chance to gain from possible favourable movements (not at present expected by the market) in the exchange rate; the chance, for example, of buying our lire more cheaply by a spot deal on day 90.

The negative premium can be illustrated in the following example. We might find that the spot rate at which the bank would sell us lire for delivery on the second working day from now is Lire2200 = £1, and that the 3 months forward rate is 12 lire higher, Lire2212 = £1. So if we bought 110 million lire now (for delivery the day after tomorrow), they would cost us £50,000, but if we bought them for delivery in three months' time, they would only cost us £49,728.70. We are 'saving' £271.30. We shall go more deeply into forward contracts and rates later, but for the moment just note that we can make a contract with the bank today under which no cash passes today; we owe the bank £49,728.70 three months from today, and it must on that same day deliver Lire110m to us. It is also the day on which we have to pay the sum of Lire110m to the supplier of the machine.

DO FORWARD DEALS ELIMINATE TRADING RISKS?

At first sight it looks as though trading risk need not be a problem. If I telephone my Italian supplier today and ask him for a price for the machine, he quotes Lire110m; and if, while I am on the line to him, I see on the video terminal that a bank will give me a forward rate now of Lire2212 = £1; and if my calculator tells me that this means a cash cost to my business of £49,728.70, compared with the lowest competitive cost from any other supplier of £52,500, then all I have to say to my Italian supplier is va bene, grazie, ring off and do the forward deal with the bank. The purchase of the machine and the exchange deal have been concluded on line and I have run no risk of a trading currency loss. The sterling cost of the machine is firm.

LIFE-CYCLE OF A TRADING RISK

In 5.1 we looked at a large contract for which a price of $15m was tendered with the aim of receiving £10m cash in sterling. If we look more closely at the biography of that risk, we find it strangely similar to the life-cycle of a human being. The important stages are:

1 Conception:	We quote a price, but have not yet achieved a sale. Our customer is not yet committed to our price.
2 Birth:	We attain commercial certainty that we have a sale.
3 Anniversaries:	Annual reporting dates on which the contract receivables (and payables) in foreign currencies are translated into the reporting currency.
4 Death:	The (spot or forward) exchange deal which sells the foreign currency receivables for the currency of cost or buys the foreign currency payables for the currency of sale.

The death of a trading risk can of course occur before some of the anniversaries, if a forward contract is entered into before those anniversaries.

The critical period for a trading risk is the antenatal period between conception and birth. In big contracts this is the tender period, during which the tenderer is committed to a price, but the customer is not. The present definition of trading risk hinges upon the exchange rate used in the pricing decision.

Tenders for large contracts are the most dramatic illustration of antenatal trading risk, but they are by no means unique: antenatal risk occurs in a much more common case where sales are made from a price-list issued perhaps some months earlier. In all these situations the **seller** is committed to a price, and therefore to the exchange rate built into his pricing decision, whereas the **customer** is not committed to that price.

There are in fact only two cases where a seller who has quoted a price in a currency other than the currency of cost, has no antenatal trading risk whatever:

(1) the on-line case, considered earlier, where a British exporter rings up, say, an Italian supplier and settles his lire buying price simultaneously with his forward contact: here the risk is not antenatal;
(2) a case where the selling price is fixed by the market and not by the seller, as in commodity trading when the seller makes no active pricing decision.

Birth was consciously defined not as some formal event, like contract signature, but as the point at which the seller becomes commercially certain that he has a sale. Is he certain enough to commit himself to a forward contract? The seller needs to be committed to his own quoted price: it is not normally a commercial option to go back on a price quoted in a price list. Why must antenatal risk be distinguished from post-natal risk? Because it is unsafe to cover forward before birth.

THE CASE AGAINST ANTENATAL FORWARD COVER

EXAMPLE

In our $15 million tender we quoted that price because at that time the spot rate was $1.50 = £1, and we knew no better than to convert our desired £10m price into US dollars at that rate. Suppose we had instead decided to use the three-year forward rate of $1.40 = £1 to compute a price of $14m. (The three-year forward rate shows a wider difference from the spot rate than for example the three-month forward rate). We chose the three-year rate because we expected to receive our cash in month 36 after month 0, the date of our tender. We assumed that the contract would be awarded in month 6 and completed and paid for in month 36 after a 30-month construction period. Our idea was that we could neutralize the exchange risk by an immediate forward sale in month 0 of the $14m for £10m, for month 36.

In fact, however, we lost the award to a competitor. We heard this bad news in month 9. By then the spot rate had moved to $1.20 = £1 and the 27-month forward rate to \$1.12 = £1. In month 36 we were committed to deliver \$14m to the bank, which were no longer due from the customer. Any exchange deal with a bank is binding. So in month nine we bought \$14m 27 months forward for month 36 at the forward rate of 1.12 = £1; the aim was to close out our original forward contract.

That forward purchase of \$14m at \$1.12 cost £12,500,000. The original forward contract will only produce a receipt of £10,000,000. So we suffer a straight cash loss in month 36 of £2,500,000, and without winning our commercial contract.

The example illustrates how antenatal forward cover actually creates a worse risk than the one it was intended to hedge: worse in that its worst outcome can be combined with the loss of the commercial tender. We might well have incurred a similar loss if we had not covered forward, but only if we had won the contract. The fatal error is to lock into an exchange rate before we are certain that we have the exposure. We shall presently discover some better solutions to antenatal risk than antenatal forward cover.

MANAGING TRADING RISK

MANAGEMENT BY SUCCESSFUL FORECASTING?

People outside the currency markets tend to believe that the sophisticated management of currency risk is accomplished by clever treasurers who are better informed than the market and outperform it. This possibility is discussed in 5.3 where position risk is considered. At this point it must be noted that this type of currency risk management takes us outside the field of trading risk management as here defined.

WHEN DOES TRADING RISK CEASE TO BE TRADING RISK?

A trading risk at some stage after birth becomes a receivable or payable, and therefore part of the net position in its currency which, in its turn, is part of the position risk of the business in that currency. If the trading risk is a dollar receipt, it is part of the position in dollars unless it has been sold forward for another currency such as sterling. In the latter case its amount would be determined in sterling, not in dollars, and would form part of the sterling position. On the face of it therefore a risk can be both a trading risk and part of the position risk. Which is it?

This turns on the aim in managing the risk. When that aim is to protect the currency outcome assumed in the pricing decision, it is being managed as a trading risk. On the other hand, if the aim is to obtain the best possible outcome regardless of the pricing decision, the receivable is being managed as part of the position risk. The decisive criterion is the benchmark against which the risk is being managed.

So what starts as a trading risk, can become part of a position risk, and that transformation occurs if and when the purpose changes. At what stage then should that mental transition be made?

The practical answer is when it ceases to be realistic to be concerned with the rate used in the pricing decision. There must come a time at which the actual market rate at which we could hedge the risk for the maturity concerned is **either** so much **better** than the pricing rate that we should no longer be content just to achieve that pricing rate, **or** so much **worse** that it is no longer realistic to aim for that rate — the priority now is to minimize the loss.

The best practical answer is that this transition occurs at birth. If birth is the earliest point at which it is possible to cover forward so as to protect the pricing rate, then it may well also be the latest point. Once we have passed the point of birth, the timing decision is one of market judgement, unrelated to trading risk. In other words, if we do not hedge a trading risk at birth, then we should treat it as part of the position risk from that point.

RISK MANAGEMENT DEVICES TO NEUTRALIZE TRADING RISK

Attitudes to currency and other risks vary from 100% aggressive to 100% defensive. An aggressive view sees currency risk as an opportunity to make gains by outperforming the market. The defensive view treats that risk as a trap from which to escape with zero or the least possible loss. Without making value judgments within this range of choices, it will be assumed, for the sake of greater clarity, that the objective is wholly defensive. This assumption will be relaxed later.

Devices to neutralize trading risk can be classified as being available (a) at birth and (b) at conception, that is in the antenatal period. The devices are:

postnatal	antenatal
1 spot deal	1 avoidance
2 forward deal	2 ECGD's TTC cover*
3 futures deal	3 currency options
	4 costing the risk

*Cover by the (British) Export Credits Guarantee Department's Tender to Cover policy.

HEDGING DEVICES USABLE AT BIRTH

Disastrous effects of covering a trading risk forward in the antenatal period have been demonstrated. Once we have reached the point of birth, however, the way to stop loss from further unfavourable changes in the exchange rate is to lock into the then prevailing structure of rates. This can be achieved by doing an exchange deal at that point. The deal can be either:

(1) a spot exchange contract, or
(2) a forward contract.

Either of these locks the exchange rate in, and thus establishes the currency outcome of the risk.

(NOTE: financial futures are described in other parts of this handbook. A brief reference to currency futures in 5.3 explains the reasons why corporate hedgers normally prefer the forward to the futures markets.)

The spot deal always involves a change in the balance sheet. By selling the currency of a future receivable (say dollars) spot for the base currency (sterling), it is possible to:

(1) increase a sterling position, by either repaying an overdraft or other sterling debt, or by increasing sterling cash or investments, and
(2) reduce our dollar position, by either borrowing dollars or liquidating dollar assets.

EXAMPLE

Our currency of cost is the US dollar, and we are hedging a future receipt in Italian lire. The *Financial Times* of 6 August 1987 quoted the closing rates for three months eurocurrency deposits on 5 August as (% per annum):

Lire $12\frac{1}{2} - 12$
Dollars $7\frac{1}{16} - 6\frac{15}{16}$

The higher of the two rates in each currency is the fixed interest rate at which a bank would lend for three months, and the lower that at which it would accept deposits. The quoted rates are fixed, not variable, and they apply to eurodollars or eurolire transactions, not to domestic loans or deposits in theUnited States or Italy.

The same page of that issue of the *Financial Times* also quotes the closing spot exchange rate for lire against dollars as Lire$1359.\frac{1}{4}$— $1359.\frac{3}{4}$ = \$1. Again, $1359.\frac{1}{4}$ is the rate at which the bank would sell lire, and $1359.\frac{3}{4}$ the rate at which the bank would buy lire for dollars. (The difference or spread in all these cases is the bank's margin of dealing profit).

A payment of Lire300m in three months from 5 November 1987 is expected. It has already been shown that the London interbank offered rate (LIBOR) for borrowing lire was $12\frac{1}{2}$ % per annum (most non-banks pay a higher spread, but that will be ignored here). To hedge the expected lire receipt, it is necessary to borrow Lire300m at 12.5% and simultaneously to sell those lire spot for dollars. At the bank's buying rate for dollars of Lire1359.75, this will produce \$220,628.79. It so happens that we can use these dollar proceeds to repay an existing eurodollar borrowing. In that case we shall for the three months pay $12\frac{1}{2}$ % per annum for the lire, and save $7\frac{1}{16}$ % per annum on the dollars. That is a difference per annum of $5\frac{7}{16}$%. The extra interest cost is therefore 3/12 × 5.4375 × 1/100 × \$220,628.79 = \$2,999.17. The net total dollar proceeds from this hedge are therefore \$220,628.79-\$2,999.17 = \$217,629.62.

When the customer pays his Lire300 million on 5 November, we use this to repay the borrowing. To sum up, the spot deal hedge consists of borrowing the lire, selling the lire spot for dollars, and repaying the lire debt from the customer's payment of lire.

A forward deal would have a very similar financial result. The closing quotation for 5 August 1987 for three months forward lire in the *Financial Times* of 6 August was '15.00 — 18.00 dis'. This quotes the forward discount. If we add this to the spot quotation of Lire 1359.25 — 1359.75, we get an outright forward quotation of Lire 1374.25 — 1377.75. This means that if (as an interbank party — a simplifying assumption) we had asked the bank to sell Lire300m forward for three months against dollars, maturing 5 November 1987, we might have obtained a rate of 1377.75, producing $217,746.32 cash on 5 November against delivery of the Lire300m due on that day from our customer. This is just $116.70 more than our alternative net result from the spot hedge.

RELATING SPOT AND FORWARD HEDGES

$116.70 in this case amounted to a difference of about 0.017%. This is within the accuracy of our calculation, and of the fractions and decimal points in which the eurocurrency interest and exchange rates are quoted in the *Financial Times*. If the reader were to repeat the experiment with other spot and forward rates quoted in any given issue of the *Financial Times*, he might find greater differences, but still a very high correlation between the financial outcomes of spot and forward hedges for the same pair of currencies at a given maturity of 1 or 3 months. This is not a coincidence, but the result of the interrelation of the currency and eurodeposit markets.

If Bank A did not take care to equate its quoted forward rates with its quoted eurocurrency interest rate differentials, it would allow other operators to make arbitrage profits from that discrepancy. Another bank B could simply deposit one of the currencies, borrow the other and cover it forward, doing all three deals with B to realise a riskless profit. Actual or feared arbitrage therefore systematically keeps forward rates very close to those differentials for each pair of currencies at given maturities. For practical currency management purposes we need, however, to note that the close correspondence of forward premiums or discounts with interest differentials holds only as long as the deposits or loans are:

(1) eurocurrency,
(2) fixed interest instruments for the quoted period to maturity.

If we were to use the dollars to repay a United States domestic debt, or to borrow lire at variable rates, we should obtain very different results. Moreover, if we used the dollar proceeds of the sale of lire to earn deposit rates instead of saving interest on existing debt, we should also lose the banks' spread between borrowing and lending rates. The forward deal is essentially a deal in the market for **fixed rate** eurocurrency funds.

This explains one restriction on the use of forward cover: for many currencies forwards are only quoted for relatively short periods like 6 or 12 months, whereas for some major traded FX rates, like dollar and sterling, maturities of up to five or even fifteen years are often available. The reach of the forward market is limited to the reach of the fixed interest market in the currencies. Consequently, spot deals with borrowings or deposits at variable interest rates (rollovers) can be arranged for much longer periods.

The main differences between spot and forward hedges are:

(1) forward deals involve significant diary and other administration costs.
(2) in this wholesale market banks will only deal at amounts of (say) $100,000 or more, depending on the bank and the relationship.
(3) if we deal spot, cash passes at the time of hedging. If we deal forward, no cash passes until the maturity date.
(4) the spot hedge can thus change the gearing of our position, by raising the absolute and relative amount of debt.
(5) a forward deal also increases the bank's credit exposure on its customer. It therefore eats into the customer's credit limit, but by less than an actual borrowing. This comparison with the spot deal thus depends on whether the spot deal causes the bank's customer to borrow. If not, the forward deal uses up more credit limit than the spot deal.

TIMING FORWARD CONTRACT MATURITIES. WHAT IF THE CUSTOMER PAYS LATE?

We may not know exactly when our customer's remittance of Lire300m will reach us. The customer may not be punctual, our own delivery may be delayed or the customer's bank may be slow to get the funds to us. At one time a popular solution was to enter into a forward option contract which the bank's customer was free to implement not on a single date, but on any day during a period such as 15 days: a when option. This is nowadays thought to be too costly.

Spot or forward exchange contracts are strictly binding on both parties and must be honoured. So whatever happens, if we have sold lire forward to the bank for 5 November, we must deliver the lire to the bank on that day, and the bank the dollars to us.

If the customer's 300 million lire have not by then reached us, we can either borrow them, overnight from day to day if we wish, or for several days or weeks at a time, or we can enter into another forward contract, say for 7 days; this last option is called rolling over the forward contract. In other words, we have the same option as before; on 5 November we can either take out a spot or a forward contract to bridge the remaining forward period. The final outcome will not be dramatically different from an original forward contract, taken out with perfect foresight to mature on the correct date when the customer's remittance is actually received. However, it is only the **final** outcome that is so similar. The **interim** period from 5 November to the final closing out of the whole transaction may well show a substantial temporary cash surplus or deficit, and therefore a balance sheet effect. The size and direction of that cash effect depend on how the spot rate has moved since the original forward contract or since the last rollover date.

Similarly, if the customer's Lire300m arrive **before** the first (or a subsequent rollover) forward contract matures, then we may have to deposit the lire at interest in the eurolire market until we can use them to discharge the forward contract.

RISK MANAGEMENT TOOLS AVAILABLE BEFORE BIRTH

The requirement before birth is that we must not lock ourselves into an exchange rate and must therefore not do an exchange deal, spot or forward, before we are certain that our quoted price will result in a sale.

AVOIDANCE

This is the most neglected, most obvious, most unglamorous and downright boring tool. Yet in practice it is much more useful than many business managers believe. We can avoid trading risk altogether by selling in the currency or currencies of cost. In many situations it is the only available device against antenatal risk. Nor is avoidance always a sign of a defensive or a risk-paranoid attitude. An active currency trading policy does not passively have to accept the task of making money out of every single risk that happens to turn up in trading. Expert currency dealers are scarce, and they will make the most gains if allowed to concentrate on those currencies in which they happen to excel. Even among antenatal risks it may pay us to concentrate on those which are unavoidable rather than accept every single avoidable risk.

Avoidance sounds simple, but it involves quite a few complications in practice. If we tender in $ for a contract to be performed in Kuwait, where our costs are 25% of the price in DM, 20% in yen, 30% in Kuwait dinars and 25% in our home currency sterling, avoidance means tendering a price in four currencies (25% DM, 20% Yen, 30% KD and 25% £).

Sometimes customers tolerate avoidance better if we quote their preferred currency subject to a currency adjustment clause for the tender period. A very simple form of such a clause runs as follows:

> Our price of $15,300,000, was calculated using a rate of $1.50 = £1. Our price will be adjusted up or down pro rata to the difference between this rate and the middle closing spot rate quoted in the *Financial Times* of the day prior to the date on which this contract is signed.

This formula effectively fixes the price in sterling at £10,200,000 during the antenatal period, that is from tender to contract. At the time of contract the dollar receipts need to be sold forward for their expected dates of receipt some months or years later. If the $1.50 rate in the above clause was itself the average (see below) forward rate ruling at the time of tender for a similar average time lag between contract and receipt of cash, the only risk left is the difference between the forward premiums (discounts) at tender date and those at contract date. The difference is seldom a major one, because interest differentials are much less volatile than spot rates. This residual risk could only have been eliminated if we had tied the currency adjustment clause to the average closing **forward** rate instead of the spot rate. Not every customer is sophisticated enough to feel comfortable with that technical concept. The word average refers to the weighted average delay between contract date and the various dates on which parts of the contract price are expected to be received from the customer.

INSURANCE IN BRITAIN BY THE EXPORT CREDITS GUARANTEE DEPARTMENT'S TENDER TO CONTRACT COVER

The principal function of the Export Credits Guarantee Department (ECGD) is to insure export credit risks for UK exporters. However, like for example its French counterpart, COFACE, it offers cover against the antenatal currency risk, called the tender to contract (TTC) cover. The cover is available subject to some fairly restrictive conditions. There must be a minimum of £10m United Kingdom export content in the tender, the contract must be covered by one of the Department's normal facilities for cash or credit contracts (supplemental extended terms guarantee, specific guarantee or buyer credit), the cover does not protect a tender period of more than nine months before a contract is awarded, and the cover is available only for exports from the United Kingdom priced in United States or Canadian dollars, Deutsche marks, Swiss francs or yen. The key restriction is the nine months time-limit. If we are not free to revise our quoted price by the end of that period, we are locked into the cover with a fresh set of exchange rates: this negates the protection for which we are paying a heavy premium. For each **tender** the premium is just 0.1% of insured receipts. If our tender is successful we must pay a further premium of between 2.5 and 4.0% of insured receipts.

At the time of tendering, the exporter receives from the Export Credits Guarantee Department a set of forward rates which will apply if he wins his contract and which he will have taken into account in his pricing decision. When the contract is won, the exporter must enter into actual forward contracts. The difference between the Department's schedule of forward rates and the cash receipts from the actual forward contracts will give rise to an overall gain or loss. If it is a gain, the Department takes the whole of this. If a loss, the exporter must bear the first 1% and the Department any excess up to a ceiling of 25% of the total insured sterling receipts. The Department's maximum tender to contract liability is therefore 24% of total insured receipts.

THE CURRENCY OPTION

This became widely available in December 1982; it is traded on a number of formal open outcry exchanges, especially Philadelphia, and also over the counter by a number of banks.

The option is a true yes or no option. The hedger pays a premium to the option-writer, for which he obtains the right (but **not** the obligation) to buy or sell a specified amount of one currency against another at a specified future exercise date, and at an agreed strike price. Let us assume that on 1 September we could buy an over the counter option to sell $s for £s at the rate of $1.55 (strike price) on 20 January (exercise date), and that at 20 January the spot rate turns out to be $1.65 or $1.45. If it is $1.65, the option strike price gives us a gain and we shall exercise it. If it is $1.45, we do better to sell spot; so we allow the option to lapse. Our worst loss is the cost of the premium, but our potential gain is unlimited.

If we have used the option to hedge the risk of an antenatal loss, that loss too is potentially unlimited, and it is compensated by the gain on the option, less the cost of the premium. In fact, the antenatal offer of a commercial US$ price, representing sterling costs, is akin to a currency option written for our customer.

Here is an example of the neatness of the option as a hedge against antenatal risk. The simplified matrix of possible outcomes is as follows:

The commercial tender is	Between tender and contract the tender currency	
	(1) rises	(2) falls
(a) WON	option lapsed antenatal gain realised **less** premium cost	option exercised antenatal loss offset by option gain **less** premium cost
(b) LOST	option lapsed loss restricted to premium cost	option exercised option gain realised **less** premium cost

In cases (1a) and (1b) the option turns out to be unprofitable: (1a) results in antenatal gain less premium. (1b) is the case of the disastrous example considered earlier under 'the case against antenatal forward cover', where the dollar tender price was sold forward at conception, the tender was lost and the tender currency rose sharply. The option limits the damage to the cost of the premium.

In cases (2a) and (2b) the option turns out to be profitable in its own right. In (2b) the option does the job for which it was taken out: it compensates for the antenatal loss. In (2b) it yields a financial gain (less premium), with no commercial contract won.

Options are expensive because they confer such a valuable right. The premium is determined by the expected volatility of the spot rate, and by the time to expiry. An option market is essentially a market in the volatility of the underlying instrument, in this case exchange rates.

Whether the corporate hedger finds the option economic, therefore, depends on the size of the premium. Premium rates began very low in 1982. Option writers burned their fingers badly by underestimating the volatility of exchange rates, especially in 1984. Over the counter premiums then reached a peak around 3% for three months, and 6% for twelve, for United States dollar and sterling options. The cost of a 6-month option has since then come down to nearer 4%, but that can still be very costly. 4% for a tender with even a nine months' validity is a high cost to a contractor who wins only one such tender in ten: this is a 40% loading on his successful tenders, less any allowance he can afford to make for outcomes in box (2b), which prove profitable in their own right when the tender is unsuccessful. A contractor needs to use options selectively. If the choice is between the straight currency option and the Export Credits Guarantee Department's tender to contract cover, a contractor with a low success rate in tendering must prefer the tender to contract cover.

To overcome the problem of cost, it was always possible to buy less protection by buying an out-of-the-money option. An option is described as 'out of the money' when the strike price stands at a loss against the current spot rate. However, since the mid-1980s, a number of option derivatives have come on the market which can significantly reduce the premium cost, often by modifying the risk profile. Some of these are tailored to the problem of the chances of the commercial tender succeeding. Also worth considering are the compound option, an option on an option, and the knock-in option, which can only be exercised if the spot rate reaches a predetermined trigger value. Both of these can be significantly cheaper than the straight option.

COSTING THE RISK

This tool amounts to a form of self-insurance. The risk is treated as a cost. The cost is evaluated at the premium cost of a notional currency option. This cost is then built into the cost estimate.

For an example we assume that the original cost estimate was £10m, so that the contractor desires a minimum selling price of £11m, a gross margin of £1m. The cost of the antenatal risk is calculated at £1.5m, making the total cost £11.5m. The minimum price should now be £12.5m. The commercial manager believes that a competitive price is \$15m when the period from contract to average date of receipt of cash is three years, and the current 3-year forward rate is \$1.40 = £1. \$15m @ 1.40 gives an expected outturn of £10,714,000. Can the company live with a price which gives it a mere £214,000 instead of £1m above the adjusted cost? That is the decision to be taken.

The decision process is complex and multidisciplinary. The currency manager has to evaluate the cost of the risk, the commercial manager has to assess the competitive price and the minimum margin which his trading account can stand.

Both have an interest in ensuring that their judgments are right, because neither will have a job if the company goes bankrupt or fails to win contracts.
This method is not suitable if a worst-case move in the exchange rate would cause a size of loss which would be catastrophic to the contractor. In that case the cost of the risk must be equated with that same worst-case loss: it cannot be taken at the notional option premium.

This method of costing the risk crystallises the issue of antenatal risk most satisfactorily. If it ends up with an unwelcome answer, the team must review again whether one of the other tools, and especially avoidance, is not less painful in the circumstances. Yet none of the other tools may in fact be available, and the final decision must be whether to abandon this tender altogether.

ANTENATAL RISK FROM PRICE LISTS

A typical time-sequence is that a price list is **prepared** on 1 December so as to be in distributors' hands on 1 January and to be in force for the three months to 31 March. On 1 December when the British exporter with sterling costs decides his DM prices, he may believe from his commercial experience that his sales will be not less than DM7m, nor more than DM9m. In that case he is commercially certain of DM7m, which he can sell forward. He has:

(1) a postnatal exposure (certain sales at committed prices) of DM 7 million which he can sell forward, and
(2) an **antenatal exposure of DM2m** (uncertain sales at committed prices), for which he might wish to buy currency options or derivatives.

SUMMARY: TRADING RISK

Antenatal risk is the big problem. Avoidance, tender to contract cover, the currency option or pricing for the risk may solve the problem up to the point of birth, where the trading transaction becomes a commercial certainty. At that point of birth it can be hedged by a spot or a forward deal. If none of the four tools provide an acceptable solution, the risk, that is the attempt to win the contract or business, has to be abandoned.

ALFRED KENYON

Vindale Ltd

5.3
Position risk

DEFINING AND QUANTIFYING POSITION RISK

In 5.1 position risk was explained as the risk of loss from exchange rate movements between the base or benchmark currency and any other currency in which the business has an imbalance or mismatch of assets and liabilities or of future cash in- and outflows. More searching questions about this explanation must now be asked.

It was also noted in 5.2 that postnatal items covered forward now belong to the position in the currency for which they have been bought or sold forward: they are no longer part of the position in the currency in which they are denominated. For example, a US$ receivable sold forward for DM is now part of the DM position; its value is now known only in DM and no longer in dollars.

This defines the effect of a **forward** hedge. What is the effect where a **spot** hedge has been used to hedge an imbalance in a currency? In the same example a spot hedge of a US$ receivable requires selling the US$ spot for DM, borrowing the US$ and depositing the DM.

The resulting position will contain a dollar receivable, a dollar liability and a DM deposit.

As the first two cancel out, we are left with a DM asset, which was also the effect of the forward hedge.

DOES THE CONVENTIONAL BALANCE SHEET CORRECTLY COVER THE ITEMS WHICH MAKE UP POSITION RISK?

Not quite. We must add any postnatal trading risks which have not yet become receivables or payables. If we have yesterday won a contract for $16m, and have decided not to sell the dollars forward, then none of it is part of our receivables yet (for we have made no deliveries), but we certainly have a risk. Moreover this is no longer a trading risk; for we decided in 5.2 to treat birth as the cut-off point after which it ceases to make sense to manage a risk against the exchange rate used in the pricing decision.

So adjusted, the conventional balance sheet covers the items in any one currency which make up an exposure, leaving only the problem of valuation. Expressly excluded are future trading transactions at prices to which the business is not yet committed (contractually or commercially) at known prices. We may know that we shall sell a minimum quantity of garments next quarter, but as long as we are still free to quote or vary our prices, the items do not yet constitute a financial risk.

IS POSITION RISK TO BE SEEN IN ACCOUNTING OR FUTURE CASH FLOW TERMS?

This is one of the major issues. Position risk can be seen in terms of either assets and liabilities, as defined and valued in conventional accounts, or future committed cash in- or outflows. In practice these two views conflict on only two topics:

(1) the values placed on the items, such as historical cost or current values,
(2) the maturity dates at which the items are seen to be at risk; in other words whether the position risk is regarded as ending at our next reporting date or when the transaction is due or expected to become a cash in- or outflow.

NON-MONETARY ASSET VALUES

Our first dilemma was whether we accept asset **values** as they are stated in financial statements even when these are shown at historic cost values, that is unadjusted for inflation.

This dilemma would for practical purposes go away if all financial statements were drawn up on a current value or inflation accounting standard. Most people would accept that current cost asset values are close enough to their notion of future cash flow asset values.

The sharpest conflict arises with fixed assets. Fixed assets have the longest life and therefore tend to include the most outdated values in historic cost accounts.

EXAMPLE

A British company in year 0 bought an Italian hotel for 1.5bn lire, buying that sum spot at Lire1500 = £1 for £1m. In year twelve, the hotel still stands in the local books at Lire1.5bn, but the currency translation is now at the closing rate of Lire2400 = £1, producing a historic cost book value of £625,000. Assuming that the current (replacement) cost of the asset is Lire2.4bn = £1m, do we value our risk at £625,000 or at £1m? Is it necessary to borrow Lire2.4bn or Lire1.5bn to neutralize the lire exposure?

The other main non-monetary asset is inventory, but inventory is not often held for long enough to cause major valuation conflicts. Fixed assets are a much bigger issue.

Monetary items are of course always correctly valued because by definition they are claims — and therefore future cash receipts — at their contractual face values.

The problem boils down to the case where fixed assets are shown in financial statements at historic cost values, where significant inflation has occurred since their acquisition, and where the accounting standard requires their translation at the closing rate. It is the combination of old historic cost values and a new closing rate that does the mischief.

If we take the cash flow view of the Italian hotel and create a hedge at the current value of Lire2.4bn = £1m, we cause a substantial short position in lire in our historic cost accounts. If the lira were then to rise substantially, a large accounting loss would appear in our next annual report. Now assume that we take the accounting view, and restrict our lire borrowing to the historic cost value of Lire1.5bn; assume further that the lira then drops to Lire2700 = £1, and that we suddenly need to sell the hotel for Lire2.4bn. Our hedge was too small to cover the exposure, leaving a substantial currency loss. This is the first serious dilemma between managing the accounting and the cash flow risk.

WHEN DOES POSITION RISK END?

This is the other principal dilemma in the accounting issue.

EXAMPLE

A British company borrows, in June of year 0, DM2m for repayment in June of year 5. It has no D-mark assets. Do we look upon this risk as one which now concerns us only up to our next annual reporting date on 31 March of year 1, or up to the maturity of the loan in June of year 5? Many well managed companies have taken contrary views on this. Yet the two views can imply very different courses of action with dramatically different short- and long-term effects. The controversy brings home the need for a clearly thought out policy on risk management which explicitly adopts one view or the other. Position risk ends therefore at the **perceived** maturity of each risk:

(1) On the **cash** view, when we have many assets or liabilities in a given currency, the total imbalance must be subdivided by maturities. Even properties do not have an infinite life in a given business, and can be allotted realistic lives. The subdivision is usually done by months for the first 12 months, then by quarters, then by years, and finally in two-and-a-half and five-year groupings.

(2) On the **accounting** view all risks mature at the next accounting date or at their earlier contractual due date. On this view too, this shorter period to maturity needs to be subdivided into perhaps monthly maturities for the purpose of management.

Thus position risk has only one risk per currency, subdivided by maturities, whereas trading risk has one per pricing decision.

WHEN DOES POSITION RISK BEGIN?

The practical importance of this question concerns the benchmark exchange rate for measuring gains and losses. In trading risk we distinguished the two stages of conception and birth. Antenatal position risk is in fact rare. Whenever a decision is taken on major investments, loan repayments or capital issues, the company is free to neutralize or control its currency effect at the same time.

In practice, however, position risk is very often perceived for the first time not when a major change is imminent, but on a review of the net balance in each currency. If so, that perception becomes the starting point or birth, and the spot exchange rate at the time becomes the benchmark against which gains, losses and risks need to be measured from then on.

THE BENCHMARK CURRENCY

This is usually the company's reporting currency, but more strictly it is the currency in which each company measures its performance. Many a financial institution whose competition is international and whose market share depends on the ranking of its net worth among its main competitors, uses as its benchmark currency an international currency like the dollar, or a basket of currencies like the Special Drawing Rights (SDR) or European Currency Unit (ECU), or a weighted average of its competitors' currencies.

A similar issue is whether a foreign subsidiary measures its performance in the home currency of the parent, or in its own local currency. This last practice predominates, but subsidiaries of many United States parent companies use the dollar.

DOES POSITION RISK INCLUDE FIXED AND OTHER NON-MONETARY ASSETS? ARE FIXED ASSETS AT RISK AT ALL?

This has caused much debate; but many companies regard fixed assets as part of the exposure, mainly because the purchasing power parity theory at best holds in the very long run, and is subject to wide deviations. Real exchange rates fluctuate widely, as was shown in figure 5.2.1. All assets contribute to risk.

THE EFFECT OF TAXATION

Taxation greatly complicates currency risk management. The total position in currency X is likely to include items on which gains or losses are tax effective (that is taxable or tax deductible as the case may be) and others which are not, such as financial foreign currency liabilities of a British trading company. The currency manager must treat these differently. If corporation tax were 35%, the tax-ineffective item needs to be valued at 100/65 as much as a tax-effective item like a trade receivable. We return to taxation issues below.

THE ACCOUNTING CONVENTIONS

The United Kingdom currency translation standard SSAP 20 became effective on 1 April 1983. It is broadly in harmony with the US SFAS 52. Here is a brief summary of its main features:

In individual companies:

(1) Foreign currency items should be **recorded** at the spot rate on the date of the transaction (the transaction date of a receivable is the date of its invoice).

(2) Non-monetary items will normally stay at the local currency value thus translated and recorded.
(3) At each balance sheet date **monetary** items in foreign currencies are translated into local currency at the closing rate. However, if trading items have been specifically covered forward, they may be translated at the rates of the forward contracts.
(4) Gains and losses, realised or unrealised, on monetary items, should be disclosed in the profit and loss account as part of the result of the year from ordinary activities, subject to the exceptions set out in (5), (6) and (7) below.
(5) If the gains or losses on monetary items stem from transactions which themselves are extraordinary items, they must be disclosed as part of extraordinary items.
(6) Where the monetary items are long-term, it may be imprudent to allow them to create gains or net gains in the profit and loss account if the convertibility of the currency is in doubt.
(7) The important **cover method** rule is not restricted to monetary items; this rule lays down that on certain conditions exchange differences on matching assets and liabilities may be taken to reserve and there netted. This is where the company has borrowed foreign currency to finance or to hedge its foreign equity investments. The exchange differences on borrowings which can be so treated must not exceed the exchange differences on the carrying amount (book value) of the equity investments. The equity investments are defined as the net assets of the investee company plus, in appropriate circumstances, any intragroup borrowings. The foreign currency borrowings, to which the cover method is applied, must not exceed the total cash (including profits) expected to be generated by the investments concerned. The intention of the cover rule is to ensure that the accounting rules do not undo the hedging actions taken by companies.

In consolidated financial statements:

(1) The normal method of translation is the closing rate/net investment method. The investment in a subsidiary is viewed not as a collection of different assets and liabilities of the parent company, but as a single long-term investment. (Exceptionally, the closing rate/net investment method may be replaced by the temporal method, provided that the subsidiary is viewed not as a separate entity but as an extension of the parent company's operations so that the parent currency is also the functional currency of the subsidiary — we shall not describe this unusual case further).
(2) Exchange differences arising from the retranslation of the opening net investment are treated as reserve movements, and therefore not as part of the profit and loss account.
(3) The foreign subsidiary's profit and loss account should be translated at the closing rate or at an average rate for the period. In the latter case the difference

arising from the discrepancy between those two rates gives rise to another movement on the reserves.

(4) The **cover method** applies subject to the same restrictions as for the individual company, but it is worth noting that in SSAP 20 the loans do not have to be liabilities of the same group company which holds the investments, nor do they have to be in the same currency (foreign means non-sterling or non-British).

The main terms of SSAP20 have been summarised to bring out the principal accounting issues which may affect risk management: fixed assets values; the time-horizon (maturities); and what exchange differences affect the ordinary results. The largest issue is to what extent hedging action is undone by the accounting conventions.

THE MANAGEMENT OF POSITION RISK

THE FUNDAMENTAL PROBLEMS

Position risk management calls for some complex policy decisions. Trading risk causes some more painful problems when a company badly needs business; but the issues of position risk management are harder to grasp. Five main issues are singled out and tentative answers suggested to each:

(1) Is our approach aggressive (to make money out of FX rate movements) or defensive (to avoid losses), or where do we stand between the extremes of 100% aggressive and 100% defensive? Possible answer: A very clear-headed corporate policy is to treat zero risk as the norm, subject to deliberate and controlled deviations. One of its many virtues is that it concentrates scarce risk management resources where they can do the most good.

(2) How far are we concerned with cash flow rather than accounting risk? Possible answer: Not without misgivings, we should give the cash flow view priority over the accounting view, without however ignoring effects on matters like gearing and borrowing powers. Stock markets in any case see through unrealistic accounting conventions.

(3) Should we manage risk in each group company or only globally for the group? Possible answer: We should manage currency risk both for the group and at least in each thinly capitalised overseas subsidiary, where a currency loss can result in its technical insolvency. A gain in another country does not cure this.

(4) Must we be on our guard against conflicts between ordinary financial and financing policy (like minimizing the cost of finance) and currency risk management? Possible answer: Care is particularly needed to watch for the effect of currency risk management action on the gearing of the group or of a subsidiary. This could for example result in breaches of loan covenants or borrowing limits. We must also beware of the **interest rate trap**, described below.

(5) How centralised should currency risk management be? To what extent, if any, should it be an exception to decentralized organization structures? Possible answer: The issue of centralization is very complex. Very few international companies leave currency risk to be managed in a wholly decentralized manner, without some group instructions, or without some central dealing services, or without some responsibility on the part of the finance director or his treasurer to watch and control the consolidated position. On the other hand very few groups centralize currency dealing for all their foreign subsidiaries or decisions about the currencies in which units sell, or decisions about the exchange rates used to calculate export selling prices.

Many give guidance and advice, but few practise direct interference. The markets and products of the company have some influence on the way it organizes itself for currency risk. There is no simple and universal rule.

THE INTEREST RATE TRAP

All companies aim to minimize the cost of interest. This can become a trap if a company is tempted to finance say sterling assets with a Swiss franc debt because it costs (say) 4% compared with 10% for sterling. The interest rates would not be in market equilibrium at those rates of 10% and 4% if the market did not expect the Swiss franc to rise against sterling at the rate of 1.10/1.04 per annum. If this market consensus turned out to be correct, then the loss on the rise in the repayment burden would cancel out the saving in interest. However, whereas the interest saving is taxable, under United Kingdom law the loss on the principal attracts no tax relief. After tax, therefore, the company would have been substantially better off with sterling debt. Famous companies have lost their solvency or their independence by ignoring these points.

MANAGING THE EFFECT OF TAXATION AND EXCHANGE CONTROL

Tax laws are generally chaotic in this field. A single cross-border transaction is unlikely to receive equal and opposite treatment in the two countries, and similar tax asymmetries in the treatment of exchange differences exist within countries. If there were a prevailing pattern, it would be that the dice are loaded against taxpayers who transact business across the exchanges.

It has already been noted that tax-effective transactions must be distinguished from tax-ineffective ones in the process of computing the amount of position risk in any one currency. Unfortunately the matter does not end there. We must also carefully explore how each of the market hedging instruments will affect the tax liability in various countries. This is particularly true of the more recent innovations like currency swaps and currency options, but it applies also to the more traditional ones like spot and forward contracts.

A simple example is where the only asset to be hedged by a British company with a marginal tax rate of 35% is a French franc receivable of FF100,000. Any currency gain or loss on this would be reduced by tax to the sterling equivalent of a gain or loss on FF70,000. Whether we should hedge this by borrowing FF70,000 or FF100,000, depends on whether we can establish to the Inland Revenue that the borrowing was undertaken for a trading purpose.

The currency manager's task is of course also complicated by exchange control restrictions which make many currencies inconvertible, and restrict the operation of free money and exchange markets and access to local currency borrowings.

DEVICES FOR MANAGING POSITION RISK

The main devices are netting, spot exchange deals, forward exchange deals, currency futures, currency options, currency swaps and leading and lagging. Netting and leading and lagging are internal measures, the remainder are market instruments.

Netting. Netting is an adjunct to all the other methods. Transactions must be grouped so as to compute a single net position for each maturity, and it is usual to group all maturities in each of the early months, then in the subsequent quarters, years and finally two-and-a-half and five-year periods. If we use such a netting matrix for periodical formal decisions to cover each maturity position nil, 25, 50, 75 or 100 per cent forward, then we are by implication taking an aggressive approach — we imply that we sometimes know better than the forward rate. Currency accounts or rollovers are used to bridge mismatched dates within each netting period.

The spot hedge. This is the device of adding a monetary item to one or the other side of the balance sheet so as to balance the position in a given currency. This will have to be done with an eye on the subdivision by maturities or even separately for each maturity. For the shorter maturities the action would be taken in the eurodeposit market, for long ones in the bond market. A spot currency deal must be combined with it and it is this, not the borrowing or depositing, that creates the hedge.

The forward hedge. The reach of the forward market for many currencies is only six or twelve months, and for many heavily controlled currencies there is no forward market at all. However, where forward cover is available, it is useful and convenient. One variant of it is the short-term interbank swap which combines a forward contract with a simultaneous spot deal.

Combined example. We have a receivable in French francs of FF200,000 due in two months, a loan repayment to make of FF100,000 on that same day and a payable in three months of FF300,000. This constitutes a net FF short position of FF200,000, consisting of a long two month position of FF100,000 and a short three month position of FF300,000. To hedge this we could:

(1) buy FF300,000 for 3 months fixed, place it on deposit, and also borrow

FF100,000 for 2 months fixed, preferably with the same bank with a right of set-off, or

(2) buy and deposit only FF200,000 for 3 months, and arrange a forward swap under which we sell FF100,000 in 2 months and repurchase them 3 months from now, or

(3) buy FF300,000 3 months forward and sell FF100,000 2 months forward.

Currency futures. Currency futures have the same effect as forward contracts, but the market and its mechanics are very different. In a currency futures contract A buys from B the obligation to deliver a standard amount of a non-dollar currency such as British pound sterling at a fixed dollar price on a fixed delivery date. Futures markets are formal open outcry markets in which instruments are traded in standard form, not unlike exchange-traded currency options. The exchange has a clearing house which guarantees the transaction. Each party must make a security deposit (margin) of around 1%. This is maintained at or near its original value by daily cash adjustments representing daily gains and losses from fluctuations in spot rates in the cash market each day. Futures contracts are tradeable in the secondary market until delivery date. This feature and the low dealing costs are an attraction, but the standardized restrictions and the administrative effort of margin transactions explain why most non-financial businesses prefer the forward to the futures market for their currency hedging. The futures market is however useful to a business which is too small to obtain forward dealing limits from banks, and for transactions too small for the wholesale markets.

Currency options. Currency options are now used by many companies as a hedge against position risk. They have been described in 5.2, because their most spectacular use is against antenatal trading risk. Against position risk they are better, but also costlier, than a strict hedge; they carry a chance to make unlimited gains as well as avoid losses. Option derivatives (briefly referred to in 5.2) are often very useful variants. They can be used either to save cost or to modify the risk profile as desired.

Currency swaps. Currency swaps have developed from, and largely superseded, a series of bilateral hedging instruments like reciprocal and parallel loans. Two parties agree to exchange an agreed amount of two currencies spot, and to reverse the deal some years later. For an effective hedge, the front-end spot leg must be neutralized with an equal and opposite spot deal with a bank. Currency swaps must be distinguished from interbank swaps. Interbank swaps are short-term, mainly between banks as principals, and involve no interest payments. Currency swaps on the other hand are usually for two or more years, preponderantly between non-bank principals, and involve mutual interest payments on the currencies that each party owes to the other on maturity. Although the principal parties are typically non-banks, banks often intervene as intermediate principals so as to guarantee the two end-parties' mutual credit risks, and also increasingly as market-makers. Banks are thus arrangers, marriage brokers, guarantors and market-makers in swaps; all this in order to earn front-end fees.

The main caution about swaps is that their tax and accounting effects are open to serious uncertainty because tax laws and accounting standards lag a long way behind the wave of financial innovation which has swept through these markets in the 1980s. Subject to that reservation, the currency swap — with front leg counteracted — can be the perfect hedge against position risk. It suffers neither from the maturity limitations of the forward hedge nor from the potential gearing effect of the spot hedge. Moreover a swap can normally be terminated or neutralized if circumstances change, for example by another swap in the opposite direction.

LEADING AND LAGGING

Leading and lagging is a shortening or lengthening of the period of credit, usually of intragroup credit within a group of companies. It was very popular in the Bretton Woods era when currency risk was essentially one-way. A given currency like the Deutsche mark or sterling was either under or overvalued, so that all participants had a clear idea of the direction, if any, in which an exchange rate might move. An overvalued currency could either stay within its intervention points of around + or −1%, or be substantially devalued. A substantial rise of its parity was not a serious runner.

Leading and lagging shifts the **group** exposure towards the perceived stronger currency. If we instruct our Spanish subsidiary to pay the Dutch subsidiary faster, or to give it longer credit, we shift the group position away from the peseta and towards the guilder. Under the Bretton Woods system this was relatively riskless, restricted only by exchange control constraints on trade credit. Under a floating regime however, forward rates are by definition in market equilibrium; it is not nearly so easy to be confident about the direction, if any, in which the future spot rate will deviate from the present forward rate.

Leading and lagging does however affect the liquidity of each subsidiary; with the modern tendency to monitor the cash flow performance of managers, leading and lagging has come to be seen as central interference with and demotivation of decentralized management responsibilities. For all these reasons there has been a marked decline in its use as a currency risk management device.

REVIEW OF ISSUES IN THE MANAGEMENT OF POSITION RISK

Every company needs to define what it means by position risk and its aims in managing it. Position risk needs to be measured for each currency and managed for each maturity, normally both in the parent currency and in each overseas subsidiary, in accordance with clearly defined objectives. The main types of objective are (a) aggressive: to optimize the effect of exchange rate movements, (b) defensive: to avoid losing money, and (c) smoothing: to keep the effect even over the years.

PERFORMANCE MEASUREMENT AND THE TIMING PROBLEM

It is difficult to find a company which is satisfied with its monitoring of currency risk management performance. Some excellent theoretical models exist which take each risk, and measure performance against the benchmark of an available alternative course of action, using both hindsight comparison and a measure of the risk taken (Cooper and Franks, *Midland Corporate Finance Journal*, Vol 5 No 2, summer 1987). One of the principal difficulties is that it is seldom practicable to evaluate particular decisions against their **direct** effect on the wealth of the shareholders. Most decisions in business are directed towards the attainment of **intermediate** corporate objectives. These are often commercial, marketing or organizational, and have priority in the pursuit of maximizing shareholder wealth. Currency risk management decisions tend to be lower level decisions in such companies, and subordinate to these intermediate objectives. Examples can be the motivation of decentralized managers, or the need to avoid distracting top managers from their strategic problems and opportunities.

In trading risk there is the mechanical difficulty of capturing in the system the rate used in the pricing decision, and to compare the dealing rate with that pricing rate. Where companies sell from price lists, currency movements introduce an often mystifying volatility into gross margins on sales.

In position risk the hardest decision tends to be the **timing** of hedging action. Between our first perception of a risk and each maturity (perhaps only a few days away) there may well be thousands of possible dealing rates even with a single bank. One of those will with hindsight turn out to have been the best rate at which we could have done the deal, but we cannot realistically expect to achieve that. So what is the benchmark rate that we should be content to achieve, that we can ascertain without unreasonable effort, and against which we can therefore sensibly monitor performance?

Some use the 'hedge everything' standard, others 'hedge nothing'. The first of these is the forward rate to maturity available at the time of our review of the risk, the other is the spot rate at which we could in fact deal at maturity. There are a multitude of different situations, but the following illustration serves as an example of a long-term hedging problem. Shorter-term risks present the same kind of problem, but within a shorter time-frame.

EXAMPLE

A dollar-based company noticed in June 1978 when the dollar/sterling spot rate was $1.82 = £1 that it had a long-term surplus of sterling assets over liabilities amounting to £50m. It looked upon its British subsidiary as an island, a single net asset with an arbitrary life (maturity) of 25 years. Corporate policy was risk averse, and required the risk to be hedged by raising long-term sterling debt. But the risk had been there unnoticed for some years. Figure 5.3.1 shows the monthly average $/£ exchange rates over the period since currencies began to float (source: Datastream).

Source: *Datastream.*

Figure 5.3.1 US dollars OL to £1 sterling – exchange rate from 1/1/73 to 9/3/90 monthly

In June 1978 it was open to the company to realise $72.8m by doing an instant spot deal at the rate of $1.82. Had it noticed the sterling mismatch in March 1975 at $2.42, it could then have sold sterling spot and realised $96.8 million. In January 1981 it would again have been able to realise $96 million at the rate of $2.40, but this could not have been predicted in June 1978:

	Summary of possible outcomes, with benefit of hindsight	
Month	spot rate per £1	Cash result $ million
March 1975	$2.42	96.8
June 1978	$1.82	72.8
January 1981	$2.40	96.0

Without the benefit of hindsight, what was the right thing to do in June 1978? Broadly, there seem to be two options:

(1) Take a doctrinal stand that every risk must be hedged instantly when perceived. In this case we immediately do a spot deal at $1.82, realise $91m and borrow this for a short period from the banks whilst mounting our eurosterling bond issue. There is no monitoring to do, except perhaps an inquest on how we failed to recognize the risk for some years.

(2) Identify the dilemma as an exception to normal company disciplines. Top managers might think it unwise to take a blind doctrinal approach after negligently ignoring the exposure for some years. This £50m asset was regarded as semi-permanent. The company could and should take a long-term perspective.

The question was whether a rise of sterling above $1.82 was on the cards at **some** time in the future. If with some expert advice they conclude that there are no good grounds for expecting that rise in sterling, then they should of course deal spot at $1.82. That decision is justifiable as long as it was not taken blindly. On the other hand if they reach the belief that sterling will at some time rise above $1.82 again, and assuming that the worst case loss would not be catastrophic, then they might look at alternative decisions like the following:

(1) to sell £25m spot for dollars now, and the remaining £25m when sterling reaches $2.00 (a 10% rise) or $1.73 (stop-loss for a 5% fall),

(2) to sell the entire £50m if sterling should either rise to $2.00 or fall to $1.73.

If the worst loss is of catastrophic size, then the position must be closed out now (sold for dollars) to the extent needed to reduce the worst loss to tolerable proportions.

In any case, as long as any part of the position is left open, the company should hold regular monthly reviews of the outlook for the dollar-sterling rate of exchange. There should be no blind policy of keeping it open.

The example illustrates how hazardous the timing problem is and why many companies hedge instantly rather than wait and watch for good timing. The latter can easily come to look like gambling. Yet the stockholders would not be entirely unfair if they were critical of a management which locks itself into an outcome of $91m after missing the opportunity to realize $121m. It takes strong nerves to manage this type of situation.

CORPORATE POLICY ISSUES REVIEWED

Finally, here is a brief checklist of topics to be addressed in any corporate policy framework.

(1) Definitions of the various risks.
(2) Is currency risk seen in accounting or cash flow terms?
(3) The benchmark currency for measuring gains and losses.
(4) To what extent is currency risk to be managed centrally for the group? Is currency risk an exception to normal decentralization principles?
(5) To what extent is dealing to be centralized?
(6) Is risk to be managed also for each overseas subsidiary, or just globally for the whole group?
(7) How defensive or aggressive is our policy?
(8) What matters have to be referred and reported to top management or the board? What are the authority levels?
(9) Who takes commercial decisions, like currency of sale or purchase and the exchange rates to be used in pricing?
(10) Are such decisions to be managed by teams combining commercial and exchange market skills? How would such teams be formed, and responsibilities allocated?
(11) Are any of these matters to be differently handled in respect of some or all overseas subsidiaries?
(12) In corporate financial policy, how is currency risk related to other financial management issues like funding, debt capacity and borrowing limits?
(13) How will currency issues be taken into account in strategic marketing and planning?
(14) How do currency issues affect capital investment criteria?
(15) What exchange rates (such as spot or forward) will be used in budgets and performance reporting? In performance monitoring against budget, how will currency movements be treated: will managers of overseas subsidiaries be monitored in local currency terms?

The mere asking of these questions may result in better handling of this important topic.

ALFRED KENYON

Vindale Ltd

5.4
Forecasting

It is the business of business, so to speak, to take risks. Companies of whatever size exist to bring together the various resources necessary to produce and distribute goods and services. However rarely, if ever, is this process achieved instantaneously on a once-and-for-all basis. A crucial feature of business activity is that it takes place over time. This is where risk enters the equation: for business activity to be successful, entrepreneurs and managers must tackle the problem that over a period of time all the relevant operational criteria may change. Of course some aspects of the business environment may change much more slowly and less radically than others, but conceptually the problem remains the same.

Most businesses are now subject to foreign exchange risk, whether directly or indirectly, and therefore must tackle it in the appropriate way if continuing business success is to be achieved. This chapter provides an overview as to the problem of foreign exchange risk, and thus how it can be managed. First, a brief discussion of the recent changes in the business environment and the reasons for exchange rate volatility indicate the nature and scope of the problem.

Secondly, some notes on the approach to business forecasting highlight the conceptual methodology and the limitations of any kind of forecasting. The techniques of foreign exchange forecasts are analysed, thirdly, to give the businessman some insights into what the 'experts' on forecasting exchange rates actually do. Finally, a discussion of some current, practical issues in foreign exchange is offered. Clearly in a short chapter full justice cannot be done to such a vast subject. Nevertheless the important points will be covered and will provide a framework within which business can assess and use foreign exchange forecasts effectively.

THE NATURE OF THE PROBLEM

Foreign exchange can be one of the biggest risks faced by business. While exchange rates between currencies were fixed in the 1950s and 1960s it was, more or less, the case that a business making the right decisions about input sourcing, labour relations, marketing strategy, plant investment, pricing policy and all the other aspects of corporate activity could rely on profits at the end of the day. Nowadays profits can easily be turned into losses by movements in exchange rates even if all the other aspects of a firm's activities are correct. An important distinction in this context is the controllability of risk. All the factors mentioned above are, in large part, ones which an individual firm has discretion over. Foreign exchange risk is essentially outside the control of one firm as, in general, its activities will be only an infinitesimally small part of the total array of influences on the foreign exchange markets and the traded rates of exchange.

THE PERVASIVENESS OF FOREIGN EXCHANGE RISK

Not only is foreign exchange risk a fact of life which firms must face, it also crucially influences most aspects of a firm's activities. The most direct effect of exchange rate fluctuations is felt on costs and revenues from existing overseas operations but indirect effects are also important in:

(1) marketing strategy between, on the one hand, domestic and foreign markets and, on the other, between different foreign markets;
(2) competition from foreign firms in the domestic market;
(3) long-term product and corporate diversification;
(4) long-term investment policy.

INTERNATIONAL LINKAGES

It might be tempting for many firms, faced with something which is uncontrollable and all-pervasive, to seek to avoid all activity involving foreign exchange risk. Although at the margin this may be possible, the trends in the world economy over the last thirty years suggest that, for most companies, it is impracticable. Over this period the growth of world trade has consistently outstripped the growth of world output, suggesting that trade links between countries have grown substantially.

If it is accepted that this risk is outside the control of each firm and that its effects can reach almost all aspects of corporate activity, then managing foreign exchange risk becomes essential and, within foreign exchange management, some form of forecasting becomes inevitable.

THE SCOPE OF THE PROBLEM

The Bretton Woods system of fixed exchange rates gradually broke down in the early 1970s as it became clear that the underlying conditions which had contributed to its success in the two previous decades no longer held. First, confidence in the US dollar as the fulcrum of the system, with a fixed parity against gold, declined following the inflationary impact of the Vietnam war. Second, a tendency towards higher inflation in most advanced economies, which had begun to emerge in the late 1960s but became more serious in the 1970s, allowed a wider divergence of inflation rates between countries. In many cases the national economic policies required to maintain a fixed external currency value became too onerous to be politically acceptable.

The Bretton Woods system was patched up in 1971 with a devaluation of the dollar against gold, but in 1972 even the new Smithsonian parities became inappropriate. Gradually a system of generalized floating exchange rates became established. It is important to remember, however, that, even today, the majority of the world's currencies are not totally free to float. A large number of (more or less) formal exchange rate arrangements still exist, taking a variety of forms.

(1) National authorities attempt to influence the value of their exchange rate through ad hoc intervention in the foreign exchange markets.
(2) Many currencies (around forty) maintain a fixed parity with another currency, mainly the US dollar.
(3) Some groups of currencies have formed new exchange rate arrangements between themselves which limit fluctuations. The Exchange Rate Mechanism of the European Monetary System (EMS) is the best known currency bloc.
(4) A large number of countries target the value of their currency against a currency basket, usually a weighted average of the currencies most important to the country from an international trade viewpoint.

Nevertheless, most major currencies do float against each other and the degree of potential movement in cross rates between currencies is large.

EXCHANGE RATE VOLATILITY

Prior to the introduction of flexible exchange rates, Professor Milton Friedman argued (in his Essays in Positive Economics):

> The ultimate objective is a world in which exchange rates, while free to vary, are in fact highly stable. Instability of exchange rates is a symptom of instability in the underlying economic structure.

Friedman went on to argue that a floating exchange rate regime would encourage overall stability of economies and exchange rates. The experience of the 1970s and 1980s shows that the underlying economic structure has not been consistent with stability in foreign exchange markets and that floating currencies have provided little, if any, incentive to correct imbalances in the underlying factors. Moreover, the scale of observed fluctuations has been considerably greater than even the most pessimistic opponents of a floating exchange rate regime had anticipated.

Table 5.4.1: Exchange rate volatility

	Range (high-low)		Annual average	
	$:£ (cents)	DM:$ (pfennings)	$:£	DM:$
1970	2.78	21.06	2.40	3.65
1975	41.62	39.61	2.22	2.46
1980	31.50	31.10	2.33	1.82
1985	43.60	86.50	1.30	2.94
1986	18.50	54.75	1.47	2.17
1987	40.75	35.65	1.64	1.80
1988	23.80	33.40	1.78	1.76
1989	30.80	34.30	1.64	1.88

Source: Fixpoint Database.

Table 5.4.1 shows the degree of fluctuation for two major cross rates since 1970. Compared to virtually no movement under the Bretton Woods system (a small fluctuation band around the central parity was, in fact, allowed), the scale of exchange rate volatility has been enormous. For the sterling:dollar cross rate the range (the difference, in currency units, between the high and the low values) in one year has been as high as 33.5% of the year's average, and 35.91% for the deutschmark:dollar exchange rate. The table also shows that on average there has been no tendency for the degree of volatility to fall; indeed, if anything, it is on an upward trend. An analysis of most major currency cross rates over the period would show broadly similar results.

THE WORLD ECONOMIC STRUCTURE

Volatility of exchange rates on the scale observed in the last fifteen years or so owes much to the changes in the world economic structure over the period. Clearly, any analysis of exchange rates and attempts to forecast them must include an evaluation of the key trends in the world economy. The following points are not exhaustive but they do cover the main aspects of the international economy.

(1) For most of the post-war period the United States has been a net exporter of capital. From the early 1980s, the role of the United States, in this respect, changed dramatically. Economic expansion, involving a burgeoning Federal government budget deficit and huge current account shortfalls, had to be financed. Hence the eighties role of the United States as a net capital importer.

(2) During the 1970s the oil market emerged as a major influence on the world economy and exchange rates. The sharp oil price rises of 1973/74 and 1979/80 and subsequent nominal and real price falls of 1984/86 resulted in historically

unprecedented reallocations of resources. The most visible changes were the movements in current account positions between oil producers and oil consumers. From a rough global balance on current account in 1970, the industrial countries' current deficit totalled $63bn in 1980 while the oil-exporting countries' surplus had reached $103.4bn. The current account deficit of the non-oil developing countries amounted to $94.5bn in 1981. By 1989, both the Organization of Petroleum Exporting Countries and the non-oil developing countries were close to balance on current account while the Organisation for Economic Co-operation and Development group were in deficit to the tune of $85bn.

(3) The early 1980s witnessed the beginning of the so-called Third World debt crisis. For many of the countries involved this was a direct result of the willingness of the commercial banks, during the 1970s, to lend on the security of expected oil revenues. Non-oil developing countries suffered from a diminishing ability to service existing debts, both on the revenue side — via declining markets and falling prices for their own commodity exports — and on the payments side from the high value of the dollar (in which a large proportion of debt was denominated) and rising interest rates. By the end of the decade, developing country debt totalled, approximately, £1280bn compared with $633bn in 1980.

(4) Prompted by global financial imbalance — initially the need to recycle the massive Organization of Petroleum Exporting Countries surpluses — a plethora of new financial instruments emerged. The 1970s saw the development of the syndicated loan market and increasing usage of the eurodollar and eurobond markets. In addition, exchange rate fluctuations necessitated the development of new means to insure against currency risk. During the 1980s deregulation of financial centres followed in the wake of the new instruments and the use of computerized trading systems increased substantially.

(5) Exacerbated by the world recession of 1980/83, protectionism has again come to prominence as technological change has contributed to shifts in international comparative advantage and international trade patterns have altered.

In view of these dramatic changes in the world's economic structure, a high degree of exchange rate volatility is understandable. Further, recent theoretical economics has shown that, under certain conditions, the foreign exchange markets would be expected to overshoot the equilibrium values of currencies consistently, even without underlying structural changes.

A common reaction to the dramatic changes in world economic structure and the related wild fluctuations in exchange rates is that it is impossible to forecast exchange rates. In fact, in a business context, as discussed above, some form of forecasting is inevitable and the scale of the problem merely emphasises the importance of adopting the appropriate method. The next two sections concentrate on forecasting methods, both at the broad level and with specific reference to foreign exchange. It will become clear that there are methods and techniques which have proven of value in a business context.

THE ELEMENTS OF BUSINESS FORECASTING

Thomas Robert Malthus (1766 to 1834) was born in Surrey, ordained in 1797 and, as a curate, anonymously published (in 1798) his Essay on the Principle of Population as it affects the Future Improvement of Society. Malthus' forecasts of gradual impoverishment (as a result of a predicted geometric increase in population compared with a predicted arithmetic decrease in food supplies) can arguably provide a claim that he was the first systematic business forecaster. It is clear, however, that the letters of his name do summarise the principal issues that confront the business forecaster:

Methods, models and motivation
Assumptions, accuracy
Lags, lack of data
Trends, turning points
Horizons, hypotheses
Uncertainty
Scenarios

It is useful to consider each of the main points in turn.

METHODS, MODELS AND MOTIVATION

All forecasters of the business environment employ a variety of methods and models in generating their forecasts. The principal methods of forecasting that are available include the following.

(1) Unsystematic judgment. Guessing the future values of relevant variables without any systematic attempt to ensure that the various independent guesses betray much in the way of logical consistency. It is a method favoured by certain groups in the City, the press and senior management. It has to be acknowledged that the gut feelings of the experienced can produce remarkably successful forecasts. The obvious problem with this approach is that it is not really susceptible to rigorous ex-post analysis. When the predictions are correct it is never really clear why; and when they are incorrect it is difficult to ascertain why not.

(2) Systematic judgment. Forecasts based upon this approach are still fundamentally judgmental, but the individual forecasts are constrained to satisfy:
(a) logical interrelationships; and
(b) the better known behavioural relationships between important variables.
This is a method much favoured by the better press commentators, and used (to a greater or lesser extent) by all professional business forecasters.

(3) Econometric forecasts. The application of systematic methods of statistical inference to the logical propositions of economic theory. It should be noted that a good econometric equation will only produce successful forecasts if the so-called independent variables are themselves forecast accurately. Thus if we

establish a very strong relationship between exchange rate movements and, say, the relative growth in real money supply, our forecasts of the exchange rate will depend critically on our forecasts of nominal money supply and prices.

(4) Statistical time series analysis, that is, the attempt to forecast the future behaviour of a variable on the basis of nothing but its past behaviour. Everyone has used a rough and ready form of time series analysis in terms of applying a simple extrapolation of previous trends in, say, sales. Modern mathematical time series analysis can provide a very strong framework for short-term forecasting of some variables.

All available forecasts of the likely development of exchange rates use one or the other (or, more usually, a combination) of the approaches described above. A model of an exchange rate is an attempt to use the methods outlined above (principally, although not exclusively, the econometric approach) to produce a system of behavioural relationships (such that the value of sterling depends upon other variables such as interest rates or inflation) that can be used to mimic the behaviour of the actual exchange rate and, on the basis of given assumptions, produce forecasts.

It is widely recognized that various alternative methods and models of business exchange rate forecasting are available. It is often forgotten that the choice of the appropriate method or model depends upon the motivation for requiring a forecast. A business forecast can be compared with a map. A rough sketch map may well be sufficient to direct a friend to a favourite bar or restaurant. A much more detailed map is required for a hill-walking expedition in Snowdonia. But nobody would demand a map of London at a scale of 1:1! The very usefulness of a map is the means whereby it can wipe away extraneous detail so as to achieve the object at hand. The usefulness of the map cannot be judged independently of the objectives that led to its acquisition. The same is true of business forecasts.

ASSUMPTIONS AND ACCURACY

The role of assumptions in generating business forecasts is often as, or more, important than the actual models and methods employed. First, it is important to distinguish between forecasts and assumptions. For example, forecasts of Gross Domestic Product, the oil price, interest rates and the current account (amongst other things) become assumptions for an exchange rate forecast. Second, the importance of any assumption will differ depending upon the forecast which it underlies. For example, any forecast for the sterling exchange rate would include an assumption about the oil market. If, in 1984, a sterling forecast did not have an assumption to the effect that oil prices would fall in 1985 the sterling forecast made for that time would probably have been wrong (although not necessarily so). On the other hand, a forecast for the deutschmark, with exactly the same oil market forecast, could well have still been fairly accurate — as the price of oil, although important to German economic performance, does not have the direct impact on the deutschmark that it does on sterling.

All forecasters are concerned with the accuracy of their forecasts, but it is not generally appreciated that a large variety of measures of accuracy are available and, moreover, in a business context accuracy will typically need to be judged in terms of the objectives of utilising the forecast. A couple of examples will serve to highlight the potential ambiguities and conflicts in judging accuracy. Consider figure 5.4.1.

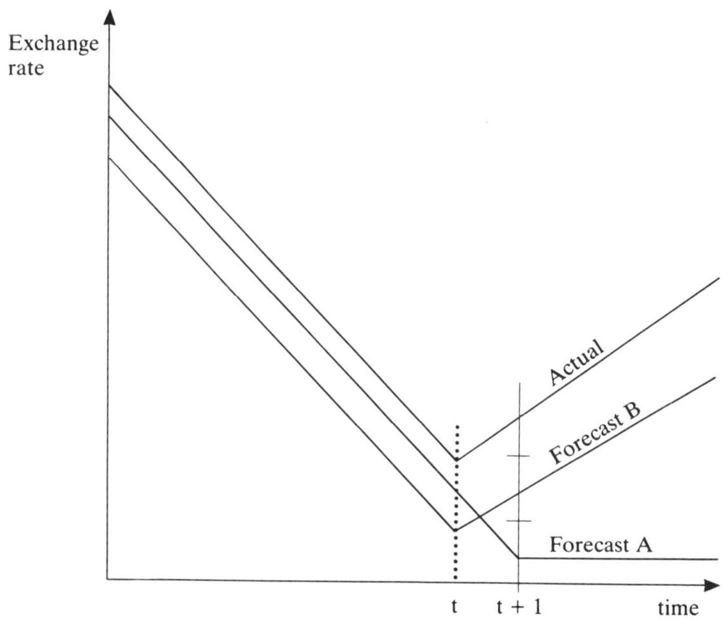

Figure 5.4.1

Which is the better forecast, A or B? Until time t, forecast A tracks the actual substantially better than forecast B and, on many conventional measures of forecast accuracy, would be judged clearly superior to forecast B. It is evident, however, that in a large number of real business contexts forecast B would be more useful because it accurately picks up the turning point in the exchange rate. Notice that even at time t+1 almost any measure of forecast accuracy would still rank forecast A above forecast B, even though, in business planning terms, forecast B would now be indisputably more useful. Table 5.4.2 provides a numerical example of a similar case.

Table 5.4.2: Forecasts of exchange rates

$:£ exchange rate	Actual	Forecast A	Forecast B
September	1.47	—	—
December	1.44	1.33	1.49

Which is the better forecast, A or B? On almost all statistical criteria, forecast B wins — its divergence from the actual is only 5 cents compared with 11 cents for forecast A. It should be noticed, however, that a corporate treasurer who took a hedge or no hedge decision in September 1986 would (other things being equal) have preferred to make the decision on the basis of forecast A (which suggested a depreciation of sterling) compared with forecast B (indicating an appreciation of sterling).

Perfectly accurate forecasting of the business environment is an impossibility, but useful forecasts can provide a guide to both risks and opportunities.

LAGS, LACK OF DATA

Most economic relationships are subject to time-lags. Thus, for example, so-called monetarists have been prone to assert that there exists an eighteen-month to two-year lag between control of the money supply and diminution of the rate of inflation. Attempts to identify the lags can be crucial in a practical business forecasting context: 'The economists are generally right in their predictions, but generally a good deal out in their dates' (Sidney Webb). Similarly, a lack of adequate data leads to the situation in which the first task of the business forecaster is, quite literally, to forecast the present and recent past. The extent to which crucial data (for example, money supply, consumer spending, balance of payments) are subject to major revision is not generally appreciated. Moreover, in the United Kingdom the discrepancy between the output, income and expenditure estimates of gross domestic product has become very large, making for even more ambiguity in setting a starting point for any forecast. The practical business forecaster is attempting to forecast what will actually happen rather than what is implied by official statistics (which will be subsequently revised), and this leads to the necessity for systematic reconciliation of the official data.

TRENDS AND TURNING POINTS

In a large variety of contexts, business forecasts are critically dependent on a correct assessment of what actually constitutes a trend. A large part of the art of forecasting revolves around distinguishing between the temporary and the permanent in the business environment. A former chief economic adviser to the government has put it succinctly:

> A trend is a trend is a trend
> But the question is, will it bend?
> Will it alter its course
> Through some unforeseen force
> And come to a premature end?

Alec Cairncross ('Economic Forecasting', *Economic Journal*, December 1969).

The assessment of trends and turning points is particularly important when the analyst attempts to move outside the conventional economic sphere of analysis and tries to forecast changing political behaviour.

HYPOTHESES AND HORIZONS

All systematic business forecasts are based upon hypotheses about the relationship between the relevant variables. As with trends and turning points it is necessary to monitor the chosen hypotheses so that they can be rejected if they do not fit changing circumstances. Thus, for example, it was historically possible to hypothesize that individuals saved a more or less fixed fraction of their personal disposable income. Indeed, for almost all developed economies the hypothesis of a constant saving rate seemed to work very well over long periods of time. The experience of the 1970s, when savings rates increased dramatically, forced the rejection (or modification) of the hypothesis.

The explicit choice of time horizon for a business forecast is often crucial in terms of:

(1) the methods to be employed — for example, time series analysis is typically much more appropriate for short-run forecasts;
(2) the sensitivity of the forecasts to the assumptions.

UNCERTAINTY

Uncertainty lies at the heart of systematic business forecasting. At a formal level, the analyst uses statistical methods that provide measures of confidence in the forecasting relationships being employed. Thus, for example, a typical econometric relationship relating, say, the deutschmark or dollar exchange rate to a variety of other so-called independent variables would typically be characterised by:

(1) a measure indicating the proportion of the variance in DM:$ cross rate that is explained by the independent variables;
(2) measures that indicate the degree of significance attached to each of the independent variables, for example whether a particular variable really is part of the explanation of the level of the DM:$ cross rate;
(3) confidence intervals on the forecasts produced by the econometric model.

At a less formal level, a practical approach to business forecasting is invariably based on an initial concentration on the areas of certainty or near certainty, because this approach necessarily highlights the areas of strategic uncertainty and can therefore provide a checklist of warning signals as to the outcome that is developing.

SCENARIOS

The nature of the uncertainties of the early 1980s produced an increased demand for alternative scenarios of the future as opposed to point forecasts. Thus, companies are increasingly using a most likely scenario, but also undertaking contingency planning on the basis of alternative sets of assumptions. Scenario techniques can be very useful in defining the likely boundaries of the future, but if employed in an undisciplined fashion they can degenerate into a forecast that anything can happen.

THE TECHNIQUES OF FOREIGN EXCHANGE FORECASTING

INTRODUCTION

The preceding two sections of this chapter have outlined the changing structure of the world economic environment and the conceptual aspects of forecasting. Both sections are relevant to a wide variety of problems (including interest rates, commodities and market growth) but the examples chosen have been from the foreign exchange field — one of the most important uncontrollable elements in business activity. This section describes some of the principal methods of exchange rate forecasting. The guide cannot be comprehensive in a short chapter but the main features of each technique are outlined, together with notes concerning their validity or effectiveness. Although the techniques are discussed individually, it should be emphasized that the more sophisticated forecasters employ a combination of them to generate their forecasts. In addition, the description is presented in a discursive or qualitative manner as a technical or algebraic approach is inappropriate in an introductory chapter. The reader should be aware, however, that in applying the techniques serious forecasters develop highly complex and detailed mathematical expressions to utilize the underlying ideas.

RELATIVE INFLATION

The use of relative inflation rates as a tool for forecasting currency movements is based upon the so-called purchasing power parity (PPP) approach to exchange rate determination. The purchasing power parity approach can be developed formally in various ways but the essential feature is the idea that the exchange rate between any pair of currencies will move so as to equate the purchasing power of units of the currencies in two countries. Thus, if one country experiences a higher inflation rate than another, the purchasing power parity theory predicts that the currency of the first country will depreciate on the foreign exchange markets. Almost all serious approaches to medium — and long-term forecasting of exchange rates are based (at least in part) on some variant of a purchasing power parity approach.

A large body of empirical evidence has been found which lends significant support to the purchasing power parity theory. One problem, however, is that empirical research has shown the theory to be of use mainly in longer-term exchange rate forecasting. For example, a study by H.J. Gailliot in 1970 (see *Journal of Money, Credit and Banking*) showed that if the major currency cross rate from 1902/04 are extrapolated forward on the basis of relative inflation rates alone, by the late 1960s (following two world wars, the Great Depression and the disappearance of the Reichsmark) the ratio of actual exchange rates to that implied by the theory is sufficiently close to unity for Gailliot to conclude that the theory receives significant support from the empirical evidence. For short periods, however, exchange rates can, and often do, move in a direction contrary to that suggested by the theory — and this tendency was particularly noticeable in the case of some of the principal currencies in the course of the 1980s.

BALANCE OF PAYMENTS

For much of the post-war period the state of a country's balance of payments on current account has been seen as an important determinant of the value of the country's currency on the foreign exchange markets. The theory underlying this proposition is a straightforward extension of basic Keynesian macroeconomic analysis. In essence, the theory suggests that a country with a balance of payments deficit (surplus) will experience an exchange rate depreciation (appreciation) to restore equilibrium on the balance of payments.

There are two main difficulties with the balance of payments as a foreign exchange forecasting tool, however.

(1) In the 1970s the theoretical basis of the method was shown to be seriously deficient.
(2) Statistics on the balance of payments for all countries are notoriously unreliable. The extent of data revisions over even long periods of time in practice reduce the reliability of exchange rate forecasts based on the balance of payments trends.

Nevertheless, various research results have indicated that even in the 1970s the balance of payments had many merits as a forecasting tool. In particular, major changes in the medium-term trends of exchange rate movements have often been well explained by changes in countries' balance of payments positions.

INTEREST RATES

Interest rates clearly have a large influence on exchange rate movements, particularly in the relatively short term. A rise in interest rates in one country, while others' remain unchanged, induces capital inflows which cause the currency to appreciate, and vice versa. However although this approach appears simple, practical attempts to build interest rate models for exchange rate forecasting have encountered many difficulties.

(1) Many of the difficulties in the 1970s stemmed from the theoretical debates between, broadly, the Keynesian and monetarist schools of economic theory.
(2) The causality of the simple relationship described above is not always observed in practice. In the 1970s the trends in exchange rates often determined movements in interest rates, frequently because of official policies towards exchange rates by national governments.

The authors' research into interest rate relationships has suggested some useful forecasting models. On a technical level, the research indicates that the rate of change of interest rate differentials is well correlated with future exchange rate movements. At the practical level, however, interest rates remain an elusive tool for currency forecasting and constant awareness and monitoring of causality and forecast time horizons is essential.

MONEY SUPPLY

In the 1970s the use of relative money supply movements enjoyed some popularity as a method of forecasting exchange rates. As part of the so-called monetarist revolution, the exchange rate can be seen as being determined exclusively by the supply and demand for money. Thus a monetary expansion in one country will lead to a proportionate depreciation of the currency. While the theoretical basis of the monetarist approach has many attractions, its usefulness as a forecasting device is relatively limited. Most importantly, the evidence suggests that the theory is effective only in the very long run, and that it adds little to insights from the purchasing power parity theory.

TECHNICAL ANALYSIS

Interest in the technical or chartist approach to short-run exchange rate forecasting grew in the course of the 1980s. This approach seeks to forecast on the basis of patterns in the time series of the exchange rate alone, with no explanatory variables.

Although the logical basis for this approach seems somewhat shaky (particularly when it is appreciated that exchange rates, unlike stock market prices, do not only represent the demand for an asset), it is often suggested that the track record of technical analysts is sufficient to justify the method. This claim is difficult to test since the technical forecasters rarely produce unambiguous forecasts of the exchange rate at some clearly defined future date, instead preferring vague conditional statements along the lines of strong potential for upside movement in the near-term. The authors have, however, conducted a partial investigation of the track record of technical forecasters and two major conclusions emerge. First, a small number of technical analysts do appear to have a remarkable record for short-run foreign exchange forecasting. Secondly, although the method is described as technical it is easy to demonstrate a high frequency of occasions on which technical analysts generate totally opposite conclusions on the basis of exactly the same historic exchange rate data. Recent research by the Bank of England (in Allen, H. and Taylor, M.P., '*Charts, Noise and Fundamentals: A Study of the London Foreign Exchange Market*', Centre for Economic Policy Research Discussion Paper, No. 341) has come to similar conclusions — although it did unearth one technical practitioner who had a remarkable forecasting record. Moreover, the survey undertaken by the Bank in the London market (still the world's most important foreign exchange market) revealed that a majority of participants considered both technical and fundamental analysis in coming to a view on the likely direction of exchange rate movements. The evidence still suggests that it seems sensible to remain neutral about the method while recognizing the relative success of some practitioners.

MARKET FACTORS

The advent of floating exchange rates in the 1970s led to an increasing awareness of market factors in exchange rate forecasting, particularly in the short run. It is almost true to say that at a point in time in a normal trading day the foreign exchange markets can determine any exchange rate they like. Certainly anyone with knowledge of how foreign exchange dealing rooms work will know the potential for instability in the markets, and sharp swings in exchange rates have often been observed in practice. Dealers react almost instantaneously to news of economic and political events whether real or imaginary (rumours). Moreover, these reactions can often be prolonged and form trends in exchange rate movements lasting, in extreme cases, over several months. Clearly a vital element in exchange rate forecasting in the 1990s is an understanding and awareness of foreign exchange market mechanics and market factors.

For the forecaster there are few rules of thumb, let alone formal models, to aid this understanding. Clearly a high level of information is required and good contacts with market participants but, ultimately, the forecaster's judgment and experience in assessing market confidence plays an important role in the production of forecasts. The recipient of forecasts must be aware of this element, of course, and constantly question the forecaster's objectivity and independence from bias.

CURRENT FOREIGN EXCHANGE ISSUES

INTRODUCTION

The last three sections of this chapter have thrown some light on the techniques of business forecasting in general, and foreign exchange forecasting in particular. It is clear, however, that the use of foreign exchange forecasts as a means of assessing and counteracting foreign exchange risk requires a knowledge of the overall world economic environment, the conceptual approaches to forecasting and the techniques applied to generate forecasts per se. A final ingredient is also essential — a knowledge of the key foreign exchange issues relevant to business activity today. There are, of course, many issues that are relevant and they can stem from the institutional, legal or historical spheres, as well as from the more definably economic sphere. Many of these issues are covered in other chapters, but the rest of this chapter is devoted to an analysis of the key, current issues which are crucial to regular foreign exchange management and planning in a business context.

THE UNITED STATES DOLLAR

Despite the decline in the importance of the US dollar as the fulcrum currency of the world economy since the breakdown of the Bretton Woods fixed exchange rate system, it still has a dominant role. Around 80% of reserves held around the world are still in the form of dollar assets, and the bulk of international trade is still carried out in dollar terms. Moreover, the United States economy remains the largest in the world and it has a major impact on the economies of the other industrial countries and the Third World. Although the external sector is still only a small part of the United States economy it represents the most important market for many countries' exports. Clearly, therefore, the movements of the dollar on the foreign exchange markets form one of the most important issues in exchange rate analysis.

From the early 1980s until the autumn of 1985, the dollar was hugely over-valued against most currencies. This was apparent on the basis of any kind of purchasing power parity analysis as outlined above — and travellers between the United States and Europe could experience directly the over-valuation in terms of the relative cheapness of United States goods. At the end of 1984, most analysis suggested that an appropriate (based on relative competitiveness) rate for the US dollar was about DM1.80:$ compared to the DM3.10 rate then ruling. Following the Plaza Agreement of September 1985, concerted action by the principal central banks of the world led to a sustained decline of the dollar towards more rational levels — and this decline accelerated at the time of the global stock market crash in October 1987.

In view of the dollar's importance, it is useful to assess why the overvaluation persisted for so long. This is especially the case since the United States posted a deficit on current account of $106bn in 1984 after a deficit of $47bn in 1983. To put the current account deficit in perspective, the previous record deficit was little more than $15bn. Normally, this would have led to expectations of a weaker currency rather than a stronger one but, for the dollar, the reverse occurred. Not until the autumn of 1985 (with the help of the monetary authorities of the major industrial economies agreeing to joint intervention in foreign exchange markets in order to lessen the value of the dollar) did the dollar weaken in any sustained way.

Since 1985 the dollar has performed more in line with economic theory, with a serious current account deficit being associated with a weakening currency. Nevertheless, the period of overvaluation is still worthy of further analysis. At its simplest, capital inflows to the United States during this period were more than sufficient to offset the current account deficit. This implied that the demand for dollars was greater than the available supply; hence the price of dollars, the exchange rate, rose. All this is very well, but it merely shifts the question to the reasons for the escalation of capital inflows to the United States.

A major insight is gained by an analysis of the national accounts statistics and, in particular, the government sector. The data show that the financial position of the United States government worsened significantly during the early 1980s. From a deficit of $78.7bn (Federal budget) in 1981, the shortfall reached $178.3bn in 1984. Of course, part of this deficit was met by internal borrowing but in view of the low level of savings in the United States, foreign borrowing became increasingly important in financing the United States Federal Government deficit. Capital inflows amounted to roughly $80bn to $90bn in both 1984 and 1985.

The United States authorities had little difficulty attracting this capital. A number of reasons can be highlighted which explain foreigners' willingness to finance the United States deficit:

(1) high interest rates in the United States in both nominal and real (that is, inflation adjusted) terms;
(2) relatively low United States inflation;
(3) the role of the United States as a safe haven for funds;
(4) the vitality of the United States economy in the mid-1980s (with a rapid growth rate) compared to other major economies;
(5) the sweeping deregulation of financial markets in the United States and the reduction of taxes on foreign deposits in 1984;
(6) high net savings in other major economies (for example, Japan).

It is difficult to rank these reasons in order of importance as effective data on each of them are unavailable. It is clear, however, that a combination of them created a climate which was very favourable for the dollar's value.

Consideration of the behaviour of the dollar in the second half of the 1980s — and particularly in 1987 — highlights the relationship between the domestic deficit, the need to attract foreign savings and the exchange rate. The constant borrowing need of the United States was broadly satisfied by high interest rates attracting primarily Japanese savings until the summer of 1987. Even a faltering in the Japanese purchases of United States Treasury instruments in August and September 1987 was sufficient to raise United States bond yields and make the relationship between bond and equity yields in the United States appear absurd — which was a major fundamental reason behind the Wall Street crash in October.

President Bush was elected on the basis of a pledge not to increase taxes ('watch my lips') — but the reality of the continuing United States Federal Deficit means that something will have to be done. Similarly, despite some improvement, the United States current account deficit is at levels that would have been thought inconceivable during the term of office of the hapless President Carter.

So, many of the inter-related issues linking the United States twin deficits to the exchange rate of the US dollar in the course of the 1980s are still central to an assessment of exchange rate movements at the beginning of the 1990s.

THE EUROPEAN MONETARY SYSTEM

The European monetary system (EMS) and the Exchange Rate Mechanism (ERM) officially began operations on 13 March 1979. The immediate aim was to restore currency stability between members of the system in a world of generally floating exchange rates. At the time this was an ambitious goal, following the experience of the 1970s when exchange rate movements had been on a scale unprecedented in the post-war era. Further, the revolution in Iran early in 1979 had already threatened to destabilize the oil market and with it the world economy. Almost as a reflection of these omens, the official commencement of the European Monetary System in March was behind schedule. The original target date had been 1st January 1979 but negotiations late in 1978 had run into difficulties. In practice, however, the events in the foreign exchange markets in the first two months of 1979 followed a pattern that would have been expected if the system had been launched on time.

The parity grid. For the majority of practical purposes the most important manifestation of the European Monetary System is the parity grid. Each currency has central cross-rate parities vis-a-vis the other member currencies; these are usually referred to as the central rates. The central rates are derived from the European currency unit (ECU), a basket of currencies including all formal members of the European Monetary System. Thus the European Currency Unit value also includes sterling as an input despite the non-participation of sterling in the exchange rate and intervention mechanism of the European Monetary System.

On any particular day the market rate for each currency is allowed a degree of fluctuation. For most currencies the permitted band of fluctuation is 4.5%, that is 2.25% on either side of the central rate; the Italian lira, however, had a wider fluctuation band of 6% above and below its central rates until January 1990 and the Spanish peseta has adopted the wider bands. The fluctuation bands give rise to upper and lower intervention limits. These limits, and hence the European Monetary System as a whole, are maintained by the willingness of each central bank to buy or sell their currency in unlimited amounts at the intervention limits. Thus the intervention limits are the main exchange rate benchmarks in the day-to-day workings of the foreign exchange markets.

Clearly, under this arrangement the currencies of the European Monetary System are only loosely fixed, at least in comparison with the much narrower fluctuation bands allowed under the old Bretton Woods exchange rate regime. The European Monetary System has another intervention mechanism, however, which tends to limit the actual fluctuation of participating currencies. This involves the divergence indicators which are based on the European Currency Unit. The main feature of this mechanism is that the burden of intervention does not fall solely on the central bank of each currency, intervention being shared and co-ordinated by central banks in the system.

Parity realignments. The early years of European Monetary System operations were marked by relatively frequent parity adjustments despite the various intervention mechanisms, interest rate changes and fairly wide fluctuation bands. Table 5.4.3 shows the diary of major events in the lifetime of the European Monetary System. There have been six realignments, and five occasions when currencies have unilaterally devalued.

The occasion of a realignment or a devaluation gives rise to some interesting effects in the short-term workings of the foreign exchange markets. An important one is the apparently perverse behaviour of exchange rates immediately following a parity exchange — the weak currencies become the strong, and vice versa. This effect is caused by a mixture of exchange rate expectations and interest rates. For example, if the Irish punt devalues against the deutschmark by 3%, the foreign exchange markets would not usually expect a further devaluation, at least in the short term. Thus after a devaluation or realignment the risk of exchange rate losses on punt assets is sharply reduced. In this situation short-term capital would tend to flow in favour of the punt, especially as, in practice, Irish interest rates are usually higher

Table 5.4.3: European Monetary System parity adjustments

1979	13 March	EMS commences operations	
	25 September	Realignment	DM rises 2%
			Dkr falls 3%
	29 November	Devaluation	Dkr falls 5%
1981	22 March	Devaluation	Lira falls 6%
	5 October	Realignment	DM and Dfl rise 5.5%
			Lira and Ffr fall 3%
1982	22 February	Devaluation	Bfr falls 8.5%
			Dkr falls 3%
	14 June	Realignment	DM and Dfl rise 4.25%
			Ffr falls 5.75%
			Lira falls 2.75%
1983	21 March	Realignment	DM rises 5.5%
			Dfl rises 3.5%
			Dkr rises 2.5%
			Bfr rises 1.5%
			Lira and Ffr fall 2.5%
			Punt falls 3.5%
1985	19 July	Devaluation	Lira falls 8%
1986	6 April	Realignment	DM rises 3%
			Guilder rises 3%
			Bfr rises 1%
			Dkr rises 1%
			Ffr falls 3%
	2 August	Devaluation	Punt falls 8%
1987	12 January	Realignment	DM rises 3%
			Guilder rises 3%
			Bfr rises 2%
1988	June	Spanish peseta joins Exchange rate mechanism	
1990	January	Italy changes to narrow bands	

than those prevailing in Germany. The punt would therefore rise towards its (new) upper intervention limit against the deutschmark. Further, this effect would be accentuated if capital had left Irish assets prior to the devaluation, in expectation of it.

Causes of realignments. That realignments of the European Monetary System have occurred is not surprising. At the time the System began operations most foreign exchange analysts correctly predicted that the initial parities would need to be changed before long. This view stemmed from elementary economic theory which suggests that unless economic performance between countries is similar it is impossible, in the context of a relatively unfettered world market economy, to fix the exchange rates between currencies in the long term. Thus one of the key issues for the European Monetary System if it is to achieve its goal of currency stability is the problem of convergence of economic performance.

While the Bretton Woods system of fixed exchange rates had achieved much success in accommodating divergent economic performance in short periods of time, for example concerning fluctuations in countries' balance of payments, it was never seriously tested, until the 1970s, with accommodating large long-run disparities in inflation rates. Since inflation was the economic problem of the 1970s it was clear in 1979 that the System's parities could only be maintained if the members' inflation rates converged to a common level.

Table 5.4.4 shows the inflation rates of members since 1980. The system began from a position where the differential between the highest and the lowest inflation rates, in 1978, was 9.4%, between Italy and Germany respectively. In 1979 and 1980 the differential between these two diverged rather than converged, to 10.7% in the first year of the system's operations and 15.7% in 1980. The trend was reversed slightly in 1981, since when substantial progress has been made.

Table 5.4.4: EMS inflation rates

	1980	**1983**	**1985**	**1986**	**1987**	**1988**	**1989**
Germany	5.5	3.3	2.2	–0.2	0.2	1.2	2.8
France	13.6	9.6	5.8	2.7	3.1	2.7	3.7
Belgium	6.6	7.7	4.9	1.3	1.6	1.2	3.1
Netherlands	6.5	2.8	2.2	0.1	–0.7	0.7	1.1
Italy	21.2	14.6	9.2	5.9	4.7	5.0	6.3
Denmark	12.3	6.9	4.7	3.6	4.0	4.6	4.8
Ireland	18.2	10.5	5.4	3.8	3.2	2.1	4.1
Spain	15.6	12.2	8.8	8.8	5.2	4.8	6.8

Source: OECD Paris.

In the second half of the 1980s, general re-alignments became much rarer — as a result, by the end of the decade many economies were beginning to behave as though the rates were fixed within the relevant bands in perpetuity — as though anticipating the proposed European Monetary Union. The long period between the re-alignments of 1983 and 1986 was primarily a result of the strength of the dollar and its impact on the linchpin of the system — the deutschmark. While the exchange rates were stable, the inflation differentials led to a divergence of competitive positions in trade among the members with obvious implications for their payments' balances. Thus, the strains created by the weakening of the dollar made the 1986 re-alignment inevitable — followed by the further re-alignment in 1987. But the degree of convergence of inflation rates in the last few years of the decade coupled with the growing recognition, particularly in France, of the anti-inflationary discipline of sticking with existing rates meant that the Exchange Rate Mechanism entered the 1990s hailed as a success — particularly in comparison with the faltering progress in the early years of the 1990s.

A number of issues are of obvious relevance to the System in the early years of the 1990s.

(1) The likelihood of British membership of the Exchange Rate Mechanism.
(2) The impact of German monetary union from 2nd July 1990.
(3) Potential progress towards the kind of European Monetary Union envisaged in the Delors Plan.
(4) The implications for exchange markets of the Single European Market and of 1992.

Although the United Kingdom took part in the original negotiations on the formation of the European Monetary System, the then Labour Government of 1979 decided not to join the Exchange Rate Mechanism — primarily because of memories of sterling's embarrassing departure from the original European snake in the early 1970s. Mrs Thatcher's Conservative government took the same view throughout the 1980s — and Mrs Thatcher's well-known hostility to the European Monetary System was the principal reason behind Mr Lawson's resignation. But the Government is now committed to joining the system — and this will almost certainly occur by the summer of 1991 (on the basis of the wide bands for rate fluctuations currently utilized by Spain).

The pace of change in Eastern Europe has astounded most observers. The demise of the Communist charade had a certain inevitability — but the speed with which the pack of cards collapsed is astonishing. German monetary union has scared many market participants — because of reasonable fears of the kind of inflationary pressures that will be associated with the Federal Republic's attempt to re-structure East Germany. But the traditions, prejudices, experience and expertise of the Bundesbank are being underestimated. They are determined to make re-unification a success — and their track record in the past forty years suggests that pessimism is unfounded.

The possibility of European Monetary Union — and a single European currency — obviously implies that concern about exchange rate movements may become a thing of the past. The rationality of the concept of a single currency is transparent. But the implications for national governments of such a system are profound. Would the Bundesbank be happy for Greece and Portugal to have a decisive influence on German economic policy? Could France concede officially that its economic policy is made in Germany? Could Denmark — with 28 years of current account deficits — have the same currency as the Netherlands? Although large numbers of influential people are committed to European Monetary Union, the difficulties in implementing such a system are so deep-seated that it is reasonable to presume that national currencies will continue to exist into the mid-1990s.

THE OIL MARKET

Since the last sharp rise in oil prices in 1979 to 1980, induced by the Organization of Petroleum Exporting Countries (OPEC), the gyrations of the oil market have played a large part in various observed currency movements. Since 1983, when the oil price began to fall, currency fluctuations related *directly* to oil price movements have been less dramatic. Nevertheless, the experience of the pound sterling during the early 1980s is worth recording.

In the late 1970s, as production of oil from the United Kingdom sector of the North Sea grew steadily, the pound took on some of the characteristics of a so-called petrocurrency. In 1979-1980, when the price of oil rose by around 150%, sterling also rose sharply, reflecting the positive impact on the United Kingdom's balance of payments and the increasing value of a key strategic economic asset — oil. The pound's strength was maintained until February 1981 when, among other events, the oil market first stabilized and then began to weaken progressively. In late 1982 and especially in early 1983, when the prospect of oil price cuts became real, sterling weakened sharply against most major currencies. Although the sterling exchange rate did not reflect (for any length of time) the full extent of oil price declines after 1983, the currency always responded positively to expectations of oil market stability. At the beginning of 1987, as the oil price appeared to be settling at around $17 to $18 per barrel, from a low of close to $10 per barrel in 1985, the pound's dependence on oil prices was, almost certainly, somewhat reduced. This is not, of course, to discount the very short-term impact on sterling that could undoubtedly occur in the event of a further disagreement amongst the principal members of the Organization of Petroleum Exporting Countries. As the economic importance of North Sea oil declines, the more fundamental determinants of exchange rate movements will reassert themselves.

Other currencies. For other currencies the oil market has had an influence on their movements but the effects have been much more diverse. Interestingly, recent academic research has suggested that there is no clear link between oil market developments and balance of payments trends for many countries, and thus the link between the oil market and exchange rate movements in oil-importing countries is somewhat obscure. What is clear, however, is that the oil price fluctuations of the 1970s and 1980s have exposed the differences in the structures of many Western industrial countries, whether this is expressed through relative inflation or balance of payments performance, or, indeed, government policy. Thus, once again, a key element in currency forecasts for oil-importing countries must be an evaluation of oil market prospects.

JENNY FOSTER-SMITH

Fixpoint Ltd

Originally drafted by John Sharples, revised and updated by Jenny Foster-Smith.

5.5 Political risk

The management of political risks by evaluation, monitoring and mitigation is a relatively new science. Corporations and Banks have been forced to incorporate this subject in the way in which they manage the risks affecting their business. A systematic approach has been adopted by many entities engaged in international business for the assessment of political risk. Like any new subject, the contents and methods of political risk assessment and ultimate management are still in the process of being defined.

The incidence of political risk has always been familiar to large multinational corporations. They have had to live with almost thirty years of antagonism from host governments while operating in lesser developed countries. From 1960 to 1980, a total of 1,535 individual firms from 22 different capital exporting countries were expropriated in 511 separate actions by 76 nations. Banks have been affected more recently by the incidence of political and country risk with the repudiation or rescheduling of external loan obligations by lesser developed countries worldwide.

The need for political risk management has increased with the changing patterns of international trade and investment. The motivation behind the need for international business and the sources of its financing have changed dramatically. New trading patterns, trends and opportunities have emerged which need to be carefully evaluated by any corporation wishing to exploit these situations. The reluctance on the part of corporations and banks to assume more exposure in lesser developed countries has increased. With the continuing need for these countries to attract new lines of credit, new trading partners and direct investment need to be addressed. One result has been that corporations are now expected to adopt new contracting techniques, for example countertrade, industrial offset and build-operate-transfer projects, or to participate in joint venture agreements or privatizations; these all have significant, but indigestible, levels of political risk attached which must be evaluated and rated by any corporation before it becomes involved.

The example of recent events in Eastern Europe, the Soviet Union and other countries emerging from the yoke of communism only serves to demonstrate the need for political risk management and control if corporations and banks are not to be caught by the tide of events.

Political risk is often used as a synonym for country risk. This is erroneous. Confusion surrounds the idea of country risk. Country risk, sovereign risk and political risk are sometimes regarded as interchangeable expressions. They are not.

Risks can only be managed following evaluation and assessment. By political risk management is meant the systematic means of assessing and managing the political risks of foreign direct investment or international business. The scope of political risk can be quite broad, in capital market theory, for example, political risk is often defined as unsystematic risk (alpha risk) or all non-business risk. This definition is sufficiently loose to include such unrelated factors as the work habits of foreign labourers or the incidence of internal violence. Other definitions are equally broad, ranging in their emphasis from foreign exchange exposure to the probability of expropriation.

In practice the term political risk refers to the legal and social environment in which the firm has to operate. In assessing political risk, we are not concerned with the likelihood of change in itself or even of discontinuous change; we are concerned with the criterion that the rules by which a firm determines its calculation of risk and return will not change in such a way as to obviate its original assumptions and calculations.

The usefulness of political risk management is threefold. First and foremost, it is meant to identify those elements of political risk associated with foreign direct investment. In short, to identify those countries which have a potential of becoming the Nigerias, Nicaraguas, Irans, Lebanons or Cubas of tomorrow. At the very least, it is meant to provide sufficient warning of mounting political risks to allow a firm to protect itself or to minimize its exposure.

Secondly, it helps in identifying those countries which have been unnecessarily discounted for political risks or where the political risk of foreign direct investment has decreased.

Finally, political risk management serves to provide a framework in which to compare those countries where the political risk is significant, but not enough to automatically rule them out for foreign direct investment or international business. Such a framework however will at best only serve to systematize what are in essence subjective judgments. This limited step goes a long way in creating a basis for comparing political risks among different countries.

POLITICAL RISK MANAGEMENT

Political risk management is often reduced to an exercise in political risk forecasting. A firm would endeavour to predict political trends in a host country over a 1–5 year period and then adjust its business plans accordingly. The forecast can have varying degrees of sophistication from internal assessments to the use of outside consultants and advisors.

To be effective, any political risk management plan should consist of three inter-related parts. Firstly to identify those elements of the business which might be susceptible to political risk and to develop an intelligent system to monitor and evaluate changing political conditions. Secondly to integrate the system with the corporation's strategic planning function so as to enable them to deal with any changing conditions. Thirdly to devise strategies to protect or reduce the impact of political risk, especially for expropriation and default.

Political risk should not be confused with political stability. The elements of political risk will vary widely between different countries and different corporations. Even within the same country, political risk is usually industry specific and, in many cases, project specific. Rural insurgency, for instance, might pose a problem to a commercial farming operation but its impact on a financial services company would be minimal. It has been suggested that, if political risk were equivalent across all firms and projects, the level of risk — that is the risk premium — could be determined by studying the discount rate on the host government's long term bonds. This discount rate would reflect the business risk existing in the host country.

POLITICAL RISK EVALUATION

Assessing political risks involves the analysis of those elements of aggregate or countrywide risk and those elements of political risk specific to the business being performed. Countrywide factors can be conveniently grouped under three headings.

(1) Domestic Climate: level of national violence, subversion, rebellion, political turmoil. Extreme tendencies among the political parties or recurring government crisis.
(2) Economic Climate: likelihood of government intervention in the economy, rate of inflation, persistent balance of payment deficits, external debts, rate of gross fixed capital formation.
(3) Foreign Relations: level of inter-nation facilities. Size of defence budget, evidence of participation in arms race, incidence of conflict with neighbours.

Specific project risk factors are more varied.

Unlike commercial risk evaluation, the evaluation of political risk cannot be reduced to the analysis of balance sheets and one or two key ratios. It involves the consideration and forecasting of a multitude of variables (some analysts list over 350) and an understanding of how these interact in affecting the risk. It requires the use of specialist techniques and considerable analytical ability to draw the correct conclusions from observed and predicted variables. This if often beyond the scope of many corporations.

Risk is an exposure to a peril. From a bank or a corporation's point of view, risk is an exposure to a loss.

COUNTRY RISK

Country risk is exposure to a loss in cross border lending or investment caused by events in a particular country. These events must be, at least to some extent, under the control of the government of that country. They are definitely not under the control of the investor or lender.

The risk of foreign lending is quite different from the risk of foreign direct investment, and so is the approach to the assessment of the risk. As most large banks and other corporations are exposed to both types of risk, there is a case for making a clear distinction between the two by reserving the term country risk for the risk of foreign lending. Thus a loan in US$ to a Brazilian borrower by the Sao Paulo Branch of the foreign bank is exposed to country risk, whereas the branch itself (the building, furniture, equipment, cash in hand, goodwill, ability to conduct business) is exposed to the risk of foreign direct investment, or political risk.

All cross border lending in a country, whether to the government, bank, private enterprise or an individual is exposed to country risk. Country risk is thus a broader concept than sovereign risk, which is the risk of lending to the government of a sovereign nation.

Only events that are, at least to some extent, under the control of the government can lead to the materialisation of country risk. A default caused by bankruptcy is country risk if the bankruptcy is the result of the mismanagement of the economy by the government. It is commercial risk if it is the result of the mismanagement of a firm.

LENDING AND DIRECT INVESTMENT

In a case of both lending and direct investment abroad, an asset and the income produced by that asset are at risk. However, in the case of a loan, the asset is money, which directly produces income in the form of interest. In the case of direct investment, apart from the goodwill, the asset is real in the form of plant and equipment and the income is generated through the production and sale of goods or services. It is thus the plant and equipment and the ability to use them for the production and sale of goods or services which are at risk.

Loans vary in period from one day to fifteen years and country risk evaluation encompasses these periods. It is highly unusual to contemplate a direct investment with a life of less than five years. This is the minimum time horizon for risk assessment. The maximum period often goes out to 30 years, especially with large capital intensive investments like mineral extraction.

There are also significant differences in the kind of situations that can lead to the materialization of risks and in the probability of losses between these two sectors. Once a particular risk has been identified there are considerable differences in the options facing the lender or investor. Assuming that the bank has a fixed spread, he can either take the risk or decline the loan. The potential investor has the additional option of being able to restructure the project to minimize in advance the impact of the risk. The difference in this respect is even more pronounced if the risk is identified after the enterprise has been commenced. The bank can do virtually nothing to minimize the risk of outstanding loans other than to sell them off at a significant discount from face value whereas the investor can actually adopt suitable strategies to minimize the risk.

Direct investors thus have longer time horizons than lenders and they are mainly concerned with a limited number of political variables. This is why they usually refer to the political risks of foreign investment. Lenders' time horizons are much shorter, but when they lend to the public sector they have to look at many other variables which might affect a country's debt servicing ability. This is why the term political risk can be too restrictive and they often refer to country risk.

The management of political risks should be adopted in a coherent fashion. The first concern is to identify the risks associated with the particular trade transaction, loan or investment. Those risks should then be assessed and evaluated with the corporation or bank when deciding if it is worth the risk to proceed. If the answer is in the affirmative various strategies and actions should be adopted to mitigate any possible exposure.

One of the immediate consequences of international trade is that a company is forced to develop a certain degree of in house political expertise. It may choose to educate existing management or to hire local management to oversee the investment or contract. Furthermore, it may wish to develop an intelligence system to collect and distribute relevant information. This would serve to supplant the information provided by line management while providing an alternative source of analysis.

STRATEGIC PLANNING

It is imperative to integrate the assessment of political risk into any company's strategic planning. The economics of a contract, loan or project may often be distorted by dramatic changes in the perceived and actual level of political risk. Two tasks are paramount in integrating political risk assessments with strategic planning. The first is to establish hurdle rates for proceeding with the transaction under different conditions of political risk. The second is to design capital budgeting plans to reflect changes in the level of political risk. These two will differ from banks to corporations undertaking long term equity investment.

A company can adopt a number of strategies in the actual mitigation of political risk. This will differ from contract to contract, loan to loan and investment to investment. Let us assume that a company wishes to mitigate the political risks associated with a general transaction with a less developed country.

The company has the option either to absorb the risks internally or to transfer them to a third party. The avenue adopted will depend on the company's assessment of the risk together with the willingness of third parties to acquire such exposure and at what price. Many companies are unwilling to take significant political risk exposures on to their own balance sheets. The reasons for this are the strain it can place on a balance sheet, stockholder pressure and the impression this might give to industry analysts if a company has over-exposure to politically sensitive countries. Some companies have adopted the philosophy of transferring all country risk both for developing as well as developed countries. They perceive political risk as being not just about third world indebtedness and instability but also actions by developed nations who are as capable as other countries of imposing restrictions on foreign corporations doing business in their country. If a company is unable to absorb a risk itself, it has two alternatives.

Firstly it can endeavour to cover the exposure by devising sophisticated strategies. The principal ways are to increase a company's political leverage, for example by seeking broad international financing for a transaction rather than by relying on single country sources. Or to make their assets difficult for a host government to interfere with. The common way is to form joint venture investment projects with foreign companies or foreign nations or to incorporate local investors or the host government itself. Another way for investment is to retain control of the distribution and marketing network for a firm's products. The reliance on overseas technology and expatriate personnel is another way of controlling the level of risk.

If this is not feasible, or if it is inappropriate, the second principal method of risk management is to transfer the exposure to a third party. Such third parties are likely to be independent guarantors, banks and insurers.

TRANSFERRING RISK EXPOSURE

The use of independent guarantors can either transfer or enhance the underlying political risk. Ideally guarantors outside the host country should be sought; but these may only be available in a limited number of circumstances. Typically the guarantee from the host government or a relevant ministry can be available. The company still has the political risk associated with that guarantee, but its profile has been changed.

The cleanest and most efficient method of transfer is the use of banks. By this is meant the sale of a commitment or obligation, usually under a contract of sale to banks, for a premium usually catered for in the discount from the face value of the debt — forfaiting or factoring. However, this is only relevant for trading transactions where there is a discountable and transferable payment instrument, whether it be a Bill of Exchange, Letter of Credit or Promissory Note. Long term equity investments would by nature be ineligible. However many of the banks that are active in this market have incurred significant problems with their portfolios of external debt from less developed countries; this has resulted in a marked reluctance to take on additional exposure beyond conservative country limits. This does cause problems for certain countries particularly when the payment terms might be on a medium to long term period. The use of recourse financing, even if it is on a limited basis, is often of little interest to a company as it will continue to have a residual political risk exposure even if it is only on a contingent basis.

The use of insurance is a new concept. The insurers are the 'New Boys on the Block'. The frequent unacceptability of the independent guarantors because of political risk, or the reluctance of banks to assume these exposures, has resulted in a boom for insurers willing to cover political risks.

Insurers have traditionally been seen as being complementary rather than competitive with the banks. This is still true but to a much lesser extent. Banks will still try to offer support for the better countries with insurers remaining the victims of adverse selection. However the problems that many banks now face, with large non-performing portfolios of less developed country debt and new constraints imposed by central banks and regulatory authorities on capital adequacy and underlying ratios, means that for many countries banks are increasingly uncompetitive. Insurers, who do not have such constraints, have been able to fill this gap and either replace these banks or cooperate with them to a significant degree.

Insurers are, in many ways, better equipped to assume political risk than banks or other third parties. If a company or a bank suffers a loss due to political risk, it is seen as a catastrophe where the bank and its risk control processes have failed. Insurers on the other hand are in the business of taking risks. If they suffer a loss, it is perceived as a normal function of their business. They are equipped to absorb these incidents and adopt strategies for recovery.

The insurance market is divided into two distinct areas: government agencies, which include national export credit schemes, government investment insurers and supra-national agencies, and the private market consisting of commercial insurers.

The government agencies are experiencing a Big Bang. This has been caused by the increasing use of the commercial insurance market to provide extra capacity as well as the impending privatization of many agencies. The latter is particularly applicable to the European Community where, with the arrival of the single market, many agencies will compete for business outside of their own country. It is too early to predict the exact impact that this will have on the purchaser of cover but it should result in a major increase in the capacity available for both supplier and buyer credit facilities as well as a beneficial impact on cost.

The private or commercial market has also gone through its own Big Bang. This market has been in operation for the last 20 years. However it is only in the last five that there has been a dramatic increase in the number of companies underwriting the business, together with an expansion in capacity. The covers that these underwriters now offer are extremely diverse. The market started and developed out of a need for flexible cover. This is still their philosophy and covers are structured to cover particular risks and exposures.

ASSET RISK COVER

The programmes divide into two broad areas of cover. First there is cover for asset risks. This includes both direct investment as well as assets located in the country of risk. The covers encompass confiscation, seizure, expropriation, nationalization and deprivation. In essence, the underwriters are indemnifying the insured against acts, actions or events in the country of risk which deprive them of the full economic use of their asset, whether it be an equity investment, a ship, a truck or an aircraft.

CONTRACT FRUSTRATION

The second area is that of contract frustration. This relates to losses under a contract of sale due to various political events. The covers are extremely wide and can be adapted for almost every type of transaction. They range from non-payment by government buyers or guarantors, import or export embargo, war, exchange transfer embargo, unfair calling of on-demand bonds and standby letters of credit, force majeure termination, contract repudiation and non-ratification. These covers have been used for both contracts of sale, service agreements, barter, counter trade, indirect offset and pre export financing agreements. The insurance can be assumed by the contracting party or a financing institution.

CONCLUSION

The management of political risks is a relatively new science. However it has developed rapidly into one where the risk manager has access to proven technology for the minimization and mitigation of such exposures. However, it is a hybrid area which many corporations have difficulty in controlling. It encompasses a number of different disciplines which are often undertaken by separate departments. Political risk management falls within the scope of both the treasury, insurance, country analysis, operations and policy planning departments. A corporation ignores it at its peril.

ANDREW LEASOR

Lloyd Thompson Ltd

5.6
Financial Futures

Financial futures came into existence in the wake of the breakdown of the Bretton Woods exchange rate system in the early 1970s. Currency futures led the way followed by interest rate, bond, and stock index futures. Chicago remains the dominant centre for financial futures but exchanges have been emerging throughout the world. London has a flourishing market in the form of the London International Financial Futures Exchange (LIFFE — pronounced life). The futures contracts traded on LIFFE reflect the types of contract traded elsewhere. The LIFFE currency contracts are for sterling, deutschmarks, yen and Swiss francs against the US dollar plus the US dollar against deutschmarks. Short term interest rate futures are traded in the form of three month sterling and three month eurodollar contracts. Bond (long term interest rate) futures are based on United Kingdom Gilts, United States Treasury Bonds, plus German and Japanese government bonds. There are also futures based on the Financial Times Stock Exchange 100 amongst the range of contracts traded on LIFFE.

CURRENCY FUTURES

A currency futures contract notionally binds the buyer (seller) of the contract to the purchase (sale) of a specific amount of currency at a specified price on a particular date in the future. The majority of currency futures contracts available price currencies in terms of US dollars. For example, the sterling currency futures traded on LIFFE (the London International Financial Futures Exchange) are for blocks of £25,000 priced in US dollars. The holder of a currency futures contract may take delivery of currency through the contract. However there is a limited number of possible delivery dates; in the case of LIFFE sterling currency contracts the dates on which delivery of the currency can take place are the third Wednesdays of March, June, September and December. Only a very small proportion of contracts are held to delivery, most are closed out beforehand. Closing out a contract involves undertaking a transaction opposite to the original one — if a September delivery date contract had been sold it could be closed out by buying a September contract.

HEDGING

The ultimate economic purpose of futures is hedging. Hedging is risk reduction. Hedging with futures involves taking a position in the futures market that would generate a profit in the event of a loss on the underlying exposure (and a loss from futures when there is a profit from the underlying exposure). A British company expecting US dollar receipts is at risk from the possibility of a rise in the pound against the dollar. If sterling were to appreciate fewer pounds would be purchased with the dollar receipts. To offset this the company treasurer could buy sterling currency futures. A rise in sterling against the US dollar would tend to generate a profit from the futures contracts that offsets the loss on the underlying exposure (the futures contracts could be sold at a higher price than that at which they were bought).

Example 1 depicts the case of a British company that on 28 October anticipates the receipt of $2,000,000 on 18 January. At this stage it is assumed that the exchange rate in the (March delivery) futures market is equal to the spot exchange rate.

EXAMPLE 1

Cash Market	*Futures Market*
28 October	
Anticipates receipt of $2,000,000 on 18 January. Fears a rise in sterling against the US dollar. At the spot exchange rate of £1 = $1.60, $2,000,000 would buy £1,250,000.	Buys fifty March sterling currency futures at a rate of £1 = $1.60. This is a (notional) commitment to buy £1,250,000 for $2,000,000 on the third Wednesday in March.
18 January	
Sterling has risen to £1 = $1.7391. $2,000,000 now buys £1,150,020.	Closes out by selling fifty March sterling currency futures at a rate of £1 = $1.7391. This is a (notional) commitment to sell £1,250,000 for $2,173,875.
Outcome	
Loss of £99,980 ($173,875).	Profit of $173,875 (£99,980).

The profit from the futures market precisely offsets the loss of the cash market in Example 1. Such precision is unlikely. Perfect offset may fail to occur because of (i) a discrepancy between the spot and futures prices, and (ii) differential changes in the spot and futures prices. The latter possibility will be examined first.

The difference between the spot and futures prices is known as basis. If basis changes while the hedge is in force then the hedge will be imperfect in the sense that the profit from the futures contracts will not precisely match the loss on the position being hedged. Example 2 is identical to Example 1 except for the fact that basis changes from zero to one cent over the period of the hedge (as opposed to remaining at zero).

EXAMPLE 2

Cash Market	*Futures Market*
28 October	
Anticipates receipt of $2,000,000 on 18 January. Fears a rise in sterling against the US dollar. At the spot exchange rate of £1 = $1.60 $2,000,000 would buy £1,250,000.	Buys fifty March sterling currency futures at a rate of £1 = $1.60. This is a notional commitment to buy £1,250,000 for $2,000,000 on the third Wednesday in March.
18 January	
Sterling has risen to £1 = $1.7391. $2,000,000 now buys £1,150,020.	Closes out by selling fifty £1 March sterling currency futures at a rate of £1 = $1.7291. This a (notional) commitment to sell £1,250,000 for $2,161,375.
Outcome	
Loss of £99,980 ($173,875).	Profit of $161,375 (£92,792).

The profit from the futures market is insufficient to offset completely the cash market loss (note that a futures profit in excess of what was required would also be deemed to be an imperfect hedge, albeit a preferable one).

The alternative way of calculating futures profits and losses is in terms of ticks. A tick is the smallest futures price movement that is recorded. In the case of LIFFE sterling currency futures it is 0.01 cents per £1 (amount to $2.50 for each £25,000 contract). In Example 2 the futures price rose by 1291 ticks. The profit from fifty contracts thus amounted to

$$50 \times 1291 \times \$2.50 = \$161{,}375.$$

The other reason for imperfect hedges mentioned above is the possibility of a discrepancy between the spot and futures prices at the time of establishing the hedge. This is a particular case of basis change since the discrepancy between spot and futures prices will disappear as the delivery date of the futures contract is approached. It can be regarded as a predictable change in basis. This needs to be taken into account when ascertaining the effective exchange rate that is expected to be locked in (guaranteed) by the use of futures contracts.

THE EFFECTIVE EXCHANGE RATE LOCKED IN BY THE USE OF CURRENCY FUTURES

It is unlikely that spot and futures prices are equal. When they are not equal some change in basis can be expected because of convergence. Convergence refers to the tendency for spot and futures prices to move towards equality as the delivery date approaches (on the day on which delivery of currency can take place through the futures contract the spot and futures prices will become the same). The exchange rate that the hedger attempts to lock in falls between the spot and futures rates. If the futures contract were closed out immediately after being entered into then the spot price of sterling would be the effective price. If the futures contract is held to delivery the futures price (at the time of taking out the contract) is the effective price. Between these two points in time the effective exchange rate falls between these two values and is a linear function of the period of time between entering and closing out the futures contracts. This is illustrated by figure 5.6.1 which assumes (for the sake of clarity) that the spot price remains unchanged throughout the period of the hedge.

At time T, when the hedge is entered into, the spot price of sterling is $1.50 whilst the futures price is $1.49. By time T + 4 months (the delivery date) the futures price has converged on the spot price. If the futures contract is to be closed out at time T + 1 month the effective exchange rate would be $1.4975, if it is to be closed out at T + 2 months the rate would be $1.4950, and at T + 3 months $1.4925.

These effective exchange rates would be unaffected by changes that move the price of sterling without altering the basis. For example a rise in the price of sterling matched by an equal rise in the futures price (leaving basis unchanged) would entail cash profits or losses and futures losses or profits that offset each other.

Profits and losses arising from futures contracts are realized daily as they occur. If a futures position makes a loss during a trading day the respective payment must be made the following morning, likewise any profits would be forthcoming the following morning. This process is known as Marking to Market and the cash flows are referred to as Variation Margin. If a futures contract is held to delivery the currencies would be exchanged at the spot exchange rate on the delivery date, the effective exchange rate would be rendered equal to the futures rate at the time of taking out the contract by means of the variation margin cash flows that would have

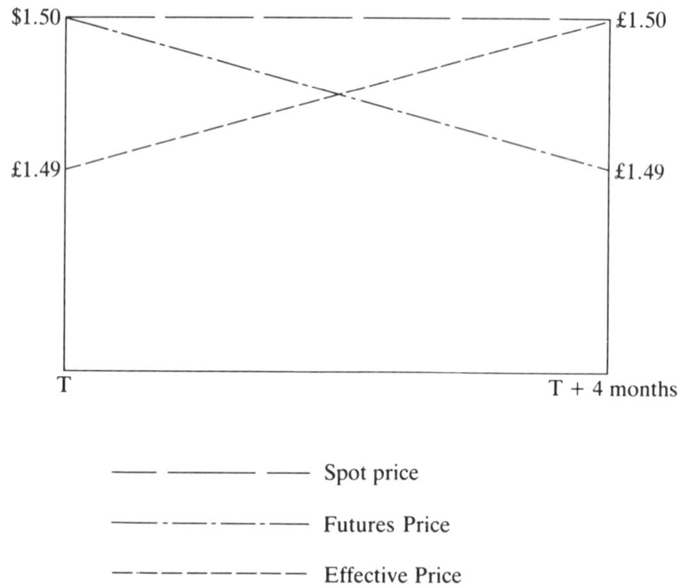

Figure 5.6.1 Significance of the effective price

occurred during the period of the hedge. Likewise the effective exchange rate of \$1.4975 achieved at time T+1 is based on exchanging currencies at £1 = \$1.50 after cash flows equivalent to \$0.0025 have taken place during the preceding month.

The price of currency obtained by interpolating between the spot and future prices may determine the number of futures contracts that need to be used. Suppose that it is 28 October, \$2,000,000 is to be received on 18 January, the spot price of sterling is \$1.55, the March futures price is \$1.5350, and the March futures delivery date is 18 March. 82 days separate the present and the exposure date whilst sixty days separate the exposure date and the delivery date. The expected effective price of sterling for 18 January is calculated thus:

$$\$1.5500 - (\$1.5500 - \$1.5350) \times \frac{82}{(82 + 60)} = \$1.5413$$

It is expected that on 18 January \$2,000,000 will be sold for sterling at an effective exchange rate of £1 = \$1.5413. In other words \$2,000,000 are to be used to buy £1,297,606. Since the futures contracts relate to the purchase of £1,297,606, the appropriate number of contracts is

$$£1{,}297{,}606/£25{,}000 = 51.9,$$

which is approximated by 52 contracts. If the exposure were in terms of sterling rather than US dollars the requisite number of contracts would be the sterling sum divided by £25,000; there would be no need to ascertain the appropriate exchange rate at which to translate the dollar exposure into sterling.

This case provides an example of another source of hedge imperfection namely the failure of a discrete number of contracts (contracts are indivisible) to match the exposure being hedged.

THE PRICING OF CURRENCY FUTURES CONTRACTS

Futures prices are determined by arbitrage, which involves making riskless profits by buying cheaply in one market and selling at a higher price in another. The arbitrage relevant to currency futures is known as covered interest arbitrage. This arbitrage becomes possible when profits can be made from borrowing in one currency, exchanging that currency for another, and then depositing the second currency. Risk is avoided by selling the second currency forward, possibly through the use of currency futures. Figure 5.6.2 illustrates covered interest arbitrage.

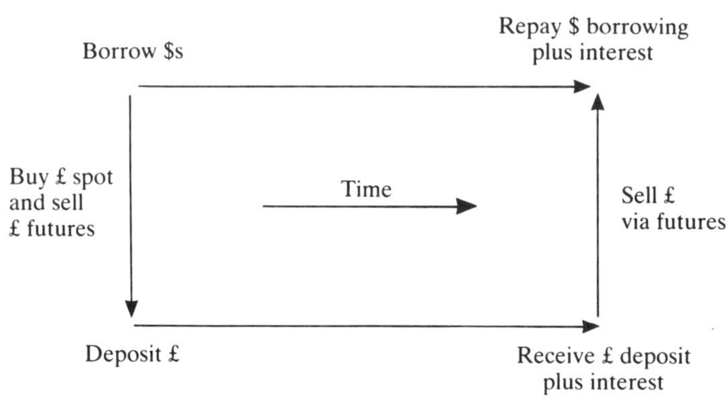

Figure 5.6.2 Covered interest arbitrage

There will be an opportunity to profit from such arbitrage if the premium or discount between the currencies differs from the interest rate differential between them. For example, if sterling was at a 3% per annum futures discount against the US dollar while sterling interest rates were 4% per annum higher than US dollar rates, the arbitrage illustrated by figure 5.6.2 would be profitable. There would be a 4% per annum gain from borrowing dollars and investing pounds which would be offset by a guaranteed (via futures contracts) depreciation of sterling against the US dollar of 3% per annum leaving an arbitrage profit equivalent to 1% per annum.

As with all arbitrage, the process of taking arbitrage profits will tend to eliminate the arbitrage possibility. In particular the sale of sterling currency futures will lower sterling futures prices; the futures discount of sterling against the US dollar will then widen. This discount will widen until the benefit from the interest rate differential is completely offset by sterling's depreciation against the dollar. The position attained is one in which the rates of premium or discount between currencies matches the difference between the interest rates on those currencies. (The arbitrage process that brings this about may influence interest rates and spot currency prices as well as currency futures prices, but the net result will always be the equality of the premium or discount and interest rate differential).

So a currency futures price is determined by the spot exchange rate and the difference in interest rates between the currencies concerned. The majority of currency futures are priced against the US dollar so that their prices are determined by the spot US dollar price of the currency and the difference between the short term interest rates on that currency and the short term interest rates on US dollars (to be more precise, eurodollars in most cases).

SHORT TERM INTEREST RATE FUTURES

Short term interest rate futures provide notional commitments to deposit or borrow for three month periods commencing on specific future dates known as delivery dates. 'Delivery dates' is somewhat misleading since these futures contracts cannot involve delivery in the sense of depositing or borrowing sums of money when the contracts mature. Instead there are cash flows that compensate for discrepancies between the futures price (interest rate) at the time of closing out the contract (which may or may not occur on the delivery date). These cash flows take the form of variation margin payments or receipts and occur on a daily basis according to whether the day's price change has produced a loss or profit for the holder of the futures contract.

Prices of short term interest rate futures are quoted on an index basis. The index is one hundred minus the (annualized) futures interest rate. So if sterling three month interest rate futures were quoted at a price of 86.50 they would imply an interest rate of 13.50% per annum. The tick, the smallest permissible price movement, is 0.01 for LIFFE three month sterling interest rate futures. Since the contract size is \$500,000 the monetary value of a tick is £12.50.

HEDGING

Hedging interest rate risks with futures involves taking a futures position that will provide a profit in the event of an unfavourable interest rate movement (and a loss that offsets an otherwise favourable interest rate change). A hedger at risk from a fall in interest rates (a lender) will buy futures whilst those who would lose from a rise in interest rates (borrowers) would sell futures. Example 3 illustrates the case of a potential borrower using futures to provide protection against a rise in interest rates.

EXAMPLE 3

Cash Market	*Futures Market*
3 January	
Intends to borrow £1,000,000 for three months on 3 February. Fears a rise in interest rates from the current 13% per annum.	Sells two March three month sterling interest rate futures contracts at a price of 86.75.
3 February	
Borrows £1,000,000 at interest rate of 13.5% per annum.	Closes out by buying two March three month sterling interest rate futures contracts at a price of 86.25.
Outcome	
There is an additional interest cost of 0.5% per annum on £1,000,000 for three months of £1,250.	The buying price of the futures contracts is fifty ticks less than the selling price. The profit on two contracts at £12.50 per tick is $2 \times 50 \times £12.50 = £1{,}250$.

The profit from the futures contracts precisely compensates for the loss arising from the higher interest rate. The hedge was perfect because basis remained unchanged. Basis was –0.25% per annum on both 3 January and 3 February. Such constancy of basis is not usual. Convergence provides one reason for a change in basis. Basis converges to zero as the delivery date is approached. So a basis that is initially non-zero can be expected to move towards zero. This introduces an imperfection into the hedge but, since this source of basis change is predictable, it can be interpreted as an interest change that cannot be hedged against (in other words the locked in interest rate differs from the current interest rate).

THE LOCKED IN INTEREST RATE

The interest rate that a hedger expects to be guaranteed by means of futures will be between the spot and futures rates, dependent upon the time period elapsing prior to closing out. This is illustrated by figure 5.6.3.

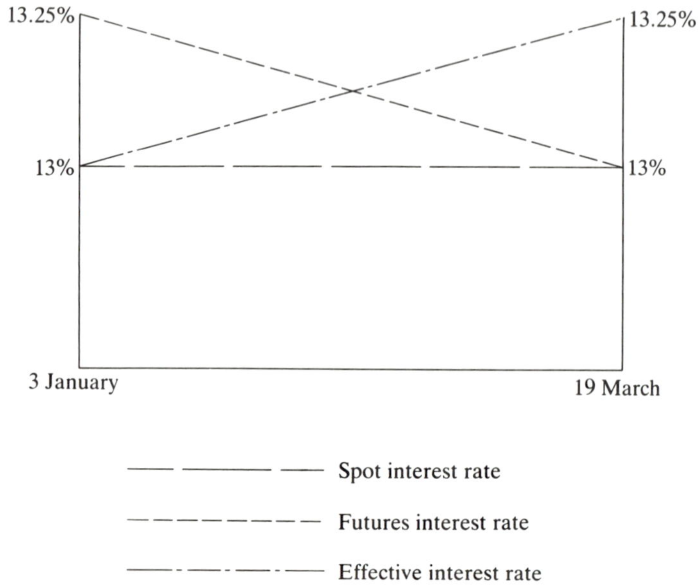

Figure 5.6.3 The locked in interest rate

Figure 5.6.3 reflects the initial data of Example 3. The spot three month interest rate is 13% per annum, the rate implied by the March futures price of 86.75 is 13.25% per annum, and 19 March is the delivery date of the March futures contract. The figure assumes that the spot rate remains constant. The futures rate will converge on the spot rate so that they will be equal on the delivery day.

The effective interest rate that is expected depends upon the time elapsing. For example the effective rate anticipated for 3 February is: 13% + 0.25% (31/75) = 13.10% per anum.

When borrowing on 3 February the interest rate payable will be the spot rate of 13% per annum. The additional 0.10% per annum will be incurred by way of variation margin payments during the period of the hedge (a rising futures price will cause a short futures position to be loss making).

The 13.10% per anum achieved is inferior to the spot rate of 13% per annum, however there is protection from any rise in the spot rate. A rise in the spot rate would be accompanied by a rise in the futures interest rate and hence a fall in the futures price. A fall in the futures price would generate a profit from a short futures position. This profit would offset the increased interest payable on the borrowing. The futures profit would accrue by way of variation margin receipts.

A remaining source of risk is the possibility of a change in the slope of the yield curve. There is protection against a rise in the spot interest rate if the futures rate moves in line with it. A shift in the slope of the yield curve implies that futures rates do not move to the same extent as the spot rate. Basis would change and the hedge would be imperfect. Protection against a change in the slope of the yield curve can be obtained by using a futures straddle.

HEDGING AGAINST CHANGES IN THE SLOPE OF THE YIELD CURVE

A futures straddle involves buying futures contracts for one delivery month and selling an equal number of contracts for another delivery month. This allows profits to be made from a change in the relative prices of the futures contracts. Changes in the slope of the yield curve cause relative movements in futures prices.

The straddle employed in the case illustrated by Example 3 and figure 5.6.3 would involve March and June futures contracts. A rise in the spot interest rate that is not accompanied by a rise in the March futures interest rate (a decline in the gradient of the yield curve) would not be offset by a futures profit. Avoidance of this would involve hedging against the change in the slope of the yield curve by means of futures straddles.

Selling March futures while buying June futures would provide a profit from a rise in June futures prices relative to March futures prices. In other words a fall in distant interest rates relative to earlier ones (a decline in the gradient of the yield curve) would generate a profit from the straddle.

So hedging against both a shift in the position and a change in the slope of the yield requires the addition of a futures straddle to the hedge of the example (which provides protection from a shift in the position of the yield curve). The complete hedge involves selling more than two March futures contracts while buying June contracts. A straddle involving the sale of two March contracts and the purchase of two June contracts would relate to a three month (91 day) stretch of the yield curve. The risk faced related to a forty-four day stretch of the yield curve. The appropriate number of straddles would be: $2 \times (44/91) = 0.97$, which is approximated by one. So the complete hedge would involve selling three March contracts whilst buying one June contract.

This example has had an exposure date (3 February) that falls outside the two futures delivery dates. If the exposure date falls between the futures delivery dates the complete hedge takes the form of a combination of the two futures with their relative weighting being dependent upon the proximity of the exposure date to the delivery dates. This can be seen by means of changing the initial date in Example 3 from 3 January to 3 November (other data in that example remain unchanged).

The exposure date of 3 February falls between the December and March delivery dates (taken as 20 December and 19 March). The hedge against the shift of the yield curve would again involve the sale of two March contracts. Hedging against a change in the slope of the yield curve would require selling December contracts while buying March contracts. Again the ideal number of straddles would be: $2 \times (44/91) = 0.97$, so that the appropriate straddle is the sale of a December contract and the purchase of a March contract. This purchase of a March contract cancels the sale of one of the contracts required for hedging against a shift of the yield curve. The complete hedge thus entails selling one December contract and selling one March contract. If futures contracts were divisible, the straddle would involve selling 0.97 December contracts and buying 0.97 March contracts so that the complete hedge consisted of selling 0.97 December and selling 1.03 March contracts. In other words a total of two contracts would be sold with the composition between December and March contracts being dependent upon the proximity of the exposure date to the delivery dates, the slightly higher emphasis on March contracts reflects the slightly greater proximity to the March delivery date.

STRIPS AND ROLLS

A hedger may be concerned with a number of future exposure dates. For example money may have been borrowed on the basis of an interest rate that is reassessed periodically. £1,000,000 might have been borrowed on the basis of the interest rate being adjusted in line with a market rate three-monthly on 1 May, 1 August, 1 November, and 1 February. Alternatively there could be a six-monthly reassessment on 1 May and 1 November.

A strip hedge would involve selling two June, two September, two December, and two March contracts (for the sake of clarity protection against changes in the slope of the yield curve will be ignored). In the case of the three-monthly interest reassessment this involves hedging three-month exposures with the three-month interest rate futures contracts whose delivery dates fall soon after the exposure dates.

The same strip might be used in the case of the six-monthly interest rate reassessment. A six-month interest rate could be looked upon as a compound of two successive three-month rates. Correspondingly a six-month interest rate exposure might best be hedged by means of futures contracts with two successive maturities. To take the extreme case of the exposure date coinciding with a futures delivery date on 19 June the six-month rate on 19 June could be looked upon as a 19 June three-month rate compounded with the expected 19 September three-month interest rate. The appropriate hedge would appear to be equal numbers of June and September futures contracts.

The strip requires adequate liquidity in the markets for contracts with relatively distant delivery dates. In the absence of such liquidity a hedger may be forced to use the contracts for which there is adequate liquidity. Rolls are used in situations where the liquidity is inadequate beyond the next delivery date.

A rolling hedge uses only those contracts with the nearest delivery date. The hedge may use either a simple roll or a piled-up roll. A simple roll hedges only the next exposure date. Suppose that a £1,000,000 borrowing is subject to interest rate reassessment on 1 May and 1 November. A simple roll on 31 March would be to sell four June contracts (a £1,000,000 borrowing for six months requires four £5,000,000 three-month contracts). There is no hedge against the 1 November risk.

A piled-up roll attempts to hedge more than one exposure date with the earliest maturing contracts. Continuing the previous example, an attempt to hedge both the 1 May and 1 November risks would involve the sale of eight June contracts, four for each of the two exposure dates. When the June delivery date is reached four September contracts would be sold in respect of the 1 November risk. The September contracts would subsequently be replaced by December contracts. Hedging strategies limited to contracts with a common delivery date are vulnerable to changes in the slope of the yield curve.

VARIATION MARGIN LEVERAGE

Compensation for adverse interest rate movements accrues over time by way of receipts of variation margin. The profit from futures contracts is received as the futures prices move. The higher interest rate payable on a borrowing is incurred at a point of time in the future. Until that point of time is reached interest can accrue on the variation margin receipts.

Suppose that, on 31 March, a hedger decides to hedge a six-month deposit to be made on 31 May by buying June and September three-month interest rate futures contracts. In the event of a decline in interest rates between 31 March and 31 May the hedger would receive variation margin payments during that period. The loss arising from the reduced interest receipts is not realized until 30 November. The variation margin receipts can earn interest between the time of their receipt and 30 November. Taking these interest receipts on variation margin into account suggests that the numbers of futures contracts used can be scaled down, otherwise variation margin plus interest would overcompensate for the interest rate change being hedged (more of a problem when a cash market profit is offset by a futures market loss). The factor by which the number of contracts is scaled down is referred to as the variation margin leverage.

Two problems encountered when calculating variation margin leverage are (1) knowing the appropriate interest rate to use since the whole exercise arises from interest rate uncertainty, and (2) dealing with the unpredictability of the rate at which variation margin will accumulate prior to 31 May. It might be decided to use the current six-month interest rate and to assume that variation margin accumulates at a constant rate.

If the current six-month interest rate is 15% per annum and there are 61 days between 31 March and 31 May and 183 days between 31 May and 30 November the variation margin leverage would be given by the following calculation: 1 = 0.15 (30.5 + 183)/365 = 1.088.

The figure 30.5 comes from dividing 61 days by 2 and is consistent with the assumption that the variation margin receipts accrue at a constant rate over the 61 day period. The number of futures contracts would be scaled down by dividing the number of contracts by 1.088.

THE DETERMINATION OF SHORT TERM INTEREST RATE FUTURES PRICES

As with other futures contracts the prices of three-month interest rate futures are determined by arbitrage. In this case the arbitrage is against forward-forward interest rates. Forward-forward interest rates are the rates for future periods implied by spot rates relating to differing maturities. For example, the spot three-month rate and the spot six-month rate imply a three month rate for a period beginning three months hence.

A six-month interest period can be looked upon as two successive three-month periods. If someone were to deposit money for six months while borrowing the same sum for three months the borrowing would need to be rolled over after three months. There will be a rate of interest for the second three-month period at which the total borrowing costs match the interest receipts from the deposit.

Suppose £1,000,000 is deposited for six months at 16% per annum while £1,000,000 is borrowed for three months at 15% per annum. The receipts from the deposit would be £1,080,000 after six months while the sum owed after three months would be £1,037,500. At the end of the first three months the sum of £1,037,500 would need to be borrowed in order to pay off the first debt. The interest rate which turns £1,037,500 into £1,080,000 over three months is the forward-forward rate. That interest rate is 16.39% per annum. One might intuitively expect the forward-forward rate to be 17% per annum so that the six-month rate is the average of the two three-month rates. If continuous compounding were used to calculate the forward-forward rate 17% per annum would be the result. 16.39% per annum, rather than 17% per annum, arises because short term money markets use simple interest rather than compound interest.

Since three-month interest rate futures contracts can be used to lock in three-month interest rates for future periods they can be used to guarantee the interest rate for the second period in the above example. This can provide opportunities for profitable arbitrage. If the forward-forward interest rate differed from the futures rate it would be possible to make a profit from depositing via the one yielding the higher rate whilst borrowing via the one with the lower rate. Pursuit of arbitrage profits would bring the forward-forward and futures rates into line with each other.

For example it might be possible to guarantee, via a forward-forward transaction, a deposit rate of 16.39% per annum for a three-month period starting three months from the present. If the futures prices were such as to provide a guaranteed borrowing rate, via futures, of 16% per annum there would be scope for arbitrage profits based on the futures borrowing rate and the forward-forward deposit rate.

The arbitrage above would involve selling futures contracts. The sale of futures contracts would tend to reduce futures prices. A futures interest rate of 16% per annum corresponds to a futures price of 84.00 (100.00 – 16.00). A fall in the futures price amounts to a rise in the futures interest rate. The sale of futures in order to make arbitrage profits would tend to move futures interest rates into line with forward-forward rates (there would simultaneously be some downward movement of the forward-forward interest rate in the process of bringing the rates into line with each other). So futures prices are determined by an arbitrage process that brings futures interest rates into line with forward-forward interest rates.

The theoretical price of three-month interest rate futures is ascertained by calculating the corresponding forward-forward rate. A popular formula for this is the following one.

$$\left(\left[\frac{1+(R_1 \times T_1/365)}{1+(R_2 \times T_2/365)}\right]-1\right) \times \frac{365}{T_1 - T_2}$$

where

R_1 = interest rate (as a decimal) to the far end of the forward-forward period
R_2 = interest rate (as a decimal) to the near end of the forward-forward period
T_1 = days to the far end of the forward-forward period
T_2 = days to the near end of the forward-forward period

The existence of bid-offer spreads means that there would be different forward-forward rates for depositing and borrowing. Consider the case of a six month offer rate of 15.125% per annum and bid rate of 15% per annum together with a three month offer rate of 14% per annum and bid rate of 13.875% per annum. Depositing for six months at 15% per annum while borrowing for three months at 14% per annum gives a forward-forward rate of:

$$\left(\left[\frac{1+(0.15 \times 182/365)}{1+(0.14 \times 91/365)}\right]-1\right) \times \frac{365}{91} = 0.1546 \text{ (15.46\% p.a.)}$$

whereas borrowing for six months at 15.125% per annum and depositing for three months at 13.875% per annum implies

$$\left(\left[\frac{1+(0.15125 \times 182/365)}{1+(0.13875 \times 91/365)}\right]-1\right) \times \frac{365}{91} = 0.1583 \text{ (15.83\% p.a.)}$$

It can be seen that the forward-forward deposit rate is 15.46% per annum while the forward-forward borrowing rate is 15.83% per annum. It follows that the no arbitrage range is large. Futures would need to provide a borrowing rate of less than 15.46% per annum or a deposit rate in excess of 15.83% per annum before arbitrage profits became available. In other words the interest rate implied by futures prices must fall outside the 15.46% to 15.83% per annum range before arbitrage became profitable. So, although futures prices are determined by arbitrage against forward-forward rates, what is actually determined is a feasible range of prices; the arbitrage does not determine which price within the feasible range is observed in the market.

BOND (LONG TERM INTEREST RATE) FUTURES

The contracts available on LIFFE are based on Long Gilts, Medium Gilts, Short Gilts, United States Treasury Bonds, Japanese Government Bonds and German Government Bonds. General principles relate to all of the them and will, for the most part, be explained with reference to just one leaving the reader to extend the analysis to the others.

Gilt futures are commitments to buy or sell gilt-edged securities during specified future months. There is a limited number of gilts eligible for delivery in fulfilment of futures contracts and the seller has a choice as to the specific gilt. Contracts are commonly not held until maturity but are closed out by means of the holder taking out an opposite contract; for example a buyer can close out by selling gilt futures in an amount and for a delivery month corresponding to those of the contracts previously bought. There are cash flows by way of variation margin to reflect the change in futures prices between the dates of buying and selling. Long gilt futures contracts are based on notional twenty year gilt-edged securities with 9% per anum coupon yield.

Those using these financial futures for hedging may wish to safeguard either the value of securities or the cash flow arising from them.

HEDGING THE VALUE OF A PORTFOLIO

A portfolio manager may fear an increase in long term interest rates, an occurrence that would reduce the prices of gilts held in a portfolio. He could attempt to avoid this effect on the value of the portfolio by taking a position in futures that would provide an offsetting gain from a fall in gilts prices. To achieve this he would sell futures contracts. A fall in gilt prices should be accompanied by a fall in the prices of gilt futures. If a loss was made from a decline in the value of gilts the portfolio manager would be compensated by profits from the futures position. He would be able to buy gilt futures at a lower price than that at which he sold.

This process is illustrated by Example 1, which needs to be preceded by details of the specification of a long term interest rate futures contract traded on LIFFE. Each

Long Gilt contract has a nominal value of £50,000 and the prices of contracts are expressed as pounds per £100 nominal value. The price of the notional long gilt would be 100 when the long run interest rate is 9% per annum but would rise above 100 when the interest rate is lower; and vice versa for higher rates. The tick, the minimum price movement, is £1/32 for Long Gilt futures.

In Example 4 a portfolio manager with gilts worth £1m on 2 January is anxious about the possibility that interest rates might rise and thereby reduce the value of his gilts. He hedges by selling twenty long gilt futures contracts.

EXAMPLE 4

Cash Market	*Futures Market*
2 January	
The 20 year interest rate is 9% per annum. The £1 million Gilt portfolio is vulnerable to an increase in long term interest rates.	Sells twenty March Long Gilt futures contracts. Futures price is 100, reflecting a 9% per annum interest rate.
15 February	
The 20 year interest rate has risen to 11.25% per annum. Correspondingly the value of the Gilt portfolio has fallen to £850,000 (this figure could be anywhere between £800,000 and £1m dependent upon the maturities of the Gilts held).	Closes out by buying twenty March long gilt futures contracts. The price of the contracts has fallen to 82.22 reflecting an 11.75% per annum futures interest rate.
There is a loss of £150,000 in the value of the gilt portfolio.	There is a profit of £177,812.5 from the futures position.

The portfolio manager has been more than successful in offsetting the fall in the value of his gilts. The reason for this over compensation is the fact that the average maturity of the gilts in his portfolio is less than twenty years (the LIFFE Long Gilt futures contract is based on a gilt with a twenty year maturity). The value of a portfolio responds less to interest rate changes as the average maturity declines. In the light of this he could have chosen to hedge with fewer than 20 futures contracts; 17 would seem appropriate, particularly when it is borne in mind that with twenty contracts a fall in interest rates would have entailed a futures loss greater than the increase in the value of the gilt portfolio. Alternatively the hedging might have involved a mixture of Long and Medium Gilt futures contracts.

Anxiety about the volatility of interest rates may not be specific to a particular period. It is possible that a portfolio manager is consistently nervous about the instability of interest rates and the possibility that it might involve a fall in the value of his gilt portfolio. The holding of futures positions, to hedge against changes in the value of a portfolio, could thus be permanent with new futures positions being entered into as old ones are closed out.

HEDGING CASH FLOW

In this case the hypothetical example is that of a corporate treasurer intending to raise money by the sale of securities with a fixed coupon yield. His anxiety is that interest rates might rise before the sale is made with the result that the raising of a particular sum of money would then entail a greater future cash flow commitment to the security holders.

EXAMPLE 5

Cash Market	*Futures Market*
2 January	
The corporation intends to raise £1m on 15 February by the sale of irredeemable debentures. The interest rate on undated stock is 9% per annum. The treasurer wants to ensure that the cost of servicing the debt will be limited to £90,000 per annum.	Sells twenty March Long Gilt futures contracts. Futures price is 100, reflecting a 9% per annum interest rate.
15 February	
The interest rate on undated stock has risen to 11.25% per annum.	Closes out by buying twenty March Long gilt futures contracts. Futures price is 82.22 reflecting an 11.25 per annum futures interest rate.

The cost of servicing a £1 million debt would now be £112,500 per annum.

There is a gain of £177,812.5 from the futures position.

The treasurer could use the £177,812.5 futures gain to reduce his borrowing requirement from £1,000,000 to £822,187.5 and hence reduce the annual servicing cost to £92,496. A perfect hedge would have provided a futures gain of £200,000 so that the cash flow required to service the debt returned to £90,000 per annum. The futures gain was less than £200,000 because the notional gilt is of a twenty year maturity and only the price of irredeemable stock responds proportionately to interest rate changes. A more effective hedge would have been obtained by using 22 gilt contracts, which would have provided a futures gain of about £195,593.75.

In both of the examples the hedger would be able to ascertain the appropriate number of futures contracts required, seventeen and twenty-two respectively, before selling the contracts. The ratio of the value of futures contracts required to the sum of assets or liabilities to be hedged is known as the hedge ratio. Even with the correct hedge ratio hedging may not be perfect. Imperfections would arise if the cash market and futures interest rates did not change to the same extent. However this basis risk tends to be much less than the outright risk of unhedged positions since the difference, between cash and futures interest rates, fluctuates less than cash market rates.

DELIVERY

The months during which the gilts may be delivered are March, June, September and December. The seller chooses the day of the month on which delivery takes place. Gilts with between fifteen and twenty-five years to maturity are eligible for delivery upon maturity of the Long Gilt futures contracts. The seller chooses which gilt to deliver.

PRICE (CONVERSION) FACTOR

The price factor will be described in relation to the Long Gilt futures contract, and the description can be readily extended to the other long term interest rate contracts.

The Long Gilt futures contracts each have a nominal value of £50,000. Likewise the gilts delivered when a contract matures must amount to £50,000 in nominal value. Gilts with the same nominal value may, however, have a higher market value than one with a 9% per annum coupon despite identical nominal values. A £50,000 bond issued when the market rate was 12% per annum would provide a coupon of £6,000 per annum whereas a £50,000 bond issued at a rate of 10% per annum would yield £5,000 per annum. The market value of bonds will vary according to the size of the coupon yield. A bond yielding £6,000 per annum is worth more than one with a coupon of just £5,000 per annum. If the seller delivers high coupon gilts he expects to receive more money than if he delivers lower coupon gilts. To ensure that this happens, price factors are used in the calculation of the sums for which buyers are invoiced. The relevant adjustment is made by means of multiplying the futures price by the price factor.

To obtain the price factor for a Long Gilt, its price is ascertained as if it were to have a gross redemption yield of 9% per annum. This price is then divided by the nominal value of the gilt and the result is the price factor. Higher coupon yields are reflected in higher price factors.

If the bonds were perpetuities the price factor would equal the ratio of the percentage yields. The price factor for an 11.25% per annum bond would be 1.25 since an 11.25% per annum yield into perpetuity would render the bond 25% more valuable than one yielding a perpetual 9% per annum. However, most Long Gilts have maturity dates (as does the notional gilt upon which futures contracts are based). Since the bonds are not perpetuities, the price factor tends to differ from the ratio of the percentage yields, with the factor approaching one as the period of maturity declines towards zero.

INVOICE AMOUNT

The futures price upon which the invoice amount is based is known as the Exchange Delivery Settlement Price, which is the LIFFE market price at 11.00 am on the second business day prior to delivery. The principal invoice amount is the exchange delivery settlement price multiplied by the price factor. The sum for which the buyer is invoiced is equal to the principal invoice amount plus accrued interest on the gilts. The resulting invoice amounts would normally differ from the market values of the corresponding gilts.

THE CHEAPEST TO DELIVER GILT

The seller chooses which gilt to deliver in fulfilment of the contract. It is in the interests of the seller to deliver the gilt whose invoice amount exceeds the market price by the largest margin (or whose invoice amount falls short of the market price by the smallest margin). This is the cheapest to deliver gilt.

CASH AND CARRY ARBITRAGE

This refers to the process of simultaneously buying gilts spot and selling futures contracts. If the invoicing amount, inclusive of accrued interest, at maturity exceeds the sum of the purchase price and financing cost arbitrage profits are available. Arbitragers can buy spot and simultaneously guarantee a profitable future selling price by selling futures contracts. Buying spot and selling futures raises the spot price, lowers the futures price, and thus tends to remove the scope for arbitrage profits. The arbitrage activity will bring about a situation in which the capital gain (loss) is equal to the excess (shortfall) of the cost of financing the long gilt position over the running yield on the gilt. If the yield on the gilt falls short of the financing cost of holding that gilt the spot price will be lower than the futures price since some capital gain will be necessary to offset the excess financing cost. The benefits from holding a gilt, in terms of running yield and capital gain, should equal the cost of financing the holding of the gilt in terms of the interest payable on money borrowed in order to finance the purchase of the gilt.

Thus cash and carry arbitrage serves to keep spot and futures prices close to each other, with the relationship between them being dependent upon the financing costs. Since the arbitragers would gain most by using the cheapest to deliver gilt it is this stock whose value is reflected by the invoicing amount for maturing futures contracts. This implies that the futures price itself is based on the cheapest to deliver gilt. It is to be expected that the cheapest to deliver is the gilt most accurately hedged by the futures contract. Changes in spot gilt prices may, however, change the cheapest to deliver gilt.

BASIS

The market price of a gilt has two components, the clean price and the accrued interest. The latter refers to the right to interest receipts accumulated since the last interest payment date. A purchaser of a gilt realizes the interest receipts that accumulated while the seller was holding the gilt. The price paid for the gilt will include compensation for the accrued interest unrealized by the seller. The remainder of the price is known as the clean price.

Division of the clean price, per £100 nominal, by the price factor renders the price comparable with the futures price. The difference between the price thus obtained and the futures price is known as basis. In the case of the cheapest to deliver gilt, basis is determined by the difference between the yield on the gilt and the interest paid (or foregone) on the money required to finance the purchase of the gilt. Basis converges to zero as the maturity date of the futures contract is approached. As maturity is approached the period over which interest is paid and received shortens and hence the monetary value of the interest differential declines towards zero.

Suppose that it is 2 October and a December long gilt futures contract has been sold as part of a cash and carry arbitrage operation. The cost of financing the holding of the gilt exceeds the running yield obtained from the gilt. This implies that the arbitrager will choose to deliver (the seller chooses the delivery date) at the earliest possible date (1 December) since there is a net loss to be expected from holding the gilt after that date. It also implies that the futures price is at a premium to the spot price.

If the clean price of the cheapest to deliver gilt is 121–00 and the price factor is 1.1 while the futures price is 112–00, the basis will be given by

$$\text{Basis} = \frac{121}{1.1} = 112 = -2$$

Figure 5.6.4 illustrates the expected erosion of basis over time.

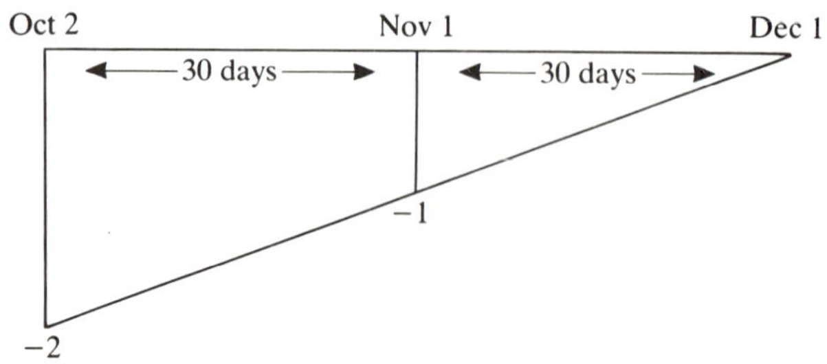

Figure 5.6.4 The expected erosion of basis over time

So basis is expected to change over time. This means that the price that a hedger seeks to guarantee may differ from the spot price at the time of taking out the futures contracts. The greater is the time lapse between agreeing the contracts and closing out the higher will be the expected guaranteed price. Closing out soon after 2 October tends to provide an effective spot price close to the spot price whereas closing out shortly before 1 December give a price close to the futures price at which the contract was agreed.

If the risk being hedged occurs halfway between the present and maturity date the locked in price will be the average of the spot price and the price implied by the futures price, if it occurs after only a quarter of the time has elapsed the price guaranteed would equal three quarters of the spot price plus a quarter of the price implied by the futures price, and so on.

A holder of a futures contract may hold it to maturity. By so doing he guarantees being able to buy or sell the cheapest to deliver gilt at the price implied by the price of the futures contract bought or sold. In most cases contracts are not held to maturity. This might be because the risk being hedged does not fall in a delivery month or because the gilt (or other instrument) being hedged is not the cheapest to deliver gilt.

In the case of a gilt other than the cheapest to deliver its value relative to that of the cheapest to deliver also affects basis. Variations in the relative values of the two gilts would cause movements in basis.

CASH FLOWS

It is useful to consider what type of cash flows might be involved in producing an effective price of the cheapest to deliver gilt along the lines shown in figure 5.6.4. Consider two extreme possibilities.

First, suppose that the futures price corresponds to the expected price and that expectations prove to be correct. In such a case the sum paid for the gilt will change over time, while the futures price remains unchanged. If the price is expected to change in a linear fashion the profile shown by figure 5.6.4 will indicate the amount payable at each point in time.

Second, suppose that the spot price remains constant. In this case the futures price may not represent an expectation but be merely based on the spot price, running yield, and financing costs. Whenever the contract is closed out the same price is paid for the gilts. However the futures price moves towards the spot price at a constant rate over time, becoming equal to it at maturity. This involves the payment (or receipt) of variation margin spread evenly over time. The spot price plus variation margin paid (or received) equals the price implied by the spot and original futures price and which draws closer to the futures price as the maturity (delivery) date of the contract is approached. So, for example, if the contract were held to maturity the difference between the initial futures price and the unchanged spot price would have been paid (or received) in the form of variation margin.

BASIS RISK

As mentioned above, basis, the difference between the futures price and the adjusted spot price (clean spot price divided by the price factor), reflects the financing cost relative to the yield on the gilt. A change in the interest rate on money borrowed to finance the purchase of a gilt in cash and carry arbitrage would alter the basis. Such a change in basis introduces a degree of imperfection into the hedge. The profile suggested by figure 5.6.4 is deviated from. This possibility is known as basis risk.

Fortunately basis risk is likely to be low when the cheapest to deliver gilt is being hedged. As the characteristics of the instrument being hedged diverge further and further from those of the cheapest deliverable gilt basis risk progressively increases. To the basis risk arising from the possibility of changes in financing costs must be added the basis risk from possible changes in the relative prices of the cheapest to deliver gilt and the instrument being hedged. The greater the difference between the cheapest deliverable gilt and the gilt (or other instrument) being hedged the greater is the basis risk arising from this latter source. When basis risk is so large that there is not a close relationship between changes in the futures price and changes in that of the instrument being hedged then this particular futures contract does not provide a suitable means of hedging.

HEDGE DESIGN

The hedger must decide upon the number of contracts required to accomplish the desired hedge. This calculation is simplest when hedging the cheapest to deliver gilt.

$$\text{Number of Contracts} = \frac{\text{Nominal Value of Gilt Position}}{\text{Nominal Value of a Contract}} \times \text{Price Factor}$$

The multiplication by the price factor is necessary to adjust for the price difference between the cheapest to deliver gilt and the notional gilt. A high coupon yield gilt has a higher value to be hedged than a low coupon yield gilt and will require a correspondingly larger number of contracts for the hedging (this difference will be greater the more distant are the maturity dates of the gilts).

Suppose that for the December 1985 contract month the cheapest to deliver Short Gilt was the Exchequer $12\frac{1}{2}$% 1990 whose price factor was 1.0858888. If the hedger wished to hedge £10,000,000 nominal of this Short Gilt the requisite number of contracts would have been calculated thus:

$$\text{Number of Contracts} = \frac{£10{,}000{,}000}{£100{,}000} \times 1.0858888 = 108.58888$$

The hedger would have used either 108 or 109 Short Gilt futures contracts to hedge the position.

When hedging gilts other than the cheapest to deliver account must be taken of the relative volatility of the gilts. Relative volatility can be measured in terms of the money value of a (say) 1% yield change per £100 nominal. If the gilt being hedged is more volatile than the cheapest to deliver a correspondingly greater number of contracts will be required for the hedge (and vice versa for less volatile gilts). In this way the larger price movements of relatively volatile gilts are dealt with. The formula becomes:

$$\text{Number of Contracts} = \frac{\text{Nominal Value of Gilt Position}}{\text{Nominal Value of a Contract}} \times \text{Price Factor of Cheapest to Deliver Gilt} \times \text{Relative Volatility}$$

Thus if the money value of a 1% yield change per £100 nominal were £5 for the gilt being hedged and £3.50 for the cheapest to deliver gilt then the number of contracts necessary to hedge £10,000,000 nominal of the gilts, in an example parallel to the previous one, would be:

$$\text{Number of Contracts} = \frac{£10{,}000{,}000}{£100{,}000} \times 1.0858888 \times \frac{5}{3.5} = 155.13$$

The appropriate number of Short Gilt contracts is 155. A large number of futures contracts is necessary so that the profits or losses on futures succeed in offsetting the relatively large losses or profits on the gilt being hedged. Without adjusting for relative volatility only £3.50 of every £5 price change would be offset. (Note that the difference between the price factor of the hedged gilt and that of the cheapest to deliver is reflected in the relative volatility, a relatively high price factor indicates a relatively expensive gilt — per £100 nominal — and this is reflected in a correspondingly larger price movement for each 1% change in interest rates, and vice versa for a low price factor gilt.)

Changes in relative volatility can reduce the effectiveness of the hedge. This occurs when the relative volatility experienced over the period of the hedge differs from the relative volatility predicted from previous observations. Although this, together with basis risk, tends to reduce the efficiency of hedging an imperfect hedge is better than no hedge at all. Besides it is likely that these imperfections in hedging are not too serious when hedging diversified portfolios of gilts. In such cases the inefficiencies in hedging specific gilts tend to be offsetting.

Sterling bonds, other than gilts, can be hedged with gilt futures; it must be borne in mind that the more dissimilar are the cheapest to deliver gilt and the bond being hedged, the less effective is the hedge likely to be.

The definition of volatility used above is known as perturbation. This uses the impacts of a specific interest rate change (for example 1%) on the prices of the gilt to be hedged and the cheapest deliverable.

There are other approaches to generating the hedge ratio. One is to use the price factor of the gilt being hedged,

$$\text{Number of futures contracts} = \frac{\text{Nominal Value of Cash Gilt}}{\text{Nominal Value of Gilt Future}} \times \text{price factor of hedged gilt}$$

This reflects the fact that relative volatility and relative price factors both emanate from particular characteristics of the gilts, in particular coupon yield and maturity.

A popular approach is to use duration. The duration of a gilt is a measure of the sensitivity of the price of the gilt to changes in the rate of interest. To be more specific duration is the relationship between the proportionate (or percentage) change in the value of the gilt and the proportionate (percentage) change in (1 + r) that caused it, where r is the redemption yield. Although the percentage change in (1 + r) is closely related to the change in the percentage rate of interest the two are not identical.

Relative duration might be used as the relative volatility in the hedge ratio. It is more likely, however, that relative duration is rendered closer to the concept of perturbation when it is used in the calculation of a hedge ratio. In particular the following expression might be used.

$$\frac{\left[1 + \text{Redemption Yield of Cheapest to Deliver}\right]}{\left[1 + \text{Redemption Yield of Hedged Gilt}\right]} \times \frac{\left[\text{Clean Price of Hedged Gilt}\right]}{\left[\text{Clean Price of Cheapest to Deliver}\right]} \times \frac{\left[\text{Duration of Hedged Gilt}\right]}{\left[\text{Duration of Cheapest to Deliver}\right]}$$

The first term in this expression effectively changes the formulation

$$\frac{\textbf{Proportionate Change in Price}}{\text{Proportionate Change in } (1 + r)} \quad \text{into} \quad \frac{\textbf{Proportionate Change in Price}}{\text{Absolute Change in } (1 + r)}$$

The second term in the expression converts proportionate changes in price into absolute changes in price.

In these ways relative duration is turned into the expression

$$\frac{\text{Change in Price}}{\text{Change in } (1 + r)}$$

which differs from perturbation in using the change in (1 + redemption yield) rather than the change in interest rate as the denominator.

STOCK INDEX FUTURES

In May 1984 LIFFE introduced a futures contract based on a stock market index, the Financial Times Stock Exchange (FTSE) 100 index. When using FTSE 100 futures to reduce stock market risk the anticipation is that any losses arising from movements in equity prices are offset by gains from parallel movements in futures prices. An investor might be anxious about the possibility that the prices of his equities might fall. He could reduce the risk of a reduction in the value of his portfolio by taking a position in the futures market that would provide him with a gain in the event of a fall in equity prices. In such a case the investor would take a short position in FTSE 100 futures contracts. By taking a short position he guarantees a notional selling price of a quantity of stock for a specific date in the future. Should equity prices fall and FTSE 100 futures behave in a corresponding fashion the notional buying price for that date would be less than the predetermined notional selling price. The investor could close out his short position in futures by taking a long position in the same number of contracts. The excess of the selling price over the buying price is paid to the investor in cash in the form of variation margin. This gain on the futures contracts is received on a daily basis as the futures price moves (a procedure known as marking to market). Had the prices of equities risen the investor would have gained from his portfolio of equities but lost on his futures dealings. In either case the investor has succeeded in reducing the extent to which the value of his portfolio fluctuates.

FINANCIAL TIMES STOCK EXCHANGE 100 CONTRACTS

The FTSE 100 futures contract is a notional commitment to buy or sell a given quantity of stock on a specified future date at a price determined at the time of taking out the contract. The quantity of stock is a basket of shares in 100 companies. With a few exceptions these are the largest 100 companies in the United Kingdom. The contribution of each company to the total is weighted in proportion to that company's market capitalization. The FTSE 100 index was given a base value of 1,000 on 3 January 1984. Each futures contract is valued at £25 per full index point (so on 3 January 1984 the contract value was £25,000). There are just four delivery dates each year. These are the first business days following the last business days of the months of March, June, September and December. FTSE 100 contracts do not involve delivery of stock if they are held to the delivery day. There would be a final settlement in cash on the delivery day, which together with the variation margin flows that would already have occurred provide compensation for any difference between the FTSE 100 index ruling on the last trading day (the average level of the index between 11.10 and 11.20) and the futures FTSE 100 when the futures contract was entered into. The tick is the smallest price movement allowed by LIFFE. Its size is 0.5 FTSE index points and it has a value of £12.50.

The use of futures to hedge the risk of a fall in stock prices does not require any alteration of the original portfolio. It is thus preferable to any form of hedging that involves changing the composition of the portfolio, for example liquidating part of it. Also, futures trading is off balance sheet.

HYPOTHETICAL EXAMPLES

In Example 6, the portfolio holder fears a generalized fall in equity prices and wishes to avoid a fall in the value of his portfolio.

EXAMPLE 6

Cash Market	*Futures Market*
5 April	
Holds a balanced portfolio of equities valued at £1,000,000 but fears a fall in its value. The current FTSE 100 index is 2000.	Sells twenty June FTSE 100 contracts at a price of 2000 each. He has thus committed himself to the notional sale of £1,000,000 of stock on the June delivery date at the level of equity prices implied by the futures price on 5 April.

10 May

The FTSE 100 index has fallen to 1900. Correspondingly the value of the portfolio has declined to £950,000.

Closes out the futures position by buying twenty June FTSE 100 contracts at a price of 1900. The notional buying price of each contract is thus 100 below the notional selling price. There is a gain of 200 ticks on each of the twenty contracts.

Loss on the portfolio = £50,000.

Gain from futures trading = £50,000 (200 × 20 × £12.50).

By 10 May the portfolio holder feels that the fall in equity prices is complete and chooses to close out his futures position. Should he wish to insure against adverse market movements on a permanent basis he could maintain a permanently open futures position, rolling over contracts as they reach maturity. Of course this strategy is one that reduces variations in the value of the portfolio holder's assets. If, in Example 6, the FTSE 100 index had risen there would have been a cash market gain offset by a futures market loss.

Example 7 shows how a long position in futures can be used as a hedge. In this case a fund manager anticipates receipt of £1m on 10 January and intends to use it to buy a balanced portfolio of United Kingdom equities. He fears, one month earlier, that stock prices will rise before the money is received.

EXAMPLE 7

Cash Market

Rise in the index

10 December

Anticipates receipt of £1m on 10 January. Current FTSE 100 index is 2200. Fears a rise in the index.

10 January

The new FTSE 100 index is 2300.

Requires an additional £45,455 in order to buy the

Futures Market

Buys eighteen March FTSE futures contracts at a price

quantity of stock that £1 million would have bought on 10 December.	of 2200. He thereby notionally commits himself to paying £990,000 (18 × £55,000) for stock on a future date.
	Closes out by selling eighteen March FTSE futures contracts at a price of 2280. He notionally guarantees a receipt of £1,026,000 (18 × £57,000) upon maturity of the contracts.
	Profit from futures of £36,000.

In Example 7 futures prices did not move precisely in line with the FTSE 100 index and as a result the hedge was imperfect. In other words there was a change in basis, which had initially been zero. Of course, if basis had changed so as to establish futures prices in excess of cash market prices the fund manager could have gained more from the futures market than he needed for the hedge.

CROSS-HEDGING

Cross-hedges involve hedging risk on one instrument with futures in another. For example, 3-month sterling certificates of deposit might be hedged with 3-month sterling interest rate futures; or movements of a single share price might be hedged by using FTSE 100 futures. Cross-hedging is subject to greater basis risk and there is a level beyond which basis risk becomes unacceptable. Basis risk can be measured by correlating the changes in the relevant cash market and futures prices. The nearer is the correlation to 1 the closer are the movements of the two instruments. A correlation coefficient of 1 indicates that the cash and futures instruments have moved precisely in line with each other so that changes in the price of the cash market instrument could have been hedged perfectly by the futures instrument. The correlation coefficient of 1 indicates an absence of basis risk in the past and that bodes well for the future. A correlation coefficient of 0 indicates that the two instruments have moved in completely unrelated ways in the past and therefore basis risk is high. Low values of the correlation coefficient suggest that the futures instrument is unlikely to be suitable for hedging risk on the cash instrument. A rule of thumb might be that a correlation coefficient of at least 0.6 is required to suggest that the hedging would be reasonably successful (a correlation coefficient of 0.6 indicates that the proportion of the risk eliminated is 0.36, that is $(0.6)^2$).

The more dissimilar are the cash market instruments, and the instruments upon which the futures are based, the lower would be the correlation coefficient and the higher the basis risk. 3-month sterling CDs and 3-month sterling deposits are very similar and hence futures on the latter (that is 3-month sterling interest rate futures) could safely be used to hedge risk on the former. There is less similarity between, say, a portfolio of shares in financial companies and the portfolio represented by the FTSE 100 so it may be expected that the correlation coefficient is lower and basis risk higher. Reasonable effectiveness of the hedge would be less certain.

HEDGE RATIOS

Hedge ratios become necessary when the volatility of the futures contract is likely to differ from that of the instrument to be hedged. If the instrument to be hedged shows relatively large variations, it is appropriate to use more futures contracts than in the case of a more stable instrument. It is unlikely that a portfolio of equities, for which hedging is required, precisely corresponds to the composition of the FTSE 100 index. It is thus probable that it will show more or less volatility than the index.

The beta factor of a share is a measure of the extent to which it has moved in line with share prices in general. A balanced portfolio is likely to have a beta factor of about 1. A share with only half the movement of the market as a whole would have a factor of 0.5 while one with double the degree of change has a factor of 2. The beta factor of a portfolio of shares is the weighted average of the beta factors of the shares that constitute the portfolio.

If the calculation indicates a beta factor of 1.2, the portfolio tends to change by 20% more than balanced portfolios of shares. Hedging the portfolio would require the value of the FTSE 100 futures contracts used to exceed the portfolio value by 20%. The relatively large losses (or profits) arising from the high volatility require correspondingly large offsetting profits (or losses) from futures contracts, and this necessitates a relatively large number of futures contracts.

DETERMINATION OF FUTURES PRICES

In the chapters on currency and interest rate futures the prices of futures contracts were seen as being determined by arbitrage. Covered interest arbitrage to establish interest rate parity in the case of currency futures, arbitrage based on forward-forward calculations in the case of short term interest rate futures, and cash and carry arbitrage in the case of long term interest rate futures.

Financial Times Stock Exchange 100 futures prices are also affected by cash and carry arbitrage. This arbitrage activity tends to produce futures prices that are at a premium or discount (against spot cash market prices) that is dependent upon the yield on equities relative to the financing cost of holding those equities. However, it is to be expected that this arbitrage effect will be weaker in the case of FTSE 100 futures than in the case of long term interest rate futures, because of the expense of acquiring balanced portfolios of equities, while the gilt arbitrageur needs to acquire only the cheapest to deliver gilt, the FTSE 100 arbitrageur needs to purchase a weighted portfolio of 100 different equities.

Thus factors other than arbitrage acquire significant influence in determining the prices of FTSE 100 futures contracts. Expectations of future share prices are likely to be important. If traders expect share prices to be higher than those suggested by futures prices they will buy futures so as to make profitswhen futures prices rise into line with the expected share prices. These purchases of futures contracts will tend to pull up their prices towards the expected levels. Conversely, if equity prices are expected to be lower than those implied by futures prices, trading for the purpose of obtaining speculative profits would tend to pull down futures prices (futures contracts would be sold with a view to closing out by buying at lower prices). Thus there will be some tendency for FTSE 100 futures prices to reflect expected share prices.

Indeed expectations of future cash market prices are likely to have some influence in the determination of the prices of other futures contracts. This is likely to be the case for the more distant delivery months. Arbitrage opportunities may be more fully taken in the nearer contracts than in the more distant ones so that the prices of the latter become more influenced by expectations of cash market prices. In fact futures prices are often used as indicators of market expectations.

Arbitrage and expectations cannot provide a complete explanation of futures prices. Futures prices are established by demand and supply (offers to buy and sell in the pit). Arbitrage, and trading based on expectations, influence prices by way of their impacts on demand and supply. Anything that impacts on offers to buy and sell will affect prices. In the absence of substantial arbitrage and speculation the desired purchases and sales of futures contracts by hedgers would tend to determine futures prices.

SPECULATORS AND ARBITRAGEURS

These types of transactor serve to render the market liquid and stable. It is unlikely that hedgers' demand for contracts will exactly equal hedgers' supply of contracts for a particular delivery month. Speculators and arbitrageurs fill the gap between demand and supply thereby ensuring the marketability of the contracts and reducing the price fluctuations that result from imbalance between demand and supply.

If there is a temporary excess demand for the contracts of a particular delivery month there would be a tendency for the price of those contracts to rise. The speculator would take a short position in those contracts in anticipation of closing out by taking a long position when the price has fallen back to its normal level. He thus sells at the higher price and buys at the lower price. In so doing he fills the gap between the long and short positions desired by hedgers. Speculators thus help to ensure that hedgers can take the positions required and simultaneously prevent the abrupt price movements that might otherwise result from mismatching of desired short and long positions.

Arbitrageurs may operate between the futures market and the market for the underlying financial instrument. By doing so they help to create liquidity in the futures market and dampen excessive divergences between futures prices and the prices of the underlying financial instruments. Thus if hedgers sought to take a net long position for a particular delivery month there would be a tendency for the price of the contract to rise. The arbitrageur could sell futures and buy equities with a view to subsequently closing both positions and making a profit. Such might be the case if the premium of the futures price over the cash market price gave a return that exceeded the excess of the financing cost of holding equities over the running yield of those equities. Thus tendencies for futures prices to diverge too far from the underlying equity prices would be tempered by arbitrage. This means that arbitrage reduces basis risk.

This arbitrage process is likely to be less than complete for several reasons. First, the arbitrageur faces uncertainty in the equity market. He may incur costs represented by the difference between interest paid on money borrowed to finance the equity purchases and the return on the equities, which takes the form of dividend receipts. These costs are subject to considerable uncertainty arising from the possibility of unexpected changes in dividends. The arbitrageur would therefore look for a risk premium. Secondly, buying a portfolio of equities that correlates strongly with the FTSE 100 is likely to prove expensive since a large number of individual purchases would be involved. Furthermore it is unlikely that they could all be purchased simultaneously with the sale of the futures contracts. The arbitrageur faces the risk of price movements while making his purchases. An arbitrageur seeking to take a long position in the futures market and a short position in the cash market faces the additional problem of how to sell something that he does not have. So arbitrage might operate only weakly in the opposite direction.

KEITH REDHEAD

Lanchester Polytechnic

5.7
Swap financing

The international financial markets have been characterised in recent years by the introduction and growth of a wide range of new products, driven by the needs of the various players to respond to the much increased volatility of interest and foreign exchange rates. At the shorter maturities, these requirements are mainly satisfied by forward foreign exchange contracts, future rate agreements, financial futures and interest rate or currency options. There exists, however, a large number of players with a need to manage their interest rate or foreign exchange exposures in a greater volume or for a longer maturity than is currently practical using these instruments, and it is in response to their needs that the swap market as we know it today has come into being.

Interest rate and currency swaps have grown from a negligible volume to a US$2,000bn market in the space of a few years, and as such now represent one of the major products of the financial world. As this volume has grown, so too has realization of the possibilities inherent in the techniques. By using swaps, participants in the market can, for example:

(1) obtain funds at costs significantly below those otherwise possible, borrowing in those areas of the capital markets in which they possess a competitive advantage, and swapping the proceeds into the desired form;
(2) change the nature of their liabilities, from fixed to floating rate or vice versa, or between currencies, without having to prepay or alter existing underlying borrowings; or
(3) perform similar transformations on asset portfolios, producing assets of a different nature or at better rates than are available directly.

This chapter first describes the nature of the various types of swap transactions, followed by examples of the use of the technique. The mechanics of entering into a transaction are outlined, with comments on typical documentation approaches. Finally, the risk aspects of swaps are discussed, including a description of the nature of the credit risk generated, the effect of recent regulatory action on the market, and issues raised by recent events.

HISTORY

The creation of the swap market is usually regarded as an evolution of the back-to-back loans arranged between British and American organisations during the period of United Kingdom exchange control. Typically, a non-resident company with a British subsidiary would borrow sterling from a British organization in return for lending its own currency (typically dollars) to the British entity's overseas subsidiary. Although this structure satisfied the then prevailing United Kingdom Exchange Control Regulations, it resulted in either party having on its balance sheet both an asset and a liability resulting from the back-to-back loan transaction, in addition to the original borrowing in its own currency. The search was on for a technique to remove this balance sheet expansion, which resulted in the creation of the currency swap at the end of the 1970s.

By defining the cash flows not as a borrowing and offsetting lending, but as a simple exchange of payments to be made between the two parties, the requirement to report the transaction on the balance sheet was avoided. As realization of this possibility spread, the number of deals concluded grew rapidly, as did the number of participants in the market. The basic concept of the exchange of payments was then extended to cover not only different currencies, but different interest rate bases — hence the interest rate swap. Simultaneously, the applications were extended from the original provision of access to restricted currencies, to the varied arbitrage and asset or liability management techniques used today. Thus, in the space of four to five years, a transaction that would originally have been arranged on a customised, on-off basis has become an established and widely understood market technique, with generally-accepted conventions as to definitions, quotation bases, documentation procedures, and dealing practices.

This is not to say that the innovatory process has ended. As the growing number of participants increases competition and reduces profits in the now common conventional transactions, many banks are moving on into new areas, creating such developments as forward swaps, zero-coupon swaps, options on swaps, commodity swaps, and the like. Each of these extends the original concept to address the increasingly sophisticated requirements of the banks' clientele, and thus widens further the range of instruments available.

PRINCIPLES

The underlying principle of a swap is, then, that it is an agreement to make exchanges of payments between two counterparties. Although differing terminology can be used to refer to specific structures, there are two basic types of swap of which the others are essentially variations:

(1) the *interest rate swap* in which the payments exchanged are in the same currency, but calculated on a different basis. The most common type is the

fixed rate/floating rate swap, in which one counterparty agrees to make periodic payments calculated on the basis of interest accruing at LIBOR (the London Interbank Offered Rate) on a notional principal amount in exchange for the receipt of payments calculated using a fixed rate. However, transactions are also arranged between fixed rate and other floating rate indices, such as the US dollar prime rate or a commercial paper index, or between two floating rate indices.

(2) the *currency swap* in which the payments are in different currencies. The most common transactions now involve exchanges of floating rate US dollars for fixed rate Swiss francs, Yen, Deutschmarks or sterling, although a large range of other possibilities exist, whether in terms of alternative currencies, fixed rate:floating rate structures, or floating rate:floating rate swaps.

To illustrate the structure of an interest rate swap, consider a US dollar transaction with a maturity of five years, based on an amount of say $10m. Suppose that the terms of the swap are for interest payments at a fixed rate of 8%, paid semi-annually, to be exchanged for semi-annual payments calculated at six month LIBOR, set by some mutually agreed mechanism at the beginning of each six-month period. Thus, if six month LIBOR is 7% at the beginning of the period, a payment of 3.5% (or US$350,000) will be due from the floating-rate payer and 4% (or US$400,000) from the fixed-rate payer at the end of the period. Commonly, where payments are due on the same date, they will be netted off, resulting, in this case, in a single payment of US$50,000 being made by the fixed-rate payer. The same calculation and payment will then be made at the end of each six-monthly period of the transaction.

This structure represents the usual form of interest rate swap, in which fixed-rate payments are made semi-annually, against floating-rate payments of six-month LIBOR. Variations such as annual or quarterly payment of the fixed rate, or the use of three-month LIBOR, are reasonably common, with other structures being possible, but less widely available.

The mechanics of a currency swap are slightly more complicated due to the introduction of the principal exchange. To create the transformation of an asset or liability from one currency to another, it is necessary for the two parties to exchange payments of the principal amounts at maturity, in a way comparable with the final repayments of offsetting back-to-back loans. This exchange also normally occurs at the start of the transaction, or may be assumed to have taken place (a notional exchange), since it amounts only to a spot foreign exchange trade.

To illustrate the structure, consider a five-year Swiss franc to US dollar currency swap for an amount of Swiss francs 100 million. The spot exchange rate at the commencement date is assumed to be SwFr2.0:$1, the Swiss franc rate to be fixed at 5.0% per annum (payable annually in arrears) and the US dollar rate to be floating at six-month LIBOR (payable semi-annually in arrears).

On the commencement date, the Swiss franc payer will receive SwFr100m from, and pay US$50m to, the US dollar payer (note that payer and receiver are defined in terms of the interest payments, not the initial amounts). Each six months thereafter,

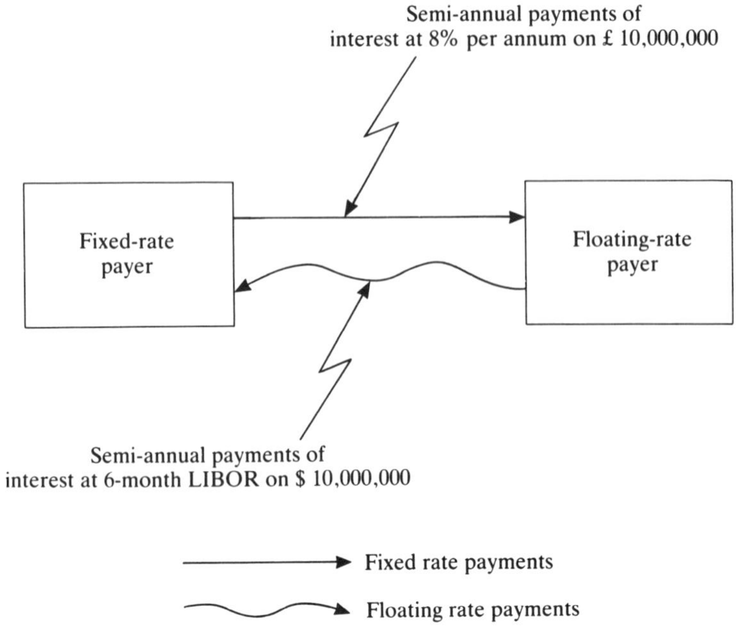

Figure 5.7.1 Interest rate swap

the US dollar payer will pay interest, in dollars, calculated at the six-month LIBOR rate on US$50m. Annually, the Swiss franc payer will pay SwFr5m, being interest at 5% on SwFr100m. At the maturity date, in addition to the final interest payments, the Swiss franc payer will pay the SwFr100m principal amount, and receive US$50m. Thus, the cash flows exactly reproduce those of the back-to-back loan, in which the counterparties would have lent one another SWFR100m and US$50m respectively.

THE MECHANICS — CLOSE-OUT AND DOCUMENTATION

During negotiations prior to closing a deal, swap rates may be quoted either as a spread to government bond yields, or as absolute levels. Although these spreads may be relatively stable, the transaction can only be fully defined, and thus closed out, in terms of the absolute rate of interest. Due to the volatility of interest rates, it is therefore normal for a swap to be concluded by telephone, followed by an exchange of telexes. At this stage, the following details are generally specified:

(1) the identity of the two counterparties;
(2) the type of swap transaction;

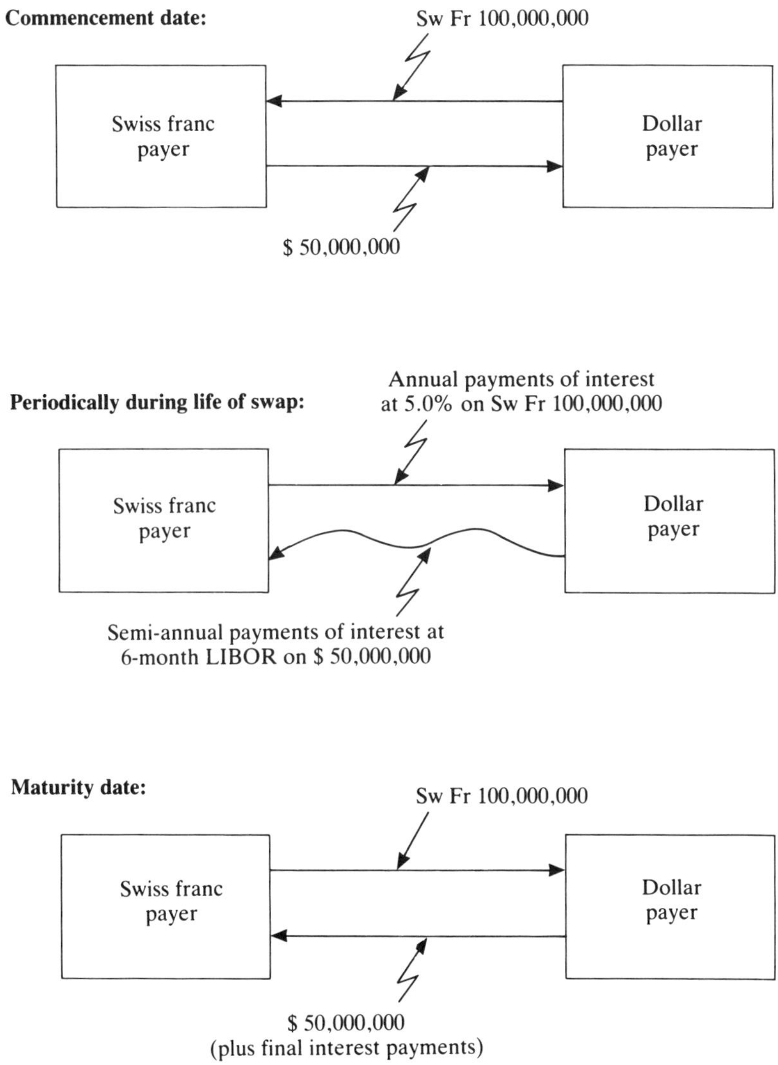

Figure 5.7.2 Currency swap

(3) the notional principal amount;
(4) the agreement, commencement and maturity dates;
(5) the nature of the payments to be made by each party;
(6) the method of calculation and dates of these payments;
(7) the basis on which documentation will be agreed.

In certain circumstances, for instance where the two counterparties have dealt frequently before, or for interbank trades conducted under standard terms and conditions (of which more below), documentation may already be in place and the exchange of telexes will suffice to confirm the details of the transaction. Historically, however, trades were done subject to documentation, to be agreed subsequently between the two parties negotiating in good faith. Where standard documentation is not being used, each bank will tend to have its own document to use as a base for any deal which it undertakes. Although the exact form differs, there are general features in common, usually including:

(1) initial recitals defining the two counterparties, and setting out the basis of the exchange of payments;
(2) the timing and nature of these payments, with specifications of the method of calculation of the amounts, and of the definition of floating rate indices. Typically, these indices will be taken from screen pages such as the Reuters or Telerate services, or failing this from reference banks, or (in the case of non-LIBOR indices) from recognised publications;
(3) specification of events of default, and the action to be taken in such cases;
(4) other causes of early termination (generally including the imposition of withholding taxes, or subsequent legislation rendering the swap illegal);
(5) representations and warranties as to the parties' good standing, and ability to enter into the transaction;
(6) definitions of governing law, and any undertakings necessary to allow the application of this jurisdiction.

Recently, increasing use has been made of standard documentation so as to facilitate the trading of swaps between financial institutions. Both the International Swaps Dealers Association (ISDA) and the British Bankers' Association (BBA) have published documents for this purpose. Whereas the BBA version is widely used in the London interbank market (especially for short-term deals), the ISDA publication is more internationally recognised and is generally used for cross-border transactions, and in particular by United States institutions. Furthermore, the ISDA document is a master agreement which provides for netting (offsetting of exposures in the event of default) between transactions. In view of concerns about credit risks (discussed further below), this has significant potential benefits.

TYPICAL APPLICATIONS

(1) THE CAPITAL MARKETS.
One of the major uses of swaps is as an arbitrage technique in the capital markets, allowing certain borrowers to achieve rates significantly below those otherwise available. Suppose, as an example, that a company wishes to raise fixed rate US dollar funding for five years. One route by which this could be done would be

directly, via a bond issue. If the company's name were not well-known, however, or its credit quality not well perceived, such an issue would require a relatively large spread over the yield of US Treasury bonds. Although such spreads vary, suppose that at the time of issue a margin of 1.50% was required, and that five-year treasury yields were 7.50%, giving a total cost of 9.0% per annum.

It is often true that credit spreads in the floating rate market are significantly lower than those applied to fixed rate funding. Thus, the company might be able to obtain floating rate funds at LIBOR plus 0.25%. Simultaneously, a fixed/floating interest rate swap could be available at United States Treasuries plus 0.85%, or 8.35% per annum, against LIBOR. The company can, therefore, borrow floating rate at LIBOR plus 0.25%, but receive LIBOR payments under the swap against fixed rate payments of 8.35% per annum. The total cost is then 8.35 + 0.25 = 8.60% per annum, or 0.40% per annum below the cost of borrowing fixed rate dollars directly.

The party on the other side of this swap would, typically, be a borrower of good credit standing, who might be able to issue a five-year fixed-rate bond at a cost of United States Treasuries plus 0.40%, or 7.9% per annum. This borrower, however, might really desire floating rate funding for which it would usually have to pay LIBOR flat. By issuing the bond at 7.9% and receiving 8.35% under the swap against payments of LIBOR, the borrower can achieve a net cost of LIBOR minus 0.45% per annum — a saving of 0.45% per annum.

Thus, in this admittedly simplified example, both parties can achieve significant savings compared to their direct costs of borrowing in their desired format. Explaining this seemingly paradoxical result is perhaps the key to understanding the functioning of the swap market as applied to capital market transactions. Essentially, the swap provides an arbitrage between the fixed rate and floating rate markets. Thus, in this example, whereas the cost differential between the two counterparties for fixed rate borrowing was 1.1% per annum, for floating rate funding the difference was only 0.25%. The swap enabled each party to borrow in the market in which it possessed the comparative advantage, and the two to share the mutual benefit.

The currency swap provides an extension to this technique, to provide a similar arbitrage between capital markets denominated in different currencies. Here, competitive advantage in borrowing can often derive more from the recognition value of a borrowers name than from pure credit quality. An example is provided by the rapid growth in the late 1980s of the Australian dollar eurobond market. A fair proportion of bond issues denominated in Australian dollars were placed with retail investors on the Continent who were attracted by the relatively high coupons available, and who were prepared to take the risk of currency depreciation. However, these investors preferred to purchase bonds issued by organisations with which they were familiar. Hence, German banks, for example, were able to issue fixed rate Australian dollar Eurobonds at competitive rates, although having no requirement for Australian dollar funding. Simultaneously, an Australian borrower which did require such funding may have found that its costs for raising fixed rate debt in the domestic Australian markets were unattractively high. This organization could,

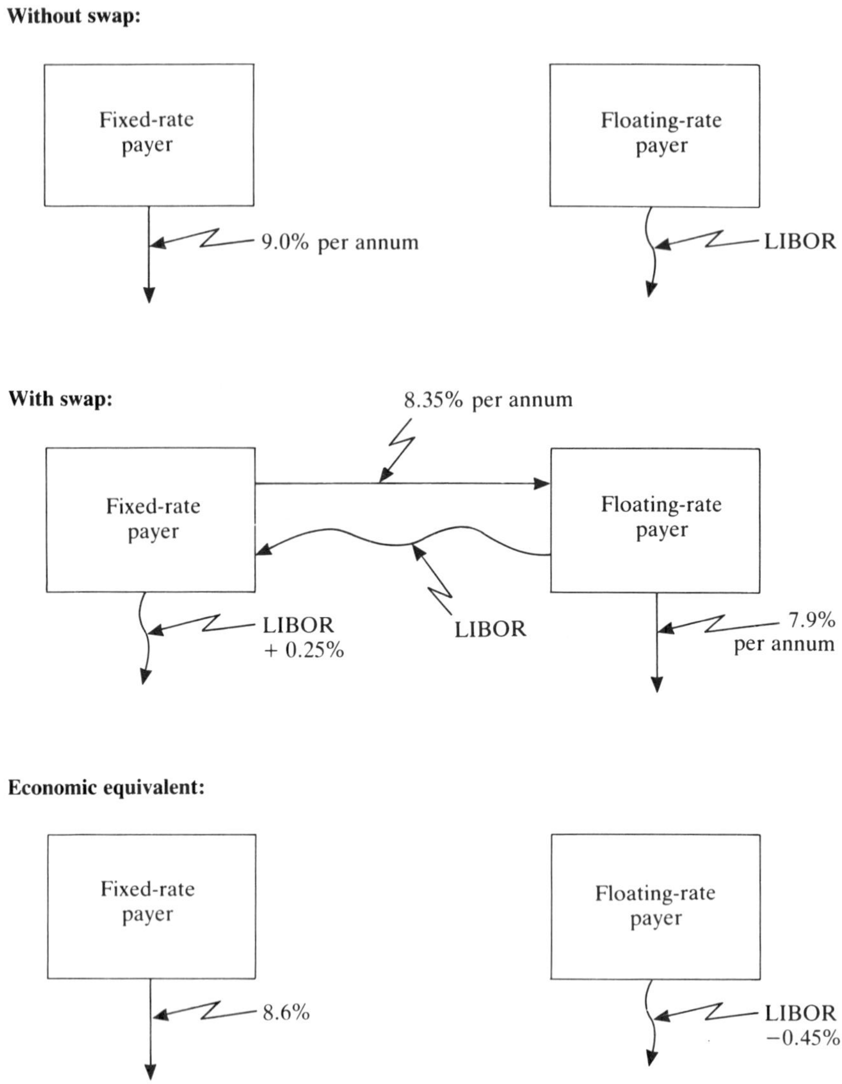

Figure 5.7.3 Use of swaps in capital markets

however, raise floating rate US dollar debt (through bank lending or a floating-rate note issue) at a comparatively cheap rate.

The opportunity then again arose for each party to raise debt in its area of comparative advantage, and for the two to swap the proceeds to mutual gain. Thus, the Australian dollars raised by the German bank would be passed to the Australian counterparty which would meet the coupon payments on the bond, while the German bank would have the use of and pay interest on the Australian's US dollar proceeds. In this way, it was possible for parties to such transactions to achieve savings of 0.50% to 0.75% per annum on their respective borrowing costs.

(2) LIABILITY MANAGEMENT.

Prior to the development of the swap market, borrowers could attempt to match their liabilities to the nature of incoming cash flows, and in accordance with their views on interest rates, only by taking decisions at the outset to which they would be largely committed for the lifetime of the transaction, unless willing to pay prepayment penalties.

Using swaps allows the net economic nature of liabilities to be altered as desired, without necessitating changes in underlying borrowings. Thus, a corporate treasurer with an established source of floating-rate funding might, after a period of falling interest rates, take the view that rates have fallen far enough that the replacement of all or part of this finance with term fixed-rate funds would be desirable. By paying the fixed rate on an interest rate swap, against receipt of floating rate payments which offset his existing interest costs, he can achieve this switch without having to cancel his existing borrowing arrangements. Should he then be correct in his view, and rates subsequently rise, he would later be able to arrange another offsetting swap in which he would receive a higher fixed rate. He would thus return to making a net floating rate payment, but receiving in addition the benefit of the increases in rates, in the form of the difference between the two fixed payments. Currency swaps extend the same concepts to foreign exchange exposure, allowing international organizations who find that the currency mix of their operations has changed, or who are willing to take a view on exchange rate and relative interest levels, to adjust their liabilities accordingly.

It should be noted, however, that the extent to which activities of this type are undertaken varies markedly amongst organisations. Although many are interested in relatively straightforward transactions such as locking in their borrowing costs following falls in interest rates, relatively few (perhaps unsurprisingly) consider their role to encompass the continual view-taking (and consequent risk of being wrong) that aggressive liability management would entail. The point here is rather to demonstrate the possibilities provided by the swap technique.

(3) ASSET SWAPS.

Just as swaps can be used to change the nature of liabilities, so similar transformations can be performed on assets. Such an operation is commonly referred to as an asset swap.

A common example of this is the creation of a synthetic floating-rate asset from a fixed-rate bond. Due to the differing preferences of typical investors in the fixed and floating-rate markets, it is sometimes possible to obtain fixed-rate issues at a sufficiently high yield that they can be sold, along with an interest rate swap, as an

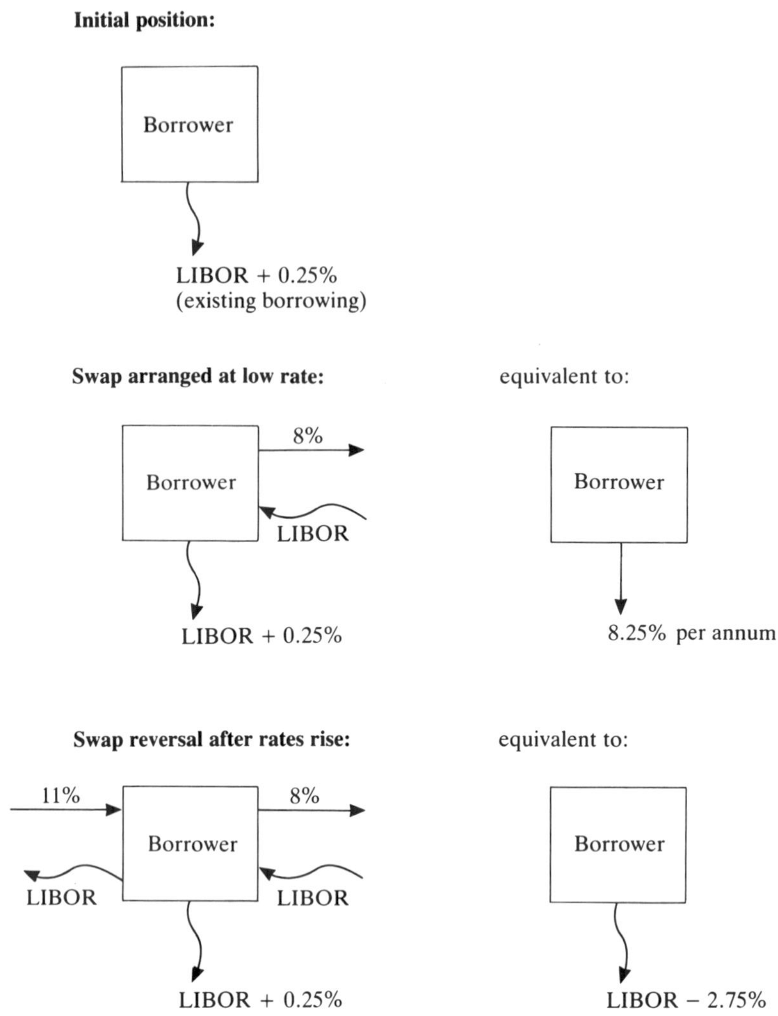

Figure 5.7.4 Liability management

attractive package for floating-rate investors. Thus, a bond issued by, say, a corporate borrower may be trading at an annual yield of 10%. If at the time swap rates are such that 10% fixed-rate swaps into LIBOR plus 0.30%, the bond plus swap may be packaged together and sold to a floating-rate investor (typically a bank) as an asset yielding a net LIBOR plus 0.30%.

This yield will generally be rather more than that available on FRN's or other

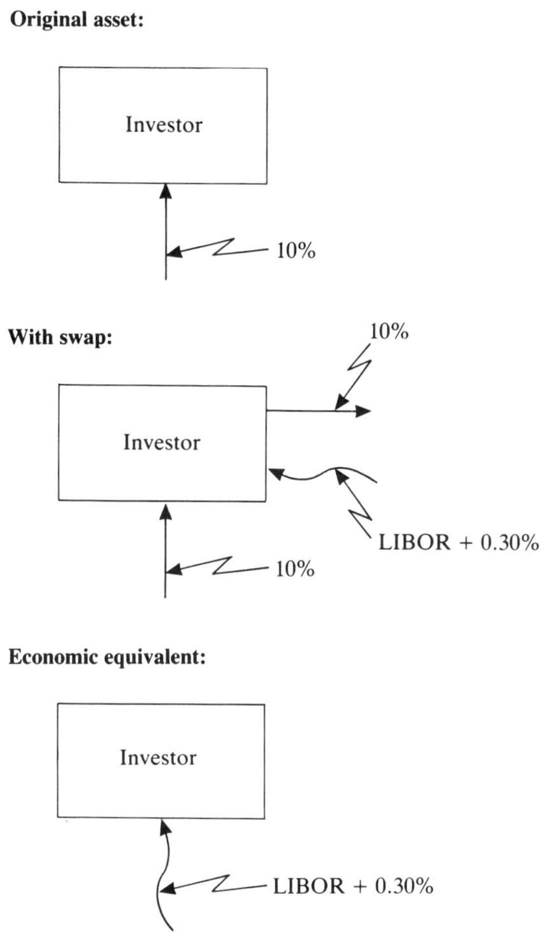

Figure 5.7.5 Asset swap

floating rate borrowings by the same issuer. Although part of this pick-up will represent recompense to the investor for the illiquidity of the package, many banks are actively searching for floating-rate assets as traditional lending activities diminish, and are prepared to accept this loss of flexibility.

Although technically possible, the opposite process of the creation of synthetic fixed rate assets from floating rate is rarer. As opposed to the banks looking to invest at floating rates, fixed-rate investors place a much higher premium on liquidity. They are, therefore, generally unwilling to purchase such non-tradeable synthetic packages.

ROLE OF THE BANKS IN THE SWAP MARKET

This variety of application of the swap technique is aided greatly by the fact that banks now act as principals in a large proportion of transactions. This in turn reflects the way in which the market has grown. Initially, banks simply acted as arrangers of deals between large counterparties of good credit standing. As the market grew, problems began to arise as either an offsetting counterparty could not be found in time for a particular client, or two non-bank parties would be reluctant to take each other's credit risk. This led banks to begin acting as intermediaries, in the latter case to effectively guarantee (for a fee) the credit standing of their clients, and in the former case, to position a swap (that is to enter into a deal with one counterparty before finding the other) so as to allow the completion of the deal with the first client.

A bank which has a positioned swap on its books carries the risk of rates moving before the other side can be closed out. This led to the development of techniques for hedging the risk, using government bond, futures and foreign exchange markets to offset losses resulting from such fluctuations. For example, a bank which positions a swap in which it pays a US dollar rate of 8.3%, or 0.8% over the current five-year US Treasury yield of 7.5%, could hedge its risk by buying the five-year Treasury bond. Then, if five-year rates were to fall, the resultant decline in the rate at which the position could be closed out would be offset by a profit realised on the Treasury bond holding. The bank's exposure is thereby reduced to a risk on the spread (here 0.8% per annum) between swap and Treasury rates.

This ability to position and hedge swaps led to some banks beginning to make markets continuously, quoting fixed rates which they would receive and pay for a particular maturity. This was originally primarily in US dollars, but has now spread to other currencies, despite the greater difficulty in hedging due to the lower liquidity of the Government bond markets, and the greater volatility of swap rates relative to Government bond yields.

Hedging techniques have been developed beyond the simple methods described above, using ideas originally generated for the management of fixed-rate bond portfolios. In particular, duration analysis, and the calculation of present values based upon zero-coupon interest rates, are now used by most major players to allow complete flexibility in the handling of complex cashflows. Thus, most large institutions are now able to quote for transactions with almost any desired structure of interest rates, or principal amounts.

A full description of these techniques is outside the scope of this book. However, they are essentially based upon the analysis of each payment generated by the swap book as a separate cash flow. The present value of each of these flows can then be found, and the sensitivity of these present values to changes in interest rates examined. Adding across the whole book gives the total picture for the portfolio. These methods, by analysing cash flows rather than transactions, treat the swaps simply as generators of payments. Thus, almost any transaction structure can be analysed.

CREDIT RISK

The question of credit has represented a major area of uncertainty in the swap market. As the volume of transactions completed grew so rapidly, concern was expressed as to the potential risks being run by commercial and investment banks active in the market. As swaps do not need to appear on the balance sheet, they escaped capital adequacy requirements imposed by central banks, thus giving rise to the possibility of large exposures being generated, without requiring a corresponding increase in the institutions' capital base. Furthermore, swap documentation and associated termination clauses have yet to be fully tested in a court of law.

The risk involved in a swap transaction is a contingent one: for a loss to occur, firstly a counterparty must fail, and secondly this failure must occur at a time when interest or foreign exchange rates have moved so as to prevent the replacement of the defaulter by a new counterparty, except at a less favourable level. For example, a bank may have two offsetting transactions, arranged at a time when five-year interest rate swap levels were around 12% fixed against LIBOR. Thus, the bank receives 12% per annum from and pays LIBOR to one party, while paying say 11.9% per annum to, against receipts of LIBOR from, the other. If now the counterparty paying the fixed rate were to fail, the bank would be left with an open position, exposed to declines in interest rates, and would seek to replace the fixed-rate player. If rates had fallen since the deal was arranged, this would be possible only at a lower level, say 9% per annum. Hence, the bank's original profit of 0.1% per annum becomes a loss of 2.9%.

In the case of a currency swap, the potential exposure becomes greater, due to the introduction of the foreign exchange element in addition to the possibility of changes in interest rates.

The calculation of the size of these potential counterparty risks is somewhat subjective, since it is a function of the possible movements in rates during the life of the deal, which can of course only be estimated. Although each institution will have its own procedures, the contingent exposure recognised is generally, except perhaps for longer-maturity currency swaps, considerably less than the notional principal amount of the deal, as it is the value of the interest and principal exchange payments, rather than the principal itself, which is at risk.

This process has been formalised by the imposition by regulators of capital adequacy requirements on off-balance sheet instruments. Statistical work has been performed to assess the degree of risk which could be incurred on various types of contract, giving rise to formulae for calculating the potential exposure which should be recognised. Under the capital adequacy rules, this potential exposure is then added to the current replacement cost of the transaction. The total exposure thus calculated will then count as part of the institution's risk assets, against which it will be required to maintain a minimum level of capital. Although it was envisaged that the imposition of the requirements would be a gradual process, certain countries (including the United Kingdom) are moving more quickly and are using the new framework as of the beginning of 1990.

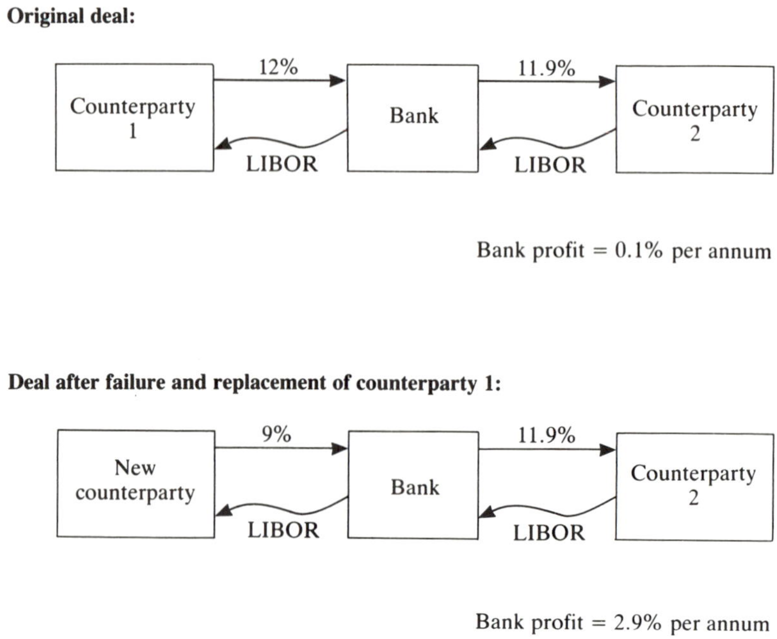

Figure 5.7.6 Credit risk

The developments have had an effect on swap market practices. Although many institutions had already had in place procedures for monitoring the degree of counterparty exposure incurred through swap activities, the introduction of capital adequacy requirements forced banks to control this more closely, and to assess the returns being generated on the capital thus needed. Although for short-term interest rate swaps typical spreads were sufficiently large to provide adequate returns, for long-term transactions and currency swaps this reassessment is generally understood to have resulted in a widening of spreads, and some reduction in liquidity.

Events in the United Kingdom during 1989 served to further increase this focus on the potential counterparty risks of swap transactions, when the legality of local authority business was challenged. The situation is unresolved at the time of writing, however possible bank losses should their agreements with local authorities indeed prove unenforceable have been estimated at several hundreds of millions of pounds. Although more a legal than a strict credit issue, this experience has graphically illustrated for many institutions the importance of risk analysis.

MARKET DEVELOPMENTS

Despite these problems, however, the swap market has continued to develop. The development of hedging techniques and the ability to handle complex cash flows, as described above, have not been the only areas of progress. There has, for example, also been significant growth in the application of options theory to swaps, to allow banks to offer an increased range of option products. An option on a swap is in principle the same as any other kind of option, in that in exchange for a premium, the buyer obtains the right to enter into a transaction at a predetermined cost (in this case, the swap rate).

Thus, a buyer might obtain the option, on or by a certain date, to enter into a swap in which he is paying or receiving a predefined fixed rate against LIBOR on a specified notional principal amount. Alternatively, he might enter into a swap, but obtain the option to cancel it (without penalty) at some future time. The development of the theory has been such that major players are today able to offer almost any desired structure of swap and option, to suit a counterparty's particular needs.

Another notable recent development has seen the extension of swap techniques to the commodity markets, through the introduction of commodity swaps. Although commodity futures or forwards have been in existence for some time, trading is typically concentrated in contracts maturing within three or six months. Such markets could not provide long-term hedges to exposures to changes in commodity prices.

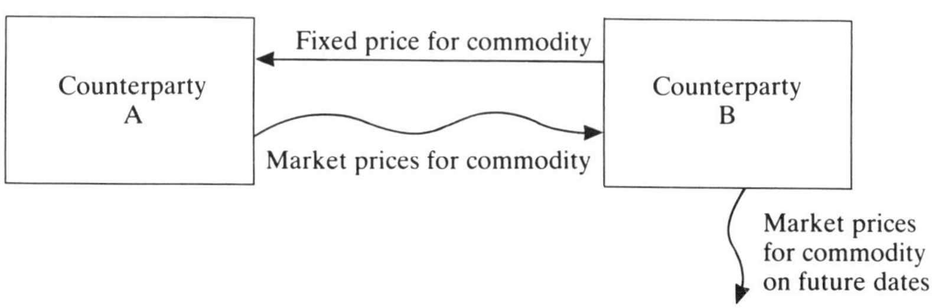

Figure 5.7.7 Commodity swap

The commodity swap is based upon exactly the same principles as an interest rate swap, except that instead of interest rates, commodity prices are used. Thus, a fixed rate would be defined, being a defined price which one party would pay at regular periods for a specified amount of the commodity. The floating rate would be the current market price at each future repricing date, set by some agreed formula relating to published prices. At each settlement date, an amount equal to the difference between the fixed and current prices would be paid. This structure allows an organization which will need to buy the commodity in the future to fix its future costs by physically buying in the cash markets, receiving the costs of those market purchases as one leg of the swap, and paying a fixed rate as the other leg.

CONCLUSION

This chapter can only be a brief discussion of a sophisticated and rapidly evolving area. As already mentioned, new swap products are continually being developed, and the approaches of the various players to the market changed or redefined. Thus, what is today standard practice, may in a short time be replaced by new methods or different perspectives.

In an environment of such change, categoric prediction is rash; the swap, however, seems now to be a permanent feature of international financing techniques, and to have a major role in the increasing integration and globalization of the financial markets.

COLIN R.B. SMITH

KPMG Peat Marwick McLintock, Management Consultants

BIBLIOGRAPHY

Bank of England (October 1988), paper, '*Implementation of the Basle Convergence Agreement in the United Kingdom*'.

Bank for International Settlements (April 1986), paper, '*Recent Innovations in International Banking*'.

Basle Committee of Banking Supervisors (July 1988), paper, '*International Convergence of Capital Measurement and Capital Standards*'.

British Bankers' Association (August 1985), book, 'Interest Rate Swaps ('BBAIRS' terms)'.

International Financing Review (November 1985), '*Inside the Swap Market*', book, IFR Publishing.

International Swap Dealers Association, Inc. (1985), book, '*Code of Standard Wording, Assumptions and Provisions for Swaps*'.

ANTLE, B. (ed.), (1983), book, '*Swap Financing Techniques*', Euromoney.

International Swap Dealers Association, (1987), book, '*Interest Rate and Currency Exchange Agreement*'.

5.8
Options and other derivative products

The opening theme of any discussion on derivative products is usually their increasing importance as hedging and speculative tools. The need for these instruments is explained by the increasing volatility of global markets and the inescapable need to protect income streams and balance sheets in order to remain competitive in this environment. This environment encompasses the vast array of foreign exchange, interest rates, equities and commodities. The unspoken implication is that traditional hedging products, such as forward foreign exchange, have suddenly lost their efficiency, and cannot cope with the needs of a modern treasury. The treasurer's salvation, we are told, like with the second and third generation of evolved products.

The majority of treasurers have long been operating with traditional products and find them both adequate and efficient; skipping lightly over that fact, corporate treasurers are now told that, to achieve any sort of modern day credibility, it is their fiduciary duty to trade a six month US$ call sterling put with strike at the money, or better still a 5–7 swaption to protect interest costs in the light of the glaringly obvious intentions of the Chancellor of the Exchequer!

Today's cornucopia of products creates its own problems. Competing financial institutions, with the inability to differentiate their products except by name, deluge the treasurer with a downpour of scouts, cylinders, zero cost, participation options, firms, Foxes, break forwards, Back Ratio Spreads, Bero's, and all the rest, claiming that this or that tailor-made product, and it alone, will solve the client's risk management concerns. Compounding the problem, the sales approach may include the claim that product X enhances reward without an equivalent gain in risk — a free lunch — an obvious nonsense.

Look at the whole issue again from a slightly different, more intuitive viewpoint. The framework for discussion considers the following:

What are derivatives?
Uncertainty and activity: reasons for growth and influence.

The tools of risk: the practicalities of the markets.
Use: active financial management, yield enhancement.
The politics of risk.
Customer-driven innovation

Treasurers and finance directors need to understand the interrelated forces that shape and move financial markets in order to understand the products that are available, and to analyze objectively these risk management tools in relation to cost and effectiveness. The analysis includes not only risk exposure, but also internal accounting treatment and control procedures. Finally, the politics of risk and how the use of hedging tools are aligned with corporate structure and operational culture must be borne in mind.

WHAT ARE DERIVATIVES?

All off-balance sheet products are derivatives, which are also defined as highly margined products, either directly margined as in futures trading or by premium payments from the option markets. Also there is always the element of leverage or gearing. Leverage occurs when profit and loss projections are not in a straight line, but increase dramatically depending on certain future events occurring, for example favourable spot movements. This deliberately generalized definition is important because it illustrates the size of the universe of derivative products: futures to forward rate agreements, options to forward exchange agreements. It indicates that trading foreign exchange spot or forwards on a margin basis is using a derivative product. This is true for any contract where principal amounts are not exchanged at the inception of the deal.

This brings us to the second implication. It is not the product but the method of transaction that determines a derivative product. Derivative products are not instruments created in isolation: they must also have a basis in known products. A forward contract that can be reneged on is a foreign exchange option. A forward-forward contract with no exchange of principal is a forward rate agreement (FRA). A three month deposit or loan without payment of principal is a zero-threes forward rate agreement.

The third point is slightly more subtle but again evolves from the former points. The definition of derivation implies that options, FXAs, FRAs and the rest are built up from traditional products. This assumption is incorrect. The purchase of a FX Option to buy US$ against sterling and the sale of an equivalent option to sell US$ against sterling results in a simple forward position. However, we cannot create any option product using a forward position. Which one then is the building block, the primary unit — the option or the forward? The creative nature of options is not limited to replicating forwards with a combination of purchased or sold puts and calls at different strike levels. Options can create any loss or reward profile required by a company and this powerful attribute should never be underestimated. Despite their abundance they can all be arbitraged through known products, and options in particular can be used as the building blocks of all other financial products.

In short there are two kinds of derivative product. There are the products that are margined directly: futures, forward rate agreements, and others, and there are the option products such as FX options, IR options, and warrants, which provide other advantages apart from the initial non-payment of principal. It is the second group of derivatives and their attributes that will form the main thrust of this chapter. This is because the building block aspect of options sets this risk management tool apart from all other financial instruments. It is not the limited loss, unlimited gain sales pitch beloved by the institutional salesmen. Treasury managers have been replicating this limited loss and unlimited gain scenario for years by stop and loss orders. An option does provide an automatic stop or loss, but how often does one encounter a market crash in which the automatic stop or loss capability of an option is required?

As stated above, option products can provide the treasurer with any risk or reward profile he might require at any market level for any time period. For example, a treasurer might require protection against a dollar appreciation against sterling in three, six or nine months time between 1.45-1.50, 1.47-1.53, from1.56 down and so on. The same is true for options on all other products. Single options or options in various combinations can produce the arbitrage against the forward contract. The forward contract is only a combination of options as is the spot contract. Therefore, if there were no transaction or administrative costs, a treasurer would be indifferent between trading options or forwards.

To take it to its logical conclusion, the forward contract is just one particular option profile and there is a universe of profiles on either side of the contract.

If a treasurer's needs can be satisfied by a straightforward purchase or sale of currency, then his choice is only between the real-world transaction costs of the option combination and a forward. Naturally the forward contract with its one market spread against the two option spreads will win ninety-nine times out of a hundred. It is when you consider the universe of alternative forward positions that we approach an option combination whose extra costs, but maybe more applicable benefits, overcome the convenience of doing a forward contract.

The decision process becomes more complicated, however, when the treasurer's needs become more complex. In particular, when they involve not just hedging but the active use of treasury resources to increase revenue: that is when the treasurer wishes to take advantage of complex arbitrages or transitory windows of opportunity. Options can provide more than this to the treasurer. The treasurer can lock into an average rate Asian option; a maximum or minimum rate Lookback option, or can initiate or leave a contract depending on some pre-determined level being activated using Knockout options. He can even decide to do all this in the future with an option on an option.

Consider the profiles in figure 5.8.1.

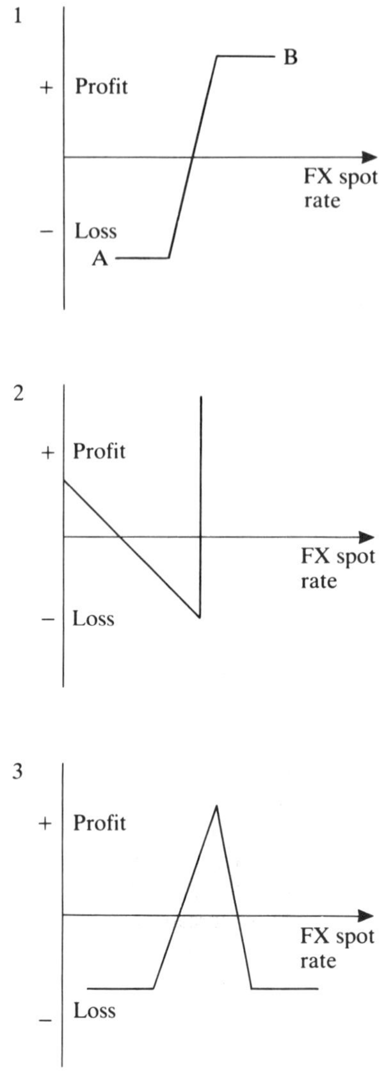

Figure 5.8.1 FX Profiles

Against which benchmark can a treasurer analyse the FX profiles? In (1) he wishes to take advantage of the market trading between A and B but does not expect to enjoy any further gains above B. In (2), usually before the release of major economic figures, the treasurer expects a violent move one way or the other, but biased on the upside. In (3) the treasurer expects no move in the market, but if he is wrong there is a very limited downside.

These are profiles that take account of not only upward or downward movements but also of ranging markets, quiet markets and so on. The main point resurfaces yet again. The treasurer can take full advantage of his views no matter how specific they are. The problem is of analysis and finding true worth, and the forward market is not too far removed for easy comparison. There is no simple way, but as we try to formalize a decision process let us not be distracted by jargon and irrelevant theory. The simple issues we will be emphasising throughout are real needs of treasurers, and the costs of fulfilling those needs, in terms of premium and acceptable risk.

To summarize, derivatives are a universe of instruments which can always be related to known traditional instruments. There are two kinds of derivatives. The first are the direct margin instruments which only differ from the traditional on balance instruments in the non-payment of initial principal, FRA and others. The second, or true derivatives, are option based and must be considered purely in the light that they can be used to reproduce not only every known financial product, but also every and any risk, reward or time profile that is desired.

EFFECTIVE SPOT

Figure 5.8.2 shows an example of the specific risk profiles now available through derivatives. This company issued 5 year Yen debt swapped into US$ with attached foreign exchange Yen/US$ options. The coupon payments were hedged in the forward market but the principal was hedged via a derivative package. The addition of these options allowed the company to ignore the actual spot rate at expiry, and instead convert their Yen principal at the Effective Spot Rate. For example, with spot at 160 Yen/US$ the company effectively trades at 150 Yen/US$ while with actual spot above 190 Yen/US$ the embedded options have no effect and actual spot is equal to the effective spot rate.

The loss on the option principal when the Yen is purchased is compensated for by the fact that repaying the Yen debt is now considerably cheaper. Lower down the profile the converse holds true. The higher cost of repaying the debt is now set against the profit on the option exercise. This profile gave this company the potential to enhance yields, and protect their principal, while hedging away unacceptable areas of risk. In practice the company discusses their requirements and exposures with the financial institution. They both make compromises on risk and reward until a final profile is achieved.

UNCERTAINTY

The rapid growth in options usage stems from the problem of uncertainty. Not only volatility and unpredictability in the markets, but also uncertainty of companies' own cash flows. Whenever there is uncertainty in size of cash flows, the timing of cash flows and the level of requisite hedging, then the option products outweigh the traditional products in benefit.

Option products also enhance financial management. More companies are

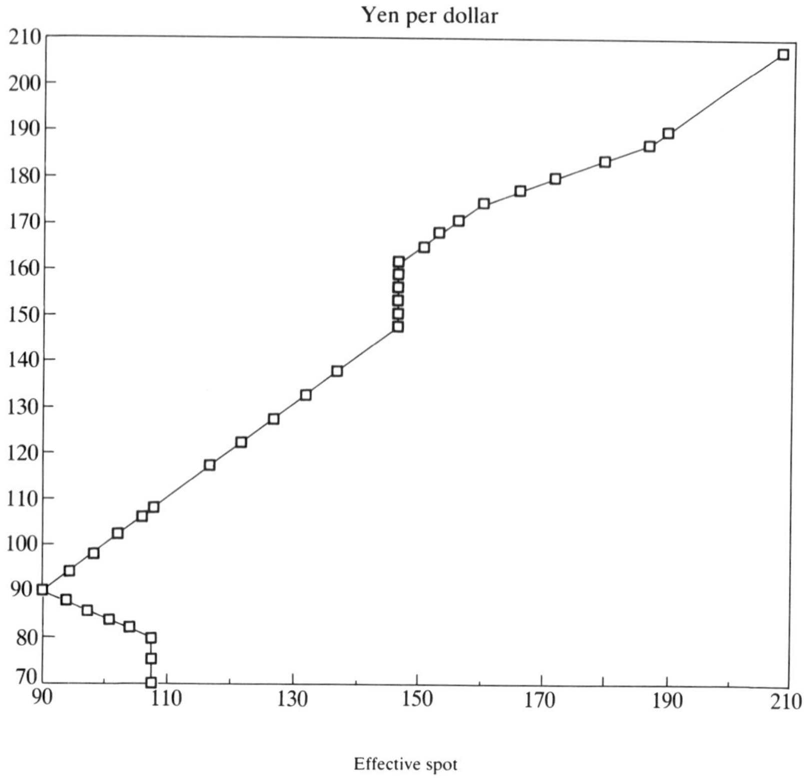

The above is an example of the specific risk profiles now available through derivatives. This company issued 5yr Yen debt swapped into US$ with attached foreign exchange Yen/US$ options. The coupon payments were hedged in the forward market but the principal was hedged via a derivative package. The addition of these options allowed the company to ignore the actual spot rate at expiry, and instead convert their Yen principal at the "Effective Spot Rate". For example, with spot at 160 Yen/US$ the company effectively trades at 150 Yen/US$ while with actual spot above 190 Yen/US$ the embedded options have no effect and actual spot is equal to the effective spot rate. The loss on the option principal when the Yen is purchased is compensated for by the fact that repaying the Yen debt is now considerably cheaper. Lower down the profile the converse holds true. The higher cost of repaying the debt is now set against the profit on the option exercise. This profile gave this company the potential to enhance yields, and protect their principal, while hedging away unacceptable areas of risk. In practice the company discusses their requirements and exposures with the financial institution. They both make compromises on risk and reward until a final profile is achieved.

Figure 5.8.2 Spot versus effective FX

finding it possible to increase revenue by employing the strength of their cash flows to leverage into more profitability. Corporate treasurers, instead of fully locking in profit or losses immediately, are now taking more risk but of a very specific nature — specialized risk — between set levels, over certain periods which is not possible with traditional instruments. There is a strong argument that corporates should look only to their traditional business for revenue. On the other hand a different approach to risk can increase corporate revenues. Closer co-ordination between sales, manufacturing and treasury can provide virtually risk-free arbitrages for the resourceful treasurer to exploit. This taking on of specific risk is proving increasingly popular and is utilized through all option products: in foreign exchange selling away currency gains; in equities selling covered warrants, and decreasing costs in debt structures by attached warrants.

THE TOOLS OF RISK

The nature and behaviour of options is fundamentally identical for foreign exchange, interest rates, debt and commodities. This basic uniformity is altered only by the peculiarities indigenous to the particular underlying contract. A US$:DM option will follow the peculiarities of that FX contract and an option on equities will to the same extent be sympathetic to the liquidity factors and trading rules of the underlying stock.

These indigenous factors mean that you cannot trade the option contract without a comprehensive understanding of the underlying instrument. If the latter is illiquid outside the year, the option will be even more illiquid. The first source that the option trader looks to for hedging is the underlying instrument and any problems in the price of this will be reflected in the option price. Strike levels that are a long distance away from the equivalent forward contract on either side become increasingly illiquid. Short-dated options are also illiquid because of the closeness to a spot position and the risk of being whipsawed around the strike levels.

There are two main markets for trading option products — the Over The Counter market and the exchanges. The larger market is the Over The Counter where all the products are derived. The exchanges provide alternative markets for the more liquid products and, in some products, with the exception of foreign exchange, may provide tighter pricing and liquidity. A further benefit of the exchanges is the lack of credit risk, but this is often offset by the structured nature of the market and the payment of brokerage charges.

USE

Options come into their own when there is uncertainty in cash flows. Let us take an example of a tour operator who is subject to fluctuating currency rates. The effect of these, if detrimental, is passed on to the customer in terms of a surcharge or other such penalty. The operator's main exposure is to US$ appreciation, which will affect the costs of transport and accommodation included in his holiday packages. The tour operator can protect himself via the purchase of a US$ call/sterling put for the relevant period. He can either choose to pay his premium up front or sell away any potential sterling appreciation, which he is in effect indifferent to, as his revenue is based in this currency. The options are shown in figure 5.8.3.

The advantage over the forward is that between A-B the tour operator is not obliged to hedge as he would have if he had traded the forward contract. In the forward-

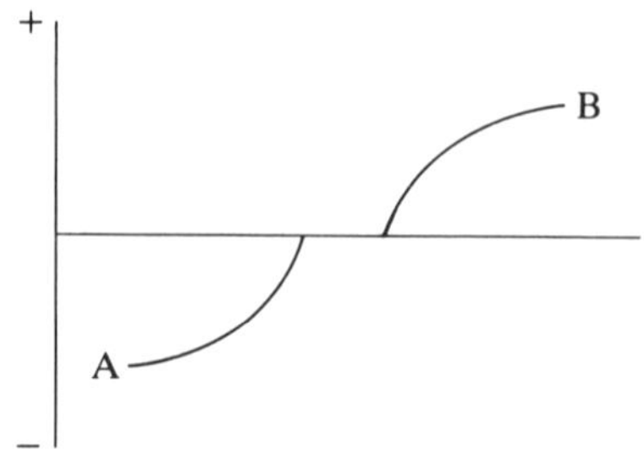

Figure 5.8.3 A tour operator's options

contract he would have lost the points immediately. The option combination costs nothing but has best and worst case levels of A and B. The decision is the treasurer's. Does he lock in his forward rate now and run the risk of being uncompetitive or does he achieve more benefit by setting a range outside which he is automatically hedged?

Conversely, idle funds can generate more revenue by selling covered options. Advantage can be taken of fundamentals. For example, buying a sterling cap to take advantage of appreciating interest rates. The careful treatment of this activity can result not only in straight profits but also in pre or post tax arbitrages. In a simple example, the treasurer sells a three month option to lend sterling at L%. For three months the cost is X basis points. In the best case we have improved our lending level by X basis points and in the worst case we have targeted a maximum level of L% + X basis points today for the next three months. This may suit corporate treasurers for other less obvious reasons — to lock in funding costs in the run up to the end of their financial year.

THE POLITICS OF RISK

Despite the numerous applications of options, there is resistance in some institutions not to go down the learning curve in terms of administration, control and accounting. Adoption of derivative products can often go directly against the culture of a company. The emergence of *zaitech* problems in Japan is cited as an example where the lure of financial activity resulted in the companies either ignoring their core business or adopting risk not commensurate with the business. But the trading of traditional products in itself is a decision. Locking in a forward price is a profit or loss decision — particularly in terms of missed profit potential. Not trading derivative products is not a breach of fiduciary duty, but the consideration of all trading alternatives must always be in the treasurer's interest. Treasurers may have further battles to fight in terms of board approval. The control and monitoring of these products involve a software and hardware commitment. There are back office and settlement issues. There is also the issue of accounting and tax treatment on products where there are often no clear guidelines. It is no wonder that corporate boards balk at the commitment required, or are slow to believe that all support mechanisms are in place.

ASIAN OR AVERAGE RATE OPTIONS

An Asian option is an option whose strike price is not compared to the exchange rate at maturity, but to the average exchange rate over the period of the option.

For example, an option giving the right to buy US$ 10m against Yen over a three month period at the rate of Yen 135:US$1.

	Standard Option	*Asian Option*
Strike	135.00	135.00
Exchange rate at expiry (ER)	137.50	137.50
Average exchange rate over period	—	141.21
Payment to option buyer	10m (137.50–135)/ER = US$182,000	10m (141.21–135.00)/ER = US$ 451,600
Premium (% of US$ principal)	= 0.61	= 0.52

The above example shows the Asian option with a higher return than the standard option but it is clear that depending on the spot price at maturity the standard option could offer a better return. This option can be 10 to 20% cheaper depending on the frequency of sampling.

ADVANTAGES

Standard options are effective when hedging single cash flows at a known future date. Standard options and forwards are certainly not effective when hedging a large number of cash flows distributed uncertainly over time.

But the typical institution with foreign exposures has exactly this type of fluctuating cash flows even though it will know the approximate total cash flow over a given period. Asian options are perfectly designed to cover this exposure.

Most accepted accounting treatments of foreign exchange exposure depends on the average foreign exchange rate — and as such this is ideal for accounting.

Cheapness. The hedging institution is only concerned about the average exchange rate and not the exchange rate when each of his separate cash flows come due. Naturally this option will cost less than the sum of the separate options for each period — usually 15% less.

Comparison to forwards. For the same reason transaction costs (spread costs) incurred by hedging each cash flow makes forward dealing impractical and unnecessary. Institutions that regularly engage in forward dealing should examine this as a possible alternative to cut down their hedging cost.

HOW IT WORKS

The buyer of the option now decides not only the principal amount, strike price, and period for the option, but they also agree the data source to compute the average and the time period between samples, for instance Reuters ERAX daily, weekly or monthly basis.

The option settles net cash at the end of the option's life, the average exchange rate is computed and compared to the strike price. A cash payment is made to the buyer of the option equal to the face amount of the option multiplied by the difference between these two rates, assuming that the option is in the money. Otherwise the option expires worthless.

OPTION ON AN OPTION

Many corporate customers are involved in bidding for contracts in foreign currencies. As an integral part of the bidding process future levels of spot FX rates must be estimated in order to arrive at the bid price (of the contract) and expected profit margin from the deal if the work is won.

It can thus easily be observed that corporates would like a cheap way of insuring this FX risk. They almost all refuse to buy an FX option outright for fear of losing the contract and then the option premium because of unfavourable spot movements.

An alternative solution involves the corporate and bank agreeing on the probability of the corporate winning the contract. If this chance is estimated to be 25% then the corporate pays only 25% of the fair FX option premium. On winning the contract the corporate enjoys the full benefits of the FX option, on losing the contract the FX option is deemed worthless. In theory this is a reasonable strategy but in practice because the probability of winning the contract cannot be accurately jointly estimated this route is not popular.

The solution offered by an option on an option relies only on spot FX rate movements and thus the chances of winning the contract are not a relevant factor.

First the option required, should the corporate successfully tender for the contract, is identified and priced. For example, a two year, at the money spot, Sterling call at a fair price of 2.9% is chosen. The time remaining before the outcome of the tender is made known is 30 days.

Next, the bank sells the customer a 30 day, American in style call option containing the right to buy the two year FX call option described above at a fixed premium of 2.9%.

The instrument is thus a short-dated American call option on a longer-dated European style FX call option. The premium for this call on a call would be 0.39%.

The outcomes and position of the customer are set out in order of likelihood below.

(1) Contract lost. Market price of two year call is 2.0%. Customer takes no action and premium of the call on the call is lost.
(2) Contract lost. Market price of two year call is 3.8%. Customer buys 2 year call at 2.9% from the bank and sells it at 3.8% to produce profit of 0.51% (3.8%–2.9%–0.39%).
(3) Contract won. Market price for two year call is 2.0%. Buy this call in the market for an effective price of 2.39%.
(4) Contract won. Market price of two year call is 3.8%. Buy this call from the bank at an effective price of 3.29%.

This style of instrument does provide insurance against the contract being awarded coupled with unfavourable FX rate movements at a walk away cost. In fact if the customer is willing to purchase out of the money call on a call the cost becomes very small indeed.

It goes without saying that all combinations of styles and types are available (such as short Euro put on a long-dated American call) to satisfy any customer's requirement.

CUSTOMER-DRIVEN INNOVATION

In terms of derivative products it is clear there is no easy way to compare true value. Competition between financial institutions to provide the product is often an effective method of ensuring price competitiveness. For the more esoteric products, however, the comparison of need to cost remains subjective and it is treasurers' needs that now drive the continuing innovation in derivative products. Corporates that have an accounting treatment that depends on the average market rate expressed a need that resulted in the Asian option. The need to achieve the optimum exchange rate over the trading period brought about the Lookback option. Knockout options were invented as an enhancement for clients who sold options frequently, but also required the ability to eliminate the option and rethink their positions when a new market level was achieved.

But the primary market between client and institution is not a zero sum game. There is profit to be made for both parties, with the zero sum game occurring only in the secondary market. Hence the crucial importance of relationship for financial institutions to make a profit for both themselves and their corporate clients. This profit is not made through the taking of a spread. Particularly in the more innovative products, one primary institution can provide a corporate with a better price for the total package than if the corporate traded a variety of transactions across the market.

Profit is due to the establishing of true value and the advantages the primary financial institution has from the exclusivity and knowledgeof the impending cash flows. This valuable primary relationship can only be achieved by trust: it is those financial institutions and corporates that can build these links with each other which will benefit fully from the derivative revolution that is upon us.

K. DUKER

Senior Executive, Midland Montague

6
TAXATION

Part 6 is about taxes and consists of three chapters by an international taxation consultant. The first covers the general subject of tax planning. The second looks at the various corporate taxation regimes in Europe, and the third at tax havens — concluding that, while the conventional view of tax havens is rapidly becoming obsolete, a sophisticated global review of corporate taxation discovers that many countries offer facilities for specialized objectives.

6.3 Tax havens in international corporate tax planning

Definitions of tax haven
United Kingdom corporation tax: basic principles
Choice of tax haven
Bermuda
Cayman Islands
Bahamas
Liberia
Panama
Hong Kong
Singapore
Conclusion

6.1 International tax planning

Because of the rapid developments in communication (such as telex and telephone) the world, from a business perspective, can no longer be viewed as being composed of totally separate countries. It is in fact one interacting and interdependent market place.

As a consequence, any decision taken by a company relating to some particular aspect of its operations may have repercussions and consequence not only on other aspects of its operations within the same country but also beyond the national boundaries within which the decision was taken; a company interacts with its environment and the company's environment interacts with it. Inevitably, as this degree of communication increases across national boundaries, competition amongst companies increases which in turn leads to cost and price cutting.

What is important for a company is the aggregate *after-tax* return that it can produce. As a consequence, as part of every decision, whether that decision relates to the pros and cons of leasing versus outright purchase of plant and equipment, the setting up of an overseas branch or subsidiary, or the compensation package, the implications of taxation have to be considered. Taxation is complex enough for the company which operates only within its home country. For the company which operates beyond national boundaries the issues and implications become dramatically more complex and the cost of getting it wrong rises exponentially.

International tax planning is concerned with seeking to identify and analyze the overall effect and interaction of different countries' tax systems on the operations of a company with a view to improving the after-tax return to the company.

TYPICAL COMPANY GROWTH

Consider the case of a company with a product line which has primarily been sold to customers in the home or domestic market, with minimal exports to foreign customers or export merchants in overseas countries. Assume that such exporting has arisen without any sales promotion effort on the part of the company itself. Typically for such a company, its invoicing policy will be unsophisticated and the foreign customers will almost certainly, as a consequence, be invoiced in the company's domestic currency and not that of the country of the customer.

If the company forms the view that overseas markets represent a viable opportunity the company may seek to make contact with other potential customers, representatives and agents. It is at this stage that the first real involvement with problems of an international flavour arise. It may then be necessary to comply with different legal requirements, to understand foreign customs procedures, to understand a foreign language and to be prepared to invoice the customer in his own currency. However, even at this stage, there is unlikely to be any involvement with foreign tax systems as such (that is, there is unlikely to be an exposure to foreign tax on any profits arising. However, the company would typically find itself exposed to foreign Value Added Tax, customs duties and other import or sales charges).

The next stage may be for the company to set up some form of presence outside its own country and in the overseas market. Though this may initially be no more than a sales office with one person, a secretary, telephone and telex, it can at once create international tax problems; the country in which the sales office is located may well claim the right to tax the profits of that office.

Even if it has no income of its own (and thus by implication no profits), merely acting as a representative sales office, the expenses of which are paid for by head office, the tax authorities of the country in which the presence has been established may still attempt a reallocation, to that presence, of some of the profits resulting from the sales made in or to that country.

It may be that something more than just a sales office becomes necessary and that if the market is to be served adequately actual production must take place in that country. The product may be one which is expensive or even impossible to transport over long distances, or there may be significant differences in the tastes and requirements of different markets. In addition, local manufacture may be necessary to bypass high customs duties, quotas or prohibitions on imports.

If there is to be manufacturing overseas this can be structured in a number of ways. The most obvious, though not always the best, is to set up a wholly-owned manufacturing subsidiary or branch in the country or countries concerned. Another approach would be to set up in association with local partners who, in addition to finding part of the capital, might contribute their knowledge of local markets and possibly also of financial and political conditions, to the technical expertise of the overseas partner. It may also be that a local joint venture partner *has* to be found under local domestic law. This is typical in Middle Eastern countries and a number of developing countries.

Another approach could involve the use of licensing. As a route to overseas profits, licensing has many advantages. If the right licensee is chosen a substantial flow of royalties can be generated with little or no financial risk and without much strain on limited management resources. However, this is usually only feasible for technology-based industries or where there is an internationally-known brand image. Although licensing profits arising from direct operations, it may represent the only viable option by which the company with limited resources can effectively exploit overseas markets. The above represent just three options open to the domestic company in relation to expanding its operations overseas. The tax consequences of each option are different and would need to be considered before taking any decision. However it should be appreciated that tax factors should be secondary and not primary considerations. The starting point must be the *commercial* considerations — what are the opportunities and how can they be converted into profits most effectively?

Nevertheless particular care is needed where, as under the above options, more than one country may have a claim to tax the same flow of profits. A United Kingdom company with a French branch would in principle be liable to tax in both countries on the profits of the branch. A United States company would be liable to United States tax on dividends received from a German subsidiary, even though the profits out of which the dividends were paid had been taxed locally in Germany. This area of possible double taxation is typically resolved either by the existence of an appropriate double taxation agreement between the countries or by unilateral credit relief. Thus in the above two examples the United Kingdom company would be able to offset, by way of credit, the French tax paid against the United Kingdom tax to be paid on the same profits; the United States company would also be able to take a credit for the German taxes paid. However not all foreign taxes are eligible for credit relief and the problem of double taxation is not always in practice completely removed, particularly where the taxes in the two countries are not comparable.

In short it is necessary for any company operating in foreign markets to consider *first* what (if any) is the foreign tax exposure arising as a consequence of the foreign operations (trading *with* versus trading *within*) and, *second*, how do the foreign taxes and the home country taxes interact (double taxation).

TRADING WITH VERSUS TRADING WITHIN

In the above description of the typical company growth pattern the point at which the domestic company may become liable to foreign taxes on its foreign profits is not always an easy one to identify. The principal distinction to note is that between *trading with* a country and *trading within* that country. Generally speaking, the former gives rise to no foreign tax liability on profits, whereas the latter does.

If a United Kingdom company sells to a German customer without having an office or other presence in Germany, it is merely trading *with* Germany, and is thus not liable to German corporate income tax on its income or profits which arise through the sale to the German customers. Import duties and Value Added Tax may, however, be in point. If the United Kingdom company sets up a branch factory and warehouse in Germany to carry on manufacturing and sales there, the United Kingdom company is then regarded as trading *within* Germany and it will thus become subject to, *inter alia*, municipal trade tax and federal corporation tax on some proportion of its profits. If, on the other hand, the United Kingdom company was to set up a sales office in Germany with, say, one salesman (but with no manufacturing there), whether this situation is one of trading with or within is more difficult to ascertain and will in fact depend upon the *precise* activities carried on by, and through, the office. In some cases the result will be trading *with*, in others *within*.

Each country has its own rules about what activities by foreigners are and what are not taxable. The definitions can be, and often are, very vague. It is rare to find a clearly worded and unambiguous statute. It is often necessary to look not only at tax statutes but also at court cases and actual revenue practice. Double taxation agreements between countries often provide a more clearcut approach — where the sales are being made via a tax haven company, there will generally be no double tax agreement. See chapter 6.3 on tax havens.

Generally, all that can be said with any assurance is that a straight sale to a completely independent purchaser in another country will not give rise to a tax liability on profits in the second country if the sale is negotiated from the first country and the goods are supplied therefrom. Potential complications begin when the selling company starts to have salesmen or an office in the country of residence of its customers or when it appoints an agent there. Most advanced-countries only tax non-residents on trading profits which arise from trading within *and* through what is known as a *permanent establishment* in the overseas country. This expression is, rather surprisingly, not to be found in the domestic tax statutes of the United Kingdom but *is* included in most of the double tax agreements to which the United Kingdom is a party.

In 1977 the fiscal Committee of the Organisation for Economic Cooperation and Development (OECD) published a *Draft Double Taxation Convention on Income and Capital* (an update of its 1963 model). This model forms the basis upon which most countries (certainly the leading industrialized nations of the world) conclude agreements, although it is essential to look at the actual text of a particular agreement as in most cases some differences from the model do exist; more often than not the provisions will be found to be broadly in line with the OECD model. For present purposes the two key articles found in a typical agreement are the business profits article and the permanent establishment article.

Article 7 of the OECD model provides:

> Business profits. The profits of an enterprise of a Contracting State shall be taxable only in that State unless the enterprise carries on business in the other Contracting State though a permanent establishment situated therein. If the enterprise carries on business as aforesaid, the profits of the enterprise may be

> taxed in the other State but only so much of them as is attributable to that permanent establishment.

What this means is that a company will be liable to taxation on its profits in the foreign country only if it has a permanent establishment there *and* carries on a part of its trade through it.

For the definition of what constitutes a permanent establishment Article 5 of the OECD model provides that:

> 5(1) For the purpose of this Convention, the term 'permanent establishment' means a fixed place of business in which the business of the enterprise is wholly or partly carried on.

This is the basic definition. More specific guidance is then given in paragraphs (2) and (3) of the Article:

> 5(2) The term 'permanent establishment' shall *include* especially:
> (a) a place of management;
> (b) a branch;
> (c) an office;
> (d) a factory;
> (e) a workshop;
> (f) a mine, quarry or other place of extraction of natural resources;
> (g) a building site or construction or assembly project which exists for more than twelve months.

It should be appreciated that the above list is *not* exhaustive but merely provides examples of what constitutes a permanent establishment.

Paragraph (3), on the other hand, lists those categories of presence which would *not* constitute permanent establishments.

> 5(3) The term 'permanent establishment' shall *not* be deemed to include:
> (a) the use of facilities solely for the purpose of storage, display or delivery of goods or merchandise belonging to the enterprise;
> (b) the maintenance of stock of goods or merchandise belonging to the enterprise solely for the purpose of storage, display or delivery;
> (c) the maintenance of a stock of goods or merchandise belonging to the enterprise solely for the purpose of processing by another enterprise;
> (d) the maintenance of a fixed place of business solely for the purpose of purchasing goods or merchandise, or for collecting information, for the enterprise;
> (e) the maintenance of a fixed place of business solely for the purpose of advertising, for the supply of information, for scientific research, or for similar activities which have a preparatory or auxiliary character, for the enterprise.

In this case the list *is* exhaustive. However, it should be noted that any combination of activities (a) to (e) would equally not, *per se*, constitute a permanent establishment.

These exceptions, it should be appreciated, permit a fairly wide range of activities to be carried on in the foreign country without any foreign taxes being levied. It is thus, for example, possible for a United Kingdom company to maintain a stock of its goods in a warehouse in the overseas country and to carry on general sales promotional activities in that overseas country *without* being taxed as trading *within* that country on any part of its profit. However an office in the overseas country through which orders were *accepted* and processed from the overseas customers is likely to result in trading *within* profits being taxed in the overseas country, providing such activity did not fall within any of the let outs in subparagraphs (a) to (e) of paragraph (3) set out above.

It is subparagraph (e) of paragraph (3) which has allowed companies resident in one country to open up what are commonly referred to as 'representative offices' in foreign countries. So long as the overseas office restricts activities to those which can be regarded as 'preparatory or auxiliary', no foreign tax liability will generally arise. The costs of running the office will, however, almost certainly qualify as tax deductible expenses of the head office. The key to falling within subparagraph (e) is to ensure that none of the office personnel in particular have the power to conclude sales contracts with customers and to ensure that the office performs its functions only for its head office and not for any third party.

Problems will arise with agents. Strictly speaking an agent is someone who acts for or on behalf of another person. A distributor who imports goods at his own risk and on his own initiative, with the object of reselling them at a profit, is strictly speaking a principal rather than an agent, though he may often in commercial practice be referred to loosely as an agent. As a consequence the mere appointment of a foreign distributor to whom sales were effected would not precipitate any foreign tax liability. The supplier is in the position of having a straight sale to an independent principal (the distributer) and would not be taxable in the country of residence of the distributor.

A true agent, in the strict sense of the word, does not take the commercial risks of owning the goods as does the distributor. He simply acts as a representative of the supplying firm and will earn a commission on any sales that are made (the distributor makes a profit on the buying and reselling). It does not usually matter whether the procedure is for him to be paid by the ultimate customer and then for the agent to pay the supplier after deducting his commission, or whether the supplier collects payment direct from the customer, subsequently paying over any commission due to the agent. The point is that the agent does not take a commercial risk, and any goods he has in stock are not his property but the property of the original supplier until sold.

The importance of the distinction between agent and distributor is that, as indicated as above, the use of the latter, *per se*, will involve no foreign tax exposure but this will not necessarily be the case with the appointment of an agent.

The supplier *can* be subject to tax on profits derived through a *dependent* agent. Paragraph (4) of Article 5 of the OECD model convention provides:

> 5(4) A person acting in a Contracting State on behalf of an enterprise of the other Contracting State — other than an agent of an *independent* status to whom paragraph (5) applies — shall be deemed to be a permanent establishment in the first mentioned state if he has and habitually exercises in that state an authority to conclude contracts in the name of the enterprise, unless his activities are limited to the purchase of goods or merchandise for the enterprise.

Paragraph (5) of Article (5) provides:

> An enterprise of a Contracting State shall not be deemed to have a permanent establishment in the other Contracting State through a broker, general commission agent or any other agent of independent status, where such persons are acting in the ordinary course of their business.

As a consequence a sales agent who was given a general authority to conclude sales contracts for his principal could render his principal liable to foreign tax. It is generally accepted that even where the agent solicits contracts but may only accept them subject to confirmation by his principal, the act of acceptance by the agent may still expose the principal to a foreign tax liability. Note, however, that *purchasing* agents do not give rise to any problems (see Article 5(3)(d) above).

As with *purchasing* agents, the use of an overseas *independent* agent does not give rise to foreign tax problems. It is important that the agent is in fact of independent status and that the activities it does perform are those which it holds itself out as being willing to perform. As a general guide an *independent* agent would act for a *number* of different principals and would not be related, by way of shareholding or otherwise, with any of the principals for which it acts. It is therefore not normally possible for a company to set up an overseas subsidiary and to argue that the latter is in fact an agent of independent status.

It is primarily because of the accepted status of independent agent that non-United Kingdom principals can use United Kingdom-based estate agents, stockbrokers, insurance brokers and others who may even conclude contracts for the overseas principal without that principal being subject to any United Kingdom tax on the profits made.

DOUBLE TAXATION

In some cases (as discussed above) only the country of residence of the company will have any claim to tax and foreign source profits of the company. This could occur where the profits arise from trading *with* rather than *within* a foreign country. Equally, certain royalty, interest and technical assistance payments may also be exempt from tax in the country of source, either because of the domestic law of that country or because of the provisions of a double tax agreement. On the other hand, trading through a permanent establishment, a branch or an agency will result in a profit taxable in the source country concerned.

For current purposes the term double taxation is intended to refer to international juridical double taxation as opposed to economic double imposition of comparable taxes in two (or more) countries on the same taxpayer in respect of the same subject matter and for identical periods.

Such a situation may arise in one of three possible ways:

(1) dual residence;
(2) source versus situs concept;
(3) computational base differences.

The taxability of a company within a jurisdiction will usually depend upon its residence. Depending upon the criteria adopted to determine residence, a company may find that more than one jurisdiction claims it to be resident in its particular territory. The profits of that company would then become subject to tax in each of those jurisdictions. If each country imposed a 50% tax charge the company would find itself with zero *after-tax* profits.

Perhaps the classic example of the dual resident company is the company which is incorporated in the United States but which is managed and controlled from within the United Kingdom. In this case both the United Kingdom and the United States would regard the company as resident in each country.

Taxability may, in addition to depending upon residence of the taxpayer, depend upon the location of the source of the income accruing to the taxpayer. Thus a company which is resident in one country and receiving income from another may find that the income is subject to tax in both countries. For multinational companies this problem is particularly applicable to the flow of dividends between members of the group and in respect of interest payments. The situation may also arise where a company carries on a trade or business within a country via a branch operation.

With respect to double taxation which arises due to computational base differences, this situation occurs where each country in which a company is carrying on business not only has the right to tax a particular quantum of profits but where each country, for whatever reason, on the same set of facts produces different profit figures. This may arise where, for example, one country permits the whole of any capital expenditure incurred to be written off in one year, whereas another country only permits the write-off over a number of years.

The two key ways in which a country attempts to resolve double taxation, however it arises, are by way of exemption or credit. Under the principle of exemption the state of residence of the taxpayer company does not tax the income which could be taxed in the state in which the source of income arises. However, the state of residence may take into account the income arising in the other state when determining the tax to be imposed on the rest of the income of the taxpayer; this is the exemption with progression system used, for example, in the Netherlands and Switzerland. Alternatively the state of residence may *not* take such income into account, a method referred to as full exemption.

Under the principle of credit the state of residence of the taxpayer computes the tax due on *all* the income due to the taxpayer, including the full amount arising in the other contracting state (*before* deduction of that other contracting state's taxes). The state then allows a deduction (credit) from its own *tax* in respect of tax paid in the other state; this is the system used in the United Kingdom. The distinction between the exemption and the credit systems is very important and the example below illustrates the two systems.

EXAMPLE

Consider a company resident in country B with pre-tax profits in country A of 100 units, the tax rate in country A being 40%. All after-tax profits arising in A are reunited to country B, where a 50% tax rate is applicable. The situation under the two systems would be:

Exemption	
Profits subject to tax in B	0
Total tax borne (in A)	40
Net after-tax profits receivable in B	60
Credit	
Profits subject to tax in B	100
Tax in B	50
Less tax in A	(40)
Net tax in B	10
Net after-tax profits in B	50

BRANCH VERSUS SUBSIDIARY

Once a decision is taken to set up business operations in a particular country the typical choice of legal presence will be between setting up as a separate legal entity (a subsidiary) or as an unincorporated branch. A subsidiary can be a direct subsidiary or can be a subsidiary of an intermediate company in a third country. In the same way the branch can be a direct branch of the parent company or of a company either in a third country or indeed in the country of residence of the parent company. One of the *features* of a foreign subsidiary is that in general no tax is payable by the parent company until dividends are distributed to it. Branch profits, in contrast, may be taxable in the country of residence of the principal company as they arise. There are exceptions to both statements. Thus, United

States companies may be subject to United States tax on the undistributed profits of certain foreign subsidiaries, while French and Belgian parent companies may not be subject to tax even on the remitted profits of overseas branches. Typically, withholding taxes are levied on dividends paid by a subsidiary to its parent whereas withholding taxes do not apply to a remittance of branch profits to head office.

However in, for example, the case of French and Canadian branches of foreign companies withholding taxes *are* levied on all branch profits whether remitted overseas or not. This is not, of course, true in the cases of subsidiaries in those countries.

It is not, in general, possible to claim a deduction for interest or royalties paid by a branch to its head office against the liability to tax in the country of operation of the branch. This is based upon the principle that such a payment is in effect an internal notional payment only (the parent and the branch being the same entity). On the other hand it is not unusual in computing the profits of a branch for executive and general administrative expenses incurred, on behalf of the branch, at the head office to be allowed as deductible expenses. In the case of a subsidiary it is usually possible for such interest and royalty payments to be treated as legitimate deductions on the grounds that a subsidiary is an independent corporate entity; there are normally restrictions on the level of payments which are accepted as tax deductible expenses.

Consider a United Kingdom parent company which is considering setting up an operation in Belgium. The choice is whether to operate as a branch or a wholly owned subsidiary. A Belgian branch of a United Kingdom company would pay Belgian tax of 48% on its profits, whereas a Belgian subsidiary would pay 43%. In the case of dividend remittances to the United Kingdom by the subsidiary, a withholding tax rate of 15% would apply whereas no such tax would be imposed on a remittance of branch profits.

	Branch	**Subsidiary**
Belgian taxable profits	100	100
Belgian corporate tax	48	43
Net profit	52	57
Withholding tax	–	(8.55)
Net receipts in United Kingdom	52	48.45
Total Belgian tax	48	51.55

The United Kingdom corporate tax liability in the case of the subsidiary's dividend remittance would be zero since the total Belgian rate of tax exceeds the United Kingdom rate (currently 35%), the United Kingdom granting a full tax credit for the Belgian taxes levied. However, United Kingdom tax would have been levied on the Belgian branch profit in the past with a United Kingdom corporate rate of 52%; with a current rate of 35% no additional United Kingdom tax would arise in this case either. Thus, where a full distribution policy is to be followed, a branch operation would appear preferable. If no distributions were to be made for a number of years the subsidiary option might be preferable, particularly when the cash-flow advantage is taken into account. Tax postponement, even at a cost of an eventual higher tax, can be valuable.

Of course, the comparison of branch versus subsidiary will involve a consideration of factors other than tax. In many cases the formalities necessary to form a branch operation are less onerous than is the case for a subsidiary. On the other hand the foreign country may require that the head office company file certain information, such as its annual accounts, which could be avoided by setting up a separate local legal entity, a subsidiary. It may also be the case that no home country consents are needed from any authority to set up an overseas branch, whereas consents would be required to establish a subsidiary. In the United Kingdom, for example, no permissions are required to set up an overseas branch but the consent of the Treasury under section 765 of the Income and Corporation Taxes Act 1988 *may* be needed before an overseas subsidiary can be set up.

INTERMEDIARIES

It is thus clear that for the company with overseas operations it is not only the taxation system of its home country and those of the countries in which it does business that are important, but also the interaction between the two.

These issues are further complicated where intermediary companies are employed in the corporate structure. Thus, for example, a United Kingdom company may wish to own the shares in all its foreign subsidiaries not directly from the United Kingdom but via some non-United Kingdom subholding company. Classically such a subholding company would be sited in the Netherlands or sometimes in Switzerland. Other locations which could be used would include Luxembourg, Liechtenstein, Panama (for South American subsidiaries) or possibly Hong Kong.

The reasons for using the overseas subholding company are many. However the common thread for all holding companies is that a country of residence will treat certain categories of income and gains in a tax favourable manner. A Netherlands resident company is subject to corporation tax on its income from both domestic and foreign sources. However the Netherlands (like Switzerland) follows the method of exemption with progression. Under this system foreign income of a Dutch company is included in the company's total taxable income but only in order to determine the rate of tax which is to be applied to the *domestic* income. As Dutch companies are subject to corporation tax at a flat rate of 35% the exemption with progression system is tantamount to an outright exemption for foreign source income. (See chapter 6.3 for a more detailed discussion of the Dutch tax system.)

Where a resident Dutch company owns at least 5% of the paid up capital of another resident or non-resident company, it is referred to as a participation *(deelneming)* holding company. Where in addition the shares have been held from the beginning of the recipient's financial year, exemption from corporate income tax (and Dutch withholding tax on dividends) is granted on dividends received from a qualifying participation and on any capital gains realized on the disposal of such participations.

A participation in a foreign (non-Dutch) company only qualifies for the above exemptions if two additional conditions are fulfilled. The first condition is that the company paying the dividend to the Dutch company must be subject to some foreign tax on its profits. Thus, for example, a subsidiary of a Dutch company — resident in a classic tax haven like Bermuda, the Cayman Islands or the Bahamas and which is paying a dividend to its Dutch parent — would give rise to a charge to Dutch corporate income tax: the profits of the tax haven subsidiary would not have borne foreign tax on its profits. On the other hand, for a subsidiary company in, for example, Cyprus (where the local tax for an offshore company is only 4.25%), dividends received would be exempt from Dutch tax. The second condition is that the participation should not be less than 25% of the stock of the foreign paying company or, if the shareholding is less than 25% but more than 5%, it must be in addition shown that the participation is held for business rather than portfolio reasons. In practice it is not normally difficult to establish this, provided the business activity of the foreign company bears some relationship to the business activities of the Dutch parent company or its other subsidiaries.

In addition to favourable tax treatment on receipts in the country of residence of the holding company, the country will also typically reduce to nil any withholding taxes on the payment of dividends to non-residents. In the case of the Netherlands the country is a party to a considerable network of double taxation agreements which further enhances the attraction of the Netherlands as a country in which to locate a holding company. This arises as many of the agreements have the effect of reducing substantially the rates of withholding tax on dividends, interest and royalties flowing from various countries into the Netherlands. In this regard the Netherlands can be contrasted with the position in Luxembourg.

In the case of a Luxembourg holding company, although dividends received are in principle exempt from Luxembourg corporate income tax (and dividends can be paid out without local withholding tax), a company is specifically forbidden to take advantage of any of the double taxation agreements to which Luxembourg is a party. Typically speaking, therefore, the Luxembourg holding company would be used only where withholding taxes on income flows from various countries are in any event minimal under the domestic laws of those countries.

For the United Kingdom parent company the use of an overseas sub-holding company also enables the company to maximize its foreign tax credit position by the use of averaging. The United Kingdom adopts a source-by-source basis of calculating foreign tax credits, with no facility for the company to surrender, carry back or forward any surplus foreign tax credits which might arise.

The Belgian subsidiary example above produces a surplus of 16.55% on a full distribution to the United Kingdom. The overseas subholding company can be used to mitigate this problem by permitting what is referred to as dividend mixing. Changes in British domestic law now permit the offsetting of foreign tax credits before advance corporation tax, thus reducing the risk of surplus unusable foreign tax credit.

In addition to the concept of the holding company, an intermediary may also be used for other purposes. For example, a United Kingdom company may wish to enter into a contract with a Middle Eastern customer. Under the contract it may be that the United Kingdom company will be involved in seconding personnel out to the Middle East for perhaps between a two and five year period. Depending upon the precise nature of the venture, there may be some logic in the company setting up an offshore subsidiary which could in some part get involved in the Middle Eastern venture. A Cyprus company could be set up as a direct subsidiary. The Cyprus company would then either directly contract with the Middle Eastern customer and then subcontract to its parent or, alternatively, the parent company would be the main contracting party with the Middle Eastern customer, with the subsidiary Cyprus company becoming involved in some form of subcontract work by, for example, providing some form of technical enterprise, acting as a procurement agency or generally providing some support services. The broad effect is that the Cyprus company would be in a position to earn profits from the venture which under Cyprus law would only be subject to local income tax at 4.25% as opposed to a *United Kingdom* corporate tax rate of 35% were those profits to fall to the parent company.

Another example of the use of an intermediary would be in the case of licensing arrangements. A company may have invented some secret process or have patented some invention which it now wishes to exploit. The company may not have the resources to manufacture the product on a worldwide basis. Licensing agreements provide a possible part solution. However, instead of the company directly licensing various licensees throughout the world, it may either sell the invention outright to an offshore subsidiary company or grant a licence to such an offshore company. The offshore company would then in either situation itself act as a sub-licensor to various licensees around the world.

To achieve this a Netherlands Antilles company could be used as the head licensor. This company could then grant a sub-licence to a Dutch company in the group. The Dutch company would then itself sub-license various licensees throughout the world. Under this arrangement the Dutch company would receive royalties or fees from the various world licensees, with minimal withholding tax suffered as a consequence of the Netherlands' excellent array of double taxation agreements. The Netherlands company would itself be under an obligation to pay over certain royalties to the head licensor, that is, the Netherlands Antilles company.

A small profit would remain in the Netherlands and thus be subject to Dutch corporate income tax at the 35% rate. For the Netherlands Antilles corporation, however, a local rate of some 2% or 3% only would then be payable on the gross receipts. The result would be that the overall net after-tax return as a consequence of the structure will be greater than if the company located in the high-tax country was itself to license the various licensees throughout the world.

ANTI-AVOIDANCE PROVISIONS

It is to be appreciated that these possible uses of intermediaries are something with which the tax authorities of the high tax countries are increasingly concerned. The view of such tax authorities ranges from mild concern to one of paranoia. The typical approach adopted by the high tax countries in seeking to combat the use of intermediaries has been to seek to levy tax on the profits of the offshore controlled subsidiary, whether that subsidiary remitted any part of its profits back to the parent company or not. In the case of the United States this legislation is referred to as the subpart F legislation and has been in effect since 1962. Other countries which have similar legislation are Canada, France, Germany and Japan. In the case of the United Kingdom, similar draft legislation was contained in the Finance Bill 1983, for implementation with effect from April 1984, but the announcement of a general election on 9 June 1983 resulted in the legislation being withdrawn from the Finance Bill. However the legislation did finally emerge and is contained in sections and schedules to the Finance Act 1984. Under this Act the profits of 'controlled foreign companies' or CFCs as they are commonly called will fall within the charge to United Kingdom corporation tax whether remitted to the United Kingdom or not unless one of a number of let-out tests can be satisfied.

For the purpose of the legislation, a controlled foreign company is a company which is controlled by United Kingdom residents, is resident outside the United Kingdom, and whose profits are subject to a lower level of taxation. In turn, the profits of a controlled foreign company are subject to a lower level of taxation if the tax actually paid in the country of residence of the company is less than one half of the United Kingdom corporation tax which would have been paid on those profits if the company had in fact been resident in the United Kingdom.

In broad terms, therefore, companies located in tax havens and which are controlled by United Kingdom residents, will find their profits subject to corporation tax on an arising basis (whether remitted to the United Kingdom or not) unless, as indicated above, one of the let-out tests can be satisfied. Thus the effect of the legislation is to prevent United Kingdom resident companies from seeking to set up tax efficient offshore subsidiaries, the profits of which would fall outside the charge to corporation tax.

Three key letouts are as follows:

(1) acceptable distribution test;
(2) exempt activities test; and
(3) motive test.

The acceptable distribution rest requires that the controlled foreign company for each accounting period remits at least 50% of its profits available for distribution to the United Kingdom. To the extent that such a distribution is made, the controlled foreign company will be deemed to have satisfied the acceptable distribution test, and to this extent the balancing 50% of its profits which remain outside the United Kingdom will not fall within the charge to United Kingdom corporation tax.

In the case of the exempt activities test, the controlled foreign company has to satisfy a number of strict conditions. These conditions require that the controlled foreign company has, within its country of residence, real premises, real effective control, and thirdly, does not carry on certain restricted activities nor receive the majority of its income from related parties.

The exempt activities test is designed to exempt from the legislation those companies which are performing bona fide commercial activities; in practice the application of the strict conditions is likely to catch tax haven subsidiaries which, in a layman's terms, could be regarded as carrying on bona fide commercial operations. It should not therefore be assumed that a company resident in a low tax country, carrying on normal commercial operations, will be able to satisfy the exempt activities let-out. Foreign subholding companies may, in particular, not satisfy this let-out.

In the case of the motive test this broadly requires that the reasons for setting up the tax haven company are such as not to achieve a reduction in United Kingdom tax nor in fact have as a primary purpose the avoidance of such tax. The Inland Revenue have produced a list of countries in which companies resident there and deriving at least 90% of their gross income from sources within that country will in fact be deemed to have satisfied the motive test. As is to be expected, the countries listed are primarily the high tax countries and do not include any of the countries which would commonly be regarded as tax havens.

It can therefore be seen that the proposed legislation on controlled foreign companies is extremely far reaching and seeks to prevent companies from setting up tax haven subsidiary operations with a view to avoiding tax unless the controlled foreign company can satisfy one of the let-out tests.

In addition to the general approach of seeking to levy tax on the offshore companies' profits (whether remitted or not), the high tax countries have also used provisions in their domestic legislation which seek to ensure that prices charged for goods and services between companies under common control represent what is referred to as an arm's length amount.

The broad effect of this legislation is that the tax authorities have the power to obtain information relating to transactions between common controlled parties with a view to ascertaining whether those prices charged are those which would be charged between independent entities and are not designed to extract profits out of high tax countries for accumulation in low tax countries. Where the result of an investigation is that prices charged have been deemed either to be too high or too low, depending upon which way the transaction operates, the effect is that the excess payments are disallowed as deductions in computing the taxable profits of the payor company; alternatively, depending upon the shareholding relationship, the excess charged is treated as a dividend distribution, with all the attendant tax consequences including the disallowance of the payment as a taxable deduction. The legislation in the case of the United Kingdom is contained in section 770 of the Income and Corporation Taxes Act 1988 and, in the case of the United States, in section 482 of the United States Code.

CONCLUSION

The art of international tax planning is to ensure that in the first instance commercial considerations are paramount. Having decided what action is required commercially, the next step is to try to structure the operation in the most tax effective manner. In so doing the fact that an investment is being made from country A to country B should not preclude the possibility of routing the investment via country C or possibly countries C, D and E. In addition, the flow of financing need not follow that of shareholding structure. Whatever form is adopted, however, it is *after-tax* profits which should be maximized.

MALCOLM J. FINNEY

Malcolm J. Finney & Partners

6.2 Corporate taxation in Europe (major countries): a guide

BELGIUM

Resident corporations are subject to Belgian corporate tax on their worldwide income. A corporation is subject to resident tax liability if it has its registered office, principal business establishment or place of management in Belgium. Corporations that do not fulfil one of these criteria are subject to non-resident income taxation, that is only on income having a Belgian source (foreign, non-Belgian source income is exempt from Belgian tax in such circumstances).

CORPORATE INCOME TAX

The corporate income tax is levied on worldwide income of resident corporations and is payable by assessment. The normal rate of corporate income tax is 43%. Reduced, but progressive rates of tax apply if taxable income is below Bfr16,600,000.

The basic rate of 43% applies to all profits of subsidiaries (50% ownership by Belgian or foreign corporations) and financial companies. Under certain circumstances Belgian corporate tax on income from foreign real estate or a foreign permanent establishment may be reduced by 75%. Profits derived by a non-resident corporation from Belgian immovable property or from a Belgian permanent establishment are subject to income tax assessment at the rate of 48% unless otherwise reduced by a double taxation agreement.

TAXABLE INCOME OF RESIDENT CORPORATIONS

Generally, taxable income corresponds to financial accounting income. However, there are significant exclusions from taxable income:

(1) exempted dividends;
(2) exempted capital gains;
(3) tax-free reserves for probable losses;
(4) Exempted profits used in favour of employees.

Generally, all legitimate business expenses are deductible provided they are provable expenses paid or accrued during the taxable period.

A dividend received by a resident corporate shareholder on a permanent participation is subject to corporate income tax on a reduced amount of income. The reduction depends upon the type of shareholder, the holding period for the shares and the source of the dividend. A general rule of Belgian tax law is that 90% of a dividend, domestic or foreign, received by a resident constitutes a permanent participation in the distributing entity. Generally, this means that the recipient has held the shares during its entire fiscal year. If the recipient is a financial corporation – a corporation holding certain participations in subsidiary companies exceeding 50% of its capital – the exemption is reduced to 85% of the dividend received. If the corporate recipient's shareholding does not constitute a permanent participation, the full amount of the dividends received must be included in its taxable income. Similar rules applies where a foreign source dividend is derived from a permanent participation (that is 85% or 90% of the dividend is exempt).

Depreciation is generally calculated on the straight-line or declining balance method. A change to the straight-line or declining balance method can be made whenever straight-line depreciation would exceed the amount of declining balance depreciation. The period over which an asset can be depreciated is normally fixed by agreement between the taxpayer and tax administration. Commonly authorised straight-line rates are as follows:

(1) commercial buildings at 3%;
(2) industrial buildings at 5%;
(3) office equipment at 10%;
(4) machinery and equipment at 10% to 33.3%;
(5) know-how and patents at 20%.

The taxpayer can postpone tax depreciation for a particular year. This will usually extend the depreciation period since the taxpayer is never permitted to deduct more than one year's depreciation in any one year. Realized capital gains and losses are treated as ordinary business income or loss except in certain circumstances.

LOSSES

A loss of any taxable period may be carried forward to the succeeding five taxable periods. No carry back of losses is permitted. Losses incurred during the first five taxable periods of new companies (formed after 31 December 1971) can be carried forward indefinitely.

ARM'S LENGTH PRICING

When a Belgian enterprise has any direct or indirect links or inter-dependency whatsoever with a foreign enterprise, any charges in excess of an arm's length amount are added to the profits of the Belgian enterprise.

FOREIGN TAXES

Foreign income and withholding taxes paid by Belgian corporations are deductible and cannot be credited against Belgian income tax.

TAXATION OF NON-RESIDENT CORPORATIONS

The taxable income of a non-resident corporation includes profits and gains of a Belgian branch or other permanent establishment. In certain cases it is recommended that a non-resident agree in advance with Belgian tax authorities as to the basis for determining such profits and gains.

The basic rate of tax is 48% on taxable income of a Belgian branch or other permanent establishment. Tax treaties concluded by Belgium usually reduce this rate to the basic corporate tax rate of 43% except for Luxembourg, the Netherlands and France, for which a 45.85% rate applies. Tax treaties, with, among others, the United Kingdom and the Republic of Ireland, provide for no reduction. The transfer of branch profits from Belgium to another country is not subject to a system of withholding (*précompte mobilier*) on investment income. Unless otherwise provided by a double taxation agreement, tax is withheld at the standard rate of 25% on Belgian source dividends, interest, royalties and rents from moveable property. The amount withheld is not refundable and constitutes the final tax liability.

DENMARK

Resident corporations are subject to Danish taxation on their worldwide income, although the taxable income attributable to a foreign permanent establishment and certain other types of foreign source business income of a resident corporation is reduced by 50% before calculating corporate tax. Resident corporations are those that have been entered into the Companies' Register as Danish corporations.

Non-resident corporations are subject to Danish taxation on profits arising from permanent establishments in Denmark and on income from real property located in Denmark.

CORPORATE INCOME TAX

A corporate tax comprising national and local taxes is assessed on taxable income of Danish and non-resident corporations at a flat rate of 50%.

TAXABLE INCOME OF RESIDENT CORPORATIONS

Taxable income is based on financial accounting income with adjustments as provided by law. The general rule contained in the Corporate Tax Act is that expenses incurred to obtain, ensure and maintain the corporation's income may be deducted in determining net taxable income.

Dividends received by a resident corporation from another resident corporation are tax exempt provided the recipient owns 25% or more of the outstanding stock of the distributing corporation for the entire financial year in which the dividend is payable. A resident corporation owning 25% or more of the outstanding stock of a non-resident corporation for the entire financial year in which a dividend is payable is in principal exempt from Danish tax (subject to certain conditions). For holdings of less than 25% the dividend income (whether domestic or foreign) is subject to tax with an appropriate tax credit.

All machinery and equipment are depreciated on a pooled declining balance method. The amount deductible is at the taxpayer's option but is subject to an annual limitation of 30% (35% in the year of acquisition) of the current written-down value of the pool, adjusted for acquisitions and disposals and adjusted by an amount that reflects the annual increase in the cost of living index.

The depreciation basis of buildings and installations used in buildings in the year of acquisition is the acquisition price, reduced according to certain rules to a deemed cash basis. Office buildings are not depreciable unless they are part of premises that otherwise qualify for depreciation and are employed in that enterprise.

In certain cases, advance depreciation on qualified ships, machinery and buildings may be available before delivery or completion of such assets. The advanced depreciation may be allowed on the cost of machinery and industrial buildings when such cost exceeds DK700,000. Goodwill acquired on or after July 1982 is not depreciable. Patents can be depreciated over their useful lives on a straight line basis.

Generally, capital gains realized by a corporation on the disposal of business assets are taxed in the same manner as trading profits. Capital gains on other assets are taxed only in cases where taxation is specially warranted by law. Capital gains realised on the sale or disposition of shares, including shares of foreign corporations, are subject to taxation in Denmark. Capital losses regarding real property and most other capital losses are not deductible.

LOSSES

Operating losses of one year may be carried forward and set off against profits of the succeeding five years. No carry back of operating losses is permitted.

ARM'S LENGTH PRICING

The Corporate Tax Act provides that if a controlled Danish corporation or Danish branch conducts commercial or economic transactions with its parent or head office which do not reflect arm's length dealings, then profits shall be attributable to the Danish corporation or Danish branch to reflect an assumed arm's length profit.

FOREIGN TAXES

Relief from international double taxation is provided in the form of tax credit. The tax credit is calculated on a country-by-country basis and is limited to the lesser of the amount actually paid in the foreign country or the Danish corporate income tax (*before the tax credit*) deemed allowable to taxable foreign source income. If the provisions of a tax treaty are applicable, the taxpayer has a choice between the treaty provisions or the above credit.

TAXATION OF NON-RESIDENT CORPORATIONS

A non-resident is assessed at the normal Danish corporate tax rate of 50% on profits derived in Denmark from the operation of a branch or other permanent establishment, including income from immovable property situated in Denmark. In addition, a non-resident is assessed on capital gains derived from the sale of business assets (except goodwill) and real property in Denmark.

There is no withholding tax on profits remitted by a registered branch or other permanent establishment to a non-resident.

FRANCE

Corporate income tax is based on the principle of territoriality. Resident and non-resident corporations are generally taxable on income derived from French sources. The territorial principle exempts foreign source income earned through foreign permanent establishments or a cycle of commercial activity carried out abroad (for instance a purchase and resale abroad) until these profits are distributed to shareholders. Income derived by a non-resident corporation from a complete cycle of operations in France, such as a purchase and resale of property in France, is deemed French source income subject to corporate tax, even if the corporation has no French branch.

There are several exceptions to the territorial principle as it applies to resident corporations, including foreign source interest and dividends, foreign source income deemed taxable through tax consolidation, and income allocated to France by double taxation agreements. For tax purposes, resident corporations are those that are either incorporated in France or that have their centre of management and control (*siège social*) in France.

However, where a firm subject to French corporate tax owns at least 25% (direct or indirect) of the shares of a company established in a foreign country in which there is a preferential tax regime, it may be subject to tax in France on its proportionate interest in the profits of that foreign company. In this case the firm may credit tax paid by the foreign company against its French tax. The provisions do not apply if the foreign company engages principally in industrial or commercial activity and carries out business transactions with firms with which no dependent ties exist.

CORPORATE INCOME TAX

Corporate income tax is levied at a rate of 39% on net income with some exceptions. Certain capital gains are taxed at a reduced rate until the proceeds are distributed to shareholders, when a further charge is made.

TAXABLE INCOME OF RESIDENT COMPANIES

Taxable income is based in principle on financial accounting income; that is the difference between the value of net assets at the beginning of the accounting year and at the close of the accounting year, adjusted for contributions and withdrawals of capital and distributions to shareholders. Financial accounting income is adjusted as provided by law; certain accounting profits are exempt, operating losses can be carried forward and certain timing differences are required.

A French company owning at least 95% of another company's capital can include the profits or losses of such a subsidiary with the results of its own operations; this means that consolidated tax returns are permitted. Not all companies must be included but the rules are elective — a specific election must be made and is valid for five years.

No withholding tax is levied on dividends paid by a French recipient company to another. Where the recipient French company owns less than 10% of the shares of another French company, broadly speaking, the dividends are subject to full corporate income tax albeit with a form of double tax relief, that is a tax credit (*avoir fiscal*) of 50% of the dividends received, subject to the satisfaction of certain conditions. The avoir fiscal is granted to non-residents of certain countries with which France has a relevant double taxation agreement.

However, where a French company qualifies as a parent company (*Société Mère*) and holds a substantial participation (for instance 10% or more or cost of shares Ffr.150 million or more) 95% of the gross amount of the dividends received is exempt.

The above rules apply whether the dividends are domestic or foreign source.

The rate of straight-line depreciation applicable to fixed assets is determined by reference to cost (less value added tax) and useful life. Typical straight-line rates are as follows:

(1) industrial buildings at 5%;
(2) office and residential buildings at 2% to 5%;
(3) machinery and equipment at 10%;
(4) office equipment at 10% to 20%; and
(5) vehicles at 20% to 25%.

In certain cases taxpayers may elect to use the declining balance method of depreciation. Short-term gains (gains realized on the transfer of fixed assets held for less than two years) are treated as ordinary income and taxed at the regular 39% rate, but may be spread over three years. Net short-term losses are first set off against ordinary income. Unused short-term losses can be carried forward for five years. All other capital gains are long term gains.

LOSSES

Generally, operating losses may be carried forward for five years. To the extent that an operating loss is attributable to depreciation charges properly deducted, that portion of the loss can be carried forward without time limit. With effect from 1 January 1985 loss carry back relief has been introduced. Under certain conditions the carry back is permitted over the previous three years.

ARM'S LENGTH PRICING

Charges made by a related foreign entity are normally subject to careful examination by tax authorities. Charges in excess of arm's length are subjected to the 50% corporate income tax rate and are treated as distributions of profit on which withholding tax is payable. French tax authorities may arbitrarily regard administrative charges to French subsidiaries of foreign companies as profit distributions by asserting that the French entity is a separate and independent business unit.

FOREIGN TAXES

Unless otherwise provided by a double taxation agreement, foreign taxes are not allowed as a deduction. However a credit for foreign taxes is permitted when a corporation obtains the consent of tax authorities to be taxed on worldwide income (*bénéfice mondial*) or to consolidate worldwide income with that of its French and foreign subsidiaries (*bénéfice consolidé*).

TAXATION OF NON-RESIDENT CORPORATIONS

A non-resident company is subject to French corporate income tax at the rate of 39% on profits derived in France from the operation of a branch. In addition, unless otherwise provided by treaty, branches must pay withholding tax at the rate of 25% of net profits after reduction by corporate income tax. Branch profits are considered separately from those of the non-resident parent company. Thus a French Branch may have taxable profit even though its non-resident home office realized an overall loss for the tax year.

Unless otherwise provided by treaty, dividends paid by a French resident corporation to a non-resident are subject to a withholding tax of 25%. Interest from bonds is also subject to a withholding tax of 25%; other interest is subject to a withholding tax of 45%. Unless otherwise provided by treaty, royalties and fees paid to a non-resident for the use of patents, trademarks, copyrights or know-how are generally subject to a withholding tax of 33.3%. Rental income from real property located in France is subject to regular corporate income tax. A 3% annual tax is levied on French properties owned by non-resident corporations, subject to treaty relief on the use of the property.

FEDERAL REPUBLIC OF GERMANY

The corporate income tax distinguishes between corporations subject to unlimited tax liability *(unbeschrankte Steuerpflicht)* and limited tax liability *(beschrankte Steuerpflicht)*. Corporations with unlimited liability are subject to tax on their worldwide income and are referred to as resident corporations. A corporation is deemed to be a resident if its place of management or its place of registration is located within West Germany. Non-resident corporations have limited tax liability and, unless otherwise provided by tax treaty, are subjected to tax only on West German source income such as business profits from the operation of a registered branch or other permanent establishment in West Germany, including sales of investment, profit arising from the sale of a qualified interest in a resident corporation, West German source dividends, royalties, certain interests and rents, and gains on sale of real estate.

CORPORATE INCOME TAX

Resident corporations are subject to corporate income tax at a rate of 50%. To the extent that profits of the resident corporation are distributed, the tax burden is reduced to 36% of the distributed profits, before tax. Resident shareholders (corporate entities and individuals) are permitted to claim a credit against their own tax liability (or a refund) for the full amount of 36% tax paid by the distributing corporation. Furthermore, the cash dividend is subject to 25% withholding tax, which is also allowed as a credit against the shareholder's tax. For non-resident shareholders the tax credit is available only if provided by treaty or by the tax laws of the shareholder's country. The trade tax or municipal trade tax is regulated by federal law and collected by the various municipalities. The tax is based on business profit and business capital (net worth). Basic rates are set by federal law. The trade tax varies between 11% to 20%.

TAXABLE INCOME OF RESIDENT CORPORATIONS

Taxable income is determined by comparing the net assets of a company as reflected on special tax balance sheets at the beginning and at the end of the accounting year. The difference in net assets, adjusted for dividend distributions, capital paid in or withdrawn, and certain other items (such as losses carried back and forward) constitutes taxable income or loss. The law contains special rules for deductions such as expenses directly connected to the formation of a company not covered by share premiums and donations to charitable and other organisations. Certain expenses are not deductible, such as corporate and net worth tax and half of the compensation paid to members of the supervisory board. Dividend received by a resident corporate shareholder are taxed as normal profit. Foreign source dividends are generally exempted by tax treaties from German taxation if the receiving resident corporation owns at least 25% (10% under domestic law) of the payor's stock. Some of the newer treaties grant this exemption only if the dividend is derived exclusively or almost exclusively from 'active business'.

If tax-free foreign dividends are redistributed, the resident corporation has to 'establish the distribution of tax burden', that is pay 36% corporation tax in order to enable the receiving shareholder to claim this tax as credit against his own tax liability. This tax may also be refunded if the shareholder is non-resident. Depreciation of fixed assets may be calculated on the straight-line, declining balance, units-of-production, or the hours-of-production method. Typical straight-line rates are as follows:

(1) buildings at 2% (higher rates if actual life of less than fifty years can be shown);
(2) machinery and equipment at 10% to 20%;
(3) office equipment at 10% to 20%;
(4) vehicles at 20% to 33.3%;
(5) patents at 12% to 20%;

Building and other immovable fixed assets must be depreciated on a straight-line method. Capital gains from the sale of business assets are taxed in the same manner as operating profits.

LOSSES

Operating losses are required to be first carried back to the two preceding years with any excess available for carry forward indefinitely.

ARMS LENGTH PRICING

Charges may be made by a related foreign entity for management and technical service fees, intercompany purchases and sales, royalties, interest or any other payments, or charges are deductible to the extent they are reasonable to the business of the West Germany entity. When charges for the service fees cannot be traced to specific identifiable services rendered and when any charge exceeds an amount that would have been determined at arm's length, the tax authorities many disallow all or part of the deduction. The law views an excessive charge paid to a shareholder corporation as a hidden profit distribution. Under the tax system such distribution is treated as a dividend and is thereby subject to 36% corporation tax, withholding tax and trade tax.

FOREIGN TAXES

If foreign income of a resident corporation is not tax exempt by treaty, the foreign tax paid on such income is permitted as a direct foreign tax credit. The tax credit is calculated on a country-by-country basis and is limited to the lesser of the foreign tax actually paid or the German corporate income tax that is attributable to the foreign source income. Alternatively, the foreign tax may on application be deducted from taxable income. A deduction is also permitted in certain cases in which the foreign tax does not qualify for tax credit.

In the case of dividends received from a non-resident corporation engaged in an active business, credit can also be claimed for foreign income taxes paid by the foreign company on profits from which such dividends were paid if the recipient corporation owns 10% or more of the stock of the non-resident corporation. This indirect foreign tax credit also extends to taxes paid by a second-tier foreign corporation in which the recipient corporation owns 10% or more of the shares.

TAXATION OF NON-RESIDENT CORPORATIONS

A non-resident corporation is assessed at a flat rate of 50% on profits derived from the operation of a permanent establishment in Germany. Profits remitted by a permanent establishment to a non-resident are not subject to withholding tax. Dividends, certain interest income, royalties, know-how and similar payments from German sources are subject to a 25% withholding tax when paid to a non-resident through a permanent establishment. Such amounts are again taxed as ordinary profits of the permanent establishment, but the withheld tax is applied as a credit against the tax assessed to the permanent establishment. Unless otherwise provided by treaty, dividends, interest on bonds and royalties are subject to a 25% withholding tax. Normal business interest payments are not subject to tax.

ITALY

Resident corporations are subject to corporate income tax on worldwide income and to local income tax on Italian source income. A corporation is deemed to be a resident if its registered office, place of management, or principal business activities are located in Italy.

Non-resident corporations have limited tax liability and, unless otherwise proved by tax treaty, are subject to corporate income tax on income derived from Italian branches, Italian permanent establishments, and on certain other Italian source income. For purposes of local income tax, a non-resident corporation is taxable on Italian source income only.

CORPORATE INCOME TAX

Corporate income tax (IRPEG) is assessed at a flat rate of 36%. Unless otherwise provided by tax treaty, a resident company is taxable on its worldwide income. Local income tax (ILOR) is assessed at a flat rate of 16.2%. Taxable income for purposes of local income tax only includes income produced within Italy. However, income arising from direct commercial activities abroad and not attributable to a permanent establishment is deemed to be produced in Italy. Local income tax is an allowable deduction for the purposes of computing corporate income tax.

TAXABLE INCOME OF RESIDENT CORPORATIONS

Taxable income is based on financial accounting income as reflected in the profit and loss statement, with adjustments as provided by law. Taxable income is the basis for determining both the corporate income tax and local income tax liabilities.

Gross dividends, including tax withheld at source, are included in taxable income for purposes of corporate income tax (IRPEG). Dividends paid by a resident to a resident corporate recipient are subject to an Italian withholding of tax of 10%. In addition the person receiving the dividend is entitled to a tax credit equal to 56.25% of the gross dividend. The amount of the tax credit is also considered as income and, therefore, included as part of the total taxable income. The tax credit and the withheld tax are credited against corporate income tax and any amount in excess of corporate income tax is refundable. Dividends from associated foreign companies are taxed on 40% of their gross amount.

Only the straight-line method of depreciation is permitted according to a table of maximum rates published by the Minister of Finance. Depreciation must commence in the financial year in which the asset is first available for use and must be recorded in the financial statements in order to be an allowable deduction for tax purposes. Rates vary depending on the category of industrial activity. Typical straight-line rates are as follows:

(1) buildings at 3.5% to 7%;
(2) plant and machinery at 6% to 17.5%;
(3) office equipment at 12%;
(4) vehicles at 20% to 25%.

In addition to normal depreciation, accelerated depreciation may be claimed on fixed assets based on up to 45% of cost taken over the first three years, subject to a maximum of 15% in any one year. Capital gains are treated as normal income for both the corporate income tax and local income tax.

LOSSES

Operating losses may be carried forward for five succeeding taxable years for corporate tax (IRPEG), but not for local tax (ILOR), purposes. Carry-back of losses is not permitted.

ARM'S LENGTH PRICES

Generally, charges made by a related foreign entity for management and technical services, intercompany purchases, royalties, interest, or any other payments or charges are deductible to the extent they are reasonable and the arm's length concept has been followed. When an Italian corporation undercharges a related foreign entity for sales or services, the amount of such hidden distribution is deemed to be income to the Italian corporation.

FOREIGN TAXES

Unless otherwise provided by tax treaty, resident corporations may claim a partial credit against corporate income tax for foreign income taxes paid on taxable profits provided that the foreign taxing authority grants a similar credit for Italian tax on Italian source income. When similar relief is not granted for the foreign tax authority, the credit against Italian corporate income tax cannot exceed 90% of the Italian tax allocable to foreign source income. The credit is calculated on a per country basis; foreign taxes that cannot be claimed as a credit because of the above limitations are not deductible.

TAXATION OF NON-RESIDENT CORPORATIONS

Profits derived from the branch of a foreign company or other permanent estalishments are subject to corporate income tax and local income tax at the same rates as those for a resident corporation. Capital gains realized on the sale of business assets of a permanent establishment or on the sale or liquidation there of are also taxed. Profits remitted by a permanent establishment to a non-resident are not subject to withholding tax. Unless otherwise provided by tax treaty, dividends paid to non-residents are subject to a 32.4% withholding tax. If the foreign non-resident company owns a 'permanent establishment' in Italy, the withholding tax, amounting to 10%, is on account and does not represent the final tax liability. The foreign company may deduct the tax credit from corporation tax (IRPEG) due on the profits of a permanent establishment.

INTEREST ON BONDS ATTRACTS WITHHOLDING TAX OF 12.5%

A 25% withholding tax is charged on interest paid by banks and other credit institutions on deposits and current accounts. This withholding constitutes the final tax liability if the non-resident does not have a 'permanent establishment' in Italy.

Patent royalties are subject to a withholding tax at an effective rate of 21%, unless otherwise provided by treaty. The withholding tax constitutes the final tax liability.

LUXEMBOURG

Resident corporations (except holding companies) are taxable on their worldwide income. However dividends from a substantial holding may be wholly exempt. A corporation is considered to be resident if either its statutory seat or principal establishment is located in Luxembourg. The term statutory seat refers to the place specified in the corporate charter as the domicile of the company; principal establishment refers to the place of management of the company. A corporation that does not have its statutory seat or principal establishment in Luxembourg is considered to be a non-resident, and unless otherwise provided by tax treaty, is liable to tax only on its Luxembourg source income.

CORPORATE INCOME TAX

The corporate income tax is levied at the national level at a rate of 34% if profits exceed Lfr1,312,000. Taxable income less than this amount is taxed at one of the following graduated rates:

Taxable income (Lfr)	Tax rate (% Lfr)
Up to 400,000	20%
400,000 to 600,000	80,000 plus 50% of excess over 400,000
600,000 to 1,000,000	30% plus 180,000
1,000,000 to 1,312,000	300,000 plus 46.8% of excess over 1,000,000

Non-resident corporations are liable for corporate income tax at the rate of 34%. The graduated rates will be applied on request of the non-resident corporation if it establishes to the satisfaction of the taxing authorities that its worldwide income was less than Lfrl,312,000.

TAXABLE INCOME OF RESIDENT CORPORATIONS

Taxable income is determined by comparing the net assets at the beginning and the end of the accounting year. The difference in net assets, adjusted for dividend distributions, changes in capital, losses carried forward and other significant adjustments required by income tax laws, constitutes taxable gain or loss.

Profits arising from abroad are fully included in the taxable base. However foreign income tax paid is creditable against tax liability to the extent of the Luxembourg tax on such foreign income. Dividends paid by a resident company are normally taxable to a resident recipient and are subject to 15% withholding at source *(retenue d'impôt sur les revenus des capitaux)*. Withholding is creditable against the corporate tax liability of the resident recipient.

If the resident recipient owns for at least twelve months prior to its year end 25% or more of the issued capital (a substantial holding) of the resident distributing corporation, dividends received will be exempt from corporate income tax and withholding at source. When the resident recipient owns 25% or more of the issued capital of a foreign corporation for the same qualifying period, dividend income received from such foreign corporation is tax exempt if the foreign distributing corporation is subject to a corporate income tax. Foreign withholding tax is creditable against income tax liability.

The straight-line method is normally used for most depreciable assets. Depreciation by the declining balance method is now permitted for tangible assets other than buildings. Gains on the sale of business assets are taxed on the same basis as operating profits.

LOSSES

Operating losses may be carried forward for five succeeding taxable years. Carry-back of losses is not permitted.

ARM'S LENGTH PRICING

Generally, charges made by a shareholder that are unreasonable in amount will be treated as a hidden distribution of profits to the extent that the charge exceeds an amount that would have been determined at arm's length. A hidden profit distribution is treated as a constructive dividend to such a shareholder; therefore, such an amount cannot be deducted as a corporate expense and is subject to withholding at source. The substantial holding privilege can apply to a hidden distribution.

FOREIGN TAXES

Unless otherwise provided by a tax treaty, income from abroad is taxed on its gross amount, but credit is given for foreign taxes similar to Luxembourg tax on income. The foreign tax credit, however, cannot exceed the amount of Luxembourg tax attributable to the foreign income. Any excess of foreign tax paid is deductible from the tax base. Tax treaties normally extend the tax credit method to other than income taxes.

TAXATION OF NON-RESIDENTS

The taxable income of a non-resident corporation includes all profits derived by a registered branch or other permanent establishment in Luxembourg. Royalties, interest and technical fees paid to the head office are not deductible in arriving at taxable income. Non-resident corporations are subject to the same tax rates as resident corporations. Profits remitted by a permanent establishment to its head office are not subject to any withholding tax.

Unless otherwise provided by tax treaty, certain income received by a non-resident is subject to withholding tax at source:

(1) dividends and interest from profit-sharing bonds at 15%;
(2) interest on other bonds at 0%;
(3) other interest at 0%;
(4) copyright royalties at 10%;
(5) patent royalties at 12%.

THE NETHERLANDS

Corporations resident in the Netherlands are subject to Dutch taxation on their worldwide income. Resident corporations are those that are incorporated under Dutch law or actually situated in the Netherlands. The principal factor in determining where a corporation is situated is the location of its central management. Other relevant factors include the location of general shareholder meetings and the situs of business activities.

Non-resident corporations are subject to Dutch taxation on profits arising from undertakings carried on in the Netherlands (such as profits arising from a Dutch branch or other permanent establishment) and on any income subject to deduction of tax at source.

CORPORATE INCOME TAX

The corporate income tax is levied on the worldwide income of resident corporations at the rate of 35%. Profits derived by a non-resident corporation from a branch or other permanent establishment or from real property located in the Netherlands are taxed at the normal rates of corporate tax applicable to resident corporations.

TAXABLE INCOME OF RESIDENT CORPORATIONS

Taxable income is based on net profits computed on the basis of sound accounting principles consistently applied.

If a resident corporation owns substantially all of the stock of another resident corporation, both corporations may apply to the Minister of Finance to be taxed as a fiscal unit, that is, parent and subsidiary are considered as one entity for tax purposes. The Minister of Finance cannot refuse to recognise the fiscal unity provided the corporations meet certain statutory conditions. The concept of fiscal unity is significant since taxable income is determined on a combined basis (inter-company profits are exempt from assessment), and assets and liabilities of the subsidiary are considered for tax purposes as actually held by the parent company (reorganisations, liquidations and rearrangements of assets can be achieved without adverse tax consequences).

Normally, dividends paid by a resident corporation are subject to withholding tax *(Dividendbelasting)* at the rate of 25%, which is an advance payment of corporate or income tax liability by the shareholders. Domestic and foreign source dividends received by resident corporations are taxed as ordinary business income.

In the event that a resident corporation owns a substantial holding (a minimum of 5% of the paid-up share capital), dividends from such holdings are exempt from corporate income tax and from Dutch withholding tax. The exemption is conditional upon continuous ownership of the substantial holding from the beginning of the tax year. In the case of dividends received from a non-resident, the exemption is only available if the non-resident is subject to a foreign tax on income or profits and the holding is more that a mere portfolio investment (that is, there must be some active business purpose).

Depreciation may be calculated by various methods provided the method selected reflects sound business practice and is consistently used. There are no official guidelines and depreciation rates are normally accepted by tax authorities unless clearly erroneous. Typical rates for straight-line depreciation are as follows:

(1) commercial and industrial buildings at 2% to 3%;
(2) machinery and equipment at 10%;
(3) office equipment at 10%;
(4) vehicles at 20%;
(5) know-how and patents at 25%;
(6) good will at 20%.

Generally, gains from the disposal of business assets are taxed as ordinary income at normal corporate rates; losses are fully deductible. Gains on the disposal of a substantial participation in another corporation are not normally taxed and losses on such disposals are not normally deductible.

LOSSES

Losses incurred during a taxable year must be carried back for offset against income of the preceding three years and then carried forward to the eight following years. Losses incurred during a corporation's first six taxable years can be carried forward indefinitely.

ARM'S LENGTH PRICING

Charges made by related entities are normally subject to careful examination by tax authorities. Charges in excess of arm's length are treated as concealed distributions of profit (constructive dividends). Such charges are not deductible in arriving at taxable income of the Dutch company and, as constructive dividends, are subject to withholding tax at a rate of 25% unless the recipient is a Dutch company with a substantial holding or unless otherwise provided by tax treaty.

FOREIGN TAXES

Generally, foreign withholding taxes are deductible from gross income unless the income is exempt from Dutch taxation. A tax credit is granted unilaterally for withholding taxes on interest and royalties from developing countries, and provision for a tax credit on foreign source income is contained in most tax treaties.

Unless otherwise provided by tax treaty, the Dutch taxation system provides unilateral tax relief to Dutch residents by reducing or eliminating Dutch taxation on foreign income earned by a permanent establishment or permanent representative that is subject to income taxation by a foreign state. Dutch tax on total taxable income is reduced by that portion of Dutch tax attributable to net foreign income earned through such permanent enterprises. The relief is in no way dependent on taxes actually paid to the foreign state.

TAXATION OF NON-RESIDENT CORPORATIONS

A non-resident is assessed at normal Dutch rated on income derived through a Dutch branch or permanent establishment. When a non-resident derives dividends through a Dutch permanent establishment and the 25% dividend tax is withheld, the withheld tax is creditable against the corporate income tax of the permanent establishment. A permanent establishment may qualify for the substantial holding privilege.

Profits remitted by a branch or other permanent establishment to a non-resident are not subject to withholding tax. Unless otherwise provided by treaty, dividends paid by a Dutch resident corporation to a non-resident are subject to a withholding tax of 25%, which is not refundable and constitutes the final tax liability. Royalty payments and normal business interest payments are exempt from withholding tax.

SPAIN

The total income or net profits earned in each taxation period by companies resident in Spain are subject to income taxes, regardless of source. Resident companies are those established under Spanish law or which have their head office in Spain. Companies resident abroad, but doing business in Spanish territory through a permanent establishment, or deriving from Spanish sources are subject to tax on such income.

CORPORATE INCOME TAX

This tax is levied on the whole amount of the net income or profits earned by companies and other legal entities. Foreign companies are liable for the payment of this tax in Spain, provided they are carrying on business in Spanish territory through a permanent establishment or are deriving income in the said territory. The taxation rate is 35%.

TAXABLE INCOME OF RESIDENT CORPORATIONS

The basis of assessment is determined by reference to the company's books and records, which are subject to verification by the tax administration. When a company's income includes dividends or participation in the profits of other companies, corporate income tax to the extent of 50% is deducted from the result obtained by applying to the amount of dividends or participation received the effective average tax rate which has been applied to the distributing company. In the case of a controlling company receiving dividends from a controlled company, the percentage mentioned in the preceding paragraph may reach as high as 100%. Control exists when the controlling company holds more than 25% of the share capital of the controlled company. The rate of straight-line depreciation applicable to fixed assets is determined by reference to cost and useful life. Typical straight-line rates are as follows:

(1) industrial building at 3%;
(2) office and residential buildings at 2%;
(3) machinery and equipment at 10%;
(4) furniture and fixtures at 10% to 12%;
(5) and vehicles at 14%.

Authorization can be requested from the administration for accelerated depreciation to be applied in special cases due to the nature of the particular assets. Assets acquired after 9 May 1985 and within the fiscal year 1985 may be freely depreciated. Capital gains are treated as normal income for the corporation income tax. Tax on such gains may, however, be avoided if the gain is reinvested by the company in other assets related to the company's normal activities.

LOSSES

Operating losses may be carried forward for five succeeding fiscal years. Carry-back of loss is not permitted.

ARM'S LENGTH PRICING

Charges for management and technical services, intracompany sales, royalties, interest or any other payments or charges made by a related foreign entity can be deducted to the extent they are reasonable. When a Spanish corporation under-charges a related foreign entity for sales or services, the amount of such hidden distribution is deemed to be income to the Spanish corporation.

FOREIGN TAXES

As a unilateral measure for avoiding double taxation, the law concerning taxation of the income of companies and other legal entities (article 24.4) provides that, in the case of foreign source income which has been subject, in the country of origin, to taxes similar to the Spanish company tax, the lesser of the following two amounts shall be deducted from the tax payable in Spain:

(1) the amount of the tax paid abroad;
(2) the amount of the tax which would have had to be paid in Spain on the profits or income in question had they been obtained in the national territory.

The Decree-Law 15 of 1977 introduced the concept of a group for Spanish accounting and tax purposes. A 'group' consists of a controlling company and one or more subsidiary companies. A controlling company is a corporation (*sociedad anonima*) resident in Spain which owns, directly or indirectly, more than 50% of the capital of another corporation (or corporations). The subsidiaries may or may not be resident in Spain.

The Decree-Law does not permit the consolidation of:

(1) companies that are not *sociedades anonimas*;
(2) two or more *sociedades anonimas* resident in Spain which are subsidiaries of the same foreign company.

The controlling company may request the Ministry of Finance to be taxed on the basis of group consolidated financial statements. Alternatively, the Ministry of Finance may require certain groups to file consolidated financial statements, but this does not necessarily imply being taxed on the basis of consolidated profits. Consolidation will only apply in the case of:

(1) profits tax;
(2) withholding taxes on dividends, royalties, interest and other remittances.

In a group that consolidates, this means that intercompany dividends will be exempted from the withholding tax. However dividends received from unconsolidated companies, such as a limited liability company or a corporation in which the controlling company does not have a majority interest, remain subject to withholding tax.

The same principle is applicable to royalties and interest paid within the consolidated group.

Notwithstanding the consolidation, other taxes applicable to the transactions with the group remain effective, such as turnover tax and transfer tax. The consolidated tax basis is assessed under the individual assessment method. Intracompany transactions are eliminated in determining the taxable income of a group. Losses in group companies must be offset in the year in which they occur. Consolidated tax losses may be offset against profits obtained in the succeeding five years in accordance with conditions established by the tax authorities.

TAXATION OF NON-RESIDENT CORPORATIONS

Unless otherwise provided by treaty, a registered branch or other permanent establishment of a foreign company is subject to Spanish corporate income tax in the same manner and at the same rates as local companies.

In arriving at the taxable income, the following items are not deductible: any payments, directly or indirectly made, involving the transfer of profits abroad by means of increases or reductions in purchase or sales prices; royalties or similar charges for technical assistance or for the use of patents and trade marks; interest, commissions or any other payments to the head office of the foreign company or to any controlled affiliate outside Spain.

If the operations carried out in Spain do not constitute a complete business activity with specific financial results, the profits normally obtained by other companies resident in Spain, and engaging in the same or similar activities, may be taken into account in estimating the income to be attributed to the Spanish permanent establishment.

Foreign companies, that carry on business in Spain through a permanent establishment, may deduct management and general administrative expenses that are reasonably allocated to the Spanish establishment. Income paid by companies resident in Spain to non-residents is subject to withholding tax (creditable against corporate income tax), unless such income is paid directly by a permanent establishment abroad of a company resident in Spain.

SWITZERLAND

Federal and cantonal tax ordinances provide that corporations domiciled in Switzerland are subject to federal, cantonal and municipal taxes on their worldwide income, except for income derived from foreign real estate and from business establishments located abroad. Domicile refers to place of incorporation and registration; however this definition is sometimes expanded to the seat of corporate management and control. Corporations not domiciled in Switzerland have limited tax liability and, unless otherwise provided by tax treaty, are subject to tax only income that has an economic attachment to Switzerland, such as income derived from a permanent establishment, immovable property or on loans secured by mortgage on real property situated in Switzerland.

CORPORATE INCOME TAXES

The national defence tax (federal income tax). The federal income tax is imposed by federal ordinance but is assessed and collected by cantonal tax authorities. Corporations are taxed at effective rates ranging from 3.63% to 9.8% of net income. Tax liability is based on taxable income and net worth (paid-in capital and surplus) and is determined in three parts:

(1) the basic tax is 3.63% on taxable income;
(2) a tax of 3.6% on taxable income that exceeds 4% of the corporation's net worth, or if net worth is less than Sfr50,000, tax of 3.63% of taxable income that exceeds Sfr2,000;
(3) a tax of 4.84% on taxable income that exceeds 8% of the corporation's net worth, or if net worth is less than Sfr50,000, tax of 4.84% on taxable income that exceeds Sfr4,000.

Cantonal and municipal income taxes. Cantonal and municipal income taxes are normally assessed by the cantonal authorities. Each of the twenty-six cantons has its own income tax system that is generally based on the principle of capital yield. Nevertheless, income tax laws and tax rates vary significantly between cantons. The combined effective rates of cantonal and municipal tax can range from 10% to 35% of taxable profits. In most cantons a minimum rate and a maximum rate of tax on net profits is fixed. Between these limits, the applicable rate is determined according to capital yield, that is the percentage relationship between taxable profit and capital.

Special tax concessions are granted by many cantons and municipalities to pure holding companies (*Holdinggesellschaft*) and domiciliary companies (*Domizilgesellschaft*).

Federal net worth tax is levied at a rate of 0.0825% of corporate net worth and is generally based on the amount of paid-up capital, surplus and reserves at the beginning of the assessment period. The portion of net worth allocable to foreign permanent establishments or foreign real estate is not subject to tax.

A similar tax is levied by cantons and municipalities, at varying rates, which are sometimes reduced for holding companies. Combined rates generally do not exceed 1%.

TAXABLE INCOME OF RESIDENT CORPORATIONS

Taxable income is based on financial accounting income with adjustment as provided by law. The federal income tax law and the tax laws of most cantons permit all federal, cantonal, and municipal taxes to be deducted. Generally, the remaining cantons do not permit the deduction of federal, cantonal and municipal taxes.

Dividends received by a resident corporation are subject to a 35% federal anticipatory tax (*Verrechnungssteuer* or *impôt anticipé*), which is withheld by the paying corporation and can be recovered by the resident shareholder.

If the recipient is a corporation owning a substantial holding in the distributing corporation, federal tax liability is reduced in the proportion that gross dividends derived from substantial holdings bear to total adjusted gross income (this rule applies in many cantons). A substantial holding means either a 20% or greater equity interest in the paying corporation or a shareholding therein with a book value of at least Sfr2,000,000.

For purposes of federal and cantonal taxation, resident corporations include net foreign source dividends on gross income unless otherwise required by treaty. If such recipient owns a substantial holding in the paying company, it may reduce its tax liability as if such dividend were received from a domestic source.

Fixed assets may be depreciated on the straight-line or declining balance method to the extent 'commercially justifiable'. Official federal guidelines have established the following maximum declining method rates:

(1) commercial buildings at 4%;
(2) industrial buildings at 8%;
(3) furniture and office equipment at 25%;
(4) Machinery at 30%;
(5) vehicles and office machines at 40%; and
(6) patents and goodwill at 40%.

For federal income tax purposes, capital gains from the sale of business assets are taxed in the same manner as operating profits.

LOSSES

The federal income tax permits losses arising in one year to be set off against profits of the other year in the same period of assessment (normally two years). The average loss for the period of assessment may be set off against the average net profit of the three subsequent periods of assessment (six years).

ARM'S LENGTH PRICING

Charges made by a related foreign entity are normally subject to careful examination by tax authorities. Charges in excess of arm's length are treated as hidden profit distributions which are subject to income and withholding taxes.

When debt financing exceeds more than six times a Swiss corporation's equity capital and retained earnings, the tax authorities will refuse to allow the benefits of double taxation agreements, disallow part of the deduction for interest paid, and levy withholding tax on the 'constructive dividend'.

FOREIGN TAXES

Unless otherwise provided by treaty, no credit for foreign tax is permitted. However income from a foreign permanent establishment and foreign real property is exempt from Swiss taxation. For the purposes of federal and cantonal income tax, other foreign source income (such as business or investment income) is reported net of income and withholding taxes imposed by the source country, unless a tax treaty provides for refund for such foreign taxes. In such a case this amount must be included in gross income.

TAXATION OF NON-RESIDENT CORPORATIONS

A non-resident is assessed at normal federal income tax rates on profits derived in Switzerland from the operation of a branch or other permanent establishment. While the tax is based on income and net worth attributed to Switzerland, the rates are calculated on the basis of worldwide income and net worth. Dividends paid by Swiss resident corporations, bond interest and interest on bank deposits from Swiss sources are subject to withholding of a 35% federal anticipatory tax when paid to a Swiss branch or other permanent establishment. This anticipatory tax is recoverable provided the Swiss branch or permanent establishment is subject to Swiss income tax and provided this investment income is derived from assets held by such branch or permanent establishment.

Profits remitted by a resident branch or other permanent establishment to the non-resident head office are not subject to anticipatory tax. Unless otherwise provided by treaty, the amount withheld is not refundable and constitutes the final tax liability. Royalty payments are exempt from anticipatory tax. Rental income from real property located in Switzerland is subject to income taxation, as is interest income from a mortgage-secured loan.

MALCOLM J. FINNEY

Malcolm J. Finney and Partners

6.3 Tax havens in international corporate tax planning

DEFINITIONS OF TAX HAVEN

There is no *absolute* definition of the term tax haven. In many ways a tax haven is similar to an elephant, difficult to describe but easy to identify.

In the publication *Tax Havens Encyclopedia* the editor defines a tax haven as:

> . . . a jurisdiction:
> (a) where there are no relevant taxes;
> (b) where taxes are levied only on internal taxable events; but not at all, or at low rates, from foreign sources; or
> (c) where special tax privileges are granted for certain types of taxable persons or events.

In another publication, *Tax Havens* by Edward Chamboust, the term tax haven is referred to as follows:

> The term conjures up the image of a safe harbour. The French call it *un paradis fiscal* — a tax paradise. In German it is *ein Steueroase* — a tax oasis. Each term is apt. The businessman may be compared with the seaman seeking shelter. He crosses the perilous seas of tax legislation, finding his way through the storms of audits and deemed remittances, and finally docks in the harbour of the paradise he is seeking. As all seamen know, each port has its own special features. The same is true of a tax haven, which is rarely a paradise in all aspects.

In a definitive work produced by Richard Gordon for the United States Internal Revenue Service, entitled *Tax Havens and their Use by United States Taxpayers — an Overview*, a tax haven is defined as:

> . . . any country having a low or zero rate of tax on all or certain categories of income, and offering a certain amount of banking and commercial secrecy.

It may be, however, that even high tax countries possess some of the characteristics normally associated with tax havens. For present purposes it is the intention to concentrate on tax havens as generally understood; this will cover countries such as those listed in the appendix to this chapter. In this regard, most of the countries listed possess one or more of the following attributes:

(1) low tax rate;
(2) high level of bank and commercial secrecy;
(3) extreme importance of banking and related financial activities to the country's economy;
(4) availability of modern communication facilities;
(5) lack of currency controls; and
(6) self-promotion as an offshore financial centre.

In order to appreciate fully the possible advantages which a tax haven may offer to a company based in the United Kingdom, it is important in the first instance to appreciate the basic principles of United Kingdom corporation tax.

UNITED KINGDOM CORPORATION TAX: BASIC PRINCIPLES

The United Kingdom operates what is called the *worldwide* system of taxation as opposed to the *territorial* system of taxation. Under the worldwide system, a company which is resident in the United Kingdom for United Kingdom tax purposes is subject to United Kingdom corporation tax on its worldwide profits on an arising basis, whether profits arising overseas are remitted to the United Kingdom or not. Thus, a United Kingdom resident company which manufactures and sells its products to customers outside the United Kingdom will bear United Kingdom corporation tax on any profit arising therefrom even if the customer is in, for example, Australia and pays for the goods purchased by arranging funds to be credited into the United Kingdom company's bank account in an Australian bank.

The criterion by which the residence of a company initially was to be determined for the purpose of United Kingdom taxation has been established by judicial authority as follows.

> A company resides, for purposes of income tax, where its real business is carried on . . . and the real business is carried on where the central management and control actually abides *(De Beers Consolidated Mines Ltd v. Howe (1960) 5 TC 198)*.

The central management and control of a company is in turn by its constitution vested in a board of directors, and the place where the directors meet regularly as a board and take decisions relating to the central management and control of the company's business is where the central management and control of the company actually abides.

Typically, therefore, where the majority of the directors of a company are individuals resident in the United Kingdom and the company's board meetings are held in the United Kingdom (at which strategic decisions relating to the company's operations are taken) the company under current United Kingdom law would almost certainly be regarded as being United Kingdom resident with the above tax consequences. (For further clarification on the United Kingdom Revenue's views on what constitutes residence of a company for United Kingdom tax purposes, reference should be made to Inland Revenue Press Release dated 27 July 1983 (SP 6/83).) However with effect from 1988 there is now also a statutory test of residence; a company will also be resident in the United Kingdom if it is incorporated there.

Because of the worldwide system of taxation adopted by the United Kingdom it is clear that, for a United Kingdom resident company to avoid United Kingdom tax on any part of its profits, it would be necessary for the relevant activities to be carried on by company resident *outside* the United Kingdom. Therefore a United Kingdom company could in effect hive off that part of its trading activity on which it wished to avoid United Kingdom tax to a company which it owns and which was *not* resident in the United Kingdom. To avoid any overseas tax on those profits (since clearly to avoid United Kingdom tax only to pay tax elsewhere achieves very little) it would be necessary to set the company up in a tax haven location where the local tax rate on profits would be low or even nil. The company could then accumulate profits not sourced in the United Kingdom in a tax free form.

As a non-United Kingdom company the only exposure to the United Kingdom corporation tax would be if the tax haven company remitted any part of its profits back to its United Kingdom parent company, for example, by way of dividend (see, however, Anti-avoidance provisions in Chapter 6.1). In such a case, the United Kingdom parent company would, of course, be liable to United Kingdom corporation tax at 35% on the dividends so received.

Not surprisingly, United Kingdom legislation contains provisions designed to limit the ability of resident companies to make extensive use of tax haven operations. Originally, one of the major provisions was section 482 of the Income and Corporation Taxes Act 1970. (Now section 765 Income and Corporation Taxes Act 1988). This section was, however, modified by the Finance Act 1988 and is today far less onerous. Nevertheless the section cannot be dismissed.

Following the Chancellor's Speech on 15 March 1988 the Treasury issued the Treasury General Consents 1988. These New Consents apply to transactions effected on or after 15 March 1988, that is with immediate effect, following subsections (1)(c) and (d) of section 765 (historically, more commonly known as subsections (1)(c) and (d) of section 482 ICTA 1970).

The previous General Consents which had been issued under section 482 ICTA 1970 by the Treasury were formally revoked with effect from the same day.

In the past, a United Kingdom resident company could not permit non-resident companies, over which it had control, to create or issue shares or debentures without specific Treasury consent except under certain circumstance. Nor could a United Kingdom resident company transfer shares or debentures owned in non-resident controlled companies without first obtaining Treasury consent. General Consents had nevertheless been issued which did permit the effecting of such transactions in certain limited instances without the need to obtain specific consent. However, under no circumstances did these General Consents apply to the creation, issue or transfer of shares or debentures where the resident controlling company lost control over the relevant non-resident company following the transactions.

This is, however, not so under the New Consents under which the range of permitted transactions pursuant to subsections (1)(c) and (d) of section 765 which may now be carried out (without the need to obtain specific Treasury consent) is broader. Unfortunately, in achieving this desirable end product the New Consents are somewhat more complex than those of old.

Under the New Consents the creation and issue of shares or debentures by a non-resident company *or* the transfer of the shares or debentures in such a company may now be effected even where the result is that the original resident controlling company no longer controls the non-resident company. In addition, the New Consents permit the creation and issue of shares or debentures and their transfers to recipients or transferees who are not resident in the United Kingdom (transactions not possible under the Old Consents).

The easiest way to obtain a feel for the New Consents is to consider some simple examples.

EXAMPLE 1

United Kingdom resident company (UK) owns Swiss resident company (S1) which in turn owns Swiss resident company (S2). The issue of shares by S1 to UK, S2 to S1 or S2 to UK would all be permitted under the New Consents (see paragraphs 3(b)(i) and (ii) of New Consents).

EXAMPLE 2

UK resident company (UK) owns directly in parallel two Swiss resident subsidiaries (S1 and S2). One of the Swiss subsidiaries wishes now to issue shares to its sister company. It is arguable that pursuant to paragraph 3(b)(i) of the New Consents such creation and issue can be effected as both Swiss companies would satisfy the requirement of being members of an overseas group (a newly introduced term). However, this conclusion involves reading and interpreting parts of Chapter IV of Part X ICTA 1988, previously section 258 ICTA 1970, as modified by the New Consents. It may be that the Inland Revenue will hold the view that in fact the two Swiss companies do not form an overseas group and that specific Treasury consent will be required for the share issue. (A straight issue of shares by either Swiss company to UK would, however, be covered.)

EXAMPLE 3

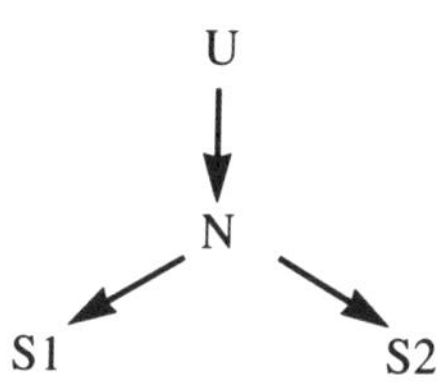

UK resident company (UK) owns a Dutch subsidiary (N) which in turn owns two Swiss subsidiaries (S1 and S2) as brother and sister companies. It is again arguable that the issue of shares by either Swiss company to the other (but not to the Dutch parent) is permitted by the New Consents. It would seem that the two Swiss companies do form an overseas group even though the UK company and the Dutch company are not themselves part of the group for the purposes of Chapter IV of Part X of ICTA 1988 (previously of section 258 ICTA 1970) as amended by the New Consents.

EXAMPLE 4

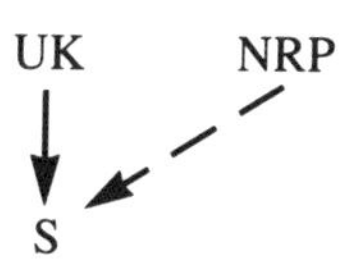

UK resident company (UK) owns a Swiss resident subsidiary (S). The issue of shares by the Swiss company to a totally non connected person (NRP) would be permitted under the New Consents. Such would also be the case even if the shares so issued were of such number as to result in the UK original resident parent company losing control over the Swiss Company (to the non connected person).

In all the above examples it is also necessary that certain additional conditions are satisfied if the transactions are to fall within the New Consents. Among other considerations, the shares so issued may need to be issued for full consideration whether paid in cash or some other form; it may be necessary that no arrangements exist under which, in effect, the person to whom the shares are issued is under an obligation, or otherwise, to hold or transfer such shares to a third party; or it may be that the shares so issued must not be of a redeemable nature. However, it should be noted that not all these conditions need to be satisfied in, for example, each of the examples cited above.

The above examples related to the *creation and issue* of shares (pursuant to subsection (1)(c) of section 765). The examples below, however, relate to the *transferring* of shares (pursuant to subsection (1)(d) of section 765).

EXAMPLE 5

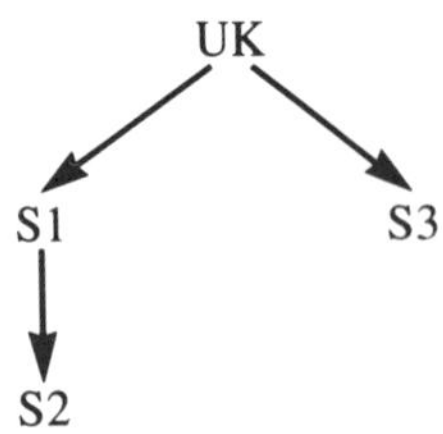

(S1, S2 and S3 are Swiss resident)

The transfer of the shares in S2 by S1 to S3, either in whole or in part, would be covered by the New Consents. This is so because S1 and S3 would be regarded as being members of a territorial group (a newly introduced term) and paragraph 8(c) of the New Consents would apply.

EXAMPLE 6

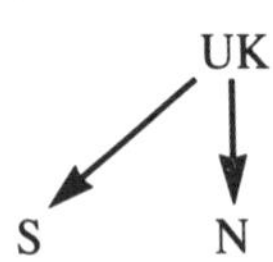

(S is Swiss resident, N is Dutch resident)

The transfer of the shares in S by UK to N would *not* be permitted without specific consent from the Treasury. A transfer by a UK resident transferor of shares in a non UK resident company is only permitted by the new Consents where the transferee is also UK resident (and forms part of a resident group) *or* the transferee is non-connected with the transferor.

EXAMPLE 7

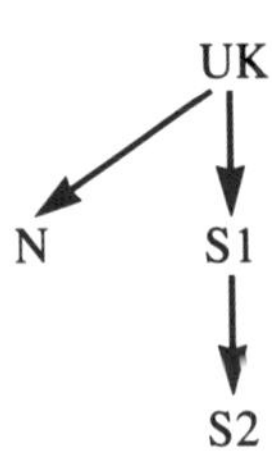

(S1 and S2 are Swiss resident, N is Dutch resident)

The transfer of shares in S2 by S1 to N would require specific Treasury consent and is not covered by the New Consents. For the New Consents to apply the transferor and transferee must, among other things, be members of the same territorial group which requires that both be liable to tax in the same territory outside the United Kingdom.

As in the case of the first four examples it is also necessary, if the transactions are to fall within the New Consents, for additional conditions to be satisfied which, among other things, include that any transfer is for full consideration paid to the transferor and that no arrangements exist under which, effectively, the transferee is under some form of obligation to transfer the shares on to a person-connected with the United Kingdom resident controlling company.

It can be seen from the above examples that the major area of doubt relates to the definitions of overseas group and territorial group. Looking in particular at examples 2 and 3 it is highly likely that the author's conclusion will not be accepted by the Revenue as it would seem that the intention (even if the wording does not already achieve the desired result) is to permit share issues and transference between companies comprised in what might be referred to as a foreign subgroup and not to permit cross-border issues and transference.

In view of this possible area of doubt it is suggested, pending clarification, that specific consent be obtained from the Treasury (in the old format) for transactions such as those referred to in examples 2 and 3.

With respect to subsections (1)(a) and (b) of section 765, the old General Consents have been withdrawn and, as yet, the only information as to the future is the 15 March 1988 Inland Revenue Press Release. This release has indicated that Treasury Consent will no longer be necessary to effect company migration or transfers of trades. However, where migration (but not trade transfers) is intended it will be necessary for notification to be delivered to the Inland Revenue (not Treasury) providing a notice of intention of migration and ensuring that adequate provision is made with regard to any payments of tax due at that time.

In conclusion, with respect to the creation and issue of shares (or debentures) by non United Kingdom resident controlled companies and transfers thereof, the New Consents appear to have broadened the old consents in effect now permitting foreign subgroup transactions previously not possible. However, the reconstruction of a United Kingdom company's overseas interests which result in the transfer of direct ownership in foreign subsidiaries to, say, an intermediate non-resident holding company would, it seems still require the specific consent of the Treasury, as has always been the case. In the case of debentures the New Consents have now removed many types of transactions all of which previously required the specific consent of the Treasury.

In addition to section 765, section 770 of the same Act must also be noted. Section 770 seeks to prevent the United Kingdom revenue from suffering as a consequence of transactions being effected between connected parties (one of which is a United Kingdom resident company) in a manner which is not at arm's length.

Thus, for example, where a United Kingdom parent company sets up a tax haven subsidiary and sells (or buys) goods to it at a price below (or above) that which it would normally sell (buy) to an independent third party, the United Kingdom Revenue may (in computing the taxable profits of the British company) impute, under section 770, the true and proper sales (or purchase) price, not those actually charged (or paid). It is thus not possible for a parent company to syphon off profits outside the United Kingdom tax net by setting up and operating a tax haven subsidiary. It is in this area of invoicing and reinvoicing between companies in a group — one or more of which are located in tax havens — that much of the United Kingdom Revenue's interest under section 770 has centred.

CHOICE OF TAX HAVEN

In deciding upon which tax haven to use, the first and foremost factor must be to base the decision on some commercial basis. For example, if a company in a tax haven is to be used for buying and reselling goods, or for supplying services, and the buyers of the goods and services are located in North America, siting the company in Liberia, Andorra, Gibraltar or Cyprus, for example, would not appear to be very commercial. The Bahamas, Bermuda or the Cayman Islands would appear to represent a far more sensible choice because of, for example, their geographical convenience to the North American market.

It is, of course, sometimes the case that the geographical location of the tax haven is unimportant as the company's activity is in any event to be carried on outside of the tax haven concerned. However, in view of an increasing trend in the high tax countries to introduce complex anti-avoidance legislation designed to counteract the use of tax havens, the latter idea is becoming particularly vulnerable to attack primarily on the premise of non-commerciality. In practice, however, it would not be uncommon for a company registered in a tax haven to be managed and operated by personnel in a third country (for instance, Switzerland or Monaco).

TAXATION

Assuming that there are a number of tax haven locations which present commercially viable options, a factor of importance to be compared for each of the options is the rate of tax imposed and its means of imposition. In this regard it is interesting to categorise the world's tax havens as follows.

Havens imposing virtually no direct taxes: Bermuda, Bahamas, Cayman Islands, Turks and Caicos, New Hebrides, Nauru, Monaco, Campione and others.

Havens which impose tax at relatively low rates: Channel Islands, Isle of Man, Hong Kong, Switzerland, Liechtenstein, Netherlands Antilles, British Virgin Islands, Montserrat and others.

Havens which impose tax only on domestic source income: Liberia, Panama, Hong Kong, Costa Rica, South Africa and others.

Countries whose double tax agreements permit their use as tax havens: Netherlands Antilles, Netherlands, Switzerland, Cyprus, Denmark, South Africa, British Virgin Islands.

Countries granting special tax privileges: Antigua, Barbados, Grenada, Luxembourg, Switzerland, Liechtenstein, Jersey, Guernsey, Isle of Man, Gibraltar.

LEGAL

In addition to the rate of taxation, the local legal requirements relating to the setting up of companies can be important.

In particular it is often important for bona fide commercial reasons that the true promoters and beneficial owners of a tax haven company are kept entirely out of the picture. Costs of incorporation, the time involved and whether this period of time may be accelerated are also often of material consideration.

Limits on the powers of the company may be important, particularly where borrowing rights are concerned, and limitation of liability is something to be investigated.

Certain provisions governing the share capital of the company may have to be taken into account; these include the minimum issued and paid-up capital and the types of classes of shares which may be issued — in particular whether bearer shares, no par value shares, preference shares, redeemable shares, shares with special (or no) voting rights or classes of shares with different rights as to income or capital are permitted.

The rules applying to the organs and officers of the company are often material from the point of view of the nationality of residence of shareholders and directors, the requirements for and the place of the holding of meetings, and the disclosures of names. The fees of local officers or nominees where these are required or desired should also be ascertained in advance as in some cases such fees can be relatively substantial. Government and professional (including banking) fees payable not merely on incorporation, but annually and on winding-up, usually merit close scrutiny.

Requirements with regard to the maintenance of a local registers office and of statutory records, and the duty to file information returns, in particular financial statements, should be noted.

Requirements with regard to auditors vary considerably, as does the extent of the need for an audit.

In certain cases the ease with which a company can be wound up is valuable. Winding-up rules should generally be checked for possible problems.

It is sometimes advantageous to make use of a company incorporated in one location but effectively run from another location. In such cases it is necessary to know whether there are any special requirements in order to carry on business or to have a branch or permanent establishment of such foreign company in the country concerned.

COMMERCIAL INCENTIVES

In addition to differences between the tax rates and legal infrastructure it is important to identify those tax havens which do tend to be associated with certain types of transactions and activities and which may thus be preferable to other tax havens.

Virtually every country in the world could qualify as a tax haven or finance centre for at least some purposes. Many countries have industrial and export incentives. They grant long-term tax deferrals, reductions, or exemptions to corporations that set up new manufacturing plants within the country. These tax holiday benefits are believed to create new jobs within the country and to increase exports. Sometimes the benefits are limited geographically to a particular section of the country, which may called a free zone or free port. Examples include the Colon Free Zone in Panama and Shannon Airport in Ireland.

The United States itself, although in the past a country with one of the most aggressive anti-tax haven stances, encouraged the exporting of home-manufactured goods under DISC (Domestic International Sales Corporation) legislation that came into effect in 1972. This law permitted, broadly speaking, an indefinite deferral of United States income taxes on approximately one-half of any profits generated from export sales. (However, the DISC legislation has now been effectively repealed and replaced with what is referred to as the FISC — Foreign International Sales Corporation — legislation.)

INTERNATIONAL BUSINESS COMPANIES

Antigua, Barbados, Grenada and St Vincent all impose taxes at high rates (40% or more) on companies resident there. However, each of them also permits what are termed international business companies. An international business company must be owned and controlled by non-residents of the particular country in which it is incorporated. It cannot carry on any local business or invest in local securities. The purpose of the legislation is to serve as an incentive to corporations with international activities to use these islands as a base from which to conduct operations.

The Barbados International Business Companies Act is still fairly typical of Acts found in other tax haven jurisdictions. An international business company must file an annual tax return on which it must claim its exempted status.

There is nothing to prevent a Barbados international business company from availing itself of treaty benefits under the income tax treaty between the United Kingdom and the United States. However, such a corporation has been excluded from obtaining benefits under the double taxation agreement between Barbados and the United Kingdom.

An international business company (that is not an investment company) is completely exempt from income tax. Dividends paid by such a corporation to its non-resident shareholders are also exempt from income tax. Profit repatriation in the form of dividends is therefore not a problem.

Although the shares of an international business company incorporated in Barbados are subject to Barbados death duty when the non-resident owner of the shares dies, this is not the case where the international business company is owned by a foreign corporation.

It is interesting to note that an international business company need not be incorporated in Barbados. For example, a Bahamian corporation could qualify as a Barbados international business company.

Despite their advantages, international business companies in the above jurisdictions are few.

BERMUDA

Bermuda has always been regarded as a leading tax haven. It has traditionally enjoyed a complete absence of direct taxation and is not a party to any double tax treaties. It has what are referred to as exempted companies which are granted long-term guarantees against possible future taxes. However, it does impose relatively substantial government fees on the incorporation of companies and yearly thereafter.

Bermuda has traditionally been the leading place in the world to set up a captive insurance company (see Chapter 4.5). It is also an excellent place to incorporate a holding company (if tax treaty benefits are immaterial). On the other hand, unlike certain other tax havens (such as the Cayman Islands) it cannot be used as a base for the establishment of an offshore bank.

An exempted company may not carry on business in Bermuda except in the furtherance of its offshore activities, although it can use a local Bermudian office from which to conduct its offshore business.

Bermuda, unlike a number of tax havens, carefully screens persons seeking to form exempted companies. In many ways Bermuda does not regard itself as a tax haven.

An exempted company formed by non-Bermudians routinely obtains a written guarantee from the Governor-in-Council, guaranteeing against the imposition of possible local taxes until the year 2006. It is believed that Bermuda now has more that 3,000 exempted companies.

As indicated above, Bermuda is an excellent base for insurance companies, including captive insurance companies. It has a new Act regulating insurance companies providing a relatively non-regulated environment for captives. Broadly speaking, a captive must have an authorised share capital of at least B$120,000 and at least that amount must be paid up. Bermuda has experienced insurance personnel and an excellent relationship with other reinsurance markets, including those of London and Switzerland.

A Bermuda exempted company can own or charter ships. If it directly owns a ship, it must be a British ship and will generally have to meet British crew requirements. However, it can charter or subcharter ships of any nationality. Thus, a Bermuda shipping company is often used to charter Liberian or Panamanian flag ships.

CAYMAN ISLANDS

The Cayman Islands have emerged as one of the world's leading tax havens. Cayman has traditionally enjoyed a complete absence of direct taxation. Like Bermuda it is not a party to any tax treaties, and its exempted companies are granted long-term guarantees against possible future taxes and, again like Bermuda, Cayman imposes substantial government fees on the incorporation of companies and yearly thereafter.

An exempted company incorporated in 1980 will not be subject to taxes in Cayman (even if such taxes are eventually imposed) until at least the year 2000. In addition to its twenty-year guarantee, an exempted company has several other advantages that are not available to an ordinary company. It can have bearer (as opposed to registered) shares and no-par value shares. It need not include Limited or Ltd as part of its company name. The company name may be in a foreign language in addition to English. The names of its shareholders are not a matter of public record.

It is possible to set up a Cayman offshore captive bank which must be licensed under the Banks and Trust Companies Regulations Law 1966. Cayman is also attractive as a base for setting up captive insurance companies because, while it lacks some of the expertise of Bermuda, the restrictions on formation are extremely limited.

BAHAMAS

The Bahamas has traditionally enjoyed a complete absence of direct taxes. The country imposes government fees on companies, but does not have exempted companies or offer guarantees against possible future taxes. It is not a party to any tax treaties.

The Bahamas allows foreign-owned vessels to register under the Bahamian flag, using the Bahamas as a flag of convenience, the Merchant Shipping Act providing certain ground rules. The Bahamas has, however, suffered as a tax haven over recent years, due to a general concern over its long-term political stability.

LIBERIA

Liberia is the only active tax haven in Africa today. It has been particularly successful in attracting a large number of shipping companies and ship registrations. It has now the world's largest merchant shipping fleet: over 50 million gross tons of shipping are registered in Liberia.

Unlike many other tax havens, Liberia imposes an income tax on domestic-source income only; this means that, unlike the United Kingdom, it adopts the territorial basis of taxation. It is a tax haven because all the foreign-source shipping income of a Liberian corporation are exempt from income tax if more than 50% of the shares are held by non-Liberians. Although no long-term guarantees are available, this exemption is likely to continue indefinitely.

Liberia has negotiated some tax treaties, but they do not affect non-resident Liberian corporations. Liberia has a 15% withholding tax on dividends, but this does not apply to offshore Liberian corporations whose dividends are paid out of tax-exempt foreign source income or shipping income.

PANAMA

Panama has for many years successfully exploited its status as the major Latin American tax haven despite the fact that it has an income tax with rather high rates. It has based its status as a haven primarily on the fact that all foreign-source income is exempt (as is the case with Liberia). Its law governing corporations is extremely liberal. Corporations can be formed quickly (sometimes in hours) and cost less to form and run thereafter than most other tax havens.

Panama has become an important international banking centre with over 100 banks; there are also a number of reinsurance companies based there.

Panama is a major haven for shipowners from all over the world. In particular, hundreds of American-owned ships have registered under the Panamanian flag.

The Colon Free Trade Zone (referred to earlier) is widely used for warehousing and trans-shipping merchandise coming from all parts of the world. It is a segregated area where foreign merchandise may be landed without payment of customs duties. The Colon Free Trade Zone is located in Colon on the Caribbean side of Panama, near the entrance to the Panama Canal, and does about $1 billion worth of business per year.

Most corporations doing business in the Colon Free Trade Zone receive a 90% discount from Panamanian income taxes payable on their profits earned from export sales. The discount reduces the effective Panamanian income tax rate on these export sales to about 3%.

Panama has a 10% withholding tax on dividends. However, there is no withholding on the distribution of foreign-source earnings.

Whereas the Netherlands is often used in international tax planning as a location in which to set up a holding company, Panama has also often been used as a base for holding companies that invest in operating subsidiaries located throughout Latin America.

HONG KONG

Hong Kong is certainly one of the most important, if not the most important, financial centres of the Far East, and it is the leading manufacturing and trading centre of South-east Asia. Its importance as a financial and commercial centre makes it useful as a tax haven for certain types of activities.

Hong Kong uses the territorial principle of income taxation. Thus it taxes only domestic-source income. Even income from local sources is taxed at the relatively low rate of 17%. There is no tax on foreign-source income even if remitted to the Colony. There is no tax on dividends or capital gains. Hong Kong is not a party to any tax treaties, and has no exchange-control restrictions.

Interest income is subject to the 15% interest tax (nil in the case of Singapore) which is generally withheld at the source. As a result, large amounts of bank deposits are placed in Singapore, which does not tax interest paid by banks to non-residents. Hong Kong banks frequently act as agents in placing deposits with affiliates and correspondent banks in Singapore.

SINGAPORE

Singapore has become the principal banking centre in South-east Asia and the centre of the asiadollar market, despite the fact that it is basically a high-tax country. It does not tax interest on bank deposits paid to non-residents, whereas Hong Kong does. For most purposes, Singapore would be classified as a high-tax country. It has, however, made a concerted effort to attract offshore bank deposits by offering tax incentives both to banks and to their customers, and income from offshore reinsurance business is taxed at only a 10% rate.

As in the case of the United Kingdom (but not typically many other countries as their test of residence is based on the place of incorporation/registration and not on the location of management and control), it is possible to use a corporation incorporated in Singapore but non-resident for Singapore tax purposes as a tax haven company so long as the corporation has its central mind and management outside Singapore. Such a corporation is not taxed on its offshore income unless that income is actually remitted to Singapore. Dividends paid by such a corporation out of its unremitted offshore income are also free of Singapore income tax. Singapore has no exempted corporations with tax guarantees.

Unlike Hong Kong and, indeed, most other tax havens, Singapore does have a number of double tax treaties. Treaties exist with Australia, Belgium, Canada, Denmark, France, West Germany, Israel, Japan, Malaysia, the Netherlands, New Zealand, Norway, Philippines, Switzerland and the United Kingdom.

GENERAL OBSERVATIONS

As is clearly evident from the above small sample of countries which would typically be regarded as tax haven locations, there are many and varied options available to a United Kingdom company which wishes to set up operations in an appropriate tax haven country. It is therefore important when looking at possible geographical locations that a detailed investigation be carried out into the particular attributes of specific locations. Typically the geographical size of the countries which fall to be regarded as tax havens tends to be relatively small, and as a consequence the costs of renting office space, attracting suitably qualified labour and of providing other services tend, in many cases, to be prohibitively high. This, however, has not in the past presented an insurmountable problem as many of the operations which are to be carried out by the company in the tax haven have been carried out effectively at locations other than the tax haven itself.

However, over time, the tax authorities of the high tax countries (such as the United Kingdom, the United States, Canada, Germany and France) have become increasingly concerned about what they regard as the use of tax havens by corporations purely for tax avoidance and, in some cases, tax evasion purposes. As a consequence, a number of countries have now in effect extended their jurisdiction so as to be able to impose tax on the profits of companies located in tax haven countries. The countries which have adopted this approach are Canada, France, Germany, Japan, the United States and, most recently, the United Kingdom.

Although the approaches adopted in each of the above countries differ in detail, the basic approach has been the same in each case. In essence, where a company is resident in a tax haven and is controlled by persons in the relevant high tax country either the whole or a specified proportion of the profits of the tax haven company are taxed by the high tax country. This occurs whether the profits of the tax haven company are remitted to its high tax country parent company or not. The basic objective of the legislation is quite simply to remove any possible tax advantage which the high tax country company might gain from seeking to shift some of its profit to a tax haven company.

In the case of the United Kingdom, draft legislation was contained in the Finance Bill 1983, which was designed to achieve the above objective. Due to the June 1983 general election, the relevant provisions were deleted from the Finance Bill and did not appear in the Finance Act 1983. However, the legislation is now contained in the Finance Act 1984.

CONCLUSION

The attitudes of the high tax countries to corporations using tax havens are hardening and in many situations the advantages previously available have now been substantially reduced, due to the introduction of legislation. In some cases they have been removed altogether. Nevertheless, with careful planning and a commercial approach a company should be in a position to improve its overall net after-tax return by the judicious choice and use of some of the world's tax havens.

MALCOLM J. FINNEY

Malcolm J. Finney & Partners

APPENDIX: LIST OF TAX HAVENS

Andorra
Anguilla
Antigua
Bahamas
Barbados
Bermuda
British Virgin Islands
Campione
Cayman Islands
Costa Rica
Cyprus
Gibraltar
Guernsey
Hong Kong
Isle of Man
Jersey
Liberia
Liechtenstein
Luxembourg
Monaco
Montserrat
Nauru
Netherlands
Netherlands Antilles
New Hebrides
Panama
St Vincent
Seychelles
Singapore
Switzerland
Turks and Caicos Islands
Vanuatu

7.1
Index of topics

7.2
Index of names